IMPERIALISM AT BAY

Ingrid Antonsen
2310 Plymouth Dr.
Champaign, Ill.
4/4/79

Other Books by the same Author

Ruanda-Urundi, 1884–1919   (1963)

Great Britain and Germany's Lost Colonies, 1914–1919   (1967)

(with Jean Stengers) *E. D. Morel's History of the Congo Reform Movement*   (1968)

British Strategy in the Far East, 1919–1939   (1971)

———

Ed. (with Prosser Gifford) *Britain and Germany in Africa: Imperial Rivalry and Colonial Rule*   (1967)

Ed. (with Prosser Gifford) *France and Britain in Africa: Imperial Rivalry and Colonial Rule*   (1971)

Ed. *The Origins of the Second World War: A. J. P. Taylor and his Critics*   (1972)

Ed. *Imperialism: The Robinson and Gallagher Controversy* (1976)

Ed. *National Security and International Trusteeship in the Pacific*   (1972)

Ed. (with William S. Livingston) *Australia, New Zealand and the Pacific Islands since the First World War*   (in press)

Imperialism at Bay

THE UNITED STATES
AND THE
DECOLONIZATION OF THE
BRITISH EMPIRE
1941-1945

by

Wm. Roger Louis

NEW YORK
OXFORD UNIVERSITY PRESS
1978

Library of Congress Cataloging in Publication Data

Louis, Wm. Roger.
    Imperialism at bay.

    Bibliography: p.
    Includes index.
        1.   World War, 1939-1945—Diplomatic history.
2.   United States—Foreign relations—Great Britain.
3.   Great Britain—Foreign relations—United States.
4.   Great Britain—Colonies—History.   5.   International
trusteeships.   I.   Title.
D753.L67   1978   940.53'22   78-1068
ISBN 0-19-821125-2

TO

MY PARENTS

Printed in the United States of America

PREFACE

THIS book is about American and British wartime planning for the future of the colonial world. The themes are American anti-colonialism and American expansion; and British reactions to American 'informal empire' as well as American ideas about the future of the British Empire. I am concerned with the moral regeneration of British purpose in the colonies and with American as well as British 'imperialism'. These matters were controversial at the time and remain so today. One cardinal source of controversy was the issue of international trusteeship. The book may also be read as a history of the origins of the trusteeship system of the United Nations.

The main narrative is in the chronological parts II–IV. I must ask the reader's indulgence for the lengthy introductory part in which I attempt to deal with a number of complex problems in relation to the themes of the book. The question of the French and Italian colonies, as well as that of the Japanese mandated islands, and the salient issues of international trusteeship, are all essential in understanding the general 'colonial problem' of the Second World War. I have linked the discussions together by an inquiry into the economic element of trusteeship in relation to strategic and ethical considerations. Americans and other critics of the British Empire tended to see 'trusteeship' as the opposite of 'imperialism'. To them trusteeship meant international machinery for advancement of colonial peoples towards independence. The British regarded the concept rather as the morality of empire. Trusteeship to them meant the ethical standards of colonial administration insisted on by Parliament. In brief, the introductory chapters deal with the ideas of trusteeship and the relative importance of the ethical, military, and economic drives to imperialism.

I have also used the introductory section as an opportunity to discuss the way in which the wartime bureaucracies made decisions about these problems. Here and elsewhere I am concerned with the question of motive and coherence in American planning and with the ways in which the President, the State Department, and the military branches of the government contributed to American policy (or lack of it). On the British side the focus is primarily on the Colonial Office, Foreign Office, and Dominions Office, and the interaction between London and the Dominions.

The book is mainly based on archival material and private papers that have only recently become accessible in the United States, Britain, Australia, New Zealand, and Canada. I would like to thank the archivists and holders of copyright of the collections listed on p. xv for their assistance and, where appropriate, for permission to publish material in their possession.

Surely one of the greatest pleasures of historical research is the opportunity to discuss one's work in progress with friends and colleagues. My list is long and my thanks many. The research for this volume was made possible by Admiral Stansfield Turner and Vice Admiral Julien J. LeBourgeois, who, as Presidents of the United States Naval War College, authorized support under the terms of the Naval War College Advanced Research Program. I am supremely grateful to James E. King, who was Director of the Advanced Research Program when the project was initiated; and I am indebted to those in Newport who have given me criticism and suggestions, including Commander William R. Pettyjohn, John Lewis Gaddis, J. Kenneth McDonald, David F. Trask, Robert F. Delaney, and Raymond G. O'Connor. I also wish to thank William R. Emerson, Colonel Clinton E. Granger, USA, and Captain John L. Butts, USN. Needless to say my views are entirely my own and do not necessarily reflect those of the President of the Naval War College or those associated with the Advanced Research Program.

A major advantage in teaching at the University of Texas is a treasure trove of colleagues: Hartley Grattan on the Pacific and British Empire, William S. Livingston on the Commonwealth, William R. Braisted on the Far East, Walt W. Rostow on economic history and affairs of the world generally, Robert A. Divine on American diplomatic history, and Claudio Segre on the Italian colonies. My thanks also to Elspeth Rostow, Warren Roberts, and Clarence Lasby.

In England I owe a special debt to St. Antony's College, Oxford, and to the members of the Imperial History Seminar, the latter including David Fieldhouse and Colin Newbury. To

Kenneth Kirkwood, Max Beloff, Jack Gallagher, and Dame Margery Perham I am indebted in a variety of ways. Those who have helped me generally and on particular points include David J. Morgan, Leslie Pressnell, Agatha Ramm, Sally Chilver, Ian Nish, Christopher Thorne, Ronald Hyam, and Alison Smith. My list of gratitude extends to Scotland to John D. Hargreaves and George Shepperson and to Switzerland to Zara Steiner and Rudolph von Albertini. I also wish to thank Sir Hilton Poynton for reading part of the manuscript. Sonia Argyle has edited it with patience and good cheer.

In Australia and New Zealand I am especially grateful to Bruce Miller, David McIntyre, Keith Sinclair, and Allan and Jean Martin. Sir Alister McIntosh and George Corner of the New Zealand Ministry for Foreign Affairs, and Sir Alan Watt in Canberra, have been gracious in their assistance.

Stephen Koss, Walter LaFeber, Richard Dale, Akira Iriye, and Maynard W. Swanson have aided me with their general knowledge and with suggestions on particular points. Alfred Gollin, Arthur S. Link, James MacGregor Burns, Bruce Marshall, Robert Dallek, Ralph Austen, Richard H. Ullman, Robin W. Winks, Leonard Thompson, Ernest R. May, and Richard W. Leopold have helped me in different specific ways.

Three of the protagonists of the wartime trusteeship saga have given me the benefit of their memories and their detailed criticism: Kenneth E. Robinson, Benjamin Gerig, and W. D. Forsyth. All of them are scholars in their own right as well as former officials; with Kenneth Robinson I was able to spend many hours reviewing the colonial problems of the wartime period. The book would be poorer without these first-hand accounts.

With Ronald Robinson I have also enjoyed countless hours of discussion and because of him a certain raciness of approach to these problems has no doubt crept into the manuscript. To my friends Jean Stengers and Prosser Gifford I am similarly indebted. Not least I am immensely grateful to my wife Patricia.

When I was in the last stage of this book I asked A. J. P. Taylor, who had read the manuscript, whether he might now have second thoughts about one of the concluding passages of *English History, 1914–1945*. The passage is: 'Future historians may see the war as a last struggle for the European balance of power or for the maintenance of the Empire. This was not how it appeared to those who lived through it.' His reply, I think, will be of general interest: 'The archives now reveal that Great Britain was fighting the Second World War in order to recover the British Empire and even (as with Libya) to add to it. Those who did the actual fighting had simpler aims. They fought to liberate the peoples of Europe from Germany and those of the Far East from Japan. That spirit dominated after the war. The British did not relinquish their Empire by accident. They ceased to believe in it.'

CONTENTS

PART I. INTRODUCTORY AND PARALLEL THEMES

1. Trusteeship and Imperialism   3

2. The Future of South-East Asia and the Question of the French Colonies   27

3. The Defence of the Middle East and the Fate of the Italian Colonies   48

4. American Security and the Controversy over the Japanese Mandated Islands   68

5. International Trusteeship   88

PART II. FROM THE ATLANTIC CHARTER TO THE CAIRO DECLARATION

6. Article III of the Atlantic Charter—Self-Determination   121

7. The Fall of Singapore and the Future of the British Empire: Trusteeship versus Partnership   134

8. Roosevelt and the American Public's Attitude towards the Colonial Issue from Pearl Harbor to the Anniversary of the Atlantic Charter   147

9. Trusteeship and the State Department's Post-War Foreign Policy Advisory Committee in 1942   159

10. Cordell Hull and the State Department's Trusteeship Planning   175

11. The British Response to the Developing American Anti-Colonial Campaign. Lord Cranborne's Policy of 'We Hold What We Have'. The Beginning of the Colonial Office's Regional Co-operation Schemes   187

12. The Crescendo of American Criticism and Churchill's 'First Minister' Speech   198

13. London and the Dominions in the Winter of 1942–1943. Parent States. The Position of India in Regional Commissions. International Accountability   211

14. The Three Dimensions of American Trusteeship Diplomacy in 1943   225

15. The British Reaction to the 'Declaration on National Independence'. The Colonial Secretary's Policy Statement of the 13th of July 1943   243

16. The Military Element in Roosevelt's Trusteeship Planning   259

17. The Cairo Declaration: the Dismemberment of Japan's Empire   274

PART III. FROM CAIRO TO YALTA

18. The Australian–New Zealand Agreement of January 1944   289

19. Regional Planning in the Colonial Office   309

20. Isaiah Bowman's Colonial Mission to London, April 1944   327

21. The Dominion Prime Ministers' Conference of May 1944   337

22. Roosevelt and the State Department in the Winter and Spring of 1944: the Question of a Growing 'Spirit of Imperialism'   351

23. The American Military's Stand on the Annexation of the Pacific Islands   366

24. The Colonial Question at the Dumbarton Oaks Conference on International Organization. The Advent of Hilton Poynton and Kenneth Robinson in Trusteeship Affairs   378

25. The Colonial Office takes the Initiative. The Poynton–Robinson Project on 'International Aspects of Colonial Policy'   392

26. The Australian–New Zealand Conference of November 1944   409

27. Washington in the Winter of 1944–1945. The Advent of Sir Frederick Eggleston as Australian Minister. Arthur Creech Jones and the Institute of Pacific Relations Conference at Hot Springs   422

28. Prelude to Yalta: the Colonial Secretary's Visit to Washington in January 1945   433

29. Yalta: Agreement on the Trusteeship Formula   448

PART IV. THE COLONIAL SETTLEMENT OF 1945

30. The Aftermath of Yalta: London   463

31. The Aftermath of Yalta: Washington   475

32. The International Conference before San Francisco: the Commonwealth Meeting in London, April 1945   497

33. San Francisco: the Resolution of the 'Strategic Trust' Controversy and the Foundation of Colonial Accountability   512

34. San Francisco: the Question of Colonial Independence   532

35. Strategic Security and the Colonial Situation in 1945   548

Index   575

ABBREVIATIONS AND LOCATIONS OF MANUSCRIPT COLLECTIONS

Public Record Office, London:
CO	Colonial Office
DO	Dominions Office
FO	Foreign Office
CAB	Cabinet Office
PREM	Prime Minister's Office

National Archives, Washington:
USSD	Decimal Files of the State Department
USSD NF	'Notter Files' (Post-war Planning) of the State Department
JCS	Joint Chiefs of Staff
OSS R&A	Office of Strategic Services, Research and Analysis

Washington Navy Yard:
USN GB	United States Navy, General Board
CNO	Chief of Naval Operations

Australian Archives, Canberra:
AA	Australian Archives, Department of External Affairs

National Archives, Wellington:
NZ PM	Prime Minister's Department
NZ EX	External Affairs
NZ IT	Island Territories

Public Archives, Ottawa:
CAN	Department of External Affairs

League of Nations Archives, Geneva:
LN	Mandates Section of the League of Nations

Anti-Slavery Society Papers. Papers of the Anti-Slavery and Aborigines Protection Society, Rhodes House, Oxford.

Blakeslee Papers. Papers of George H. Blakeslee, Clark University, Worcester, Mass.

Bowman Papers. Papers of Isaiah Bowman, Johns Hopkins University Library, Baltimore.

Eggleston Papers. Papers of Sir Frederick Eggleston, Australian National Library.

Evatt Papers. Papers of H. V. Evatt, Flinders University Library, Adelaide.

Fabian Papers. Papers of the Fabian Colonial Bureau, Rhodes House, Oxford.

Forrestal Papers. Papers of James V. Forrestal, Princeton University Library.

Forsyth Papers. Papers of W. D. Forsyth, Canberra, privately held.

Hailey Papers. Papers of Lord Hailey, Rhodes House, Oxford.

Hopkins Papers. Papers of Harry L. Hopkins, Roosevelt Library, Hyde Park, N.Y.

Hornbeck Papers. Papers of Stanley K. Hornbeck, Hoover Institution, Stanford, Cal.

Hull Papers. Papers of Cordell Hull, Library of Congress.

IPR Papers. Papers of the Institute of Pacific Relations, Columbia University Library.

Jones Papers. Papers of Arthur Creech Jones, Rhodes House, Oxford.

Lugard Papers. Papers of Sir Frederick (Lord) Lugard, Rhodes House, Oxford.

Roosevelt Papers. Papers of Franklin D. Roosevelt, Roosevelt Library, Hyde Park, N.Y.

Stettinius Papers. Papers of Edward R. Stettinius, Jr., University of Virginia Library, Charlottesville, Va.

Stimson Papers. Papers of Henry L. Stimson, Yale University Library.

Taussig Papers. Papers of Charles W. Taussig, Roosevelt Library, Hyde Park, N.Y.

Watt Papers. Papers of Sir Alan Watt, Australian National Library.

PART I

INTRODUCTORY AND
PARALLEL THEMES

I

TRUSTEESHIP AND IMPERIALISM

'TRUSTEESHIP', according to a New Zealand official at the close of the Second World War, should be conceived of as the *antithesis* of 'imperialism'.[1] By focusing on the trusteeship controversy during the war, this book is concerned generally with the nature of imperialism and specifically with the conflicting colonial aims of the British Empire and the United States. As in earlier times, 'imperialism' was popularly believed to be the exploitation of the non-western world. During the First World War, Woodrow Wilson identified the struggle for overseas markets and raw materials as a cause of war. At American insistence, the former German colonies and parts of the Ottoman Empire were not annexed as colonies but administered as mandated territories under the League of Nations. They were held as a 'sacred trust of civilization'. During the Second World War, Franklin D. Roosevelt viewed the continued existence of the colonial empires as a possible cause of future wars. He favoured the eventual independence of the colonies. Again at American insistence, the mandates of the League of Nations became trust territories under the United Nations and the system was expanded to include enemy colonial territories of Japan and Italy. The anti-colonial attitude of the United States gave powerful impetus to the decolonization of the European colonial empires, which is one of the great transformations of our age.[2]

The nineteenth-century historian François Guizot once wrote that history presents us, in each epoch, with predominant ideas and events that decide the fortune and character of a long series of generations. When one studies the colonial question of the twentieth century, the events of the two world wars and the principle of *self-determination* come immediately to

[1] C. G. R. McKay, Secretary of the Island Territories Department, Miscellaneous Notes, June 1945 to July 1946, NZ IT 25/1/3.
[2] For the best survey, see Rudolph von Albertini, *Decolonization: the Administration and Future of the Colonies, 1919–1960* (New York, 1971).

mind. During the Second World War, those who dealt with the future of the colonial empires began to reap the harvest sown in 1914–18. Self-determination *for whom?* President Wilson believed that the peoples of the disintegrating empires in Europe should themselves decide the sovereignty under which they would live. In Africa he probably had in mind above all the prevention of exploitation and abuses attributed to the Germans. As for the prospect of eventual self-determination, he thought that sound colonial rule might lead to consolidation within the colonial regimes. 'If successful administration by a mandatory should lead to a union with the mandatory, he would be the last to object', the President is recorded as saying in 1919.[3] Wilson belonged to the tradition of colonial reform, not liberation. He believed that the European powers should be held accountable for the political development and social and economic progress in the colonies. Over a period of decades or even centuries, the peoples of 'backward' areas in Asia and Africa might reach a stage of development where they could stand on their own. Self-determination would come in due course. In any event Africans and Asians would be heard as to their own fate.

Franklin D. Roosevelt also belonged to the epoch of the great European colonial empires and he held essentially the same outlook as Wilson two decades earlier. He also was a gradualist. He foresaw the possible independence of colonial peoples only after a period of tutelage by the 'parent' states. He spoke of places such as New Guinea as existing in the stone age. He differed from the European view on tropical Africa only in emphasizing the need for greater economic and social progress. Roosevelt was appalled at the standards of living in places such as the Gambia. He talked about possible independence for Korea and Indo-China after twenty or thirty years of western or international 'guardianship'. Nevertheless he was quite certain that *independence* should be the ultimate goal for the colonies generally. In studying the 'colonial question' during the war, Roosevelt and many other Americans increasingly believed that the principle of self-determination would work in favour of the creation of independent states out

---

[3] *Papers relating to the Foreign Relations of the United States: the Paris Peace Conference, 1919*, iii. 740–2.

of the European colonial empires. Though he did not foresee the fragmentation that would occur in the period of decolonization, Roosevelt should be regarded as one of the fathers of the post-war world of politically independent nations.

Winston S. Churchill held the extreme view among Englishmen that the future world order would be based in large measure on the power, prosperity, and prestige of the British Empire, as it had in the nineteenth century. His ideas often reflected the experience not only of the earlier period of the First World War but also of the Victorian age, when he had spent his formative years in India, in the campaign in Africa against the Mahdi, and in the Boer War. He had witnessed, in his view, the benefits of peace and progress conferred by England on the Indian subcontinent, a war against the forces of barbarism in the Sudan, and the struggle at the turn of the century which tested the resilience and the magnanimity of the British Empire. British reconciliation of the Afrikaners proved to be one of the political cornerstones of the twentieth-century Commonwealth. Now, during the Second World War, Churchill as Prime Minister faced the supreme challenge of collaborating not only with the leaders of South Africa, Australia, New Zealand, and Canada, but also the United States and the other Allied powers. Churchill is remembered, above all, as a great champion of the English-speaking world. But it is equally important to bear in mind that he was a British Imperialist. Though Churchill was not an especially creative or forward-looking colonial statesman, he had a strong sense of guardianship of the dependent peoples in the Empire.[4]

At the time of the Paris Peace Conference in 1919, Lord Milner, then Colonial Secretary, represented *par excellence* the ideals of enlightened British Imperialism. In his own phrase he was 'a British race patriot' in much the same sense that Cecil Rhodes had in mind when he founded the Oxford scholarships. One of Milner's key ideas was to draw the United States into the colonies, possibly as a mandatory power in Africa or the Middle East, and to bring certain Americans with pro-British sympathies into the affairs of the British Empire. It was the vision of an Anglo-American colonial alliance. The two most

[4] For the shaping of Churchill's views on colonial questions, see Ronald Hyam, *Elgin and Churchill at the Colonial Office, 1905–1908* (London, 1968).

powerful components of the English-speaking world would work together to secure the peace and provide a benevolent guardianship over backward peoples. This idea appealed especially to Americans who believed that there existed a kinship between the United States and the British Empire based on race and common culture. There were specific manifestations of this impulse of the British to promote American involvement in the colonial world and an alacrity on the part of some Americans to accept the responsibilities. At Milner's instigation, for example, George Louis Beer, the Columbia University historian of the old British Empire and the American adviser on colonial questions at the Paris Peace Conference, was invited to become the director of the mandates section of the League of Nations.[5] Beer admired Lord Milner, and the appointment would have been a concrete step towards Anglo-American colonial friendship. It came to nothing because of the refusal of the United States to join the League of Nations. But there existed throughout the inter-war years and the Second World War a substantial sentiment on the part of Americans in prominent positions who believed that Britain managed her affairs in Africa and Asia with a sense of justice and fair play that distinguished her from the continental colonial powers. Americans might be critical of some aspects of the British Empire, but the British were old friends and natural allies. During the wartime period the theme of collaboration developed in a new way as the American military began to study the problem of post-war security and the question of bases. In contrast with some officials of the State Department who favoured decolonization and independence, the General Board of the Navy and the Joint Chiefs of Staff Strategic Survey Committee saw good reasons for the continued existence of the British Empire. British withdrawal from colonial regions would create areas of instability and uncertainty. Throughout the war there was a similarity of ideas about the post-war world

---

[5] On Milner, Beer, and Anglo-American colonial relations at the close of the First World War, see folder marked 'Mandates' in the Milner Papers (Bodleian Library, Oxford); letters in the Lothian Papers GD 40/17/75, Scottish Record Office, Edinburgh; memoranda and correspondence in the archives of the League of Nations (Geneva), LN R1/2062/248 and R2998/248; and Beer's Diary, copy in the Library of Congress. On Beer see Wm. Roger Louis, 'The United States and the African Peace Settlement of 1919', *Journal of African History*, 4. 3 (1963).

held by the United States Navy and the British Colonial Office.

The wartime archives amply reveal that the sense of historic antagonism between Britain and the United States continued to exist along with the spirit of co-operation generated by the war. In the relations between the two powers, the loss of the British Empire in the Far East was of cardinal importance. It made clear the reality of the balance of power in Asia. With the fall of Singapore in February 1942, British prestige in the Far East suffered an irreparable collapse. The future of British colonies such as Hong Kong depended on the American war effort against Japan. Hong Kong itself became a major issue of contention between Roosevelt and Churchill. The President hoped that China would emerge from the war as one of the great powers of the world. Together with Russia and Britain, the United States and China would serve as policemen of the world's peace. Roosevelt feared that Hong Kong would jeopardize friendly relations with the Chinese. It virtually symbolized the old system of imperialism which should be ended. Roosevelt wanted the colony returned to China. Churchill's perception of the problem was entirely different. In his view China had neither the military force nor the internal cohesion to be rated as a great power, and, far from emerging as a major nation, China would probably lapse into civil war. Churchill thought that Roosevelt was putting forward China as a puppet. Speaking to the American Ambassador to China in 1945, the Prime Minister said in regard to Hong Kong, 'never would we yield an inch of the territory that was under the British flag'.[6] Churchill scarcely disguised his contempt for the American 'sentimental' attitude towards the 'pigtails', 'Chinamen', or 'Chinks'—phrases which irritated Roosevelt.[7] When the President spoke of trusteeship regimes in the Far East and other parts of the world, the Prime Minister immediately

---

[6] Note by Churchill, 11 Apr. 1945, FO 371/46325.

[7] For an example of Roosevelt's distaste for Churchill's use of these words, see the diary of Sir Frederick Eggleston (Australian Minister in Washington), 14 Nov. 1944, Eggleston Papers. See also e.g. Lord Moran, *Churchill: Taken from the Diaries of Lord Moran* (Boston, 1966), p. 594: 'when Roosevelt used to say that it was better to be friends than enemies with a country of four hundred million souls, he [Churchill] would listen in silence, but later he spoke scornfully of "little yellow men".'

suspected that the United States was trying to dismember the British Empire. Throughout the entire war, Churchill regarded the question of 'trusteeship' as merely a cloak for American expansion. When he made his famous speech in November 1942 that he had not become the King's First Minister in order to preside over the liquidation of the British Empire, Churchill in part meant that under no circumstances would trusteeship regimes be created out of British colonies.

During the first half of the war, roughly to the time of Churchill's 'First Minister' speech and the turn of the tide against the Axis powers, an explosive colonial situation existed in India. The Viceroy wrote to Churchill in August 1942, 'I am engaged here in meeting by far the most serious rebellion since 1857, the gravity and extent of which we have so far concealed from the world for reasons of military security.'[8] To add to their burden, British officials faced the prospect of what they referred to, again in the Viceroy's words, as visits by 'well meaning sentimentalists from the U.S.A. to India'. Perhaps the most famous of the unofficial American peripatetics was Wendell Willkie, the Republican Presidential candidate in 1940. In 1942 he made a world-wide tour. His speeches created a sensation in England. His central message to the American people on his return can be summed up by the title of his book *One World*—one world against the forces of imperialism and behind 'the orderly but scheduled abolition of the colonial system'.[9] Though he did not actually visit India, Willkie criticized the British handling of the Indian nationalist crisis. He was shocked at Churchill's 'First Minister' speech, which he rightly interpreted as a resurgence of old-fashioned British imperialism. With prominent Americans such as Willkie stirring up the colonial issue in the United States, India became a sensitive political problem for Roosevelt. The President made it no secret that he deplored British Imperialism in India and

[8] Linlithgow to Churchill, 31 Aug. 1942, *Constitutional Relations between Britain and India: the Transfer of Power, 1942–7*, ii. 853. For the United States and India during the war, see Gary R. Hess, *America Encounters India, 1941–1947* (Baltimore, 1971).

[9] Wendell L. Willkie, *One World* (New York, 1943), p. 185. Ten years later Lord Hailey assessed Wilkie's tour in terms of symbolic significance. 'Ever since the world tour of the late Mr Wendell Willkie, the United States has been urging the need for the liquidation of the colonies.' Hailey, 'A Turning Point in Colonial Rule', *International Affairs* 28. 2 (April 1952).

in all other parts of the world. He found it easier to talk to Stalin and Chiang Kai-shek than Churchill about the future of the British Empire. Roosevelt's sentiments were genuine. With an 'almost boyish relish' he would speak of American constitutional history and how the problems of India might be solved by learning the lessons of the American revolution.[10]

To Churchill, and most other Englishmen, Roosevelt's ideas about India were not only sentimental but fatuous. They thought he knew nothing of the complexity of the situation in India or the grave nature of British responsibilities. For his part, Roosevelt made his views entirely clear. He took a definite stand throughout the war on behalf of India and colonial peoples everywhere. But he did not intervene directly. His scheme for the creation of trusteeship regimes in places such as Indo-China and Korea represented one of the few concrete ways in which he attempted to alter the colonial *status quo*. In the view of Roosevelt's biographer, James MacGregor Burns, Roosevelt treated Churchill and the question of India in the same way that he dealt with Southern Senators and the issue of the American Negro. He subjected them to monologues and proclaimed his liberal intentions, but his words were greater than his deeds.[11] Roosevelt had a shrewd sense of what might and might not be politically possible, and he refused to pursue an issue that would interfere with wartime co-operation. He aimed at stabilizing, not undermining, the colonial world. He wanted a peaceful transition to independence. Time and again in conversation, Roosevelt would dwell on the question of *timetables for independence* in India and in all European colonial areas.[12] The demand for timetables was a distinctly American contribution to the process of decolonization.

Partly as a result of the crisis in India in 1942, a wave of anti-colonial sentiment swept through the United States at a critical stage of the war. Americans generally did not distinguish between India and the Colonial Empire, or for that matter between the Empire and the Commonwealth. Much of the British colonial propaganda (or, to use the British word, 'en-

---

[10] Note by Graham Spry, 15 May 1942, *Transfer of Power*, ii. 90.

[11] James MacGregor Burns, *Roosevelt: the Soldier of Freedom* (New York, 1970), p. 549; conversations with the author.

[12] e.g. Memorandum by Charles Taussig (Joint Chairman, Anglo-American Caribbean Commission), 16 Jan. 1945, Taussig Papers.

lightenment') during the war sought to make clear the nature of the dependent Empire administered by the Colonial Office. India and Burma apart, the Colonial Empire consisted of fifty-five territories scattered throughout the world with a population estimated at 60 million. The Colonial Office regarded some of the peoples of the Empire as so backward and some of the territories so geographically isolated or with economic prospects so bleak that it would be impossible for some colonies ever to be capable of self-government, much less of independence. One had only to think of the primitive tribes of Borneo, the desert wastes of British Somaliland, or the geographical isolation and barren economies of some of the Pacific islands to see that the catchword 'independence' would not bear serious scrutiny. On reflection, American officials and opinion as expressed through the newspapers tended to agree with the British that the 'colonial question' (or the problem generally of dependent peoples, especially in Africa and the Pacific) boiled down to benevolent guardianship and long-range development.

To some extent the issues were rhetorical because the Americans no more than the British foresaw the liberation of colonies in anything approaching the scope and speed with which decolonization actually occurred in the two decades following the war. But genuine controversy did exist in other areas. With memories of their own colonial past, Americans wondered whether the British would grant freedom to colonial peoples who could stand on their own. To a significant segment of the American public, the history of Ireland was hard ly reassuring. What were British intentions in India? After Churchill's speech saying that the British meant to hold their own, Americans could legitimately question British motives. So far as Churchill was concerned, American suspicions were justified. 'Keep a bit of India' for the Empire, an unrepentant Churchill said in a final remark to the Viceroy in August 1945.[13] The burden of less reactionary British statesmen throughout the war was to prove the genuineness of British intent to grant Dominion status to India and to prepare the colonies generally for self-government.

The Englishman who spoke to Americans with greatest authority and persuasiveness was Lord Hailey. A retired

[13] Penderel Moon, ed., *Wavell: the Viceroy's Journal* (London, 1973), p. 168.

Governor of the Punjab and the United Provinces in India, Hailey before the war had launched into a massive research project on Africa. When he published *African Survey* in 1938 it represented a monumental accomplishment. He possessed an analytical mind capable of systematically organizing scattered information and often recondite bodies of knowledge. The synthesis presented in *African Survey* served as the basic guide for both academics and officials to the resources and economic and social problems of the African continent and the colonial policies of the European powers as well as the British. He had travelled extensively in Africa. He had served as the British representative on the Permanent Mandates Commission. And during the war in a semi-official capacity he directed the research of the Colonial Office. In short he was a key figure in the 'colonial question'.

In December 1942 Hailey led a British delegation to a conference sponsored by the Institute of Pacific Relations at Mont Tremblant, Canada. This episode is mentioned here because it occurred when American anti-colonial sentiment reached its wartime peak, and because it gives insight into the British response to foreign criticism. Representatives of all of the major powers in the Pacific basin attended the conference in an unofficial capacity. They met in an anti-British atmosphere, in part because of the situation in India. One of the British delegates, Arthur Creech Jones (later to become a Labour Colonial Secretary), gave this description:[14]

The temperature about Britain is pretty low. The references in the Willkie speeches about British colonial policy, colonial status and the rest, are widely held by men everywhere and by practically all the Americans and many of the Dominions representatives at the Conference. Indeed, the subject is hot and one of the most canvassed. I say nothing about the feeling regarding India which also holds the field but the ignorance about colonial policy in the past four or five years is profound.

14 Arthur Creech Jones to Harold Macmillan, 17 Dec. 1942, Creech Jones Papers 12/1. Creech Jones's writings and speeches which seem especially relevant to the trusteeship controversy are: 'The Colonies in the War', *Political Quarterly* (Oct.–Dec. 1940); 'The Colonial Office', ibid. 14. 1 (Jan.–Mar. 1943); 'International Trusteeship of Colonies', an Address to the Anti-Slavery and Aborigines Protection Society, 7 June 1945; review of Institute of Pacific Relations, *Security in the Pacific*, in *Political Quarterly*, 16, 4 (Oct.–Dec. 1945); (with Rita Hinden) *Colonies and International Conscience* (London, 1945), ed., *New Fabian Colonial Essays* (New York, 1959).

It is difficult to discuss the subject with Americans because they are not only uninformed about it but they picture an almost semi-feudal Britain and society nearly 100 years out-of-date. They love idealistic generalisations, glowing phrases, which ignore the actualities of the colonial situation and seem impatient of the practical approaches to policy making, so common with Englishmen.

It was the necessity for a pragmatic approach to colonial problems that Hailey above all emphasized as he explained the circumstances of dependent peoples, their aspirations and the policies of the colonial powers, and the influence of 'world opinion'. A generation earlier, he stated on one occasion, he would not have attached much importance to the question of world opinion. But no one now could deny its importance. Humanitarian sentiment in England and elsewhere had manifestly helped to bring about the end of notorious colonial conditions such as the abuses of the rubber regime in the Congo Free State and the use of Polynesian labour in the Pacific sugar plantations.

Hailey also stressed the publicity given to colonial questions by the Permanent Mandates Commission. In these public debates he would develop with considerable powers of persuasion the idea that backward peoples were now generally regarded as trusts. The doctrine of 'trusteeship' had increasingly gained recognition as a principle of administration, in the United States no less than in the European colonies. In pursuit of this argument Hailey would cite evidence such as the case of *The Cherokee Nation vs. the State of Georgia*, in which the Chief Justice defined the position of the federal government as one of a trustee. Using such examples, and presenting them with exceptional lucidity, Hailey would demonstrate that the problems facing the British were essentially the same as those of all nations with dependent peoples. He would go on to argue that the key to British policy was the development of self-governing institutions. The British, far from being motivated by 'Imperialism', genuinely wished to see colonial peoples attain self-government and freedom.

Hailey was an effective propagandist. Indeed he was a godsend for the defence of the British Empire. According to the Colonial Office representative at the Mont Tremblant Conference, whose account portrays some of the emotional content of the issue from the British side:

> Hailey throughout was truly superb . . . [H]e was too obviously head and shoulders above anyone at the Conference: even his accomplished technique could never quite conceal the fact that much of the time he was tucking up his mental trousers to step gingerly through a great deal of intellectual ditch-water. . . . He achieved it in spite of himself, without a trace of condescension.
>
> I was lost in admiration at the whole ten-day performance and many times as I watched him cross swords with the American 'Professors' and gracefully prick one balloon after another, I thought what a stupid tragedy it would be to take the management of great affairs from men like Hailey and give them over to the boys with thick-lensed glasses, long hair and longer words nasally intoned.[15]

No one can study the colonial question during the war without becoming aware of the immense influence exerted by Lord Hailey. During his visit to America in the winter of 1942–3, for example, in only three months he wrote major articles on the colonial issue for *Foreign Affairs* and the *Reader's Digest*.[16] He gave a major series of lectures at Princeton University which resulted in the best single account of the colonial problem written during the entire war.[17] In addition he lectured at various other universities: Yale, Brown, Toronto, and Columbia; and he talked to private groups such as the Council on

[15] D. M. MacDougall to Noel Sabine (Colonial Office), 22 Dec. 1942, copy in Hailey Papers. One of the Canadian delegates wrote about the general atmosphere of the conference: 'American suspicions regarding British colonial policy are so widespread that nothing short of a major step will allay them.' Louis Rasminsky (Foreign Exchange Control Board) to Hume Wrong, 16 Dec. 1942, CAN 180(S).

[16] Lord Hailey, 'India in the Modern World', *Foreign Affairs* 21. 3 (April 1943); for reasons that have not become clear in the course of my research, the article for the *Reader's Digest* never appeared. This must have been a disappointment to Hailey and especially to the Ambassador in Washington, Lord Halifax, who had gone to considerable trouble to arrange for its publication. It was to have appeared anonymously. Perhaps the editorial board took fright. It would have looked odd to have seen a loftily written defence of the British in India along with the run-of-the-mill *Reader's Digest* articles. Hailey received $1,500, a lot of money for an essay in 1943. Correspondence in the Hailey Papers.

[17] Lord Hailey, *The Future of Colonial Peoples* (Princeton, 1944). Hailey was a prolific writer. Here are merely a few of his speeches and essays relevant to the trusteeship controversy during the war: *The Position of Colonies in a British Commonwealth of Nations* (Romanes Lecture, London, 1941); 'A New Philosophy of Colonial Rule', *United Empire* 32. 8 (Nov.–Dec. 1941); 'Capital and Colonies', *Journal of the Royal Society of Arts* 91. 4645 (6 Aug. 1943); *Britain and Her Dependencies* (London, 1943).

Foreign Relations in New York and Chicago, to members of religious organizations brought together by John Foster Dulles, and to officials of a foundation especially interested in the problems of the American Negro, the Phelps-Stokes Fund.

On one memorable occasion Hailey dined with Hamilton Fish Armstrong, the editor of *Foreign Affairs*, and Wendell Willkie. They talked at great length about India. Willkie later thanked Hailey for his help in comprehending the colonial problem. 'You were so patient, tolerant and helpful I shall never forget it', he wrote.[18] His words were not perfunctory.[19] Hailey conveyed the idea that the problem of dependent peoples was universal and one which could be solved by men of goodwill working together. No less important, those who listened to him usually were left with the sense that the British Empire stood for progress, self-government, and freedom.

One way or another, Englishmen generally held strong feelings about the Empire. Churchill's sentiments approached a religious fervour. On one occasion during the war he remarked that the danger of Communism in part lay in the religious zeal of its followers. 'The truth is', observed the Canadian Prime Minister, Mackenzie King, 'as he [Churchill] speaks of Communism . . . being a religion to some people, the British Empire and Commonwealth is a religion to him.'[20] Members of the Labour Party also held strong convictions. In one of the sharpest rebukes to American critics, Herbert Morrison, the Home Secretary, stated in January 1943, 'It would be ignorant, dangerous nonsense to talk about grants of full self-government to many of the dependent territories for some time to come. In those instances it would be like giving a child of ten a latchkey, a bank account, and a shot-gun.'[21] On a later occasion Morrison referred to the 'jolly old Empire'—a remark which infuriated the wing of the Labour Party associated with the Fabian Colonial Research Bureau.

[18] Willkie to Hailey, 20 Jan. 1943, Hailey Papers.

[19] 'The setting you gave the Indian problem in your talk with Mr. Willkie that evening at my house impressed him very much.' Hamilton Fish Armstrong to Hailey, 8 Feb. 1943, Hailey Papers.

[20] J. W. Pickersgill, *The Mackenzie King Record* (Toronto, 1960), i. 679.

[21] *Manchester Guardian*, 11 Jan. 1943. For the Labour Party and colonial problems generally, Partha Sarathi Gupta, *Imperialism and the British Labour Movement, 1914–1964* (London, 1975).

With a fervour equal to that of their Tory counterparts, the Fabians believed that the colonial system gradually should be *ended*. There was nothing 'jolly' about colonial oppression. Irresponsible politicians might distort the intention of the majority of the Labour Party, making them liars and hypocrites in the eyes of millions of Indians and Africans, but, according to the Fabians, it should be beyond dispute that the Labour Party stood against the Tory conception of the Empire as personified by Churchill. Nevertheless even the Fabians tended to respond to American criticism in the same way as Herbert Morrison. Creech Jones was one of the founders of the Fabian Colonial Research Bureau, and, in Parliament, one of the most persistent critics of the Colonial Office. At Mont Tremblant, however, he had rallied in defence of British colonial policy. According to the report to the Colonial Office, on one notable occasion Creech Jones reacted with anger to a Canadian delegate who accused the British of complacency:

Well, all this was too much for Creech-Jones. He'd been extra-good throughout the Conference—so patently progressive, so obviously sincere, so manifestly not one of the 'old gang'. He caught the Chairman's eye at about the third attempt and rose to his feet, looking just right—rather red in the face and very angry, not well-dressed with a rather dark and crumpled shirt—looking, in fact, like a labour leader and not in the least like a 'sahib'. Hands on hips, he rounded on the whole lot of them in his best House of Commons manner and barked a bit in a very forthright way.

It was a wonderful scene and I wish some others from Downing Street [at the Colonial Office] besides myself could have been present to witness the strange spectacle of him defending the Colonial Office and its administration. . . . I thought it was magnificent: here was the loud and living proof that England was not effete nor spiritually bankrupt.[22]

No less than the First World War, the Second World War brought about a revival of the sense of Britain's imperial mission. The Secretary of the Fabian Colonial Bureau, Dr. Rita Hinden, said in May 1944, 'I was a rabid anti-Imperialist at one time, but one cannot ignore the fact that there is a certain sympathy, an intangible something, which holds the British

[22] D. M. MacDougall to Noel Sabine, 22 Dec. 1942, Hailey Papers.

Empire or Commonwealth together and which cannot be wholly explained in terms of material advantage.'[23]

When Mackenzie King wrote about Churchill's zeal for the Empire and Commonwealth, it would have been more accurate to have noted that the Prime Minister's real enthusiasm lay with the Empire. It is true that he used the terms interchangeably, depending on the occasion. The British Ambassador in Washington, Lord Halifax, once recounted an anecdote about Churchill addressing a group of Americans which included Senator Arthur Vandenberg. The Senator's eye twinkled when the Prime Minister mentioned the phrase 'British Empire'. 'Churchill . . . as the phrase again became due to round off the peroration, said " . . . British Empire, or British Commonwealth of Nations", and, with a side squint at Vanderbergh [sic], "we keep trade labels to suit all tastes".'[24] Churchill's conception of the Commonwealth, as he once described it to Mackenzie King, was 'this congeries of states and peoples, all brought together as one'.

Probably none of the Dominion Prime Ministers would have taken exception to Churchill's definition, and he was certainly careful in all formal speeches not to imply that the imperial government in London possessed any more authority than the equal members of the Commonwealth in Ottawa, Cape Town, Canberra, and Wellington. But in fact a powerful tension existed between London and the Dominion capitals. What was the future direction of the Empire and Commonwealth? Was it a Commonwealth as envisaged by Churchill, with the white Dominions and perhaps India on more or less equal terms with the imperial government, but with the Empire as a permanent institution? Or was the British Empire and Commonwealth

[23] *Hampstead and Highgate Express*, 5 May 1944, clipping in the Fabian Colonial Bureau Papers. For a sample of Rita Hinden's writings especially relevant to trusteeship, see 'Colonial Blind Alley', *Fabian Quarterly* 28 (Winter 1940); *Plan for Africa* (London, 1941); 'Imperialism Today', *Fabian Quarterly* 45 (April 1945); ed., *Fabian Colonial Essays* (London, 1945); *Socialists and the Empire* (Fabian Colonial Bureau Pamphlet, 1946—an account of the work of the Bureau since its founding in 1940); and *Empire and After* (London, 1949). Especially important publications of the Fabian Colonial Bureau include: *Downing Street and the Colonies* (pamphlet, London, 1942); *International Action and the Colonies* (pamphlet, London, 1943), perhaps the most important publication of the Bureau during the war; *Four Colonial Questions: How Should Britain Act?* (pamphlet, London, 1944); and *Strategic Colonies and their Future* (pamphlet, London, 1945).

[24] Earl of Halifax, *Fulness of Days* (London, 1957), p. 273.

evolving towards greater freedom on behalf of all its members, at least its white members? This was the vision most clearly seen by the Prime Minister of South Africa, General J. C. Smuts. He once defined the Commonwealth as the greatest example of organized freedom the world had ever seen. The Commonwealth was a dynamic institution in a constant state of evolution. Smuts referred to the 'Empire' as a relic of the nineteenth century. In his view the Colonial Office needed to reform its centralized system of administration, just as the imperial government generally needed to continue the devolution of authority to the Dominions. The question of central control overshadowed all aspects of the colonial debate during the war. Mackenzie King once told Churchill, 'You know, the minute I cross to England, immediately there is a cry raised that I have gone into the imperialist camp. . . . What people are really afraid of is the imperialist idea as against the complete independence of the parts.'[25]

If there was tension between London and the Dominions on the nature of the Empire and Commonwealth, there existed outright disagreement about the future of dependent peoples. In this debate the Canadians took little part. 'This is not a subject on which we shall take a strong line', wrote the Canadian official who followed the issue most closely during the war.[26] An excerpt from a despatch of the Canadian High Commissioner in March 1945 gives one of the underlying reasons: 'Canada is interested in seeing that the colonial problem is not a source of friction between the United States and the United Kingdom or a cause of ill-will towards the United Kingdom on the part of the Canadians.'[27] Though the Canadians were sensitive to the way in which a general declaration on dependent peoples might affect the Indian tribes, Canada alone of the Dominions did not administer a mandated territory.

For South Africa the problem of international control over South-West Africa posed a unique problem. In May 1945 Smuts wrote from the San Francisco Conference, which established

[25] Pickersgill, *Mackenzie King Record*, i. 508.

[26] H. Hume Wrong (Department of External Affairs) to L. B. Pearson (Canadian Ambassador in Washington), 8 Mar. 1945, CAN 180(S).

[27] High Commissioner to Secretary of State for External Affairs, 20 Mar. 1945, CAN 180(S).

the provisions of the trusteeship system: 'The idea about mandates is to continue the system under a new form of administration and to extend its scope to dependent peoples generally.'
At any cost, Smuts wanted to avoid international measures that
might interfere with the race laws of South Africa. 'I am
formally reserving our rights, including incorporation,' he continued, 'as far as South West Africa is concerned.'[28] Smuts in
short wanted to terminate the mandates system.

South Africa's position was the diametric opposite of
Australia's and New Zealand's. Both of the antipodean powers
worked to strengthen and extend the mandates system. Peter
Fraser, the Prime Minister of New Zealand, and H. V. Evatt,
the Minister for External Affairs and Attorney-General of
Australia, believed that the principles of trusteeship should be
extended to *all* colonies. They pressed for rigorous colonial
accountability to the future international organization. Each
holding strong individual opinions on the subject, both spoke
from the tradition of the Labour Party. Dependent peoples
should be protected and not exploited, and their welfare could
be promoted by international supervision. On this vital point
the antipodeans held the opposite view to that of the imperial
government. The Colonial Office passionately resisted international supervision of any part of the Colonial Empire. The
imperial government thus found itself in tacit alliance with
South Africa, the only power in fact that gave whole-hearted
support to the Colonial Office on the question of the mandates.
The Australians and New Zealanders found themselves more
in agreement with the American officials in the State Department. In sum, the colonial question was a divisive issue.

The colonial issue similarly divided the military and civilian
branches of the American government. The General Board of
the Navy surveyed such questions as the future of the Pacific
with a memory of Anglo-American naval rivalry and sharp
distrust of any form of international supervision. Admiral E. J.
King, Chief of Naval Operations, was an Anglophobe. Though
other officers certainly were less anti-British, the Navy generally
aimed to prevent British claims to any part of the Japanese
Empire. By restricting European participation in the war

[28] Jean van der Poel, ed., *Selections from the Smuts Papers* (Cambridge, 1973),
vi. 534.

against Japan, the United States would be in a better position to determine the future not only of the Japanese colonial empire but also of the European colonies occupied by the Japanese. This strategy suited the officials of the State Department who wanted to set the terms of European reoccupation. To get the colonies back, the Dutch and French, at the very least, would have to agree to self-government and eventual independence.

So far as the British were concerned, there is much truth in the view of Chester Wilmot that, for the officials of the State Department and for Roosevelt, it was the case of an enlightened son and a wayward father.[29] With considerable pro-British sentiment, members of the State Department conceded that the British pursued their colonial policy with a sense of progress and humanity which distinguished them from the Europeans. Nevertheless the British Empire was still an *Empire* with all of the inherent evils of European colonialism. It had to be reformed. The pace for self-government and measures for education, health, and welfare had to be accelerated. One specific way of ensuring progress in the colonies was to make the colonial regimes accountable to an international organization in which the United States would have a major voice. Thus the doctrine of trusteeship should be applied as universally as possible. The officials of the State Department logically saw that if they placed the territories of the former Italian colonial empire under international supervision, they would have to do the same for the islands of the Japanese Empire. Here the State Department came into head-on collision with the military. The Joint Chiefs of Staff absolutely opposed any form of international supervision over the Japanese mandated islands. When Roosevelt died in April 1945, he was holding the lid on one of the most explosive controversies within the American government.

To what extent can one generalize about American motives? What is the nature of the evidence? To take Roosevelt as an example, until the opening of the wartime archives historians have had to rely in large part on the account of Roosevelt's ideas about the colonial question given by his son, Elliott, in a book published in 1946, *As He Saw It*. As historical evidence the book is unsatisfactory. It is written in the tone of gossip

[29] Chester Wilmot, *The Struggle for Europe* (New York, 1952), p. 633.

and melodrama. Churchill glowers and bites his cigar and
de Gaulle gives wordless grunts. On a major point of importance
for the colonial question, Elliott injects the theme of colonial
liberation into the talks at the time of the signing of the Atlantic
Charter when, by all other accounts, it was not discussed.[30]
In general Roosevelt is portrayed as believing that the future
threat to the world's peace would not come from Russia but
from the European colonial powers, especially Britain.[31] It
clearly is important to establish whether or not Roosevelt
believed this, and, if he did, why he held these views.

In 1952 Sir Norman Angell, a lifelong student of the causes
of war and one with a particular interest in Anglo-American
relations, addressed himself precisely to those questions. His
views are intrinsically valuable on the question of American
motive as well as illuminating in regard to Roosevelt. As he
had done in *The Great Illusion* published in 1910, Angell pondered the reasons why rational men could not stop the drift
towards war. He wrote about tragic misunderstanding and
moral misconceptions which had produced catastrophic results
during the Second World War. Churchill's grand strategy,
according to Angell, could be summed up by stating that the
military situation at the end of the war should enable the
western Allies to block the expansion of Soviet Russia. Roosevelt, in Angell's view, had opposed this strategy. The President
of the United States, to whom the British owed more than to
any other foreign statesman, held suspicions about the British
Empire rather than about Russia. Angell quoted a review essay
by Arthur M. Schlesinger, Jr., of *As He Saw It* in support of
this interpretation:

The thesis of this curious and lively little book is that Franklin

[30] See below, ch. 6.
[31] This interpretation tends to fall in line with that of some of the leading British
critics of the book, and it is possible that, because of Elliot's melodramatic style,
it is somewhat too strong. In any case he was an Anglophobe (like others of the
military with whom he associated), but he was not an extreme Russophile. Nor
was F. D. R. By the war's end, Roosevelt and other Americans probably were
thinking of their own country as replacing the British Empire as a global power.
Yet they and their post-war successors always viewed this prospect with considerable ambivalence. For Roosevelt's concern to sustain Britain as a world power,
despite his anti-colonial sentiments, see Martin J. Sherwin, *A World Destroyed: the
Atomic Bomb and the Grand Alliance* (New York, 1975), p. 123. I am indebted to James
E. King for extended discussions of these points.

Roosevelt, anticipating a mortal struggle between Great Britain and the Soviet Union, regarded Britain as much the greater menace to the world in which he believed. . . . He reports—in direct quotes —the President's consistent and detailed suspicions of British perfidy. Churchill figures as combined buffoon and villain, endlessly scheming—generally to the detached amusement of the President and his son—to divert the United States from the war against Germany to the war against Russia. Hearing the British military and naval leaders on board the 'Augusta', Elliott found himself wondering— this was before Pearl Harbor—'whether it was the British Empire's purpose to see the Nazis and Russians cancel each other out, while Britain grew strong'.[32]

Angell pointed out that one of the most perceptive contemporary observers of the war, Chester Wilmot, also concurred generally in Elliott's interpretation.[33]

Scholars investigating Roosevelt's anti-colonial attitude have also found that, though Elliott may have been occasionally inaccurate (as in the case of the colonial issue at the time of the Atlantic Charter), his general account holds true.[34] The opening of the wartime archives and private papers now gives further and ample confirmation that Elliott Roosevelt's account is essentially correct. Roosevelt did indeed believe in the danger of British power, as did many of his military and political advisers. How can this be explained? According to Norman Angell:

How could a man like Franklin Roosevelt, of all people, come to hold the views he did? His view was that of so many of his countrymen who differentiate sharply between the British people and the British government. The British people are regarded generally as decent, honest, law-abiding, freedom-loving. But their government is represented usually as a class or caste rule, maintaining, often against the will of the people, a world tyranny compounded of

---

[32] Quoted in Sir Norman Angell, 'A Re-Interpretation of Empire', *United Empire*, 43. 5 (Sept.–Oct. 1952). Schlesinger's review appeared in the *Nation*, 2 Nov. 1946.

[33] 'Some critics of this book [*As He Saw It*] have suggested that it misrepresents Franklin Roosevelt's ideas, but it is abundantly clear from the Memoirs of Cordell Hull, the Hopkins Papers and other first-hand American sources that Elliot was not an inaccurate reporter of the views his father held on the colonial question.' Wilmot, *Struggle for Europe*, p. 633, n. 1.

[34] See especially Willard Range, *Franklin D. Roosevelt's World Order* (Athens, Georgia, 1959); and Foster Rhea Dulles and Gerald E. Ridinger, 'The Anti-Colonial Policies of Franklin D. Roosevelt,' *Political Science Quarterly*, 70. 1 (March 1955).

imperialism, colonialism and power politics which violates all political morals and, in particular, denies the elementary human rights of all peoples to be independent like the United States.[35]

The dichotomy between the benevolent nature of the British people and the vicious system of government might have been made between any people and their government, but during the war it seemed especially true for the British. The British Empire was the foreign Empire that Americans knew best of all. Angell's interpretation catches the moral conviction of the Americans fighting the war in part as an anti-imperialist crusade.

There is a further explanation. R. F. Harrod, in his biography of John Maynard Keynes, writes about one persistent American belief:

According to this myth, the British are a wily and cunning people, diabolically astute in international finance, the British Empire always occupying the first place in their thoughts and plans, determined at all costs to advance its interests, and easily able to make rings round anyone who would oppose their Machiavellian projects. This mythology exerted some influence during the Second World War. . . .[36]

Harrod was certainly accurate in saying that some Americans believed that economic imperialism motivated the British, and, more specifically, that the British sought to increase the economic autarchy of the British Empire and Commonwealth by strengthening the Ottawa tariff system. To some Englishmen the opposite seemed true. The Americans appeared to be taking the opportunity of the war to create a new American Empire, mainly at British expense. Here then are two central and basic interpretations, both of which are rooted in the historiography of 'imperialism'. Within the context of this volume, two key historical works immediately come to mind which illuminate the general problem. Shortly after the close of the First World War, Leonard Woolf published *Empire and Commerce in Africa*, a savage indictment of British officials who often unwittingly espoused the principles of economic imperialism.[37] In the historical literature of the British Empire, Woolf's work

[35] Angell, 'A Re-Interpretation of Empire', p. 255.
[36] R. F. Harrod, *The Life of John Maynard Keynes* (London, 1951), p. 539.
[37] The book was published by the Labour Research Department, no date, but 1920. There is no adequate scholarly appraisal of it.

stands as a classic inquiry into the economic springs of British policy, and its themes are as relevant for the British statesmen of the Second World War as for the First. The other work is by Gabriel Kolko, whose *Politics of War* was published in 1968.[38] This work also may be seen in the tradition of John A. Hobson writing against the background of the Boer War. For what reasons are wars fought? In part for profit? Were the public speeches of the wartime leaders at variance with the true motivation? To what extent was American motivation economic? To what extent was it strategic, as for example in the case of the Pacific islands? Can a distinction be drawn between strategic and economic imperialism? If so, does an examination of specific strategic problems throw light on the general nature of economic imperialism? To ask the key question for the present work, how important was the economic element in trusteeship, especially in relation to the ethical factor?

The purpose of the following sections will be to examine these questions in relation to three major colonial issues of the war: (1) the future of the French colonies, especially Indo-China, (2) the disposal of the Italian colonies, and (3) the fate of the Japanese colonial empire. These commentaries are also intended as an introduction to some of the main themes of the book, and they will include a brief analysis of the bureaucratic business of making decisions within the American and British governments.

Although the following discussion will be mainly concerned with the economic element in trusteeship (and with the notion of 'strategic' imperialism), a word needs to be said about one prerequisite in estimating the motive, or cause, of imperialism in general. It is essential to distinguish between what men *thought* was happening and what was *actually* occurring. In retrospect it is clear that the system of Imperial Preference established by the Ottawa agreements of 1932 was not an

[38] Gabriel Kolko, *The Politics of War: The World and United States Foreign Policy, 1943–1945* (New York, 1968). For a sympathetic and important assessment of the issues at stake in Kolko's work, see Barrington Moore, 'Of Predatory Democracy', in *Reflections on the Causes of Human Misery and upon Certain Proposals to Eliminate Them* (Boston, 1970). For comment on other radical historians dealing with these issues see especially Robert W. Tucker, *The Radical Left and American Foreign Policy* (Baltimore, 1971); and Richard M. Abrams, 'United States Intervention Abroad', *American Historical Review*, 79. 1 (February 1974).

effective or comprehensive means of achieving Empire self-sufficiency.[39] A few stalwarts of autarchy saw this at the time. L. S. Amery (who served as Secretary of State for India and Burma during the war) not only thought that the Ottawa provisions were insufficient but also believed that the very existence of the British Empire would depend on the British being able to protect the trade and commerce of the colonies and Dominions from an economic takeover by the United States. On the American side, Cordell Hull and Sumner Welles regarded the question of Imperial Preference as one of the vital issues of the war, and, if their own words are to be believed, a threat to the future peace of the world. They wanted 'Free Trade' and the 'Open Door', clichés meaning, in practice, equality of economic opportunity, and access to colonial raw materials.[40] Amery wanted to keep this door closed and if possible to lock it even tighter. He once commented that he would prefer the 'New Order of Hitler' to the 'Free Trade' of Cordell Hull. Such were the flights of rhetoric.

No doubt some Englishmen seriously believed that the United States stayed out of the war until 1941 in order to be able to pick up the pieces of the British Empire, just as some Americans suspected that beneath the idealism of British war aims lurked the familiar beast of British economic imperialism. For those actually making the decisions about economic policy, there is a good deal of truth in the words of Keynes's biographer: 'All turned on whether adequate measures could be devised . . . to create a prosperous world, in which discrimination could be disposed with.'[41] At Bretton Woods and later during the period of the Anglo-American loan, both sides displayed a keen sense of economic self-interest which enabled critics to see the rise of a new American informal Empire, or to hear the death

---

[39] See Ian M. Drummond, *Imperial Economic Policy, 1917–1939* (London, 1974); and an especially important critique, Max Beloff, 'The Political Blind Spot of Economists', *Government and Opposition* 10. 1 (Winter 1975).

[40] Here again the restrictions to raw materials in British colonies were fewer and less effective than many American observers believed. For the American response to the various economic problems of the British, see especially Warren F. Kimball, 'Lend-Lease and the Open Door: The Temptation of British Opulence, 1937–1942', *Political Science Quarterly*, 86. 2 (June 1971); also Alfred E. Eckes, Jr., 'Open Door Expansionism Reconsidered: The World War II Experience', *Journal of American History*, 59. 4 (March 1973).

[41] Harrod, *Keynes*, p. 517.

rattle of British Imperialism. Such are the dialectics that have to be borne in mind in attempting to get at the economic element in trusteeship.

For the colonial issues of substance dealt with in this book, there are two developments in the wartime experience that are of fundamental importance. (1) *The depletion of British economic resources.* By the end of the war Britain had overseas debts of £3,355 million.[42] There was a huge deficit in balance of payments. Though the problem of the wartime debt never directly impinged on the negotiations about the future of the colonies, British planners had good reason to fear that it might. (2) *The relative decline of British power in relation to that of the United States and Russia.*[43] This was a theme especially apparent in the deliberations of the Strategic Survey Committee of the Joint Chiefs of Staff and their counterparts in London, though to the latter the significance seemed more debatable. Did the advent of air power signify the erosion of Britain's traditional basis of power at sea? Men caught up in the events of the war had different answers to such questions. They had varying perceptions of the gigantic transformation. The reactions will become apparent in the discussion of the specific problems they faced.

The advantage of case studies is that the historian can reconstruct the economic and political ingredients as they were seen at the time by those making decisions. In the view of the theorists of economic imperialism, there may be disadvantages in selecting the cases of the French, Italian, and Japanese colonies. On the whole these were hardly areas where 'capitalism' could expect to extract a profit. The same could be

[42] For the cost of the war to Britain, see W. K. Hancock and M. M. Gowing, *British War Economy* (London, 1949), ch. xix. For the wartime economic negotiations the standard account is by Richard N. Gardner, *Sterling–Dollar Diplomacy: Anglo-American Collaboration in the Reconstruction of Multilateral Trade* (Oxford, 1956); see also the recent major work by Alfred E. Eckes, Jr., *A Search for Solvency: Bretton Woods and the International Monetary System, 1941–1971* (Austin, 1975).

[43] It might be noted that, though American leaders did explain and forecast Britain's post-war decline economically and militarily, very few appear to have detected the decisive change in British *values*. See Harold and Margaret Sprout, ' "Retreat from World Power", Processes and Consequences of Readjustment', *World Politics* 15. 4 (July 1963); and 'The Dilemma of Rising Demands and Insufficient Resources', ibid. 20. 4 (July 1968). The latter essay especially reflects the changing conditions (including the rising costs of armaments) that resulted in Britain's becoming a welfare state. See A. J. P. Taylor's comment in the preface to this volume for a succinct statement of the transformation.

said of tropical Africa in the late nineteenth century. 'It is easier to acquit nineteenth-century bankers of unlawful desires in the Sahara than anywhere else except at the North and the South Pole.'[44] With the desert wastes of the Italian colonies and the barren atolls of the Japanese islands, the imperialists might truly be said now to be scraping the bottom of the barrel.[45] In fact this increases rather than diminishes the value of these case studies for the illumination of the particular type of imperialism designated 'strategic'.[46] Roosevelt once said to Churchill: 'the British would take land anywhere in the world even if it were only rock or a sand bar.'[47] Churchill might have reversed the accusation, saying that the Americans were now attempting the same thing indirectly.[48] Strategic 'trusteeship' as a cloak for American expansion is a theme that runs throughout the British wartime documents.

[44] Victor Kiernan, *Marxism and Imperialism* (London, 1974), p. 82. By 'theorists of economic imperialism', I mean those historians who are concerned above all with such questions, in Leonard Woolf's words, of economic control through political means. How did the men of the Second World War era regard that proposition? By directing the discussion to 'the economic element in trusteeship' it is hoped that points of interest can be added to the debate about the nature of Imperialism without flogging 'the decrepit beast of economic imperialism' (Ronald Robinson's phrase) and, at the same time, without ignoring some of the questions raised, e.g. by Harry Magdoff and Bob Sutcliffe. Harry Magdoff's *The Age of Imperialism* (New York, 1966) is one of the key works by an American Marxist dealing with questions of expansion with which the present volume is also concerned. Bob Sutcliffe, in a lucid and fair-minded commentary in (eds.) Roger Owen and Bob Sutcliffe, *Studies in the Theory of Imperialism* (London, 1972), examines questions of concern to both Marxist and non-Marxist historians. For an example of the way in which the two sides can have meaningful, if rather sulphurous, exchanges on the subject of Imperialism, see [Eric Stokes], 'Comrades All' (unpublished Cambridge History Faculty Commonwealth Seminar paper, December 1975). For a review of the recent literature, see especially Ralph Austen, 'Economic Imperialism Revisited', *Journal of Modern History*, 47. 3 (September 1975).

[45] John Gallagher and Ronald Robinson, 'The Imperialism of Free Trade', *Economic History Review*, 2nd ser. 6. 1 (1953).

[46] As David S. Landes points out in similar cases in 'Some Thoughts on the Nature of Economic Imperialism', *Journal of Economic History*, 21. 4 (1961).

[47] Edward R. Stettinius, Jr., *Roosevelt and the Russians: the Yalta Conference* (Garden City, New York, 1949), p. 237.

[48] Churchill's suspicion is similar to the argument of 'Open Door Imperialism' put forward by Williams A. Williams in *The Tragedy of American Diplomacy* (New York, 1951); see also Lloyd C. Gardner, *Economic Aspects of New Deal Diplomacy* (Madison, Wis., 1964), especially ch. 9, 'America and the Colonial Empires'. For a balanced interpretation concerned more with the political issues of the war, John Lewis Gaddis, *The United States and the Origins of the Cold War, 1941–1947* (New York, 1972); and a work of lasting value, William H. McNeill, *America, Britain, and Russia: Their Co-operation and Conflict, 1941–1946* (New York, 1953).

2

THE FUTURE OF SOUTH-EAST ASIA AND THE QUESTION OF THE FRENCH COLONIES

FOR General de Gaulle as for Churchill, the question of the future of the colonies was a touchstone of the post-war world. The preservation of the colonial empires formed a bond between them. There was, however, an important fundamental that distinguished the French colonial empire, at least theoretically, from the British Empire and Commonwealth. To de Gaulle as to most Frenchmen, Free French and pro-Vichy alike, there existed *an indissoluble link* between the metropole and the colonies.[1] Roosevelt was keenly aware of the attitude of the French towards their colonies, which he described as one of a landowner towards his property. He asked his son Elliott:

> *How* do they [the colonies] belong to France? Why does Morocco, inhabited by Moroccans, belong to France? Or take Indo-China. The Japanese control that colony now. Why was it a cinch for the Japanese to conquer that land? The native Indo-Chinese have been so flagrantly downtrodden that they thought to themselves: Anything must be better than to live under French colonial rule![2]

With a sense of outrage, Roosevelt denounced the oppressive colonial rule by France, a nation he held generally in low

[1] The key work for French colonial problems in this period is D. Bruce Marshall, *The French Colonial Myth and Constitution-Making in the Fourth Republic* (New Haven, 1973); see also especially Raoul Girardet, *L'Idée coloniale en France de 1871 à 1962* (Paris, 1972); and Brian Weinstein, *Éboué* (New York, 1972).

[2] *As He Saw It*, p. 115. On American policy see Gary R. Hess, 'Franklin Roosevelt and Indochina', *Journal of American History*, 59.2 (Sept. 1972); also Edward R. Drachman, *United States Policy toward Vietnam, 1940–1945* (Rutherford, N.J., 1970). I have greatly benefited from an unpublished paper by Walter LaFeber, which has now appeared as 'Roosevelt, Churchill, and Indochina: 1942–45', *American Historical Review*, 80. 5 (Dec. 1975). See also Christopher Thorne, 'Indochina and Anglo-American Relations, 1942–1945', *Pacific Historical Review*, 45. 1 (Feb. 1976); R. E. M. Irving, *The First Indochina War: French and American Policy, 1945–54* (London, 1975); and Akira Iriye, *The Cold War in Asia* (Englewood Cliffs, New Jersey, 1974).

esteem. Decadent is not too strong a word to sum up his estimate of the people who not only collaborated with the Germans
in Europe but also gave the Japanese the airfields in northern
Indo-China in 1940. To Roosevelt the French were corrupt.
France could no longer be counted among the great powers.
These views coloured his ideas about the future of the French
colonies, about which he held stronger feelings than any of
the other European colonial empires. In order to encourage
resistance against the Nazis, Roosevelt in public speeches would
assure the French people that their empire would be returned
to them; but in his private conversations with his political and
military advisers, and with foreign leaders, including Churchill,
Stalin, and Chiang Kai-shek, he made it explicitly clear that
the French colonies, and Indo-China in particular, would not
be restored to France but placed under international trusteeship. His plans were no secret to de Gaulle, who, like Churchill,
viewed the scheme for trusteeship as a disguise for American
expansion.

For his part Roosevelt nourished an abiding distrust of de
Gaulle. When the President, shortly before his death in 1945,
conceded that Indo-China and other French colonies should
be restored to France, his contempt for French colonialism had
not abated. What had changed was Roosevelt's optimism about
the 'Big Four'. By then it was becoming more clear that China,
for example, would not emerge as a great power to assist in
the business of trusteeship. He also faced the practical problem
of how to prevent de Gaulle from eventually re-establishing
French control in Indo-China. In yielding to the reality of the
situation, Roosevelt was also influenced by the hope that
France, like the other colonial powers, would encourage self-
government and other measures that in time would foster independence. In the realm of French colonial affairs, the
decisions made at the Brazzaville Conference of January–
February 1944 symbolized, at least in American eyes, the
progress already made by the Dutch and the British. The
declaration of liberal intent did much to influence American
attitudes. Did the rhetoric conform to the reality? In both the
British and American wartime archives there are assessments of
French aims. Were the French in fact motivated by principles
of 'trusteeship'? The British? And, not least, the Americans?

An examination of the evidence will at least help to put the elements of trusteeship into the perspective seen by the British and the Americans at the time.

One of the minor revelations of the wartime archives is the extent to which the Dutch, and not the British and still less the French, took the lead in anticipating the possible consequences of American intervention in South-East Asia. In June 1942, only a few months after the Japanese invasion, the Dutch Colonial Minister, H. Van Mook, paid a visit to Lord Cranborne, the Colonial Secretary. The Dutchman pointed out that the fate of the European colonies under Japanese occupation would be inseparably linked, and much would depend on the American attitude. The Dutch in fact were extremely apprehensive. According to Cranborne's record of the conversation:

He [Van Mook] wanted to counter the vigorous propaganda which was going on in the United States and in China to the effect that recent events had shown the Dutch—and the British—not only to have been Imperialists but bungling Imperialists at that, whose day was now over.

He evidently thought that, taking a long view, the danger from the United States and China was far greater than that from Japan. They would come to the Peace Conference claiming to have won the war in the Pacific, and would demand a say in the post-war set up over the whole of that area. He wanted to forestall their interference, so far as the Netherlands East Indies were concerned.[3]

The Dutch therefore proposed to announce that the Netherlands East Indies in the future would have equal status with the Netherlands itself. So it transpired.

In December 1942 Queen Wilhelmina proclaimed that the political union between the Netherlands and the Netherlands East Indies would be reconstructed 'on the solid foundation of complete partnership'. With emphasis on 'national evolution', the Dutch would create a Commonwealth in which 'the Netherlands, Indonesia, Surinam and Curacao will participate, with complete self-reliance and freedom of conduct for each part regarding its internal affairs, but with the readiness to render mutual assistance'. Officials in the State Department interpreted the declaration as a response to American

[3] Memorandum by Cranborne, 12 June 1942, CO 825/35/55104.

anti-colonial criticism, and perhaps as a move towards greater autonomy (though they also noted that the Dutch were silent on the central questions of greater native participation in the government and foreign access to colonial raw materials).[4] Roosevelt greeted the development as an indication of a European power at least attempting to improve the colonial relationship. Throughout the rest of the war he held out to the British and the French the example of Holland. He would point out that the Dutch were even trying to educate the head-hunters of New Guinea. The Dutch thus managed to tell Roosevelt what he wanted to hear. Roosevelt made astute use of it, urging the British and the French to march in the same direction.

If the Dutch appeased the Americans by announcing plans for reconstruction in the Netherlands East Indies, would there be an advantage for the British to do the same for Malaya? If the French refused to reform, might there be a danger at the other extreme that the Americans would attempt to resolve the future of South-East Asia by themselves—and for themselves? As far as 'Trusteeship' is concerned, there did exist in British official circles the suspicion that the Americans would attempt to use the war to their economic advantage—in the words of a key Colonial Office official concerned with the future of the Far East and South-East Asia, Gerard Gent, the head of the Eastern Department, there could be no doubt that the question of raw materials in Malaya and the Dutch Indies was 'responsible for a good deal of hopeful thinking in New York and Washington'. Gent went on to defend the British record in this regard, and from his vantage point in the Colonial Office it is important to note that he was not unduly alarmed about the revival of the old question of Anglo-American trade rivalry in Asia. 'Certainly in such matters as freedom of access to the raw materials of Malaya, or freedom of the port of Hong Kong, the Americans can have no serious grumble at our record, nor need they be apprehensive of our post-war policy.'[5]

---

[4] See especially the analysis prepared by the Division of Far Eastern Affairs, 'Post-War Status of the Netherlands Indies', 2 Feb. 1943, USSD 840.50.1351.

[5] Minute by Gent, 29 June 1942, CO 825/35/55104. For Gent and some of the problems with which he was concerned see A. J. Stockwell, 'Colonial Planning during World War II: The Case of Malaya', *Journal of Imperial and Commonwealth History*, 2. 3 (May 1974). For the question of the Far Eastern trade during this

If 'economic imperialism' suggests in part the attempt to secure markets and raw materials, then it came as no surprise to the officials of the Colonial Office, for example, that the United States would continue the quest for overseas profit and resources, perhaps under the guise of internationalization.

As they debated 'trusteeship' and the ethics of empire, British officials readily acknowledged the economic basis of the British Imperialism. A revealing exchange on this point once took place between Ashley Clarke, the head of the Far Eastern Department at the Foreign Office, and Stanley Hornbeck, the Adviser on Far Eastern Affairs at the State Department. 'I know that some American critics', Clarke wrote to Hornbeck, 'think that the British Empire exists in order to keep the holders of rubber, tin and oil shares in immense comfort in the West End of London; and I don't deny that we derive economic advantages from our system.'[6] Clarke found it ironic that officials of the two powers fighting for their survival against Germany and Japan could harbour mutual suspicions of economic imperialism. As he had pointed out on a previous occasion, it was 'economic nationalism of the most improvident character' that in part had caused the war.[7] It was a common enemy. Officials such as Clarke and Hornbeck saw a clear distinction between themselves as civil servants and the private financiers whose actions and excessive profits should be deplored. Legitimate economic gain was not in question. Some of the staunchest opponents of 'economic imperialism' (and upholders of 'trusteeship') were the career civil servants.

In any discussion of motives of imperialism (in the sense of policies pursued and not an economic system) a good deal turns on the individuals chosen as examples. In England during the

period, Paul A. Varg, *The Closing of the Door: Sino-American Relations, 1936–1946* (East Lansing, Mich., 1973).

[6] Clarke to Hornbeck, 25 Nov. 1943, Hornbeck Papers Box 118.

[7] Clarke to Hornbeck, 23 Nov. 1942, ibid. In this letter Clarke also protested against the interpretation given by a former British official, Simon Harcourt-Smith, about the meaning of the war for Britain's Far Eastern Empire. Among other things, Clarke believed that Harcourt-Smith should have concentrated on the record of Japanese imperialism 'rather than dilating with relish on the extent to which "whisky and syphilis" followed in the wake of the British raj and on the extent to which British policy towards China was dictated by old [British] China hands "hiccoughing with suffused faces at the longest bar in the world"' (see Simon Harcourt-Smith, *Japanese Frenzy*, London, 1942). Hornbeck noted on this letter, 'Perhaps the "Lady doth protest too much"?'

war a strong case could be made for Leo Amery as one of the pre-eminent 'Imperialists'. Of all British statesmen Amery waged the fiercest battle for Imperial Preference.[8] He viewed the preservation and bolstering of the economic system of the British Empire as one of the essential stakes of the war. To him the war was a continuation of the Great War and he had essentially the same goals in mind: the strengthening of Imperial lines of communication (this time making a greater effort to secure the airways as well as the sea lanes), the tightening of Imperial Preference, and the bulwarking of crucial points of Imperial Defence.

To Amery the disaster at Singapore indicated the necessity for proper fortification in the future. When he learned that Roosevelt might try to create an international 'trusteeship' base at Singapore, Amery indignantly responded:

[T]he President seems to have assumed that the old situation cannot possibly be restored in Malaya and that some sort of joint trusteeship of Great Britain, China and the United States should take its place. . . . I should have thought . . . that Singapore is going to be even more essential to us as a base after the war than before, that the war has shown the necessity for holding the whole of Malaya effectively as a protection to Singapore, and that we mean to hold it more firmly than ever. As for joint trusteeship, we might consider that when the United States are prepared to concede to us a joint trusteeship over the Panama Canal and the adjoining Central American States.[9]

One of the principal British war aims, according to Amery,

---

[8] Amery wrote in 1945: 'Imperial Preference is a subject which we are [not] even prepared to discuss with any outsider. That is the key of our own household which we cannot hand over to strangers. That is our birthright which we cannot sell for any mess of pottage.' *America and Imperial Preference* (pamphlet reporting a speech made by Amery at a meeting of the Institute of Export at the Royal Empire Society, 2 Oct. 1945).

[9] Amery to Cranborne, 26 Aug. 1942, CO 825/35/55104. The other Empire Crusader was Lord Beaverbrook, who, according to A. J. P. Taylor, took an even fiercer stand than Amery: 'Beaverbrook offered a clear . . . policy he had preached before the war. The sterling bloc should be maintained as a world-wide trading community. It should be sustained by imperial preference. . . . In this matter Beaverbrook stood virtually alone with no supporters except Leo Amery and [Brendan] Bracken. The economists led by Keynes were all against him, and Churchill, understanding nothing of the subject, came down on the American and supposedly Free Trade side.' A. J. P. Taylor, *Beaverbrook* (New York, 1972), p. 563.

should be to ensure that one form of imperialism would not be substituted for another:

> After all, smashing Hitler is only a means to the essential end of preserving the British Empire and all it stands for in the world. It will be no consolation to suggest that Hitler should be replaced by Stalin, Chiang kai-Shek or even an American President if we cease to exercise our power and influence in the world.[10]

Amery was among the foremost of British statesmen who not only ranked Roosevelt as an enemy of the Empire but also attached paramount importance to the economic factor. Above all he was an economic nationalist. But to stop there would do Amery a great injustice. He also believed in the Imperial mission. To repeat his own words, he worked to preserve the British Empire 'and all it stands for in the world'. During the Second World War Amery continued to be the true disciple of Lord Milner: 'What I think is needed to-day more than anything else', he wrote in August 1942, 'is a vigorous reaffirmation of our faith in our destiny as an Empire and of our determination to make good that destiny afterwards, regarding the war merely as a step in the process.'[11]

It should be said at once that not all British statesmen shared Amery's views by any means. Within the Cabinet, the leader of the Labour Party, Clement Attlee, protested against the holding of colonies for the financial advantage which 'mainly accrued to a capitalist group'.[12] In the Labour tradition, he believed that colonies were an economic burden to the British electorate. Sovereignty could not be maintained in colonial territories without expenditures for defence. Defence meant armaments. Armaments led to wars. The alternative might be *the renunciation of national sovereignty in colonial areas and their development by a system of international administration*. These words were anathema to Leo Amery, who above all upheld the principle of British sovereignty. In the clash of views between Attlee and Amery can be seen two entirely different judgements about the value of colonies. They may be roughly called pre-war and post-war. According to Amery's pre-war outlook, colonies were a source of national power, profit, and prestige.

---

[10] Amery to Cranborne, 26 Aug. 1942.   [11] Ibid.
[12] Minutes of Ministerial Meeting, 11 Sept. 1942, CO 825/35/55104. For Attlee's further views in this regard, see below, ch. 11.

The post-war disposition, which had long antecedents in radical and Labour thought, on the whole held that colonies were a burden. In the words of John Strachey, after the war a Secretary of State for War (whose academic writings affirmed the value of Marx and Marxist assessments of imperialism), 'Exactly contrary to popular prejudice, a nation is likely to-day to be strong or weak in inverse ratio to her imperial possessions.'[13] In the wartime period of transition, both views were profoundly important. Within the government the older outlook tended to predominate. Not only did Churchill and Amery ardently espouse the value of colonies but two other high Tories also held posts of commanding importance in colonial affairs: Lord Cranborne (Colonial Secretary, 1942, Dominions Secretary, 1943–5), and Oliver Stanley (Colonial Secretary, 1942–5).

The policies of Lord Cranborne will be discussed below. He is mentioned here in relation to the economic element in trusteeship and the future of South-East Asia. Like his grandfather, the 3rd Marquess of Salisbury, the principal architect of the partition of the African continent, Cranborne had no affection whatever for the jobbers and freebooters who represented the seamy side of imperialism. He accepted his duties for the Colonies and the Dominions with the refined passion of an aristocrat whose responsibility for the Empire was almost a family concern. He was a Cecil. John Maynard Keynes once noted that in Cranborne's presence he felt the spirit of A. J. Balfour hovering near.[14] Balfour's views on economic imperialism in fact were similar to Cranborne's. At the close of the First World War, Balfour, then serving as Foreign Secretary, had remarked that much of his troubles as a public servant had arisen out of looking after the 'twopenny-halfpenny and very corrupt interests' of the petty imperialists.[15] The Cecils also considered themselves above the vulgar world of high finance.[16] They hardly fit into ringing generalizations about capitalistic exploitation, though no doubt Leonard Woolf was right when he observed that the 3rd Marquess, like

---

[13] John Strachey, *The End of Empire* (London, 1959), p. 194; quoted by Max Beloff, 'Empire and Nations', *Government and Opposition* 9. 4 (Autumn 1974), which contains a trenchant analysis of the two outlooks.

[14] Harrod, *Keynes*, p. 619.

[15] Quoted in Wm. Roger Louis, *Great Britain and Germany's Lost Colonies* (Oxford, 1967), pp. 127–8.   [16] See Kenneth Rose, *The Later Cecils* (London, 1975).

most statesmen of the time, allowed himself to be duped by promoters of chartered companies who argued that British capitalism in Africa would elevate the natives to a higher level of civilization. It is certainly true that Cranborne seldom questioned similar assumptions about the British Empire as a force for good in world affairs. He wrote in June 1942 about Britain's achievement in Asia:

[T]aken by and large, our record of administration is not one of which we need be ashamed. We created Singapore and Hong Kong, two of the greatest ports in the Pacific, out of nothing. We made of Malaya one of the richest and most vital producing areas of the world. We brought to her peoples law and order, happiness and prosperity. These are no mean achievements. Where we did fail was in giving them protection from Japan, and this criticism may equally be levelled against the Dutch and the Americans.[17]

On the question of defence against Japan, Cranborne differed fundamentally from Roosevelt's interpretation of French weakness in Indo-China being in part responsible for the catastrophe in the Far East. '[I]t is in fact the United States who have above all brought about the present situation in the Far East by their refusal to shoulder their responsibilities and co-operate with other nations in restraining Japan in the years before this war.'[18] Just as Roosevelt's view of history brought the conviction that the French colonies should not be restored to France, so Cranborne's lesson of the past influenced his estimate of the best future course. Like most other British statesmen, Cranborne was extremely sceptical about Roosevelt's proposal for a trusteeship regime in Indo-China.

Colonel Oliver Stanley ('Colonel' because of his military service in the First World War) was the second son of the Earl of Derby, a fact that impressed Roosevelt. Sumner Welles, American Under Secretary of State, in November 1942 described Stanley as the 'most narrow, bigoted, reactionary Tory' he had met in his official career.[19] Charles Taussig, Roosevelt's confidant

[17] Minute by Cranborne, 14 July 1942, later expanded into a letter to his colleagues. See below, ch. 11.   [18] Cranborne, loc. cit.

[19] Memorandum by Charles Taussig recounting a conversation with Welles, 11 November 1942, Taussig Papers. This was written at the time of Stanley's appointment as Colonial Secretary, which Welles interpreted as 'a clear indication that Churchill had decided to dominate post-war planning and it would be along reactionary lines'.

on colonial questions, described Stanley as 'hard-boiled', meaning in this case a mixture of realism and cynicism which marked
his true personality. Outwardly Stanley was urbane, witty,
and gracious. Some of his friends regarded him as a possible
Tory Prime Minister.[20] He was a realist, one who could look
dispassionately at such emotional issues as the future of Hong
Kong and ask whether the British post-war position would be
'tenable or at any rate valuable with a bitterly hostile China'.[21]
If calculations of economic gain and the dismissal of more lofty
motivation are the mark of a cynic, then Stanley was a cynic
par excellence in regard to American imperialism. He regarded
the talk about 'trusteeship' as cant. To him the obvious hypocrisy of it was not only irritating but boring.[22] Stanley was
entirely convinced that the Americans would not be putting
forward 'trusteeship' proposals except for the economic benefit
and strategic advantage of the United States.

These remarks should not be interpreted to mean that
Stanley was cynical about his responsibilities at the Colonial
Office. On the contrary, he regarded his paramount job as
Colonial Secretary as protecting the true interests of the
colonial subjects from meddlesome American schemes such
as international trusteeship and capitalist exploitation alike.
These were only two of the danger points. He also perceived
a threat from within the government. 'I suppose the F.O. were
horrified', Stanley once wrote sarcastically about the problem
of the French colonies and the general future of the Far East,
'. . . that a colonial policy should be directed in the first place to
the benefit of the Colonies & only after that to the appeasement
of U.S.A.'[23]

An examination of the attitudes of the British bureaucracy
can help to throw light on the question of trusteeship and
colonial appeasement. Stanley detected a disposition of the
Foreign Office to feel slightly embarrassed about the Colonial

---

[20] Historians however have not been so generous in their assessment. Maurice
Cowling has recently described him as 'This vast, sly figure . . . [who] had created
a sybaritic, secular Conservatism which differed markedly from that of his eccen-
tric grandfather.' *The Impact of Hitler: British Politics and British Policy 1933–1940*
(Cambridge, 1975), p. 334.

[21] Minute by Stanley, 23 Aug. 1943, CO 825/42/53104.

[22] See e.g. memorandum by Stanley, 18 Apr. 1944, CO 323/1877/9057B.

[23] Minute by Stanley, 8 Aug. 1944, CO 825/42/55104.

Empire and to make concessions to the Americans and others, as if bending over backwards to prove that the British were not 'economic imperialists'. This was a traditional view of the 'official mind' of the Colonial Office, which had a long memory of the 'supine' or 'spineless' policy of the Foreign Office. According to Gerard Gent, Assistant Under-Secretary and former head of the Eastern Department:

There is a kind of defeatism in the Foreign Office Far Eastern outlook which is not a new phenomenon. They suffer from what to my mind is a quite fatal lack of confidence themselves in our position in the Colonies, and they seem to be fascinated by the belief that H[is] M[ajesty's] G[overnment] must be subservient to the supposed American policy of preventing the restoration of British sovereignty in Malaya, Hong Kong, and possibly Burma too.[24]

Gent went on to point out the need for vigilance. Otherwise Foreign Office 'appeasement' might lead to the end of Britain's Far Eastern Empire rather than merely a lapse in British authority caused by the temporary Japanese occupation. 'It is certain that the Foreign Office need stimulating,' Gent wrote, 'in order that their phobia in these urgent practical questions of the formulation of post war policy in the Far East, including the restoration of British Authority in Malaya and Hong Kong, may be removed.'[25] About the mentality of the Foreign Office regarding colonies as pawns in the game of international politics, Gent later observed: 'our attitude towards British territories— fully-going communities and concerns at the moment when our military weakness cut them off from us—must be . . . based on what we believe to be right rather than solely on what would be best moves from the point of view of foreign politics.'[26] This was an attitude shared by virtually all officials in the Colonial Office. In the words of Sir George Gater, the Permanent Under-Secretary, when the question of the French colonies was coming

[24] Minute by Gent, 17 June 1942, CO 825/35/55104. Gent himself had been mainly responsible for a proposal to keep an open mind on the question of Hong Kong, arguing that unless they kept a flexible position the United States or China might force the issue of restoration and the British might find themselves powerless to prevent it. Lord Cranborne however took a hard line: 'we should not decide now to lower our flag there after the war. To put it on no higher plane, that would be to surrender one of our main bargaining counters before the negotiation begins.' Minute by Cranborne, 14 July 1942, ibid.

[25] Minute by Gent, 17 June 1942, ibid.

[26] Minute by Gent, 1 July 1942, ibid.

to a head in mid-1944: 'If, in formulating our policy, we are to be governed by the caprices of the U.S.A., we shall never develop a policy worthy of the name.'[27] In the case of the French colonies, an international regime as urged by the Americans definitely would not be to the advantage of the inhabitants, as amply proved to Colonial Office satisfaction by the unhappy history of the condominium in the New Hebrides. International trusteeship in Indo-China furthermore might give the Americans ideas about international control over British colonies. Therefore the Colonial Office would resist appeasement of the United States at any cost.

On the question of Indo-China, the stand of the Foreign Office was not as wobbly as the Colonial Office suspected. This may be demonstrated by the response to Roosevelt's pronouncements at a crucial time, when he returned from the Cairo and Teheran conferences in December 1943. Having discussed colonial issues with Chiang Kai-shek and Stalin, and having largely circumvented Churchill, Roosevelt was stirred up about the future of the colonial world. He summoned the representatives of China, Turkey, Persia, Egypt, Russia, and Britain. He told them he was working 'very hard' to prevent Indo-China being restored to France. According to the British Ambassador reporting Roosevelt's words:

[The] poor Indo-Chinese had nothing done for them during a hundred years of French responsibility, no education, no welfare. They were just as poor as they had ever been, and there was no reason why this state of affairs should be allowed to go on. His idea was that the Indo-Chinese who were not yet ready for elective institutions of their own, should be placed under some United Nations trustee-ship whose duty it would be to educate them on towards the ability to govern themselves.[28]

This was, to say the least, a sweeping indictment and drastic solution. A Foreign Office official observed:

President Roosevelt is suffering from the same form of megalomania which characterised the late President Wilson and Mr. Lloyd George (the latter to a lesser extent) at the end of the last war and proved the former's undoing. . . . If Indo-China is not

27 Minute by Gater, 17 June 1944, CO 825/42/55104.
28 Halifax to Eden, No. 5714, 19 Dec. 1943, FO 371/35921.

restored to France on the ground that 'the poor Indo-Chinese' have no education and no welfare (I have never heard that the Indo-Chinese were any more unhappy than the share-croppers of the Southern United States), the Dutch and ourselves may later on be told that the oil resources of the Netherlands East Indies and Borneo have never been properly developed, nor the rubber resources of Malaya, that the natives are insufficiently educated according to Washington standards and that these territories must be placed under United Nations trusteeship (perhaps with United States oil and rubber controllers).[29]

Thus the Foreign Office clearly identified the economic element in Roosevelt's trusteeship policy.

Was there substance to Roosevelt's charge that the French had done nothing to improve the colony they had occupied for a hundred years? According to Geoffrey Hudson, a scholar attached to the Foreign Office's Research Department during the war (and later the Director of the Far Eastern Centre of St. Antony's College, Oxford), the French took great pride in Indo-China. He quoted Albert Sarraut, a colonial statesman of the stature of Lord Lugard, as saying that it was 'the most important, developed, and prosperous of the French colonies'. With an analytical eye by no means blind to the shortcomings of the French regime, Hudson credited the French with certain economic and social achievements:

The French have a notable record in the building of road and rail communications, dyke construction and irrigation, and agricultural and industrial development. Exports and imports have risen remarkably and the population has increased considerably, while the standard of health has been much raised since a service of direct medical assistance to the natives was begun in 1904.

Educational progress has been notable, the use of the French language as the language of the educated is definitely established and is the only common vehicle of expression as between Annamite and Cambodian intelligentsia. There is a University at Hanoi, there are four Pasteur Institutes in the Union; and various special and technical colleges; while the 'École Française d'Extrême Orient' has made important contributions to archaeology and linguistics.[30]

Clearly this was a more positive assessment of the French record than Roosevelt's, and one by a scholar who had devoted his

[29] Minute by Cavendish Bentinck, 22 Dec. 1943, ibid.
[30] Minute by Geoffrey Hudson, 14 Jan. 1944, FO 371/41723.

life's work to the affairs of the Far East. It reinforced the dis-position of the Foreign Office to believe that the President's judgement was misguided. The Permanent Under-Secretary, Sir Alexander Cadogan, for example, believed that on this particular question the President was not only wrong but also that his solution would jeopardize the colonial possessions of Britain as well as France. In the following minute Cadogan summarized the British objections to Roosevelt's Indo-China policy:

> I have heard the President say that Indo-China shd. not revert to France, and he is on record as saying that the French, in that region, 'were hopeless'. I have not had the advantage of hearing him develop this theme. We'd better look out: were the French more 'hopeless' in Indo-China than we in Malaya or the Dutch in the E. Indies? In what way were they 'hopeless'? When stricken at home, they could not, of course, defend it. But was their peace-time record so bad? . . .
>
> [I]f the French are to be turned out, what is to be put in their place? A multinational Condominium? A mandatory? (France could hardly be excluded from any Commission to which a manda-tory wd. be responsible, and what fun France wd. have). China?! And who would be better off?[31]

Cadogan concluded that this was 'one of the President's most half-baked & most unfortunate obiter dicta'. The Foreign Secretary, Anthony Eden, noted, 'I agree.'[32]

Churchill was shrewd enough to let events take their own course.[33] 'Let this sleeping dog lie' were the words of one Foreign Office official on the subject of British policy towards

---

[31] Minute by Cadogan, 2 Feb. 1944, FO 371/41723.   [32] Ibid.
[33] Churchill was also wary of further friction with de Gaulle, e.g. in May 1944 he wrote to Eden on the subject of the French war effort in Asia: 'It is hard enough to get along in S[outh] E[ast] A[sia] C[ommand] when we virtually have only the Americans to deal with. The more the French can get their finger into the pie, the more trouble they will make in order to show they are not humiliated in any way by the events through which they have passed. You will have de Gaullist intrigues there just as you now have in Syria and the Lebanon. Before we could bring the French officially into the Indo-China area, we should have to settle with President Roosevelt. He has been more outspoken to me on that subject than on any other Colonial matter, and I imagine it is one of his principal war aims to liberate Indo-China from France. Whenever he has raised it, I have repeatedly reminded him of his pledges about the integrity of the French Empire and have reserved our posi-tion. Do you really want to go and stir all this up at such a time as this?' Churchill to Eden, 21 May 1944, FO 371/41719.

Indo-China.[34] With the hope that the French would eventually argue their own case against the Americans, the British aimed at the restoration of the French colonial empire, which they regarded as a concomitant to a strong metropolitan France whose strength in Europe would be a keystone to the future peace. If France and the United States should break into an open quarrel, the British planned to give powerful support to France.[35] As it turned out, a direct stand proved unnecessary because the wartime developments in this area worked in favour of Churchill and de Gaulle and against Roosevelt. The President shifted accordingly.

Roosevelt was responding to domestic as well as to international tensions. To the American people, the restoration of Indo-China was a much more unpopular idea than the thought of the British or the Dutch returning to their colonies in South-East Asia. This explains part of Roosevelt's caution in finally giving way. He also felt the pressure of both the State Department and his military advisers. Some influential State Department officials such as James Clement Dunn (in charge of European affairs) believed that antagonizing the French on the colonial issue would jeopardize Franco-American relations in Europe. Henry L. Stimson, the Secretary of War, pressed on Roosevelt the post-war military importance of a resuscitated France. Not least, Roosevelt felt the pressure from de Gaulle, who in the spring and summer of 1944 increased his demands for American recognition of the legitimacy of the Free French colonial aspirations. After his meeting with Roosevelt in July 1944, de Gaulle stated that Roosevelt would not bar the way to Indo-China. When the United States officially recognized the provisional government of de Gaulle in October 1944, it signified, among other things, the waning of Roosevelt's hopes for international trusteeship in the French colonies.

[34] Minute by Sterndale Bennett (Head of the Far Eastern Department), 10 Jan. 1945, FO 371/46304.

[35] They also hoped to appease the Americans on the issue. For example, the inter-departmental Post-Hostilities Planning Sub-Committee in January 1944 concluded: 'our policy for Indo-China should be to encourage American co-operation in its defence, without prejudicing our friendly relations with France by laying ourselves open to the charge of conniving at an infringement of her sovereignty on the mainland of Asia. This might be achieved by the establishment of some system of United Nations bases in Indo-China, rather than by depriving France of her possessions.' 'French Possessions in the Pacific', 22 Jan. 1944, P.H.P. (44)2, o, CAB 81/45. See also War Cabinet Conclusions 25 (44), 24 Feb. 1944, CAB 65/41.

The ultimate deathblow to the trusteeship schemes came in March 1945, when the Japanese assumed direct control from the Vichy regime. The Americans could hardly refuse the Free French assistance against the Japanese, which meant ultimately the opening of the way to restoration of French authority. But Roosevelt persevered. To the time of his death he insisted that the French should at least promise 'independence' as a goal of their policy in Indo-China. And secondly he wanted assurances that they would not slam the door on American trade. 'It was more in the economic field that the President meant to get his views adopted', Roosevelt's adviser, Harry Hopkins, told the British in reference to raising standards of living, but certainly also implying the 'Open Door'.[36] To the Americans no less than to the British, the lingering memory of French colonial protection was a potent force.

When the American experts in the State Department examined the history of the French administration in Indo-China, they arrived at roughly the same conclusions as had Geoffrey Hudson in the Foreign Office. By contrast with the President, the State Department acknowledged that the French had made contributions to the economic and social development of their colonies. In Indo-China they had established a public order where none had existed before. According to the Territorial Subcommittee in November 1944: 'the government which the French had set up was the glue which held French Indo-China together and that without the French administrative system it would not be possible to conduct any government in this area'. The French had created a transport system. They had increased the production of rice at least tenfold and had

[36] Cited by LaFeber, 'Roosevelt, Churchill, and Indochina' (p. 1294), which has a good discussion of all these points in relation to broader issues such as the deteriorating situation in China and the eventual intervention of Russia. LaFeber's main themes are appropriate in concluding the present discussion: 'The President's Indochina policy in 1943–44 is a case study of how supposed idealism, in this instance anticolonialism, can blend perfectly with American self-interest. If such colonial areas as Indochina and Hong Kong were placed under international trustees who pledged to carry out the Atlantic Charter's principle of "free access" to markets and raw materials, it was obvious that the United States, emerging from the war as the globe's economic and military giant, would be best able to take advantage of the "free access" opportunity.' The American position was thus similar to Britain's championing of 'Free Trade' in the nineteenth century. See John Gallagher and Ronald Robinson, 'The Imperialism of Free Trade', *Economic History Review*, 2nd ser., 6. 1 (1953).

raised the general standard of living. 'They had done very well in many of the technical aspects of their administration and in particular in such matters as snake farms where they had gone a long way in combatting one of the great menaces in that part of the world.' On the other hand the Americans disapproved of French *moral conduct*. Striking a theme that is virtually absent in the British records, the minutes of the Territorial Subcommittee read:

[C]orruption was rife everywhere. In the inhabited areas every form of licensing and control was made the occasion for a small racket, whereas on the frontier areas between French Indo-China and Thailand the less said about the officials the better. The use of alcohol and opium by the lower officials was so common it attracted no attention and many of their practices were unprintable.[37]

If the State Department officials were willing to grant a greater achievement in economic development than Roosevelt was prepared to admit, it is also true to say that Americans generally made moral judgements. They found the French morally deplorable. In American eyes, the French had not proven themselves worthy as 'trustees' of colonial peoples.

It is one of the major themes of this book that the conception of colonial trusteeship had a substantial and intrinsic meaning quite apart from trusteeship as an issue in power politics. Writers of international history tend to regard the Second World War trusteeship schemes as a sort of international receivership or makeshift device to block the takeover of a colonial territory by a rival. There is a good deal of truth in this partial view, if only because de Gaulle and Churchill both saw it as the essence of American colonial designs. For de Gaulle's part, it is paradoxical that he regarded the Brazzaville Conference of January–February 1944 as a step towards tying the colonies more firmly to the metropole, while in fact the conference stands in colonial history as one of the seminal events in the resurgence of French colonial trusteeship (and in French decolonization).[38] This was not necessarily the way the French

[37] T. Minutes 55, 5 Nov. 1943, USSD NF Box 42.
[38] According to one of the authorities on the Brazzaville Conference: 'In the end, the reforms of Brazzaville did indeed contribute both to the desire for independence within the colonies and to the creation of a political system that tended to legitimate the pursuit of that aim. Yet nothing could have been further from the intentions of

saw it at the time. The conference was attended mainly by French colonial Governors and administrators, and, it should be added, by the Governor-General of the Belgian Congo, Pierre Ryckmans.[39] The discussion was restricted to Africa, though the conclusions had a definite impact on the future of Indo-China.

Much of the agenda of the Brazzaville Conference dealt with technical questions of tropical medicine, colonial agriculture, and economic self-sufficiency.[40] Some of these topics had broad significance. To what extent, for example, would economic self-sufficiency transform the traditional economic relationship with the metropole? On larger political issues there was a critical ambiguity. Meeting in a general spirit of optimism, the French colonial authorities agreed that the colonial administrations should be modernized, that there should be more Africans involved in administration, and that the colonies should seek 'their own identity'. The general significance of the conference is that it held out the prospect of political change. On the ambiguous key issue where the recommendations of the conference could be interpreted in two ways, *would it be change towards increasing local autonomy or towards the reassertion of metro-*

those responsible for free French policy, especially Charles de Gaulle. To him, the unity of the Empire and the metropole appeared, in that prenuclear era, to hold the key to the restoration of French grandeur and to provide tangible evidence of her rank as a world power.' D. Bruce Marshall, 'Free France in Africa: Gaullism and Colonialism', in Prosser Gifford and Wm. Roger Louis, eds., *France and Britain in Africa: Imperial Rivalry and Colonial Rule* (New Haven, 1971), p. 748.

[39] According to the British records, the Belgians as well as the French indicated a sensitivity to the question of 'international trusteeship'. The British Consul-General in Leopoldville wrote in late 1943: 'There has been a tendency recently for Belgians to defend the gradual nature of their native policy, and there is a sign of Belgian awareness of the international interest that is being shown, particularly by the United States, in the trusteeship of the colonial Powers. The political education of the Congo native has long been postponed to a comfortably indefinite future, and its irruption into the present would be likely to involve both the Congo and Belgian Governments in difficult and far-reaching problems.' F. M. Shepherd to Eden, No. 183, 30 Nov. 1943, copy in CO 852/502/18930. According to the United States Office of Strategic Services, the American proposals for international trusteeship held no attraction at all for the Belgians: 'it is generally believed that Belgium would favor the removal of the Mandate [for Ruanda–Urundi], probably by its incorporation as the seventh province of the Belgian Congo'. OSS R&A 3030, 'Official and Unofficial Opinion in the Mandatory Countries as to the Future of the African Mandates', 10 Apr. 1945.

[40] For the proceedings of the conference published by the French Colonial Ministry, *Conférence Africaine Française de Brazzaville, 30 janvier–8 février 1944* (Paris, 1945).

politan authority? This was one of the central questions asked by American officials attempting to assess the significance of the Brazzaville Conference.

The archives of the State Department reveal that the Americans did not confuse the rhetoric of the conference with the colonial reality. The most far-reaching evaluation was written by Ralph J. Bunche, an official of particular interest within the context of this volume because of his work in the Dependent Areas division of the State Department and later in the trusteeship affairs of the United Nations. Bunche pointed out that General de Gaulle had by no means struck a new note when he opened the conference by saying that France would not neglect her duties in elevating the native peoples of the French Empire. Even when the delegates stated that the natives would be brought step by step to manage their own affairs, this again was nothing new in French policy. 'The implication is very strong', Bunche wrote, 'that Brazzaville clung tenaciously to conventional French policy of integration and assimilation of the colonial territories and their peoples.'[41] Bunche also noted that the French at Brazzaville did not stray from Sarraut's classic formula of *mise en valeur* (a co-ordinated program of economic development for the benefit of both the metropole and the colonies). On the other hand they did make statements against excessive protectionism, and against the economic subordination of the colonies to the metropole. Bunche attached importance to the emphasis on *decentralization*. The key conclusion of the conference, however, was extremely limited:

> The goals of the task of civilization accomplished by France in her colonies rule out any idea of autonomy, any possibility of evolution outside the French bloc of the empire; the eventual creation, even in the distant future, of *self-government* [sic] for the colonies is to be set aside.

The phrase *self-government* had been rendered in English, as if it had no equivalent in the French language nor in the French conception of the proper relationship between the colonies and the metropole. Nor did the French seem inclined to seek external advice. This led Bunche to conclude that the results

[41] Ralph J. Bunche, 'The French African Conference at Brazzaville', 6 April 1944, USSD NF Box 36. I am grateful to Professor Jacques Berque, who attended the Brazzaville Conference, for discussing this document with me.

of the conference on the whole should be interpreted as the rejection of the idea of international trusteeship.

[T]here was no compromise with the basic principle that French Africa belongs solely to France and is an exclusively French affair. There was no recognition that France owed any accountability to the international community in the conduct of her colonial affairs nor that the international community had any valid interest in such affairs.

On the contrary, Bunche wrote, the French had reaffirmed their own colonial mission. 'The French were clearly thinking in terms of strengthening the bonds of empire, of drawing the natives into closer communion with France and French institutions. It would seem that the French dream of a united France, with one hundred million Frenchmen, has not been dissipated.'[42]

Nevertheless the French did demonstrate a sensitivity to political pressure. Following his meeting with Roosevelt in June 1944, de Gaulle mentioned the word *autonomy* in regard to Indo-China, which did not necessarily contradict the recommendations of the Brazzaville Conference in the sense he used it. Though there remained a fundamental ambiguity about the word 'autonomy', increasing decentralization and 'HOME RULE IN INDO-CHINA' seemed to be remarkable developments to American and British observers.[43] No less important, the French appeared to have rediscovered their own colonial heritage. For the French as well as the British, the Second World War marked a rejuvenation of the French colonial mission, a mission that would be controlled *by France*. At the San Francisco Conference, the Foreign Minister, Georges Bidault, spoke indignantly about 'a campaign of ignorance and calumny' against the French colonial empire. With words that can truly be said to mark the end of the schemes to place French colonies under international trusteeship, Bidault said in March 1945, '*France would be her own trustee.*'[44]

One final observation might be made about trusteeship schemes and the French colonies during the war. The differences between the European colonial empires do not now seem so great as they did to contemporary and post-war com-

---

[42] Bunche, loc. cit.
[43] As e.g. the *Manchester Guardian* emphasized it on 26 Mar. 1945.
[44] Quoted in OSS R&A 3030, 10 Apr. 1945, italics added.

mentators.[45] With the benefit of thirty years perspective, it is possible to say that the French as well as the British—and one should add the Americans—were *gradualists* who in general believed that in a period of roughly half a century the more advanced colonies might be able to manage their own affairs. The Brazzaville Conference, despite its ambiguity, held out promise for decentralization and the improvement of economic and social conditions in the colonies. It greatly helped to counter American criticism. When one studies French colonial history, however, one of the most striking paradoxes is the Brazzaville Conference as a basis for decolonization. It was not the intention of the participants. And when one considers the American pressure to decolonize, the French must surely regard the outcome as ironic. Today there are only remnants of the French Empire. As the French and other foreign observers frequently pointed out during the war, the Americans also possessed a dependent empire. The present-day status of Puerto Rico, the Virgin Islands, Guam, and American Samoa (not to mention Hawaii and Alaska) is remarkably similar to de Gaulle's vision of the proper relationship between France and her colonies.

[45] This is the theme of Leonard Thompson, 'France and Britain in Africa: A Perspective', in *France and Britain in Africa*. The argument is given further force if Ireland is considered as a British 'colony'. Since this appears to be the present trend in the historiography of the subject, it seems all the more important to remember that contemporary British observers saw substantial differences. The British did have self-governing Dominions; and the degree of autonomy in India after 1919 far surpassed that of any French dependency.

3

THE DEFENCE OF THE MIDDLE EAST
AND THE FATE OF THE ITALIAN
COLONIES

FOR the defence of the British Empire, the problem of the disposal of the Italian colonies was the equivalent of the question of the Japanese mandated islands for the security of the United States. During the course of the war, international trusteeship emerged as a common solution to the problems of both the Italian and Japanese colonial territories, though with important qualifications and exceptions. This chapter comprises a brief examination of the British post-war planning for the Italian colonies within the larger context of the problems of the Middle East; it is followed by a case study of American policy-making towards the Japanese islands within the broader setting of the Pacific basin. Particular attention will again be paid to the economic element in trusteeship as viewed by the wartime protagonists.

If the minutes of British officials during the war are to be believed, the desert sands of Libya and Somalia were as worthless as the 'light soil' of the Sahara in the days of Lord Salisbury. Particularly for this reason, however, the area of the new partition is of especial interest. Why did the Italian colonies appear to have such vital importance to some British statesmen? If it was for the protection of imperial lines of communication, for what reasons were these lines being protected? For the Suez Canal and beyond that India and the Empire in the East? Was then the essential stake not indirectly economic? Or was it the protection of oil resources and supply lines in the Middle East, where the motive was clearly economic, at least in large part? If so, how did British officials reconcile these thoughts with the doctrine of 'trusteeship'?

The answers to such sweeping questions vary dramatically if they are associated with Imperialists such as Amery or with the intellectual heirs of the nineteenth-century 'Little

Englanders' who regarded colonies as economically undesirable burdens. Attlee, for example, had no use whatever for the Italian colonies and described the territories in the Red Sea areas as an 'incubus'.[1] The vision of the Middle East also appeared different from the vantage-points of the Colonial Office and the Foreign Office, and, of course, the wartime outlook of the military authorities. During the latter part of the war the Middle East came to resemble a giant military arsenal, and this development had an important bearing on possible post-war organization. The Middle East Supply Centre, which controlled shipping, supplies, and production, provided a unity for British control that some Imperial statesmen hoped would carry over into the post-war period to consolidate defence and administrative responsibilities.[2]

Apart from the military and the question of the Middle East Supply Centre's future, there existed two types of British Empire in the Middle East. The formal dependent empire of the Colonial Office consisted of the Mandate of Palestine and Transjordan, the Somaliland Protectorate, the Crown Colony of Aden, and the Crown Colonies of Cyprus and Malta (the latter two, though technically in the Mediterranean Department of the Colonial Office, were caught up directly in many Middle Eastern questions). The other was the informal empire of the Foreign Office, which rested on treaty relations with the Arab states, notably Egypt and Iraq. Here then is a direct contrast between formal and informal empires, complicated by one overriding consideration: the future of Palestine. The Foreign Office officials tended to be pro-Arab and anti-Zionist, while the Colonial Office officials, if not pro-Zionist, were certainly less pro-Arab.[3]

Shortly after the close of the war, Lord Altrincham, or, as he

[1] Attlee's views on the Italian colonies are discussed below, ch. 35. In this chapter I am especially indebted to Professor John DeNovo of the University of Wisconsin for giving me the advantage of reading part of his work in progress on British and American oil rivalry in the Middle East during the war. For background see especially Elizabeth Monroe, *Britain's Moment in the Middle East* (London, 1963).

[2] See Martin W. Wilmington, *The Middle East Supply Centre* (State University of New York Press, Albany, 1971).

[3] See e.g. the comments of the head of the Palestine Department of the Colonial Office, E. B. Boyd, on the 'anti-Zionist sentiments of many of the British authorities in the Middle East', 4 Jan. 1945, CO 732/88/79238.

was better known, Sir Edward Grigg, wrote a memorable analysis of British policy which helps considerably in giving one set of answers to the general questions of British purpose, including 'trusteeship', in the Middle East. Like his friend Amery, Grigg took a broad view of Imperial issues. Another of Milner's disciples, he had served as one of Lloyd George's Private Secretaries at the time of the Middle Eastern Empire's creation following the First World War. He had been a Governor of Kenya and a Member of Parliament. In 1944 he published *The British Commonwealth: Its Place in the Service of the World*, a book which immediately took its place in the literature of enlightened British Imperialism and also served to counter American criticism of the Empire.[4] In the last stage of the war Grigg became Minister Resident in the Middle East. Writing in September 1945, he now surveyed the meaning of the war for the future of the British Empire in that part of the world. His opening sentence clearly places the economic factor in the Middle East into the perspective seen by most Imperially minded Englishmen of the time.

As a funnel of communication between the western, eastern and southern peoples of the British Commonwealth, as their richest reservoir of lubricant and motive oil, and furthermore as an area in which, without desiring to dominate ourselves, we cannot allow any other Power to dominate and must preserve for ourselves the maximum of friendship and goodwill, the Middle East is no less vital to Britain than Central and South America to the United States, or than the eastern and western glacis of the Russian landmass to the Soviet Union.

From this premise there followed, in Grigg's view, the strategic lesson to be learned from the entire war: 'It was not for nothing that we sent to Egypt in 1940, when this island was in imminent jeopardy of invasion, the only armoured division of which we stood possessed. It was no mere accident that the whole face of the war began to change after our victory, two years later, at Alamein.'[5] Granted the central economic importance of the oil reserves, the question of the Middle East as a centre of Imperial communication had a logic of its own. 'The loss of

---

[4] See the New York edition, 1944, with an introduction by Lord Halifax.
[5] Altrincham, 'British Policy and Organization in the Middle East', 2 Sept. 1945, C.O. copy, CO 732/88/79338.

primacy in that region would deprive the Commonwealth of its coherence and much of its power.' How was this system of communication held together? Here Grigg candidly discussed the problem of the formal and informal Empires: 'We have relied in this war upon our mandatory rights in Palestine and Transjordan and our treaties with Egypt and Iraq. They have served us well.' But the treaty system, which made the Middle Eastern states appear as British clients, was now obsolescent. In a world in which the United Nations more or less guaranteed national independence, Britain would have to find a new basis for British power in the Middle East.

In Grigg's view the key—and here he voiced the governing principle of British post-war colonial policy—was economic development on a regional basis. The war had 'transformed the primitive economies of the Middle Eastern States'. This raised the question of trusteeship. It would now be up to the British to stand by with men of 'quiet wisdom' who possessed 'true creative enthusiasm'. This is the passage in which Grigg outlined the master solution for the problems of the Middle East and for Britain's continuing paramountcy:

> Britain will stand or fall in the Middle East by her influence upon the promotion of social justice and betterment, claiming no arbitrary power over or even open influence upon its national Governments, but helping and advising unobtrusively at request, so that all parts of the population can feel the benefit of progress in opportunity, education, living conditions and health.[6]

Did Grigg also see the purpose of this British presence as securing the oil resources of Iraq or, more remotely, the rubber and tin of Malaya? Certainly yes, for the wealth and prosperity of the British Empire were inseparably linked in his mind with its power as a force for good in the world. Like Leo Amery, for Grigg the economic factor was sublimated into a higher purpose of trusteeship.

> Britain is no longer the equal of the United States or Russia in material resources and capacity for war; but she can still be the greatest of all countries in her power for helping the smaller and more backward peoples towards greater abundance and freedom under law in a world at peace . . .

6 Ibid.

[S]he is not an exhausted and declining but still, as of old, a creative and pioneering influence, stronger by her character than dollars can ever be, stronger also by her appeal to normal human aspirations than those who serve the Communist ideal. Britain still has a powerful attraction for the weak of which her great Allies are not as yet possessed.[7]

In the Middle East, as in other parts of the world, the British Empire would revive to bind its peoples together in 'its tolerant and human way of life'.

Another reason for the significance of Grigg's thoughts is that they stirred up comment in the Colonial Office, in particular by an economist who played an important part in the trusteeship question, (Sir) Sydney Caine, later Director of the London School of Economics. His observations are of value in getting the economic perspective of the Colonial Office. Caine valued Grigg's analysis because it was first and foremost a political commentary 'and treats economic questions as definitely subsidiary'. Many other officials, in Caine's view, erred in seeking an economic unity in the Middle East that did not exist.

The Colonial Office have always held the view that economic unity [in the Middle East] is a complete myth, and that in so far as the area has a substantial community of interest, it is because of common political feelings and aspirations and because of a common relationship to the main communications routes which run through the area.[8]

Political considerations gave a unity to problems of economic policy, according to this economist, and not the other way round. Caine and other Colonial Office officials also held a contemptuous view of commentators who saw the Colonial Empire as an instrument of economic exploitation. For them economic questions were often quite technical ones such as agricultural development and, to use a Middle Eastern example, funds to be allocated for such projects as locust control. This is not to say by any means that Caine or his colleagues were oblivious to larger questions of political and economic control, but rather that as Colonial Office officials they tended to see economic problems in terms of development of the specific territories which concerned them. A common purpose held them together, but individually they held independent and

[7] Altrincham, 'British Policy and Organization in the Middle East', 2 Sept. 1945, C.O. copy, CO 732/88/79338.   [8] Minute by Caine, 8 Sept. 1945, ibid.

often conflicting views. Caine, for example, was the only Colonial Office official during the war who came out in favour of international trusteeship and he held an open mind on the question of the future of Palestine.

This book will not delve into the intricacies of the Palestine mandate. Like the question of the future of India, the complexity of the problem merits a separate volume. And there is an additional reason. Palestine, despite its status as a mandated territory, fell outside of the mainstream of trusteeship affairs during the war. It was *sui generis*. The question of international control over Palestine was always present in the minds of those dealing with trusteeship in Africa and elsewhere, but it was treated separately as a unique problem. In the commentary below, the Palestine question will appear as it intruded, rather infrequently, into the general discussions about trusteeship. Here it will be dealt with briefly in order to illustrate the difference between the Foreign Office and Colonial Office approach to trusteeship, and because the Palestine problem was connected with the fate of the Italian colonies.

The basis of Churchill's Palestine policy during the war can be traced to the time he was Colonial Secretary in 1922 and the issuing of the Palestine White Paper of May of that year. It represented Churchill's effort to reconcile the conflicting claims of the Jews and Arabs by (a) stating that the Balfour Declaration of 1917, which promised the Jews a national home in Palestine, did not apply to Trans-Jordan; and (b) affirming the definite promise of a national home *in* Palestine. This formula rested on the assumption, as Leo Amery pointed out during the war, that Jews and Arabs could co-exist within a single state just as French and English-speaking peoples lived together in Canada and those of British and Dutch descent accepted the framework of a single state in South Africa.[9] The history of the

---

[9] See memorandum by Amery, 'Palestine', 31 July 1943, P. (M) (43) 3, CAB 95/14. For Colonial Office thought antecedent to the Ministerial Committee, see e.g. CO 732/87/79238. The High Commissioner in Palestine, Sir Harold MacMichael, had pressed for a federation of Palestine, Trans-Jordan, and the Levant states under the 'supreme supervisory control' of Britain, France, and the United States. Neither the Colonial Office nor the Foreign Office responded favourably. The Americans, Cranborne noted, were showing too much of a tendency already 'to intervene in our affairs, and it will be better not to take them into our confidence till we have fully made up our minds as to the lines of our future policy'. Minute by Cranborne, 18 June 1942.

Palestine question in the inter-war years did not vindicate this optimism, but Churchill regarded the famous White Paper of 1939, which restricted Jewish immigration while barely appeasing the Arabs, as a breach of faith with the Jewish people. In July 1943 as Prime Minister he appointed a Ministerial Committee to deal with the future of Palestine. The work of the committee remained one of the best-kept secrets of the war, which even the United States Office of Strategic Services failed to crack.[10] The committee of six ministers reported in December 1943. With one exception, they all favoured the solution of a clear-cut partition. In the words of the report, 'partition offers the best and possibly the only final solution of the Palestine problem'.[11] The committee urged utmost secrecy so that when the cut came, it would be 'swift and clean', ending, so it was hoped, once and for all the Palestine problem by reconciling, in so far as humanly possible, the differences of the Jews and Arabs. The sole dissenter was Richard Law, who represented the Foreign Office. Law warned that partition 'will provoke such violent opposition throughout the Arab world as will jeopardise our whole position in the Middle East'.[12] The War Cabinet approved in principle the view of the majority in January 1944. The Foreign Secretary reserved judgement until he could receive the advice of the Ambassadors in the Middle East. This was the stage of the Palestine question when, in April 1944, an American delegation arrived in London to discuss, among other things, international trusteeship in Palestine.

The American mission, led by Edward R. Stettinius (an Under Secretary who became Secretary of State in late 1944), included the Director of the State Department's Office of Near Eastern and African Affairs, Wallace Murray, and a person of extraordinary interest for the history of international trusteeship, Isaiah Bowman. Bowman was the President of Johns Hopkins University and a distinguished geographer. He had attended

---

[10] A. Ilan makes this point on p. 158 of 'The Origin and Development of American Intervention in British Palestine Policy, 1938–1947', unpublished Oxford D.Phil. thesis, St. Antony's College, 1974, which I have greatly benefited from reading. I am also especially indebted to Elizabeth Monroe and Max Beloff for discussion about the Palestine question.

[11] Report of the Committee on Palestine, P. (M) (43) 29, 20 Dec. 1943, CAB 95/14.

[12] Ibid., 10 Dec. 1943.

the Peace Conference in 1919 as one of Wilson's advisers. From first to last he figured prominently in the trusteeship question during the war. As Chairman of the State Department's Advisory Committee on territorial questions, he had a large influence in 'The Strategy of Territorial Decisions'.[13] And he served as Roosevelt's adviser on Jewish and other settlement schemes. Though Bowman was not a precise thinker, he gave the President hard and definite advice on the question of Palestine. It boiled down to making no commitments to either side. '[K]eep the Palestine question in abeyance, so far as possible, until the end of the war', Bowman had written to Roosevelt in May 1943.[14] Similar recommendations from other Middle Eastern experts, notably one of his other trouble-shooters, Colonel Harold Hoskins, probably helped to alter Roosevelt's easy-going optimism about Palestine during the first part of the war when he wanted to solve the problem by installing three 'trustees', a Jew, an Arab, and a Christian. During the latter part of the war Roosevelt became increasingly wary about Palestine.[15] At the time of the Stettinius mission, his advisers were attempting to give specific content to the President's sweeping and, at least to the British, unrealistic ideas. In the case of Palestine, 'trusteeship' to the Americans meant the extension of the mandate under the auspices of the United Nations, but with much more rigorous international control than that of the mandatory regime.

Certain Foreign Office officials regarded international trusteeship as a possible solution to the Palestine problem, though by no means with the amount of international control specified by the American scheme. These included Sir Maurice Peterson,

[13] This is the title of Bowman's article in *Foreign Affairs* 24. 2 (January 1946). For the Stettinius mission, see Thomas M. Campbell and George C. Herring, eds., *The Diaries of Edward R. Stettinius, Jr., 1943–1946* (New York, 1975). Campbell, *Masquerade Peace, America's UN Policy, 1944–1945* (Tallahassee, Florida, 1973), and Herring, *Aid to Russia, 1941–1946: Strategy, Diplomacy, the Origins of the Cold War* (New York, 1973), are both major works on themes related to those of the present volume.   [14] Bowman to Roosevelt, 22 May 1943, Bowman Papers.

[15] e.g. Colonel Hoskins wrote in September 1943: 'In regard to Palestine, the President seemed well informed on the complications with the Arabs not only in Palestine but throughout all the Middle East if a Jewish State were established in Palestine. I had the opportunity to emphasize again what he had already been told —that the establishment of a Jewish State in Palestine can only be imposed by force and can only be maintained by force.' Memorandum by Hoskins, 27 Sept. 1943, Stettinius Papers Box 725.

who conducted the talks on Palestine with the Stettinius mission. Peterson and his colleagues were obliged to be less than candid. Restrained by the secrecy of the Ministerial Committee, the Foreign Office officials could not reveal the plan for partition. Peterson listened to Murray and Bowman sympathetically and at one point stated that *officially* he could not comment on the American proposal for trusteeship but that *personally* he thought it a good idea. Bowman's words are explicit on this point: Peterson 'dwelt on the necessity in any event of a mandatory power and an international undertaking with respect to Palestine'.[16] Thus the Americans were led to believe that the British favoured trusteeship, which was in fact the opposite of the Ministerial Committee's line of thought. Since Peterson's remarks stirred up controversy between the Foreign Office and the Colonial Office about the meaning and desirability of 'trusteeship', here is the British account of the exchange:

He [Peterson], personally, would see advantage in a Palestine State, under some form of United Nations mandate, into which further Jewish immigration would be allowed, but with a provision that the Jewish population should not come to within, say, 50,000 or 100,000 of the Arab population. But, he repeated, it was all a Cabinet matter.[17]

Wallace Murray responded by saying that he of course could not speak for the White House. At least there seemed to be a meeting of minds between the Foreign Office and the State Department.

The Foreign Office's handling of the Stettinius mission on the question of trusteeship drew the wrath of the Colonial Office. Oliver Stanley noted 'with great surprise' that Sir Maurice Peterson 'had seen fit to propound to the Americans as a personal view, a solution of the Palestine problem which was at variance with the policy recently approved by the War Cabinet . . .'.[18] Among other things, a Colonial Office representative had not even been present at these discussions about a critical Colonial Office concern. One official, (Sir) Gerard Clauson, whose minutes reflect a high moral tone, resented the

[16] Memorandum by Bowman, 'Palestine', 11 Apr. 1944, Bowman Papers.
[17] 'Conversations with Mr. Wallace Murray regarding the Middle East', 11 Apr. 1944, C.O. copy, CO 732/88/79303.
[18] Minute by E. B. Boyd, recording Stanley's remarks, 17 Apr. 1944, ibid.

Foreign Office's high-handed practice of 'conducting conversations about our affairs without our being there'. This was a traditional Colonial Office complaint. Clauson went on: 'Our presence on this occasion, for instance, might have deterred Sir M. Peterson from making such a deplorable exhibition of himself; an exhibition, I hasten to add, which wd. not have surprised me in an American officer, but which we must do all we can to stop in future on our own side.'[19]

There was however a certain freedom of bureaucratic action sustained by the Colonial Office by not being present at such discussions. Under the circumstances, it is difficult to imagine how the British could have rebuffed the rather vague American proposals for trusteeship without creating further friction. Sir William Battershill, Deputy Under-Secretary in the Colonial Office, noted: 'Personally I think it was just as well that the Colonial Office was not represented at these talks. There is . . . little "identity of view" at present on various M[iddle]. E[astern]. topics between the C.O. and the F.O. and it is most unlikely that we should have been able to put up a united front . . .'[20]

The major point of disagreement which Battershill pointed out was the essence of international trusteeship—some form of accountability to an international organization. This the Colonial Office absolutely deplored. It proved to be an unending source of controversy between the two offices, in the Middle East as in other parts of the world. As for the specific problem, the Colonial Office and Foreign Office remained divided even after the British representatives in the Middle East, united in their opposition to the partition scheme, began to swing the balance in favour of an international solution.[21] For Churchill, the assassination in November 1944 of the Resident Minister of State in Cairo, Lord Moyne, brought home the apparent

[19] Minute by Clauson, 9 May 1944, ibid.
[20] Minute by Battershill, 10 May 1944, ibid.
[21] For the division of the two sides as of September 1944, see memorandum by Stanley, 11 Sept. 1944, arguing 'The Case for Partition', P. (M) (44) 10, CAB 95/14; and memorandum by Eden, 'The Case Against Partition', P. (M) (44) 11, 15 Sept. 1944, ibid. The latter memorandum contains a despatch by the British Ambassador in Bagdad which includes a passage on what he believed to be 'President Roosevelt's Idea of a Permanent Trustees State'. (Sir Kinahan Cornwallis to Eden, 24 Feb. 1944.)

futility of it all. Towards the end of his wartime career the
Prime Minister had grown pessimistic. 'I am not aware of the
slightest advantage which has ever occurred to Great Britain from
this painful and thankless task', he wrote to Oliver Stanley.[22]
Many other British statesmen shared Churchill's disillusionment
with the Palestine question. Nevertheless throughout the wartime files about Palestine there runs the continuous theme of
genuine humanitarian concern for the Jews.

In July 1943 Churchill circulated to the War Cabinet a moving statement by General Smuts on the plight of the Jews.
Smuts expressed his strong feeling that their position in the
world would call for drastic action at the end of the war. 'If
we continue to forget or ignore Jewish claims,' Smuts argued,
'we shall fail in our larger efforts on behalf of a fair and just
settlement at [the] end of this war. . . . If we fail the Jews it
means Hitler's triumph in the fundamental of his satanic creed.'[23]
Smuts assumed that it probably would be impossible to send
refugees back to the countries where they had been persecuted.
Therefore the solution would have to be found, in part, in
a Palestinian state or liberated areas such as Libya—or both.
The idea of 'satellite settlements' exerted a powerful appeal.
They might relieve the immigration pressure on Palestine, and
they might put to good use the Italian colonies. This possibility
raised a host of questions. Would the Italian colonies, or at least
some of them, be returned to Italy? Or would part of them be
annexed by Britain? Or would all of them be placed under
a trusteeship regime? These questions could only be answered
after a full examination of the economic and strategic importance of the Italian colonies for Britain and their potential as
areas of Jewish settlement. Once more this is a complex subject
which can be dealt with here only in passing, but a brief
examination again helps to isolate the economic factor and the
clash over trusteeship within the British government.

There were three Italian colonies: Somaliland, Eritrea, and

[22] Churchill to Stanley, 6 July 1945, quoted in Ilam, 'The Origin and Development of American Intervention in British Palestine Policy', p. 194.

[23] W.P. (43) 337, 26 July 1943, CAB 95/14. Churchill had also given the following directive in April: 'A careful examination should be made by the Departments
concerned of the possibilities of making Eritrea and Tripolitania into Jewish
colonies, affiliated, if desired, to the National Home in Palestine.' W.P. (43) 178,
28 Apr. 1943.

Libya. Somaliland was never seriously considered as a potential 'satellite' colony for the Jews. As for Eritrea, the Foreign Office Research Department took note that the Italians had developed the cultivation of cotton in the western part of the colony, near the Sudan border, and that the amount of arable land might be extended by irrigation. The Foreign Office Research Department also observed that the colony 'contains no valuable mineral deposits'. Therefore the British had nothing to gain, but could anticipate considerable expenditure in making the settlement schemes a viable solution. There were also political difficulties. Part of Eritrea, geographically, politically, and ethnically, was an extension of Ethiopia. The Emperor of Ethiopia could not be expected to look favourably on the establishment of a Jewish colony of any substantial size. The British would have to be prepared to back the Jewish settlement schemes in the face of Ethiopian opposition.[24]

The most attractive prospect appeared to be Libya, made up of the three provinces of Cyrenaica in the east, Tripolitania in the west, and Fezzan in the south-west.[25] The Foreign Office Research Department observed that there were approximately 30,000 colonists in Libya as of 1940. The Italian populations of Cyrenaica and Tripolitania were unevenly divided, but the resources of the latter were already so fully exploited that any future agricultural development would have to be planned mainly in Cyrenaica. The British noted that capital expenditure for the establishment of the Italian colonies had been extremely high and that they had benefited from a protected market in Italy. The majority of the inhabitants in both Cyrenaica and Tripolitania, somewhere between 84 and 89 per cent, were Arabic-speaking Muslims. There could be no doubt, according to the Foreign Office Research Department, that they would feel 'menaced by the threat of militant Zionism' in the event

[24] F.O.R.D., 'Possibility of Jewish Settlement in Cyrenaica, Tripolitania and Eritrea after the War', circulated by Richard Law to the Committee on Palestine, CAB 95/14. For the background of this report see FO 371/35414 and CO 323/1859/9067/2.

[25] For the historical background see especially *Fourth Shore: The Italian Colonization of Libya* (Chicago, 1974) by Claudio G. Segrè, to whom I am indebted for discussion on the problem of the Italian colonies. See also Majid Khadduri, *Modern Libya: A Study in Political Development* (Baltimore, 1963), and, especially for the theme of trusteeship, Adrian Pelt, *Libyan Independence and the United Nations* (New Haven, 1970).

of the establishment of Jewish colonies. There was also an important political commitment. In a Parliamentary declaration of January 1942, Britain pledged to the Senussi of Cyrenaica that in no circumstance would they again fall under Italian domination. If the British now promoted a Jewish colony, this 'would be regarded by the Arabs as a breach of the spirit of this undertaking'.[26] Thus the British faced all of the possible contradictions of the commitments made to the Arabs and Jews during the First World War. Despite this gloomy possibility, the principal author of the Foreign Office's Jewish settlement schemes, the historian Arnold J. Toynbee, at this time attached to the Research Department, on the whole regarded the prospect as a definite *possibility*, though one fraught with economic and political hazards. Richard Law circulated Toynbee's estimate to the Ministerial committee. In spite of the difficulties laid before them, the members of the committee noted in their report of December 1943, 'In principle, we favour the idea of satellite settlements . . .'[27]

Various Colonial Office officials were highly sceptical about the Jewish settlement schemes. Christopher Eastwood, who superintended the issue, was extremely critical from beginning to end. This official is of particular interest because as head of the General Department he supervised the trusteeship question until mid-1944. He had previous experience in the Middle Eastern Department, which he brought to bear on the problem of the Italian Colonies. Eastwood was an intelligent and humane official, and there can be no doubt that he sympathized with the Jews as much as anyone else. But he was sensitive to the Palestine problem in all its ramifications. He reeled in dismay at the thought of creating 'another Palestine' somewhere in northern Africa. When the issue arose in April 1943, he wrote that the Foreign Office seemed to be speculating on the basis that the Italian colonies would be placed under some form of international trusteeship. In Arab eyes this would mean a continuation of the mandates system. 'Certainly the Arabs would not like any extension of the Mandates, which stink in their nostrils,' he noted, especially 'if it meant that the Mandate was to go to a European power.' Eastwood was also appalled at

[26] F.O.R.D. memorandum cited p. 59 n. 24.
[27] Report of the Committee on Palestine, 20 Dec. 1943, CAB 95/14.

the easy assumption that the Italian colonies could be made economically self-sufficient:

> It seems to be agreed that the economic future of Italian colonization was still very chancy. It was primarily a piece of Fascist window-dressing on which a great deal of money had been spent. The nature of the country and climate [in Libya], and the difficulties in regard to the supplies of underground irrigation water (much of which is highly saline) made its ultimate success very problematical.
>
> Things looked all right for the first few years, since the settlers were guaranteed a livelihood, but what would have happened if they had not had strong Government support and an assured and protected market for their products, is more uncertain. It seems very doubtful whether settlement in Tripolitania could ever be an economic proposition.[28]

As Eastwood continued to study the question he found no reason to alter his pessimism. His opinion about the economic prospects of the Italian colonies, and their potential as areas for Jewish settlement, can be summed up in a single phrase—'pretty damning'. He wrote in October 1943:

> It is obvious that Europeans can only be settled in Cyrenaica and Tripolitania with a heavy capital expenditure. . . . The really important point seems to be whether, once settlers have been established, they can continue to support themselves. On that such evidence as has been produced seems to show that the prospects are very doubtful.[29]

Eastwood placed his finger on the key weakness of the Jewish settlement schemes when he posed the question, 'In point of fact would the Jews ever consider Jewish settlement in Tripolitania?' He was also well aware of 'the disastrous reaction on Arab opinion' and 'Arab good will . . . [as] a factor of considerable strategic importance'.[30]

[28] Note by Eastwood, 20 Apr. 1943, CO 323/1859/9067/2.

[29] Minute by Eastwood, 10 Oct. 1943, ibid.

[30] Minutes by Eastwood, 20 Apr. and 29 June 1943, ibid. Eastwood's views were similar to those of the principal F.O. official presiding over the issue, Lord Hood, who wrote: 'The necessary capital is unlikely to be forthcoming from Jewish sources as the Zionists would be opposed to any such diversion from their goal. The hostility to Jewish settlement would, moreover, be by no means confined to the local inhabitants of the two areas. The Arab world as a whole would bitterly resent Jewish intrusion; and the Emperor of Abyssinia probably has designs on Eritrea. . . . If we were to sponsor the scheme we should land ourselves with two further Palestines without even obliging the Zionists.' Minute by Hood, 12 July 1943, FO 371/35414.

The Foreign Office Research Department's more optimistic view became embodied in the Ministerial report on Palestine, but the judgement of the head of the Palestine Department in the Colonial Office ultimately proved to be accurate: 'the political objections to a Jewish settlement in the Italian territories of Africa . . . are so weighty that the scheme for a Jewish satellite State in any of the territories is not likely to commend itself . . .'[31] When the Palestine partition scheme cracked in 1944, the Jewish settlement project died with it. But trusteeship as an over-all answer to the problem of the Italian colonies refused to dig its own grave. 'I do wish the Foreign Office would emancipate itself from this conception of international trusteeship', wrote Sir George Gater. To another Colonial Office official the Foreign Office in this regard seemed to be 'merely beating in the air'. To which Oliver Stanley noted, 'I agree.'[32]

What appeared to the Colonial Office as the glib and dangerous assumption of 'international trusteeship' seemed to the Foreign Office an unavoidable fundamental premise. In the Atlantic Charter of August 1941, Churchill and Roosevelt had declared that Britain and the United States were not fighting the war for territorial aggrandizement. Only at the risk of repudiating wartime idealism and appearing as cynical as the Axis powers could the British directly annex enemy territory. What were the alternatives? Though some sentiment did exist for the restoration of part of Italy's colonial empire,[33] the military and civilian authorities overwhelmingly concurred that the Italian colonies would be a strategic menace to British lines of communication in the eastern Mediterranean and Red Sea areas. There remained but one choice: some sort of an international regime. Here the Foreign Office espoused the conservative tradition of international trusteeship versus what

[31] Minute by Boyd, 20 Dec. 1943, CO 323/1859/9067/2.
[32] Minutes by Gater, Battershill, and Stanley, 24 and 25 Aug. 1943, ibid.
[33] e.g. (Sir) George Seel, at this time head of the East African Department in the Colonial Office, wrote in January 1943: 'indeed it seems to me that if we want to keep the whip hand over Italy for the future, the most promising line would be to debar her return to North Africa but to allow her to re-occupy Eritrea. There, she would be dependent upon our good offices for access to her Colony via the Suez Canal, without being in a position to threaten our position in the Mediterranean, and I should imagine she would hesitate long before again entering the field against us.' Seel admitted that his thoughts on this matter were 'heretical'. Minute of 20 Jan. 1943, CO 323/1859/9067/2.

might be called the more liberal American interpretation of the concept. The Americans were willing to experiment with genuine international administration. The Foreign Office thought more along the lines of 'annexation in all but name', though those officials who dealt with the Americans were well aware of the dangers of trusteeship as a legal fiction rather than a reality. The head of the American Department of the Foreign Office, Nevile Butler, wrote in August 1943:

The political point we are up against, vis-a-vis the United States is that after the last war large new sections of the map [the mandated territories] became virtual British possessions, or at least were painted pink on the map. The United States acquired no fresh territory; it is not sufficient to say that she did not want any for the abiding impression has been that whereas the British Empire made a very good thing out of the war, the Americans were had for 'suckers'.[34]

Taking a broad political view of the problem, the Foreign Office officials saw that the colonial peace settlement would have to satisfy the Americans. On the other hand the Foreign Office certainly was not oblivious to cries of 'appeasement' from the Colonial Office. Nor was the Colonial Office the only other interested party. The military authorities, of course, were acutely aware of the strategic issues at stake.[35] And in Ministerial circles Leo Amery, for example, kept a sharp eye on the Italian colonies. Amery easily disposed of the argument of the Atlantic Charter. There could be no question of territorial aggrandizement, after all, if the inhabitants of the country concerned wished to live under the Union Jack. With the assumption that the natives of the Italian colonies would welcome the British with open arms, Amery wrote a letter to the Colonial Secretary on the subject of the Italian islands in the Mediterranean, a copy of which was forwarded to the Foreign Office: 'we should insist in the terms of peace on keeping Pantellaria and Lampedusa. From the defence point of view Pantellaria would be invaluable as affording much better air

[34] Minute by Butler, 2 Aug. 1943, FO 371/35414.
[35] e.g. Admiral Bellairs (Military Sub-Committee) to Toynbee, 25 June 1943, FO 371/35414, in which the military disadvantages to the Jewish settlement schemes were pointed out. 'It is . . . of great moment from the strategic aspect that we should not do anything or allow anything to be done by others, which would adversely affect our present good relations with the Arab world.'

protection of the Sicilian Strait . . .'[36] The Foreign Office was thus caught in the crossfire of American insistence for inter-nationalization and in the other direction from Amery and Stanley. Believing both sides to err in the extreme, the Foreign Office officials attempted to impose a creative solution of trusteeship that would meet minimal American requirements without sacrificing British security.

The concluding passages of this chapter will be devoted to the way in which the British attempted to reach agreement among themselves about the fate of the Italian colonies—through inter-departmental committees. Since an entire book could be written about the inter-departmental committee system and the Italian colonies alone (by including a thorough examination, for example, of the strategic considerations of the War Office, and Air Ministry), this brief comment will restrict itself to the major point at issue between the Foreign Office and Colonial Office, that of international trusteeship. The Foreign Office began to give sustained attention to the prob-lem after the turn of the tide in the North African campaign in late 1942. The group charged with this responsibility was the Ronald Sub-Committee (of a committee dealing with armistice and peace proposals), named after the chairman, Sir Nigel Ronald, an Assistant Under-Secretary. On the 30th of December 1942 this Foreign Office group reached two major conclusions. First, they agreed that the Italian colonies east of Suez should not be restored. They discussed the possibility of a 'Greater Somalia' to be created by the merger of the Italian, British, and French territories, though they observed that the French might object to giving up the strategic port of Djibouti. '[I]t was thought that there would be no inherent difficulty in arranging for some sort of mandatory, or even international, régime which would be founded on the terms of the Atlantic Charter.' Eritrea might be given to the Ethiopians, with an 'international' base retained at Massawa. Secondly, in regard to Libya, the

---

[36] Irrepressible as always in Imperial affairs, Amery proceeded to suggest another improvement in the Mediterranean: 'I believe it would be a source of great satisfaction to the Maltese, and possibly to the Gibraltarians, if they were taken out of the Colonial Office and put under the Home Office on the same footing as the Channel Islands and the Isle of Man—in other words, that they should become part of the "British Isles".' Amery to Oliver, 11 June 1943, CO 323/1859/9067/2; copy in FO 371/35414.

committee members noted the pledge to the Senussi not to allow the Italians back into Cyrenaica. They also observed that the Greeks were interested in Cyrenaica as a place to settle some of their 'surplus population'. Not least they pointed out the strategic importance of possible naval bases, especially if the Egyptians eventually pushed the British out of Egypt.

Turning to Tripolitania, there appeared to be two choices: handing over the territory to the French, in order to buy them out of Syria ('where they would be likely to be a thorn in our side so long as they remained'); or allowing Tripolitania to revert to Italy. 'The "Italian" solution was . . . preferred by the Egyptian Department on the grounds that a large French bloc continuous [sic] to Egypt might possibly be a menace in 50 years time.' Here then was a broadly political solution to the problem of the Italian colonies, one by no means Carthaginian and one moreover that included a proposal for international trusteeship that would please the Americans.[37]

The Colonial Office responded to the Foreign Office solution with outrage and deep concern. To Gerard Gent, an Assistant Under-Secretary, three points were immediately obvious:

(1) The Mediterranean sea-route shd. not again be exposed to interruption by Italy, nor the safety of Malta. . . .

(2) Italian territory & influence in the Red Sea shd. *not* be allowed to revive. We have had enough experience of the dismal effects of this in the Yemen, for instance.

(3) We do not want to promote anywhere the idea of International Régimes as administrative bodies—not only are they ineffective (Tangier, N. Hebrides etc.), but it wd. be a dangerous precedent for Colonial territories.[38]

The Deputy Under-Secretary, Sir William Battershill, regarded the whole business as a preview of a new Scramble for Africa:

We shall be faced after this war with many claims for territories in the Mediterranean. Greece wants the Dodecanese, Cyprus and part of North Africa. Turkey wants the Dodecanese, Egypt wants a slice of North Africa and I have little doubt that there will be Arab claims in North Africa, while the French will expect something. There clearly isn't enough to go round and it would seem

[37] Committee minutes, 30 Dec. 1942, C.O. copy CO 323/1859/9067/2.
[38] Minute by Gent, 26 Jan. 1943, ibid.

advisable not to assume that even a small part of the small cake available should be given back to its former owner.[39]

The Permanent Under-Secretary, Sir George Gater, noted angrily: 'The Foreign Office seem to have indulged in a little family party, leaving us out in the cold.'[40] And last, the Colonial Secretary concluded that the Foreign Office's generous attitude could only be explained by 'the Xmas spirit'. Stanley wanted to make it clear beyond any possible doubt that on this issue he would take a firm stand. 'I should like it to be made clear to the F.O. representatives that their consistent policy . . . of treating bits of the Colonial Empire as cheap & convenient gratuities is neither my policy nor I believe the policy of H.M.G.'[41]

The Foreign Office and Colonial Office now began to consider the problem together. At the first meeting the Colonial Office representatives made it clear that policy towards such territories as Somaliland should be based on traditional Colonial Office safeguards for native welfare. The Foreign Office members of the committee noted that 'if British Somaliland were transferred to an international body under the aegis of the United Nations' then the natives would be even more adequately protected. The Colonial Office members of the committee thought this was a preposterous proposition. What could provide better protection than British guardianship? George Seel observed that there was no evidence that the Somalis would be enthusiastic about international trusteeship, and he 'assumed that the Colonial Office might be regarded as the authority'.[42] There was no agreement at all, in other words, about the basic principle at issue.

There is no need to dwell on the inter-departmental proceedings because the Colonial Office and Foreign Office remained fundamentally at odds.[43] During the rest of the entire war the Colonial Office regarded the trusteeship scheme, among other things, as a Foreign Office device to appease the Americans.

[39] Minute by Battershill, 26 Jan. 1943, C.O. copy CO 323/1859/9067/2.
[40] Minute by Gater, 26 Jan. 1943, ibid.
[41] Minute by Stanley, 26 Jan. 1943, ibid.
[42] Minute by Seel, 28 Jan. 1943, ibid.
[43] There was also the strategic factor, for which see, e.g., the deliberations of the Post-Hostilities Planning Sub-Committee, CAB 81/40–2. For résumé of developments on the American side and exchanges between the two governments, USSD NF Boxes 32 and 65.

By contrast the basic Colonial Office goal was to end, not extend, the mandates system. The official superintending the issue in the Foreign Office, Lord Hood, noted in May 1944:

> If we are to accept the Colonial Secretary's view that there can be no international trusteeship and that the mandatory system must be brought to an end, then we shall have to forget about the Atlantic Charter and enlarge the British Empire. . . . If, however, our consciences or our purses rule this out, then we must, I submit, continue to think in terms of some international supervision. . . .[44]

Later in 1944 the same official noted that no progress had been made in reconciling the two views: 'The C.O. attitude on the future of the Italian Colonies has up till now been unconstructive. They oppose the return of any of the Colonies to Italy; they oppose any idea of International Trusteeship . . .'.[45] Until the Yalta conference forced the Colonial Office to concede the principle of international trusteeship as a basis for the resolution of the problem, there remained fundamental disagreement within the British government.

Despite the quarrel between the Foreign Office and the Colonial Office, there was a consensus that trusteeship, whether international or purely British, would promote Britain's political and economic position in the Middle East. With the exception of some Labour statesmen such as Attlee, British statesmen and officials generally agreed that, though the areas were economically worthless, the Italian colonies possessed immense strategic importance.[46] The strategic benefits of these particular colonies would carry with them the obligations of trusteeship. Here was the basis of British post-war policy. To the official mind, strategic and economic positions could be maintained only if Britain promoted the economic and social progress of the inhabitants.

[44] Minute by Hood, 11 May 1944, FO 371/40601.

[45] Minute by Hood, 20 Oct. 1944, FO 371/40601. For the Italian colonies in the last stage of the war, see below, chap. 35.

[46] Gerard Clauson, a Colonial Office economist, once emphasized the economic point in a way that connects with the problem of Japanese imperialism: 'Italy . . . is not now in control of any Col. territory & has never been in control of any important piece, but it will be essential in the Japanese armistice for us to obtain direct control of the Japanese banks, firms etc., which have been playing merry hell with Malaya.' Minute by Clauson, 10 June 1943, CO 323/1859/1967/2.

4

AMERICAN SECURITY AND THE CONTROVERSY OVER THE JAPANESE MANDATED ISLANDS

W AS American policy animated] by a determination to reorganize the world in line with the economic interests of the United States? In this chapter I shall examine that question with an eye towards some of the problems of the Pacific basin, particularly those of the 'trusteeship' of the Japanese islands.[1] Since one of the main themes of this volume is the controversy over the Japanese mandates, the present discussion does not attempt to deal comprehensively with the military and civilian exchanges on the subject, but to illuminate the way in which a certain body of experts assessed the problem. This group was known as the 'Security Subcommittee' of the State Department's Advisory Committee on Foreign Policy.[2] The reason for the emphasis on this particular committee is that the wartime planners viewed the question of the Japanese islands as essentially strategic. Like the Italian colonies, the mandated islands did not appear to have any intrinsic economic value. Here again however there arises the question of economic motivation in relation to 'trusteeship'. If the Japanese islands were to be retained by the United States for the sake of security (and perhaps secondarily for humanitarian reasons), did the estimate of 'security' include making the world, or in this context the Pacific and Far East, safe for American trade and

[1] By the phrase 'Japanese islands' I mean in this context only the mandated islands of the Marianas, Carolines, and Marshalls. The other parts of the Japanese Empire such as the Ryukyus and the Kuriles will be referred to specifically. For discussion about the Japanese Empire I am especially indebted to my colleague William R. Braisted, whose work *The United States Navy in the Pacific, 1909–1922* (Austin, 1971) provides a comprehensive background for American naval thought on the subject.

[2] For the subject of post-war planning for Japan, see especially Hugh Borton, *American Presurrender Planning for Postwar Japan* (Occasional Papers of the East Asian Institute, Columbia University, 1967). For the State Department's committees, the indispensable guide is [Harley Notter], *Postwar Foreign Policy Preparation, 1939–1945* (Department of State Publication 3580, Washington, 1949).

investment? The American wartime officials would probably have given a generally affirmative answer to that question. Their calculations carried them into long-range speculation about the economic future of Japan and parts of the Pacific basin that would form the hub of a post-war system of commercial aviation. Like the British officials examining the problem of the Italian colonies, the American planners saw questions of 'security' ineluctably bound up with the broad political and economic foundations of the post-war world.

In order to clarify the nature of the American wartime committee system, and its importance and influence, a useful contrast can be made with the way in which the British used committees to decide definite points of policy. When aspects of the colonial question, for example, assumed such importance that they needed to be resolved by heads of departments, the Colonial Secretary, Dominions Secretary, and Foreign Secretary might meet together to reach agreement. Having arrived at a consensus, their recommendation would go forward to the War Cabinet. If accepted, this advised opinion would become the policy of the British government. Even at lower levels the inter-departmental committee system worked effectively and the views of those working in a research capacity were taken into consideration (an outstanding example being Toynbee's report on the Jewish settlement scheme). The point to be emphasized is that advisory reports were at least taken into account through usual channels by those making actual decisions. In some instances, such as minutes by Geoffrey Hudson in the Foreign Office and Lord Hailey in the Colonial Office, advisory influence could be decisive.

Comparable lines of communication within and between branches of the American government did not exist in practice, though they did on paper. This is especially noticeable in the vast committee network of the State Department, where advisory committees of various experts established principles of foreign policy and recommended solutions to specific problems. Many of the members of these committees were academics on leave from their universities for the duration of the war, or who were able to devote large amounts of time to governmental work in addition to their usual academic responsibilities, as in the case of Isaiah Bowman. It is difficult to assess the importance of these committees. In terms of hours of discussion, the amount of talk and paperwork must have surpassed the British equivalent a hundredfold.[3] The discussions were often shrewd. But they often had no impact whatever on actual decisions. Nevertheless it would be a mistake for the historian to ignore these voluminous deliberations. One remarkable fact that emerges from a study of them is the degree of consensus among American wartime officials. When controversy did exist it is all the more remarkable for the light it throws on the mode of official thought as it existed in the State Department, as opposed, for example, to that of the Navy and War Departments. In the question of trusteeship this was a split that ultimately divided those who believed in the post-war world based upon co-operation of nations through an international organization, and those who believed in military security as the basis of the future. The proceedings of such groups as the Security Subcommittee are invaluable because military representatives participated in the debates.

There is another reason why the committee system is important to the historian. In particular instances the President might ignore the laborious work and advice of the committees, as Roosevelt did at the time of the Cairo Conference in late 1943, when he not only failed to take into account the recommendations of the specialists but did not even allow a State Department representative to accompany him. Nevertheless the work of the committees and the staff of the Division of Special Research (as well as the studies by the Office of Strategic Services) formed a part of a vast pool of accumulating information and advice. When it came to actual territorial decisions, for example, the American representatives at international conferences tapped this reservoir of knowledge by reading the briefing books. In this way there was a continuity of official thought; it might even be said that the officials and academic advisers who spent endless hours toiling on reports about such questions as the future of the Japanese islands ultimately exerted a great influence indeed. In the case of trusteeship, for example, the briefing book definitely made an impact on the decisions at Yalta.[4]

---

[3] For a British example see the work of Lord Hailey's 'Post-War Problems Committee' in the Colonial Office, CO 323/1858/9051.   [4] See below, ch. 29.

The work of the Security Subcommittee focused mainly on problems of international security in relation to ex-enemy states, as foreseen in the period immediately following the cessation of hostilities. These issues included control of armaments and general security arrangements in the light of broadening conceptions of strategy. Problems of air power and lines of communication thus fell directly within the scope of the committee's business. So also did security aspects of civil aviation, which extended the purview of the committee into the southern as well as the northern Pacific. The work of the Security Subcommittee must be studied in conjunction with the task of the closely allied Territorial Subcommittee, whose chairman, Isaiah Bowman, frequently attended sessions of the former committee because the subject-matter was closely related and sometimes identical. The responsibility of the Territorial Subcommittee was to consider the historical, economic, and social forces at work in the territories whose fate would be determined by the peace settlements, and to integrate the work of other groups such as the Security Subcommittee into a fuller view of post-war problems. Thus the social consequences of military occupation, for example, was one concern of the Bowman committee.

The Security Subcommittee, in Bowman's opinion, took an over-restricted view of the problems of the future peace 'and tended to ignore the political implications, while the military and naval experts thought only in terms of military installations without regard for political considerations'. The Territorial Committee, in contrast, tried to take a wider outlook. Again in Bowman's words:

[I]t was necessary for the Territorial Subcommittee to think of the position . . . after the war. The various experts, military and economic, each had their own closed systems in which they lived; whereas it was the function of the Territorial Subcommittee to bring together all of the considerations advanced by the various groups of experts.[5]

One member of the Territorial Subcommittee deserves special mention in relation to the work of the Security Subcommittee. This is George Blakeslee of Clark University, who had been

[5] T Minutes 52, 16 July 1943, USSD NF Box 42.

the State Department's expert on the Pacific islands since the days of the Paris Peace Conference. During the war he served as chairman of the Interdivisional Area Committee for the Far East. He attended sessions of the Security Subcommittee when it dealt with problems of the Pacific. His voice carried great influence on the question of the Japanese mandates.[6] Of the (approximately) ten members of the subcommittee itself, those who displayed a particular interest in the Pacific islands included Grayson Kirk (later President of Columbia University), Hugh Borton (later Professor of Japanese and Director of the East Asian Institute at Columbia and subsequently President of Haverford College), Colonel James Olive of the United States Army, and Captain H. L. Pence, head of the Occupied Areas Section of the Navy Department.

From the beginning the committees optimistically worked on the assumption of ultimate Allied victory. With the awareness that the victors might disagree on the terms of the peace, the Security and Territorial Subcommittees gave full consideration to the problem of the Japanese Empire at an especially interesting time, during the spring and summer of 1943—in other words, not long after the proclamation of 'unconditional surrender' of January of that year and after the beginning of the sweep towards the defeat of the Axis powers. The assumption of Allied victory now seemed warranted. Realistic decisions had to be made about such problems as the future of the post-war Pacific. What security requirements might dictate the territorial limits of post-war Japan? What would become of Korea? Should Korea be placed under international trusteeship? What plans should be made for Formosa and the other island territories of the Japanese Empire? What would be American base requirements in the Pacific following the war? These were the sorts of questions to which the members of the Security Subcommittee addressed themselves in May 1943.

The nature of the peace imposed upon Japan clearly would

[6] For Blakeslee's background see Lawrence E. Gelfand, *The Inquiry: American Preparations for Peace, 1917–1919* (New Haven, 1963), pp. 63–4. Letters between Hornbeck and Blakeslee in the Hornbeck Papers throw considerable light on the wartime committees—e.g. even though Blakeslee was a principal adviser on international relations in the Far East, his access to secret documents was restricted. There is also much material of interest in regard to the Pacific and Far East in the Blakeslee Papers.

determine the degree and type of post-war military control. On this point there arose fundamental disagreement. Captain Pence believed in a harsh peace in which Japanese power would be crushed once and for all time. He adopted the extreme view that a lasting peace could be achieved only by a permanent ring of bases around Japan. A man of straightforward views, he held that the entire problem would be 'simplified' if Japan's power were entirely destroyed. When one nation became an 'international bandit', he said to the committee, it should be eliminated. The minutes of one meeting of the Security Sub-committee read: 'Captain Pence emphatically expressed his view that the Japanese should be destroyed. We were too kindly disposed towards them. They were international bandits and not safe on the face of the earth.'[7]

Other members of the committee were by no means convinced that this extreme solution was either possible or desirable. The alternative hypothesis was that Japan should eventually be restored to a status of equality. This could not be done if the willingness to co-operate were destroyed. 'Security can be imposed or security can be cooperative', Grayson Kirk once told the committee. To obtain Japanese participation in a stable and safe post-war world, there would probably have to be some degree of Japanese economic strength and self-sufficiency. The political regime would have to be genuinely Japanese and not a puppet government (though of course the members of the committee debated long and hard about the amount of control to be retained over the Japanese). All the members of the Security Subcommittee believed in the recuperative power of the Japanese people (not least Captain Pence, but in the negative sense that they must be kept down as long as possible). To men of moderate minds the question was how best to channel Japan's revival in a direction that would not menace American security and that would generally contribute to the world's prosperity. Even Captain Pence, who was less dogmatic when he gave thought to specific problems, eventually agreed that a lasting peace would to some extent depend on an economically and politically healthy Japan. With words that proved to be historically accurate, Grayson

[7] ST Minutes 16 and 17, 7 and 12 May 1943, USSD NF; for Pence's further views see below, ch. 23.

Kirk said: 'At some time in the future, and perhaps in the not too distant future, Japan will regain its full liberty of action.'[8]

The historical records entirely absolve the officials of the Security Subcommittee of any possible charge that they failed to take into account the economic well-being of the United States as they speculated about the future of Japan. It is illuminating to examine the thought of the committee members as they projected optimal post-war circumstances. It seemed reasonable to assume that Russia might remain co-operative after the war, and might be awarded parts of the Japanese Empire in accordance with the Russian contribution to the war in the Far East (Captain Pence, for example, at one point suggested the Kurile islands and southern Sakhalin, depending on the amount of Russian assistance).[9] China would continue to be friends with the United States, though the status of China as a great power would depend on industrial development, which some committee members foresaw as a long and difficult process. If Japan were resuscitated as a 'civilized' power, then the post-war economic prospects of the Far East and Pacific looked bright indeed. With that prospect in mind, the committee members on one occasion speculated about the commercial potential of Asia as they gazed at a map of the Pacific basin. They foresaw the advent of the air age. It is important to note that they calculated the operational radius of airbases at 700 miles. This therefore meant the establishment of numerous key bases which would form a network connecting, for example, San Francisco with Tokyo, Manila, Singapore, and Sydney. Colonel Olive pointed out that these networks would be established along military lines of communication being developed during the war, and could serve in both a military and commercial capacity.

Japan would hold a central place in this grand design. In Grayson Kirk's words, Japan would be ' "the Grand Central station" of the Far East'. According to Colonel Olive: 'At the end of the war various powers would wish to have bases in Japan for commercial purposes. Japan would hold a key position on long-run commercial lines. . . . Japan would be the nerve center of lines branching in all directions.'[10] Captain

8 ST Minutes 17, 12 May 1943, USSD NF.
9 ST Minutes 18, 19 May 1943, ibid.   10 Ibid.

Pence expounded on the importance of Manila as another strategic air center, which in his view would be even more important than Tokyo. 'Manila would be the air center of the East because the wealth of that area was centered in the lands of southeastern Asia. The wealth of Northern China and Siberia was not comparable to that of Sumatra, Java, and India.' The idea of the United States benefiting from the wealth of Asia, if only in the sense of raw materials, raised further ideas. The increase of air traffic would not diminish the use of shipping. 'Colonel Olive pointed out that the shortest distance from Chicago to the Philippines was the great circle route to the north. There was a difference between air and ship cargoes. The products of southeastern Asia, such as oil, will continue to be transported by ship.'[11]

Colonel Olive also felt certain that the arctic air routes would be used increasingly after the war. The committee members moreover considered the importance of the great southern arc, on which Clipperton island and the Marquesas in the South-East Pacific held out promise as links to America's commercial bases in the Far East. According to Captain Pence, 'the United States should control a string of islands from Clipperton by way of the Marquesas to the Far East'.[12] Throughout these discussions there was a conspicuous absence of any mention of the British Empire and an assumption (which proved to be entirely false) that the European powers would be willing to hand over islands in the South Pacific to the United States. The Pacific, to use a memorable phrase of Captain Pence, was 'our lake'.

The future of the Pacific basin looked entirely different if the worst rather than the best of circumstances were chosen as the basis of the estimate. Suppose that Russia emerged from the war as America's foe instead of friend. According to Captain Pence (who was not especially consistent in his views), if Russia gained access to a warm water port, 'Russia would become an important commercial nation' and an economic rival in the Far East. Moreover, 'Captain Pence mentioned the possibility of Russian expansion to the Yangtze.'[13] What about the Chinese?

[11] Ibid.
[12] ST Minutes 20, 16 June 1943. The South Pacific routes are discussed below, ch. 16.   [13] ST Minutes 18, 19 May 1943.

Suppose that China, as some committee members genuinely believed, would not remain an ally of the United States but would become hostile, demonstrating, in one member's words, 'violently anti-foreign' sentiment? Suppose furthermore that the war would irretrievably weaken Britain's basis of power, so that even her anchor of defence at Singapore would be negligible. Suppose above all that Japan would remain bellicose. If one took a cataclysmic view, as did Captain Pence on occasion, then the yellow races of the East might eventually unite against the white races of the West. In sum, these hypotheses might seem improbable if taken together, but individually each appeared possible (except perhaps Captain Pence's racial theory, to which some of the committee members strongly dissented).[14] All in all, the various possibilities seemed to lead to one inescapable conclusion: American security would depend on keeping control over Japan, and in a broader sense all of the Far East, by the establishment of strategic bases.

The Security Subcommittee as a whole refused to take either an excessively optimistic or an alarmist view. Grayson Kirk guided the deliberations on to middle ground. 'It could be assumed', he said on the 19th of May 1943, 'that there would be an ultimate restoration of a considerable measure of Japanese strength. . . . Bases would be an important factor in the interval before Japan regained its military strength, and that interval would be a long one.'[15] Where would these strategic bases be located? The Security Subcommittee emphasized the importance of control over Korean airfields, which might be facilitated by placing that country under international trusteeship. Formosa also appeared to be another obviously important location for the control of Japan. 'Formosa would be desirable both as a military base and as a staging point on a commercial airline', according to Colonel Olive.[16] Apart from the Philippines, the other major bases in the northern Pacific would be developed, in the view of the Security Subcommittee, at the old American bastion at Guam, and at Truk in the Carolines.[17] Though the committee had taken the problem of the Korean airfields into consideration, on the whole the thrust of thought

[14] ST Minutes 18, 19 May 1943.   [15] Ibid.   [16] Ibid.
[17] For historical perspective on the island groups see especially Earl S. Pomeroy, *Pacific Outpost: American Strategy in Guam and Micronesia* (Stanford, 1951).

was the control of strategic bases in the Pacific rather than bases on the Asian mainland.[18] Here the members of the Security Subcommittee found themselves in accord with the Territorial Subcommittee. Everyone concerned wanted to correct one of the errors of the peace settlement following the First World War. So important did this point seem to Isaiah Bowman that he read into the record, 'at the Peace Conference in 1919, Mr. Hornbeck had written many memoranda protesting vehemently against the cession to Japan of important strategic islands. Since 1919 Mr. Hornbeck had been proved to be right a thousand times over . . .'[19]

Some members of the Territorial Subcommittee, taking a broader political view and attempting to assess the economic consequences of a regenerated Japan, placed a different emphasis on a vital point. While the Security Subcommittee stressed the importance of strategic bases, the Territorial Subcommittee tended to believe that Japan's post-war future could be regulated through economic means. Stanley Hornbeck above all thought that Japan's economy and thereby the Japanese state could be controlled by restricting imports:

> Mr. Hornbeck expressed a distrust of the views which he had heard stated in the Security Subcommittee to the effect that while they regarded it as necessary to disarm Japan, at the same time they were agreed that a series of bases should be established around the Japanese Islands. . . . [On the contrary, Hornbeck argued,] it seemed clear that one could prevent Japan from rearming by merely controlling her imports, since one could be sure that she would not have certain materials at all unless she imported them.[20]

Here then were two fundamental views on how to control Japan. One stressed the primacy of strategic bases. The other emphasized the control of Japan's economy. The two views were not necessarily contradictory, and both had ramifications that went far beyond Japan. Captain Pence, for example, was well aware of the economics of the 'island Empire': 'If Japan is deprived of the approaches to its empire it will be deprived of its life-blood. Being an island, it is dependent on commerce for its existence. If its trade were cut off it would become a

---

[18] For the historical development of this stategy see W. W. Rostow, *The United States in the World Arena* (New York, 1960), chs. 4–6.
[19] T. Minutes 52, 16 July 1943, USSD NF Box 42.　　　　　　　　[20] Ibid.

sixth- or eighth-rate power.'[21] The strategic and the economic
plans would interlock. By creating strategic bases out of some
of the Japanese islands, for example in the Bonins, Japan, in
Pence's words, would be kept 'crippled'. After the war, he said
on another occasion, Japan would wish to establish commercial
airlines. By depriving Japan of her islands, the commercial lines
of communication 'would be cut'.[22]

There was a further, vast economic dimension to the idea of
strategic bases. By giving economic aid to the European powers
to establish American or international bases in the colonies,
American influence would be greatly extended. Again according to Captain Pence, who assumed that the British and Dutch
would have no objections to sharing their bases:

> [I]f British bases were placed at our disposal, they would be suitable
> for the units of the American fleet. . . . Seerabaja [in the Netherlands
> East Indies] would probably be developed by the Dutch as an excel-
> lent international base, with the aid of American money and
> equipment. It would be very similar to an American base.[23]

What a splendid idea for the defence of the entire world! According to Grayson Kirk, the contribution of the smaller states
to a general security system 'might take the form of furnishing
bases'. Thus in the Bismarck archipelago, for example, 'there
was an excellent port at Rabaul', in Captain Pence's ebullient
words.

Expanding these ideas to the antipodes, one member of
the research staff, James F. Green, commented that the two
Dominions would be in a weak economic position after the war:
'Australia and New Zealand were not in a financial position to
maintain the necessary naval and air establishment. They could
not defend themselves against a powerful enemy. A major
power would have to shoulder the financial burden.'[24] As
students of the subject of economic imperialism always immediately point out, with economic aid goes some measure of
political control. Grayson Kirk responded to Green's comments
by saying he felt 'that the responsibility would be increasingly
that of the United States and less of Great Britain'. To the
officials of the Security Subcommittee in mid-1943, at least, the

21 ST Minutes 17, 12 May 1943.   22 ST Minutes 20, 16 June 1943.
23 ST Minutes 17, 12 May 1943.   24 ST Minutes 20, 16 June 1943.

United States was becoming the heir incumbent to the British Empire. The ideas blossoming at this time, both of strategic bases and economic assistance, profoundly influenced the course of post-war American policy.

The principle governing the discussion of the future of the Japanese colonial empire was Wilsonian. As George Blakeslee explained it to the Territorial Subcommittee, it meant the recognition of 'the right of nationality and self-determination'. It thus appeared axiomatic that Japan would lose Manchuria, which would revert to China. The principle of self-determination, especially in the case of Formosa and Korea, would work to America's strategic advantage. These were the two key areas from which Japan would be guarded. They would also provide two of the anchors of the American defence system in Asia. Since a clear-cut case could be made for the return of Formosa, like Manchuria, to China, there appeared to be no great obstacle to the establishment of a stable regime which would welcome American military assistance (though it was recognized that the Chinese would have to be handled with tact in order not to revive memories of the treaty ports on the China coast[25]).

Korea was an entirely different case. Here was an ancient kingdom with its own distinct civilization, yet apparently unable to govern itself. Russia as well as China clearly would show a great interest in the fate of Korea. Hugh Borton suggested that a negative approach might yield answers about the future government:

It appeared clear that Korea was not capable of self-government. If some power was to control Korea until it was ready for independence, the question arose as to which power was to exercise that function. Both Russia and China had interests in Korea. If China were sufficiently strong to exercise a predominant position in Korea, Russia would be suspicious, and China would likewise be suspicious of Russian control. His own view was that the only feasible solution was international control . . .[26]

Borton had specifically in mind international trusteeship under the auspices of the future international organization. This was the prospect embraced by American official thought throughout the latter part of the war. It held promise for a provisional

[25] T Minutes 52, 16 June 1943.   [26] ST Minutes 18, 19 May 1943.

regime that would enable the Koreans eventually to stand on
their own. The Americans did not underestimate the difficulties. According to Grayson Kirk, 'It was a delicate problem
since the international authority must possess sufficient power
to fulfill its functions while the native administration must not
be a mere puppet regime.'[27] The trusteeship government would
be supervised by the United States, China, and Russia (with
Britain mentioned from time to time as a possible additional
trustee). The scheme had a fatal flaw. To the Koreans 'trusteeship' savoured of foreign domination. Moreover it implied to
the Koreans that they were being treated in the same way as the
'barbarians' of the South Seas. In 1945 the United States
learned that the Koreans did not intend to exchange Japanese
'guardianship' for American 'trusteeship'.[28]

With American military installations on Formosa and in
Korea, the other parts of the Japanese Empire such as the
Ryukyus (Liuchius) and the Kuriles could be easily neutralized,
or, alternatively, developed into key salients of the defence
perimeter. As for political control, Grayson Kirk said at one
point in these discussions, 'It might be possible to place the
[Ryukyus] islands under an international administration in
which China was represented, and which would satisfy Chinese
amour propre.'[29] The Security Subcommittee also considered
internationalization as a possibility for the chain of islands
north of Japan, the Kuriles. The Territorial Subcommittee as
well devoted considerable attention to this idea. On one occasion a member of the latter committee said, 'if the northern
islands were internationalized there would not be much the
Russians could do about it'. Another powerful line of thought
that influenced these weighty geopolitical discussions was expressed by Adolph Berle (Assistant Secretary of State): 'it would

---

[27] ST Minutes 18, 19 May 1943.
[28] See below, ch. 35; the key work on Korea for these problems is Robert
A. Scalapino and Chong-sik Lee, *Communism in Korea* (2 vols. Berkeley, 1972).
[29] ST Minutes 18, 19 May 1943. On the Ryukyus at this time see also memorandum by John W. Masland, Jr., of the Research Staff, T 343, 2 July 1943, USSD
NF Box 35. The memorandum argued: 'the strategic significance of the islands
would largely disappear if Japan should lose Formosa at the close of the war. . . .
If the islands should be retained by Japan, however, provision might reasonably
be made for . . . a system of periodic investigation of the islands by an international
agency, to prevent the utilization for military purposes of such facilities as may be
required for legitimate commercial enterprise.'

be possible for the United States, if it had transit rights on the Kuriles, to establish an air route from this country to the mainland of the Far East without touching on either Canadian or Russian territory'.[30] American control and (or) internationalization did not necessarily mean renunciation of Japanese sovereignty, though at all stages in these discussions the committee members recognized that future events in the war and technological developments might change their views. With regard to the Kuriles and other parts of the Japanese Empire, Hugh Borton expressed the moderate Wilsonian consensus of the two committees when he stated that if 'the Japanese dismantled their military bases . . . there was no objection to their retaining sovereignty over the islands [especially if] principles of nationality and of economic stability supported the Japanese claim'.[31]

The part of the Japanese Empire with which the present volume is particularly concerned is Micronesia (derived from the Greek, signifying small islands). In a broad geographical and ethnic sense, Micronesia is one of the three divisions of Oceania and extends over an area approximately the size of the continental United States. The three principal groups are the Marshalls, Carolines, and Marianas, known collectively in the inter-war years as the Japanese mandated islands. Their strategic value predominated in all debates about their future. In George Blakeslee's words, 'They have been called anchored aircraft carriers which largely control the Pacific Ocean between Hawaii and the Philippines.'[32] The islands form an

---

[30] T Minutes 52, 16 July 1943. See also memorandum by Masland, T 322, 24 May 1943, USSD NF Box 34, in which he had argued as he had in regard to the Ryukyus, 'If Japan is deprived of the mandated islands and of Korea and Formosa, and if she is disarmed, her ability to threaten the security of the Pacific will be very limited. Possession of the Kuriles will have little, if any, effect upon this situation.'

[31] T Minutes 52, 16 July 1943. For Borton's further ideas, see his important memorandum dated 10 Jan. 1945, in which he discusses the possibility of trusteeship for Southern Sakahalin, in *Foreign Relations: the Conferences at Malta and Yalta 1945*, pp. 385–8.

[32] Blakeslee, 'Japan's Mandated Islands: Description and History', T-328, 27 May 1943, USSD NF Box 34; other important papers written by Blakeslee at this time include: 'Japan's Mandated Islands: Legal Problems', T-345, 8 July 1943, ibid., Box 35; 'The Mandate Under Japanese Administration', T-365, 9 Aug. 1943, ibid., 'Japan's Mandated Islands: The Maintenance and Use of Commercial Airfields', T-370, 1 Sept. 1943, ibid. See also especially his memorandum on 'Japan: Territorial Problems: the Kurile Islands', 28 Dec. 1944, in *Foreign Relations: Yalta*, pp. 379–83. There is important background material in the Blakeslee Papers, though most of his important wartime papers appear in the official files.

immense bloc of the tropical North Pacific. The total land area, however, is only 830 square miles, considerably less than Rhode Island's.[33] Many of the inhabited atolls are less than one square mile. The Marshalls in the east consist of low coral islands with a hot and humid climate. The Marianas in the north are of volcanic origin and extend to heights of 3,000 feet. The Carolines group, extending farthest to the west, consists mainly of coral islands, many with shallow lagoons. During the war George Blakeslee reported that by 1941 the Japanese had built approximately a dozen airfields, but that the bases were mainly suitable for small aircraft. In the Carolines, the Truk island group contains a great coral reef with a lagoon 30 miles in diameter.

Wartime estimates of the population roughly established the figure of 103,000 for the Japanese mandates, of which 63,000 were Japanese and 50,000 were indigenous inhabitants. As American officials studied the islands, they noted the Spanish influence in the Marianas, where the inhabitants resembled the Filipinos. The Micronesian inhabitants of the area as a whole appeared to be of Melanesian, Malay, and Polynesian stock.[34] According to Blakeslee, the economic value of the islands was slight. He did note in 1943, however, the Japanese discovery of bauxite and manganese ore.[35] Since the military experts always discounted the economic potential in order to emphasize the purely strategic reasons why the islands should be retained, perhaps it is noteworthy that the principal civilian authority did take account of the economic factor, though it was one he never rated highly. To Blakeslee as to most Americans, the significance of the islands could be summed up in the phrase 'strategic outposts'.

During the war the history of the mandated islands was reviewed extensively both by officials within the government and by writers presenting the great issues of the war to the

[33] These and other figures concerning population are those which recur in the American wartime documents and are slightly at variance with present-day knowledge.

[34] In fact the ethnic and linguistic diversity is extremely complicated. For the peoples and cultures of Micronesia, see Daniel T. Hughes and Sherwood G. Lingenfelter, *Political Development in Micronesia* (Columbus, Ohio, 1974).

[35] Blakeslee, 'Japan's Mandated Islands', 27 May 1943. The mineral resources did not prove to be important.

American public. How did the Japanese get hold of the islands in the first place? George Blakeslee examined the records of the State Department to give a definite answer.[36] During the period of the scramble for colonies in the mid-1880s the United States did not move to extend political control over the Pacific. In 1885 the State Department merely protested vigorously when Germany seized the Marshalls and Spain reasserted old claims to the other two groups. In 1898 the Spanish-American war altered American attitudes. During the peace negotiations the American delegates became convinced of the desirability of acquiring not only Guam but also the Carolines. An American offer of $1,000,000 was actually made for the island of Kusaie in the Carolines. Instead of accepting it, the Spanish sold all of the Carolines and Marianas to Germany for a little over $4,000,000. Guam, of course, became an American possession, but one that could be held as hostage by the power controlling the island groups or otherwise dominant in the western Pacific. In 1914 Japan occupied all of the German islands north of the Equator. In 1917 the British, French, and Italian governments assured Japan that her claims to the islands would be supported, in return for Japanese support of Allied claims. To the Americans this was a deplorable example of 'secret diplomacy'. The General Board of the Navy pressed for annexation of the islands by the United States.[37] According to Blakeslee, whose comments are particularly valuable because of his official capacity at that time as the adviser to the State Department on problems of the Pacific islands: 'President Wilson . . . made no effort to obtain them for this country, although he was disturbed at the thought of Japan's possessing them and was opposed to permitting Japan to use them as naval bases.'[38] By the terms of the mandate, the islands could not be fortified. This was a solution to the problem that seemed reasonable enough in 1919.

[36] Blakeslee, 'Japan's Mandated Islands'.

[37] The General Board of the Navy stated on 24 Jan. 1918: 'The General Board is of the decided conviction that the Marshall and Caroline Islands should be acquired by the United States; and this object should be kept in view and prepared for by the Department of State as a preliminary to future peace negotiations and settlements. In the same manner, the Mariana Islands, north of Guam, should be similarly acquired.' Quoted ibid. The views of the General Board are discussed at length by Braisted, *The United States Navy in the Pacific*, ch. 25.

[38] Blakeslee, 'Japan's Mandated Islands'.

During the Second World War it now appeared obvious to almost all Americans that there was a historical lesson to be drawn from these episodes. According to an essay in the *Yale Review* (which is of especial interest because Stanley Hornbeck called it to the attention of the Secretary of State):

It is now painfully clear that no power can hope to hold the Philippines and Guam unless it holds also the enveloping archipelago of Micronesia. Any strong nation with bases in the Carolines, which approach to within 500 miles of the Philippines, or the Marianas, of which the nearest to Guam is less than fifty miles distant, can take both of these objectives within the first few weeks of war.

[In 1898] We took the lock, the Philippines and Guam, but would not accept the key, Micronesia.[39]

Since some of the fiercest and bloodiest battles of the entire war were fought to wrench the Pacific islands from the Japanese, the question of the mandates became a highly emotional and patriotic issue. Over 38,000 Americans suffered casualties in the capture of Micronesia in 1944 and 1945. One of the foremost historians of the American territories in the Pacific, Earl S. Pomeroy, has astutely noted that, by the end of the war, no one doubted the continuation of American control over the mandated islands, but merely debated the form of legal jurisdiction. 'Micronesia had emotional values aside from those of victory. It was the collective Louisbourg, the multiple Heligoland of the 1940's—the enemy's fortress.'[40] Admiral Ernest J. King stated publicly in April 1945:

These atolls, these island harbors will have been paid for by the sacrifice of American blood . . .
Failure to maintain these bases essential for our own defense raises the fundamental question—how long can the United States afford to continue a cycle of fighting and winning and giving away, only to fight and build and win and give away again?[41]

He spoke those words on the eve of the San Francisco Conference, at a time when the public had also learned that the State Department had elaborate plans to place the islands under 'international trusteeship'. Admiral King voiced a power-

---

[39] Willard Price, 'The Island Road to Tokyo', *Yale Review*, 33.3 (Spring 1944); for Hornbeck's comment to Cordell Hull, 2 May 1944, USSD 890.0146/12.
[40] Pomeroy, *Pacific Outpost*, p. xix.   [41] Quoted ibid., p. 169.

ful sentiment. However noble might be the goals of the future United Nations organization, to most Americans there could be no doubt whatever that the islands won with American blood would remain under the unchallenged control of the United States.

From the President down through the echelons of the State Department there existed a sensitivity to the political problems that might be created by American claims to the islands. In particular the word *sovereignty* caused officials to pall at possible repercussions. Apart from obviously violating the Atlantic Charter, if the United States annexed the Pacific islands, might this not spark a new scramble for territory? By what right could the United States object, for example, to British claims to Italian Somaliland if the Navy appropriated the islands? The answer to the hoary question of sovereignty was to let it reside, rather vaguely, in the United Nations. The United States would still retain complete political and military control. This was a solution in which American military authorities concurred only with extreme reluctance. George Blakeslee said to the Security Subcommittee in May 1943:

[I]t would be desirable for the United States to have the islands in full sovereignty, but there were obvious political difficulties to this solution, namely, the principles of the Atlantic Charter. Perhaps it would be necessary for the United States to acquire rights in the islands by an arrangement short of full sovereignty.[42]

Captain Pence responded to Blakeslee's suggestion. In many cases the Captain held strong opinions, but on this point he faithfully represented the viewpoint of the Navy:

Captain Pence replied that the Navy was not in a position to raise its voice to any great extent on political problems; however he himself wondered whether the Atlantic Charter would be adhered to in post-war settlements. He raised the question of whether we could afford, for security reasons, to be too idealistic.

The islands were of use only for naval and air purposes. There was no reason why a long leasehold at Truk similar to that at Bermuda would not be consistent with the principles of the Charter.[43]

Thus there was a tension between the military and civilian

[42] ST Minutes 16, 7 May 1943.   [43] Ibid.

officials, but one in which both sides respected the strategic as well as the political arguments and vice versa.

There is a further passage in the minutes of the Security Subcommittee which indicates the degree of consensus reached by the spring of 1943. It also helps to place the economic factor into the perspective of the military as well as the civilian officials at the time:

> Colonel Olive observed that these islands were useful to the Japanese for the purposes which they had in view. The islands would be much less valuable to the United States. He . . . emphasized that the islands were suitable for small landing fields and not for large air bases.
>
> Captain Pence felt that in the long-term view the islands in the southern Pacific could not be considered separately from the mandated islands. Commercial air lines in the future would undoubtedly cross the southern Pacific. There were excellent air bases along the southern route.
>
> Mr. Kirk suggested that it might be assumed that the United States would have a string of bases in the southern Pacific and predominant control in some form over the mandated islands.[44]

When the Navy and War Departments finally acquiesced in the solution of 'international trusteeship' in the spring of 1945, the military authorities had made certain beyond any reasonable doubt that international supervision would not jeopardize American security. As for the economic element in trusteeship, American officials, military and civilian alike, had no trouble in reconciling security measures with those such as plans for bases that might promote American prosperity (and, as if by afterthought, native welfare in Micronesia).

To what extent did committee groups actually influence policy? In many cases it is not easy to make the connection between those who ventured advisory opinions and those who executed policy. Indeed sometimes there was no connection at all. With the membership of Stanley Hornbeck and George Blakeslee on the Territorial Subcommittee, it is possible to see in this particular case a direct flow of communication. Hornbeck and Blakeslee were close friends. Blakeslee participated in the committee sessions of the Security Subcommittee and Hornbeck followed them closely. Hornbeck as the Political Advisor on Far Eastern Affairs also allowed Blakeslee con-

[44] ST Minutes 16, 7 May 1943.

siderable latitude in chairing the Interdivisional Area Committee for the Far East. In some particular cases it is possible to trace the line of communication directly from Blakeslee to Hornbeck to the Secretary of State.[45] Here however must end the effort to analyse the American process of decision-making along British lines. The Secretary of State often had little influence on the President, and still less, for example, on the Navy. The military and civilian branches of the government negotiated with each other as if they were foreign governments. Roosevelt acted as his own Secretary of State. At the Cairo Conference in late 1943 the President and his advisers decided that Japan should be stripped of her colonial empire. This was the same conclusion arrived at by the Security and Territorial Subcommittees. But the experts had no influence at all in this great wartime decision. As Hugh Borton has written, the similarity between the Cairo Declaration and the conclusions of the committees *'was by chance, not design'*.[46]

In studying the work of the wartime committees of the State Department in relation to American policy, one is left with a sense of paradox. Within themselves, the committees reached systematic and often astute conclusions. Sometimes they did and sometimes they did not influence policy. Especially during the early part of the war, there was little success in co-ordinating State Department policy with, for example, the Navy's. The President followed his own inclinations, though it should be added that sometimes Roosevelt's attentiveness was not great and the Departments could often win their way by persisting. To foreign observers such as the British the general picture of American policy thus appeared to be one of constant improvization. The great expansion of American power during the Second World War was not accompanied by an over-all clarity of policy.

[45] See e.g., USSD 890.10146/12.
[46] Borton, *American Presurrender Planning*, p. 13, italics added.

5

INTERNATIONAL TRUSTEESHIP

THE heart of the concept of international trusteeship is accountability to an international organization. In the history of ideas, *international* trusteeship stands in contrast to *national* trusteeship. The latter concept is probably as old as the notion of overseas colonization. No colonial empire has existed without a sense of mission. Thus some scholars have identified the modern origin of trusteeship, for example, in Spanish thought of the sixteenth century.[1] In English intellectual history, the idea is usually identified with Edmund Burke's interpretation of a 'trust' as derived from Roman law. Just as the Spanish formed their ideas about trusteeship in relation to their empire in Latin America, so the British developed the concept in relation to India. Burke said in 1783: 'Every species of political dominion . . . are all in the strictest sense a trust; and it is of the very essence of every *trust* to be rendered accountable.'[2] This is a key statement in understanding British thought

[1] See, e.g., R. N. Chowdhuri, *International Mandates and Trusteeship Systems: A Comparative Study* (The Hague, 1955). For an introduction to the vast literature on the subject, see Wm. Roger Louis, 'International Trusteeship', in Robin W. Winks, ed., *The Historiography of the British Empire–Commonwealth* (Durham, N.C., 1966). The key works are: Quincy Wright, *Mandates under the League of Nations* (Chicago, 1930); H. Duncan Hall, *Mandates, Dependencies and Trusteeship* (Washington, 1948); and James N. Murray, Jr., *The United Nations Trusteeship System* (Illinois Studies in the Social Sciences, xl, Urbana, 1957). The best recent book, an outstanding contribution, is George Thullen, *Problems of the Trusteeship System* (Geneva, 1964). There have also been several excellent recent works written from regional angles. These include W. J. Hudson, *Australia and the Colonial Question at the United Nations* (Honolulu, 1970); Mary Boyd, 'The Record in Western Samoa to 1945' and 'The Record in Western Samoa since 1945', in Angus Ross, ed., *New Zealand's Record in the Pacific Islands in the Twentieth Century* (New Zealand Institute of International Affairs, 1969); and Solomon Slonim, *South West Africa and the United Nations: an International Mandate in Dispute* (Baltimore, 1973). On South-West Africa the important work of Richard Dale should also be mentioned. See, e.g., his essay 'The "glass palace war" over the international decolonization of South West Africa', *International Organization* 29. 2 (Spring 1975). For Tanganyika see B. T. G. Chidzero, *Tanganyika and International Trusteeship* (London, 1961). For the French territories, see the comprehensive bibliography by David Gardinier in Gifford and Louis, *France and Britain in Africa*.

[2] Burke on the East India Bill, 1 Dec. 1783. For an example of the way in which

through the period of the Second World War. To whom were the British accountable? With their own sense of colonial tradition, which Englishmen commonly regarded as the highest in the entire world, they saw themselves responsible above all to Parliament. Especially to those who took a true-blue Tory view of the colonial world, such as Churchill and Amery, only scorn could be poured upon the idea of international interference in the affairs of the British Empire.

The idea of international as opposed to national trusteeship is of relatively recent origin. Its birth is usually associated with the partition of the African continent in the late nineteenth century, though scholars in tracing the antecedents of the term 'mandate' have found diverse origins in, for example, the affairs of the great powers in Bosnia and Herzegovina and in such international arrangements as the control of the Danube river. For present purposes the crucial distinction is whether there existed a dual concern for the welfare of the indigenous inhabitants and the protection of free trade. At the time of the creation of the Congo Free State in 1884–5, Leopold II, King of the Belgians, proclaimed himself the trustee of civilization and guardian of equal trading opportunity in the Congo. The Berlin Act of 1885 established these two principles that later became the basis of both the mandates and trusteeship systems.[3] Native welfare and free trade are the cardinal elements.[4]

The importance of trusteeship in tropical Africa has a double significance for the present volume. First, the Berlin Act failed

British statesmen consistently identified Burke as the spiritual ancestor of the idea of trusteeship, see Lord Cranborne in the House of Lords, 3 Dec. 1942, *Parliamentary Debates*, c. 407.

[3] The Berlin Act as an antecedent of the mandates and trusteeship systems is discussed at length in Wm. Roger Louis, 'African Origins of the Mandates Idea', *International Organization* 19. 1 (1965). This has been one of my standing interests. My further investigations of the subject include 'The Berlin Congo Conference', in *France and Britain in Africa*; chs. III and IV of *Germany's Lost Colonies*; and 'The United Kingdom and the Beginning of the Mandates System, 1919–1922', *International Organization* 23. 1 (1969).

[4] In 1890 the Brussels Anti-Slavery Act amplified the humanitarian purpose of the Berlin Act. In a splendid book on the subject, Suzanne Miers has written, 'In the development of the doctrine of international trusteeship the Brussels Act was a landmark. . . . the idea had been voiced and the responsibility accepted, and the principles embodied in it were adopted by the League of Nations and eventually passed on to the United Nations.' *Britain and the Ending of the Slave Trade* (London, 1975), p. 319.

to secure free trade. The Congo State also became infamous for cruelty to the Africans. When the next major partition of Africa occurred in 1919, those who created the mandates system attempted to strengthen provisions for free trade and native welfare. Secondly, the lurid history of the Congo State was still within living memory of those who established the trusteeship system in 1945. Following both world wars, those pursuing the goal of 'International Trusteeship' were working to curtail the excesses of European imperialism as had existed in such places as the Congo.

It is possible to give a more cynical interpretation of the mandates and trusteeship systems. As seen from the Tory viewpoint, at the time of both peace settlements in 1919 and 1945, the United States imposed conditions without accepting responsibilities. In 1919 the United States insisted on creating the mandates system and then refused to join the League. In 1945, the Americans demanded the application of trusteeship principles to the Italian colonies and at the same time proclaimed the Japanese mandated islands to be an exception. The Tory interpretation is entirely consistent. By blocking the annexation of the German colonies in 1919 the United States kept the door open for American influence. By putting forward idealistic principles in 1945 the Americans sent up a smoke-screen for the annexation of the Japanese islands in all but name. Walter Long (the Colonial Secretary in 1918) no less than Oliver Stanley dismissed professions of concern about 'native welfare' as unadulterated cant. Beneath the 'diaphanous idealism' (Stanley's phrase) crouched the spectre of American economic imperialism.

No one who has studied the archival records would deny for a minute that the American officials kept a sharp lookout for the economic interests of the United States in the mandated territories. The same concern for economic advantage may be said of the Colonial Office documents. Aversion to the free-trade clauses of the tropical African mandates is a persistent theme in British official thought. The Colonial Office officials wanted freedom to shape their own economic policies. They argued that commercial restrictions worked to the detriment of the peoples of the mandated territories. Of the particular British statesmen who held strong views on the subject, Leo Amery regarded the economic clauses of the mandates as yet another example of the way in which the Americans were attempting to reduce the British Empire to the status of a satellite. Oliver Stanley also detested the obligations of free trade. Nevertheless the specific economic issue was trivial if compared with other issues at the close of the war. At the San Francisco Conference the British gave way to American insistence without feeling that a vital interest had been sacrificed.[5]

On the American side the economic issue may be put into sharp perspective by bearing in mind the ideas of the State Department official who supervised the trusteeship issue during the war, Benjamin Gerig. As a staff member of the Division of Special Research, Gerig prepared reports on all aspects of colonial problems and participated in the major State Department discussions on the subject. Throughout the war he chaired the Committee on Dependent Areas. In 1945 he acted as Harold Stassen's right-hand man on the colonial issue at the San Francisco Conference. In the same year he became Chief of the Dependent Areas Division. Until his retirement in 1962 he was directly involved in the trusteeship affairs of the United Nations. He is a figure of paramount importance for the subject of the United States and the decolonization of the European colonial empires.

Gerig had begun his career as a political economist and had served in the secretariat of the League of Nations. His first book is entitled *The Open Door and the Mandates System: A Study of Economic Equality before and since the Establishment of the Mandates System*. Here then is a principal American witness to the economic factor in American policy. In the concluding passage of the book, he wrote in 1930:

The Mandates System is undoubtedly the most effective instrument yet devised to make the Open Door effective. The mandates principle is irreconcilable with that of national economic imperialism.[6]

The statement holds true for his general outlook during the Second World War. For Benjamin Gerig the mandates and trusteeship systems in a minor way represented an effort to break down commercial barriers and restrictive tariffs. To the permanent official of the State Department who supervised

---

[5] See below, ch. 33.

[6] Gerig, *Open Door and the Mandates System* (London, 1930), p. 199.

day-by-day policy, the principles of trusteeship were the opposite of those of economic imperialism.[7]

The minor nature of the free-trade issue needs to be stressed
because the mandated territories formed only a fraction of the
colonial world. The mandates system is much more significant
as a case study in political evolution. In 1919 the non-western
peoples who comprised the 'sacred trust' were blocked into
types of 'A', 'B', and 'C'. The 'A' peoples of the Middle East
were those who appeared to be capable of standing on their
own after a period of tutelage. The 'B' mandates were those of
tropical Africa, whose inhabitants were destined for an indefinite period of guardianship. The 'C' mandates of South-West
Africa and the Pacific islands consisted of peoples so 'primitive'
that they probably never would be capable of governing themselves. The 'A', 'B', and 'C' classifications may be taken as
concepts of the non-western world. Different civilizations had
various stages of development. By 1945 these crude concepts
had vanished. 'Non-self-governing territories' became the phrase
used to describe colonial dependencies. Preparation for independence became the explicit goal of the trusteeship system. In
this sense a political revolution had occurred in a quarter of
a century. On the other hand the statesmen of 1945 were still
thoroughly paternalistic in outlook. They continued to think
of self-government in terms of decades and even centuries for
some of the more remote areas. Again, no one in 1945 would
have hazarded a prediction that New Guinea would become
independent three decades later.

It is useful to regard the actual creation of the mandates
system as a compromise between those who wanted annexation of the German colonies and those who advocated internationalization. The loudest voice in favour of annexation
in 1919 was that of the Prime Minister of Australia, William

---

[7] Some of Gerig's writings relevant to the trusteeship controversy include: 'Colonies in an Eventual World Settlement', *International Conciliation* 369 (April 1941);
'Mandates and Colonies', *World Organization: A Balance Sheet of the First Great Experiment* (A symposium of the Institute on World Organization, American Council on
Public Affairs, Washington, 1942); (with others) 'Colonial Aspects of the Postwar
Settlement', *International Conciliation* 379 (April 1942); 'Significance of the Trusteeship System', *Annals of the American Academy of Political and Social Science* 255 (January
1948). For his scholarship on the League of Nations, see Benjamin Gerig, 'Cases
under the League of Nations', in David W. Wainhouse and others, *International
Peace Observation: a History and Forecast* (Baltimore, 1966).

Morris Hughes.[8] He and his colleague from New Zealand, William F. Massey, accepted the solution of mandates only when they became convinced that international control would not interfere in any way with their defence and commercial policies. The 'C' mandates were administered as integral parts of the mandatory states. The free-trade provisions were omitted. The Dominions statesmen of 1919 made every effort to obtain the 'C' mandates as colonies in all but name. Their success in doing so caused American critics to charge that the mandates were a 'sham' or a 'fake'.[9] Nevertheless there was a real element of accountability. The mandatory regimes were required to submit annual reports to the League of Nations.

The Permanent Mandates Commission consisted of approximately ten members of different nationalities, all European except for one Japanese, who were colonial experts but who did not officially represent their governments. They offered spirited and detailed observations which caused pain and indignation in official circles, not least in the Colonial Office. With the opening of the archives, it is now possible to see that the implicit criticism of the Permanent Mandates Commission goaded British officials into articulating basic policies and caused them to be extremely circumspect in preparing the annual reports. The mandated territories became colonial showcases because of the amount of publicity given to them. The impact of specific colonial policies extended beyond the boundaries of the particular mandate. The care taken with the pronouncements of 'native policy' in the mandated territory of Tanganyika, for example, had repercussions in Kenya and Uganda. Professor Ralph Austen has written: 'the frequent statements by British mandate representatives of the manner in which they were applying the policy of Indirect Rule undoubtedly contributed to the great reputation which this doctrine achieved throughout the interwar colonial world.'[10]

[8] In 1942 Hughes got in a final jab at President Wilson, whom the Australian held responsible for the whole business of the mandates, by suggesting that the United States should bear the responsibility for the Pacific war because the Americans failed to annex the islands in 1919. This overlooked, of course, the secret agreement between Britain and Japan of 1917 which allocated the islands to the Japanese. 'Isn't this one cute?' Stanley Hornbeck wrote of Hughes (*Washington Star*, 29 July 1942, clipping and notation in the Hornbeck Papers).

[9] See below, ch. 9.

[10] Ralph A. Austen, 'Varieties of Trusteeship: African Territories under British

The extreme alternative to annexation in 1919 was thorough-going internationalization. This was the course urged by British Labour politicans as well as by various Pacifists who believed that 'imperialism' had been a cause of the war. It was almost an instinctive reaction of those who had a superficial knowledge but real concern about colonial problems. It was the way some American officials responded during the early stages of the Second World War. The reason can be explained in the following way. When one stops to ponder profound causes of war and large issues such as the presence of Europe in the non-western world, the first reaction is likely to be one of outrage. The situation appears so bad that something should be *done* about it. Why not start with a clean slate? First of all, by internationalizing the colonies they would no longer be a source of international rivalry. A cause of war would be eliminated. There would be a truly international administration. It would be composed of men of goodwill representing non-colonial states such as those of Scandinavia. They would be trained in fields such as education and tropical agriculture. Thus genuine progress could be made towards self-sufficiency and independence. Such was the logic of a supranational colonial administration.

The idea of internationalizing the colonies exerted a powerful appeal in the inter-war years, especially for those who believed that Germany had been unjustly deprived of her colonies. In the 1930s much of the talk about the 'haves' and 'have-nots' turned on whether the colonial boundaries could be redrawn so as to provide a more equitable distribution of markets and raw materials. For the British this era ended with the failure of the policy of appeasement.[11] It is noteworthy that Leonard Woolf, one of the staunchest supporters of internationalization during the First World War, had completely given up the idea by 1942.[12]

and French Mandate, 1919–1939', in *France and Britain in Africa*, p. 525. These observations are based on my study of the files of the Mandates Section of the League in Geneva and the relevant Colonial Office records. I have also benefited greatly from the collections at Rhodes House, notably the Papers of the Anti-Slavery and Aborigines Protection Society and the Lugard Papers.

[11] See Wm. Roger Louis, 'Colonial Appeasement, 1936–1938', *Revue belge de philologie et d'histoire*, 49. 4 (1971). For the German side see Klaus Hildebrand, *Vom Reich zum Weltreich* (Munich, 1969).

[12] See Woolf, *Empire and Commerce in Africa*, part III; for his ideas on the subject during the Second World War, see, e.g., Woolf to C. W. W. Greenidge (Secretary of

What is also remarkable in regard to the main themes of this book is that certain American officials such as Sumner Welles responded in the early part of the war with the same fire-eating attitude of 'reform by internationalization' that characterized British Labour thought in the First World War. According to Welles and certain members of the State Department's Advisory Committee on Foreign Policy in 1942, *all* European colonies should be placed under direct international administration.

There is a crucial distinction between international *administration* and international *control*. Those who advocated thorough-going international colonial administration soon came up against formidable questions. For example, Liberia was an independent nation but was generally considered more backward than many colonial areas. Should Liberia be placed under international administration? And why should internationalization be restricted to the eastern hemisphere? Would the Virgin Islands and Puerto Rico be internationalized? American enthusiasm for all-out internationalization soon dwindled after the implications were examined. To moderate minds, international administration appeared to be an impossible and undesirable goal, but international *control* over colonial areas, in the sense of the conditions imposed by the Berlin Act, had much to be said in its favour. The principles of the mandates system, for example, could be extended to help improve trade conditions, at least for those who wanted access to colonial markets. International standards of colonial administration would be codified. This codification might merely confirm existing policies, but it would be useful as a measuring stick to examine, for instance, Portuguese colonial practices. Would it not also be reasonable to empower the international body with the right to receive petitions from the indigenous inhabitants and to send out visiting missions of inspection? Here is the vital difference between the Permanent Mandates Commission and the Trusteeship Council.

The Permanent Mandates Commission had no powers of inspection. This was a basic innovation of the trusteeship system. It was one the British resisted to the end. They finally agreed to it at the San Francisco Conference only when they

the Anti-Slavery and Aborgines Protection Society), 31 Dec. 1942, Anti-Slavery Papers G442–3. See also especially Hailey to Amery, 6 Oct. 1942, Hailey Papers.

feared that the entire plan for the future international organization might collapse if they refused. Some officials took the line
that inspections could do no harm because the British had
nothing to hide. On the contrary, they were proud of their
colonial administration. But the Colonial Office feared the
political impact of official visitations. These fears proved justified. In the post-war era of decolonization the visiting missions
of the United Nations to such territories as Samoa and Tanganyika helped to shape the international consciousness of the
inhabitants.[13] The visiting missions were empowered to receive
petitions (another distinguishing feature of trusteeships as opposed to mandates). Though the innovation of petitions did not
prove as effective as its American sponsors had hoped,[14] the
Africans, for example, quickly saw that they had the right to
appeal beyond the colonial authority. The full history of the
influence of the visiting missions of the United Nations has not
yet been written (and cannot be until the opening of the
archives), but it is certain that they played a significant part
in the process of decolonization. For present purposes it is
important to emphasize that the visiting missions are a distinguishing feature of the trusteeship system. It was a power the
Permanent Mandates Commission never possessed, and it was
a principle that the British representative for much of the inter-
war period, Lord Lugard, thoroughly deprecated.

Sir Frederick Lugard (as he was known before being elevated
to the peerage in 1928) stands in history as one of the most famous
British pro-consuls and the philosopher of the system of colonial
administration known as 'Indirect Rule'. The cardinal principle was the preservation of indigenous institutions for British
purposes.[15] Lugard himself would probably have stressed the

---

[13] See J. W. Davidson, *Samoa Mo Samoa: the Emergence of the Independent State of Western Samoa* (Melbourne, 1967); Chidzero, *Tanganyika and International Trusteeship*.

[14] I am indebted to Benjamin Gerig for an explanation of how the American delegation at San Francisco anticipated that the right of petition would be a major step forward. In the event it proved to be unmanageable simply because of the great number of petitions.

[15] See Ronald Robinson, 'Non-European Foundations of European Imperialism', in Wm. Roger Louis, ed., *Imperialism: the Robinson and Gallagher Controversy* (New York, 1976). For an analysis of the substance of 'Indirect Rule', see especially Prosser Gifford, 'Indirect Rule: Touchstone or Tombstone for Colonial Policy?', in eds. Prosser Gifford and Wm. Roger Louis, *Britain and Germany in Africa* (New Haven, 1967).

reciprocity of British and African interests, as he did in 1922 in the work that elaborated his ideas, *The Dual Mandate*. The purpose of British rule in Africa, he wrote, was to promote the prosperity of England and to facilitate 'the native races in their progress to a higher plane'. The 'dual mandate' he defined as 'the dual responsibility of controlling powers in the tropics viz as trustees to civilization for the adequate development of their resources and as trustees for the welfare of native races'. This was a definition entirely compatible with the doctrine of the sacred trust of the mandates system. These post-First World War ideas were essentially static. Though the 'native races' were in a state of evolution, this was a long-range prospect. European overlordship would continue indefinitely with subject peoples held almost as if in perpetual trust. Shortly before and during the Second World War, Lord Hailey became a key figure in pointing out that social and political change in Africa would occur much more rapidly than Lugard had anticipated.

Lugard is a convenient figure to dwell upon not only because of his national colonial stature but also because his career spanned the crucial period in the development of international trusteeship. He acted as the British representative on the Permanent Mandates Commission from 1923 to 1936 (a length of time surpassed only by the Belgian, Pierre Orts, who served for the entirety of the inter-war period). Lugard, like most other Englishmen of official experience, regarded the mandates system as essentially a negative set of checks on colonial administration. Article 22 of the League's Covenant guaranteed that the administrative authorities would not interfere with freedom of missionary activities. It prohibited the slave trade and arms and liquor traffic. It prevented military and naval fortifications. According to the terms of the 'B' mandates, the administering authority would protect the natives from forced labour and land alienation. These were negative injunctions. Article 22 did stress the 'well-being and development' of the native peoples. This was merely the minimal requirement of any colonial administration.

Lugard painstakingly cross-examined British representatives who appeared before the Permanent Mandates Commission. He made clear to the world at large that the record of Britain as a great colonial power would bear close scrutiny. For his meticulous performance at Geneva he earned the frigid esteem of the

Colonial Office.[16] Here was a former colonial governor who appeared to have divided loyalties! He called attention to the weaknesses as well as the strengths of British colonial administration! In point of fact Lugard was keenly aware of the moral dilemma of being an internationalist and a British patriot at the same time. After his retirement from the Permanent Mandates Commission, he wrote about land alienation in Kenya in 1937: 'While things like this go on in a British Colony, we have no locus standi to criticise South Africa, or to dot the i's and cross the t's as to what Trusteeship should mean.'[17] During the war he exchanged views with numerous people on the future of the mandates. He brought to bear his lifelong experience as an authority on colonial affairs.[18] Some of his views were emphatic: ultimate control over the colonies should remain vested in the metropolitan state. There is one further point that, in all Lugard's voluminous correspondence, deserves special emphasis in the context of the present discussion. He wrote in 1930 about the possibility that the East African mandate might be transferred to another power: 'this has a disastrous effect in unsettling the minds of people in Tanganyika.'[19] To Lugard as to most other officials, Tanganyika could not be properly developed unless it were treated for all practical purposes as a permanent British possession.

Impermanence—a single word summarizes the repugnance of many Imperially minded Englishmen to the mandates system, especially those of Tory persuasion. 'The chief objection to the Mandatory system', Oliver Stanley wrote in 1945, 'was not, as some people suppose, the amount of supervision which it entailed.' It was, above all, 'the sense of impermanence which the absence of permanent British sovereignty gave in the territories concerned'.[20] At least during the inter-war years the

[16] I am indebted to Margery Perham for numerous discussions about Lugard. For his work in Geneva see the second volume of her biography, *Lugard: the Years of Authority, 1898–1945* (London, 1960). For the long-standing hostility of the C.O. to Lugard, see the review of this work by Kenneth Robinson, *Journal of African History*, 2. 2 (1961). For a sample of Lugard's view on international supervision, see 'The Mandate System and the British Mandates', *Journal of the Royal Society of Arts* 72 (27 June 1924).

[17] Lugard to Sir John Harris (Secretary of the Anti-Slavery and Aborigines Protection Society), 26 May 1937, Anti-Slavery Papers G442–3.

[18] e.g. Lugard to Greenidge, 15 Jan. 1943, ibid.

[19] Lugard to Harris, 16 May 1930, ibid., G510.

[20] Memorandum by Stanley, 19 Mar. 1945, W.P. (45) 200, CAB 66/63.

mandates were treated as though they were British colonies. They were provided with economic assistance as if they were British possessions. They were painted British red on maps of the world. Their affairs might be examined by a body of experts in Geneva, but the discussions were not political. These facts led critics of British imperialism to believe that the mandates were a legal fiction. During the war American officials began to talk of putting teeth into the mandates system. They asked the question, why should the future of the colonies not be discussed in the general assembly of the future world organization? Oliver Stanley, for one, recognized this possibility as a vital danger. He spoke of the hazards of debating the affairs of the British Empire in a *'motley international assembly'*. Churchill also perceived the same peril. Never so long as he was Prime Minister, he stated emphatically at Yalta, would he allow the British Empire to be put *'in the dock'* to have its affairs discussed by others to see if it measured up to their standards.[21] Stanley and Churchill had an accurate premonition of things to come, though they probably would have gasped at the extreme political attacks on the colonial powers that characterized the United Nations colonial debates of the late 1950s and 1960s. This political transformation marks the greatest difference between the mandates and trusteeship systems.

The fact that the Colonial Empire did not prove to be a permanent institution does not mean that the British wartime vision was unrealistic. In view of contemporary beliefs and the vigour of the arguments, in 1945 it was just as reasonable to believe that there would be evolution towards self-government within a lasting British Empire–Commonwealth as it was to hold the American view that there should be self-determination and independence. Despite the clash of British and American views about the future, what strikes one with the benefit of thirty years' hindsight is the common assumption of gradual evolution: neither the Americans nor anyone else foresaw the speed or the fragmentation of decolonization. Broadly speaking the British and Americans did emphasize different political goals. But if one looks to the economic dimension of trusteeship, there is a striking similarity of outlook: in both England and America there was a common belief that without economic

[21] See below, ch. 29.

development other problems such as poverty, illiteracy, and disease could not be ameliorated and political development would lack substance.

The foundations of British economic trusteeship were the Colonial Development Act of 1929 and the Colonial Development and Welfare Acts of 1940 and 1945. A brief examination of their purpose and scope will help to see the points of consensus about national versus international trusteeship. Just as the modern genesis of the international idea can be associated with the promise of free trade in tropical Africa in the late nineteenth century, so can the modern development of the national side of the concept be identified with Joseph Chamberlain's famous statement that the colonies should be regarded as undeveloped estates. This is a powerful theme in British colonial thought; it must be considered along with another strong tradition, that colonies should pay their own way. The Act of 1929 constituted a recognition that many of the smaller and poorer colonies could not be developed without economic assistance.[22]

In 1929, for the first time, Parliament allocated regular funds amounting to £1 million a year for development in such areas as tropical agriculture, forestry, fisheries, water supplies, irrigation, and transport. The economic depression of the 1930s demonstrated the need for more and not less economic aid. In particular, the unrest in the West Indies dramatically called attention to the need for larger expenditures in social services, especially in such ways as slum clearance and health programs. When the next development Act was passed in 1940, one of the recurrent themes in the debates and newspaper commentaries was the desirability of state intervention to improve standards of living. The concept of *welfare* became the formal concomitant of development. The leading Labour politician who systematically studied these issues, Arthur Creech Jones, said in

[22] The best work on the Colonial Development and Welfare Acts is *Colonial Development* (Overseas Development Institute, British Aid, 5, London, 1964) by D. J. Morgan, to whom I am greatly indebted for discussion of these issues. See also D. Meredith, 'The British Government and Colonial Economic Policy, 1919–39', *Economic History Review* 28. 3 (1975); G. C. Abbot, 'A Re-Examination of the 1929 Colonial Development Act', *Economic History Review* 24. 1 (1971); and E. R. Wicker, 'Colonial Development and Welfare, 1929–1957: the Evolution of a Policy', *Social and Economic Studies* (Jamaica) 7, 4 (1958).

May 1940, 'This Bill marks . . . the ending of the *laissez faire* attitude towards Colonial development and, I hope, the end of platitudinous talk about trusteeship.'[23] British guardianship could no longer be attacked as sanctimonious. Britain as a great colonial power had now recognized her social as well as economic responsibility in the colonies. The 1940 Act provided up to £5 million a year by grant or loan and one-half million for research (£55,000,000 over ten years). It included an explicit emphasis on education, on which the 1929 Act had been silent. When American critics talked about British 'Imperialism' during the war, Creech Jones and other Englishmen who spoke to American audiences would cite the Colonial Development and Welfare Act of 1940 as evidence of concrete measures to advance the prosperity and social welfare of British colonial subjects.

The 1945 Act renewed and extended the purpose of the CD&W Act of 1940. The Act of 1945 embodied the recommendations of extensive wartime planning and laid the basis of Britain's post-war colonial development schemes. This was truly the turning point in British commitment to improving economic efficiency and production, and to raising the standards of health, education, and welfare in the colonies. It provided the total sum of £120 million for the ten years 1945–56. This was a colossal increase from the 1940 Act. When the Colonial Office negotiated the amount with the Treasury in 1944, everyone involved was keenly aware of the wartime debt, the adverse balance of payments, and the domestic financial austerity that lay ahead. So vast is the increase between the 1940 and 1945 Acts that it is legitimate to ask whether the United States had a hand in it. To revert to the subject of the economic element in trusteeship, did the Americans seize the opportunity of wartime extremity to gain control over British colonial development? This is a question, which, if answered affirmatively, might throw new light on British intent. It would also suggest a calculated plan to extend American influence in the colonial world.

There is no evidence whatever in either the American or British archives that officials of the United States in the late stages of the war attempted to influence, still less subsidize,

---

[23] *Parliamentary Debates* (Commons), 21 May 1940, c. 55.

British colonial development. What emerges from the documents is something quite different. When the Colonial Office in 1944 raised the issue of renewal of the 1940 Act, the Treasury responded with simple and direct words of concurrence: '*As regards the money we are conscious that we must justify ourselves before the world as a great Colonial power.*'[24] This was remarkable language for a Treasury official. There then followed, more characteristically, a bitter dispute between the Colonial Office and the Treasury over the amount of expenditure and the methods of financing colonial development. There is no question of ulterior motive. Oliver Stanley wrote to the Chancellor of the Exchequer in September 1944:

> I believe that the time when we must take action . . . is now upon us. The end of the fighting in Europe will, I am convinced, be the psychological moment at which to announce our intention to make fully adequate provision for the assistance from His Majesty's Government which will be necessary for a dynamic programme of Colonial development. It is the moment at which to demonstrate our faith and our ability to make proper use of our wide Colonial possessions. It is also the moment when the minds of administrators in the Colonies will be turning even more definitely towards planning for the future, and when a clear call from here will give them faith in the permanence and adequacy of our policy. . . .

The Colonial Secretary emphasized that the time had come to demonstrate the sincerity of Britain's colonial mission:

> Finally, it is the moment at which to kill the enemy propaganda lie that the policy announced in 1940 was forced on us by our critical situation and that we never mean to implement it. Nothing would better confirm faith in our sincerity than that at the height of our success we should confirm and amplify this policy which was first announced in the depth of our disasters.[25]

Stanley went on to say, among other things, that the Colonial Office had borne in mind the large increases of expenditure that the Exchequer would face in the post-war years, but that colonial development, after all, would increase production,

---

[24] Sir Bernard Gilbert (Treasury) to Sydney Caine, 13 Sept. 1944, CO 852/588/19275. Italics added. Here I am grateful to Ronald Robinson for extended discussions of these points.

[25] Stanley to Sir John Anderson (Chancellor of the Exchequer), 21 Sept. 1944, CO 852/588/19275.

which in turn would strengthen Britain's general financial position. In his ultimate argument, however, Stanley did not rest his case on economic return: 'I make no pretence . . . that this is going to be a profitable transaction on a purely financial calculation. The over-riding reason why I feel that these proposals are essential is the necessity to justify our position as a Colonial Power.'[26] A major conclusion can be drawn from this exchange between the Colonial Office and Treasury in late 1944 (and from similar documentation that will appear in the narrative below). The Americans did not take advantage of the mounting wartime debt so as to control colonial economic development. The Colonial Office secured War Cabinet and Parliamentary approval of the CD&W Act because Britain was the trustee of a great Colonial Empire. The Second World War witnessed a moral regeneration of British purpose in the colonial world.

The experience of war generates idealism as well as imperialism. Much of this book is concerned with the revival of imperial aims that resembled the territorial ambitions and plans to consolidate the colonial empires that characterized the First World War. It would be a mistake not to stress at the same time the resurgence of British 'enlightened Imperialism'. To illustrate this point, there was a remarkable meeting convened by the Colonial Secretary only a month after the outbreak of war in 1939. This was also less than a year after the publication of Lord Hailey's *African Survey*, which gave great stimulation to those working in African affairs. Hailey attended the meeting, along with Lord Lugard and several ranking members of the Colonial Office. A number of leading academic authorities were also present, including Professor Reginald Coupland of Oxford, Dr. Julian Huxley, Professor W. K. (Sir Keith) Hancock, and Miss (later Dame) Margery Perham of Oxford. Malcolm MacDonald, the

---

[26] Ibid. See also especially Stanley's memorandum of 15 Nov. 1944, W.P. (44) 643, CAB 66/57. 'I am not pretending that the assistance to the Colonies which I propose will not impose some burden upon this country', Stanley wrote to the members of the War Cabinet. 'I do, however, feel that the Colonial Empire means so much to us that we should be prepared to assume some burden for its future. . . . If these sums are wisely spent . . . there will in the long run accrue considerable benefit to us. . . . But I am not basing my argument on material gains to ourselves, important as I think these may be. My feeling is that in the years to come, without the Commonwealth and Empire, this country will play a small rôle in world affairs . . .'

Colonial Secretary, presided. He said in his opening remarks, 'during the war they could advance certain policies . . .'. The war would provide the opportunity to move ahead. Lord Hailey asked several questions that suggested the eventual Africanization of the colonial service, at least in part. 'Are Africans to be admitted to the Administration? The present uncertainty was cruel to those Africans who qualified for higher employment and failed to get it', Hailey stated. In this wide-ranging and intense discussion, Professor Coupland made a point of fundamental importance for the trusteeship controversy of the wartime period:

> The war provides an opportunity for putting the dependent Empire on the same moral footing as the rest of the Empire. Nowhere is there any acceptance of the sincerity of our expressed intentions in the dependent Empire. Left opinion in England, general opinion in the United States . . . were unable to believe that there was reality in our professions of trusteeship.

He spoke as a historian bringing knowledge to bear on the present and future:

> As a historian, he recalled that there had only been two periods when British public opinion had been interested in Africa—namely, the fight against the slave trade and the time of Livingstone. In both periods that interest had been idealistic. You could get British public opinion, with its curious affection for the under-dog behind a restatement of trusteeship.[27]

Julian Huxley was also concerned with the moral foundation of the Colonial Empire: 'Unless we could establish the dependent Empire on a firm moral basis it would be a continual source of weakness.'[28] The concern for a legitimate and inspirational moral stand characterized the British wartime debates about trusteeship.

At this meeting in October 1939 in which these authorities on Africa made a reconnaissance of problems that would arise during the war, Professor Hancock introduced a controversial thesis. He pointed out certain facts about recent British economic history. The British had ceased to export capital. How could

[27] Record of a discussion at the Carlton Hotel, 6 Oct. 1939, CO 847/17/47135.
[28] Ibid. For Huxley's further views on colonial development see his essay, 'Colonies in a Changing World', *Political Quarterly*, 13. 4 (Oct.–Dec. 1942).

Africa be developed without capital investment? 'Great Britain does not possess the resources to finance . . . all her African Empire, let alone the West Indies and other places as well.' He emphasized the magnitude of the task and the need for external assistance:

The great danger of war-time is that we shall get into monopolistic habits of thinking and carry them into the peace. There is no escape from internationalising the Empire economically, because we cannot develop it economically ourselves. It is therefore urgent to think out in economic terms the means of getting world co-operation.

Miss Perham observed that only the United States would be in a position to subsidize the economic development of the African continent.[29]

Here was a divisive issue. Two distinct views emerged during the war in regard to it. For sake of clarity they may be called the Tory and the Labour views of the future of the United States in colonial development. The Tory view held in general that the Americans should be kept out of the Colonial Empire because it was a British concern. The Labour view affirmed the desirability of co-operation with the United States in colonial development. Within the Colonial Office, where of course sophisticated discussion took place on these matters as well, there also existed a divergence of opinion. Gerard Clauson, who dealt with economic affairs, thought that Professor Hancock's views were 'great nonsense'.[30] Andrew Cohen (who in the post-war era played such a large role in the decolonization of British Africa) believed not only that the United States should undertake colonial development, but also that American economic assistance might underwrite the Colonial Empire. American aid could be used for British purposes as well as for the prosperity and welfare of colonial subjects.[31] Cohen was exceptional. In general there was a good deal of British ambivalence about the future of the United States in Africa and in all parts of the colonial world.

A similar ambivalence can be seen in British reactions to the

[29] Carlton Hotel discussion, CO 847/17/47135.
[30] Minute by Clauson, 31 Oct. 1939, ibid.
[31] Once again I am indebted to Ronald Robinson, with whom I have examined this material in detail.

problem of the future of the mandates system. In October 1944 the journal of the Royal African Society, *African Affairs*, published a symposium which presented the spectrum of ideas as held by informed Englishmen. Some of the participants had been associated with the mandates system in an official capacity. All of them had a long-standing interest in the mandates. They included Lord Harlech (W. Ormsby-Gore), who had been the first British representative on the Permanent Mandates Commission (and later High Commissioner in South Africa), Lugard, and Leonard Woolf. The editor of *African Affairs* asked them to respond to a statement made by General Smuts in April 1944: 'There is a feeling in many quarters that the Mandatory System has outlived its time and that another arrangement must be made . . .' The editor's request for a response to this statement created an especially interesting situation. No one doubted that Smuts thought the best solution for South-West Africa would be annexation by South Africa. This itself was sufficient cause for alarm for those who suspected expansionist aims of South Africa.[32] The mandates system had proved to be an effective check on the South African goal of annexation of South-West Africa.

Lord Harlech responded, 'I do not believe in direct international administration, but I do believe in international co-operation, advice and supervision, not merely of the ex-German colonies but of everyone's tropical dependencies.' This support of international supervision would hardly have given comfort to Smuts. Lord Lugard wrote: 'pressure might be put on all Colonial Powers to undertake to allow free access to all foreigners, to tolerate a free local Press, and to publish an annual report.' This was perhaps a minimal requirement for the new system of international supervision of the mandated territories. Though minimal, it was none the less more than Smuts wanted. In the view of Leonard Woolf:

> *Timeo Danaos et dona ferentes.* It is a curious fact that 'the feeling in many quarters that the mandatory system has outlived its time' seems to be troubling the souls precisely in those 'quarters' where souls have not been hitherto notably sensitive to the expressed object of the system . . .

[32] On this theme see Ronald Hyam, *The Failure of South African Expansion, 1908–1948* (London, 1972).

There may well be much better systems up the sleeves of Field-Marshal Smuts and other people, but until we know exactly what the gifts are which the Greeks are going to give us (and the Africans), we may be wise not to abandon the little which we have.[33]

Leonard Woolf was thus frankly hostile to the South African position. Rita Hinden, the Secretary of the Fabian Colonial Bureau (and of South African origin), added: 'the principle that what an imperial Power does inside its empire is the just concern of world opinion.' This was also the opposite of Smuts's view, and, it should be noted, of the Colonial Office's. But the Colonial Office and South Africa in this particular case took the stand that they were *not* responsible to world opinion. There was a fundamental difference between the Tory outlook (held by South Africa and the Colonial Office, especially Oliver Stanley) and the Labour or Fabian view (held by the Fabian Colonial Bureau, Creech Jones, and to some extent by some Labour politicians within the coalition government such as Attlee, though not strongly or consistently). Lord Hailey summed up the key point of division when he mentioned the words *international accountability*.[34] The Fabians were willing to admit some degree of international accountability. The Tories were not.

The strength of the Labour view can be most clearly seen by looking beyond England to Australia and New Zealand. In 1919 the two antipodean Dominions had taken the same attitude as South Africa, that the best course was to annex the German colonies. In 1945 Australia and New Zealand reversed their positions. They now believed that international control should be extended over all colonial possessions. This was the extreme Labour view, held quite independently by Peter Fraser, the New Zealand Prime Minister, and Herbert Vere Evatt, the Australian Attorney General and Minister for Foreign Affairs. Their ideas were highly individualistic and by no means doctrinaire. Both had been influenced by the Fabians, both were Labour statesmen of 'post-colonial' or Dominion governments, and both were anxious for peace in a predominantly

[33] 'The Future of the Mandates: a Symposium', *African Affairs* 43 (October 1944), 168.
[34] See Lord Hailey, 'Colonial and World Organisation', *African Affairs* 44 (April 1945), 54–8.

colonial region. Their alliance on the trusteeship question was
a powerful combination. By holding common ideas, Fraser and
Evatt found themselves broadly in agreement with the State
Department officials who also favoured international accountability, and with the Fabians in England. In contrast, the
affinity for autonomy created a tacit alliance between South
Africa, the Colonial Office, and, it should be added, the United
States Navy, since American naval officers no more wanted
international interference in their affairs in the Pacific than the
South Africans did in South-West Africa. The predominance of
Labour views in the antipodes proved to be a potent force,
especially since Fraser chaired the trusteeship commission
at the San Francisco Conference and Evatt emerged as the
champion of the smaller nations versus the great powers.

If there was any particular individual whom the true-blue
Tories disliked—loathed perhaps would not be too strong a
word—because of his attitude on the colonial issue, it was
Evatt. Evatt was not a gentleman. He pursued his goals by
unorthodox methods, which included rude comments about his
opponents. He had a streak of the larrikin. He took a delight
in throwing rocks at the street lamps of British Imperialism
simply because the lamps were there. He was a master at logic-
chopping. Trained in the law, he quickly saw the specious
reasoning behind much of the talk about 'trusteeship' and he
would attack his foes with savage intensity. He is the only one
of the protagonists of the trusteeship controversy who had as
part of his background the authorship of a treatise on the mandates in international law. It is a lucid, learned, and powerfully
argued essay. Since one of the great debating points among
scholars of 'international trusteeship' is always the immediate
antecedents of the idea, it is of considerable interest that Evatt
saw the foundation of British trusteeship as the Kenya White
Paper of 1923. He quoted this passage in his article published
in 1935:

In the administration of Kenya, His Majesty's Government
regard themselves as exercising *a trust on behalf of the African population*,
and they are unable to delegate or share this trust, the object of
which may be defined as the protection and advancement of the
native races.

We are the Trustees of many great African Dependencies, of

which Kenya is one, and our duty is to do justice and right between the various races and interests, remembering, above all, that *we are trustees before the world for the African population.*[35]

Evatt's article is revealing in many ways. His interpretation and emphasis on *trusteeship* indicate his belief that the mandatory powers were responsible to world opinion. He concluded that a mandatory power could not unilaterally annex a mandated territory (a conclusion of profound importance for the South-West Africa question). His sources, though by no means comprehensive, included the works by Quincy Wright and M. F. Lindley, which he obviously had thoroughly digested.[36] During the war this background gave Evatt an immense advantage over many of his adversaries. He possessed a keen legal mind and international trusteeship was one of his particular areas of interest.

Peter Fraser's contribution to the founding of the trusteeship system was no less important. In his formative years as a politician he had been greatly influenced by the publication of the Labour Party's pamphlets and books on the subject of imperialism. He had probably read, for example, Leonard Woolf's *Empire and Commerce in Africa*.[37] He had a genuine concern for raising the standards of living of the working class in New Zealand, and he easily extended this enthusiasm to the islanders of the Pacific. Fraser took concrete steps to ensure the expansion of health services, agricultural research, and education. During the war he was the only Prime Minister actually to visit a mandated territory. Fraser's journey to Samoa in late 1944 convinced him that New Zealand should move faster in preparing the Samoans for self-government.[38] Together with Evatt, he pressed for specific measures of international accountability. Fraser was a staunch supporter of the idea that the future international organization should be empowered to send visiting missions of inspection. He had his own distinct views about the problems of 'independence' which figured so

[35] H. V. Evatt, 'The British Dominions as Mandatories', *Proceedings of the Australian and New Zealand Society of International Law*, 1 (1935), p. 29, Evatt's italics.
[36] Quincy Wright, *Mandates under the League of Nations*; M. F. Lindley, *The Acquisition and Government of Backward Territory in International Law* (London, 1926).
[37] I am indebted to Sir Alister McIntosh for discussing with me Fraser's ideas and career.
[38] See Davidson, *Samoa Mo Samoa*, pp. 158 and 165.

prominently in the discussions of 'imperialism' by Americans and Englishmen. He said in 1945: 'To us of the British Commonwealth it is very difficult to distinguish between self-government and independence, for to the self-governing sovereign States of the British Commonwealth, self-government is independence and independence is self-government . . .' He then emphasized a catchword of the Second World War era, *inter-dependence*.

[W]e have also learned that there is something additional to independence . . . as well as being independent, we are interdependent, and that the future of the British Commonwealth depends upon our inter-dependence and co-operation. I go further: the future of the world depends upon our recognition of the interdependence of all nations. . . .[39]

Fraser's idea of 'inter-dependence' was shared by some members of the Colonial Office, but his notion of *independence* was very much the view of a Dominion Prime Minister. It is a word found more in the rhetoric of Dominion than of Imperial statesmen.

Some participants in the wartime trusteeship controversy held that the differences between Englishmen and Americans were mainly semantic. Lord Halifax, for instance, did not hesitate in translating the word 'independence' as 'self-government', just as Churchill used 'British Commonwealth' interchangeably with 'British Empire' to suit the occasion. H. Duncan Hall is another example. A prominent Australian scholar in Empire–Commonwealth affairs, he had served in the League's Secretariat. During the war he worked in the British Raw Material Mission in Washington. At this time he began to organize material for a book on international trusteeship. When it appeared in 1948, *Mandates, Dependencies and Trusteeship* immediately became a landmark in the historiography of the subject.[40] It is therefore of considerable interest to note Hall's views on 'American mental processes on the Empire' during the war itself. He believed it might be possible to break through 'the crust of American tradition that all colonies, and

[39] Fraser at the San Francisco Conference in 1945, quoted by W. David McIntyre in an unpublished essay, 'Peter Fraser's Commonwealth: New Zealand and the Origins of the New Commonwealth in the 1940s'.

[40] See especially the review in *The Times Literary Supplement*, 28 Oct. 1949 (the anonymous reviewer was Leo Amery).

particularly British colonies, are intrinsically bad'. In a letter
to a Colonial Office official he explained his reasoning:

> The tradition stems of course from the Revolution which produced
> fundamental attitudes, ideas and symbols that are still at the core of
> the national thinking. It is just because the attitude springs from this
> emotional source that it is so difficult to modify it by argument or
> discussion on the rational level . . .
>
> We can only by-pass this emotion by presenting our policy
> through ideas and symbols of a positive kind which are in line with
> positive American traditions. Conceptions like 'union', 'partner-
> ship', 'self-government', 'federation' fit this tradition; 'trusteeship',
> 'colony', 'Empire', 'British subject',—any words that smell of sub-
> jection—do not.[41]

This touches on an important point. Should the British attempt
to prove to the Americans the semantic irrationality of de-
nouncing British 'Imperialism'?

With an insight tempered by international perspective,
Duncan Hall privately attacked Sumner Welles's recently published book *Time for Decision*.[42] He emphasized that Welles
stated that 'international trusteeship' would not apply to the
Netherlands East Indies because the Dutch had proclaimed
'magic words' such as 'partnership'. 'It looks as though the
mental process is something like this: "The Dutch have been
nice to the American idea. Anyhow we have got nothing historically against them; and so we let them off. But not the other
unrepentant Empires."'[43] He went on to point out that in this
same type of illogical and emotional thinking 'no reference is
made to America's own dependencies—Guam, Samoa, Puerto
Rico, etc. And of course there is no reference to the colonial
fringes of the U.S.S.R.' To Hall there was an outrageous injustice in these American 'mental processes'. After all the
Dominions *were* independent. The British *did* practise what they
preached about self-government. He concluded that the British
should take care to use *the right words* 'as a means of outflanking
the still persistent mentality of 1776'.[44]

---

[41] Hall to A. H. Poynton (Colonial Office), 16 Nov. 1944, copy in the Eggleston
Papers.

[42] New York, 1944. For an important review by one of the participants in the
trusteeship controversy, see the review essay by Grayson Kirk, *Pacific Affairs*,
17. 4 (December 1944).

[43] Hall to Poynton, 16 Nov. 1944.　　　　　　　　　　　　　　　[44] Ibid.

This book places no particular emphasis on propaganda efforts. It is important to bear in mind, as Duncan Hall pointed out, that semantic confusion did exist, and that words had emotional overtones. But the issues were real and not semantic. They were certainly real to the greatest historian of the British Empire and Commonwealth of his generation, Professor W. K. Hancock. In 1943 he published *Argument of Empire*. Of all the books on the Empire that appeared during the war, this one merits special attention because of the clarity of its message and its obvious purpose as propaganda in the basic sense of the word. Hancock's objective in part was to cause American readers to ponder the ideals of the British Empire and Commonwealth. Paradoxically the book can be read as a study in semantics because the author was careful to define such terms as 'British Empire'. Like much of Hancock's writing, it is at once simple and complex. Many of its arguments are polemical and didactic. Professor Bruce Miller is quite accurate in pointing out that it distils some of the more controversial elements of Hancock's monumental *Survey of British Commonwealth Affairs*, which ranks along with Hailey's *African Survey* as one of the most influential works of the era.[45] The polemical line is anti-Empire preference. The didactic strain is that his readers should not defend or attack the British Empire until they understand the central problem that *should* be at issue. This he identifies in simple and powerful words as a concern for human liberty. It is a point of great importance because ultimately it is the same underlying issue of the trusteeship controversy of the wartime period. In Hancock's words, the debate about trusteeship and imperialism 'raises the deepest issues of human freedom'.[46]

Among the many complex themes of *Argument of Empire*, one thesis in particular has a central relevance to the present volume. This was the *concurrent* debate in England and in America.

It is difficult to conduct an argument across the Atlantic. John Bull wakes up one morning to read newspaper headlines which give

[45] J. D. B. Miller, 'Hancock, Mansergh and Commonwealth Surveys', *Historical Studies*, 13. 51 (October 1968); W. K. Hancock, *Survey of British Commonwealth Affairs* (London, 1937–42).

[46] W. K. Hancock, *Argument of Empire* (London, 1943), p. 8.

him the impression that Americans are making the liquidation of the British Empire one of their war aims. John Bull growls that it's like their cool cheek and that he won't let go.

John Bull's growl is cabled across the Atlantic and served up to the American citizen in still bigger headlines. . . . All this is grand newspaper stuff. But it isn't real. The real argument is going on *inside* Britain and *inside* America. It will merge later on with the big international discussion, but it hasn't done so yet.[47]

This is in fact what this book is about, though on a broader scale. It discusses the various facets of the arguments as they were pursued in official as well as public circles and from various vantage points, not least the antipodean. The arguments merged at the San Francisco Conference, as Hancock had anticipated.

To reduce the trusteeship controversy to one of semantics is to reduce the American and British views on the future of the colonial empires to a common outlook. To some extent this is a useful exercise. It is helpful to remember that the Americans and British were almost all gradualists and that virtually no one anticipated the speed with which the British Empire would collapse. When pressed to give extreme examples, Americans tended to admit that self-government or autonomy within the British Empire might be preferable to independence, especially in the case of remote, small, and 'primitive' areas such as the Pacific island groups. Yet it would be absurd to argue that the future of the colonial empires was not a real issue between the Americans and the British. It definitely was. In the words of Margery Perham, another British scholar of the first rank, American criticism, at least in the early stages of the war, was couched in fundamentalist terms: 'These conjure up a picture of a strong power destroying the independence of the weak and keeping under subjection nations which (in the inappropriate words applied to the Sudan by Gladstone, who tended to be fundamentalist himself when in opposition) are "rightly struggling to be free".'[48] During the latter part of the war the general emotional tone of American criticism subsided. But the issues remained. For the trusteeship controversy, would

[47] Ibid., p. 7.
[48] Margery Perham, 'African Facts and American Criticisms', *Foreign Affairs* 22. 3 (April 1944); reprinted in Margery Perham, *Colonial Sequence, 1930 to 1949* (London, 1967), p. 254.

the British agree to be held accountable for their colonies to an international organization? To those who were passionately involved in the 'colonial question' of the Second World War, the issue of accountability was a touchstone for the future of the Colonial Empires.

The precise ways in which the British and the other Europeans would be held accountable formed the subject of many meetings of committees in the State Department. Of these planning groups, foremost attention should be drawn to Benjamin Gerig's Committee on Dependent Areas. Though this committee was relatively obscure in relation to other groups and individuals making actual decisions, Gerig and his colleagues systematically analysed virtually all the major colonial problems of the wartime era. They thus provided an underlying continuity of American policy. Here again the issues can be approached by examining the semantics. Much of the work of this particular committee consisted of the drafting and redrafting (that began in 1942 and culminated in 1945) of the sections on dependent peoples in the United Nations Charter. If ever there was a persistent war effort, surely this one might be it. On the eve of the San Francisco Conference, Gerig's committee held its *ninety-ninth meeting*.[49]

Over the years the redrafting of the principal clauses of the mandates, native welfare and free trade, formed some of the main themes of American planning. In one important respect the emphasis shifted from the comparable period before the Paris Peace Conference. In 1919 American policy aimed at international agreement on non-fortification, especially for the Pacific islands. With that mixture of realism and idealism that characterizes American policy, the demilitarization approach now was found wanting. It appeared to have been ineffective against the Japanese, or so American intelligence suspected.[50]

---

[49] For the minutes of the Committee on Dependent Areas see USSD NF Box 183.

[50] In the inter-war period the Americans persistently suspected that the Japanese had violated the terms of the mandate by fortifying the islands. The charge was never proved. In one of the most far-reaching intelligence reports prepared in the late 1930s, a major conclusion held that 'there are no *Naval* air stations *known* in any of the outlying areas of the Japanese Empire' ('Secret Monograph of Japanese Mandate Islands, prepared by The Intelligence Section of the Fleet Marine Force', Washington Navy Yard). For a recent exploding of the myth (and expression of relief by a United States Marine Colonel that the islands were not fortified), see Paul B. Haigwood, 'Japan and the Mandates', in Wm. Roger Louis, ed.,

Now the Americans took the opposite line. Complete military freedom in the islands would contribute to the defence of the free world. The administering authority would be granted the power to take whatever military measures might be necessary to ensure international security (which in this case was synonymous with American security). 'Security' became the watchword of the era. The Committee on Dependent Areas laid the foundation of reconciling American strategic security with the idealism of the trusteeship system. The Americans felt they were entirely justified in creating a strategic fortress in the islands while carrying the torch of trusteeship throughout the rest of the world. If self-righteousness is a hallmark of American policy, then in the trusteeship question it found its finest hour.

The specific and general meaning of the trusteeship controversy can be established by a brief examination of the end result, the three relevant chapters in the United Nations Charter. Chapter XI is the Declaration regarding Non-Self-Governing Territories. In addition to recognizing a responsibility for the political, economic, social, and educational advancement of dependent peoples, the members of the United Nations also endorsed the principle of self-government. The word 'independence' is not mentioned. For all but a few specific 'trust' territories, 'self-government' became the general colonial goal established by the San Francisco Conference in 1945.

Article XII deals with the International Trusteeship System. The basic objective is explicitly stated as 'the progressive development towards independence'. A further article in this chapter provides for the designation of 'strategic' areas. The Japanese mandated islands became the only strategic trust territory. Military bases were permitted. Indeed two of the islands in the Marshalls, Bikini and Eniwetok, became nuclear test sites. But, unless one considers the missile test sites in the Marshalls as a centre of military power, the islands have never been fortified in a 'strategic' sense.[51]

National Security and International Trusteeship in the Pacific (Annapolis, 1972). For a different emphasis, which stresses the difficulty in differentiating between commercial and military facilities, see the important article by Richard Dean Burns, 'Inspection of the Mandates, 1919–1941', *Pacific Historical Review* 37. 4 (November 1968).

[51] See Daniel J. Morgiewicz, 'Micronesia: Especial Trust', *United States Naval Institute Proceedings* 94. 10 (October 1968).

The trust territories were (with dates of independence):

French Cameroons	1960
British Togoland	1960
French Togoland	1960
Italian Somaliland	1960
Tanganyika (Britain)	1961
British Cameroons	1961
Western Samoa (New Zealand)	1962
Ruanda–Urundi (Belgium)	1962
Nauru Island (Britain, Australia, and New Zealand)	1968
New Guinea (Australia)	1975
Micronesia (United States)	—

South Africa withheld the South-West Africa mandate.[52]

Chapter XIII provides for the composition, function, and powers of the Trusteeship Council. Until recently (at the time of writing the United States holds the only remaining trust territory) the Trusteeship Council has been composed of the members of the United Nations administering trust territories, and an equal number of nations which did not. The Trusteeship Council was given specific powers which included the authority to:

a. consider reports submitted by the administering authority;
b. accept petitions and examine them in consultation with the administering authority;
c. provide for periodic visits to the respective trust territories at times agreed upon with the administering authority . . .

The United States strategic trust territory is subject to the same economic, social, and educational provisions as the other trust territories. Periodic missions have visited Micronesia.

Since American initiative in large part led to the creation of these Chapters, it is especially noteworthy that Chapter XII contains the word 'independence', and the general declaration, Chapter XI, does not. This was because the American delegation at the San Francisco Conference, in putting forward these

---

[52] For the South-West Africa controversy, see especially Slonim, *South West Africa and the United Nations*. For further discussion of the drafting of the three Chapters, see especially Ruth B. Russell, *A History of the United Nations Charter* (Washington, 1958), a work of fundamental importance.

provisions that had matured after years of consideration in the State Department, regarded the trusteeship system as a *mechanism* to promote independence.[53] They hoped that, as colonies became self-governing under Chapter XI, the administering authorities would then place specific territories under Chapter XII for preparation for independence. This proved to be a false trail. Only later did the State Department learn that the British, for example, had no intention of placing any of their colonies under trusteeship. In the end the trusteeship system as a specific mechanism for independence worked only for the former mandates, in other words, the old German colonies, and Italian Somaliland. On the other hand the general impact of the United Nations trusteeship system has been far-reaching.

The crucial innovation of the trusteeship system was the change in composition and character of the supervisory organ from expert to political. Though the subject overreaches the scope of this volume, it is perhaps useful to bear in mind the long-range significance of the trusteeship controversy of the wartime years. The members of the Trusteeship Council were representatives of governments, and not, as was generally true for the Permanent Mandates Commission, scholars and specialists. The trusteeship representatives were political agents out to defend or attack the conduct of administration in the trust territories. This transformation raised the debate from discussion of techniques in such areas as agriculture and health to that of goals and issues such as political education and preparation for independence. The visiting missions reported on progress towards independence, or lack of it. The amount of rhetoric generated by the United Nations debates should not be allowed to obscure a basic historical fact: the trusteeship system had teeth and often bit.

[53] Here I am again grateful to Benjamin Gerig for discussing with me at length the ideas of the American delegation at the San Francisco Conference, especially the concept of the trusteeship system as a mechanism for independence.

PART II

FROM THE ATLANTIC CHARTER
TO THE
CAIRO DECLARATION

ARTICLE III OF THE ATLANTIC CHARTER—SELF-DETERMINATION

IN relating the drama of the Atlantic meeting off New-foundland between Roosevelt and Churchill in August 1941, Roosevelt's son, Elliott, depicts a fundamental clash over the colonial issue. It began with Roosevelt's insistence on freedom of trade as a precondition of a lasting peace.

Churchill's neck reddened and he crouched forward. 'Mr. President, England does not propose for a moment to lose its favored position among the British Dominions . . .'

'You see,' said Father slowly, 'it is along in here somewhere that there is likely to be some disagreement between you, Winston, and me.

I am firmly of the belief that if we are to arrive at a stable peace it must involve the development of backward countries. Backward peoples. How can this be done? It can't be done, obviously, by eighteenth-century methods. . . . I can't believe that we can fight a war against fascist slavery, and at the same time not work to free people all over the world from a backward colonial policy.'[1]

With Churchill looking 'apoplectic', Roosevelt concluded that there must be 'equality of peoples'. Unfortunately for those who prefer melodrama, Elliott Roosevelt's account is distorted.[2] But it does convey an important point fully apparent to those present at the time. Roosevelt and Churchill collided on the issue of the economic autarchy of the British Empire, a theme which per-sisted during the entire war and its aftermath.[3] Contrary to

---

[1] Elliott Roosevelt, *As He Saw It* (New York, 1946), pp. 36–7.

[2] Among many others who make this judgement, Theodore A. Wilson, the author of the exhaustive work on the Atlantic Charter, writes on the colonial issue and in particular the question of India: 'Its divisiveness at Argentia . . . is not demonstrated by extant evidence.' *The First Summit: Roosevelt and Churchill at Placentia Bay 1941* (Boston, 1969), p. 302. See also especially the classic account of the Atlantic conference in William L. Langer and S. Everett Gleason, *The Un-declared War: 1940–1941* (New York, 1953), ch. XXI.

[3] The economic controversies are examined in detail by Richard N. Gardner, *Sterling–Dollar Diplomacy* (Oxford, 1956), ch. III; see also E. F. Penrose, *Economic Planning for the Peace* (Princeton, 1953), ch. 1. See also especially Warren F. Kimball, *The Most Unsordid Act: Lend-Lease 1939–1941* (Baltimore, 1969); by the same

Elliott Roosevelt, the issue of colonial liberation was not explicit in the exchanges. Thus it is crucial to grasp clearly the intent of Roosevelt and Churchill respectively when they drafted the self-determination clause of the Atlantic Charter. As in the days of Woodrow Wilson, no other principle could be adopted so whole-heartedly and with such studied ambiguity. None other again proved to be such a Pandora's box.[4]

The point is often made, and bears repeating, that the Atlantic Charter was essentially a press release, not a formal document. The President wanted to avoid anything that might be interpreted as an alliance. At the same time he desired the public assurance that Britain had not concluded any secret treaties. If the ghost of Woodrow Wilson haunted Roosevelt on this occasion, it is equally true that Churchill in the tradition of Lloyd George found it a small price to pay to affirm noble principles in order to prove the solidarity of purpose with the non-belligerent United States. With haste and with an eye towards the value of an idealistic declaration as a counter to Axis propaganda, the two statesmen proclaimed that they sought no aggrandizement, territorial or other. They stated that there should be no territorial transfers without the consent of the peoples concerned. The next point—Article III—followed logically. All peoples should have the right to choose their own form of government. These principles to their authors in August 1941 were not controversial. Other issues, notably trade, provoked fundamental disagreement. Self-determination appeared to be innocuous, though it quickly became apparent in the

author, a major reinterpretation central to all aspects of Anglo-American relations in the early years of the war, 'Lend-Lease and the Open Door: The Temptation of British Opulence, 1937–1942', *Political Science Quarterly* 86. 2 (June 1971). Generally but tendentiously on the theme of Anglo-American economic rivalry, Gabriel Kolko, *The Politics of War* (New York, 1968).

4 For an important Second World War analysis of the Wilsonian legacy in all its complexity, see Alfred Cobban, *National Self-Determination* (London, 1944; the 1969 revised edition includes his essay 'The Nation State'). On a basic point, Cobban explains that the usage of the phrase self-determination derives from the First World War context of the belief that each nation has the right to constitute an independent state and determine its own government. For a World War II attack on the theory, see Walter Lippmann, *U.S. War Aims* (Boston, 1944), pp. 172–5. For a masterly and sceptical analysis, Rupert Emerson, *Self Determination Revisited in the Era of Decolonization* (Harvard University Center for International Affairs, 1964). See also especially Michla Pomerance, 'The United States and Self-Determination: Perspectives on the Wilsonian Conception', *American Journal of International Law* 70. 1 (January 1976).

aftermath of the conference that potentially it was perhaps the most explosive principle of all. Churchill later argued consistently that he had in mind self-determination for the conquered nations of Europe. Roosevelt subsequently stated repeatedly that the Atlantic Charter applied not only to Europe but also to peoples throughout the world.

The author of the original draft was Churchill's diplomatic adviser, Sir Alexander Cadogan, Permanent Under-Secretary of State for Foreign Affairs. When Churchill gave Roosevelt the draft on 10 August, Article III read:

> Third, they respect the right of all peoples to choose the form of government under which they will live; they are only concerned to defend the rights of freedom of speech and thought without which such choice must be illusory.[5]

Cadogan's opposite number, Sumner Welles, Under Secretary of State, immediately deleted the last part of the article. In his words, 'It was . . . more than doubtful that the American Congress would at that moment have approved a pledge by the government of the United States to "defend the rights of freedom of speech and thought" when those rights were abrogated in every Axis country.'[6] Roosevelt himself substituted the phrase 'and they hope that self-government may be restored to those from whom it has been forcibly removed'. On the 11th of August Churchill added the words 'sovereign rights' before the phrase 'self-government'. If it could be argued that Roosevelt's purpose was to make explicit the principle of self-determination, then it could also be argued that Churchill's addition of the phrase 'sovereign rights' made the clause inapplicable to the dependent British Empire. In final form the article read:

> Third, they respect the right of all peoples to choose the form of

---

[5] Winston S. Churchill, *The Grand Alliance* (Boston, 1950), pp. 433–7. Cadogan played a key role in the Anglo-American colonial negotiations throughout the entire war. At the Atlantic meeting Churchill told him, 'Thank God I brought you with me.' David Dilks, ed., *The Diaries of Sir Alexander Cadogan* (New York, 1972), p. 401. At the time Cadogan appears to have made no comment about the colonial implications of the Atlantic Charter, but later, when the American Department of the Foreign Office complained that the Charter had been of little value in winning American sympathy for the Empire, Cadogan noted: 'Have the Dept. reflected that it had its genesis in an offer by the President? And at that time (Aug. 1941) a joint declaration of any kind went beyond our wildest dreams?' Minute by Cadogan, 6 May 1943, U 2062, FO 371/35311.

[6] Sumner Welles, *Where Are We Heading?* (New York, 1946), p. 7.

government under which they will live; and they wish to see sovereign rights and self-government restored to those who have been forcibly deprived of them.[7]

Those were the words affirming the principle of self-determination that Americans and Englishmen read in their newspapers on Saturday the 16th of August 1941.

In England, officials and the informed public alike during the course of the war came to believe that Americans seized upon the Atlantic Charter from the outset as a means of attacking the British Empire. In the words of an important study by the United States Office of Strategic Services, there existed 'a widespread British impression that Americans would like to use the Atlantic Charter to "liberate" Africa and other British colonial areas'.[8] Margery Perham in *Foreign Affairs* in 1944 described the British perception of this fundamentalist American attitude:

> The American view which reaches us through war's interruptions and by way of our shrunken newspapers may be put in the following brief and therefore blunt terms: 'The British are guilty of a sin called Empire. They committed it against the American people until these broke clear of British control to become a nation. The Americans are innocent of any such a guilt. They thus are in a moral position to condemn Britain as they watch her continuing in her way of sin against other people. The situation is the more distressing to Americans as they are being asked, in this war, to defend and support the British Empire.'[9]

Miss Perham did not argue that there was a direct connection between the general attitude of the American public and the Atlantic Charter, and it would have been historically inaccurate to have done so. Though Roosevelt and certain American officials no doubt believed in the universality of their ideas, the American press in 1941 saw the Atlantic Charter almost totally as a European document.[10] Important commentaries

---

[7] For commentary on the drafting and significance of this and all other important public documents as background to the United Nations Charter, see Ruth B. Russell, *A History of the United Nations Charter* (Washington, 1958).

[8] OSS, R&A No. 1972, 'British and American Views on the Applicability of the Atlantic Charter to Dependent Areas', 30 Aug. 1944, USSD Notter Files Box 37.

[9] Margery Perham, 'African Facts and American Criticisms', *Foreign Affairs* 22.3 (April 1944); reprinted in Margery Perham, *Colonial Sequence, 1930 to 1949* (London, 1967).

[10] For detailed analysis of this point see the OSS document cited in note 8.

such as those by John Foster Dulles in *Fortune* and Carl Becker in the *Yale Review* cetainly did not emphasize the colonial significance of the Charter.[11] Nor did the immediate public response in England stress its possible non-European application—with one important exception. On the 16th of August the Labour newspaper, the *Daily Herald*, gave prominent attention to Deputy Prime Minister Clement Attlee's statement.

The Atlantic Charter

IT MEANS DARK RACES AS WELL

Coloured peoples, as well as white, will share the
benefits of the Churchill–Roosevelt Atlantic Charter

By coincidence Attlee on the day after the release of the Charter happened to be addressing a group of West African students in London. He told them that the Labour Party had always been conscious of the wrongs done by white men to races with darker skins. After assuring them that 'nobler ideas' had replaced those of exploitation, he contrasted the principles of Roosevelt and Churchill with those of the Nazis.

Our enemies, the Nazis, set up a monstrous and ridiculous racial doctrine. They declare themselves to be a master-race to which the rest of us are inferior, and if they assert that claim in respect to Europeans you may be quite assured they are going to apply it to everyone else—Asiatics, Africans, and everyone.[12]

The opposite idealistic principles of the Atlantic Charter would also apply to all the peoples of the world. Attlee used the word 'freedom'. It was a significant public indication that the Atlantic Charter might have consequences reaching far beyond Europe.

Within the secret councils of the British Empire, Churchill straight away received word from the Governor of Burma on the 15th of August that the Burmese would grasp the literal meaning of Article III in order to push for full post-war self-government. The Governor might explain that Churchill and Roosevelt did not have Burma in mind when they drafted the declaration, but the Burmese—or anyone else—could retort

[11] John Foster Dulles, 'Peace Without Platitudes', *Fortune* (January 1942); Carl Becker, 'Making Democracy Safe in the World', *Yale Review* (March 1942).
[12] *Daily Herald*, 16 Aug. 1941.

that neither did they specifically exclude any particular coun try. This development alarmed that staunchest of all British imperialists, Leo Amery, now Secretary of State for India and Burma. He wrote to the Colonial Secretary, Lord Moyne, that the declaration had 'let loose a lot of questions about its application to the Empire'. These questions in Amery's opinion were 'strictly irrelevant'. In his view the declaration pertained entirely to European war issues; but he thought the matter could easily be clarified. He proposed that the India Office and Colonial Office submit a joint memorandum on the subject to the War Cabinet. Amery and Moyne would merely assure everyone concerned that the British Empire, animated by a spirit of liberty, pursued the goal of self-governing institutions. However, far from clarifying the purpose of the Empire in relation to the Charter, Amery's statement plunged the imperial statesmen into controversy. The Colonial Office could not accept the ideal of self-government. Moyne replied to Amery:

Self-governing institutions would probably be interpreted in many quarters to rule out all [imperial] reserve powers. Some Colonies are so small, or strategically so important, that complete self-government seems out of the question; and I cannot, for instance, imagine any conditions under which we would give Dominion status to Aden, Gibraltar, the Gambia or British Honduras.[13]

The Atlantic Charter thus immediately brought into play within high government circles divergent ideas about the future and purpose of the Empire.

So important did the authorities of the Colonial Office regard the issue of self-government that they submitted two memoranda to Churchill. These documents were drafted by Christopher Eastwood, who supervised the trusteeship question during the early part of the war. He was regarded within official circles as a man of intellectual distinction. The memoranda reveal not only the Colonial Office's confidential thought on specific colonial issues in the early stage of the war but also general reflections on imperial progress. Despite observations to the contrary in both America and the Dominions, the

---

[13] Copies of telegrams from Burma in PREM 4/42/9; Amery to Moyne, 25 Aug. 1941, enclosing draft memorandum; Moyne to Amery, 26 Aug. 1941, CO 323/1858/9057.

Colonial Office officials did not regard themselves as reactionary. In fact Eastwood warned Churchill's private secretary that the views of the Colonial Office 'may appear a little bald and frightening to those whose thoughts have moved along conventional lines on these matters'.[14] Among other things, the Colonial Office believed that it should be clear that in the British Empire no one race was superior to another.[15] There might be technical differences, for example, between protected persons and subjects of the Crown; but all were loyal members of the Empire. They had their right to participate in the life and government of the Empire. If this view seemed unconventional, the next step of the argument must have appeared almost revolutionary: each part of the Empire must be allowed to develop in its own way and at its own pace. The growth of local institutions in some colonies might be healthy, but this development should not *necessarily* mean eventual self-government as separate units. Even if self-government were possible 'in the far distant future' in such places as East Africa, this was not necessarily the best solution. Self-government for many colonies was clearly impossible. Expanding on the point already made to Amery, self-government clearly could not apply to the following territories:

Gibraltar, Aden, Mauritius, Seychelles, Fiji, the Western Pacific islands, the Falklands, British Honduras, Bermuda, the Gambia, Hong Kong. All these Colonies, and probably others (Cyprus, Malta, the dependencies in Borneo, and even Malaya) are too small or too important strategically ever to become independent self-governing units.[16]

Nor did federation provide a solution. 'It may make full self-government possible in the West Indies, though local jealousies are so great there that at present it cannot even be avowed as our aim, but it would not help any of the Colonies in the list given above.' While not rejecting self-government and

[14] Eastwood to J. M. Martin (Churchill's Private Secretary), 1 Sept. 1941, PREM 4/42/9, enclosing draft memoranda.
[15] Eastwood referred specifically to the racism of the Nazis, but it could well be that he also had in mind the 'economic colour bar' of southern Africa which had been debated extensively in England in 1940–1 as a result of the 'Copperbelt Riots' in Northern Rhodesia.
[16] 'The Constitutional Future of the British Empire', enclosed in Eastwood to Martin, cited in n. 14 above.

federation as a possible goal for some colonies, other colonies would develop in different (unspecified) ways. 'We have always been rather proud of the degree of variation that our colonial system, or absence of system, permits.'[17] Such was the gist of some of the more advanced and unconventional views of the Colonial Office.

The Colonial Secretary tried to convince the War Cabinet of the dangers involved in endorsing the principle of self-determination, even in the limited sense of self-government. Allowing colonial peoples to choose their own form of government, he stated, would be 'difficult' for the Colonial Office. He had no doubt about the way in which Churchill and Roosevelt had intended the application of the principle. Surely it was not for peoples still in need of political tutelage.

It was, of course, used, as is obvious from the context, with the nations of Europe in mind. But in the Colonies we cannot admit a right of unfettered choice to those who, in the words of the League of Nations Covenant, are 'not yet able to stand by themselves under the strenuous conditions of the modern world'.[18]

Moyne went on to explain that the Colonial Office supported the healthy growth of local institutions, a restatement of one of the basic themes of 'Indirect Rule' without the overtone of larger philosophical issues. He drove home the persistent Colonial Office theme of diversity of peoples and geographical units and the impossibility of eventual self-government for some of the smaller or strategically important parts of the Empire.

The development of local institutions to the fullest practicable extent has been and is our policy. But I am certain that it would be premature to commit ourselves to the belief that this will eventually lead to fully responsible government for every unit within the Empire. There are at least fifty governmental units in the Colonial Empire and, although the number might be reduced by federation, many would still remain too small, while others are strategically too important, for them ever to become completely masters of their destiny.[19]

[17] 'The Constitutional Future of the British Empire', in Eastwood to J. M. Martin (Churchill's Private Secretary), 1 Sept. 1941, PREM 4/42/9.
[18] 'Interpretation of Point III of Atlantic Declaration in respect of the British Empire', 2 Sept. 1941, W.P. (G) (41) 89, CAB 67/9.   [19] Ibid.

Moyne therefore in some cases advocated the indefinite continuation of Britain's paternal authority. He urged rejection of Amery's proposal to establish self-government as the Empire's goal of political development.[20] The Colonial Office's solution to the difficulties raised by the Atlantic Charter thus read:

> The Colonial Empire comprises peoples and territories of many different types and with a wide variety of institutions, which have evolved in accordance with the particular history and circumstances of each case. That evolution must continue on lines that accord with British conceptions of freedom and justice.[21]

Churchill was unimpressed, or failed to take fully into account the paradoxes of the dependent empire. Or his political sense guided him in the direction of making a more powerful political declaration *vis-à-vis* the United States and the Atlantic Charter. When the War Cabinet discussed the issue briefly on the 4th of September, Churchill aligned himself with Amery. As for the attitude of the War Cabinet in general towards the Atlantic Charter and self-determination:

> The view generally expressed in discussion was that it was clear that the Atlantic Charter . . . was directed to the nations of Europe whom we hoped to free from Nazi tyranny, and was not intended to deal with the internal affairs of the British Empire, or with relations between the United States and, for example, the Philippines.[22]

Churchill accordingly prepared a statement for Parliament.

The Prime Minister's oration in the House of Commons on the 9th of September 1941 was one of his masterly performances. He recapitulated the major topics of the Atlantic Conference, which of course included not only the statement of broad principles but also the measures to aid Russia against 'the hideous onslaught which Hitler has made upon her', policy towards Japan to prevent the spread of the war to the Pacific, and some indication of highly secret military and naval topics. Having established the Atlantic Charter as only one of several

---

[20] Memorandum by Amery, 'Interpretation of Point III', 29 Aug. 1941, W.P. (G) (41) 85, CAB 67/9. In a letter to Moyne of 27 August, Amery had explained that a suggestion of qualifying self-government 'would send both India and Burma right off the deep end, for they would at once begin thinking that the qualifications . . . were meant to apply to them'. CO 323/1858/9057.

[21] Colonial Office War Cabinet paper cited above, p. 128, n. 18.

[22] 4 Sept. 1941, W.M. (41) 89th Conclusions, CAB 65/19.

important items of business, Churchill went on to stress the danger of formulating precise peace aims at a time when the end of the war was not in sight. The Joint Declaration was a statement of common principles on which to build a better world—'*after the final destruction of Nazi tyranny*'.[23] Having emphasized the importance of postponing a specific formula for the peace and having established the European context of the Charter, Churchill said that he could not as a single party to a two-party agreement put special interpretation on particular clauses. He could however speak in an exclusive sense. He could explain what the President and he had *not* had in mind. They had not intended to qualify in any way the commitments or pledges Britain had made to India, Burma, or other parts of the Empire.

We are pledged by the Declaration of August, 1940, to help India, to obtain free and equal partnership in the British Commonwealth with ourselves, subject, of course, to the fulfilment of obligations arising from our long connection with India and our responsibilities to its many creeds, races and interests. Burma also is covered by our considered policy of establishing Burmese self-government and by the measures already in progress.

He then put in a positive way the application of the self-determination principle. 'At the Atlantic meeting, we had in mind, primarily, the restoration of the sovereignty, self-government and national life of the States and nations of Europe now under the Nazi yoke and the principles governing any alterations in the territorial boundaries which may have to be made.' Clearly to Churchill this had nothing to do with the British Empire.

So that is quite a separate problem from the progressive evolution of self-governing institutions in the regions and peoples which owe allegiance to the British Crown. We have made declarations on these matters which are complete in themselves, free from ambiguity and related to the conditions and circumstances of the territories and peoples affected.

Churchill thus had stated explicitly before Parliament that Britain was committed to self-government in the colonies, and

[23] *Parliamentary Debates* (Commons), 9 Sept. 1941, cols. 67–9. Churchill was emphasizing the wording of the Charter.

moreover, that these commitments were 'complete in themselves' and 'free from ambiguity'.[24]

To most Englishmen, self-government within the Empire
probably appeared to be an excellent answer to the American
cry for independence. Nevertheless the endorsement of this
principle was a step the Colonial Office had not been willing
to take. And with good reason. Could the Colonial Office
actually prove in general that progress had been made towards
self-government by declarations free from ambiguity and complete in themselves? The challenge began with comments in
the House of Commons regretting the absence of a forthright
statement by the Prime Minister saying that the war was being
fought to promote the political and economic advancement of
the peoples of Asia and Africa no less than those of the democracies.[25] Despite the drama at Pearl Harbor and Singapore,
the colonial issue by no means lapsed. Political organizations
such as the Fabian Colonial Bureau began to make inquiries
as a result of Churchill's statement.[26] What did the Prime
Minister have in mind when he had given the assurance of
progress towards self-government? 'We are somewhat at a loss
to know precisely what it is to which they refer', stated a
Labour Member of Parliament, Arthur Creech Jones, who
later became a post-war Colonial Secretary. In July 1942 he
asked the Under-Secretary for Colonies whether the Colonial
Office could now publish 'as a White Paper the past declarations
of Colonial policy upon which our relations with the Colonial
peoples of the Empire are to develop'.[27]

Even the Colonial Office regarded the request for evidence
as reasonable, but it threw the Office into pandemonium trying
to find suitable declarations. Christopher Eastwood set out to
make a comprehensive list of statements about general policy
and achievements in particular colonies. He first of all discovered that they had failed to keep systematically a list or
index of papers concerning political progress. 'As a result we

[24] Ibid.
[25] Dr. Leslie Haden Guest (author–journalist–doctor and frequent commentator on colonial affairs), *Parliamentary Debates* (Commons), 30 Sept. 1941, c. 538.
[26] The manuscript material most helpful in this regard is: Fabian Papers, Box
129; Creech Jones Papers, Box 15; Anti-Slavery Society Papers, G442–3; and the
Hailey Papers, *passim*.
[27] *Parliamentary Debates* (Commons), 24 June and 1 July 1942, cols. 2122 and 199.

are dependent largely upon the memories of people in the Office.' Furthermore, though he found good value in certain Command Papers on education, colonial development, and welfare, there simply were no general statements about political advancement towards self-government. Nor could he make much progress with particular colonies. For example, he recalled from memory that the Windwards and Leewards had introduced unofficial majorities in their Legislative Council. Would such information be of general interest? Or the proposal to introduce adult suffrage in Jamaica? Or the fact that the Legislative Council of Northern Rhodesia had created a finance committee? Much of the documentation was tied up with other matters extraneous to self-government and if everything were included the Colonial Office might be accused of introducing irrelevant information—it might even make the Colonial Office appear ridiculous. 'The document is going to be a thin one and poor one anyhow', Eastwood concluded. Having conscientiously tried to document the Prime Minister's assurance to Parliament, he wrote in despair:

> I am afraid . . . it reflects the confusion in my own mind on the whole subject. . . . Whatever document we produce will not, I am afraid, be very impressive and will be likely to lead to criticism. That may perhaps be a good thing. . . . The very great difficulty of making an authoritative collection of past statements of policy seems to me to show up a great weakness in the Office machinery.[28]

Harold Macmillan, at this time Parliamentary Under-Secretary for the Colonies, took the matter in hand. He fully grasped the importance of the issue at stake, and he also despaired. 'I do not think the P.M. can have realised the true nakedness of the land when he made the statement. . . . The declarations are not complete in themselves, nor are they free from ambiguity. They are scrappy, obscure and jejune.'[29] Since for many years historians have wondered about the inner thought of the Colonial Office in regard to the general colonial issue during the early stages of the war, it is of great interest that the archives reveal Macmillan's observation about bankruptcy: 'We have no complete list of our pledges and commitments. In private

---

[28] Minute by Eastwood, 5 Aug. 1942, CO 323/1848.
[29] Minute by Macmillan, 1 Sept. 1942, CO 323/1848.

life, this leads inevitably to bankruptcy.'[30] Macmillan wrote of the failure to record pledges, but the Colonial Secretary, now Lord Cranborne (Salisbury), clearly saw a poverty of policy: 'Declarations on Colonial Policy seem to have been mainly conspicuous by their absence, and, when any have been made, they are vague in the extreme.'[31] Cranborne summed it all up by saying that they were in 'an embarrassing situation'.

The Atlantic Charter thus led to a recognition within the Colonial Office that Britain's basic colonial policy would have to be examined and defined. The anguish of the Colonial Office was part of the general and agonizing reappraisal of the future of the Empire, a reappraisal that became especially searching and intense after the disaster at Singapore.

[30] Ibid. In his memoirs Macmillan gave quite a different impression of the Colonial Office's march towards self-government. Reflecting on the Atlantic Charter, he wrote: 'President Roosevelt, like President Wilson, was fond of generalisations. The British tradition is more practical, and we were already considering the positive steps in the evolution towards self-government of the different territories, having regard to their history and background.' Harold Macmillan, *The Blast of War* (London, 1967), p. 178.

[31] Minute by Cranborne, 4 Sept. 1942, CO 323/1848.

7

THE FALL OF SINGAPORE AND THE FUTURE OF THE BRITISH EMPIRE TRUSTEESHIP VERSUS PARTNERSHIP

SHORTLY after the surrender of Singapore on the 15th of February 1942, Walter Lippmann wrote a column in the *Washington Post* entitled 'The Post Singapore War in the East'. Lord Moyne and Lord Hailey deprecated it in Parliament.[1] The Foreign Secretary, Anthony Eden, regarded it as 'most depressing' and as evidence that 'American opinion is hopelessly ill-informed of world politics'.[2] Lippmann argued that, stupendous as the military defeat might seem, it was the long-range political future of Asia that had to be viewed in different perspective. The loss of Britain's Far Eastern Empire transformed overnight an imperialist's war into a war of liberation.

[T]he western nations must now do what hitherto they lacked the will and the imagination to do: they must identify their cause with the freedom and the security of the peoples of the East, putting away the 'white man's burden' and purging themselves of the taint of an obsolete and obviously unworkable white man's imperialism. In this drastic reorientation of war policy, the leadership of the western nations must be taken by the United States . . .

For such a war we are, fortunately, not unprepared. Though we have dabbled in empire, we have had no stomach for it. Though we have many grievous sins and follies of our own to expiate, it is not self-righteousness to say that in this particular field it is not the case of the devil was sick when we identify our cause with the freedom of the Asiatic peoples . . .

General MacArthur leads an Army of Americans and Filipinos in a struggle which is as noble as it is glorious. For the Filipinos

---

[1] *Parliamentary Debates* (Lords), 6 and 20 May 1942, cols. 902 and 1090. Though Cranborne succeeded Moyne as Colonial Secretary on 22 Feb. 1942, the latter continued to take a prominent part in the colonial debates of that year.

[2] Minute by Eden, 2 May 1942, F 2947, FO 371/31777.

know that under American law, their own independence is assured to them. When they fight in the Bataan Peninsula side by side with our men, they are fighting for their independence.[3]

The implication was galling. The peoples of Malaya had not fought because they were subjected to British imperialism. In the spring of 1942 those Englishmen concerned with the dependent Empire engaged in a searching debate about what they believed to be the true lessons of Singapore. Publicly the discussion led to concrete statements defining trusteeship, or, in the new phrase, 'partnership'. This reappraisal took place against the background of momentous events. To those especially involved in colonial affairs, the loss of Singapore was the blackest day in the war.[4] At Singapore alone the Japanese took 130,000 prisoners. In addition to Malaya, Japan's dominion extended over Hong Kong, the Straits Settlements, Northern Borneo, Sarawak, and eventually Burma. Outrageous though Walter Lippmann's thoughts might have seemed to British Imperialists, he had seen a basic truth. As Michael Howard has written in his brilliant survey of British strategy in the inter-war years, 'The charisma on which British rule in the East had rested for a hundred years and which British defence planners had been so anxious to preserve was destroyed forever.'[5]

While the press and Members of Parliament searched for the military reasons for the catastrophe, colonial experts asked whether the Malayan experience revealed weaknesses in the British colonial system. Margery Perham in two major articles in *The Times* reviewed the colonial situation in the light of

---

[3] *Washington Post*, 21 Feb. 1942. On the theme of Filipino loyalty, Hailey, among many other Englishmen, warmly denied the legitimacy of comparison with the British colonial empire. In the 20 May Parliamentary debate cited in n. 1, he spoke of false analogies and said, 'the Filipino people are in fact very much more akin to the people of a South American State in every way than they are to that mixture of peoples found in Malaya—one-third Indians, one-third Chinese and one-third a people who are subjects of their own native rulers'. In explaining the failure to resist the Japanese, Hailey, Cranborne, and others emphasized that Britain had given Malaya the *Pax Britannica*, which, with its benefits of peace and prosperity, did not include military training.

[4] See, e.g., Sir Cosmo Parkinson, *The Colonial Office From Within, 1909–1945* (London, 1947), p. 87.

[5] Michael Howard, *The Continental Commitment: The Dilemma of British Defence Policy in the Era of the Two World Wars* (London, 1972), p. 144.

Singapore. She wrote on the 15th of March 1942:

The Malayan disaster has shocked us into sudden attention to the structure of our colonial empire. Events such as we have known in the last few weeks are rough teachers, but our survival as a great power may depend upon our being able to learn their lesson. . . . most people in this country have been startled into a sudden questioning, or rather into an intuitive certainty that our colonial administration needs adjustment to the new conditions of our world.[6]

Likening the structure of colonial administration to a 'steel frame', Miss Perham used this metaphor to connect the problems of South-East Asia and those of Africa. The colonial communities emerging under western imperialism could be described as 'plural societies'.[7] Though many colonial territories shared the characteristics of plural societies, Malaya and Kenya were the most striking examples—Malaya with its Indian, Chinese, and indigenous components, and Kenya with its African, Arab, Indian, and British inhabitants. The steel frame of the colonial administration held the societies together while each of the separate groups pursued their material interests. In J. S. Furnivall's classic phrase, they mingled but did not mix. Miss Perham projected the lesson of Singapore to East Africa.

It needs the brutal hammering of war to make us fully realize the weakness of such communities. Since we ought not now to shrink from applying this test in anticipation, let us imagine—what is not unimaginable—that Japanese transports and aircraft carriers appear outside Mombasa harbour.

How would the 'plural society' of Kenya respond? The small settler community would know very well what they were fighting for. The disciplined professional African troops would show the same remarkable bravery as they did in Ethiopia. But would the Indian community, in its political and social segregation, find it possible to rally shoulder to shoulder with the Europeans and join with them in common discipline and sacrifice? Would the Kikuyu, still unsatisfied about their land and with some of the leaders of their political societies in prison, give the wholehearted co-operation that would be needed? Would the coastal Arabs, or the Kavirondo

---

[6] 'The Need for Stocktaking and Review', *The Times*, 13 Mar. 1942, reprinted in Margery Perham, *Colonial Sequence, 1930 to 1949* (London, 1967), pp. 225–8.

[7] The phrase is indelibly associated with the work of J. S. Furnivall, whose writings had an immense influence on the wartime writers on colonial affairs. See, e.g., J. S. Furnivall, *Progress and Welfare in Southeast Asia: A Comparison of Colonial Policy and Practice* (New York, 1941).

dock labourers, who not long ago rioted against the admittedly indefensible conditions in which they had to work, carry on in the face of hardship and danger?[8]

Even to imagine Kenya in the throes of Japanese invasion caused one to wonder about the grand philosophy of 'Indirect Rule', according to which the components of the plural society should be allowed to develop along their own lines.[9] 'Can we afford the assumptions that a common citizenship is impossible and that the steel frame will be there to hold the groups in their uneasy suspension for all time?' Clearly the times demanded a drastic reorientation of colonial policy to hold out hope for a more egalitarian society.[10]

In her concluding article, entitled 'Capital, Labour and the Colour Bar', Miss Perham continued to examine the economic and racial policies of the Empire that had to be altered substantially if the Empire were to be egalitarian. The essay is remarkable for its summation of the major issues of colonial rule as seen from the immediate vantage point of the fall of Singapore. In essence the problem consisted of economic control and planning, the absence of which allowed the unhealthy growth of 'plural' or stratified societies. Uncontrolled economic forces had interacted with sociological prejudices. *Laissez-faire* had produced the *economic colour bar*. The impact of the western industrial world on indigenous societies had created vicious 'tropical East Ends' throughout much of the Empire. The resulting and deep-seated racial attitudes could not be easily modified except through long-range colonial economic policies; in the short range it was imperative to bridge the human gap developing between Britain's colonial rulers and the African and Asian élites. In her analysis she used the word 'partnership':

Differences of race, colour, language and customs *are* barriers; backwardness *is* a dividing fact. But there is a level of education and of potential common interests upon which we are held back only by our prejudices from co-operation and friendship. Yet, without these,

[8] Perham, 'The Need for Stocktaking'.
[9] For a brilliant summation of the doctrines of British colonial administration especially helpful in regard to the Second World War debate, see R. E. Robinson, 'Why "Indirect Rule" has been replaced by "Local Government" in the Nomenclature of British Native Administration', *Journal of African Administration* 2.3 (July 1950).   [10] Perham, 'Need for Stocktaking'.

imperial rule cannot change into the working partnership which the coming age demands.[11]

In broader perspective the war would inevitably and profoundly influence the future of race relations.

This question of racial attitudes has wider relevance. Japan's attack in the Pacific has produced a very practical revolution in race relationships. An Asiatic people has for the moment successfully challenged the ascendancy of three great white imperial Powers. Indian troops, towards whom a changed India may develop a more direct connexion, are fighting for our colonial empire; Chinese, Indonesian and Filipino soldiers, as well as American and Dutch, are all in the same battle.

Will our colonies, saved from Japanese conquest by this alliance in arms, revert to the same status of imperial possessions with all their links gathered exclusively to Whitehall? Yet, if the alliance of arms is to develop into a Far Eastern co-operation for defence and development, what an energetic exercise in racial understanding with the Asiatic Powers, including Russia, must be built up almost from nothing in the next few years![12]

Miss Perham called for reform; and she identified Lord Hailey as the moving spirit behind the substance of colonial reforms in progress despite intolerable official delay and incompetence. The next day *The Times* responded to these sweeping assessments by taking its own stock of the colonial situation in a leading article. *The Times* defended the 'integrity, humanity and progressiveness of British administration'; but it concurred in the economic and racial defects of the colonial system:

Misguided conceptions of racial prestige and narrow and obsolete interpretations of economic interest are grave obstacles. But they must be surmounted if democracy is to have any meaning or appeal for the colonial peoples. The price of failure is the perpetuation of those 'plural' societies whose fissiparous tendencies and inherent weaknesses, luridly revealed by the Japanese assault, make them unfit for survival in the modern world.[13]

The future depended on Britain's capacity to reform the social and economic inequalities especially apparent in colonies with

[11] 'Capital, Labour and the Colour Bar', *The Times*, 14 Mar. 1942; reprinted in *Colonial Sequence*, pp. 228–31.
[12] Ibid.   [13] 'The Colonial Future', *The Times*, 14 Mar. 1942.

'plural societies' but present in varying degrees throughout the colonial Empire.

For such a challenge of basic economic and social as well as political reform, 'trusteeship' was not enough. The formula of merely protecting Africans and Asians from economic exploitation had been tried and found wanting. 'Trusteeship' implied paternal protection and the safeguarding of native rights—essentially a negative concept which failed to meet the need of progressive economic development and social reform. 'Trusteeship' had become associated with the sterile legalism of the League of Nations. It had failed to promote the development of self-governing institutions. In Harold Macmillan's words, the concept of trusteeship in 1942 appeared to be obsolete or at least obsolescent. In his memoirs he remarks that in the parliamentary debates in the spring of 1942 he deferred to Lord Hailey's insistence on the phrase 'partnership' in place of the old notion of trusteeship.[14] The dynamic idea of Britain's working together with colonial peoples to solve these mutual problems emerged as an inspiration worthy of the dire times in which they lived.

As Chairman of the Colonial Office's Post-War Problems Committee, Hailey wielded official as well as public influence.[15] The Colonial Office kept him fully informed on issues of broadest importance.[16] When he spoke on colonial questions he brought to bear the experience of his career in India and the insights of comparative research on the colonial policies of France, Belgium, and Portugal as well as of Britain—a research effort that had culminated in the monumental *African Survey.*[17] He possessed a rare ability to synthesize great amounts of

[14] Macmillan, *Blast of War,* p. 177.

[15] For the work of this committee I am indebted to discussion with J. M. Lee, whose forthcoming book deals with post-war planning. For an indication of his work in progress, '"Forward Thinking" and War: the Colonial Office during the 1940s', paper presented at the Anglo-French Colloquium on Independence and Dependence (Paris, 6–8 May 1976).

[16] See, e.g., notations in the files on the Atlantic Charter (CO 323/1858/9057 and CO 323/1848) which clearly indicate that Hailey had the inside view of the difficulties in dealing with the problem of trusteeship.

[17] London, 1938. See especially the 1956 edition, which describes the relatively short usage of 'partnership' as an improvement of 'trusteeship' during the Second World War; 'partnership' later was used to describe the character of relationships which British policy sought to promote in multiracial societies in eastern and central Africa (p. 193).

material and to present general views on controversial subjects in a persuasive manner. In the spring of 1942 Hailey spoke with authority on the subject of trusteeship and partnership. The occasion was a House of Lords debate on the colonial war effort. A Labour peer, the Earl of Listowel, had given formal expression to an idea which had, in the words of a keen observer, 'been in the air since the formulation of the Atlantic Charter'.[18] Listowel recommended:

> that we need a supplement to the Atlantic Charter, which described so well the aims for which we and our Allies are fighting. This supplement might be called the British Colonial Charter, and it would add to our list of war aims the achievement of those conditions of life which are sought by the peoples of our Dependencies.[19]

Hailey responded immediately. With some exaggeration he claimed that British official declarations on colonial policy had consistently affirmed the principle of trusteeship. No government, Conservative or other, had ever departed from it. 'No one can deny that the sentiment of trusteeship has played a great and most beneficent part in the development of our system of civil administration in the Colonies.'[20] But it was no longer sufficient. As he had emphasized on a previous occasion, the old conception of trusteeship looked upon the state as a protector of rights. Now the state had to be viewed moreover as the chief agency for public welfare and economic development.[21]

Since the content of the idea of trusteeship had changed in response to the demands of the times, Hailey wished to discard the old-fashioned usage of the concept and the word itself. He pointed out a disadvantage to the legal connotation of the phrase. 'The use of the term is irritating to the Colonial people. It was intensely unpopular in India. It is becoming equally unpopular in the Colonies . . . if I were a native of the Colonies, I should equally resent [it].' Though he did not stress the analogy of development from childhood to young manhood

---

[18] The phrase is that of the Secretary of the Fabian Colonial Bureau, Rita Hinden, in a memorandum of 4 June 1942, Creech Jones Papers 15/1. In this memorandum she directly attributes the inspiration of Listowel's speech to the activity of the Fabian Bureau.

[19] *Parliamentary Debates* (Lords), 20 May 1942, c. 1088.

[20] Ibid., c. 1095.   [21] Ibid., 6 May 1942, c. 919.

(perhaps because colonial subjects would resent it also), the premise of the parent–child or senior–junior relationship remained the same as he recast it in terms of partnership:

If we need to express ourselves in a formula at all, let our relations be those of senior and junior partners in the same enterprise, and let it be said that our contract of partnership involves the progressive increase of the share which the junior partners have in the conduct of the undertaking.[22]

Hailey granted that it might not be impossible to make such a general statement about 'partnership' that would serve the purpose of clarifying British intentions. It could be drawn up in terms of a 'Colonial Charter'. Those who advocated the colonial equivalent of an Atlantic Charter must have taken heart. But Hailey's immediate qualification about the difficulties of such a Charter must have also comforted those who believed that Britain's imperial mission must not be diverted for the sake of international propaganda.

[T]he statement, if it is to avail us, must be honest. If we do not believe that a Colony of small population or resources can, standing by itself, ever achieve responsible government, let us frankly say so now. If we do not believe that a Colony with a settled European population can ever attain self-government under any form which will place the native majority under the political control of the European minority, then let us say that now also. If we do not believe that the self-governing institutions best suited to a native population are those which follow the model of our own Parliamentary institution, let us say that also.

You can, perhaps, afford to offer attractive generalizations about the future to highly-civilized people. They know the rules of the game and can draw their own conclusions. But if we are to have the co-operation of more simple people we must have their confidence, and we shall not have that if they ever have reason to feel that we have misled them or allowed them to entertain false hopes about their own future.[23]

[22] Ibid., 20 May 1942, cols. 1095–6.
[23] Ibid. Hailey's speech provoked discussion on fundamental points. For example, Lord Wedgwood commented: 'The difference between the native under British rule and the native under French rule is that the French coal-black Sengalese nigger can strike his chest and say "I am a French citizen". You do not get that same sense of citizenship in any part of the British Empire.' Ibid., c. 1098.

When the Colonial Secretary responded to the debate, he emphasized the difficulties of the proposed declaration rather than the advantages, as Hailey had outlined them. After denying that there was any particular need for a 'Colonial Charter', Cranborne stated: 'There is also a danger that, if one made such a general declaration, certain of the less developed peoples might wish to run before they could walk; and, if they were not really fit to run, and we did not think that they were, they might charge us with a breach of faith.'[24] Nevertheless Cranborne did not entirely exclude the possibility of a declaration or 'Colonial Charter'. The archives reveal that the Colonial Office gave considerable thought to it as a means of getting out of the 'embarrassing situation' created by the Prime Minister's parliamentary statement about unambiguous pledges of self-government. A new and formal declaration would remove the need to find these non-existent pledges.[25]

Shortly after the debate in the House of Lords, Hailey on the 28th of May delivered the annual address to the Anti-Slavery and Aborigines Protection Society. It attracted wide attention because it was eventually published in *The Fortnightly* with the title 'A Colonial Charter'.[26] To the casual reader it probably appeared to be an endorsement of the idea. In fact Hailey had polished his parliamentary speech into a sophisticated dialectic. Every argument had its counter argument and a Haileyan synthesis. Those who argued in favour of a Colonial Charter pointed to the need for a new vision. British ideals should be declared, thus justifying the cause of the Empire and mitigating criticism abroad. On the other hand, a declaration of some ideals such as self-government might not be appropriate for all parts of the Empire. To paraphrase his Noble Lordship, we must not make false promises. Therefore let us be practical. We can at least say that even the more primitive peoples of the Empire have hopes of eventually becoming junior partners in this great enterprise. With partnership as the dynamic idea, we can speak of specific projects on which everyone can agree: the improvement of social services in the colonies, raising the standard of living, the more rapid development of local

---

[24] *Parliamentary Debates* (Lords), 20 May 1942, c. 1127.
[25] See especially Cranborne's minute of 4 Sept. 1942, CO 323/1848.
[26] Lord Hailey, 'A Colonial Charter', *Fortnightly*, July 1942.

institutions, and the fuller participation of the colonial peoples in their administration. A 'Colonial Charter' might or might not be useful if it could be harnessed to the idea of partnership.

Hailey was looking for workable solutions to controversial problems. This is all the more apparent from his unpublished correspondence. At the same time that he was making public speeches, he wrote privately:

> It seems to me that our own outlook on colonial policy is in the process of being recast; partly because of the new conception . . . of the position which the State must occupy as an agency for social welfare, but even more because international interest is now beginning to take a somewhat different form . . .
>
> I am not sure that what we may call 'international interest' will not yield to an interest of a much more regional character. There are some signs of this in America's interest in the Caribbean colonies and I feel sure that we shall before long have to face the fact that she will develop an active interest in the policy to be pursued in the control of the Far Eastern Colonies after their recovery from the Axis Powers.[27]

To restate the significance of this passage in terms of international trusteeship, Hailey admitted that the mandates system had served a useful purpose by bringing possible breaches of principle to the court of international opinion. But Britain had her own institutions of accountability and therefore, for Britain at least, the mandates system was unnecessary. To conserve some of its useful functions, certain schemes such as analogous regional commissions might be carried over into the post-war era. Thus, as early as the post-Singapore phase of the war, some of the main lines of a colonial post-war organization scheme had clearly emerged in Hailey's mind.

Hailey's advocacy of partnership in place of trusteeship won support in many quarters, but it by no means found universal acceptance. When the House of Commons debated colonial affairs in June, Macmillan in his maiden speech as Under-Secretary for the Colonies introduced partnership as the dynamic theme of development. 'Out of partnership come

[27] Hailey to Wilfrid Benson, 27 May 1942, Hailey Papers 600.18.S.20. This and other letters to and from Benson (an officer of International Labour Organization in charge of colonial questions) in the Hailey Papers and Fabian Papers. For Benson's ideas, see, e.g., his essay 'An I.L.O. Pattern for Pacific Territories', *Pacific Affairs* 17. 3 (September 1944).

understanding and friendship.'[28] Some of the response was
hostile. Dr. Leslie Haden Guest, an outspoken Labour M.P.
with a long-standing interest in colonial affairs, immediately
attacked him. 'The present relation between the Colonies and
the Mother Country', he said, 'is not one of partnership. It is
subordination, and the Colonies have not equality of government economically or politically. Does the right hon. Gentleman mean equal partnership?' Haden Guest was a formidable
debater, even to one of such forensic agility as Macmillan.
The exchange continued:

Mr. Macmillan: That was the conception [of partnership] I was
trying to develop.
Dr. Guest: But it is a new policy and not the policy of the Government?
Mr. Macmillan: Not at all. Perhaps in the hon. Gentleman's own
relations there have been junior and senior partners. What I was
trying to convey was that this was an organization that should not
be broken up but should continue in a spirit of partnership.
Dr. Guest: Is it real partnership or just another form of words to
delude people?[29]

It was an apt question. During much of the subsequent wartime discussion about international trusteeship, the substance
of the phrase 'partnership' continued to be debated. Some, like
Haden Guest, believed it to be rhetoric and not a change of
heart. He persisted in his attack:

Is it now the policy of the Government, and is he proclaiming it
here to-day, that the Colonies are in fact to be taken into equal
partnership, or is it just a form of words, soft soap or soothing
syrup, which means nothing? What does 'partnership' mean? It
either means a share in control, economic and political—and I hold
that the Colonies ought to have an equal share—or it means nothing
at all and is just a form of words.[30]

If partnership was the policy of the Colonial Office, then
clearly it had failed in Malaya, at least in Haden Guest's view.
There the British 'had been using the place merely to exploit
its natural⌐resources, to get enormous sums of money out of
it for people in this country, a very small proportion of which

---

[28] *Parliamentary Debates* (Commons), 24 June 1942, cols. 2014–15.
[29] Ibid., c. 2106.   [30] Ibid., c. 2107.

was ever returned to Malaya itself'. In his opinion the old British Empire had died with the fall of Singapore and its old spirit should not be revived by such 'extremely academic and old fashioned' rhetoric used by Macmillan and Hailey.[31] Such was the tone of some of the hostile reception to 'partnership'.

On the other hand the Labour spokesman for colonial questions, Creech Jones, acknowledged agreement with Hailey. 'Lord Hailey . . . has admirably expressed what some of us have been saying for a long time on this matter.' The trouble with 'trusteeship', Creech Jones said, was that it had become unpopular and irritating. It suggested cant and unfulfilled promises. It implied inequality of status. 'Indeed, some of us want a new relationship with the Colonial peoples which conveys the idea of equality and fellowship, the idea of service and practical assistance and which expresses it in dynamic and constructive terms.'[32] Creech Jones privately held that Hailey did not go far enough. In the deliberations of the Fabian Colonial Bureau, in which he was a moving force, the limitations and deficiencies of 'partnership' were analyzed. The phrase seemed to pertain only to British colonies. 'It takes no account of the future interests of non-British territories' and thus it failed to measure up to the universal applicability of trusteeship. Moreover it did not provide adequate assurance for the development of self-governing institutions. 'It smacks too much of an extension of "indirect rule" which is not very popular among educated Africans.' The Fabians also criticized Hailey's economic proposals. 'They ignore all the question of ownership of land and resources and the nationalisation of colonial areas.' And, most important of all, Hailey's 'partnership' did not give any guarantee that racial problems could be ameliorated. 'There is no mention of discrimination in civil and political rights (colour bar) and no reference to the special problems in the area of white settlement.' On the whole, however, the Fabians agreed with Hailey that the concept of trusteeship had to be recast 'in more positive terms of equality of status'.[33]

[31] Ibid., c. 2108.   [32] Ibid., c. 2042.
[33] See Fabian Papers Box 129; Creech Jones Papers Box 15; the points are summed up in a memorandum by Rita Hinden of 4 June 1942. Other societies

One final point should be made about Hailey's attempt to eclipse trusteeship with his dynamic notion of partnership. Students of the international dimension of the mandates believed he was entirely wrong in describing trusteeship as a static institution in which the guardians merely guarded their wards without promoting their welfare and development. Freda White, the author of one of the better books on the mandates,[34] made this point when she described Hailey as 'a sort of majestic herald' moving the Colonial Office in the direction of progress. His progressive policies could only be welcomed, *but*:

[H]e sets up an antithesis between 'trusteeship' as a static policy, and an active planning of social betterment. This is puzzling to students of the mandatory system, for the 'trusteeship' of the mandates is specifically defined as aimed at 'welfare and development', and their application has always been judged by the criterion of progress. There is, it seems, some opposition to the mandatory system floating in the official air.[35]

She had gone to the heart of the matter. By replacing trusteeship with partnership within the British Empire, the British would be accountable only to themselves, not to an international organization. It was a point that later became fully apparent to American critics of British Imperialism.

that indicated a particular interest in the problem of trusteeship at this time included the League of Coloured Peoples, the Anti-Slavery and Aborigines Protection Society, and the League of Nations Union, which prepared a memorandum of particular importance dated 19 June 1942. It is of interest among other reasons for the specific proposals for the way in which a strengthened mandates system might assist in economic development. The best collection of this material is in the Anti-Slavery Society Papers G 442–43. See also C. W. Greenidge, 'Tasks for an International Colonial Conference', *Crown Colonist* (December 1943). Greenidge was from Barbados and Chief Justice of British Honduras, 1932–6. In 1941 he succeeded Sir John Harris as Secretary of the Anti-Slavery and Aborigines Protection Society. The Greenidge Papers at Rhodes House help considerably in throwing light on these matters. For Harris and the Society in the inter-war years, see Wm. Roger Louis, 'Sir John Harris and "Colonial Trusteeship"', Académie Royale des Sciences d'Outre-Mer, *Bulletin des Sciences*, 1968, no. 3.

[34] *Mandates* (London, 1926).
[35] Freda White, 'Colonial Outlook: Unsettled', *New Statesman*, 27 June 1942.

8

ROOSEVELT AND THE AMERICAN PUBLIC'S ATTITUDE TOWARDS THE COLONIAL ISSUE FROM PEARL HARBOR TO THE ANNIVERSARY OF THE ATLANTIC CHARTER

PROMINENT Americans shared common assumptions about imperialism as they shaped their opinions about trusteeship.[1] They tended to believe that national independence was the natural and desirable course in world affairs, though, in the case of the British, some were more willing than others to grant that self-government within the British Empire might be a satisfactory alternative. Roosevelt must be counted among the sceptics. He disliked British Imperialism, pure and simple as it seemed to him. He complained about antiquated eighteenth-century methods of British rule. British observers, including Churchill, believed that the President's own conception of the British Empire belonged to the time of George III. At least Roosevelt's general attitude was comprehensible. His anti-colonialism was clearly apparent to the British no less than to his American peers, many of whom shared his antipathy. At the same time he held sophisticated views about the replacement of imperialism by trusteeship. In this realm his ideas were almost idiosyncratic and not readily discernible by the British. The same may be said even of his own advisers, if only because the President did not keep them fully informed. Even before the American entry into the war Roosevelt began to develop the concept of trusteeship in a distinctive sense—one that went far beyond the context of the debate about 'partnership' in England. He used the idea as a solution to the world's political

---

[1] For a general analysis of common principles of American decision-making, see Frederick S. Dunn, *Peace-Making and the Settlement with Japan* (Princeton, 1963), which is especially helpful on the subject of this chapter.

problems. Shortly after the signing of the Atlantic Charter, he wrote:

[T]here seems no reason why the principle of trusteeship in private affairs should not be extended to the international field. Trusteeship is based on the principle of unselfish service. For a time at least there are many minor children among the peoples of the world who need trustees in their relations with other nations and peoples, just as there are many adult nations or peoples which must be led back into a spirit of good conduct.[2]

Here was the embryo of the 'Four Policemen' scheme by which the United States, Britain, Russia, and China would patrol the world to keep the peace. 'Trusteeship' to Roosevelt meant far more than the guardianship of colonial peoples. It embraced the entire organization of the post-war world. Having stressed this important application of the concept in a way that he did not divulge publicly, it is no less important to emphasize that Roosevelt espoused the idea in a traditional sense shared by many Americans. He believed that subject peoples should be held in tutelage only until they could stand on their own feet. As in the case of many Americans, the courage and loyalty of the Filipinos during the Japanese conquest strengthened his conviction. In his message to the people of the Philippine Islands on the 28th of December 1941 he stated:

The people of the United States will never forget what the people of the Philippine Islands are doing this day and will do in the days to come. I give to the people of the Philippines my solemn pledge that their freedom will be redeemed and their independence established and protected. The entire resources, in men and in material, of the United States stand behind that pledge.[3]

To Roosevelt the colonial powers would do well to follow

---

[2] Quoted in Russell, *History of the United Nations Charter*, p. 43. For the development of Roosevelt's anti-colonial ideas, see Willard Range, *Franklin D. Roosevelt's World Order* (Athens, Georgia, 1959), ch. VIII; and Foster Rhea Dulles and Gerald E. Ridinger, 'The Anti-Colonial Policies of Franklin D. Roosevelt,' *Political Science Quarterly* 70. 1 (March 1955).

[3] Louise W. Holborn, ed., *War and Peace Aims of the United Nations* (Boston, 1943), p. 65.

America's example in the Philippines.[4] Whatever the President's inconsistencies, on this point he never wavered.[5]

At this stage of the war, Roosevelt freely offered his advice to Churchill on the future of the Empire. After Pearl Harbor, during the Prime Minister's visit to Washington, the President broached the subject of India. Churchill recorded in his memoirs, 'I reacted so strongly and at such length that he never raised it verbally again.'[6] Roosevelt later advised Stalin not to mention the word 'India' in conversation with Churchill. The President nevertheless persisted. He believed that the lessons of the history of American independence could be applied to India. When the British government in March the next year announced the Cripps mission, Roosevelt explained to the Prime Minister that, following the American revolution, a stopgap government had been formed under the Articles of Confederation. He believed a similar transitional government might be possible in India. It could be composed of the different religions, castes, and occupations representing various regions.

Perhaps some such method, with its analogy to the problems and travails of the United States from 1783 to 1789, might cause the people of India to forget past hard feelings, and to become more loyal to the British Empire, and to emphasize the danger of domination by the Japanese, and the advantages of peaceful evolution as contrasted with revolutionary chaos.[7]

Roosevelt noted that this was 'none of my business', but he wanted to help. Churchill's scathing comment indicates how

[4] 'I like to think that the history of the Philippine Islands in the last 44 years provides in a very real sense a pattern for the future of other small Nations and peoples of the world. It is a pattern of what men of good will look forward to in the future—a pattern of a global civilization which recognizes no limitations of religion, or of creed, or of race.' Roosevelt's radio address on the seventh Anniversary of the Philippines, 15 Nov. 1942, Samuel I. Rosenman, ed., *The Public Papers and Addresses of Franklin D. Roosevelt, 1942* (New York, 1950), p. 475.

[5] See Range, *Roosevelt's World Order*, ch. 8.

[6] Winston S. Churchill, *The Second World War: The Hinge of Fate* (Boston, 1950), p. 209. For American policy towards India, Gary R. Hess, *America Encounters India, 1941–1947* (Baltimore, 1971). For revealing comments on American attitudes towards the crisis, John M. Blum, ed. *The Price of Vision: the Diary of Henry A. Wallace, 1942–1946* (Boston, 1973), pp. 89–91 *et passim*.

[7] Robert E. Sherwood, *Roosevelt and Hopkins* (New York, 1948), p. 511; cf. Churchill, *Hinge of Fate*, p. 214.

little he thought Roosevelt knew of either India or the British Empire.

The President's mind was back in the American War of Independence, and he thought of the Indian problem in terms of thirteen colonies fighting George III at the end of the eighteenth century. . . . This was no time for a constitutional experiment with a 'period of trial and error' to determine the 'future relationship' of India to the British Empire.

Nor was the issue one upon which the satisfying of public opinion in the United States could be a determining factor. We could not desert the Indian peoples by abandoning our responsibility and leaving them to anarchy or subjugation.[8]

With such half-baked ideas coming from the President himself, the British had difficulty in assessing the significance or seriousness of statements made by other American officials, not to mention those produced by that amorphous phenomenon known as American public opinion.

Roosevelt's general ideas about the colonial issue in 1942 can be understood as a reflection of widespread American attitudes.[9] His own views on the subject did not harden until early 1943. Since he did not address himself publicly to the question, the analysis of public opinion was one important method used by the British as they tried to divine his thought.[10] The range of proposals about the future of colonial areas ran the gamut from an across-the-board colonial swap to schemes for international administration as a transition to independence. Since Roosevelt had a well-known liking for political geography, anything appeared to be within the realm of possibility. An article in *Colliers* magazine by a Professor of Geography at Columbia University proposed redrawing the map of Africa

[8] Churchill, *Hinge of Fate*, pp. 219–20.

[9] e.g. in a major work in progress on Roosevelt and American foreign policy, Robert Dallek holds that Roosevelt 'was more a reflector than a creator of American attitudes towards foreign affairs. Indeed, in all his major foreign actions . . . F.D.R. was more a spokesman for the American foreign policy public than an independent agent pursuing his own vision of America's role in world affairs.' 'Franklin Roosevelt's Foreign Policy Leadership', unpublished paper presented at the Mount Kisco Conference on Far Eastern History, April 1974.

[10] See in particular a despatch written by R. I. Campbell of the British Embassy in Washington, No. 493, 14 July 1942, in the Prime Minister's papers (PREM 4/42/9) as an outstanding attempt to make sense of the often conflicting patterns of opinion, and as an indication that Churchill kept a close eye on the matter.

in the spirit of colonial appeasement before the Second World War. In a view popular among demographers, wars were caused by lack of outlets for excess population and denial of markets and raw materials to non-colonial powers. Thus the Japanese should be allowed to develop a definite but limited area in the Pacific and the Germans should take over central Africa at the expense of Belgium and Portugal, nations too weak properly to exploit the area.[11] Armchair imperial geography died a hard death! Even Roosevelt's geographical imagination did not stretch so far, nor did his generosity to the Japanese —and certainly not to the Germans. At no time during the war did responsible officials either in England or in America contemplate the restoration of Germany as a colonial power. In the case of Japan, Roosevelt believed that the island empire should, in the cliché of the war years, be pared back to the bone—the Japanese home islands for the Japanese, but no more.[12]

The President's ideas about the United States acting as a trustee for colonial territories or incipient nation-states were in line with important studies by two Harvard Professors of Government, Arthur N. Holcombe and Rupert Emerson. Holcombe's *Dependent Areas in the Post-War World* appeared in October 1941 and received wide attention after the American entry into the war.[13] Though he devoted much of his commentary to German and Japanese colonial aims, he called particular attention to the Havana Convention of the 30th of July 1940. This international act was the product of a meeting of the Foreign Ministers of the American Republics. It provided for the provisional administration of European colonies in the Americas in the event that British, French, or Dutch possessions became derelict as a result of the European war.[14] More than simply a warning to Germany not to meddle with

---

[11] George T. Renner, 'Maps for a New World', *Colliers*, 6 June 1942.

[12] For the evolution of American wartime policy towards Japan, see especially Dunn, *Peace-Making and the Settlement with Japan*; and Hugh Borton, *American Pre-surrender Planning for Postwar Japan* (Occasional Papers of the East Asian Institute, Columbia University, 1967). See also Leonard Gordon, 'American Planning for Taiwan, 1942–1945', *Pacific Historical Review* 37. 2 (May 1968).

[13] Arthur N. Holcombe, *Dependent Areas in the Post-War World* (World Peace Foundation, Boston, 1941).

[14] For the Havana Convention, see Russell, *History of the United Nations Charter*, pp. 25–7.

European colonies in the Caribbean area, the Havana Convention was regarded by Holcombe as the 'analogue' of the Permanent Mandates Commission. He argued that it might provide the basis or immediate legal precedent for American participation in the reform of the mandates system into an 'International Supervisory Commission'. In the case of the 'A' mandates, he foresaw a rapid termination of the trust by the achievement of independence. In the case of the 'C' mandates, the authority of the international body would have to be strengthened in order to receive petitions, make investigations, and redress grievances. In the case of the 'B' mandates he recommended direct international administration:

> The simplest way to internationalize these administrations is to give the International Commission authority to organize the territorial administration itself and to operate it through officers of its own choice. Direct international administration would not only ensure that the doors would be kept wide open for the commerce of all the Powers, but it would also go far toward securing equality of opportunity for their labor, capital, and enterprise in the development of these territories.[15]

The scope would extend far beyond the existing mandates system:

> What the United States has proposed to do in the Western Hemisphere, it may wish to ask others to do in Africa, Asia, and the Western Pacific. The principal Powers, interested in the future development of British Malaya, the Netherlands East Indies, or French Indo-China,—to select one of the areas in which the problem of governing dependencies has become specially acute—should be willing to make similar arrangement for an international territorial administration.[16]

This was the first extensive American wartime proposal calling for reform and extension of the mandates system. Though it

---

[15] Holcombe, *Dependent Areas*, p. 90. In evaluating the degree to which the European powers had fulfilled the mandates, Holcombe concluded that the French and Belgians had accomplished the most for the physical development of the areas under their control, while the British had manifested the highest degree of the spirit of trusteeship. In this connection he stressed the observation of Negley Farson, *Behind God's Back* (New York, 1941), especially the comment that the British displayed a 'weird combination of almost absent imagination, in which the British Colonial Office was managing the affairs of the Tanganyika Mandate, and a fairness toward all nationals which could not be matched anywhere in Europe' (p. 67); cf. Farson, p. 194.   [16] Holcombe, *Dependent Areas*, p. 93.

was generally known that the President might be disposed to look favourably upon such internationalization schemes, it only gradually became apparent that he was unenthusiastic about the mandates system itself. 'I am inclined to think', he wrote later in 1942, for example, 'that the mandate system is no longer the right approach, for the nation which is given the mandate soon comes to believe that it carries sovereignty with it.'[17] More generally, Roosevelt did not want to become associated with plans to revive the League of Nations. One of the keys to his thought on the colonial issue was to avoid the mistakes of Woodrow Wilson, and the mandates system was Wilson's creation.[18]

Rupert Emerson also concluded that an international mandate in South-East Asia might be useful to protect American interests, but his proposal was more moderate than Holcombe's thoroughgoing international administration. In a study entitled *The Netherlands Indies and the United States*, published in May 1942, he calculated the amount of tin, rubber, and oil imported from South-East Asia, giving particular attention to Malaya and the Dutch East Indies. As the author of the scholarly volume *Malaysia* published in 1937, he spoke authoritatively. In the Indies alone American investments amounted to little less than 70 million dollars. Writing in the aftermath of Pearl Harbor, it would have been possible to paint an alarmist picture based on such figures. This Emerson firmly refused to do, pointing out that 70 million dollars was slight in terms of total foreign investment of $2,263,500,000 in the Indies, and of the $6,691,000,000 total American foreign investment.[19] American economic interests should not be regarded as a major determinant of policy in that part of the world. He proposed a straightforward international solution by which the Dutch would act as trustees in accordance with the conception of the mandates system. They would thus be reconciled to the loss of some part of their sovereignty and foreign economic interests

[17] Roosevelt to Smuts, 24 Nov. 1942, in Elliott Roosevelt, ed., *F.D.R. His Personal Letters* ii (New York, 1950), 1372.

[18] On Roosevelt's determination to avoid the mistakes of Wilson and the League, see especially Ernest R. May, *'Lessons' of the Past: the Use and Misuse of History in American Foreign Policy* (New York, 1973), ch. 1.

[19] Rupert Emerson, *The Netherlands Indies and the United States* (World Peace Foundation, Boston, 1942), pp. 61–2.

would be protected. By no means, Emerson stated, should the American people allow themselves to be caught up in a spirit of imperialism:

The primary and direct interest of the United States in the Indies and in the neighbouring territories with the exception of the Philippines does not extend beyond the maintenance of a situation in which they are neither controlled nor seriously menaced by a hostile power. It can be no part of the American purpose to seek to possess or to dominate the islands or the adjoining mainland strips.

With the exception of the brief period of imperialist activity at the time of the Spanish–American war the American people have shown a deep repugnance to both the conquest of distant lands and the assumption of rule over alien peoples.[20]

Emerson had expressed a fundamental point in Roosevelt's own outlook on the colonial issue: the United States was not fighting the war for purposes of imperialism. There would be no territorial annexations as a result of Allied victory. To take any other stand would have been to fly in the face of the American public concerned with foreign affairs.

By embracing trusteeship, or the opposite of imperialism, Roosevelt found a sufficiently elastic formula to exercise his freedom of action in colonial areas. Critics later charged that he twisted the meaning of trusteeship so that in substance it became identical with American imperialism; but on the basic point that Emerson had warned against—that there must be no direct territorial aggrandizement or control—Roosevelt persistently showed circumspection.

Sumner Welles made the most important public, official pronouncement on the subject of imperialism during the early part of the war in his Memorial Day address of 1942. The British took particular interest in it because they regarded the Under Secretary as one of the President's right-hand men in foreign affairs and figured that his views probably reflected Roosevelt's.[21] In dramatic language, Welles proclaimed the end of the era of imperialism. The goal was liberation.

If this war is in fact a war for the liberation of peoples it must assure the sovereign equality of peoples throughout the world, as

[20] Emerson, op. cit., p. 72.
[21] See Halifax to Eden, No. 3325, 11 June 1942, copy in the Prime Minister's files, PREM 4/42/9.

well as in the world of the Americas. Our victory must bring in its train the liberation of all peoples. Discrimination between peoples because of their race, creed or color must be abolished. The age of imperialism is ended.

As if in answer to British commentators on the limitations of the Atlantic Charter, Welles emphasized its universality. 'The right of a people to their freedom must be recognized, as the civilized world long since recognized the right of an individual to his personal freedom. The principles of the Atlantic Charter must be guaranteed to the world as a whole—in all oceans and in all continents.'[22]

The British were uncertain whether Welles's oration represented careful thought on the possible consequences of the end of the colonial system. They suspected not.[23] Indeed Roosevelt in his zeal to bolster French resistance to the Nazis in January 1942 placed himself in the contradictory position of favouring the restoration of the French colonial empire.[24] The American position, Eden wrote to Churchill, 'is becoming highly absurd, for while they apparently contemplate disappearance of [the] Dutch Colonial Empire, and perhaps our own, they have guaranteed [the] integrity of French territories which is much more than we have done'.[25] What were the President's specific ideas?

In a pattern to recur later in the war, Roosevelt chose to reveal his thoughts on the colonial question first to the Russians or the Chinese rather than the British. When V. M. Molotov, the Russian Foreign Minister, visited Washington in 1942 to discuss the second front, the colonial issue played a significant part in the exchange between him and the President. The Russian Ambassador, Maxim Litvinov, attended the conversation with Molotov. The Americans present besides Roosevelt were his adviser Harry Hopkins and the interpreter Samuel H.

[22] Holborn, *War and Peace Aims of the United Nations*, p. 90.
[23] See Ronald to Eden, No. 493, 14 July 1942, PREM 4/42/9.
[24] In a letter to Ambassador William D. Leahy in Vichy, Roosevelt had stated: '(1) It is most important for the French Government and the French people to realize that the President of the United States is about the best friend they have; that one of his greatest wishes is to see France reconstituted in the post-war period in accordance with its splendid position in history. (2). The word "France" in the mind of the President includes the French Colonial Empire.' Roosevelt to Leahy, 20 Jan. 1942, Elliott Roosevelt, *Personal Letters* ii. 1275.
[25] Eden to Churchill, 15 June 1942, PREM 4/42/9.

Cross, whose notes provide the only record. The context of the exchange on the colonial issue was the post-war disarmament of Germany and Japan and the future police activities of the four great powers who would guarantee the peace. As if almost by afterthought,[26] Roosevelt mentioned 'that there were all over the world, many islands and colonial possessions which ought, for our own safety, to be taken away from weak nations'. Here was a reflection of the line of reasoning of Lord Salisbury's famous 'Dying Nations' speech half a century earlier—with an American twist. Now the colonial possessions of the weaker powers (not least those of Portugal, a nation whose colonial longevity continued to be greatly underestimated) would be placed under international trusteeship. Molotov replied that Stalin had responded favourably to the President's other post-war proposals and had no doubt that the trusteeship idea also would be well received in Moscow. Roosevelt then explained that the scheme would supersede the mandates system. For the first time he fully developed his train of thought.

The President then pointed out that the acceptance of this principle would mean the abandonment of the mandate system. For example, after the last war the Japanese had received a mandate over the previously German islands in the Pacific, which they had fortified. These islands were small, but they ought not to be given to any one nation. The Japanese should, of course, be removed, but we did not want these islands, and neither the British nor the French ought to have them either.[27]

Thus Roosevelt stated definitely to the Russians that the United States had no ambition of annexing the Japanese mandates. If a system of international control were instituted, he believed it might apply not only to the former mandates but also to all colonial possessions in the Pacific.

Perhaps the same procedure should be applied to the islands now held by the British. These islands obviously ought not to belong to any one nation, and their economy was substantially the same everywhere. The easiest and most practical way to handle the problem of these islands over a long period would be to put them under an international committee of 3–5 members.[28]

[26] The transcript reads 'he had omitted one other point . . .', which indicates that the trusteeship question at this stage hardly held priority. Sherwood, *Roosevelt and Hopkins*, pp. 572–4; *Foreign Relations, 1942* iii. 578–81.
[27] Ibid.   [28] Ibid.

As if in jest, Roosevelt asked Litvinov, who had been the Russian representative in Geneva in the 1930s, 'whether he was ready to abandon the League of Nations'. Litvinov replied, 'Anything for the common cause.'

Taking a survey of the colonial situation in the Pacific basin, Roosevelt went on. He now clearly revealed his conviction that within a definite period of time the colonies would achieve self-government or independence.

> Turning to the question of colonial possessions, the President took as examples Indo-China, Siam, and the Malay States, or even the Dutch East Indies. The last-mentioned would some day be ready for self-government, and the Dutch know it. Each of these areas would require a different lapse of time before achieving readiness for self-government, but a palpable surge toward independence was there just the same, and the white nations thus could not hope to hold these areas as colonies in the long run.[29]

Here the transcript reads that Chiang Kai-shek had put forward the idea of trusteeship administration as a transition to independence, but in view of later exchanges with Chiang, it was probably Roosevelt's embellishment. In a highly interesting passage, Roosevelt speculated on the time-table for independence for the trust territories. He gave the impression that Chiang had a good deal to do with the idea:

> Generalissimo Chiang Kai-shek . . . had the idea that some form of interim international trusteeship would be the best mode of administering these territories until they were ready for self-government. They might, the President added, be ready for self-government in 20 years, during which the trustees might endeavour to accomplish what we accomplished in the Philippines in 42 years.[30]

In June 1942, therefore, the President's grand design for the Pacific consisted of internationalization of the Japanese mandates and further internationalization of other colonial possessions in the Pacific basin, not least the British. Molotov again gave assurance that the Russians would do their best to co-operate.

With the hope of independence for the colonial world in twenty years, Roosevelt had good reason to show more caution with the British about his trusteeship schemes. He did not con-

[29] Ibid.   [30] Ibid.

sult them at this stage. Nor did he commit himself in detail even with his advisers.[31] In the sumner of 1942 Roosevelt preserved flexibility on the colonial issue. He did not take the opportunity of the anniversary of the Atlantic Charter to press his conviction that self-determination applied to colonial peoples throughout the world.[32] His ideas on trusteeship had not yet developed into an anti-colonial campaign. He opposed annexations. He favoured solutions by internationalization. His general ideas were entirely compatible with the consensus of the American public interested in foreign affairs. In July 1942 *Fortune* magazine vividly presented a generally popular international scheme. On a map of the Pacific a 'Trans-Pacific Defense Belt' swept across the western Pacific through the Japanese mandates to the Asian 'states of the future'. With some imagination, the artist portrayed a loose federation of new states with Batavia as the capital. It could have just as well been the President's map, or that of any other enthusiastic American who looked to a future of liberated colonial areas.[33] Together with many Americans who took an interest in world affairs, Roosevelt foresaw the end of the colonial system. To repeat Sumner Welles's ringing phrase that attracted so much attention in England, so far as the American public was concerned, 'the age of imperialism is ended'.

[31] Welles did however briefly describe the result of the meeting with the Russians to a subcommittee of the Advisory Committee on Post-War Foreign Policy. 'Mr. Welles said, in great confidence to members of the committee, that the Soviet Union has agreed to the international trusteeship idea and has indicated its willingess to support the United States in that regard. The British government has not been consulted although the question may have been discussed between Mr. Churchill and the President.' P Minutes 21, 8 Aug. 1942, USSD NF Box 66.

[32] In fact Churchill easily deflected Roosevelt by insisting that one party could not elaborate the meaning of a document so carefully considered without the consent of the other party—and now parties. On 1 Jan. 1942, twenty-six nations (and subsequently more) subscribed to the Atlantic Charter, bringing with them twenty-six shades of interpretation of the meaning of self-determination. For Roosevelt's exchange with Churchill on the substance of the anniversary statement, see PREM 4/45/6.

[33] e.g. a member of the Foreign Policy Advisory Committee, Mrs. Anne Hare McCormick of the *New York Times*, mentioned the *Fortune* article as presenting 'a plan very similar to the one under discussion except that Burma is not included and Thailand is, and that Batavia is the capital instead of Manila'. P Minutes 22, 15 Aug. 1942, USSD NF Box 66.

9

TRUSTEESHIP AND THE STATE
DEPARTMENT'S POST-WAR FOREIGN
POLICY ADVISORY COMMITTEE
IN 1942

SHORTLY after Sumner Welles's proclamation of the death of imperialism, the British Ambassador in Washington telegraphed to London that Welles's views probably reflected the sentiment of a group of prominent Americans appointed by direction of the President to serve as a committee on post-war reconstruction. The proceedings and indeed the very existence of this group of foreign policy experts were secret, but the British knew that one of their purposes was to examine the future of the European colonial empires.[1] They were known as the Advisory Committee on Post-War Foreign Policy.[2] During the summer and autumn of 1942 they gave considerable attention to the question of trusteeship. By coincidence one of their first full-blown sessions on the issues of self-determination coincided with the anniversary of the press release of the Atlantic Charter. They took a fresh look at the old problems of the British Empire as they examined the new difficulties created by the war. Their debates were fundamental and uninhibited. They made sweeping recommendations about changes of sovereignty and direct international colonial administration. They believed in trusteeship as a transition to independence. Though some held more sophisticated views than others, and some were less favourably disposed towards the British than others, they all shared the belief, like the President, that the colonial regimes must be brought to an end.

---

[1] Halifax to Eden, No. 3225, 11 June 1942, PREM 4/42/9.
[2] See [Harley Notter] *Postwar Foreign Policy Preparation, 1939–1945* (Department of State Publication 3580: General Foreign Policy Series 15. Washington, 1949). The technical name of the group giving attention to the trusteeship problem at this time was the Subcommittee on Political Problems of the Advisory Committee on Post-War Foreign Policy. For changes in nomenclature, membership, and evolution of the wartime committees, *Postwar Foreign Policy Preparation* is the key reference.

Of the more or less fifteen who attended the meetings of the subcommittee on political problems that fully considered the colonial issue in 1942, five members had a particular interest in trusteeship. Stanley K. Hornbeck is important in this regard because, as the State Department's adviser on the Far East, he brought to bear not only a lifetime's knowledge of the American experience in Asia but also the immediate attitudes and policies of the Department. James T. Shotwell, the historian, had been a member of Wilson's advisory group, the Inquiry, and had a first-hand knowledge of Wilson's ideas on mandates and a keen grasp of the clashes between the British and the French on the colonial issue at the Paris Peace Conference. Isaiah Bowman, the President of Johns Hopkins University, had also been a member of the Inquiry and as a geographer had a special interest in Africa. Mrs. Anne Hare McCormick, a foreign-affairs analyst and member of the *New York Times* editorial staff, infused into the discussions a sense of indignation at European colonialism and advocated the direct international administration of the mandates. Not least, Sumner Welles chaired these sessions in 1942.[3] He guided the discussions with an imperious Wilsonian hand, convinced of the legitimacy of Wilson's vision and determined not to repeat the mistakes of the post-First World War era.

Welles pointed out in one of the committee's sessions that all their recommendations were predicated on the assumption of an eventual international organization. The remark was fundamental. Roosevelt was *not* operating on this assumption, or at least he was working towards an international organization that differed radically from that of his Wilsonian advisers. As is now clear from the accounts of his private conversations, he envisaged an international executive, not a new league of nations. It is ironic that while he talked to Churchill, Stalin, and Chiang Kai-shek about his élitist ideas of the 'Four Policemen' holding colonial territories in trust, his experts were methodically refining the mandates system and preparing draft charters which led to the establishment of the trusteeship system under the democratic auspices of the United Nations.[4]

---

[3] Welles served as Chairman until January 1943, when the Secretary of State assumed direct charge. The details are given in full in *Postwar Foreign Policy Preparation, 1939–1945*, pp. 96 ff.
[4] The irony of the difference between Roosevelt's post-war plans and the actual

During the war this distinction in regard to the colonial issue could well have seemed academic because it reflected merely a difference of means to achieve an end on which everyone was agreed. As Welles explained to the committee on the 8th of August 1942:

[T]he liberation of peoples should be the main principle. Many of these peoples cannot undertake self-government at this time. This is where trusteeship comes in. The United Nations [i.e. the Allied Powers] should endeavor to develop the ability of these peoples to govern themselves as soon as possible.[5]

On this principle there existed no disagreement, particularly in regard to Asia. 'The committee was unanimous in thinking that the United States should work for the liberation of the peoples of the Far East.' After all, as another member noted, self-determination was in line with the Atlantic Charter, at least in the way that Americans interpreted it. The question then arose, how should the United States respond if the colonial powers did not agree? What if they refused to liberate their subject peoples? What if, asked Welles, 'the Dutch, the Portuguese, the French, and the British want to go back in control of their former possessions, what attitude should the United States Government take?'[6]

Hornbeck believed the United States should employ 'moral suasion'. He doubted whether they could go any further. Turning, for example, to a case that was in everyone's mind in the summer of 1942:

If we insist on Indochina's being separated from [Vichy] France, the question arises of the position of Frenchmen in Indochina who will not want to be placed, for example, under Chinese authority if that should be the plan or the solution.

He asked if we were going to do this on the basis of self-determination of native populations, or what other principle was to be used for determining the disposal of territory after taking it away from the present owner.[7]

In a few words Hornbeck had posed the general problem in relation to a specific area. Were they to proceed on the basis

development of the United Nations is one of the themes in Robert A. Divine, *Roosevelt and World War II* (Baltimore, 1969), ch. 3.

[5] P Minutes 21, 8 Aug. 1942, p. 3, USSD NF Box 66.
[6] Ibid., p. 2.   [7] Ibid., p. 2.

of the principle of self-determination and apply it country by country? Hornbeck's comments are of great interest in this regard because his mind worked in a similar way to those of the Colonial Office officials, who, with intimate knowledge of a particular region, found it difficult to apply general principles. In South-East Asia, Hornbeck went on, there might be peoples who did not want self-government. Or they might want self-government and refuse trusteeship as the best way to achieve it. Would the Wilsonians force the hands of both the colonial governments and the indigenous peoples to accept an interim solution that neither wanted? Taking specific examples, Hornbeck could see that they manifested varying degrees of nationalism, but the only thing they had in common was their determination not to return to the pre-war colonial status.

Mr. Hornbeck presented the situation in which neither the sovereign nor the people to be liberated wished to accept trusteeship. What are we going to do in such a case? He referred here particularly to Indochina, India, and the Netherlands East Indies. Taking the latter area as an example, he thought that the people of the Netherlands East Indies were not going to be satisfied to continue to be occupied after the present war.

There is a ferment growing throughout the Far East. People are becoming politically conscious and the trend toward nationalism is increasing rapidly. A situation of that kind was, in his judgement, one which would make for instability if the United [Allied] Nations insisted on a return to the status quo existing at the outbreak of the present war.[8]

What general policy then could be pursued? The answer depended in part on whether one viewed the problem of South-East Asia, for example, from the vantage-point of the colonial powers or the emerging national states.

Shotwell tended to see the issue in the historical focus of British and French colonialism. Perhaps more than his fellow committee members, he saw the colonial issue in terms of the great powers of France and Germany because of his experience at the Peace Conference. Projecting the lesson of the past into the post-war future, Shotwell thought in the case of South-East Asia: 'It is possible that at the end of the war if Cochin China is taken from France, it would give an added political strength

[8] P Minutes 21, 8 Aug. 1942, p. 3.

to the anti-American trend of conservative circles in France. This is not enough to deter us, but this situation will exist.'[9] He urged the committee to bear in mind that it was the colonial issue, after all, that had contributed to the origins of the First World War and would require delicate handling at the end of the present struggle. 'We must remember that it was Germany who turned France into a colonizing country in order to interest it outside of Europe.' The United States could hardly dictate to the Allies on a matter of such moment. Negotiations would be difficult—it would not, he implied, be a matter that could be resolved by a group of Americans sitting in committee. As for the colonial subjects, the experience of Lord Milner in his mission to Egypt following the First World War seemed to have a meaning for the present situation.

The peoples under discussion are not now ready for self-government in our sense of the word. As Milner said in his Egypt report, there comes a time when the governing body cannot govern, even when it is good for the country. This is when the people begin to talk in abstract terms about government.[10]

Abstractions to Shotwell should not be allowed to obscure realities. Clearly the United States wanted to help colonial peoples along the road towards self-government, but co-operation could not necessarily be expected and immediate self-government seemed to be out of the question. Shotwell therefore favoured a strengthening of the mandates system as the best means of working towards the goal of eventual independence. 'He had in mind with regard to trusteeship, a revised and corrected mandate idea.'[11]

Though he did not disagree in principle with Shotwell, Welles wanted far more than a mere endorsement or extension of the mandates system. He advocated liberation. He desired the establishment of definite machinery for trusteeship that would guarantee self-government and eventual independence. He believed that the future world organization should develop the ability of dependent peoples to govern themselves as soon as possible. As to the international machinery:

The creation of an international board on which would be represented all the powers concerned in the Far East was in his mind. It would lay down certain standards applicable to all the areas and

<hr>

[9] Ibid., p. 3.   [10] Ibid., p. 4.   [11] Ibid., p. 4.

would provide for the necessary amount of administrative personnel to assure that the standards were applied in fact and not just in written reports.[12]

The establishment of an 'International Board' seemed like a reasonable measure if one considered the circumstances of the colonies. 'What has been the result of the situation we are now contemplating?', Welles asked.

> With few exceptions there has been exploitation by European powers with very little if any advantage to the peoples concerned. The control by those powers made possible the argument that some powers control all the resources of the world and that other powers are have-nots. If we do nothing about it, can we expect that the moral opinion of the world will require the governments to make some agreements with these peoples?[13]

Welles wanted to put teeth into the mandates system to make sure that the raw materials would be exploited for the benefit of the inhabitants as well as the imperialists. He made a classic neo-Wilsonian statement of the Dual Mandate:

> The international trusteeship idea was the proper solution. At the same time this system will be created to assist these peoples and to control the raw materials which are produced in these areas so that they may be of advantage to all peoples, including the local peoples.[14]

In the case of Indo-China Welles waxed especially indignant. He saw it as a moral issue and compared France's record there with Japan's in other places.

> There is a great moral question involved here and it is a question that will shape and color the history of the world after this war is over. To get right down to the question, what inherent right has France to territory which she has seized, sometimes by war, as recently as the 1880's, any more than has Japan to seize by force certain territories of China which she has now occupied? The only difference is in point of time.[15]

In Welles's demonology of imperialism, a special place was reserved for Japan: the 'Far Eastern type of imperialism as

---

[12] P Minutes 21, 8 Aug. 1942, p. 9.   [13] Ibid., p. 6.   [14] Ibid., p. 6.
[15] Ibid., p. 6. Another member of the committee, Green Hackworth (Department of State Legal Adviser) commented in this regard that he 'would have no compunction taking Indochina away from France and establishing a trusteeship'. Ibid., p. 5.

shown in Korea—the worst of all'. He did not, however, forget Portugal, apparently the runner-up. 'Of all the shocking examples of colonial administration both in Africa and Asia, Portugal is the worst. Why should that be continued in any healthy or reasonably logical world? If they are put in trusteeship, civilization will be advanced.'[16] Using an argument that recurred during the war, Welles believed that the Portuguese could be forced to accept international supervision, and that the British would be willing to place their colonies under trusteeship if only because of their own desire to bring the Portuguese up to minimal standards.

Hornbeck doubted whether trusteeship could be used as a general solution to the problems of the colonial world. He and Welles collided on the issue of universality—whether the trusteeship principle should be applied throughout the world. It was a question to be debated during the entire war.

Mr. Hornbeck asked whether this thing was going to be made a universal principle. If so, let us go ahead, but if not, should it be used in the Pacific?

Mr. Welles thought it should be regarded as universal.

Mr. Hornbeck then listed the territories to which the principle should be applied: Indochina, Hong Kong, Malaya, Burma, Netherlands East Indies, Timor, India, the Portuguese points on the Indian coast.[17]

Hornbeck began to point out the difficulties involved in particular cases. What about the mandated islands? Were they to be excluded from the general formula on grounds of security of the United States? Would that not make a mockery of the trusteeship principle? Or were the peoples of Micronesia so insignificant that they need not be included (a similar argument used by the South Africans in regard to South-West Africa)? Might this not involve special pleading? The more Hornbeck's mind ranged over the problem the more sceptical he became. In fact, it appeared to raise basic issues concerning American domestic policies. 'What is to be done with Guam? . . . the problem of our own islands is difficult, when we talk about other peoples's islands. Hawaii might make trouble on the issue of self-determination, and then what about Alaska?

[16] Ibid., pp. 6–7.   [17] Ibid., p. 11.

Any principle has a tendency to smack us as a boomerang and we want to keep this in mind.'[18] The other members of the committee apparently disliked this line of reasoning, but Hornbeck persisted. Trusteeship had a bearing on the problem of the American Negro.

On the one hand, we want to do away with imperialism and on the other we want to develop freedom and also want all peoples of the world better off in every way. Now when it comes to the economic matter the more freedom some peoples have the less well off they are economically. The average negro does enough work to get enough to live on and no more. Peoples of the South Seas are similar. He is not interested in property or culture and you have to impair his freedom to make his economic standards higher.[19]

Hornbeck had been a Rhodes Scholar and Cecil Rhodes no doubt would have agreed wholeheartedly with his remarks. Hornbeck concluded that 'there are some things to be said in favor of imperialism'.[20]

Welles protested, but not vigorously. He thought Hornbeck had posed preposterous difficulties and irrelevant cases. Therefore his objections should not be taken too seriously. 'Mr. Welles said that it seemed that Mr. Hornbeck was approaching the *reductio ad absurdum* of his argument. The problem that is before the committee is a problem which is a reality. Certain peoples of the Far East have not advanced as far as others.' He stated that they merely had to consider the question in relation to world peace: '[T]o carry it to the degree where we should have to supply an international committee for every atoll in the Pacific would be absurd. To go on and consider Hawaii or Alaska is beyond our concern. The people there are in general satisfied.'[21] Welles thus skirted the issue of where to draw the line. To an islander living on an atoll, it did not appear absurd that the principle of self-determination should not be applied, nor did it later seem obvious to everyone that some islands should be excluded from the trusteeship system on grounds of security. As Hornbeck pointed out, high-minded principles could boomerang.

On the question of the immediate post-war future of the colonies and the extent to which international trusteeship

---

[18] P Minutes 21, 8 Aug. 1942, p. 11.   [19] Ibid., p. 12.
[20] Ibid., p. 12.   [21] Ibid., p. 12.

should be invoked, the committee wavered. Such was the animus of some members towards European colonialism that they would have preferred the direct substitution of an international administration with the immediate aim of independence. Realistically they had to proceed on the assumption that the European regimes would continue in some form as an interim measure. The colonial powers would, however, have to submit to international supervision. According to Welles, trusteeship would be instituted on a world-wide scale with direct international administration in some instances. He said on the 15th of August in regard to South-East Asia:

> The best thing to do . . . probably is to permit the British and the Dutch at least to continue to administer the territories, providing they recognize their responsibilty to a higher authority to which they have to report; namely, the international trusteeship. Thus you get away from the otherwise inevitable result that the peoples will be exploited by the colonial powers.[22]

The colonial peoples would have opportunity to appeal to an impartial body, and, when the international trusteeship organization judged them ready, they would achieve independence. With this principle in mind the committee began to fluctuate in opinion as to the applicability of international trusteeship when it came to different regions and specific colonies—and whether it should apply to American territories as well.

In South-East Asia the committee projected a grandiose scheme. The trusteeship powers in the Pacific basin would constitute a miniature international organization, within which regional federations could be formed. According to Sumner Welles:

> It means for the Pacific area that the trustees will have to be the Soviet Union and China and the United States and Australia and New Zealand in cooperation and, if we apply the concept of trusteeship, representatives of the powers having colonies in that area— almost a League of Nations in itself.
>
> The question arises whether it is possible to put Indochina under the administration of a board of representatives of so many powers or whether such work should be delegated to a small group.[23]

Nor was organizational size the only difficulty. With the mention

[22] P Minutes 22, 15 Aug. 1942, p. 4, ibid.   [23] 8 Aug., p. 8, ibid.

of a particular colony, large ideas began to crack. Even the Dutch East Indies posed problems, here for the opposite reason from that of French Indo-China. To the committee the Dutch seemed to be so far ahead of the other powers in terms of enlightened administration that the Indies might be too far advanced for a federation scheme. According to the Dutch, colonial subjects would become Dutch citizens. Mrs. McCormick, a sceptic, said that 'the Dutch are doing this in an effort to keep their possessions, for they realize that the tide has turned and they cannot keep their possessions'.[24] She agreed, however, that 'the Dutch administration was the model in many ways'. What would happen if the French and the British imitated the Dutch? The result might be disastrous for American internationalization schemes.

Mrs. McCormick expressed concern regarding the integration of the Netherlands East Indies with the mother country and asked whether this might not have an effect on French and British policy as well. For example, would they do the same thing with Indochina or Burma and so in effect destroy the international plan?[25]

As for Burma, Isaiah Bowman despaired of applying any rational scheme to such 'a mess of people'.[26] As one member remarked it was not easy to 'tidy up' the map of South-East Asia. In this regard the Portuguese posed a particular problem. Welles repeated his opinion: 'the Portuguese type of control is about the lowest type which we know'. Hornbeck agreed. He thought that the Portuguese should be removed. Asked how, he said that the Portuguese held their colonies for prestige value and therefore in exchange for them 'cash would probably be the only thing acceptable'.[27] Thus the Portuguese did not qualify as a trusteeship power. High ideas were a prerequisite. When the committee members broached the idea of 'security' trusteeships for Singapore and Hong Kong, an enthusiast for international organization would have been disappointed to observe that they had no intention of extending their idealistic schemes to the Philippines or the Panama Canal.[28]

[24] P Minutes 22, 8 Aug. 1942, p. 4.   [25] 15 Aug., p. 5, ibid.
[26] Ibid., p. 3.   [27] Ibid., pp. 12–13.
[28] Welles states at one point in the discussion that he 'did not envisage that there would be any international control whatever over the Philippines' (15 Aug., p. 5), and, later, that he did not think that the United States 'could possibly agree to permit the internationalization of the Panama Canal' (29 Aug., p. 3).

In a peripheral way the theme of international trusteeship can be traced in the committee's discussions on the Middle East. Adolph Berle (Assistant Secretary of State), for example, wondered whether an international trusteeship for Palestine should 'be so loaded that they [the Jews] will tend progressively to exclude the Arabs from the region?'[29] The State Department expert on the Middle East, Wallace Murray, at another point noted that the French in Syria had 'welshed on the job and did not take their mandate as seriously as had the British in Iraq'. On the whole, however, discussion of trusteeship did not seem apposite to the problems of the Middle East because, in Welles's words, the peoples of Syria and Lebanon, for example, 'are prepared to make a good attempt at running their own show if given a chance'.[30] When Mrs. McCormick asked whether this meant 'the end of the mandate system', Welles replied 'it did in this area'.[31] Apart from the Jews and Arabs in Palestine, the peoples of the Middle East in the American view had reached the stage where they could stand on their own feet. Together with the peoples of North Africa, those of the Middle East seemed to the committee to form an advanced civilization at a stage of political development quite different from those of South-East Asia, or, looking forward on their agenda, black Africa. There was one point, however, on which the discussions of the Middle East and North Africa had a direct bearing on tropical Africa. When the committee members discussed Tangier, on the whole they were struck with the success of the international administration.[32] This however brought quickly to mind the unmitigated disaster of the international condominium in the New Hebrides which no one (not least the British and the French) wanted to repeat.[33] This comparative discussion on the merits of international government led them to conclude in Welles's words, that 'the smaller the number of territories placed under direct international control the better'.[34]

[29] P Minutes 25, 5 Sept. 1942, ibid.
[30] P Minutes 24, 29 Aug. 1942, p. 6, ibid.
[31] Ibid., p. 4.
[32] For an account of the international regime at Tangier during the war, see Graham H. Stuart, *The International City of Tangier* (Stanford, 1955 edn.), ch. 11.
[33] Unfortunately there is no satisfactory account. No other failure of internationalization is so frequently mentioned in the peace preparation of both world wars.
[34] P Minutes 26, 26 Sept. 1942, p. 14, USSD NF Box 66.

The corollary for black Africa was: direct international colonial administration for only a few carefully selected territories.

To the members of the committee, the distinguishing fact about black Africa appeared to be evolutionary backwardness. Isaiah Bowman took a prominent part in these discussions and a remark he had made earlier in the war on the subject is revealing. 'The first consideration', Bowman said, 'is that colonies are backward and that we must do something about them.' He affirmed the idea of limited progress. 'We must further assume that they are "coming up to something such as we are". These assumptions lead to the conclusion that by and large the people of backward areas are going to arrive at some stage of development to the limit of their competence.'[35] He was certain that the Africans in places such as the Belgian Congo had no conception of self-government. In discussing the problem of Africa, the committee was dealing with peoples on the lowest rung of the evolutionary ladder. Mrs. McCormick held a similar outlook. She believed that 'no black people had developed a leading civilization for Africa as China and Japan had done for the peoples of eastern and southeastern Asia'.[36] To these views should be added the opinion of Sumner Welles, who told the committee on the 2nd of October that in Africa 'the Negroes are in the lowest rank of human beings'.[37] In other parts of the world they had considered colonial peoples who desired independence and self-government. In Africa, 'we are not confronted by any such desire on the part of the native populations'. Welles asked an African expert of the State Department, Henry S. Villard, whether this view was accurate. He replied, 'that was correct—in the British territories there is a slightly more nationalistic feeling than in others, but it is still embryonic.'[38] The members of the committee tended to blame the colonial powers for this lack of political development. In Mrs. McCormick's words, 'in most of these territories' experience there has been little attempt to give the natives any experience at all in administering or governing themselves'.[39]

[35] Minutes T—5, 11 Apr. 1942, pp. 1–2, USSD NF, Box 42.
[36] T Minutes 22, 2 Oct. 1942, p. 8, ibid.
[37] P Minutes 27, 3 Oct. 1942, p. 3, ibid., Box 66. For an examination of similar attitudes, see Rubin Francis Weston, *Racism in U.S. Imperialism: the Influence of Racial Assumptions on American Foreign Policy, 1893–1946* (Columbia, S.C., 1972).
[38] Ibid., 3 Oct. 1942, p. 4.   [39] Ibid., p. 3.

To correct the lamentable lack of progress on the part of the colonial regimes, the urge ran strong to redraw the map of Africa—again in Mrs. McCormick's phrase, to make 'a general re-shuffle'. Following the South-East Asia precedent, they agreed that the colonial powers should continue to administer their territories, but subject to trusteeship supervision of regional councils. Possibly with American aid,[40] the regional councils would ensure political and economic development. The headquarters of all of western and equatorial Africa would be at Leopoldville. Liberia ('a great independent state . . . and happy as a clam', according to one member[41]) would participate. Shifting their attention to the east coast, the committee deplored the arbitrary boundaries created by the European partition of Africa. Geographically, economically, and politically it made more sense, at least to the members of the committee, to associate all of eastern Africa with southern Africa under a large regional grouping. There was one detail of the speculative sorting out of eastern Africa that vividly indicates the geographical hand of Isaiah Bowman. The committee favoured the restoration of Ruanda–Urundi to its natural East African association with Uganda and Tanganyika. In compensation, the Belgians would be given a strip of Portuguese Angola to enlarge the Congo's access to the Atlantic. Without knowing it, the committee had endorsed the secret horse-trading proposal made by the Belgians to the British in 1919.[42]

In southern Africa, Bowman and other members of the committee exercised full geo-political imaginative powers. They wished that Portugal could be made to disgorge her African colonies. Only reluctantly did they conclude that the Portuguese should be allowed to take a seat on the regional council. Bowman fancied that some sort of international body might take a part of Angola 'which can be shown to be worth developing and demonstrating to Portugal what can be done in

[40] There was no definitive agreement about the extent of American participation. Adolphe Berle thought that 'American interests—strategy and airlines and the closeness of the African shoulder would require American attention'. Welles felt that the United States should not become a direct party to any of the African regional councils and in any case 'would be heard in the executive [world] council that will run the whole show'. P Minutes 27, 3 Oct. 1942, p. 10, ibid.

[41] The words of Norman H. Davis, President of the Council on Foreign Relations and Chairman of the American Red Cross. Ibid.

[42] See Wm. Roger Louis, *Ruanda–Urundi, 1884–1919* (Oxford, 1963), ch. xxi.

that area'.[43] He elaborated at length on settlement schemes for Angola, making it clear that he recognized the dangers of creating 'another Palestine' but urging the development of irrigation projects, cattle ranches, and fruit orchards. At another time he talked of the Portuguese in Mozambique thwarting the natural course of expansion to the sea by the Rhodesians and South Africans—an implication of manifest destiny which the white communities of Rhodesia and South Africa certainly would have endorsed.[44]

Of greatest moment for trusteeship, Bowman along with Welles supported the idea that the mandate for South West Africa should be terminated and South Africa allowed to absorb the territory. Bowman hoped that this could be done 'in the most painless way'.[45] On this question Welles held especially strong views. He thought that there was 'every logical reason' why the territory should be assimilated. He wished to avoid a collision between South Africa and the post-war international organization. The minutes record Welles's insistence:

He could not see that from the general world interest anything was achieved by creating a rupture with the Union by placing Southwest Africa with its tiny population under international control . . .

He thought that the sooner a federation should come into being in South Africa, the better for all concerned.[46]

Mrs. McCormick agreed. Where mandates could not be taken under international control, in her view they should be assimilated so as to abolish 'hypocritical mandates'. The committee went on record in October 1942 as favouring South Africa's absorption of the mandate.[47]

For the other mandated territories the committee favoured direct international administration. Beginning with Togo and the Cameroons and extending their ideas to Tanganyika and

---

[43] P Minutes 33, 3 Oct. 1942, pp. 12–13, USSD NF Box 66.
[44] See Ronald Hyam, *The Failure of South African Expansion 1908–1948* (London, 1972).
[45] P Minutes 27, 3 Oct. 1942, p. 17.   [46] Ibid.
[47] The conclusions read: 'An exception to the general rule for mandated areas was thought to be justified in the case of Southwest Africa. Assimilation to the Union of South Africa was believed desirable, partly to avoid a collision with the Union if any other course were chosen, and partly because political and economic ties between the two entities had become very close in the last twenty years.' P Minutes 27, 3 Oct. 1942: Conclusions.

Ruanda–Urundi, the members of the committee talked in terms of 'fraud', 'hypocrisy', and 'fake'. They believed that the colonial powers had betrayed the sacred trust of Article 22 of the League Covenant. Mrs. McCormick held the most indignant views on the subject. She believed that the British, French, and Belgians had exploited the Africans and had flouted the world's conscience. She urged the establishment of an 'International Colonial Office', which, among other things, would provide an idealistic career for young men in countries not possessing colonies.[48] Especially in the case of Togo and the Cameroons, 'the situation presented the most perfect setup for international administration of some sort'.[49] It would be a lesson to the colonial powers for having treated the mandates as colonial property. Sumner Welles also thought it outrageous that the colonial powers had regarded the mandates as national property in all but name. He believed that true internationalization might end forever the old German argument about access to raw materials and colonial markets. He saw no reason why the other 'B' mandates should not also be administered by an international trusteeship authority. The mandated territories of Tanganyika and Ruanda–Urundi as well as Togo and the Cameroons could thus become showcases of reform and progress. Out of the great number and diversity of African colonial territories, these four seemed to be good representatives of the problems involved and the number of four seemed moderate.

In sum the African solution had three parts to it: (1) the absorption of South West Africa by South Africa; (2) general trusteeship supervision by regional councils; and (3) direct international administration of the 'B' mandates of tropical Africa. The proposal interlocked with schemes for trusteeship by regional councils throughout the entire world. During the course of the investigation, the committee had discovered that this proposal coincided with that of the British Labour Party and other groups in England. This seemed to be remarkable because some members had come to regard the trusteeship idea as more or less an American invention. When the Labour Party doctrine on the subject was read to the committee on the 3rd of October, Mrs. McCormick and another member of the committee, Norman H. Davis, remarked that this was

[48] P Minutes 27, ibid., p. 9.   [49] Ibid., p. 3.

'extraordinarily interesting since, quite independently, we have reached exactly the same point of view'.[50]

The general scheme received the approval of the committee on the 14th of November 1942. It represented a definite and important official set of American 'trusteeship aims' in 1942, though not necessarily those endorsed by the President or the Secretary of State, both of whom held different ideas.[51] Isaiah Bowman summed up the purpose of the committee's business by pointing out the shortcomings of the mandates system.

[E]veryone who had studied the mandate system was satisfied that it was an unworkable system, because rights and properties were intermingled in a way which gave the surface aspect in the matter of dominance to the power which held the mandate . . . [and] the so-called exploiting foreigner . . .[52]

The mandates system merely said, in Bowman's words, 'Be good.' This was not enough. The committee with its definite proposals for trusteeship supervision by regional councils and in some instances direct administration hoped to set colonial peoples on the path towards self-government and independence. Stanley Hornbeck, though still troubled by some of the racial implications of trusteeship,[53] praised the work of the committee as 'splendid'. A United States Senator who had shared in the committee's deliberations, Warren R. Austin, perhaps expressed the consensus of the group when he referred to the detailed proposal as 'a great beginning—a great work'.[54]

---

[50] P Minutes 27, p. 8.   [51] See below, ch. 14.
[52] P Minutes 33, 14 Nov. 1942, p. 2.
[53] Hornbeck was worried about the clause affirming equality of opportunity, which, he said, 'gets down to conclusions . . . concerning some aspects of human relationships of a very fundamental character'—e.g., if the trusteeship system guaranteed free immigration, Germans might return to the mandated territories. Moreover, 'if the principle of equality is applied, any Japanese or Negroes might also go. That might work [in some places] . . . but it would not work well in some other places.' Ultimately the endorsement of such a principle might affect the white immigration laws. Ibid., pp. 14–16.
[54] Ibid., p. 5.

10

CORDELL HULL AND THE STATE DEPARTMENT'S TRUSTEESHIP PLANNING

ONE of the notable contrasts between the development of the mandates system in 1914–19 and that of trusteeship in 1941–5 is systematic preparation. Within a year after the attack on Pearl Harbor, officials in the State Department already had penned elaborate drafts pertaining to dependent peoples that eventually were incorporated in the United Nations Charter as Chapters XI and XII on non-self-governing territories and trusteeship respectively. These projects have their own histories. They possessed a substance distinguishable from the more enthusiastic and ephemeral inspirations of *ad hoc* committees or the more erratic ideas of the President. The continuity in development of these two basic State Department policies can be associated with the Secretary of State, Cordell Hull, though such a generalization needs considerable qualification. Hull had deep convictions about colonial peoples. He believed their lot should be ameliorated so that they could eventually attain self-government if not independence. In this regard his ideas were gradualistic and he probably shared as much ground with Lord Cranborne as he did with Sumner Welles. The basis of Hull's thought on dependent peoples can be found in a radio address on 'The War and Human Freedom' delivered on the 23rd of July 1942. He stated the problem in much more moderate language than Welles had used in the Memorial Day speech proclaiming the death of 'Imperialism'. According to the Secretary of State:

We have always believed—and we believe today—that all peoples, without distinction of race, color, or religion, who are prepared and willing to accept the responsibilities of liberty, are entitled to its enjoyment. We have always sought—and we seek today—to encourage and aid all who aspire to freedom to establish their right to it by preparing themselves to assume its obligations. We have striven to meet squarely our own responsibility in this respect—in Cuba, in the Philippines, and wherever else it has developed upon us. It has been our purpose in the past—and will remain our purpose in the future—to use the full measure of our influence to support attainment of freedom by all peoples who, by their acts, show themselves worthy of it and ready for it.[1]

Such rhetoric provided the British much food for thought. Hull frequently used the word 'liberty', sometimes in the context of colonial independence. He spoke of 'freedom' without making it clear whether he recognized the existence of political freedom within the British Empire–Commonwealth. At one moment Hull could mention 'Mother Countries' and 'Parent States' in a manner highly agreeable to the British and the next moment talk of independence for the colonies. He was not precise about his ideas. It only became gradually apparent to the British that the Secretary of State quite tenaciously was developing two basic propositions: (1) specific steps should be taken to increase the capacity for self-government in all dependent territories, and (2) the more advanced colonies should become independent, in accordance with definite timetables for decolonization. To these two principles should be added a third, which was basic to all of his thought: there should be economic equality of treatment throughout the world, not least the colonial world. Hull would have been at home with some of the doctrinaire Free Traders of the British Empire. The abolition of economic nationalism was an integral part of his program for colonial freedom. He was doggedly persistent in his pursuit of these goals.[2]

Lord Halifax once made a fundamental remark about an intellectual difference between Englishmen and Americans that has a particular relevance to Cordell Hull and American trusteeship policy. 'We are accustomed to proceed from the particular to the general,' the Ambassador wrote, 'but the Americans do just the opposite.'[3] The experts of the Colonial Office, for example, attempted to generalize on the basis of experience in particular colonies within geographical regions. On the other

---

[1] Holborn, *War and Peace Aims*, p. 101.

[2] For Hull's own account, see *The Memoirs of Cordell Hull* ii, especially pp. 1234–8 and ch. 117.

[3] Halifax to Eden, No. 1916, 23 Apr. 1943, U2026/G, FO 371/35311.

hand, Hull, though taking into account geographical location and local conditions, sought universal principles applicable to all dependent territories. If he fitted the British stereotype in this respect, some of his colleagues manifested a more sophisticated approach to the problems of the colonial world. Sumner Welles, for example, attached a much greater importance to regionalism. He saw the complexity and the uniqueness of problems within particular colonies, yet he also recognized that within certain regions, problems of health, education, and transport might be conducive to regional management. In short his approach was more similar to the British method of dealing pragmatically with colonial problems on a local and then a regional level. This general outlook can be expressed as the identification of *local authority and regional responsibility*. It stands in contrast to Hull's different perception of *universal authority and world-wide responsibility*. Hull favoured a set of principles to be espoused by all colonial powers throughout the world. This dichotomy contained paradoxes on the American side. In terms of practical politics Hull recognized that the United States would be able to do little more about the remote outposts of the British Empire than about the internal colonial situation of Soviet Russia. In terms of ideological commitment Welles espoused liberation and independence but stopped short of applying an international solution to American dependencies or indeed to the western hemisphere. Nevertheless Halifax's observation holds generally true. While the British attempted to generalize from particular local colonial situations and worked up to possible regional groupings, the Americans on the whole began at the top with the general colonial situation and then proceeded downwards to regional and local problems. In terms of *Realpolitik*, the State Department's influence throughout the world would have been greater if it had been admitted from the beginning that the United States had a general responsibility in the question of the colonies' future.

The search for universal principles began in the State Department in the spring of 1942 and found concrete expression in an elaborate draft proclamation submitted to the British nearly a year later. It became known as the 'Declaration of National Independence' of the 9th of March 1943. Its genesis was an attempt by Stanley Hornbeck and the Far Eastern Division to formulate a 'Pacific Charter' or 'World Charter' explicitly extending throughout the world the principles of the Atlantic Charter. 'It is obvious that consequent upon the formulation and publication of the Atlantic Charter,' Hornbeck wrote to Welles on the 6th of May 1942, 'there has been a difference of opinion and confusion of thought regarding the character and the intended applicability of that charter.' Churchill clearly gave it a different interpretation from Roosevelt's. Quite wrongly, from the American point of view, the Atlantic Charter had become geographically associated with Europe. In an effort to make the Atlantic Charter universal in scope, Hornbeck considered and rejected the possibility of a Pacific Charter:

> [F]ormulation and publication of a Pacific Charter would certainly confirm wherever it exists the impression that the Atlantic had, as would the new Pacific Charter, simply a limited geographical applicability . . . Ought not thought be directed rather to the formulation and publishing of a *world* charter which might be built upon, which might absorb, and which might be the logical, legal and political successor to the Atlantic Charter?[4]

In one of the early drafts of the 'World Charter' Hornbeck and his colleagues stated the purpose in the context of the historical experience of the United States. In the course of human events it sometimes became necessary to dissolve political bonds. The war had clarified certain self-evident truths. In a preamble echoing the words of the American Declaration of Independence, the State Department officials reaffirmed the historic purpose of the United States and saw the opportunity of extending to other lands 'life, liberty, independence and religious freedom'. These words conveyed concepts that went far beyond the principle of peoples having the right to choose their own form of government that Churchill had endorsed in the Atlantic Charter. Not only did the American project now espouse independence but it also specifically stated that the principles applied 'to all the peoples of the world'. Citing the Philippines as the pre-eminent example of the historical process of political freedom and independence, the draft of May 1942 read:

> On November 15, 1935, the Commonwealth of the Philippines was established preparatory to final withdrawal of American sovereignty. Our gallant and indomitable [Filipino] comrades in arms

4 Hornbeck to Welles, 6 May 1942, Hornbeck Papers Box 48.

have made the world witness to the fighting spirit of freedom and the Philippines shall achieve freedom.[5]

On the assumption that the British were working towards a similar goal for India—'full dominion status with the right of succession'—the American declaration stated that the extension of political independence for the colonies should be endorsed as a war aim by the Allies. It is perhaps a measure of American exuberance at this time that no one appears to have questioned British willingness to interpret the future of the British Empire in accordance with the terms of the Declaration of Independence of 1776.

As the drafting progressed, the emphasis on independence became more insistent. By November 1942 part of one sentence of the preamble read:

> [T]hat the *independence* of those nations which now possess *independence* shall be maintained; that the *independence* of those nations which have been forcibly deprived of *independence* shall be restored; that opportunity to achieve *independence* for those peoples who aspire to *independence* shall be preserved, respected, and made more effective; . . .[6]

To aid those peoples aspiring to independence, definite dates would be established for decolonization: 'It is, accordingly, the duty and the purpose of each nation having political ties with colonial peoples . . . to fix, at the earliest practicable moment, dates upon which the colonial peoples shall be accorded the status of full independence within a system of general security . . .'[7] With timetables to mark the pace, colonial peoples progressively would be granted self-government which would lead to independence. Thus within the State Department in 1942 can be found the grand design of the United States in the post-war era of decolonization.

In the original drafts of the Declaration on National Independence, no specific territories were mentioned. Had he been privy to the documents, Lord Halifax would have confirmed his impression that the experts of the State Department worked from the general to the specific or from universal principles to

---

[5] 'Supplementary Declaration', 25 May 1942, USSD 501.BE/5-2642. This particular draft was prepared by Joseph W. Ballantine of the Far Eastern Division.
[6] 'The Atlantic Charter and National Independence', 13 Nov. 1942, Hornbeck Papers Box 48. Italics added.   [7] Ibid.

particular cases. This deductive method by no means devalued the significance of area problems and local precedents. Stanley Hornbeck tested the principles of the Atlantic Charter against the background of the Pacific and the Far East. To Cordell Hull no less than Roosevelt the Philippines stood as the magnificent example of decolonization to be followed by all the colonial powers. 'Our course in dealing with the Philippine situation', Hull wrote in November 1942, '. . . offers, I think, a perfect example of how a nation should treat a colony or a dependency in cooperating with it in making all necessary preparation for freedom.'[8] He used the example of the United States and the Philippines as he pondered the problem of Britain and India. When dealing with particular cases, he believed it important to keep in mind 'our general course and attitude toward freedom for dependent peoples, as illustrated by our attitude in cooperating with the Philippines for the purpose of their freedom'.[9] For Cordell Hull the Philippine and India were the two regions providing the key historical precedents during this time of formative thought on general colonial issues.

One other region figured particularly in American thought about colonial areas in 1942. In March of that year, as part of the lend-lease negotiations, Britain and the United States agreed to establish a joint commission in the Caribbean. The purpose was to co-ordinate shipping and increase local food production. Since the creation of naval bases caused economic dislocations, the two powers decided to consult on wages, food supplies, and other possible sources of economic and political discontent. On a broader scale the British and Americans agreed to discuss within the framework of the Anglo-American Caribbean Commission mutual problems of education and welfare. The commission had only an advisory capacity. Nevertheless it acquired considerable importance as the first functioning regional commission. Its significance in part can be attributed to the personalities associated with it, though officials in both countries throughout the war agreed that it served a useful, practical purpose by facilitating the exchange of information and ideas.

The Chairman of the Caribbean Commission was Charles

⁸ Hull to William Phillips, 19 Nov. 1942, USSD 123 P54/531.   ⁹ Ibid.

W. Taussig. He was the President of the American Molasses Company, with connections in the sugar industry throughout the Caribbean. He was a member of Roosevelt's original 'brains trust'. He had direct access to the President. He had cordial relations with both Hull and Welles. He was also on friendly terms with prominent Englishmen, including Richard Law (Bonar Law's son in the Foreign Office), Oliver Stanley (Cranborne's successor as Colonial Secretary), and the Prime Minister himself. Throughout the war he guided Anglo-American discussions about the Caribbean and he contributed directly to the ideas discussed between the President and the Prime Minister. In 1945 he served as one of the members of the delegation to the San Francisco Conference. He believed that independence was the purpose of colonial trusteeship. On this point, of course, he differed from Churchill. Taussig recorded this story after he lunched with the Prime Minister in December 1942. Churchill told Taussig:

'Nations live on their traditions, or die.' He [Churchill] continued, 'Your country has its traditions which you cherish. In Washington you have a 720 ft. obelisk erected to the memory of George Washington. When I flew to Washington last summer, I made a non-stop flight to the Potomac. As we were approaching Washington, we were flying low. I told the pilot about [the] Washington Monument. I said it would be most inappropriate if we hit it and made him climb to 1500 feet. We also have our traditions and as long as I am here, we will hold to them and the Empire. We will not let the Hottentots by popular vote throw the white people into the sea; nor let the Syrians by popular vote throw out the Jews.'[10]

In such a way did fundamental positions on the colonial issue become perfectly clear. Partly because of Taussig's stature, the Anglo-American Caribbean Commission played an important part in the general colonial discussions throughout the war as a 'model' for future regional commissions.

On the British side, Sir George Gater, Permanent Under-Secretary at the Colonial Office, took a special interest in the Caribbean. In 1942 he visited Washington to consult Taussig and other prominent officials about the work of the Commission. The reports of his mission afford an unusual insight into American thought on the colonies at this time. In October Taussig

[10] Memorandum by Taussig, 28 Dec. 1942, Taussig Papers Box 46.

accompanied Gater in separate interviews with Roosevelt, Welles, and Hull. From the President, Gater learned that all of the islands in the Caribbean might eventually be combined into a vague federation which would be 'watched over by the various nations concerned as trustees'. The President monopolized the conversation and did not allow his British visitor even a single word on the subject. For his part, Gater got an earful about Roosevelt's ideas:

> The President was emphatic in stating that there should be no interference with the existing sovereignty of the islands. The United States of America had no desire to acquire the British West Indies. He regarded the islands as headaches, and he wanted no 'British headaches.' Moreover, the West Indian islands as at present organised represented a heavy financial liability to the British and other Governments which he had no wish to shoulder.[11]

With Sumner Welles, Gater discussed in detail such problems as shipping and food production. To their mutual satisfaction they talked about general policies as well as specific issues being dealt with by the Commission. To Gater, Welles was the man at the State Department who truly knew his business.[12] Cordell Hull gave a different impression. The Secretary of State spoke in generalities. He evoked 'a spirit of co-operation'. He was concerned to know whether Gater's views coincided with the President's. Hull himself ventured nothing original. In this matter as in others, the British gathered that Hull gave general supervision but left the work of substance to his lieutenants.[13]

In the realm of trusteeship Hull's role was little more than superficial, yet he took a definite interest in the question. He encouraged Hornbeck and Green Hackworth, the legal adviser, to prepare the general statement of principle that later became known as the Declaration on National Independence and still later as the chapter in the United Nations Charter on non-self-governing territories. He also gave support to members of the State Department's Division of Special Research working as a unit in the subcommittee on International Organization who produced the draft on trusteeship. The project eventually formed a related but separate article in the United Nations

[11] Memorandum by Gater, 27 Oct. 1942, copy in FO 371/30674.
[12] Gater's 'Note of Interview with Mr. Sumner Welles', 29 Oct. 1942, ibid.
[13] 'Note of Interview with Mr. Hull', 30 Oct. 1942, ibid.

Charter. It also had its genesis in 1942. Some of the early memoranda on the subject were penned by Isaiah Bowman and others especially concerned with international organization; but the individual most intimately associated with the trusteeship article from beginning to end was Benjamin Gerig.

As an official in the League's secretariat, and the author of an important book on the mandates,[14] Gerig holds a place of particular importance in the history of trusteeship before the war and especially during it. Within the State Department, he possessed an unrivalled knowledge of the details of the mandates system. He impressed the British as intelligent and competent. He was sympathetic with the problems of the European colonial powers but kept his critical faculties. Above all he persevered. Through committee after committee and crisis after crisis, Gerig remained the expert on trusteeship. He was the key man behind the scenes on the American side.

By October 1942 the Subcommittee on International Organization had produced a full draft on international trusteeship for non-self-governing peoples.[15] Differing from the Declaration on National Independence in approach and substance, the draft reflected Gerig's familiarity with the history of the League's experience with dependent territories. In every sense the trusteeship draft should be regarded as a refinement of the mandates system. Gerig and his colleagues in the preamble extended the principles explicitly. The goal would be liberation of colonial peoples, in the sense that they would be freed from foreign subjugation. True to the dual potential of self-determination, the draft acknowledged that, as an alternative to independence, some colonial peoples might choose to remain in association with the colonial power if they were granted full rights of self-government. The subcommittee also urged that *direct* international colonial administration should be avoided except in territories such as Libya where there appeared to be no feasible alternative. The subcommittee moreover discouraged possible changes of boundaries which

[14] *The Open Door and the Mandates System*, see above, ch. 5. For a summary of his views on the mandates system written during the early part of the war, see his memorandum of 8 October 1942, P-I.O. Document 79 USSD NF Box 118.

[15] Important drafts dated 31 July, 28 Aug., 21 Oct., and 8 Dec. 1942; the Political Subcommittee considered the draft on 14 Nov. and in revised form on 5 Dec. Drafts and minutes in USSD NF Boxes 63-6 and 117-18.

might possibly be to the advantage of the colonial powers. In this the proposal seemed moderate, and non-progressive, especially to those who wished to adjust colonial boundaries to conform to ethnic and economic frontiers.[16]

The International Organization Subcommittee's draft embodied an extreme proposal in that it placed *all* colonial territories under international trusteeship. Final authority and responsibility would rest with an international executive composed of regional representatives of the colonial powers. The executive authority would judge whether self-government had been achieved to the satisfaction of the colonial peoples. Local administrations would be charged with the responsibility of education for self-government and the achievement of economic and social justice; and with the responsibility of equal economic opportunity and security measures. The administering authorities would have the duty of submitting *reports*. The international executive would have rights of *inspection*. The colonial peoples would have rights of *petition* directly to the international authority. Here truly the reformed mandates system would be given teeth. Other specific measures included the assimilation of colonial subjects into the administration. In marked contrast with the mandates system, the trust territories could be fortified if the members of the executive authority agreed that military bases would contribute to the world's security.[17]

The principles of trusteeship would be applicable throughout the world, with one important exception. Conditions were sufficiently 'different' in the western hemisphere to warrant its exclusion. From time to time committee members raised the question whether American dependencies would be placed under trusteeship, but Sumner Welles firmly rejected all proposals to place any territory in any part of that hemisphere under international supervision. Indeed he viewed all of the Americas as almost a sole United States responsibility. It appeared to him and other members of the State Department that the Caribbean area would be more stable if the British would relinquish sovereignty in Honduras and that the British along with the Dutch and the French should terminate their colonialism in the three Guianas. The State Department regarded Central and South America as an area of American

[16] Ibid.   [17] Ibid.

responsibility in much the same way that the Colonial Office felt a sense of historic duty in parts of Africa. Why should international authority in the western hemisphere be invoked when the United States performed outstanding service as guardian? No one in the State Department appears to have pointed out that the British, for example, would regard these arguments as an example of American self-righteousness, if not hypocrisy. On the contrary, the members of the advisory committees thought that the European colonial powers were in need of moral improvement. So morally debauched were the Portuguese that, in the State Department's view, they should be stripped of their colonies, though with adequate monetary compensation.[18]

Other notable features of the State Department's proposals for trusteeship in late 1942 included the recommendation that Korea should be administered directly as a trust territory. Regional councils would be established, with more latitude for great-power membership, including China's and Russia's, than the British envisaged. In Africa as in South-East Asia, regional councils would provide the machinery through which the colonial powers would be held accountable for their territories held in trust. When the Political Subcommittee considered these proposals, Welles and his colleagues displayed a concern for balance between measures for the welfare of the colonial inhabitants, on the one hand, and considerations for economic opportunity and security for the world at large, on the other. They thus found themselves attempting to achieve exactly the same equilibrium as the founders of the mandates system. It is perhaps significant as a landmark in the general relations between Africa and the West that, in the course of these deliberations, on the 5th of December 1942, the members of the State Department's committee formally recorded that the term 'local inhabitants' should be used instead of the word 'natives'.[19]

Cordell Hull approved the trusteeship proposal with a good deal of circumspection and with an eye on its feasibility. By a stroke of the pen he narrowed its scope from *all* colonial territories to merely the former mandates and colonies of the

[18] Ibid.
[19] P Minutes 36, 5 Dec. 1942, ibid.

Axis powers.[20] The President eventually approved it perfunctorily in this form. This radical transformation at least brought trusteeship within the realm of possibility in negotiations with the British. As for the other project on non-self-governing territories, Hull had told Halifax casually in August that he had in mind a declaration whereby 'Parent States' would affirm certain principles of welfare and progress for their colonial wards.[21] There is no evidence that he used this phrase with any notion of the way the British would interpret it. His careless paternal overtone plunged the British into lengthy deliberations in the hope of finding common ground with the Americans. It did not exist. Hull believed that 'Parent States' had the responsibility of preparing colonial subjects or 'local inhabitants' for *independence*. Independence was the key word the British would not accept. Hull persisted in his quest throughout his tenure as Secretary of State. In his memoirs he noted with pride that 'independence' appears in the trusteeship chapter of the United Nations Charter.[22]

[20] For discussion of this point see Russell, *History of the United Nations Charter*, pp. 84–6. There was tension between Hull and Welles on this point (see memorandum by Taussig, 15 Nov. 1942, Taussig Papers Box 46) and between Hornbeck and Welles on the priority and relationship between the general declaration and the trusteeship proposals (see the memoranda in the Hornbeck Papers Box 48).

[21] See Halifax to Eden, No. 4285, 25 Aug. 1942, printed in W.P. (42) 544 CAB 66/31; compare with Memorandum by Hull, 24 Aug. 1942, USSD 740.0011 European War 1939/24125; cf. *Foreign Relations* (1942), i. 726–7.

[22] *Memoirs of Cordell Hull* ii. 1238.

II

THE BRITISH RESPONSE TO THE DEVELOPING AMERICAN ANTI-COLONIAL CAMPAIGN LORD CRANBORNE'S POLICY OF 'WE HOLD WHAT WE HAVE'. THE BEGINNING OF THE COLONIAL OFFICE'S REGIONAL CO-OPERATION SCHEMES

ONE of the British statesmen who found himself in a key position in relation to the planning of an alternative for post-war trusteeship was Lord Cranborne, later the 5th Marquess of Salisbury. In 1942 he became Colonial Secretary for nine months, from the 22nd of February to the 23rd of November. Since 1940 he had served as Dominions Secretary, a post to which he later returned in 1943 and where he stayed until the end of the war. In 1945 he was one of the British delegates at the San Francisco Conference, where he conducted the colonial negotiations. He was thus centrally involved in the trusteeship question almost for the duration of the entire war. As the grandson of the great Prime Minister who had presided over the Empire during the zenith of its expansion in the late nineteenth century, Cranborne held attitudes similar to his Victorian predecessors. The British Empire was the concern of the British, not the Americans, and he saw no reason whatsoever to be apologetic. With the utter self-confidence of a British aristocrat he believed that 'The British Empire is not dead, it is not dying, it is not even going into a decline'.[1] Only in extremities did he regard colonial questions as a matter for negotiation. He intensely disliked the prospect of dealing with Cordell Hull, for example, because he believed the Secretary of State held simplistic views on the British Empire and would be led by

[1] *Parliamentary Debates* (Lords), 21 July 1942, c. 970.

the experts of the State Department to make embarrassing demands. Cranborne had particularly in mind Churchill's flat assertion in Parliament in September 1941 that there existed unambiguous British commitments to the development of self-governing institutions in the colonies. 'Bobbety', as he was known to his friends, knew that these pledges were in fact fictional.[2] He viewed Anglo-American negotiations on the question as a possible but dangerous means of giving the Americans assurance of the progressive nature of the Empire without having to produce past evidence. From first to last he adopted an attitude, identical with Churchill's, of 'We hold what we have'. Because of the disaster in the Far East, this policy became, optimistically, 'We shall hold what we had'. He recognized that there would be an increased American influence in Asia after the war; but he attempted to salvage the best of a bad situation by hoping to commit the Americans to the post-war defence of Singapore. There, as in all other parts of the world, he attempted to keep American interference in colonial affairs at a minimum. This meant, above all, the discouraging of American trusteeship schemes.

In the summer and autumn of 1942 the Colonial Secretary responded to American criticism (and what he believed to be the thrust of the State Department's planning) by developing a counter-strategy to international supervision. At this time the question of Hong Kong seemed especially pressing because of uncertainty about the evolving Chinese attitude.[3] Would the Chinese demand its unconditional restoration after the war? What attitude would the Americans take? Any discussion about general colonial issues thus began specifically with Hong Kong. This in turn raised questions about the post-war defence, economic development, and political organization of the Far East. While the Americans seemed to favour a regional political council that in some way would be accountable to a world organization or international executive, Cranborne believed that it might be possible to reap the benefits of regional defence and economic co-operation in the Far East without interna-

---

[2] See his minute of 4 Sept. 1942, CO 323/1848/5091; and minutes and memoranda in CO 825/35/55104.

[3] See Chan Lau Kit-Ching, 'The Hong Kong Question during the Pacific War (1941–45)', *Journal of Imperial and Commonwealth History* 2. 1 (1973).

tional accountability. Herein was the genesis of the Colonial Office's idea of regional cooperation as a counter-plan to international accountability under American trusteeship schemes.

Cranborne expressed his basic views to Anthony Eden, the Foreign Secretary, in a letter of the 18th of August 1942. Eden marked on the letter, 'This'seems cheerfully robust', a comment that well summarizes Cranborne's attitude on colonial questions. The Colonial Secretary began by emphasizing the need to take a firm line on the question of Hong Kong and the Far East in general.

> We must not allow ourselves to be manœuvred by the Chinese and Americans into the position of standing in a white sheet. Our record is not a bad one. On the contrary, over a long period, we established a reign of peace and prosperity, in the areas over which we exercised control, hitherto unknown. We created Hong Kong and Singapore. We developed the rubber and tin industries of Malaya.[4]

Cranborne went on to express a sentiment he had already voiced at length in Parliament.[5] In his view it was entirely wrong for the British to accept the entire blame for the catastrophe at Singapore. His private letter continued:

> It is true that in one vital sphere we failed. We were unable to defend our territories against Japan. But even here we were not the only nation, or indeed the main nation, at fault. As we both know, the chief sinner was the United States.

> Had she been willing to throw in her weight in the Pacific in the years preceding the war, when we were preoccupied with the deteriorating situation in Europe and she was not, the Japanese menace might have been strangled before it became really dangerous. By all means, let us shoulder our share of the blame, but not hers too.

> It is for that reason that I think it essential that any concessions that we make should not be unilateral. If we do not insist upon this, we shall be regarded as accepting sole responsibility for what has occurred. We all have a contribution to make, in the future as in

---

[4] Cranborne to Eden, 18 Aug. 1942, CO 825/35/55104; FO 371/31777. For a good discussion of Colonial Office policy and Malaya during the war, see A. J. Stockwell, 'Colonial Planning during World War II: the Case of Malaya', *Journal of Imperial and Commonwealth History* 2. 3 (May 1974).

[5] *Parliamentary Debates* (Lords), 24 Feb. 1942, cols. 16–24. Cranborne's maiden speech as Colonial Secretary was also his first in his capacity as Leader in the House of Lords. He remarked that he was the third member of his family in successive generations to hold this position.

the past, if peace is to be preserved in the Pacific. But His Majesty's Government should make it clear that our contribution should be dependent on a similar contribution being made by others, whose responsibility for the unhappy situation which exists to-day is at least as great as ours.[6]

On the question of Hong Kong, the Colonial Office was prepared to be more flexible than those lines might suggest. Cranborne proved to be much more accommodating to the Chinese than, for example, Leo Amery, who held that Hong Kong's sovereignty should be relinquished only in the last resort and only in return for a tangible strategic advantage elsewhere.[7] The Hong Kong issue lies beyond the question of trusteeship, but it should be noted that the Colonial Office co-operated with the Foreign Office in carrying forward the revision of the 'Unequal Treaties' which culminated in the Anglo-American treaties renouncing extra-territoriality of the 1st of January 1943.[8]

An easy working relationship developed between the Colonial Office and the Foreign Office on colonial issues during Cranborne's tenure as Colonial Secretary. At a meeting between representatives of the two departments on the 20th of August 1942 he persuasively elaborated the Colonial Office's point of view. He first of all emphasized the need for a full-scale propaganda campaign to educate the Americans about the true nature of the British Empire.[9] 'Convincing answers to American criticisms', according to Cranborne, 'require a conviction in England that our record was, in general, a good and progressive one, and a conviction that the Empire was not a thing to be

---

[6] Cranborne to Eden, 18 Aug. 1942, CO 825/35/55104.

[7] Throughout the war Amery brought to bear the lessons of the Territorial Changes Committee of the First World War, which had attempted to establish Britain's strategic and colonial aims. Anachronistically, he regarded the removal of the French and the Portuguese from their enclaves in India, e.g., as a priority. He saw no reason why Hong Kong should be ceded unless it were for some 'essential strategic desiderata we could obtain in return'. All things considered, he thought it probably would be best for Hong Kong to be retained. 'If China were anarchic, Hong Kong might well form a haven of refuge.' Minutes of an inter-departmental meeting of the Secretaries of State for the Dominions, Foreign Affairs, India, and the Colonies, 10 Sept. 1942, FO 371/31777; CO 825/35/55104. The F.O. minutes are more detailed than the Colonial Office's.

[8] See Chan Lau Kit-Ching, 'The Hong Kong Question'.

[9] G. E. J. Gent's record of the meeting, 20 Aug. 1942, CO 825/35/55104; FO 371/31777.

ashamed of, and that the British people had a useful mission to continue in the Colonies.' He next pointed out, in traditional Colonial Office vein when discussing such matters with the Foreign Office, that 'Colonial peoples were not peoples to be bartered round the peace table'. Britain had obligations to fulfil.

Turning their attention to American impressions of the Empire, and to Roosevelt's views in particular, Cranborne and his colleagues noted that the President 'appeared to assume that it was impossible for the British to return to their old position in Malaya'. Here they could only assume that Roosevelt suffered from lack of information about the affairs of the Far East and failed utterly to perceive the steadfast character of the British Empire. 'It was thought likely that the President, like other distinguished Americans, had only a very vague understanding of the Malayan position, and we certainly should not concede the assumption that the restoration of our sovereign position in the Colony and our Protecting position in the Malay States was impossible.'[10] The British had every intention of remaining in control of their own affairs. 'It was a matter for ourselves to decide what, if any, new grouping or constitutional arrangements in Malaya (and possibly in Borneo too) would best suit new conditions.' Nevertheless Cranborne was prepared to admit an American contribution to the affairs of South-East Asia, especially if it could be directed into defence efforts and certain types of economic development. He spoke vaguely of 'mutual defence obligations' and a 'Council for the Pacific'. For the Colonial Office it was an important concession. Foreign influence would be permitted in a British colonial area; but, Cranborne stressed, whatever the nature of the 'Council', Britain would continue to enjoy complete 'constitutional and administrative control'. This was a consistent Colonial Office line throughout the war. The British themselves would be the judge of their own actions, and they would not give the impression of acting under American pressure—in the Far East or anywhere else.

On the 9th of September 1942 the Secretaries of State for the Colonies, Foreign Affairs, India, and the Dominions met to thrash out their ideas on the colonial situation in the Far East. Cranborne and Eden held similar views on Hong Kong as

[10] Ibid.

opposed to Amery, and the three of them had very strong opinions on the general colonial question as opposed to Clement Attlee, who at this time was serving as Dominions Secretary. It should be noted that the other officials in attendance included Paul Emrys-Evans, the Dominions Parliamentary Under-Secretary. He had earlier served as Cranborne's private secretary and shortly after the meeting influenced Attlee's outlook on the colonial issue. Attlee himself had been appointed by Churchill in order to have the Dominions Secretary in the War Cabinet, not because of the Deputy Prime Minister's passion for the Dominions. On the question of Empire, Attlee held a doctrinaire Labour position on 'imperialism'. His attitude served as a catalyst for those such as Cranborne who wished to move forward in a conservative direction.

There developed an ideological split of the first magnitude. Cranborne wanted to keep Far Eastern questions separate from those of Africa. By opening the international door in Asia he did not intend to welcome the Americans into Africa. 'Conditions varied widely in the different colonies,' Cranborne stated, 'especially in regard to their capacity for self-government.' Eden wanted a statement on colonial aims for propaganda purposes and a defence scheme in which the Americans could participate. The Secretary of State for India took issue with them on Hong Kong, but found himself in general agreement with the Colonial and Foreign Secretaries. As usual Amery dwelt on strategic issues of broad concern to the Empire. 'He thought that we should not abandon any territory without at least considering what essential strategic desiderata we could have in return.' Such talk may have gone down well in the 'Territorial Changes Committee' of the First World War, but it appalled Attlee. It seemed to him to be a 'reversion to pre-war ideas, including a balance of power and uncontrolled free trade'. He took a firm stand. He resisted the suggestion that they should endorse a colonial formula to be applied only in the Far East and that could not be used throughout the world. He wanted to include Africa. He doubted whether the British public would favour the cost that seemed to be inherent in post-war colonial development and defence schemes. 'The people of this country would not wish to have the exclusive privilege of paying for the defence of all these territories at the expense of their own standard of living and for the benefit of certain privileged classes.' To cap his objections he then dropped what must have seemed to Cranborne, Eden, and Amery to be a bombshell:

[I]nstead of national armaments he favoured an international force and a general sharing of the burden of defending these colonial areas. This could be best achieved by international control and administration of these territories.[11]

Mrs. Anne Hare McCormick and other members of the American Advisory Committee almost at this very time were learning about the Labour Party's view on the colonies. They would have been intensely interested to know that such basic issues were being debated within the highest circles of the British government.

The Colonial Office minutes of the meeting give an expanded account of Attlee's protest. It clearly galled Cranborne to hear the colonies referred to in 'capitalist' terms and it seemed to him that Attlee was attacking the Colonial Office's record of reforms. While Cranborne talked about determination not to surrender any British territories, Attlee referred to their exploitation.

Mr. Attlee explained that there was an important political aspect about all this, and that in the view of the Labour Party the British electorate would not be content to go on bearing a financial burden in respect of Colonies for which the advantage mainly accrued to a capitalist group. The maintenance of national sovereignty over colonies required the maintenance of national armaments; and in respect both of armaments and sovereignty over backward peoples the political views which he shared were in favour of the substitution of an international system of responsibility and control.[12]

In Attlee's opinion a reversion to the old colonial system could lead to another war. Though colonialism was not his special interest he was vigorously putting forward one of the basic Labour ideas about the colonies:

National sovereignty and national armaments had shown poor results and would inevitably lead to renewed war in due course.

[11] Minutes of meeting at the F.O., 'Post-War Settlement in the Far East', Most Secret, 10 Sept. 1942, FO 371/31777; CO 825/35/55104. The CO minutes are slightly more full and give different emphasis. [12] Ibid., CO minutes.

A new conception of international collaboration and responsibility and a pooling of the burden, including the financial burden, of armaments was required.[13]

Cranborne objected by stressing Britain's good record with the natives. Eden again advocated the advantages of defence schemes to which the Americans and the Dominions would adhere. Of the reactions to Attlee's remarks, however, Amery's were the most agitated. Since the days of the First World War the phrase 'international colonial administration' to him had symbolized subversion of the Empire. He now found himself seriously confronted with the proposal not only by a colleague but the Deputy Prime Minister. The minutes probably do not do Amery justice, but they reflect his convictions. He dwelt first on the immorality of international colonial administration. He stressed Britain's imperial duty. In the Foreign Office minutes he is recorded as saying:

[W]e had a direct moral responsibility for the welfare of native populations in the territories with which we have been associated and . . . we must continue to bear that responsibility in our own territories . . . it was our duty to promote a higher standard of living not only in this Island but throughout the Empire.[14]

The Colonial Office minutes note Amery's belief that the highest authority to which Englishmen could owe their allegiance was the British Parliament, not a polyglot international Super-State. Moreover he deplored the inefficiency and the chaos of international colonial administration. Here however Attlee had a ready reply, knowing that the two examples always used were Tangier and the New Hebrides.

[I]t was not sufficient to condemn such a system [of international administration] by pointing to the inefficiency of the international system at Tangier or the Condominium in the New Hebrides. In neither of these cases was there an obvious effort to promote

---

[13] Ibid.

[14] Ibid., FO minutes. Amery must have taken great alarm because he wrote to Lord Hailey requesting information about the current state of proposals for full international control. Hailey wrote back at length indicating that schemes for international colonial administration appeared to be supported only by various individuals—but Attlee was one of them. (Hailey to Amery, 6 Oct. 1942, Hailey Papers 600.18.S.20.) Attlee's enthusiasm for colonial questions, however, was never strong.

efficiency. But something on a much larger scale deriving from an intention to collaborate to mutual advantage and the achievement of results is worth examination. It would not necessarily mean that the local executive in any territory would be a polyglot mixture of officials but the international authority would need to be the sovereign authority with the power of laying down standards and regulations and to carry out inspection in any way and matters thought necessary.[15]

What were the economic implications for a 'capitalist' colonial settlement, he asked?[16] Attlee was proving to be a formidable adversary of the Tory view of proper colonial development.

Cranborne somewhat feebly put forward his ideas about regional committees as an alternative to thorough-going internationalization. He had not fully formulated his plan at this stage but he got across his point that sovereignty would reside in the individual colonial powers, not in an international body. He wanted to end once and for all the indeterminate status of the mandates but nevertheless used the Permanent Mandates Commission as his model for the 'Regional Councils':

> The Secretary of State for the Colonies said that in his view the functions of the international supervisory body would be analogous to the Mandates Commission but that instead of being composed of representatives of small States having no practical experience of colonial administration it would consist of representatives of the administering States themselves and would be in a sense an expert body of which the members, in considering particular problems, would be aware of kindred problems in the territories under their own administration.[17]

He failed to convince Attlee of the horrors of international colonial administration conducted by 'Norway, Poland, Venezuela, etc.'.[18] The meeting ended with a clear division between the two rival theories of how best to run the colonies.

[15] Ibid., CO minutes.
[16] For the question of the economic aspects of the colonial settlement as it was envisaged in 1942, see especially FO 371/31527, especially for the hand of one of the leading economic authorities, Sir Frederick Leith Ross (U 1613).
[17] Ibid., FO minutes.
[18] Cranborne referred to the Permanent Mandates Commission, and he exaggerated—presumably to impress upon Attlee what a disaster it would be to have Eastern Europeans or South Americans running the affairs of the British Empire. Mlle Valentine Dannevig of the Permanent Mandates Commission was a Norwegian. There were never any representatives from Poland or Venezuela.

No one wanted an explosion in the War Cabinet on the colonial issue. Cranborne managed to find common ground between the two of them. In Cranborne's words Amery was 'really not so reactionary as Attlee thinks'. Amery proved willing to go along with the idea of regional supervision provided British sovereignty and authority remained intact. Attlee was open to persuasion, particularly by Paul Emrys-Evans and Richard Law of the Foreign Office. These two friends of Cranborne managed to convince Attlee not only that it was the wrong time of the war to bring up the divisive colonial issue but also that the Colonial Office's proposals had merit in them. In a letter of the 9th of October 1942 Cranborne thanked Emrys-Evans for help with Attlee.

You and Dick [Law] must have done wonders with the Dominions Secretary. I quite agree that it is most desirable to avoid a row in the Cabinet, if in any way possible. There is always the danger that having taken up a position in black and white, he [Attlee] might find himself unable to retire from it, and then I do not know where we should be.[19]

Cranborne went on to outline the basis of agreement or compromise between himself, representing the conservative view, and Attlee, representing the Labour or international view. Cranborne's comments are important because they provide a good summary of the Colonial Office's views as of October 1942. He yielded to Attlee's insistence that a colonial formula or supervisory machinery be worldwide and not restricted to the Far East. Cranborne then outlined his ideas about area 'consultative committees' which in later form became the Colonial Office's 'Regional Councils' scheme.

My idea is that we might propose the setting up in each main Colonial area, the Far East, Africa, and the Caribbean, of consultative Committees, composed of representatives of all the nations interested territorially in those particular areas.

For instance, in the Far East, the members would presumably be ourselves, the United States, Holland, Australia and New Zealand, and possibly France, if she is allowed to keep Indo-China. We might even stretch a point and include Russia, though her interest in the Pacific is more limited.

In Africa, the members of the Committee would be ourselves, the

[19] Cranborne to P. V. Emrys-Evans, 9 Oct. 1942, CO 323/1858.

Union of South Africa, France, Belgium, and Portugal. For the Caribbean, the members would be ourselves, the United States, and possibly France, if she keeps her Caribbean islands.[20]

Here was the key point on the way in which these committees would differ from the mandates system:

These regional committees would in one essential respect be different from the Mandates Committee which used to sit at Geneva before the war. That body was formed to ensure the application, in the mandated territories, of certain principles, and to report to an outside body, the League. The committees which I have in mind would have nothing to do with any outside body.[21]

There would be no derogation of sovereignty. There would be no accountability to an international organisation. Each colonial power would merely co-operate with other colonial powers in areas of common interest.

No doubt, the Americans would be a great nuisance to us on the Caribbean Committee, where they would constantly be interfering in the internal affairs of our West Indian Colonies. But they will do that in any case, and one cannot deny that they are vitally interested in what happens in that part of the world. From the African Committee, on the other hand, they would be excluded, and this, I think, is right. They have no territorial interests there.[22]

It seemed to be a singularly good scheme to resolve a number of difficult problems at one stroke. Superficially it resembled the area council proposals of the American Advisory Committee on Foreign Policy. For purposes of the British Left, as well as the Americans, it had in it, in Cranborne's phrase, 'the element of internationalism' which in fact, he candidly explained, 'gives away . . . nothing essential'.[23] Regional co-operation thus emerged as the grand alternative strategy to trusteeship with international accountability.

[20] Ibid.   [21] Ibid.   [22] Ibid.   [23] Ibid.

12

THE CRESCENDO OF AMERICAN CRITICISM AND CHURCHILL'S 'FIRST MINISTER' SPEECH

WHILE the officials in both England and the United States discussed the nuances of trusteeship in secrecy, the public debates on the question revealed much of the same sharp division on basic issues and caused both Roosevelt and Churchill to respond. On the 12th of October 1942 the editors of *Life* magazine published an 'Open Letter . . . to the People of England'. It was a frank message. Americans might disagree among themselves about war aims, but they were unanimous on one point:

[O]ne thing we are sure we are *not* fighting for is to hold the British Empire together. We don't like to put the matter so bluntly, but we don't want you to have any illusions. If your strategists are planning a war to hold the British Empire together they will sooner or later find themselves strategizing all alone.[1]

After a reminder that the American civil war had been fought to secure freedom for the black man, the editors of *Life* noted that they failed to find any comparable principle motivating the British in India. 'In the light of what you are doing in India, how do you expect us to talk about "principles" and look our soldiers in the eye?' With a rhetorical American flourish, the editors of *Life*, professing to speak for 134,000,000 fellow citizens, entreated the British to forsake 'Your Side of the war', which included imperialism, and join 'Our Side', which meant the side fighting for freedom throughout the world.

Our Side is plenty big. It always has been big. It is much bigger than the British Raj. It is much bigger than the British Empire. It is bigger than both of us combined. You will find Our Side on the steppes of Asia, and across the deserts of Africa, and up and down

---

[1] *Life*, 12 Oct. 1942.

the muddy banks of the Mississippi, and along the smooth-sliding waters of the Thames. Our Side is as big as all outdoors.[2]

The spiritual invocation carried a message to British readers. Clearly Americans believed that the British Empire should be liquidated.

At this time the press in both countries gave full coverage of the round-the-world tour of the Republican Presidential candidate in 1940, Wendell Willkie. In England he was generally regarded as a friendly American and, because of his presidential candidacy, Churchill, among many others, took note of his speeches.[3] Travelling in thirteen countries through South America, Africa, the Middle East, Russia, and on to China, Willkie in the autumn of 1942 confirmed American beliefs that, in his words, 'this war must mean an end to the empire of nations over other nations'. Speaking in Chunking, in one of his most important wartime speeches, he called not only for the freedom of colonial peoples but specifically for *timetables* under which they could work towards their independence. On his return to the United States his broadcast to the American people on the 26th of October included these lines:

Men and women all over the world are on the march, physically, intellectually and spiritually. After centuries of ignorant and dull compliance hundreds of millions of people in Eastern Europe and Asia have opened the books. Old fears no longer frighten them. They are no longer willing to be Eastern slaves for Western profits. They are beginning to know that men's welfare throughout the world is interdependent. They are resolved, as we must be, that there is no more place for imperialism within their own society than in the society of nations.[4]

Roosevelt was asked to respond to this part of the speech at

[2] Ibid. Subsequently on 19 October the editors of *Life* congratulated the *Manchester Guardian* for taking a similar view on the 'patently obsolete' British Empire with its 'mixture of paternalism and repression'. The *Guardian* did not, however, invoke the spirit of the universe.

[3] See PREM 4/26/6 and 4/27/1. In a conversation with Charles Taussig, Churchill said that 'Willkie knew very little about the Empire and on his trip around the world visited few parts of it and, where he did land, he saw little more than the airport'. Quoting the Prime Minister's exact words, 'I am not going to accept less favourable terms from that other German Willkie than I could get from Hitler.' Memorandum by Taussig, 28 Dec. 1942, Taussig Papers, Box 46.

[4] *Wendell L. Willkie's Report to the People* (New York, 1942); *Vital Speeches* (1942), ix. 34–9; see also Wendell L. Willkie, *One World* (New York, 1943).

a press conference. He took care to point out that Willkie had merely endorsed a well-accepted point (at least to Americans): the Atlantic Charter applied 'to all humanity'.[5] The President's remark was quoted in England as giving great force to Willkie's speech.

The British response came from Churchill in one of his most famous wartime statements. On the 10th of November 1942 he acclaimed the landing of American and British troops in North Africa. He denied that the British had acquisitive ambitions in North Africa or any other part of the world. The British had not entered the war for profit or expansion.

> *Let me, however, make this clear, in case there should be any mistake about it in any quarter. We mean to hold our own. I have not become the King's First Minister in order to preside over the liquidation of the British Empire.*[6]

Churchill's eruption seemed to be a direct rebuke to Willkie as well as a declaration of purpose. In any case it shocked Americans, including Willkie, and dedicated British Imperialists as well.

Lord Lugard greatly regretted that Churchill's remark could be interpreted as reactionary. In a letter to *The Times* he explained what the Prime Minister *should* have said explicitly. He vindicated Churchill's motives by putting the remark in the context of the Empire's purpose. The British did not hold the Empire in the nineteenth-century sense of empire for the sake of empire, or for the sake of economic exploitation, but for the welfare and progress of the inhabitants of the colonies—trusteeship. The British would not abandon their sacred trust to an international authority of dubious qualification. According to Lugard:

> The motive which seems to have been attributed to Mr. Churchill's words about standing by what we hold and refusing to liquidate the Empire is not consonant with his record and character. I am convinced that his meaning was precisely what His Majesty's Government, and I think Mr. Roosevelt also, have declared—namely that as trustees for the dependent peoples they would never surrender that trust, which they alone could fulfil, to anyone else, e.g., to an international body, well knowing that no body of super-

---

[5] Press conference of 27 Oct. 1942, *Public Papers and Addresses of Franklin D. Roosevelt* (1942), 437.

[6] *The Times*, 11 Nov. 1942. Italics added.

men could in practice carry on the administration of some scores of colonies, and perform the work which at present occupies the large expert staff of the various colonial ministries.[7]

If the Americans reflected on their own experience with dependent peoples, they would probably agree, Lugard concluded, that so serious a matter as colonial administration should not be entrusted to an 'international consortium'. In this sense the Empire would not be liquidated.

In perhaps the most searching commentary in the aftermath of Churchill's statement, Margery Perham in two articles in *The Times* examined the historical reasons for American criticism of the British Empire. She found that it arose 'from habits of thought long and deeply rooted in American minds'. Willkie's speech reflected an attitude shaped by the political experience of the United States.

It was not to be expected that Americans whose ancestors broke away from the British Empire in 1776 should march to its direct defence in 1942 without asking themselves and us uncomfortable questions. . . . America was born out of negation of the British Empire; her democracy has been bred in the tradition of anti-imperialism. When Americans wake up to find their soldiers beside ours in India and Africa, and marshalled, it may be, for the recovery of Burma and Malaya, they have to put their minds suddenly into reverse; and this jarring process has been freely reflected in their Press during the last nine months.[8]

Giving a sympathetic explanation of Willkie's views, Miss Perham also pointed out that he had seen the benevolent side of British rule. The British no less than the Americans desired an end to exploitative imperialism. Any student of American and British history would have to be struck with their common experience in dealing with dependent peoples. Certainly Americans could not claim exemption from brutality and bloodshed in their own expansion. 'In this expansion the rights and interests of Red Indians were considered as little as those of Australian aborigines. Force, bloodshed and insurrection marked the subjection of the Filipinos as it did that of the Maori or Matabele.'[9] With a willingness to acknowledge past faults

---

[7] *The Times*, 26 Nov. 1942.   [8] Ibid. 20 Nov. 1942.
[9] Ibid. 21 Nov. 1942.

on both sides, English and Americans should work together, first in understanding the problems of the colonial world, then in solving them through co-operation on a worldwide scale. She hoped that there would be scholarly investigations by Americans as well as Englishmen. She pointed to the publication by the Phelps–Stokes Foundation of *The Atlantic Charter and Africa from an American Standpoint* as 'a very well informed and appreciative analysis of our African administration'.[10] Not all American comment on the Empire was negative by any means. In her view the British could only gain by encouraging American interest in the colonies. Education about the realities of tropical Africa would convince Americans of the merit and dedication of the British colonial services.

To Miss Perham, American concern for dependent peoples was much less a danger than British sluggishness in moving forward with their own colonial affairs.

The Americans are . . . forward-looking people and we must do more than explain that, as empires go, ours is doing meritorious work. While few of them expect us to walk out of the colonies tomorrow, many feel strongly, if somewhat vaguely, that the idea of 'colonial possessions' is obsolete and dangerous. They want us to convince them that we are liquidating this idea from above by a readiness for international co-operation and from below by strenuous education in self-government.[11]

Her view on the colonial future as one of the British scholars most intimately concerned with the colonial empire thus differed drastically from Churchill's. 'Mr. Churchill's declaration of tenacity may represent a mood of justifiable self-confidence but it does not answer American doubts.' The future of the Empire as well as the reconquest of the lost territories depended on American co-operation and mutual understanding. Miss Perham above all saw this problem from the British side as one of race relations. As realistic Americans would recognize,

10 (New York, 1942.) The Secretary of the Fabian Colonial Bureau, Rita Hinden, wrote that the book 'has received very widespread attention and interest in this country'. (Hinden to Anson Phelps-Stokes, 27 Nov. 1942, Fabian Papers.) For further references and discussion of this theme, see J. Ayodele Langley, *Pan-Africanism and Nationalism in West Africa, 1900–1945* (Oxford, 1973). In this connection I am grateful to Hollis Lynch for letting me read parts of his work in progress on 'Black American Radicals and the Liberation of Africa'.

11 *The Times*, 21 Nov. 1942.

it was not an exclusively British problem. 'The Americans . . . do not expect us to accept all their criticism or to believe . . . that they have solved all their own difficult race problems.' Englishmen and Americans alike could benefit from trying to find common ground on issues that would shape both their futures. The Americans strived toward the goal of abolishing the inequalities created by imperialism. This was after all a British ideal as well. 'Taken broadly and at best, the American challenge to us to hasten the work of de-imperializing empire can lead only to good.'[12] Reflection on the meaning of the speeches of Willkie and Churchill in this case thus produced deep optimism about Anglo-American co-operation and the future of the British Empire.

In Parliament the common theme in defence of Churchill ran that Britain would hold fast to her responsibilities. Sir Edward Grigg spoke at length. His comments are of particular interest because he represented the school of 'enlightened Imperialism' associated with Lord Milner, because of his concern with racial problems of the settler communities in East Africa, and because in the next year he published a major book on the British Empire which Americans as well as Englishmen discussed extensively.[13] Grigg deplored criticism shouted 'from rooftops across the Atlantic'. He and others believed that mutual accusations on sensitive issues such as colonies impaired the military conduct of the war. Like Miss Perham he identified the racial issue as central to the future of both countries.

It is the profoundly difficult problem of the relations between the black and the white races when they have to live together in the same society. The United States have that problem right at home. . . . We have it in South, Central and East Africa. White settlement has moved up the central spine of Africa, where the greatest potential wealth is to be found and the climate is favourable, like mercury up a tube.[14]

As an indication of the support the concept of partnership had gained at this time, Grigg seized upon it as the policy the British should pursue in attempting to resolve racial conflict. The paternalism of a trustee was not enough. 'I think we have moved

[12] Ibid.
[13] Sir Edward Grigg, *The British Commonwealth* (American edn. New York, 1944).
[14] *Parliamentary Debates* (Commons), 26 Nov. 1942, c. 911.

on from the idea of trusteeship . . . to a more constructive idea still—the idea of partnership with these peoples.'[15] Grigg went on to stress the regional nature of specific colonial problems and spoke vaguely of regional co-operation and the way the United States might participate by contributing capital. The ideas advanced so lucidly by Lord Hailey thus found increasing support in the House of Commons.

In the House of Lords, Lord Samuel addressed himself to the question. His remarks are noteworthy because of his experience as the High Commissioner of the Palestine Mandate, 1920–5, and generally because of his stature as an elder statesman of the Liberal Party. Commenting on Willkie and Churchill, Samuel thought that Americans did not desire the 'liquidation' of the British Empire so much as 'the more rapid extension of self-government'. He believed that this could be accomplished best by more devolution of authority to regional administrations covering groups of colonies. He referred to Hailey as the 'unrivalled authority' favouring this scheme. He made it clear that he opposed international administration of any sort as 'notoriously inactive and inefficient'. Yet he supported the idea of international supervision.

> If, after the war, it is found possible to establish some widely-extended international authority over world affairs in general, I see no reason why all Colonial Administrations . . . should not be required to accept the supervision of such an international authority, acting much as the League of Nations had done through the Mandates Commission in respect of the Mandated Territories.[16]

Samuel now referred to his own experience as High Commissioner for Palestine:

> [A]s being the first to present a report from that particular territory to the Mandates Commission of the League of Nations, I had an opportunity of realizing and admiring the manner in which the affairs of that Commission were conducted, its impartiality, its conscientiousness and its painstaking care.[17]

As clearly as anyone else, Samuel gave the reasons why American participation would be both necessary and desirable in the international supervision of regions such as the Far East.

[15] *Parliamentary Debates* (Commons), 26 Nov. 1942, c. 909.
[16] *Parliamentary Debates* (Lords), 3 Dec. 1942, c. 392.   [17] Ibid.

It would only be through successful military and naval action by the Americans that Malaya and the other Far Eastern colonies would be restored. The United States would have every reason to insist that these territories in the future would be administered in the interests of the inhabitants and would be adequately defended. The British had no reason to fear publicity resulting from such supervision. 'We should have every reason to court it, and, if it were part of the general, normal system of supervision . . . it would be in no way derogatory to British rule.'[18] Here again this line of reasoning went far beyond Churchill's attitude of holding the Empire intact. In England also, fundamental disagreement existed about the future of the colonies.

Against this background of specific colonial controversy as well as the momentous events of the war, the eighth conference of the Institute of Pacific Relations convened at Mont Tremblant in Quebec. They met at the time of the anniversary of the attack on Pearl Harbor to discuss the problems and future of the Pacific and Far East. Although the representatives attended in an unofficial capacity, many were officials closely associated and involved in national policy such as Stanley Hornbeck. Lord Hailey led the British delegation. He was well abreast of official thought on both the general question of trusteeship and the specific territorial issues. The history of the conference itself belongs more properly to a history of the Far East during the war, but the theme of trusteeship can be traced through the proceedings. Hailey gave it particular attention. In the wake of Churchill's explosion, his voice sounded moderate. If Churchill in the realm of colonial affairs seemed to represent die-hard Tory Imperialism,[19] Hailey personified the Colonial Office's spirit of measured and pragmatic progress. To his colleagues at Mont Tremblant, he seemed to possess not only an encyclopedic knowledge of colonial affairs but a philosophical temperament as well.

In an exposition that could have served as a model for any British discussion of post-war problems, Hailey began with the

---

[18] Ibid., c. 393.

[19] See, e.g., the *New Statesman* of 28 Nov. 1942, which commented that Churchill's statement offered 'encouragement to the Tory Imperialist Diehard, a blank "What we have we hold" '.

premise of security. Without security, any talk of freedom of any kind was illusory. Security in the Far East and Pacific would have to be a cooperative venture involving not only the colonial powers but also the dependent peoples. Hence there had to be an atmosphere of goodwill and mutual trust. He illustrated how the British attempted to move toward this goal in Asia by the relinquishment of extra-territorial rights in China. He pointed to the exceptional position of Hong Kong, which in some way would have to be maintained as a key point in future defence arrangements. In South-East Asia he recognized that there were arguments in favour of the liberation of dependent peoples as part of the post-war settlement. He insisted on Britain's prerogative in taking account of this demand. In good form, Hailey made the point that Britain herself had produced the most anti-imperialist tradition, from which the Russians had borrowed.

No attack made today against the spirit of what is called Imperialism is as incisive as that provoked in England itself some forty years ago by the interlude of expansionism which marked our colonial policy during the latter part of the last century. That attack had a wide following and was adopted as a text by Lenin himself.[20]

The seed of English liberty had been planted in the colonies and British subjects would eventually pluck its fruit. Having skilfully made this point, Hailey then developed the line of argument that it could only be a question of method and timing on which critics of British rule would object.

He introduced the theme of gradualism. Some dependent peoples were more advanced than others. There was great diversity. Nevertheless the British had introduced a general principle, that of trusteeship. In the course of this part of his exposition he took care to point out the exceptional position of the Philippines, where there already existed an advanced society which, by implication, made the American task easier. He mentioned specifically that trusteeship with lesser or more advanced peoples included:

(1) establishing institutions of local self-government,

[20] Institute of Pacific Relations, *War and Peace in the Pacific: A Preliminary Report of the Eighth Conference of the Institute of Pacific Relations on Wartime and Post-War Cooperation of the United Nations in the Pacific and Far East, Mont Tremblant, Quebec, December 4–14* (New York, 1943), p. 9.

(2) the progressive substitution of natives of the country for the European element in the official administration, and

(3) the creation of legislatures which at the outset are only of a consultative character but are given increasing responsibility as their capacity develops.[21]

He thus stated that the purpose of British rule was the development of self-governing institutions. He then characteristically asked in encompassing fashion whether reluctance to surrender political control could explain slowness or failure to achieve this goal, and whether political control served agencies of economic exploitation. Or did the explanation of failure to march towards self-government lie with the indigenous peoples? Those who had studied his previous speeches probably were not surprised to find that part of his answer lay in the negative and static nature of trusteeship, which in his view should be replaced with the concept of partnership. 'If at the outset the relationship is that of senior and junior partners, that is a situation which can and must adjust itself as the experience and capacity of the junior partner grows.'[22] Here in summary fashion Hailey presented his theory of the development of the state as an agency of social and economic change as it had developed from the old days of trusteeship.

> The doctrine of trusteeship was born in the days of individualism; the State was then conceived as holding the ring while individual enterprise and voluntary effort shaped all our social and economic activity. Today the State has become the prime agency in promoting social welfare and in safeguarding the standards of life. That idea has been projected from domestic into colonial policy.[23]

This evolution of thought in regard to the colonies had produced a 'dynamic' view of British responsibilities. He made it clear that this historical development was not purely humanitarian. The British themselves stood to benefit from social and economic development in dependent territories.

Hailey's theoretical analysis led him to its practical application. He recommended a 'Pacific Zone Council'. It would have a double function. The first was the preservation of the peace through defence measures. The second was joint consultation and co-operative action.

---

[21] Ibid., p. 11.   [22] Ibid., p. 12.   [23] Ibid.

It would maintain a technical staff, available for advising the administrations concerned on health, agriculture, economic or cultural problems. It would be the agency through which areas unable to finance their own development would obtain the assistance required.

It would receive regular reports from the different national administrations in the area, and be empowered to require information and explanation from them. It would finally—and I desire to emphasize this point—be charged with the periodic review of the progress made in the promotion of self-governing institutions in the dependencies, and in the improvement of their standard of living.[24]

Hailey made clear that he did not intend any form of international administration. He listed specific examples of failure, such as Danzig and the New Hebrides. Having dismissed this possibility, he turned to another possible international formula —mandates. This he took as a serious challenge. He spoke as a former British representative on the Permanent Mandates Commission.

With no desire to underrate the value of the mandatory system, I must point out that the principles it was established to safeguard were largely negative in character. It initiated no new policies. Its existence was compatible with the maintenance of a great diversity of administration in educational, economic or political systems; it gave no guidance as to their respective merit. Its unique value was that of publicity.[25]

Publicity, the one success of the mandates system, in Hailey's view, would be the chief function of the Pacific 'Council'. By implication the Pacific Council in this respect would resemble the Permanent Mandates Commission and would not interfere with colonial administration. As if fearing that this solution of the colonial problems of the Far East might seem rather modest, Hailey emphasized in conclusion that it was best to be practical for fear of holding out false hopes. Many colonial peoples, he said, had suffered from an unfortunate past. 'Many of them are now suffering the calvary of an aggressive war. Do not let us add to that the tragedy of disillusionment.'[26]

Without the rhetorical embellishments and the dialectical extremes of argumentation, Hailey's scheme could be described as regional co-operation in defence schemes and publicity for

---

[24] Institute of Pacific Relations, *War and Peace in the Pacific* . . . , p. 14.
[25] Ibid., pp. 14–15.   [26] Ibid., p. 15.

colonial administration. The goal was self-governing institutions, not necessarily independence, even within the British Empire–Commonwealth. Hailey's proposals were exactly in line with the solution arrived at within the government and endorsed by the mainstream of the British public interested in colonial affairs. If his specific ideas did not seem to American and other critics to represent a commitment towards rapid liberation of dependent peoples, at least his demeanour differed substantially from Churchill's bluster of 'We hold what we have'. In substance his position was not so far removed.

One other public discussion about the British Empire in 1942 deserves special attention. On the 28th of December *Life* magazine featured an interview with the Prime Minister of South Africa. General Smuts, now a Field Marshal, spoke of the experience of South Africa and the British Empire as one who himself had fought on the opposing side to Churchill in the Boer War. Thus he of all people seemed entitled to say that 'the old British Empire died at the end of the 19th Century'. In the famous line of the interview he described the British Commonwealth as 'the widest system of organized human freedom which has ever existed in human history'. Referring to India, Smuts said it was bitter misfortune that the Indians themselves could not agree to win India's emancipation. 'India, if she wills it, can be free in the same way and by the same means as Canada, Australia, and New Zealand.' The interview must rank as one of the most skilful propaganda pieces of the entire war.[27] As he explained its purpose privately to the authorities in London, he chose not to stress the theme of postwar defence because 'this may frighten the U.S.A. and make them think that while they have no colonies themselves they are called in to defend the colonies of others'.[28] He therefore rested his case on the Atlantic Charter in the belief that this would appeal to American idealism. He called for international collaboration. He specifically recommended regional councils in which the United States would participate. In the words of the interview:

There should be a system of regional grouping of colonies. . . .

[27] *Life*, 28 Dec. 1942.
[28] Smuts to Dominions Secretary in Waterson to Attlee, 16 Dec. 1942, DO 35/1014/WR8/12.

While the mother countries would be exclusively responsible for the administration of their policies, the ultimate control of the general or common policy would come under a regional commission or council, on which would be represented not only the mother countries but also others regionally interested for security or economic reasons.

Thus the United States of America, although not a colonial Power, could be on the regional control council of the West Indies, or of Africa or elsewhere.[29]

On the point of accountability to an international council or control board, he went beyond any British statesman. His commitment in this regard is perhaps understandable in view of his role in the founding of the League of Nations. On another point of central importance his ideas coincided exactly with those of the authorities in London. His stand is entirely comprehensible in view of the problem of South-West Africa. 'It would be unwise to disturb the existing administrative relationship between mother countries and their colonies. Mother countries should remain exclusively responsible for the administration of their colonies and interference by others should be avoided.'[30] Apart from the point of some degree of international accountability, even the most idealistic statements about the British colonies thus in substance did not go much beyond Churchill's position of 'We hold what we have'.

[29] *Life*, 28 Dec. 1942.   [30] Ibid.

13

LONDON AND THE DOMINIONS IN THE WINTER OF 1942–1943. PARENT STATES. THE POSITION OF INDIA IN REGIONAL COMMISSIONS INTERNATIONAL ACCOUNTABILITY

O N the 22nd of November 1942 Oliver Stanley became Colonial Secretary. Lord Samuel, commenting on the rapid change-over and Cranborne's quick end of office, aptly quoted, 'They have their exits and their entrances, and one man in his time plays many parts.'[1] Cranborne returned to the Dominions Office in 1943. Stanley stayed at the Colonial Office until the end of the war. On the question of trusteeship his part was traditional. Like Cranborne he took a conservative view of preserving the colonial Empire. More steadfastly than his predecessors he set out to abolish the remnants of the mandates system. From Churchill's point of view he could be relied upon to hold the line. A witty and skilful debater, Stanley upheld conservative ideas for substantial administrative reform. He carried forward important projects of colonial development.[2] He gave shape and substance to the regional organization schemes as an alternative to international trusteeship. Under his supervision the Colonial Office followed a persistent line of rejecting any form of international control of the colonies. Among his Cabinet colleagues, Stanley was not especially forceful, in part because of a certain diffidence of character.[3] As a Colonial Secretary in the Conservative tradition, he holds a place of his own for finding common ground

---

[1] *Parliamentary Debates* (Lords), 3 Dec. 1942, c. 385.

[2] See especially David Goldsworthy, *Colonial Issues in British Politics, 1945–1961* (Oxford, 1971), pp. 182–8, which is the best discussion of Stanley and such issues as the Colonial Development and Welfare Act, constitutional developments, and progress in self-governing institutions. See also especially J. M. Lee, *Colonial Development and Good Government* (Oxford, 1967).

[3] See especially Macmillan, *Blast of War*, p. 138.

with Labour Party leaders and in laying the post-war foundations of Britain's colonial policy. In resisting international
trusteeship, he was Churchill's man.

In the winter of 1942–3 Stanley, along with Cranborne, Eden,
and Attlee, held out hope to their colleagues that the colonial
issue between Britain and the United States might be merely
a misunderstanding. They reasoned that the differences between Americans and Englishmen might prove to be semantic
rather than substantial. They seized upon Cordell Hull's use
of the phrase 'Parent States' in a conversation with the British
Ambassador in August.[4] Hull had said, according to Halifax,
that he would favour a joint declaration of purpose concerning
the colonial empires. Picking up Cranborne's unfinished business in this sphere, Stanley noted that Hull would include in
the declaration a 'very clear expression against officious intervention from outside with affairs, which were the responsibility
of the Parent State'. With a sense of urgency the Colonial
Secretary wrote to the Prime Minister on the 1st of December
1942 that this attitude seemed 'surprisingly satisfactory'.[5] He
advised Churchill that they should seize the opportunity before
the Americans changed their minds. Therewith the immediate beginning of the project for an Anglo-American colonial
declaration.

On the 5th of December 1942 Stanley, Attlee, Eden, and
Cranborne (now Lord Privy Seal) submitted a memorandum
to the War Cabinet on the need to counteract American criticism of British colonial policy. In a pattern which was to recur
during the war, British ministers bridged their ideological
differences and united against the Americans. Attlee proved
amenable to persuasion by his Conservative colleagues while
they, on the other hand, tried to find common ground to meet
his demand for international supervision of the colonies. All of
them believed that something needed to be done to correct
Wendell Willkie's 'misguided' view that 'there is something
archaic in the conception of the British Colonial Empire'.
Propaganda (or 'enlightenment' as they called it) was not
enough. They recommended a declaration on colonial policy
which would reaffirm traditional British goals and would 'keep

---

[4] Halifax to Eden, No. 4285, 25 Aug. 1942, printed in W.P. (42) 544, CAB 66/31.
[5] Stanley to Churchill, 1 Dec. 1942, CO 323/1858; PREM 4/42/9.

the initiative in our hands'. Based on the conversation of Hull and Halifax, they hoped to commit the Americans in a public statement to the paternalistic principle of 'Parent States'. If the Americans would agree that colonial administration was the responsibility of the parent state directly concerned, then the British would be willing to discuss the practical application of the concept to regions such as South-East Asia.[6] At the Cabinet meeting which approved this approach, Stanley pointed out that Roosevelt's 'personal representative' for Caribbean affairs, Charles Taussig, had arrived in London.[7] Though the British might try to restrict regional organization schemes at the beginning to South-East Asia, the Americans would soon demand discussion of other regions as well, not least the Caribbean. Indeed the Anglo-American Caribbean Commission established in March 1942 (during the arrangements for leased bases in British territories) seemed to some to be a desirable precedent for regional co-operation.[8] It was merely a consultative commission and in Stanley's opinion gave the Americans too much opportunity to inquire into the affairs of British colonies;[9] but on the whole such regional organizations seemed to hold promise as a substitute for the mandates commission. The question then logically arose, why not establish similar commissions in places such as the South-West Pacific? From the outset the British thus found themselves confronted with the global dimensions of the problem.

Having reached at least tentative agreement among themselves, the authorities in London now faced the problem of

[6] In explanation of the special consideration given to this region, the memorandum reads: 'South-Eastern Asia is in many ways a special case, since (a) it has been almost entirely occupied by Japan; (b) common defence in that area is more urgent than it is in other Colonial areas; (c) it is an area in which the United States have practical experience of Colonial administration.' 'Colonial Policy', 5 Dec. 1942, W.P. (42) 544, CAB 66/31; CO 323/1858; DO 35/1014/WR8/12; FO 371/31527.

[7] W.M. (42) 154th Conclusions, CAB 65/28.

[8] In note 7, p. 333, Russell, *United Nations Charter*, remarks from an American vantage point that the Anglo-American Caribbean Commission 'bore not the slightest resemblance to the proposed Regional Councils'. From the British point of view, however, it was an excellent model because it possessed no executive powers.

[9] Stanley's attitude is clearly revealed in reaction to Hailey's much more open approach of attempting to allay American suspicion by collaboration. See memorandum by Hailey, 5 May 1943, and minute by Stanley, 10 May, CO 323/1858/9057B.

bringing the Dominions into line. On the 11th of December Attlee and Stanley and their advisers met with the High Commissioners of the Dominions in London. Stanley candidly explained the situation. He hoped to win over American opinion; and he wanted to dispel the air of impermanence about the colonies which had been blown in by talk of international trusteeship. He stated that the ultimate purpose of British rule was 'to fit the Colonial territories to assume responsibility for their own affairs, even if in the distant future, and to train the inhabitants for that purpose'. To discharge such solemn responsibilities the British would have to be masters in their own house. This was the attraction of Cordell Hull's phrase 'Parent States'. At the same time Stanley opened the door to international cooperation. In language agreeable to Attlee and, it was hoped, to Dominion Ministers with similar views, Stanley explained that regional commissions would be an improvement upon the mandates system.

Regional Commissions would be bodies similar to the Permanent Mandates Commissions, but it was hoped that they would be more practical and be able to devise effective machinery for co-operation in a given area, particularly as, unlike the Mandates Commission, they would be composed exclusively of members who had a direct interest in the area and would be in a position to contribute something more than advice.[10]

As for the actual composition and scope of the regional commissions, Sir George Gater of the Colonial Office cautioned that it would be unwise at this stage to try to formulate detailed proposals. The warning proved to be prescient in every respect. On the 9th of December the Dominions Secretary despatched telegrams to Canberra, Wellington, Cape Town, and Ottawa.[11] Even before replies came in from the Dominions, the fragile consensus between the Americans and the British and among the British themselves had already begun to crack.

Although general agreement might be reached on broad principles, attempts at specific application brought forth divergent and basic opinions about the future of the Empire. In the winter of 1942–3 the question of India continued to preoccupy

[10] 'Note of Meeting with Dominions High Commissioners', 11 Dec. 1942, CO 323/1858; DO 35/1014/WR8/12; FO 371/31527.
[11] See DO 35/1014/WR8/12.

British statesmen and entered into all discussion about colonial affairs. What part would India play in a regional commission in South-East Asia? Amery argued that, since India was on the threshold of self-government, she obviously differed from the dependent territories to be supervised by regional commissions. India also was not a 'Parent State'. Yet if India were granted membership in a regional commission she would claim the same status as, for example, China or the United States. Pursuing this line of thought, Amery deplored any possible Chinese interference with British policy in Burma. 'One of the most important features of these proposals is, in my view, that each parent State should have the unquestioned right to administer its own territories.' He hoped China's role would be restricted to purely international questions. As for India, Amery thought she would be well represented by Britain.[12]

Ernest Bevin, Minister of Labour and National Service and a member of the War Cabinet, held an entirely different view from Amery's. Bevin wanted to do nothing to prevent India from becoming a 'Parent State' after the war. Since the regional commissions were to provide for defence schemes and economic development, India's interests certainly could be considered in the same rank as those of China. As for Amery's suggestion that Britain represent India, Bevin pointed out that India in her own right was already a member of the League of Nations and the International Labour Organization. '[W]e surely cannot neglect the status which India has secured on existing international organisations in considering what her position should be in relation to the present proposals.'[13]

Cranborne saw merit in both views. Denying India membership in a regional commission would exacerbate feeling in India and it would strengthen Chinese and American conviction of the insincerity of Britain's Indian policy. Yet Cranborne saw valid practical reasons against Indian membership. India did not seem to fit into a commission whose purpose it would be to supervise colonial affairs in South-East Asia because India was not a colonial power. Nor did India's defence requirements extend into the Far East or Pacific, where a regional defence group might consist of Britain, the United States, the Netherlands,

---

[12] Memorandum by Amery, W.P. (42) 575, 10 Dec. 1942, CAB 66/32.
[13] Memorandum by Bevin, W.P. (42) 606, 23 Dec. 1942, CAB 66/32.

Australia, and New Zealand. Cranborne admitted that India on economic grounds might have some claim to membership in a South-East Asia commission because of the Indians in Malaya. But if India were granted the chance to intervene in the internal administration of Malaya, the Chinese would also demand a voice because of the large Chinese population. 'This would rapidly bring about a situation which would embody the worst features of a condominium.' Cranborne summed up his arguments by stating that too many nations on particular commissions would impede the collaboration the commissions were designed to promote.

> We shall, I feel, fall into great error if we admit too many nations, with indirect interests, to these Commissions. After all, they are in essence Colonial Commissions, instituted primarily to promote collaboration between Colonial Powers in Colonial Areas. India is not a Colonial Power. She has no knowledge or experience of Colonial administration. Nor has she so direct a defence or economic interest in the South-West Pacific. . . . If we open the door to her, we shall have to open it to many other nations.[14]

Cranborne thus wanted to restrict the membership of the commissions to states directly concerned.

This exchange of views among Cabinet members on such a sensitive issue made Stanley, in his own words, 'particularly nervous', especially in regard to the implication that India might have some ground for interference in the internal administration of Malaya if she were made a member of the regional commission. He wrote to Cranborne: 'As you know, it was a fundamental part of our proposals that the Parent States should be solely responsible for administration and that the members of the Regional Commission would have no right of interference.'[15] In a closely reasoned memorandum circulated

---

[14] Memorandum by Cranborne, W.P. (42) 614, 30 Dec. 1942, CAB 66/32.

[15] Stanley to Cranborne, 30 Dec. 1942, CO 323/1858. Stanley thought that India might be a valuable member on the South-East Asia commission 'as a useful counterpart to China', and he did not think this would involve intervention in internal affairs of Malaya. Cranborne, however, believed that India could be included because of the Indians in Malaya, and that if the British conceded this point to India, China would also have to be admitted. 'This would be selling the pass, for it would mean legalising interference by members in the internal affairs of territories of other members, the one thing which we are both, I gather, anxious to avoid.' Cranborne to Stanley, 30 Dec. 1942, ibid..

in the War Cabinet, Stanley argued that regional commissions should be composed of (a) 'Parent States' and (b) states having an economic or strategic interest in a particular area. He pointed out that it was premature to decide on the actual composition and scope of the commissions since agreement had not yet been reached with the United States, not to mention Russia and China. The issue was becoming highly speculative.[16]

At this stage in the discussion the Viceroy of India, Lord Linlithgow, intervened by telegraphing to Churchill and at great length to Amery. According to Stanley, the Viceroy had 'a complete misconception' about the proposed colonial declaration.[17] Gladwyn Jebb, in charge of the reconstruction department at the Foreign Office, called the Viceroy's telegrams a 'deplorable effort'.[18] In any case they had a definite impact on the Prime Minister. Never enthusiastic about international trusteeship, even in the negative sense of getting a disclaimer from the United States, Churchill had his instinctive feelings reinforced by the suggestion that the Americans in colonial affairs should not be trusted. In the remote future, Linlithgow stated, there might be 'an indifferent, hostile or electioneering President'.[19] In a long, rambling telegram the Viceroy explained his views. Above all he distrusted American economic policies and feared a 'violent conflict' between the United States and Britain on the imperial tariff issue. He urged that 'we should surrender nothing that we can possibly hold on to'. He attached 'extreme importance' to excluding India from the regional commission and deprecated undue influence of the Americans or the Chinese, who he thought should be watched closely.

Americans have neither a Colonial Empire nor experience of one. We have both, and on a large scale. . . . And I should be wary of paying too high a price for a hypothetical American undertaking to take a share in defence of areas which hitherto we have held with exceedingly light forces, and the fate of which will always in practice be likely to be subordinated to the policy of Great Powers.[20]

[16] Memorandum by Stanley, 5 Jan. 1943, W.P. (43) 7. See also minutes in CO 323/1858 and CO 323/1858/9057B.
[17] Stanley to Amery, 9 Jan. 1943, CO 323/1858/9057B.
[18] Minute by Jebb, 9 Jan. 1943, U126/14/70, FO 371/35310.
[19] Linlithgow to Churchill, 2 Jan. 1943, PREM 4/42/9.
[20] Linlithgow to Amery, 2 Jan. 1943, ibid., and W.P. (43) 9, CAB 66/33.

The Viceroy's opinions do not sustain scrutiny for coherence. But, in Stanley's words, they 'sent Winston off the deep end'.[21]

Churchill had already begun to have renewed doubts about the wisdom of negotiations with the Americans on the colonial issue. On the 22nd of December the Lord Chancellor wrote to him:

> Are you satisfied that Cordell Hull's phrase 'Parent States' is the best that can be found for the proposed declaration on Colonial Policy? It seems to me that it may hereafter be exploited by critics and agitators on behalf of 'Children' States. In what sense is Britain 'parent' to Hongkong or Jamaica? *'Guardian* States' seems to me a safer expression, especially as in the future America will cast envious eyes on the West Indies.[22]

There followed a discussion on semantics and poetry. Amery favoured the phrase 'Parent States' because he thought it connoted mutual affection. 'There are some famous lines in Latin poetry describing Rome as "mother, not mistress" of the peoples which had come under her sway.' Furthermore if the word 'guardianship' were used in regard to the West Indies, the Americans might retort that they were doing the actual 'guarding'.[23] Thus there was disagreement in London about the proper phraseology. Now Churchill learned that the President himself did not like the term 'Parent States'. On the 26th of December Lord Hailey met with Roosevelt and briefly discussed the schemes for regional commissions as bruited at the Pacific Relations Conference. The President evidently had not given much thought to the project for a colonial declaration, but he 'casually observed' that he did not think the phrase 'backward peoples' a happy one, 'nor did he much like the phraseology "parent States"'.[24] Churchill was next told that in fact the Secretary of State had mentioned the phrase 'Parent States' to the British Ambassador without first reaching agreement about it with the President. On the 5th of January 1943 Hull 'emphasized that his original suggestion had been made on his own responsibility and before discussion with [the] President'.[25] To this Churchill

---

[21] Stanley to Amery, 9 Jan. 1943, CO 323/1858/9057B.
[22] Simon to Churchill, 22 Dec. 1942, PREM 4/42/9; CAB 66/32.
[23] Amery to Churchill, 24 Dec. 1942, PREM 4/42/9.
[24] As recounted in Halifax to Eden, 26 Dec. 1942, No. 6246, U1886/828/70, FO 371/31527.
[25] Halifax to Eden, 6 Jan. 1943, No. 75, U91, FO 371/35310.

erupted in a minute to the Foreign Secretary and Colonial Secretary, 'Please note how very informal and insecure is the foundation on which the "Parent States" policy is being elaborated.'[26]

In the meantime the Dominions had begun to respond. On the 16th of December 1942 General Smuts outlined his views, which were, in fact, shortly to appear in *Life* magazine. His ideas are striking evidence that the concept of the British Empire–Commonwealth at this time depended very much on one's angle of vision. While to such ministers as Stanley and Amery—and Churchill—London seemed the natural and perpetual center of the Empire, Smuts as a Dominion Prime Minister saw a continuing devolution of authority as the Empire evolved into a Commonwealth. He based his exposition to an American audience on grounds that larger units of regional organizations made more sense administratively, and also that British willingness to promote regional commissions would indicate to the Americans that the colonies were not 'run from Downing Street as private British interests'.[27] Remarkably enough, despite the different perception of the Empire–Commonwealth, Smuts and the ministers in London could agree on the idea of 'Parent States' as the basis of British policy. Smuts did not dissent. He had once remarked that South Africa's claim to South-West Africa was 'like the poor sinning girl's plea that her baby was only a very little one!'[28] Smuts was now perfectly prepared to have South Africa recognized as a legitimate 'Parent State'.

The New Zealand government replied on the 18th of December 1942. The view from Wellington, like the one from Cape Town, also derived from the experience of the Dominions' 'orderly evolution from dependent to independent status'. The New Zealanders felt that their own experience with dependent peoples would enable them to contribute to the discussion.[29] At this stage New Zealand merely wished to be kept informed, but it is of interest to note that in the telegrams between the

[26] Minute by Churchill, 7 Jan. 1943, PREM 4/42/9.
[27] Smuts to Attlee, 16 Dec. 1942, DO 35/1014/WR8/12; W.P. (43) 6, 4 Jan. 1943, CAB 66/33.
[28] Quoted in Louis, *Germany's Lost Colonies*, p. 131.
[29] New Zealand to Dominions Secretary, 18 Dec. 1942, DO 1014/WR8/12; W.P. (43) 6, CAB 66/33; NZ PM 151/2/1, Pt. 1.

High Commissioner in London and the Prime Minister that the New Zealanders wondered whether the Americans would see the connection between the development of colonial peoples and the progress of the American Negro. 'If our colonial peoples are to be raised to full status will the U.S.A. and United Kingdom give consideration to the Negro question in the States?'[30]

The Canadian government felt 'hesitant' about venturing an opinion since Canada possessed no colonies. Nevertheless Canada had a deep interest in the issue because of the effect it would have on Anglo-American relations. Like Smuts, the Canadians cautioned against putting too much emphasis on post-war defence. In a point they later developed at length, they wished to see a connection made between the colonial declaration and the Atlantic Charter. On another issue of substance, the Canadians argued that the 'Parent States' should prove their seriousness about trusteeship by making the colonies more 'international'. In moderate language they urged the establishment of an international body with its own staff and with the right to make independent investigations. They envisaged the participation of the colonial peoples themselves.

[U]nless some provision is made for representation on the commissions of the indigenous peoples themselves, the scheme might not be regarded as constructive and progressive. Some importance might also be attached to the right of the proposed international bodies to maintain their own technical staffs and to make their own investigations in Colonial territories.[31]

The proposal went beyond the ones being debated in London, but since it could be considered as a refinement or replacement

---

[30] High Commissioner in London to Prime Minister, 12 Dec. 1942, No. 2554, NZ PM 151/2/1, Pt. 1. For this and other points in regard to New Zealand's colonial policy during the war there are two useful unpublished monographs, J. D. O'Shea, 'New Zealand's Part in the Establishment of an International Security Organisation', and H. Witheford, 'Samoa, the War and Trusteeship', both 'Civilian Narratives', War History Branch, Department of Internal Affairs, Wellington.

[31] Canada to Dominions Office, 23 Dec. 1942, DO 35/1014/WR8/12; W.P. (43) 6, CAB 66/33. The Canadian official who prepared the reply to London, Hume Wrong, noted that Canada 'was not interested' in assuming colonial responsibilities because 'we had our own Colonial problems inside our national boundaries . . . but . . . we might be interested in participating in some form of international regulation in the Caribbean area with which the United States was associated'. Memorandum by Hume Wrong, 14 Dec. 1942, CAN 180(S).

of the mandates system, it did not cause anxiety. The Canadians were willing to go along with the idea of 'Parent States'.

From Australia there came a response radically different from any of the others. On the 2nd of January 1943 the Minister for External Affairs, H. V. Evatt, telegraphed to say that because of the importance and complexity of the problem the Australians could give only their 'preliminary views', which he proceeded to expound at considerable length. Evatt's policy will be analyzed extensively below, but here it is important to note that from the outset he regarded the colonial issue as linked with the universal principles of the Atlantic Charter. As a Dominion Minister much closer to the anti-white ideological impact of the Japanese co-prosperity sphere, Evatt saw the need for a reply based on the idealism of the West. To him the issue seemed of such fundamental importance that he failed to see why the British Government should be establishing virtually a new world order merely in pique at American criticism of British colonial policy. He saw *trusteeship* as the basis of this new world order. He asked—in a sentence which must have sent chills up and down the spines of the more traditional ministers in London—'the degree and extent to which parent States are prepared to relinquish sovereignty in favour of principle of international trusteeship . . .'.[32] Evatt called for no less than international accountability for the colonies.

Parent States (a better term would be mandatory, guardian or trustee States) should accept the principle of accountability for their trust to some International Colonial Commission operating through machinery analogous to the Permanent Mandate Commission which, on the whole, was regarded as successful . . .

[T]rustee States . . . [should] take immediate and practical steps to promote social, economic, and political progress of such peoples, looking to the time when they will, each at the appropriate stage, undertake the full responsibilities of self-government.[33]

Such was the ideological foundation of trusteeship on which Evatt persistently based his case for the rest of the war. It was poles apart from the position of Stanley, Cranborne, Amery, and Churchill.[34]

[32] Australia to Dominions Office, 2 Jan. 1942, DO 35/1014/WR8/12; W.P. (43) 6, CAB 66/33. From the Australian end the key file is AA A989/43/735/321.
[33] Ibid.
[34] It should be noted that the Reconstruction Department of the Foreign Office

The War Cabinet considered the views of the Dominions on the 7th of January 1943, but the larger issues became lost in what Amery described as a 'hopelessly muddled discussion'.[35] Churchill had been upset by the telegrams from the Viceroy. More than ever the Prime Minister believed that they should not give any indication that they were responding to American criticism or any other 'ill-informed clamour about our Colonial Empire'. The Cabinet agreed that regional commissions would be 'a great improvement on the system of the mandated territories'.[36] To the ministers in London here lay the true significance of the entire business. The point is clearly brought out in the private letters between Stanley, Cranborne, and Amery. Cranborne wrote to Stanley: 'Like you, I do not think that "Trustee States" is ideal. It gives too much an impression of impermanence, as if we were only to be there until our wards had grown up, and must then bundle out willy nilly. On the other hand, I have not been able to think of anything better.'[37] Amery wrote to Stanley:

'[I]t does seem to me that a declaration of this sort might afford a very good starting point, not only for getting rid of the Mandates Commission, but of the whole mandatary system and of the doubts which it created, quite unnecessary to my mind, as to the real sovereignty and permanence of authority in our African mandated territories.'[38]

Stanley wrote to Amery:

I fully agree with you that a Declaration of this sort may not only prevent any spread of the mandatory system but afford a starting point for getting rid of the existing machinery. I am with you in disliking the whole system which merely gives an air of impermanence to our authority without providing any advantages in the way of real collaboration.[39]

responded much more favourably to the Australian views than the other branches of the government. See especially minutes in FO 371/31527, which are also important for the way in which the Foreign Office foresaw the possible impact of the declaration on the Belgian, Portuguese, Dutch, and French Empires.

[35] Amery to Stanley, 8 Jan. 1942, CO 323/1858/9057B.
[36] W.M. (43) 4th Conclusions, 7 Jan. 1943, CAB 65/33.
[37] Cranborne to Stanley, Private and Personal, 4 Jan. 1943, CO 323/1858/9057B.
[38] Amery to Stanley, 8 Jan. 1943, ibid.
[39] Stanley to Amery, 9 Jan. 1943, ibid.

Stanley went on to say that he did not want to make the point explicitly because the Australians wanted 'a further extension of the mandatory system rather than its abolition'.[40] The Colonial Secretary thus wanted to gloss over points of fundamental difference.

Stanley's inclination to duck the issue stands in contrast with Cranborne's urge to meet it head-on. As a consequence of the War Cabinet meeting the Colonial Secretary began revising the draft colonial declaration. He tried to find consensus by draftsmanship. He took account of Roosevelt's dislike of the phrase 'Parent States' and substituted 'Parent Trustee States'.[41] With other rather ingenious phraseology he managed to put together a document that reflected points of agreement, so far as possible. Everyone could subscribe to principles such as states working together 'to promote the advancement of the colonial peoples and the general welfare of mankind'. The revised declaration was circulated to the Dominions. South Africa and New Zealand had no comment. Australia chose to regard it as merely a general guide for discussion with the Americans rather than a draft of a formal document. Since their view appeared to have been disregarded, the Australians reiterated the considered opinion that there needed to be 'some provision for the accountability of all trustee States to some international body as both practicable and essential if the trusteeship is to be a reality'.[42] Stanley again thought it best to ignore this view. On a point raised by Canada, Stanley also chose the course of deliberate silence. The Canadians still wanted a specific mention of the Atlantic Charter and this time they couched their language pointedly. Cranborne felt that a response was necessary. To him the Canadians had raised 'an embarrassing issue' and he believed that they should be candidly told the position adopted in London. He wrote to Stanley in a 'Secret and Personal' letter:

The truth, I suppose, is that we do not think the Atlantic Charter at present applicable in its entirety to Colonial territories, or at any rate to primitive colonial territories. There is, for instance, the principle of self-determination, which finds a prominent place in the

40 For the replies of the Dominions see DO 35/1895; W.P. (43) 33, CAB 66/33.
41 On the redrafting see CO 323/1858/9057B.
42 For the Australian side see AA A989/43/735/321.

Charter. Can it possibly be said that the African Colonies are fit for the application of this principle? Or the West Indies? Or the Pacific Islands?[43]

Cranborne thought it queer that the Canadians were not intelligent enough to see this basic point. He thought it should be frankly explained to them and the other Dominion statesmen.

Otherwise, we shall merely look shifty, and they will tend to take the American view as opposed to ours. The Atlantic Charter was originally intended, as I understand it, to be concerned primarily with the European countries at present overrun by Hitler. They are adult nations, capable of deciding their own fate. No doubt, the time may come when even the most backward of our Colonies also become adult nations. But at present they are children and must be treated as such. Ought we not to say so, so as to avoid further misunderstanding?[44]

Cranborne's views certainly had the merit of frankness. Stanley, however, thought that such points should not be made with such brutal honesty. He thought 'certain passages' of the Atlantic Charter could be made applicable to some colonial territories and that they would be looking for trouble if they stated that some parts of the Charter were not applicable to some territories.[45] Stanley's ambiguity, like Churchill's, carried the day. The Dominions were not told candidly or explicitly, though they certainly could read between the lines, that the purpose of the colonial declaration was to consolidate the position of the 'Parent States' and get rid of the mandates system— in Amery's phrase, 'that relic of the previous war'.[46]

[43] Cranborne to Stanley, 14 Jan. 1943, CO 323/1858/9057B.
[44] Ibid.   [45] Stanley to Cranborne, 14 Jan. 1943, ibid.
[46] Amery to Stanley, 8 Jan. 1943, ibid. Amery also thought that the colonial declaration might 'afford a starting point for clearing up the whole Congo Basin Treaty business which again is hopelessly out of date'.

14

THE THREE DIMENSIONS OF AMERICAN TRUSTEESHIP DIPLOMACY IN 1943

WHILE the British aimed at obtaining a declaration that would reaffirm the status of the British Empire as a 'Parent State' and perhaps terminate the mandates system, the Americans were working towards an entirely different objective. In the winter and spring of 1943 it became increasingly clear to the British that *colonial independence* was the explicit American goal. The common theme of independence ran through the thought of Roosevelt, Hull, and Welles, or what may be called the three dimensions of American diplomacy at this time, as represented by the President, the Secretary of State, and the State Department's advisory committees. The time of January–February 1943 is particularly important in the development and modification of this triangular nature of American policy. Roosevelt's ideas crystallized. His trip to West Africa and Morocco to the Casablanca Conference hardened his views on European imperialism. He dwelt increasingly on trusteeship schemes that would include such places as Indo-China and Korea as a transition to independence. His ideas did not always coincide with the Secretary of State's. More than in Britain, there was difficulty in the coordination of policy. In regard to the other two major dimensions, however, the Secretary of State imposed some degree of coherence. In January 1943 Hull himself began to chair the Advisory Committee and thus unified the two hands that sometimes had been working in different ways if not at cross purposes. The significance of Hull's closer supervision of the colonial issue is that he modified Welles's more extreme position. Although Welles and the Advisory Committee wanted to place *all* colonial territories under international supervision, Hull restricted the proposal to the much more narrow scope of former mandates and detached enemy territories. He thus closed the gap within the State Department and brought one basis of American policy at least within the realm of discussion with the British. On general colonial issues, however, a hiatus continued to exist between the policies of the Secretary of State and the President.

The journey to Casablanca profoundly influenced Franklin Roosevelt's views on the colonial question.[1] Scholars who have critically examined Elliott Roosevelt's account of the mission conclude that in some respects it may be unreliable, but that the colonial discussion rings true. The visit to European colonial areas sparked general ideas. The President told his son in Casablanca:

> [T]he colonial system means war. Exploit the resources of an India, a Burma, a Java; take all the wealth out of those countries, but never put anything back into them, things like education, decent standards of living, minimum health requirements—all you're doing is storing up the kind of trouble that leads to war.[2]

During his stopover in the Gambia, Roosevelt believed he had witnessed exploitation by British imperialism.

> This morning . . . at about eight thirty, we drove through Bathurst to the airfield. The natives were just getting to work. In rags . . . glum-looking. . . . They told us the natives would look happier around noontime, when the sun should have burned off the dew and the chill. I was told the prevailing wages for these men was one and nine. One shilling, ninepence. Less than fifty cents. . . .
> A *day*! Fifty cents a *day*. Besides which, they're given a half-cup of rice. . . . Dirt. Disease. Very high mortality rate. I asked. Life expectancy—you'd never guess what it is. Twenty-six years. Those people are treated worse than the live-stock. Their cattle live longer![3]

In Morocco he continued to gain similar impressions of poverty and disease. He began more clearly to formulate his view that France and the other colonial powers must hold colonies in trust and report to an international organization on 'how the literacy rate was improving, how the death rate [was] declining, how disease [was] being stamped out . . .'.[4] Talking with the Sultan of Morocco, the President expounded his ideas of

---

[1] See especially Range, *Roosevelt's World Order*, pp. 105–6.
[2] Elliott Roosevelt, *As He Saw It*, p. 74.
[3] Ibid., p. 75.   [4] Ibid., p. 76.

colonial development, increasingly one of his favorite topics of conversation. Like his adviser Isaiah Bowman, Roosevelt attached great value to irrigation schemes. The idea of making the Sahara bloom caught his fancy. 'It'd make the Imperial Valley in California look like a cabbage patch!' 'Wealth!' he exclaimed at one point:

Imperialists don't realize what they can do, what they can create! They've robbed this continent of billions, and all because they were too short-sighted to understand that their billions were pennies, compared to the possibilities! Possibilities that *must* include a better life for the people who inhabit this land.[5]

Though some Englishmen thought he should direct his sympathies to the Negroes of the American South, Roosevelt felt compassion for the inhabitants of the European colonies. He was also annoyed at conditions in such places as the Gambia, which he denounced to Churchill as a 'hell-hole'.[6] He had large ideas about how to remedy the colonial situation.

The global scope of Roosevelt's thoughts about the colonial world became fully apparent to the British during Anthony Eden's visit to the United States in March 1943. Of the several discussions the Foreign Secretary had with American officials, one in particular brought out the President's elaborate ideas for colonial reorganization.[7] On the 27th of March Eden met with Roosevelt (and Hull and Welles, among others). In discussing the possible structure of the post-war international organization, Roosevelt insisted on the central part of China as one of the four foundation members. This led them to talk about the future of the Far East, which included the fate of the Japanese mandated islands. Eden reported to Churchill: 'In the Far East the policy is to be "Japan for the Japanese". Manchuria and Formosa would be returned to China and southern Sakhalin to Russia. The Japanese mandated islands in the Pacific would pass under the trusteeship of the United Nations.'

Nor were the Japanese mandates the only Pacific islands to

---

[5] Ibid., p. 86.

[6] Roosevelt to Churchill, 17 Mar. 1943, *F.D.R.: His Personal Letters* ii. 1413.

[7] For the American side, an important source for these discussions is Container 329 of the Hopkins Papers. See also especially Box 284, USSD NF. For the British side, PREM 4/42/9; also FO 371/35917.

be included in the scheme. Roosevelt's ideas encompassed the entire world:

All other Pacific islands (with the exception of the two groups mentioned below) would remain under their present sovereignty, British, French, or whatnot, but would have a common economic policy such as is to be set up in the West Indies. The French Marquesas and Tuamotu Islands would pass to the United Nations, for use respectively as stages on the northern and southern air routes across the Pacific from Caribbean area to Australia and New Zealand. Korea and French Indo-China would pass under international trusteeship; for the former the trustees might be the United States, the Soviet Union and China. Timor was most important for Australia and would also have to be dealt with. . . . [the President] suggested in passing that places like Dakar and Bizerta were of the greatest importance for the defence respectively of the United States and Mediterranean. His idea was that the United States should act as policeman for the United Nations at Dakar and Great Britain at Bizerta.[8]

Eden remarked that the President 'was being very hard on the French'. Welles reminded Roosevelt that the United States had gone on record as favouring the restoration of France's colonial Empire. This contradiction did not give the President pause. He merely said that in the 'ironing out' of things this position could be 'rectified'.

Roosevelt's breezy manner disguised a shrewd grasp of some of the real colonial issues at stake. In another conversation, including Hull and Hopkins, Eden attempted to get Roosevelt to commit himself to annexation of the Japanese mandated islands. In line with Churchill's views, Eden saw that if the United States incorporated the Pacific islands, this move could only strengthen British territorial claims as a *quid pro quo*. At least American aggrandizement would greatly aid Britain's effort to salvage her Far Eastern Empire. According to Hopkins, Eden 'said he hoped that the Japanese Mandated Islands would be turned over to us, preferably in outright ownership'.

---

[8] Eden to Churchill, 29 Mar. 1943, PREM 4/42/9. This account is fuller than the American versions. See also Anthony Eden, *The Reckoning* (Cambridge, Mass., 1965), pp. 436–8. For yet another dimension of Roosevelt's trusteeship schemes, see Olav Riste, 'Free Ports in North Norway: A Contribution to FDR's Wartime Policy towards the USSR', *Journal of Contemporary History* 5. 4 (1970).

The President felt that the islands 'would be put under some kind of trusteeship'.[9] He had anticipated a British trap. Only a few days earlier he had written to the Secretary of the Navy that the British would be 'delighted' to see the discussions restricted to American embroilment in the Pacific.[10] Roosevelt kept a free hand. He returned time and again to the grand theme of trusteeship. In the specific case of the islands, he firmly resisted any suggestion of annexation and favoured an 'international' solution. Eden, for his part, made it clear that he thought 'very little of a trusteeship and would rather have the full responsibility in the hands of one country'. Roosevelt, on the larger question of the Far Eastern settlement, envisaged China as a trustee power whose duties would include the policing of Japan. Eden, again reflecting a persistent British attitude, 'did not much like the idea of the Chinese running up and down the Pacific'.[11] Nor did the Foreign Secretary respond favourably to Roosevelt's casual suggestion that Hong Kong should be restored to China as a gesture of 'goodwill'. Eden remarked that the President did not appear to be making 'any similar gestures'. Despite this divergence of views, Eden thought that his discussions with Roosevelt had cleared the way for basic understanding.

Eden, together with Halifax, also thought that common ground could be found with Cordell Hull. Here, in contrast to Roosevelt's high flying talk of global trusteeship, the discussions assumed a practical, almost mundane character. What could the two governments agree on in regard to dependent peoples? Eden and Halifax showed a greater willingness to accommodate themselves to American rhetoric than did their colleagues in London. Hull had a much more realistic idea of 'feasibility', in his phrase, of a colonial declaration than did some of his fellow Americans on the advisory committees. During the time of Eden's visit he persisted in the use of the term 'Parent States' which perhaps caused his English visitor to believe that they were closer to fundamental agreement in

[9] Memorandum by Hopkins, 'Off Record Luncheon Conference with the President, Anthony Eden and Mr. Hull in the President's Study', 22 Mar. 1943, Hopkins Papers, Container 329; Sherwood, *Roosevelt and Hopkins*, pp. 715–16.

[10] Roosevelt to Knox, 12 Mar. 1943, USN GB 450; Roosevelt Papers MR Box 167.

[11] Hopkins's memorandum of 22 Mar. 1943, cited above, n. 9.

a paternalistic sense than they actually were. Hull also tended to give the impression that the difficulty would be in getting, for example, the Belgians and Dutch to adhere to a colonial declaration rather than reaching agreement between the British and the Americans. This seemed encouraging to Halifax and Eden.[12] Hull, however, had a deep conviction of the need for what was referred to sarcastically in the British Foreign Office as a universal 'Bill of Rights'. He believed that the right to *national independence* was inherent in the natural order of nations.[13] Here was the point of fundamental difference between the British and the Americans in the wartime colonial conversations.

It is of crucial importance to note that Hull had under his supervision two distinct projects. They can perhaps best be conceived with the retrospective benefit of the United Nations Charter. One project was trusteeship, as eventually developed into the trusteeship system of the United Nations. It was limited to specific trust territories, as described in Article XII of the Charter. The other category was a declaration on dependent peoples, which forms a separate part of the United Nations Charter as Article XI.[14] This project was universal in scope. Hull, though holding deep convictions and possessing a sense of practicality, in the winter and spring of 1943 was still in the process of mastering the projects' basic distinctions and their ramifications. He responded to the advisory committee's proposal to place all colonial territories under the trusteeship supervision by limiting the scope to the former mandated and enemy territories that might become detached during the war, as in the case of the Italian colonies and the Japanese mandates. At the same time he gave enthusiastic support for the declaration on dependent peoples being drafted by Leo Pasvolsky, Stanley Hornbeck, and Green H. Hackworth, the State Department's legal adviser. This project had been variously known in the Department as the 'Pacific Charter' (as an extension of the

---

[12] On these points see especially Halifax to Eden, 5 Feb. 1943, No. 599, FO 371/35311, which brings out Hull's scepticism about the minor European colonial powers; and a memorandum by Hull, 27 Mar. 1943, USSD NF Box 284, which continues to use the phrase 'parent governments'.

[13] See Hull, *Memoirs of Cordell Hull*, pp. 1234–6.

[14] The guide to these issues in relation to the United States Charter is Russell, *History of the United Nations Charter*, chs. iv and xiii. See also especially *Postwar Foreign Policy Preparation*, pp. 108–10.

principles of the Atlantic Charter) or 'World Charter'. It was the American equivalent on a more universal scale of Lord Hailey's 'Colonial Charter'.

In March 1943 Leo Pasvolsky, who had a gift for synthesis, took the two projects of trusteeship and dependent peoples and amalgamated them. He explained to Hull the result of his draftsmanship: 'It takes from the project developed in the Subcommittee the idea of an International Trusteeship Administration. . . . It differs from the Subcommittee draft in that it gives the Administration no powers over colonial areas, as distinguished from mandated or trust areas.'[15] From the British point of view, it became a matter of debate whether the resulting draft declaration on 'National Independence' provided the basis for discussion, or whether it provided none at all. An official in the British Foreign Office made a fair comment: 'Mr. Hull has tried to cram too much into a single document and to cover areas which cannot be described as Colonial.'[16] In time, the two problems of general principles for dependent peoples, on the one hand, and specific recommendations for the former mandates and detached enemy territories, on the other, were disentangled and drafted into the separate articles of the United Nations Charter. In the conversations of 1943 they were lumped together in what appeared by any one's estimate to be a project of monumental proportions.

The declaration on 'National Independence', dated the 9th of March 1943, can be summarized in the words of its preamble. It pledged preservation of liberty, independence, human rights, and justice. It resolved to extend the principles of the Atlantic Charter to peoples of all nations. There followed two major parts of the declaration. The first enunciated specific responsibilities of the colonial powers in preparing dependent peoples for independence: education, self-government, timetables for independence, and collaboration through regional commissions. The second part dealt with the establishment of an 'International Trusteeship Administration' and the machinery to prepare trust territories for independence.[17]

---

[15] Pasvolsky to Hull, 9 Mar. 1943, Hornbeck Papers Box 48.
[16] Minute by D. J. Scott, 10 Apr. 1943, FO 371/35311.
[17] The Declaration is printed in Notter, *Postwar Foreign Policy Preparation*, Appendix 12.

The British draft declaration had been given by Halifax to Hull on the 4th of February 1943.[18] The American draft declaration, presented by Hull to Halifax during Eden's visit in late March, hinged on the word 'independence', which, as an official in the Foreign Office noted, occurred no less than six times in a single opening sentence.[19] If the phrase 'self-government' could be substituted for the word 'independence' throughout the document, then the differences might be considered rhetorical rather than substantive; otherwise the points at issue would be irreconcilable. The British response, especially at the Colonial Office, will be analyzed later, but it should be noted here that in general the declaration appeared distinctly American to British eyes, not only in content but in style. Sir Alexander Cadogan doubted whether it could be translated into English.[20] The comment reflects more than British condescension. Clarity and precision of purpose could be measured by the extent to which specific cases would fit into the general formula. Here the British thought the declaration failed utterly. Even if the premise of independence were granted, could the same principles be applied to the territories of Soviet Russia, for example, as to the colonies of tropical Africa? American experts who gave close thought to the problem had doubts as well.

Three meetings of the Advisory Committee are of particular importance in the clarification of official thought on trusteeship in its universal and particular dimensions. On the 3rd, 10th, and 17th of April, during the time that the British studied the American counterdraft, the body of foreign-policy experts thoroughly reviewed the colonial situation with the Secretary of State, and they in turn benefited from Hull's own explana-

[18] See Halifax to Eden, No. 599, 5 Feb. 1943, FO 371/35311. On the American draft, a revised version of which was submitted to Halifax on 29 Mar. 1943, see Halifax's minute of that date in which he notes that 'Mr. Hull made it plain that President had not finally approved'. U1534, FO 371/35311.

[19] Minute by Gladwyn Jebb, 12 Apr. 1943, FO 371/35311.

[20] Minute by Cadogan, 28 Apr. 1943, FO 371/35311. What Cadogan referred to as 'Horrible verbiage' can perhaps be explained by the authorship of the declaration. Pasvolsky was an economist, Hackworth a lawyer. Hornbeck was notorious in the Far Eastern Department of the Foreign Office for his cumbersome rhetoric. Someone in the Foreign Office underlined the phrases 'by and of themselves', 'between and among the nations', 'to participate and to have or to achieve representation', 'other peoples in like status', and so on.

tion of American policy. Historians have noted the antagonism between Hull and Welles which contributed to the latter's resignation later in the year;[21] but on this particular issue the different intellects and temperaments of the two men complemented each other. Welles brought to the problem of international trusteeship an intellectual acuity and moral fervour for the underdog. Hull, entirely in sympathy with 'oppressed peoples' of the European colonies, tempered enthusiasm for trusteeship with a keen sense of American public opinion and some awareness of the limits to which the European allies could be pushed on the colonial issue.

At these meetings Hull and Welles and the rest of the committee members attempted to reach agreement on generalizations about non-western emerging nations in Africa, such as Ethiopia, and in Asia, such as Korea. The more they examined particular territories the more they recognized the difficulty of applying universal formulas; at the same time they saw that some territorial problems after the war would be more immediate than others. The problem of the future of Ethiopia might appear to be incapable of an immediate solution, but the question of the Italian colonies in north-eastern Africa would demand a clear-cut answer. At first sight the Korean situation appeared analogous. Here was an incipient nation-state subjugated by an imperialist power. The more closely the two cases were examined the more they appeared to be profoundly different, but superficially they at least had in common imperialist subjugation. In time the two nations would be able to stand on their own feet. This could not be said of the Italian colonies in the neighbourhood of Ethiopia or the Japanese mandated islands in the Pacific. The question then arose, what should American policy be towards such territories as Ethiopia and Korea, on the one hand, and the Italian colonies and the Japanese islands, on the other?

Hull's own thoughts as presented to the committee illuminate a cautious progression of thought. He began by stating that Ethiopia shared with all other 'backward' territories the need for external aid—Ethiopia no less than outer Mongolia. None of these areas could be considered in isolation from

[21] See especially Robert A. Divine, *Second Chance: The Triumph of Internationalism in America during World War II* (New York, 1967), pp. 137–41.

neighbouring territories. Ethiopian exports and imports, for example, had to pass through 'the fiery furnace' of French Somaliland, in Bowman's phrase. If the port of Djibouti, which controlled the rail access to the interior, were handed over to Ethiopia, this would undoubtedly please the Ethiopians, but it would antagonize both the French and the British. The British were especially sensitive to the question of Ethiopia because it controlled the source of the Blue Nile. Bowman summed up this classical geo-political problem:

Lake Tana is the source of the flood waters of the Nile and is more important for reasons of water supply than for any inherent resources. Any hostile power which controlled Lake Tana would control the whole life of the Anglo-Egyptian Sudan and of Egypt, because most of the people in those countries depend upon plantations watered by the Nile.[22]

This summation of the problem by Bowman led to an intervention by a U.S. Congressman on the committee, Representative Charles A. Eaton of New Jersey. Hull, along with Welles, thought that Eaton's questions were 'very much to the point'.

[H]e pointed out that in this area we have lesser breeds without the law and greater breeds above the law, usually exercising their rule under some façade of philanthropy. In proposing to make changes in Northeast Africa, he inquired, are we assuming that the lesser breeds will immediately start developing self-government and that the greater breeds will undertake philanthropy on a larger scale? Is it not possible that the United States will become involved in problems which it is not prepared to meet?[23]

What seemed to Hull to be an apt question prompted him to relate the inner history of the Ethiopian crisis of the 1930s. It brought vividly to mind the constraints on American policy. 'There was not enough sentiment in Congress then to support the Administration's policy', he told the committee.

During Italy's attack on Ethiopia, the American Government sought to interfere but it was not supported by sentiment in the country. . . . We imposed a 'moral embargo' on a number of the most important materials needed by Italy—copper, oil, et cetera. It was not long, the Secretary continued, before the United States

---

[22] P Minutes 50, 3 Apr. 1943, p. 5, USSD NF Box 66.
[23] Ibid., p. 9.

was considerably ahead of the League of Nations in its efforts to foster peace. . . .

When the Senate convened in January 1936 he, himself, had gone to 'the Hill' for several weeks in order to get through the 'moral embargo' which would have restricted the sale to Italy of critical materials to the normal pre-war levels. Our friends in the Senate could not be interested at that time, he added.[24]

A Senator on the Committee, Tom Connally from Texas, doubted that the Congress would now accept trusteeship responsibilities. If past experience provided a guide to the future reaction of the public, then caution would be needed. Another Senator believed that it would be necessary to 'Be bold! Be bold! Be not too bold!'[25] Hull shared these wary sentiments. 'The Secretary declared that never in his memory has public opinion been so unsettled as it now is over the very problems which we are discussing.'[26]

Sumner Welles continued to be irrepressible in his enthusiasm for trusteeship schemes. With far more analytical acumen than Hull, he saw distinctions of territories, peoples, and circumstances. Without hesitation Welles pointed to the Italian colonies of North Africa and the Japanese mandates as territories that would fall under the trusteeship scheme. When asked whether the United States Navy might object to the Pacific islands being subjected to international control, Welles replied in a way that indicates he might well have discussed the matter with Roosevelt:

[I]t is the opinion of the highest authorities of the United States Government that the disposition of these islands should be governed solely by security considerations and that these islands should not be taken over by the United States alone but by all the United Nations for their joint use.[27]

Korea also stood out in Welles's mind as a pre-eminent example of a territory that should be placed under trusteeship.

[Trusteeship] for a considerable period of time—perhaps twenty-five years—would help in developing their muscles [of the Korean peoples], which had not been exercised for a long time. Since outside help will be necessary to prepare Korea for self-government,

[24] Ibid., pp. 9–10.   [25] Ibid., p. 19.
[26] Ibid., p. 17.   [27] Ibid., p. 14.

it would seem logical to place that country under a national trusteeship composed of the United States, China, and the Soviet Union. The expenses of this trusteeship would, very properly, be paid by the Korean people.[28]

When asked specifically *why* it would be necessary to place Korea under trusteeship, Welles stated:

[Trusteeship] would be necessary until Korea was able to become independent again. For approximately thirty-five years Korea had been under Japanese control. The native population had been supine but was nevertheless capable of regaining its capacity for self-government. In order to make self-government possible, however, some period of transition would be necessary. If Korea were immediately constituted an independent state, it might become a real danger to peace.[29]

Elaborating on possible trustees for Korea, Welles thought that the Swedes or the Swiss might aid in the effort:

In the case of Korea, he said, it was obvious that the United States, Great Britain, China, and the Soviet Union would have to join together in helping Korea get back on its feet. These trustees might select as the head of their administration a citizen of some disinterested country—perhaps a Swede or a Swiss—and give him the technical staff needed for his work.[30]

Welles drew the line for these idealistic experiments at the western hemisphere. He had no intention of including American territories in the trusteeship scheme. When asked specifically by Representative Eaton whether the Virgin Islands, Puerto Rico, and Hawaii would become trust territories, Welles replied:

[T]he Western Hemisphere has been regarded as lying outside the scope of the trusteeship program. . . . The people of Porto Rico have already achieved local autonomy and self-government—with certain exceptions to be remedied in the near future. During the past year the Virgin Islands have also received an increasing measure of self-government.[31]

Self-government would lead to independence, but the process would take longer in some areas of the world. The minutes of

---

[28] P Minutes 50, 3 Apr. 1943, p. 13, USSD NF Box 66.
[29] P Minutes 51, 10 Apr. 1943, p. 10, ibid.
[30] 10 April., p. 15.   [31] Ibid., p. 3.

the Advisory Committee contain this exchange between Welles, Representative Eaton, and Representative Sol Bloom of New York.

Representative Eaton asked how long it will take the various dependent areas—for example, the Belgian Congo—to achieve self-government. Mr. Welles replied that in the case of the Congo and many other areas, it will certainly take more than a hundred years. Representative Bloom interjected: 'Perhaps more than a thousand years'. Mr. Welles replied that in the case of Portuguese Timor it would certainly take a thousand years.[32]

Welles continued to refine his notions about European colonial rule. He had 'no illusions' about the policy of the British. But the British along with the Dutch at least had something to their credit.

He said that it was the general opinion that the Dutch have made the best administrators, and the British the second best, in parts of their Empire. Portugal would certainly come lowest on anybody's list, while France and Belgium would come somewhat higher on the scale. Italy and Japan would rank pretty low as colonial administrators.[33]

Part of the attractiveness of the trusteeship scheme was that certain territories could be used as models of administration for the enlightenment of the practitioners of imperialism, not least the Portuguese. But Welles did not rest his case ultimately on the idealistic principle of helping the less advanced peoples of the world by forcing the imperial powers to improve colonial administration. Ultimately Welles believed the American people themselves would benefit from the trusteeship program and would support it because it would contribute to American security. It would make a more stable world. '[E]verything in this [trusteeship] proposal is designed to promote world security. The project is motivated not by altruism or idealism but solely by considerations of security. To a certain extent, of course, the two objectives can be obtained at the same time.'[34] Thus security and welfare formed the two main purposes of trusteeship, as seen by the most articulate American high official. Welles's

[32] Ibid., p. 3.   [33] Ibid., p. 8.   [34] Ibid., p. 11.

views can be regarded as fully within the grand Wilsonian tradition of trusteeship. In summing up his thoughts he said:

[T]he basic concept used as the foundation for the trusteeship project is the concept that these people have not yet reached the stage of development at which they can make decisions themselves. The whole purpose of the trusteeship program is to help these people to make their choice.[35]

Woodrow Wilson might have spoken in exactly the same way.

From the minutes of the Advisory Committee in the spring of 1943, Isaiah Bowman emerges as another American expert who gave especially energetic thought to the problem of trusteeship at this time. Along with Welles, Bowman drew basic distinctions in regard to the territories where trusteeship principles might be applied. In one category were the mandated territories and the Italian colonies; in the other were the colonies of all the European powers. Perhaps to a greater extent than his fellow committee members, Bowman as a geographer and social scientist was concerned with the relationship between facts and theories. In what ways could the United States actually hope to improve the situation in the colonies? In Bowman's own words, how could the 'high-falutin' words of trusteeship be implemented? How far would it be possible, he asked, 'to promote self-government and economic development for the benefit of native peoples'? What limitations would be placed upon idealistic ideas? He concluded that the answers to those questions would depend in part on the territories which the Americans would be able directly to influence. The United States could insist on the implementation of trusteeship in the Japanese mandates or detached Italian colonies to a greater degree, for example, than in the colonial possessions of the European powers. Here an interesting point in the minutes is Bowman's insistence that Soviet Russia possessed colonies in exactly the same sense as the other European powers, but that the United States would be able to do little about the Russian colonial situation. He drew this comparison between Russia and Britain:

[I]n placing the Soviet Union and Great Britain in juxtaposition, we are dealing with things that go under different labels but which

[35] P Minutes 52, 17 Apr. 1943, USSD NF: Conclusions.

are not nearly so different as they seem. Russia is actually one of the major colonial powers; its colonies are merely internal rather than external. The Soviet Government has been dealing with peoples that are as remote from the center of power as the islands of the British Empire are remote from London.[36]

As he developed his line of thought Bowman found a similar analogy to the 'internal' peoples of the United States.

The Soviet Union merely draws a line around its Empire and governs its colonies as part of a single country. It has no more reason to subscribe to these principles of trusteeship than it would have to ask us to subscribe to certain principles relating to the Osage Indians. In other words, Russia will be dealing with her own colonies in one way and with 'outside' colonies in an entirely different way.[37]

Along with Welles, Bowman thought that the most they could hope for from Russia would be co-operation in international trusteeship projects. The Russians thereby would at least acknowledge higher principles than they applied in their own colonies.

In contrast with most of his fellow committee members, Bowman drew freely on American experience with dependent peoples as he attempted to generalize on the basis of particular cases. The Osage Indians were one of his favourite examples. What lessons about economic development and political progress could be learned from the history of the Osages? 'After oil was discovered in Oklahoma every Indian owned one motor car and every chief owned three. The way Indians wasted money became a byword in the Middle West. For example, when one tire on his car went flat the chief went out and bought another Lincoln!'[38] Bowman thought 'this fundamental problem' of reconciling 'economic facts and political situations' existed throughout the world as it had in Oklahoma. He gave other examples. In the case of Bahrein island:

[T]here is Bahrein Island in the Gulf of Persia, with a few hundred of square miles and 90,000 people. Some millions of gallons of oil are exported from Bahrein every year. Suppose, starting with our plans of trusteeship, we try to use this oil for the benefit of the people through promotion of education and self-government. These

[36] 10 Apr., p. 16.   [37] Ibid., p. 17.   [38] 17 Apr., pp. 3–4.

people are raisers of goats and fishers of pearls who have no understanding whatever of the modern oil industry in their country,
which some westerner created when he came along and bored
a hole. How, therefore, are we to relate these millions of gallons
of oil to the 90,000 raisers of goats in terms of our trusteeship
principles?[39]

The problem of responsibility for political education in areas
of economic richness was even more dramatically relevant in
the case of Nauru. Australia and New Zealand held the island
together as a mandated territory on behalf of the British
Empire.

Nauru Island, which has 3,000 natives, produced 1,265,000 tons
of phosphates in 1940. How are we to relate these 3,000 natives to
the 1,265,000 tons of phosphates? Thanks to newspaper pictures, we
are all sufficiently familiar by this time with the nature of the South
Pacific islands, and we have no illusions about them.[40]

The natural resources of Nauru were not inexhaustible. Hornbeck joined the discussion with these words:

[H]ow long will resources like phosphate last? What happens if
these resources give out after the natives have enjoyed great benefits, such as those enjoyed by the Osage Indians? This consideration
suggests that in the functioning of a trusteeship system there should
be strict regulation of the exploitation of natural resources, so that
the whole economy of a given territory would not be upset by the
exhaustion of a single mineral.[41]

The responsibilities of the trustee powers in such cases were
grave and also unique. 'Each territory', Bowman pointed out,
'is a world in itself.' He went on:

The more you generalize about your basic principles, the more
criticism you will arouse when you come to apply those principles.
Under such circumstances, you are likely to be charged with having
betrayed your principles because you have not applied them fully
to every local situation.[42]

Bowman had arrived at the identical conclusion of the experts
of the British Colonial Office. Indeed he concluded that the
more specific cases were investigated, 'we shall find striking

<hr />

[39] 10 Apr., p. 16.   [40] 17 Apr., p. 3.   [41] Ibid., p. 6.   [42] Ibid., p. 4.

contrasts and individual difficulties of the nature Britain has been encountering for generations'.[43]

The expositions by Welles and Bowman appear to have crystallized the ideas of important figures not intimately concerned with trusteeship but occupying important policy-making positions. Among these officials were Adolph A. Berle, Assistant Under Secretary of State, and Leo Pasvolsky, who headed the post-war planning staff. Berle concluded that regardless of theoretical problems about trusteeship, there would be 'certain territories for which, whether we like it or not, something will have to be done'. He mentioned the Japanese mandates and the Italian colonies. For the United States the Pacific islands would pose a great problem.

We can do one of the following three things: (1) hand them over to somebody else; (2) place them under some form of international control; (3) annex them ourselves. It is not possible for us to avoid taking a decision about these territories because, in terms of military security, we shall have them on our doorstep.[44]

The question was not, therefore what the United States *ought* to do about the islands, but *what* to do about them. Continuing later in the same vein, Pasvolsky pointed out that the territories that would demand immediate attention after the war would be the 'detached territories' whose ties with the metropole had been broken. 'These detached territories must go somewhere, either by annexation or by establishment of some mandate or trusteeship system. This problem, therefore, confronts us whether we like it or not and compels us to adopt a policy.'[45]

Pasvolsky went on to analyse the larger question raised by Isaiah Bowman, that of 'internal colonies' such as Russia's. In Pasvolsky's view, 'The test of colonial status is a test of unequal rights.' In some 'composite' states, some inhabitants might be subjected to colonial status and others might enjoy full rights of citizenship. 'The Soviet Union, as Mr. Bowman said, is a composite state of this type. There should be no objection, however, to participation by the Soviet Union or any other composite state in the trusteeship plan for "outside areas", providing they recognize the general principles of trusteeship.'[46] The distinctions thus were becoming sharp.

[43] 10 Apr., p. 17.   [44] Ibid., p. 12.   [45] Ibid., p. 18.   [46] Ibid., p. 18.

(1) Trust territories might be created out of the 'detached territories' and former mandates; there would be some advantage in encouraging powers such as Russia to acknowledge at least the principles of trusteeship by participating in the trusteeship system. (2) The European powers should be encouraged to endorse a general declaration on human rights that would apply no less to the internal colonies of Russia than to the outposts of the British Empire—in the words of the American draft submitted to the British, a declaration on 'liberty, independence, human rights and justice'.

By discussing the colonial problems in relation to specific territories such as the Pacific islands, and in relation to the Russian as well as the British Empire, the members of the committee had at least clarified the difficulties in pressing for universal independence. In this regard the thoughts of Cordell Hull were by no means as clear-cut or advanced as those of his colleagues. It is apparent, however, that he perceived some of the fundamental issues at stake. On the 10th of April 1943 he read to the committee the British draft declaration on 'Parent States'. He pointed out that the British did not accept the premise of international machinery to carry out the principles of trusteeship. Without being precise about the distinction of 'trust territories' and a general declaration, Hull hoped to progress merely by getting the British to commit themselves to a set of general principles that the Americans could insist upon at least in certain territories. Hull explained to the committee:

> [B]y the continual preachment of these policies and ideas, it would be possible to revitalize and revive the undertaking of international responsibility for dependent areas and thereby contribute to the general forward movement among the nations of the world in support of dependent peoples such as the committee had been talking about.[47]

Such was Hull's response to the lengthy deliberations of the Advisory Committee. He did not advance any more particular ideas. During the time that the British and members of his own staff analyzed the trusteeship proposals in detail, the Secretary of State merely braced himself, in his own phrase, for 'continual preachment'.

[47] 10 Apr., p. 20.

15

THE BRITISH REACTION TO THE 'DECLARATION ON NATIONAL INDEPENDENCE'. THE COLONIAL SECRETARY'S POLICY STATEMENT OF THE 13TH OF JULY 1943

ONE of the best summaries of the British reaction to the American blueprint for the colonial empires is this comment by Richard Law, Parliamentary Under-Secretary at the Foreign Office:

... I've seen Mr. Hull's draft: it's far worse than I had supposed. The whole tenour of it is to look forward to the ideal of the dissolution of the British Empire & the substitution for it of a multiplicity of national sovereignties. I don't see how we can possibly subscribe to this or anything like it.[1]

Nevertheless Law was not entirely discouraged. He believed that Hull simply had not thought through the implications of national independence for the colonies. It would mean, among other things, a multiplication of sovereign nations. Law and others held that if Hull and Roosevelt could be made to see this basic point the Americans would concur that 'self-government' should be substituted for 'independence'. The British Ambassador in Washington agreed with this interpretation. Halifax believed that the Americans and British could resolve the colonial issue if only they would put their minds to it. Lord Hailey, who had discussed the colonial question briefly with Roosevelt, also thought that men of goodwill reasoning together could surmount the problems of the colonial empires. Those who took a broad view of the question therefore did not think that it was futile to discuss the issue with the Americans. On the other hand some of the experts of both the Foreign Office and the Colonial Office believed that the American

[1] Minute by Law, 5 July 1943, U2936/G, FO 371/35311.

project was hopeless from the beginning. The Colonial Secretary himself was aghast that the subject of national independence for the colonies should even be broached. Ultimately the project came to a dead end in 1943 because Stanley proved inflexible. The internal debate in the British government at least clarified some basic notions about the British Empire's purpose and future. As a result of the deliberations in the spring and summer of 1943, later when the colonial question again raised its head the British had clearly in mind the issues at stake.

In the Foreign Office, Gladwyn Jebb, the head of the postwar planning section, first analyzed the American declaration. He noted straight away the basic departure from the Prime Minister's interpretation of the Atlantic Charter. By extending the principles of the Charter throughout the world, as Hull seemed bent on doing, there would be a direct collision between Roosevelt and Churchill as to legitimate interpretation. In any case Churchill would never agree to the use of 'independence' as Hull used it in this crucial passage: 'that opportunity to achieve independence for those peoples who aspire to independence shall be preserved, respected and made more effective.' Jebb went on to comment:

> This phrase might be interpreted in extremely unfortunate ways, and indeed it is worth while observing that if the principle had been adopted before 1863 the Southern States would have had every right to break away from the Union. It might also be interpreted as meaning that support should be given to Catalan Separatists and the Jews in Palestine, but the most likely guess is that the Americans want it to apply to India and Burma as well as to more specifically colonial areas. But equally it might be quoted as . . . support for Pakistan. In any case whatever [the] interpretation . . . it tends to encourage the notion that the hope for the future lies in a great multiplication of small national sovereignties.[2]

Jebb then complained about 'obscurities', but he did grant that, though the wording had been changed, the purpose of the body of the American declaration resembled that of the original British draft. The Americans had omitted, however,

---

[2] Memorandum by Jebb, 12 Apr. 1943, U1534, FO 371/35311. On his experience as head of the Economic and Reconstruction Department, see *The Memoirs of Lord Gladwyn* (London, 1972), chs. 8 and 9.

the phrase 'Parent States', which had been the great attraction to the British. The passage now read, 'Those of the United [Allied] Nations which have owing to past events become charged with responsibilities for the future of colonial areas.' The Americans wanted to enjoin these powers to fix definite dates for eventual independence. To British eyes this was one of the most objectionable features. The draft seemed also to suggest that the greater the wartime contribution, the greater the capacity for independence. 'This is not perhaps a bad idea in itself but it is a pretty dangerous one and might give rise to all kinds of unexpected difficulties.' He explained: 'The mere fact, for instance, that the King's African Rifles have fought toughly in this war is not necessarily a reason for giving full independence after it to Uganda.' Upon other points such as regional co-operation the two parties seemed to be closer to agreement. On the other hand the last part of the American draft dealt with specific trust territories to be created out of the former mandates and conquered enemy colonies.

All this leads up to a proposal to institute a kind of international colonial office (not it seems a kind of commission composed of representatives only but a definite *administration*) in which even ex-enemy powers may participate if they co-operate in carrying out the provisions of the Atlantic Charter. But this administration will in practice operate through 'Regional' Councils and it is not quite clear what the relations of the Regional Councils with a central administration will be.[3]

Specifically, Jebb found the Americans lamentably vague on three points. What did they mean 'in terms of geography' by: '(a) Peoples who aspire to independence, (b) Colonial peoples, and (c) Peoples "still unprepared for full independence"'?[4] If the Americans meant to apply the declaration to places such as Africa and South-East Asia, then in Jebb's opinion trouble could be anticipated from the other colonial powers, not least the Belgians and the Dutch.[5]

---

[3] Ibid. [4] Ibid.

[5] Ibid. On this point see also a minute by F. K. Roberts of 18 April in which he comments that the Belgians 'are strongly opposed to any changes in the position of the Belgian Congo in the direction of internationalisation', and that the Portuguese would resist any form of regional supervision 'for the simple reason that this would mean thinly-disguised Union control in Southern Africa'. This and other important minutes in U1753/G, FO 371/35311.

For the reasons summarized by Jebb, Eden telegraphed to Halifax on the 18th of April, 'We none of us like Hull's draft.'[6] The Ambassador was dismayed. Here was a project on which he had hoped to cement Anglo-American understanding. Why could his colleagues, despite British pride, not swallow a little American rhetoric in order to promote the common cause? 'Perhaps I am stupid,' he telegraphed to Eden, 'but I would like to put my thoughts to you.' Halifax did not interpret the declaration as an American effort to liquidate the British Empire; he rather saw it as an effort by Hull to educate American public opinion. As to the American addiction to resounding preambles, 'it does not appear to state anything that is not self-evident'. He thought his colleagues were reading a sinister intent where none existed.

[S]ince [the] object of the declaration is to satisfy public opinion (especially American public opinion) I should have hoped we might not have found ourselves unable to accept such a statement of general principles . . . even if it is presented in this Jeffersonian form so dear to the American heart.

The form adopted by Hull, the fact that you find it so repugnant, is no doubt typical of the different methods of approach of our two countries. This difference will be with us to the end of time. We are accustomed to proceed from the particular to the general but the Americans do exactly the opposite and unless there is real necessity the fact of our making difficulties about their broad statement of general principle is only to make them suspect that we do not sincerely share their laudable consideration or the desirable object that they have in view.[7]

Halifax commented on only one point of substance: timetables for independence. He dismissed the insistence on dates for decolonization as holding 'the place in American political thought that the cocktail does in their social life'. On this point Sir Alexander Cadogan commented about the American emphasis, 'silly'—'though Ld. Halifax seems to think this plays a useful part in tickling the American palate'. Cadogan, like Halifax, thought that the differences were more rhetorical than real. Basically he thought the British and Americans were attempting to say the same thing. Eventually the colonies should

6 Eden to Halifax, No. 2551, 17 Apr. 1943, FO 371/35311.
7 Halifax to Eden, 23 Apr. 1943, No. 1916, U2026/G, FO 371/35311.

be allowed a greater voice in their own affairs. In translating the document from American into English, 'independence', in Cadogan's view, should merely read 'self-government'.[8]

The Colonial Office took a far more cataclysmic view. With caustic irony Christopher Eastwood remarked that, though the word 'independence' occurred in the document no less than nineteen times, the Americans were in fact attempting to establish a sort of informal empire. 'Independence is a political catchword which has no real meaning apart from economics. The Americans are quite ready to make their dependencies politically "independent" while economically bound hand and foot to them and see no inconsistency in this.'[9] Though he did not pursue this line of reasoning, he clearly expressed what he believed would be the result of American enthusiasm for independence:

[W]hatever the exact meaning, this emphasis throughout on independence implies that the hope for the future lies in a great multiplication of small national sovereignties. Personally, I think this idea is disastrous. It is at least arguable that we are suffering at the moment from too much *in*dependence and too little *inter*dependence. The whole idea of fostering independence of individual Colonies is quite contradictory to the idea of regional association.[10]

Thus the official directly supervising the trusteeship issue in the Colonial Office believed that the United States and Britain were fundamentally at odds. Nevertheless he did not regard the matter quite so seriously as some of his colleagues. Eastwood thought it 'curious' (one of his favourite words) that the Americans would produce such a document, and 'embarrassing' that they would give such prominence to the Atlantic Charter. He thought it 'odd' that they would deliberately use such cumbersome phraseology and he saw no way to make palatable the 'highfalutin' preamble'. As for definite dates for independence, Eastwood attributed this aberration to the popularity of the

---

[8] Minute by Cadogan, 28 Apr. 1943, ibid. For a much more critical view, see especially the minute of Nevile Butler of the North American Department: 'The vital defect in Lord Halifax's telegram . . . seems to me that it ignores the obvious dangers that would arise from the Americans and we having quite different ideas in our minds as to the phrase "at the earliest possible or practicable moment".' 6 May 1943, ibid.

[9] Minute by Eastwood, 21 Apr. 1943, CO 323/1858/9057B.

[10] Ibid.

idea in the United States. He noted also that the Americans apparently wanted to create a 'super-body' over the regional commissions—'a sort of glorified Mandates Commission, only in this case with definite administrative functions'. Like his colleague Jebb in the Foreign Office, Eastwood wondered what the Americans had in mind, geographically, when they spoke of peoples not yet ready for independence but being released from political ties as a result of the war.

> I suppose this means the Japanese islands, the Italian colonies and possibly French Indo-China. Conceivably also it may mean Malaya, the N.E.I., Burma, Hong Kong, North Borneo and Sarawak. Indo-China has been exercising the Americans a good deal. . . . The idea of international trusteeship is certainly in their minds for these territories.[11]

In discussing the matter with Jebb, Eastwood said that the whole business sounded rather 'sinister'. Apart from territories of obvious concern to the United States such as the Japanese mandates, Eastwood believed that 'the Americans may in addition be aiming at certain parts of the French Empire'.[12]

The following minutes reflect the general sense of dismay in the Colonial Office. T. K. Lloyd wrote:

> [U]nless there is some prospect of getting the Americans to change the theme of their draft from 'independence' to 'self-government', the attempt to secure a joint declaration might as well be abandoned now . . .
> [T]he notion of a definite timetable of constitutional progress . . . is understood to be very dear to President Roosevelt, but it is alien to our conceptions . . .[13]

G. E. J. Gent, Assistant Under-Secretary, added:

> [T]he idea that British cols. can suitably be subject to similar treatment as enemy territories is a basic mistake. . . . the Prime Minister has already made it clear that he will not contemplate the rôle of presiding over the liquidation of the Colonial Empire . . .[14]

Sir George Gater, Permanent Under-Secretary, summed up:

> It now turns out that our initiative has been valueless. . . . The whole theme of the draft is wrongly conceived and exhibits on the

---

[11] Minute by Eastwood, 21 Apr. 1943, CO 323/1858/9057B.
[12] Minute by Jebb, 20 Apr. 1943, U1753, FO 371/35311.
[13] Minute by Lloyd, 21 Apr. 1943, CO 323/1858/9057B.
[14] Minute by Gent, 22 Apr. 1943, ibid.

part of the draftsmen ignorance of actual conditions in British Colonies. It is only necessary to think of applying its principles to Colonies like Mauritius to realize its full absurdity.[15]

After studying the American declaration, Gater wrote, he was 'left with a feeling of complete hopelessness'.

Lord Cranborne held similar sentiments to those reflected in the Colonial Office minutes. Though as Lord Privy Seal he no longer had a direct official interest in the colonial issue (in fact he wrote more than once privately that he felt uncomfortable making suggestions that technically fell within Stanley's jurisdiction) he continued to take an active part in the discussions. The American Ambassador, John G. Winant, apparently saw no breach in protocol in discussing Hull's draft declaration with him. Cranborne with characteristic candour went straight to the heart of the matter. He reported to Eden this conversation with the Ambassador:

I thought it best to be quite frank with him, and told him that though there was clearly much common ground between the two [draft declarations], there was also one essential difference. The American draft threw great stress on the word 'independence' in connection with the future of colonial peoples: the British draft never mentioned it. I thought personally that it would be impossible for us to accept any document that included that word.[16]

As if belabouring a fundamental truth, Cranborne felt it necessary to explain to Winant:

The colonial peoples were not ready for independence, and would not be ready for a very long time. If they were deprived of the protection of Britain, they would merely fall into the maw of some other country without the same experience of colonial government, and would be not better but worse off.

In these circumstances the use of the word [independence] would have deplorable results. It would have no basis of reality, and it would encourage a simmering agitation among the half-baked semi-Europeanized intelligenzia [*sic*] in colonial territories, who would try and play off the United States against us.[17]

Winant appeared to be receptive to this point of view and suggested that there might be more room for agreement on

[15] Minute by Gater, 27 Apr. 1943, ibid.
[16] Cranborne to Eden, 26 Apr. 1943, FO 371/35311.   [17] Ibid.

social and economic development in the colonies. This of course was very much what Cranborne and his colleagues liked to hear. The result of this exchange of ideas was to shift the locus of the diplomatic conversations from Washington to London, away from Lord Halifax to Ambassador Winant. As for Halifax, Cranborne thought it 'silly' that he could contemplate endorsing the American declaration on colonial independence. 'It would give the impression that we were completely on the run. Our friends would be horrified: our enemies would be jubilant: Parliament here would, I hope and think be disgusted. Why must we always toe the American line, especially on a question like this which is a British and not an American problem?'[18] Whatever his colleagues might think about Cranborne's advice on colonial matters, it was always candid. Unlike Oliver Stanley, he always met trusteeship problems head-on.

At a ministerial meeting on the 3rd of May, Stanley, Eden, Attlee, and Cranborne quickly decided not to respond to Halifax's plea for a more sympathetic understanding of the American position.[19] On the contrary, they formulated four fundamental objections. These points were incorporated into an *aide-mémoire* given to Winant on the 26th of May. The first reflected the belief that the far-reaching and ambitious scope of the American draft impaired its practicability.

1. The draft appears to relate not only to Colonial Dependencies but also to sovereign States which have lost their independence as a result of the war. It is impracticable and quite unrealistic to deal in one document with Czechoslovakia and the Gambia, Poland and Barbados.

The second point stated explicitly the objections to independence. The separatist element was a special Foreign Office concern.

2. The whole emphasis of the draft is on 'independence.' This would not be acceptable. The multiplication of small and completely independent entities all over the world could only be a retrograde step which would add to the difficulties of establishing an enduring security system. Is it really intended that every island in the West Indies should be independent and that St. Helena or

---

[18] Cranborne to Eden, 26 Apr. 1943, FO 371/35311.
[19] Minutes in CO 323/1858/9057B; FO 371/35311. Eastwood and Jebb attended this meeting.

the Seychelles should be independent? Incidentally, it is evident that the existing phrasing of the preamble—more especially the mention of peoples who aspire to independence—would encourage separatist tendencies all over the world.

Even stronger objections were put forward against timetables.

3. . . . A definite time-table of this kind would be quite unacceptable to His Majesty's Government, even if the word 'self-government' were substituted for the word 'independence.' This is not because His Majesty's Government desire for their own reasons to delay the introduction of self-government in any Colonial Dependencies administered by them as soon as they are ready for it, but because it is not possible to say when that time will be. The process of developing self-governing institutions must be one of trial and error. Many parts of the Colonial Empire are still so little removed from their primitive state that it must be a matter of many generations before they are ready for anything like full self-government. There are other parts inhabited by people of two or more different races and it is impossible to say how long it will take to weld together these so-called 'plural communities' into an entity capable of exercising self-government.

Last, the British rejoinder dealt with detached territories and possible international administration.

4. . . . Apparently international administration through Regional Commissions is contemplated. . . . It is not clear whether these Regional Commissions are intended to be separate from the purely consultative Regional Commissions. . . . It seems greatly preferable to confine the draft to general questions of Colonial administration without raising the specific question of individual ex-enemy dependencies, for which different policies may be required in different cases.[20]

Eden told Ambassador Winant that there seemed little chance for agreement, though he left the matter open.[21]

The Colonial Secretary now wanted to see the project dropped entirely. Having initially hoped to see the Americans merely espouse the concept of 'Parent States', he had witnessed Hull's attempt to transform the project into what he regarded as a muddled plan to liquidate the British Empire by trusteeship. Stanley's own ideas were clear-cut. Like Lord Cranborne,

[20] Ibid.
[21] Eden to Halifax, 26 May 1943, No. 569, U2381/130G, FO 371/35311.

he believed that the Colonial Empire was the business of the British, not the Americans. Unlike Lord Hailey, he did not especially concern himself with criticism of the Empire. He had said in a speech in Oxford in March:

> I am convinced that the first and fundamental principle is that the administration of the British Colonies must continue to be the sole responsibility of Great Britain. . . . I am going to confess that I am more interested in what Britain thinks of the British Empire than in what the United States thinks of it.[22]

This statement was hailed in the Conservative press as 'a valuable and timely service', in the words of the *Daily Mail*, which gave emphasis to the point by proclaiming '*Still Our Colonies*'.[23] The *Daily Sketch* carried a headline '*On Stanley On!*' and depicted the Colonial Secretary as a White Knight unfurling a banner, '*Let British Colonies Be British.*' Among the Labour newspapers, the *Daily Herald* commented that Stanley's echo of Churchill's determination to hold the line would do little to allay suspicions of British imperialism. 'He should realise that such arrogance contributes nothing to Anglo-American understanding.'[24] The press comments accurately portrayed Stanley's determination not to make a colonial declaration for the sake of Anglo-American understanding that might be at the expense of the British Colonial Empire.

Such bulwarks of the Empire as Halifax, Hailey, and Cranborne believed that discussions about the colonies with the Americans would at least clear the air of misunderstanding and suspicion. Halifax and Hailey thought it possible to reach agreement on a joint declaration. Cranborne was more sceptical, but he believed in frank discussion. Stanley, on the other hand, thought it better to have the British position left implicit rather than made explicit. This mode of operation eventually had unexpected consequences for the British because the Americans, believing them to be unresponsive, later in the year turned to the Russians and the Chinese to break down supposed British resistance. The colonial negotiations might have developed entirely differently had Cranborne remained Colonial

---

[22] *The Times*, 8 Mar. 1943.   [23] 8 Mar. 1943.
[24] *Daily Herald*, 9 Mar. 1943: various clippings in the Fabian Colonial Bureau Papers.

Secretary. As events transpired, Stanley stood at the helm of British colonial policy and steered a course away from Anglo-American collaboration and towards freedom of British action. It may be debatable whether another Colonial Secretary with other goals ultimately would have made any difference; but it is clear that in 1943 Stanley preferred a British rather than an Anglo-American course and deliberately chose to ignore signals from the Americans and from his colleagues.

Stanley's method of operation is vividly apparent from his handling of Hailey during the colonial discussions in the spring of 1943. Through Halifax's intervention and only because of it, the Colonial Office gave Hailey a copy of the American counterdraft and asked him to comment on it.[25] Hailey's analysis stands in marked contrast to the gloomy minutes of the Colonial Office officials. Christopher Eastwood noted, 'I gather that he does not think the [American] draft quite so impossible as we were inclined to think it.'[26] Hailey merely saw two questions of substance, the first relating to the colonies whose political ties were being broken as a result of the war.

> Mr. Hull may be thinking primarily of Korea, Eritrea or Libya, but there are some, at least among the United [Allied] Nations which will see here evidence of an intention to withdraw other areas also from the 'ties' which have bound them to colonial Powers. Nor, indeed, do I think that such an intention has been entirely absent from Mr. Cordell Hull's mind.
>
> It would be dangerous for us to agree to any declaration in the proposed form until we had some clearer indication on this point. It is one thing to propose international control for the ex-Italian areas; it is another to contemplate it for British, French or Dutch areas recovered from the Japanese.[27]

The second matter of substance pertained to the fixing of definite dates for independence. 'I have some doubt whether the President himself would insist on this; he has spoken rather about the necessity for a period of "graded education" than about the need for "liberation". . . . It is possible that the

---

[25] Halifax had requested in a telegram to Eden that Hailey give an independent view of the American draft declaration. The telegram was read at the ministerial meeting on 3 May and afterwards Stanley told Eastwood 'to show him [Hailey] the papers'. Minute by Eastwood, 6 May 1943, CO 323/1858/9057B.

[26] Ibid.

[27] Note by Hailey, 5 May 1943, CO 323/1858/9057B.

U.S.A. might accept here some alternative phrase . . .'[28] One question of 'form' disturbed Hailey. It consisted of 'the insistent repetition of the term "independence"'. Some of the Colonial Office officials were astonished that he regarded such a fundamental point as one of form rather than substance; but in Hailey's opinion it depended on one's vantage point. With breadth of view he believed that the British and the Americans had more in common than otherwise, and that common sense would render the difference rhetorical rather than substantial. Specifically, he believed that most Americans used the word 'independence' as synonymous with 'self-government'. He did not think the distinction should be pressed. Self-government in the British Empire meant the process of gaining complete autonomy. Common sense and historical precedent indicated that this meant, in effect, independence. Here was his key point: 'To imply that there is a distinction between self-government and independence suggests a refinement which will be viewed with a great deal of suspicion in the U.S.A.' Though he saw the objections to 'independence', he thought the concept might be negotiable in the manner of Churchill and Roosevelt:

> One has to admit at the same time that the use of the word 'independence' may create an awkward reaction in some of the colonies. We might perhaps endeavour to meet the difficulty by substituting in regard to the colonies the phrase 'the exercise of the right to choose the form of government under which they shall live'—the term used in the Atlantic Charter.[29]

After weighing the objections to a joint declaration, Hailey nevertheless thought it would be better to try to reach agreement with the Americans than to make a unilateral declaration.

> [T]o Americans a declaration of this nature is rather of the nature of an advertisement of the character of the party making it than a guarantee of performance. In short, it will be almost as difficult to frame a 'unilateral' declaration that would carry weight with Americans, or which would not be scrutinized with suspicion by them, as it would be to agree to a form of declaration with them.[30]

Hailey thus believed that a joint colonial declaration was both possible and desirable.

[28] Note by Hailey, 5 May 1943, CO 323/1858/9057B.
[29] Ibid.   [30] Ibid.

The Colonial Office officials believed that the question of independence was a real one and should not be confused with self-government. With due deference, Christopher Eastwood noted:

It seems to me utterly wrong to set up independence as the goal for the greater number of the Colonies and even if we had said something of this sort in the past (which I do not think we have) I think it would be a great mistake to say it again.

I do not think the phrase 'self-government' is really much better. I suppose it does leave a loop-hole for arguing that what we really mean is only local self-government, but that would not be a very honest interpretation of the phrase.

Myself I believe that 'independence' and 'self-government' both imply substantially the same goal, namely fifty different self-contained sovereignties, which would be disastrous. The sooner we start emphasizing the importance of solidarity and '*inter*dependence' the better.[31]

Here clearly was a sharp difference of opinion, the same difference, many would have argued, that existed on a larger scale between Britain and the United States. Hailey at least wanted to talk it out. Stanley would have none of it. He minuted that Hailey had contributed nothing of substance, and 'I wholly disagree with the emphasis'. He instructed that Hailey's memorandum should not even be circulated.[32]

By late May Stanley was becoming more 'pessimistic' than ever about the chances of a joint declaration with the United States.[33] The Foreign Secretary got no response from the American Ambassador about the 'Four Basic Objections' to Hull's counterdraft. Eastwood noted in late June, 'the rabbit is slow in coming out of Mr. Winant's hat'.[34] If they had known why, the reason would have appeared extraordinary to British officials: the American Ambassador had never forwarded the *aide-mémoire* of the 26th of May to Washington.

In any case Stanley saw no chance whatever of bringing the Americans round to his point of view. He believed that it was none of their business and decided to make his own declaration.

[31] Minute by Eastwood, 6 May 1943, ibid.
[32] Minute by Stanley, 10 May 1943, ibid.
[33] See Jebb's minute of 27 May 1943 recording a conversation with Eastwood FO 371/35311.
[34] Minute by Eastwood, 30 June 1943, CO 323/1858/9057B.

Unlike Hailey, who thought that a unilateral statement would merely arouse American distrust, Stanley felt it would be better to make a firm but ambiguous stand lest the Americans try to force unacceptable commitments. On the 13th of July 1943 he made a major policy statement.

The occasion was a Parliamentary debate on colonial expenditures. Since Stanley's statement set the main lines of British policy for the rest of the war, both the timing and the substance of the declaration are important. Some contemporary observers of the colonial question believed it ill timed, and both highhanded and vague. One member of Parliament stated, 'It is a bad way of making such an announcement.'[35] He referred to Stanley's method. The Colonial Secretary had introduced an issue of substance at the *end* of a long debate, as if almost in passing, and as if to give no time to have it questioned. The timing of the statement also drew the wrath of the Foreign Office officials, who had no advance notice. Nevile Butler of the North American Department sputtered:

> The failure of the Colonial Office to cooperate with us in this and other matters is really exceedingly disheartening. It is common knowledge and was commonly agreed that American misapprehensions about our Colonial Empire required exceptional and sustained counter efforts on our part . . . this did not render the procedure less amateurish or uncooperative on the part of the Colonial Office. . . . Stanley feels at perfect liberty to make speeches . . . with reference to America without any previous consultation with us.[36]

In defence of Stanley, he had consulted Churchill and Eden. 'We considered that at this juncture there would be advantage in giving public expression to our views as to the lines along which we hope progress can be made.'[37] There was nothing in the statement which of itself either of them found objectionable. As for timing, Stanley professed to have been drawn into making the statement by questions during the debate. Critics pointed out that it was highly unfortunate that, not only had the Colonial Secretary allowed his declaration to become obscured by the issues of a long debate, but he also chose to make the announcement during a major event of the war, the inva-

---

[35] *Parliamentary Debates* (Commons), 13 July 1943, c. 144.
[36] Minute by Butler, 16 July 1943, U3152, FO 371/35311.
[37] Eden to Halifax, 16 July 1943, No. 4695, U3152, FO 371/35311.

sion of Sicily. Stanley's speech at the time thus failed to attract any significant notice in the United States. There is no indication that the Colonial Secretary desired to call particular attention to the importance of his comments. As he said during the debate, 'There are no fundamental changes.'[38]

The substance of Stanley's declaration consisted of an endorsement of the idea of regional commissions. Britain would work in co-operation with neighbouring and friendly nations in colonial areas.

Developments of modern transport and modern communications have brought close together vast areas which before were widely separated. Many of the problems to-day are common problems and can only be solved in co-operation, for problems of security, of transport, of economics, of health, etc., transcend the boundaries of political units.

He proposed positive action, but without any suggestion of specific territories:

His Majesty's Government would therefore welcome the establishment of machinery which will enable such problems to be discussed and to be solved by common efforts. What they have in mind is the possibility of establishing Commissions for certain regions. These Commissions would comprise not only the States with Colonial Territories in the region, but also other States which have in the region a major strategic or economic interest.

He carefully stated a key point:

While each State would remain responsible for the administration of its own territory, such a Commission would provide effective and permanent machinery for consultation and collaboration so that the States concerned might work together to promote the well being of the Colonial territories.

Not failing to take account of colonial peoples themselves, Stanley stated:

An important consideration in designing the machinery of each Commission will be to give to the people of the Colonial territories in the region an opportunity to be associated with its work.

[38] *Parliamentary Debates* (Commons), 13 July 1943, c. 144.

In conclusion Stanley commented obliquely on the mandates commission:

> In this way it would be possible to have international co-operation which consisted of something more than theoretical discussion but would be able to grapple with realities and get down to the solution of individual problems.[39]

In response to questions, the Colonial Secretary refused to go into further detail. In the discussion he made this point, which should be emphasized because in the Colonial Office minutes it is clear that it was uppermost in his mind: '*We retain complete control of our administration.*'[40] Refusing to be drawn out by questions on international collaboration raised by Creech Jones and others, Stanley managed to steer the discussion back to such topics as the fish in Lake Nyasa. All in all he gave what one member of Parliament referred to as a 'very luminous and exhilarating speech'. He did establish unequivocally that Britain favoured regional commissions in colonial areas. Implicitly this meant the replacement of the mandates system and international accountability by regional, voluntary, collaboration.[41]

---

[39] *Parliamentary Debates* (Commons), 13 July 1943, c. 142.

[40] Ibid., c. 144. Italics added.

[41] Stanley was a great believer in keeping key assumptions of policy implicit rather than making them explicit. The question arose, what should the colonial governors be told? Sir George Gater posed the proposition directly to Stanley: should they be told that the Colonial Office had no intention of making the colonies *accountable* to either the commissions or to an international body? Even within the secret councils of the Colonial Office Stanley preferred to leave it, to use his own word, 'implicit'. Minutes by Gater and Stanley, 14 July 1943, CO 323/1858/9057B.

16

THE MILITARY ELEMENT IN
ROOSEVELT'S TRUSTEESHIP
PLANNING

JUST as the hardening of Churchill's determination to hold the imperial line can be viewed in relation to events such as the British victory in North Africa at El Alamein on the 2nd of November 1942, so the development in precision of Roosevelt's post-war planning can be seen in the context of the turn of the tide in the Pacific and the Japanese defeat at Guadalcanal two weeks later.[1] In the month following Churchill's speech resolving not to liquidate the British Empire, Roosevelt on the 23rd of December 1942 instructed his military staff to study the implementation of his idea of an international police force. In a memorandum for Admiral William D. Leahy, the President's Naval Aide wrote:

[T]he President stated that we must keep in mind the peace negotiations and that he visualizes some sort of international police force will come out of the war. Pursuing this thought further, the President stated he wished you to have a study made by the Joint Chiefs of Staff to the end that when the peace negotiations are upon us we will be decided in our own minds where it is desired that 'International Police Force' air facilities be located throughout the world; this plan to be without regard to current sovereignty.[2]

The President's directive caused consternation among the Joint Chiefs of Staff. Did he mean by 'police force' a military force to be created out of the armed services of the United States? What were the civil as opposed to the military functions of a police force? By 'international' did the President mean eventually to include the present enemies of the United States? Did he have in mind air bases for commercial use as well as

---

[1] The point about El Alamein and Churchill's 'First Minister' speech is made by Henry Pelling, *Winston Churchill* (London, 1974), p. 497.

[2] Memorandum for Admiral Leahy by Captain John L. McCrea, Naval Aide to the President, 28 Dec. 1942, Roosevelt Papers MR Box 167; JCS CCS 360 (12–9–42) Sec. 1; USN GB 450.

military aviation? Did he want a list of bases? If so, by what criteria should the bases be selected? On grounds of national security? At a meeting of the Joint Chiefs which considered the ambiguity of the directive, Admiral E. J. King reflected on the history of the British Empire: 'He cited the many British coaling stations throughout the world for commercial use which eventually became of Military importance.'[3] The President had given the Joint Chiefs a large assignment, especially since they did not have the benefit of his ideas on trusteeship as the master solution to the political and military problems of the world.

The concept of trusteeship was alien to American military thought. In the proceedings of the Joint Chiefs in 1943 it is conspicuous by its absence. On the 15th of March Lieutenant General S. D. Embick, Major General Muir S. Fairchild, and Vice-Admiral Russell Willson of the Joint Chiefs Strategic Survey Committee completed a report on the international police force. These officers are of considerable interest in regard to trusteeship because in the same month they began service as liaison officers to the State Department on general security matters which included the future of the mandated territories.[4] In their report to the Joint Chiefs, nowhere did they mention the word 'trusteeship'. Though they were prepared to make some concessions to a future international organization, 'in the last analysis national security must dominate'. Their ideas about post-war security were straightforward. The world would be divided into three zones in which the following powers would keep the peace:

American Zone—assigned to the United States.

Europe, Africa and Middle East Zone—assigned to Great Britain and Russia.

Far East Zone—assigned to Russia, United States, Great Britain, and China.

In the Pacific, they dealt with the Japanese mandated islands, among others:

From among the Japanese mandate or other islands which come

[3] JCS 65th Meeting, 9 Mar. 1943, JCS 183/1 CCS360 (12–9–42) Sec. 1.
[4] The three officers comprised the Joint Strategic Survey Committee and represented the Joint Chiefs as a single member on the Advisory Committee. See Notter, *Postwar Foreign Policy Preparation*, p. 76.

under our control in the process of defeating Japan we should assure that none is returned to Japan or given up to any other possible aggressor nation, and that we select, equip, and fortify a line of U.S. Naval and air bases west from Hawaii to and including the Philippines, and Bonins. These are required primarily for national defense, but will also be available for use by any international military forces, and for U.S. commercial purposes.[5]

Direct control was the military solution to the Japanese mandates. The three officers also emphasized certain other key areas such as the Galapagos and Clipperton Island off the coast of Mexico,[6] where the United States should obtain long term air rights for both military and commercial purposes. This was the genesis of the Joint Chiefs' master plan by which air bases in all oceans and continents interlocked in a global security system that established (a) points required for the direct defence of the United States; (b) areas or bases where defence responsibility might be shared with other powers; and (c) islands or territories that should be effectively neutralized. The system was not static. It would evolve from (a) the time that the allied powers defeated Germany but would still be at war with Japan; (b) the transitional period to peace after the defeat of both Axis powers; and (c) the period in the future when machinery for international cooperation could be established. In this painstaking scheme trusteeship played no part, but the Joint Chiefs had faithfully elaborated half of Roosevelt's equation for world peace. In his mind, military precautions did not necessarily contradict international organization and territorial trusteeships. By the time of the Cairo Conference the plan had been refined into a highly sophisticated global defence scheme.

During the formulation of defence strategy in 1943, the Navy gave particular attention to the problem of the Pacific. At the request of the Commander in Chief and Chief of Naval Operations, the General Board in February 1943 began the preparation of an independent study. The purpose was to recommend policies 'that the Navy should follow in its negotiations with

[5] 'Air Routes Across the Pacific and Air Facilities, International Police Force', JCS 183/5 CCS360 (12–9–42).
[6] There is an entire file on the question of Clipperton Island in the Roosevelt papers. It received considerable attention because of its supposed value to the British as part of a chain of bases linking the South-West Pacific, the Caribbean, and England, and by-passing the United States. Roosevelt Papers MR Box 162.

other government departments and foreign governments'.[7] The Secretary of the Navy, Frank Knox, wrote to Roosevelt that he now had a keen interest in the question. Why not make a deal with the British so that the United States could annex the Japanese mandates?

Would it be out of order or untimely for us to attempt an understanding with the British that they will support and approve after the war, our control and possession of all of the Japanese mandated islands in the Pacific and agree to work out with us, an understanding under which we would be assured the possession of a base in Northwest Africa, at a place to be mutually agreed upon by the two powers. . . . I am rather inclined to think we can get these concessions out of England far more readily and easily now than when the war is over when the British needs and reliance upon us becomes less.[8]

The President responded immediately, on the date of Eden's arrival in Washington, the 12th of March:

I think the Navy had better do nothing further in regard to understanding with the British about Japanese Mandated Islands in the Pacific—in view of the fact that I am anxious to clean up the problem of all the islands in the Pacific, and the British would probably be delighted to confine the discussions to the Japanese Mandated Islands.

I think I had better handle the discussions myself without bringing the two Navies into it, though I may later ask for naval advice on the subject of which islands should be made police stations. I think we will have no trouble about arranging for mutual use of the islands.[9]

The President wanted no interference in his negotiations with the British. He did desire precise confirmation about the value of certain strategic island groups.

Under the direction of Admiral Thomas C. Hart, the General Board study comprehensively analyzed the international policeman proposal and the related strategic issues. The Navy deeply distrusted international organization as an instrument of collec-

[7] King to Secretary of the Navy, 9 Feb. 1943, USN GB 450. For a valuable analysis of how the Air Force similarly began post-war planning, see Perry M. Smith, *The Air Force Plans for Peace* (Baltimore, 1970).

[8] Knox to Roosevelt, 10 Mar. 1943, Roosevelt Papers MR Box 162; USN GB 450.   [9] Roosevelt to Knox, 12 Mar. 1943, ibid.

tive security. About the international police force, the first of three major reports concluded on the 20th of March:

A study of the history of the League of Nations clearly shows the difficulties of creating and putting into effect such an international organization. Without skepticism as to the eventual success of some kind of an international organization for collective security, the Board's firm opinion now is that years will elapse before any such league or council can be completely organized and made effective.[10]

Rather than relying immediately on an untested international policeman, the General Board recommended caution and patience. 'To weld elements from many nations into a force having the international rather than the national viewpoint is something never before attempted. The process will be a long one and undue haste will greatly increase the risk of failure.'[11]

In regard to negotiations with other departments of the government, which the Navy regarded as in the same category as foreign governments, the General Board repeated similar advice:

The Navy must retain a background of realism in all negotiations with other Government Departments, as well as with Foreign Governments. It is submitted, that the situation, now and as is clearly foreseeable, calls for effective combination as between Britain, China, Russia and the United States, for the specific post-war purpose of keeping good order over such portions of the world as involve any danger of outbreaks that might menace the general peace. Any world security organization should be built up slowly and deliberately step by step, based on the experiences of the past and the then current problems.[12]

After recommending a general division of post-war world-wide responsibilities between Britain and the United States (in a way that could eventually include Russia and China) the General Board in an annex containing 'material which should be less widely known', projected American bases (a) in the *Pacific* area (1) to the *south*, to cover Panama by such island bases as Clipperton and the Galapagos; (2) to the *south-west*, to within easy contact with the British Dominions, by an extensive

[10] Chairman, General Board, to Secretary of the Navy, 20 Mar. 1943, USN GB 450.　　　　　　　[11] Ibid.　　　　　　　[12] Ibid.

list of eleven island groups, including the Marquesas, Samoa, New Hebrides, and the Solomons; (3) to the *west*, to within easy contact with the Dutch East Indies, China, and covering the Philippines by bases on such islands as the Marshalls, the Gilbert and Ellices, Wake, Truk, Guam, Batan, Formosa, and even Shanghai; (4) and to the *north-west*, in easy contact with Russia to include the Aleutians. Passing to the *Atlantic*, (b) the General Board (1) to the *south-east* projected bases throughout the Caribbean and in Brazil; and in Liberia and Dakar, and even Natal; and (2) to the *north-east* in Newfoundland, Greenland, and Iceland.[13] Like the British Empire, the United States found its defensive requirements were world-wide.

In the second of the three reports, dated the 27th of March, the General Board dealt in detail with the islands north of the Equator. Japan's 'flagrant and deliberate violations' of the mandate could only mean revocation.

It is scarcely conceivable that the terms imposed upon Japan as a result of the present war will permit her to remain established in any capacity in the Pacific islands mandated to her after the last war. . . . For reasons of our own security, and because we are likely to be committed to the protection of the Philippines after they have become independent, the United States is vitally interested in the form which a readjustment in control of these islands may take.[14]

For the same reasons it was undesirable to leave the Bonins in Japanese hands. Japanese control of the Bonins would menace the Philippines. Therefore the Bonins would be taken away from Japan and given to whatever power would control the Marianas.

That other power is logically the United States. Guam belongs to us and again will be administered by us when it has been wrested from enemy hands. The island is one of the Marianas and, as has been demonstrated in the past, is potentially menaced by the other islands of that group unless the same power controls them all. It follows naturally that the United States should control the entire Marianas, the control of the Bonins should also pass to the United States.

Because of their geographical position with relation to the

13 Annex A, ibid.
14 Chairman, General Board, to Secretary of the Navy, 27 Mar. 1943, USN GB 450.

Marianas, the Philippines and Hawaii, the same military principle applies in the case of all the islands mandated to Japan; the control of the whole properly belongs to the United States.[15]

With the logic of interdependence virtually all of the islands north of the Equator would become American. The General Board therefore felt it necessary to disclaim motives of imperialism.

None of the islands in question possesses natural features of value from other than the military standpoint. Both from the economic and the political standpoints they are a liability to the nation charged with their control and administration. The transfer to the United States of any or all of these islands with all that is implied therein cannot constitute territorial aggrandisement. Japan has frankly referred to them as 'unsinkable aircraft carriers' and their severance from her control will be part of her disarmament.[16]

In summary:

The General Board recommends that planning for post-war conditions provide for United States possession of:

(a) All the former German islands mandated to Japan by the League of Nations, i.e., the Marshalls, Carolines and Marianas (except Guam).

(b) The Bonin or Ogasawara Group, the Volcano Islands, Marcus Island, and Ituaba Island, at present owned or controlled by Japan.[17]

After all, these territories were being won, in the General Board's ringing words, by 'effort, blood and treasure'.

In the third report, dated the 6th of April, the General Board made sweeping suggestions for changes in status of the islands south of the Equator. Here the political situation was so complicated that only transfers of sovereignty could stabilize the area. 'The political and administrative situation is extremely complex because several nations have interests therein and there are too many governmental organizations over the small, scattered land masses and their small populations.'[18] Again, the General

---

[15] Ibid.   [16] Ibid.   [17] Ibid.
[18] Chairman, General Board, to Secretary of the Navy, 6 Apr. 1943, USN GB 450.

Board pointed out that changes in sovereignty would not be made in a spirit of imperialism:

> Since the political changes recommended . . . will not constitute territorial aggrandizement at the expense of a defeated enemy, the Board is of the opinion that such changes conform to the spirit of the Atlantic Charter. There will be little if any economic value or advantage involved, and the assumption of sovereignty will mean an increased burden of administration.[19]

Samoa was one particular island group where the United States should assume the financial and moral responsibility. The General Board felt it was unfortunate that the Samoan people were divided under the sovereignty of two nations.

> It seems clear that the Samoa Islands should be under the control of one nation and, as the United States in the discharge of its postwar military responsibilities for good order will have to continue its expenditure of money and effort in both subdivisions of these islands, it is logical that the control should be entrusted to this country.[20]

North and west of Samoa, the Line Islands, Ellice and Gilberts, and other groups near the Equator might also become American possessions. The General Board members also gave particular attention to the islands in the Pacific under French sovereignty. These groups constituted 'a military situation incompatible with the probable responsibilities of the United States in these areas'. France might not be able to regain even Indo-China, and her ties with the islands were weakening.

> The islands in question, the Marquesas, Society, and Tubuai Islands, the Tuamotu Archipelago, and the New Caledonia–Loyalty Islands group, lie in areas detached from other French interests or responsibilities. This detachment is in itself a strong argument against any future continuance of their control by the French. . . .[21]

In summary:

(a) The transfer to the United States by Britain or the British Dominions of the sovereignty of British Samoa, British Line Islands, Ellice Islands, Gilbert Islands, British Phoenix Islands, and the Union Islands.

---

[19] Chairman, General Board, to Secretary of the Navy, 6 Apr. 1943, USN GB 450.   [20] Ibid.   [21] Ibid.

(b) The transfer to the United States by France of the sovereignty of the Marquesas, Society, and Tubuai Islands, the Tuamotu Archipelago, and the New Caledonia Colony which includes the New Caledonia group, the Loyalty group, and the Wallis Islands.

(c) The transfer to Britain by France of its interest in the condominium in the New Hebrides Islands.[22]

The members of the General Board might have been able to satisfy themselves that they were not motivated by imperialism, but it is highly unlikely that they would have convinced the British, not to mention the French.

On the 12th of June 1943 the President inquired about the Navy's conclusions as to the relative strategic importance of the Pacific islands. He asked specifically what islands of the South-East Pacific might be of special value as air bases. He had in mind especially two island groups in French Polynesia, the Tuamotu Archipelago, and the Marquesas. It seemed to Roosevelt that these two particular groups held the key of control over strategic routes in the South Pacific. So advanced were his ideas in this regard that he now suggested that air transport experts actually visit the islands and report on the local geography. The President wanted 'all the facts' before final discussions took place about specific base sites the United States should seek to control after the war.[23]

The Navy responded to the President's inquiry by sending him the three reports of the General Board. Admiral A. J. Hepburn, writing on behalf of the General Board on the 18th of June, explained that the Tuamotu and Marquesas had been listed for acquisition. He also pointed out that the Board's recommendations were 'sufficiently comprehensive' to cover post-war commercial aviation as well as military requirements. When the three reports reached Roosevelt's desk, they formed, in fact, a blueprint for transforming most of the Pacific into an American lake.[24]

Roosevelt immediately curtailed the scope of the Navy's ambitions. Among other things, he saw that the cost of the

---

[22] Ibid.

[23] Roosevelt to Secretary of the Navy, 12 June 1943, Roosevelt Papers MR Box 162; USN GB 450.

[24] Memorandum for the Secretary of the Navy by Admiral Hepburn, 18 June 1943, ibid.

far-reaching annexationist program would be enormous. He wrote on the 30th of June 1943:

The sweeping changes in sovereignty recommended by the Board may not be attainable, and, from an economic point of view, all of the acquisitions recommended may not be desirable. It seems to me important, therefore, that we should make up our minds now which individual islands, because of their geography and location, promise to be of value as commercial airports in the future. After a study of charts and distances, a board of commercial aviation experts should actually visit the islands we select as having possible value in the future. Could we not spare one of the older Coast Guard cutters from a strictly war mission to this important exploration?[25]

In response to the President's suggestion about maps and charts, the Secretary of the Navy now forwarded statistical data about air routes from the Panama Canal and South America to New Zealand and Australia.[26] This information did not please Roosevelt. Among other things, the General Board based the calculations of long-distance flights upon wartime experience rather than investigating post-war possibilities. Roosevelt also thought that the Navy's preoccupation with the war in the Pacific had prevented the General Board from seeing the potential of the South-East Pacific in proper perspective. In a severely worded memorandum of the 29th of July 1943 the President criticized the General Board's assessments:

I note that all of their suggestions are based on the assumption that 2100 sea miles is the longest single leg that can be flown with profitable pay load on board.

That may be and probably is true today but the consideration of these bases must take into account the probability that the development of planes will increase this distance by many hundreds of miles in the reasonable near future. It is probably safe to say that the profitable distance twenty years ago was not much over 500 miles.

Therefore, I do not want the committee of civilians who are to make a study of this route to be bound by existing profitable distances.[27]

Roosevelt went on to say that he was not much interested in the extreme southern route via Easter Island. In his view 'the Canal Zone will become commercially a crossroads with much commerce, and the route from there via the Galapagos and the

[25] Memorandum by Roosevelt, 30 June 1943, USN GB 450.
[26] Knox to Roosevelt, 26 July 1943, with enclosures, USN GB 450.
[27] Roosevelt to Knox, 29 July 1943, USN GB 450.

Marquesas to Australia should be studied'. This route would have the additional advantage of touching Latin America in places such as Colombia and Ecuador. He rebuked the General Board for not taking sufficient account of the crucial area in the South-East Pacific. 'I do not quite know why the General Board takes no interest in the Central and South Pacific Islands from the naval point of view. Two years ago we took no interest in the Solomons or Bora-Bora, from a naval point of view, but I understand we are now doing it.'[28]

Thus by mid-1943 Roosevelt had clear-cut ideas about the future of trans-oceanic routes. It would not be possible, if only for economic reasons, to acquire islands for base sites throughout all of the southern as well as the northern Pacific. With the guarantee that American power would make the North Pacific secure by the events of the war, the President set out to establish which bases in the South Pacific would be indispensable for American military security and future commercial development. He directed that Rear Admiral Richard E. Byrd of Antarctic fame lead an expedition to make an on-the-spot inspection of possible base sites.

The Byrd mission consisted of fourteen members—six civilians, four Army officers, and four Naval officers, plus officers and enlisted men for specialized work such as surveying and photography. The civilian members of the mission consisted of representatives from Northeast Airlines, Transcontinental and Western Air, United Air Lines, Pan American Airways, American Air Lines, and the American Export Airlines. The mission left Balboa in the Canal Zone on the 5th of September aboard the *USS Concord*. As special equipment they took with them a landing barge, two aeroplanes for aerial photography, surveying and movie equipment, four rubber boats with outboard motors, and two jeeps. They first visited the Galapagos Islands and then proceeded to Clipperton. In the Marquesas group they observed 'extreme dissatisfaction with the French regime . . . among all of the native population'. In the Tuamotu Archipelago they noted the popularity of American songs such as 'You are my Sunshine' and 'Alexander's Ragtime Band'. At another group in the Society Islands they remarked that 'the natives . . . went wild with joy and amazement' as

[28] Ibid.

their jeeps rolled ashore. Though their mission was not political, anyone who read their report would have gathered that an American presence in the South Pacific would not be unwelcome to the islanders. The expedition arrived back at Balboa on the 24th of November. The subsequent voluminous report consisted of six books, the last being a 78-page geo-political review by Admiral Byrd on the strategic value of the islands.[29]

Byrd summarized his findings in a personal letter to Roosevelt. Though the date of the letter, the 14th of April 1944, falls several months beyond the chronological scope of the problems now under consideration, Byrd's ideas had been shaped during the time of the expedition in the autumn of 1943. His thought reflects an awareness of the importance of the timing and psychology of any possible American expansion or 'consolidation' in the Pacific. Byrd wrote to the President, addressing him 'Dear Franklin':

Knowing of your great interest in what islands and other areas we should get control of after the war, I went deeply into the job you gave me in the Pacific and tried to think it through to rock bottom. My study shows that you were right—that you were years ahead of all of us, even those concentrating in the overall aspects of post-war strategy and international air commerce.

Not until I had made a thorough analysis of the whole problem did I fully comprehend the reasons that brought you to consider this matter of such transcendent importance to the future of this nation.

My findings (arrived at objectively, I can assure you) show that you were entirely correct about Clipperton and the strategic and commercial value of certain key islands in the Tuamotu, Marquesas and Society Groups, as well as about the feasibility of new air routes to the Southwest Pacific. There can be no question about this.

Byrd now boiled down the significance and result of the mission:

There were 130 islands in the group that we investigated. You will recall that you asked us to assess these groups and individual islands from the standpoint of national defense as well as air commerce. . . . I knew that with your foresight you would be interested in the *permanent* value of islands and other areas throughout the

[29] The secret Byrd report, entitled 'Report of Survey of Certain Pacific Islands by Special Mission', 15 Dec. 1943, and correspondence pertaining to the mission are in the files of the Chief of Naval Operations, Washington Navy Yard.

world rather than their *temporary* value. Regarding this matter of permanent value of islands, we know that defense plans may change with the passage of time, *but that the importance of neutralizing or keeping control of certain strategic islands is not so subject to change.* . . . In this connection, there is one significant agreement we should attempt to get . . . namely, *that after this war the sovereignty of no island in the Pacific be changed without full agreement from the United States.*

Byrd dwelt on the need to avoid the stigma of imperialism.

We know that the timing of our efforts to neutralize or control island or other areas is of the utmost importance. We cannot allow ourselves to be charged with imperialism, aggrandizement or the abandonment of the tenets of democracy in taking islands from our weak or prostrate allies. Nor can we disturb the solidarity with our more powerful allies by aggressive or tactless methods. Nevertheless, in spite of those and other limiting factors in getting control of islands, our study shows that we have ahead of us unparalleled opportunities which may never come again that this war has developed for the United States.[30]

Byrd concluded his letter by advising Roosevelt to know '*exactly what air routes, islands, landing fields, strategic areas, etc., are essential for the combined purposes of commerce and political and military strategy . . .*'.

The timing of Roosevelt's acquisition of precise information can be dated exactly. On the 6th of November 1943 the Joint Chiefs completed the comprehensive study on United States military requirements for air bases, facilities, and operating rights in foreign territories. The heart of the plan was a far-flung chain of bases. To meet Roosevelt's specification, the military requirements were divided into two categories: (a) those essential for the defence of the United States; and (b) those necessary for the functions of an international police force. In fact the distinction merely meant a gradation of priorities. It also appeared to solve the politically explosive issue of arrogation of sovereignty. The United States would lease bases, not annex them, and many of them would be leased under the auspices of an international authority, not the United States. This method had the advantage, in the words of the Joint Chiefs, of enhancing 'Our reputation for integrity of international agreement and traditional lack of imperialistic

[30] Byrd to Roosevelt, 14 Apr. 1944, Roosevelt Papers MR Box 162.

ambition'. The prospective bases stretched throughout the world. On maps coloured in shades enthralling to any strategist, the bold outlines of outer and inner rims of defence areas encompassed bases in American territories, the routes of which interlocked with bases on foreign soil. In the east, the defence line ran through points in Iceland, the Azores, Madeira, the west coast of Africa, and Ascension Island. In the west, the outmost western defence line ran from Alaska through Attu, Paramashiru, the Bonin Islands, the Philippines, New Britain, the Solomons, Suva, Samoa, Tahiti, Marquesas, Clipperton, and the Galapagos to the west coast of South America. In the Atlantic area, secondary locations would exist in Greenland, Labrador, Newfoundland, Bermuda, Trinidad, French Guiana, and Brazil. In the Pacific area, bases would be required in the Gilbert Islands, Canton Island, Christmas Island, Ecuador or Peru, Guatemala, and Mexico. These were merely the outer rims which were interconnected by complex networks. The types of bases would vary, of course, depending on the need for long range super-heavy bombers, radar control, glider and rocket bombs, or whatever other weapons and defence systems might prove necessary. The Joint Chiefs recognized that the defence requirements would change in time. The periods they envisaged were:

(a) First period—Enforced peace in Europe and war in the Pacific;
(b) Second period—World-wide peace enforced . . . pending establishment of a world-wide organization for collective security;
(c) Third period—Peace maintained by formally established world-wide machinery.

Until the millennium, the United States would be prepared to repulse any attack by whatever means from any direction.[31]

Roosevelt expressed satisfaction with the Joint Chiefs' study. He thought it was 'very clear and excellent'. That he examined it with care is obvious from a memorandum to the Joint Chiefs asking them to include the Marquesas and the Tuamotu groups in the United States' sphere of influence. On the map he adjusted colors from blue to green in the area east of the Samoan

---

[31] For all this material, see JCS 570 CCS360 (12/9/42) sect. 2.

Islands, another indication of his fixation on the South-East Pacific as having a particular strategic significance.[32] On the eve of the Cairo Conferences, the President now had the precise military information he required. Though Roosevelt might talk about trusteeship territories in slapdash fashion with Churchill and Chiang Kai-shek, he knew precisely what issues were at stake for American security.

[32] Memorandum by Roosevelt, 23 Nov. 1943, ibid., and Roosevelt Papers MR Box 162 f. 5.

17

THE CAIRO DECLARATION
THE DISMEMBERMENT OF JAPAN'S
EMPIRE

LIKE the Atlantic Charter, the Cairo Declaration of the 1st of December 1943 holds a place of ambiguous importance in the history of trusteeship during the war. A Washington journalist on the political right, David Lawrence, gave one popular interpretation of the latter's significance: 'A charter for the Pacific comparable to the Atlantic Charter, now has been promulgated to all the world.'[1] If this were true, then the Cairo Declaration achieved something distinctly different from what the State Department tried to accomplish in its draft on universal national independence, which would apply to all regions of the world and not merely specific areas such as the Pacific and the Atlantic. Another prominent journalist, Walter Lippmann, gave a different interpretation:

> Military agreements . . . covering the whole basin of the Pacific are now politically and strategically feasible. In this setting the Philippines can be made secure, and questions which the unthinking have raised about the remote islands, where we have had to improvise bases during this war, will fall into their proper perspective and cease to be very interesting or important.[2]

With the benefit of hindsight it is clear that Lippmann was mistaken on one important point. The Cairo Declaration did not end the territorial questions; it intensified them. For the subject of international trusteeship, the significance of the Cairo Declaration is clear and simple: Japan would be stripped of her Empire. Among other parts, the Japanese mandated islands became a detached territory. It is important to stress this basic fact because it is easy to lose sight of it among the many other decisions and events of the time. The two Cairo conferences of November and December 1943, before and after the meeting

---

[1] *Washington Star*, 2 Dec. 1943.   [2] *Washington Post*, 2 Dec. 1943.

of the Big Three in Teheran, should be viewed as counterpoints of military and political decision-making of highest order. Militarily the allies attempted to co-ordinate their actions in all theatres of war. At Cairo they made decisions about the priority to be given the war in the Far East. Roosevelt, Churchill, and Chiang Kai-shek defined their war aims and tried to lay the foundation of the future peace. Japan would be forced to surrender unconditionally. As in the case of the Atlantic Charter, the resulting document took the form of a press release, with all of the haste and confusion that the phrase can imply.

It would be tempting to suppose that the western statesmen at Cairo saw a magnificent opportunity to create a new order in the Far East based on the goodwill and competence of China as a great power.[3] Therefore the deliberations must have been systematic if not profound. From the American side the basis for systematic planning certainly existed. The Territorial and Security Subcommittees of the State Department's Advisory Committee had given long and hard thought to the problems of the Far Eastern settlement and to the specific problem of the mandated islands. These planning sessions have an intrinsic importance to the subject of trusteeship and will be considered separately later. It is important to note them in passing here because they did *not* have any bearing on the Cairo Declaration. So far as the American mission to Cairo was concerned, the Far Eastern authorities of the State Department could just as well have belonged to a foreign government. Roosevelt took no account of their expert knowledge and, in fact, did not even include a State Department representative in the mission. A participant in the post-war planning for Japan, Professor Hugh Borton, has described how the Territorial Subcommittee was actually in session discussing Far Eastern problems when the State Department received word that a 'Declaration' would be made at Cairo. 'None of the group had any indication as to the contents of the "Declaration." In fact, the meeting was adjourned so everyone could read the Declaration as it appeared on the ticker tape.'[4]

---

[3] See Herbert Feis, *Churchill, Roosevelt, Stalin: The War They Waged and the Peace They Sought* (Princeton, 1957), p. 253.

[4] Borton, *American Presurrender Planning for Postwar Japan*, p. 12.

Nor did the Secretary of State himself have any influence on the proceedings at Cairo. Here it is important to trace the developments in the 'policy of preachment', in Hull's phrase, because, if other international conferences provided any indication, then the British could certainly have expected the matter to be raised at Cairo. At the Quebec Conference in August, Hull had explicitly asked Eden about the draft declaration on national independence for dependent peoples. According to the State Department's record of the conversation, the Foreign Secretary finally responded only after the third inquiry.

Mr. Eden said to be perfectly frank he had to say that he did not very much like the American draft on this subject. He said it was the word 'independence' which troubled him. He had to think of the British Empire system, which was built on the basis of Dominion and Colonial status . . .

He pointed out that under the British Empire system you had varying degrees of self-government in the units, mentioning the Dominion status . . . and, running from those degrees of self-government down through the Colonial establishments which had in some cases, like Malta, complete self-government, to other more backward areas which, he confessed, were never likely to have their own government . . .

Mr. Eden's position was absolutely unchanged at the end of the discussion of this subject and it was perfectly clear that it was the word 'independence' which he found could never have a satisfactory meaning which would cover what various governments might have in mind by this term.[5]

Despairing of the British, Hull turned to the Russians. At the Foreign Ministers' meeting in October he gave Molotov a copy of the declaration, asking for his favourable consideration of it.[6] The British were outraged by this tactic. Richard Law at the Foreign Office wrote to the Colonial Secretary:

It is difficult to know just what Hull is after. It may be that he is trying to get Russian support for his own draft, and thus put us in a minority of one . . . whatever the reason for it, it is apparent that the Americans are not disposed to let the draft die a natural death as

---

[5] Memorandum of conversation, 21 Aug. 1943, USSD NF Box 284; *Memoirs of Cordell Hull* ii. 1237–8. *Foreign Relations: the Conferences at Washington and Quebec* (1943), pp. 926–7.

[6] Ibid., p. 1238. Hull's statement that he 'brought it up again and again' with the British preceding the conference is a gross exaggeration.

we had hoped they would. It is clear that this is going to be brought up again and that we shall have to deal with it.[7]

In the Colonial Office the American draft declaration was now being referred to by Eastwood and others as 'the egregious document' and 'the freak' because of the way they believed it distorted the purpose of colonial rule. On the eve of the Cairo conference the Colonial Office learned that Roosevelt himself had given a copy of the declaration to Churchill during the Quebec conference.[8] The Prime Minister had not responded. But it was a dire omen. There could be no way of telling when the Americans might again 'trot out' the document, in Eastwood's phrase. Had Hull attended the Cairo conference the British probably would again have been subjected to more 'preachment'. As events transpired, the issue of trusteeship raised its head in other ways.

At Cairo Roosevelt vented his thoughts about specific territories, not least Indo-China. For this specific application of the trusteeship idea the British were prepared. In July at a meeting of the Pacific War Council (the consultative body in Washington composed of representatives of powers at war in the Pacific) the President had stated that nothing could alter his views about this fundamental question: 'Indo-China should not be given back to the French Empire after the war. The French had been there for nearly one hundred years and had done absolutely nothing with the place to improve the lot of the people.'[9] Officials in the Foreign Office exhaustively analyzed Roosevelt's comment. They concluded that Indo-China would provide one of the critical issues in the post-war settlement. Geoffrey Hudson wrote:

Roosevelt's attitude is perhaps largely due to his fear that Willkie next year will mobilize American anti-imperialist sentiment against him for the Presidential election. . . . The President no doubt estimates that a French colonial restoration would be harder to justify to the American public than a British or Dutch restoration, and that it would greatly strengthen his position if he could claim

[7] Law to Stanley, 22 Nov. 1943, CO 323/1858/9057B; FO 373/35311.
[8] See Eastwood's minute of 9 Nov. 1943, CO 323/1858/9057B; copy of the transaction at Quebec in the file; for chronology of this event in the evolution of the issue, see U6184, FO 371/35311.
[9] Pacific War Council minutes, 21 July 1943, Roosevelt Papers MR Box 168 f. 3.

that he had eliminated at least one piece of European imperialism from the Far East.[10]

After lengthy internal and inter-departmental debate, the Far Eastern Department summed up in a brief for Sir Alexander Cadogan:

[W]e feel that we should try to convince the Americans that it is right to readmit the French. It is possible that their views could be met by the establishment of bases in Indo-China under international control or under U.S. control as trustee for the United Nations without requiring the removal of French administration from Indo-China as a whole . . .

On the assumption that Anglo-French co-operation will be a vital factor in our post-war policy it would be undesirable either to weaken France by depriving her of so important a part of her Empire or to undermine at the outset the possibilities of friendship with France.

We do not believe that international control of French Indo-China would work satisfactorily. It would open the door to Chinese, and, in time, Japanese intrigues, and outright Chinese control would be both objectionable to the natives and probably menacing to ourselves.[11]

The Foreign Office thus had a thoroughly prepared case to put before Roosevelt. Unfortunately for the British, the President preferred to consult the Chinese.

[10] Minute by Hudson, 26 July 1943, F4023/G, FO 371/35930.

[11] 'Brief for Sir Alexander Cadogan', 22 Nov. 1943, F6780/G, FO 371/35930. It should be noted that a visit to London by Stanley Hornbeck in October provided the British many insights into American policy at this particular time. When asked about Roosevelt's Indo-China statement, this 'came as news to Dr. Hornbeck, who said that the Departments of the United States Government were not always kept very fully informed of what happened in the Pacific Council' (Minute by Ashley Clarke, 15 Oct. 1943, ibid.). Hornbeck's conversations with British officials focused mainly on the post-war future of China, but trusteeship occasionally came under discussion: e.g. in talking about Korea, 'Dr. Hornbeck . . . showed no eagerness for the United States to have the honour of acting as a mandatory' (Minute by Clarke, 13 Oct. 1943, FO 371/35871). Also in regard to trusteeship, Hornbeck's conversations with the Colonial Office officials about regional organization for the Far East and Pacific are of especial interest. His conception of regional organization included all of the great powers and the entire Pacific basin and was thus much larger than the Colonial Office's scheme, which embraced only South-East Asia, and, tentatively, the western Pacific. The Colonial Office officials thought Hornbeck had not thought out the matter 'at all clearly'. (See memoranda and minutes in CO 323/1858/9057B.) Hornbeck had a similar impression of vagueness of the British officials. When he asked what areas the Colonial Secretary had in mind for regional commissions in his speech of 13 July, 'no one in the Foreign Office or the Colonial Office knew specifically' (T Minutes 55, 5 Nov. 1943, USSD NF Box 42).

The conference at Cairo opened on the 23rd of November with acrimonious discussion about military operations in the China theatre. In the British view, the Americans were putting the Asian cart before the European horse. To Churchill's dismay, Roosevelt 'closeted' himself with Chiang Kai-shek to reach agreement on some of the more sensitive political issues. The key conversation occurred on the evening of the 23rd at Roosevelt's villa at 8 o'clock. Roosevelt and Harry Hopkins met with the Generalissimo and Madame. Unfortunately the only official record of the meeting is a Chinese summary which does not include all the points debated by Roosevelt and Chiang. According to Elliott Roosevelt, this free-wheeling discussion touched on the formation of a democratic government in China after the war, British 'Empire rights' in Hong Kong, Canton, and Shanghai, the use of American rather than British warships in future operations based on Chinese ports, and even the future of Malaya, Burma, and India. As for trusteeship in Indo-China, Roosevelt said:

[T]he French would have no right, after the war, simply to walk back into Indo-China and reclaim that rich land for no reason other than it had once been their colony. And he had insisted to Chiang that the most the French should have was a trusteeship of their colonies responsible to a United Nations organization, looking toward eventual independence, once the United Nations were satisfied that the colonies could manage their own affairs.[12]

Roosevelt asked Chiang whether China would assume trusteeship responsibility for Indo-China. According to another contemporary account, this one by General Joseph W. Stilwell, the conversation as related by Roosevelt had this tone and substance: 'I asked Chiang point-blank if he wanted Indo-China, and he said, "under no circumstances!" Just like that—"under no circumstances".'[13] Roosevelt himself later gave this version:

The first thing I asked Chiang was, 'Do you want Indo-China?' He said, 'It's no help to us. We don't want it. They are not Chinese. They would not assimilate into the Chinese people.'

I said, 'What are you going to advocate? It will take a long time to educate them for self-government.'

He said they should not go back to the French . . .

[12] Elliott Roosevelt, *As He Saw It*, p. 165.
[13] Theodore H. White, ed., *The Stilwell Papers* (New York, 1948), p. 253.

I suggested at the time, to Chiang, that Indo-China be set up under a trusteeship—have a Frenchman, one or two Indo-Chinese, and a Chinese and a Russian because they are on the coast, and maybe a Filipino and an American—to educate them for self-government.[14]

The official Chinese account amplifies some of the more specific points. Foremost among these, China would assume international responsibilities as one of the Big Four. On other questions, Chiang showed restraint. When Roosevelt raised the issue of Hong Kong, for example, Chiang suggested that the British should be brought into the conversation.[15] In regard to the territorial settlement, Roosevelt and Chiang agreed:

that the four Northern provinces of China, Taiwan and the Penghu Islands [*Pescadores*] which Japan had taken from China by force must be restored to China after the war, it being understood that the Liaotung Peninsula and its two ports, Lushun (Port of Arthur) and Dairen, must be included. The President then referred to the question of the Ryukyu Islands and enquired more than once whether China would want the Ryukyus. The Generalissimo replied that China would be agreeable to joint occupation of the Ryukyus by China and the United States and, eventually, joint administration by the two countries under the trusteeship of an international organization.[16]

On the same day that the British and American military authorities in consultation with the Chinese had debated the priority of the Asian theatre in the global war, Roosevelt and Chiang had redrawn the political map of the Far East—without Churchill's help.

On the next afternoon, the 24th, Harry Hopkins drafted the press release that eventually became known as the Cairo Declaration. So fresh in his mind were the items of agreement

[14] Press conference of 23 Feb. 1945, *Public Papers and Addresses of Franklin D. Roosevelt* (1944–5), p. 562.

[15] The Hong Kong issue did not arise formally at the conference (see Chan Lau Kit-Ching, 'The Hong Kong Question during the Pacific War'). Roosevelt however did expand on the subject informally: e.g. he said to General Stilwell, 'Now, we haven't the same aims as the British out there. For instance, Hongkong. Now, I have a plan to make Hongkong a free port: free to the commerce of all nations—of the whole world! But let's raise the Chinese flag there first, and then Chiang can the next day make a grand gesture and make it a free port. That's the way to handle that!' *The Stilwell Papers*, p. 252.

[16] *Foreign Relations of the United States: The Conferences at Cairo and Tehran* (Washington, 1961), pp. 323–5.

that he dictated the communiqué without notes.[17] He framed it as a clear-cut piece of propaganda. Roosevelt, Chiang Kai-shek, and Churchill would bring unrelenting pressure against their brutal enemy. Japan must be made to surrender unconditionally. The territories treacherously stolen with violence and greed by Japan would be returned to China. No one at the conference questioned the historical accuracy of the indictment.[18] The Chinese raised no objections to the draft. It was enormously generous to China.

Throughout all this business, Roosevelt and Hopkins dealt with the Chinese first and only later with the British. It was a humiliating experience for the representatives of the British Empire, but in view of the military situation in the Far East they could not effectively resist American political overtures.[19] They did, however, manage to convert the declaration from a highly objectionable draft favouring China (and ignoring Britain) into a statement minimally acceptable to the government in London. Hopkins gave Cadogan the draft on the morning of the 26th of November. It is a curious commentary on the business methods of Roosevelt and Churchill that the former had not brought a single representative of the State Department to Cairo, while the latter's entourage included not only the Foreign Secretary but also the Permanent Under-Secretary who had originally drafted the Atlantic Charter. Cadogan immediately noted that the Americans wanted to strip Japan's Empire in favour of China, but they made no mention at all about the restoration of British possessions. He also observed that Hopkins's draft failed to state that the Allies were not fighting for territorial aggrandizement.[20] The tacit corollary of

[17] William M. Franklin, 'The Cairo Declaration of 1943: Origin and Significance', paper presented at the American Historical Association, San Francisco, 1973.

[18] It subsequently fell to the experts in the State Department to ascertain whether there could be a distinction between territories taken by 'violence and greed' and those acquired by other means. The chronology was also a problem, since 1914 was the only date mentioned in the declaration. When the Territorial Subcommittee on 3 December surveyed the problems raised by the Declaration, Professor George Blakeslee remarked that 'the exact year in which virtue ceased for Japan was an academic matter' (T Minutes 58, USSD NF Box 42). For discussion of the historical accuracy of the Cairo Declaration, see Robert J. C. Butow, *Japan's Decision to Surrender* (Stanford, 1954), p. 40 *et passim*; and F. C. Jones, *Japan's New Order in East Asia* (London, 1954), p. 464.   [19] See Eden, *Reckoning*, p. 493.

[20] See PREM 4/72/2 part 2; *Diaries of Sir Alexander Cadogan*, pp. 577–8.

this proposition, to the British at least, was that neither would any territory be given up. Churchill's reactions were the same as Cadogan's. He submitted a revised draft to the President, while he also telegraphed the draft for approval by the War Cabinet. It is another contrast in the methods of the two statesmen and governments that, while Churchill was in close touch with London, Roosevelt did not bother even to keep a record for the benefit of the State Department. Churchill's draft carried the day. It very closely resembled the final communiqué. The Prime Minister's version ran:

President Roosevelt, Generalissimo Chiang Kai-shek and Prime Minister Churchill, together with their respective military and diplomatic advisers, have completed a conference in North Africa. The following general statement was issued:

'The several military missions have agreed upon future military operations against Japan. The three great Allies expressed their resolve to bring unrelenting pressure against their brutal enemies by sea, land and air. This pressure is already rising.

'It is their purpose that Japan shall be stripped of all the islands in the Pacific which she has seized or occupied since the beginning of the First World War in 1914, and that all the territories Japan has stolen from the Chinese, such as Manchuria, Formosa & the Pescadores, shall be restored to the Republic of China. Japan will also be expelled from all other territories which she has taken by violence and greed. The aforesaid three Great Powers, mindful of the enslavement of the people of Korea, are determined that in due course Korea shall become free and independent.

'With these objects in view the three Allies, in harmony with those of the United Nations at war with Japan, will continue to persevere in the serious and prolonged operations necessary to procure the unconditional surrender of Japan.'[21]

From the British point of view the Declaration still seemed generous to China, but at least it could not be interpreted as adversely affecting British possessions. It gave Churchill the basis on which to argue, as he had consistently, that the British had no imperialist ambitions, but, on the other hand, neither did they intend to liquidate the British Empire. Eden explained to the War Cabinet on the return to London: 'the Prime Minister had on several occasions said that we asked for no increase of territory for ourselves at the end of the war, but likewise we were not going to give any up.'[22]

At Teheran Roosevelt and Churchill consulted with Stalin about the Cairo Declaration and indeed discussed the whole range of colonial issues raised by it. For the subject of trustee-ship the significance of these exchanges among the 'Big Three' is the extent to which Roosevelt and Stalin saw eye to eye on the colonial question and the way in which Churchill sus-piciously viewed their collaboration on trusteeship as a threat to the British Empire. When Roosevelt first met Stalin on the 28th of November, the President talked freely, in Churchill's absence, about trusteeship schemes. The two of them im-mediately agreed that Indo-China should not be restored to France. Stalin remarked that the Japanese had to be fought in the political as well as in the military sphere, 'particularly in view of the fact that the Japanese had granted the least [sic] nominal independence to certain colonial areas'. Roosevelt emphatically concurred.

The President said he was 100% in agreement with Marshal Stalin and remarked that after 100 years of French rule in Indochina, the inhabitants were worse off than they had been before. . . . He added that he had discussed with Chiang Kai-shek the possibility of a system of trusteeship for Indochina which would have the task of preparing the people for independence within a definite period of time, perhaps 20 to 30 years.

Marshal Stalin completely agreed with this view.[23]

It was during this conversation that Roosevelt suggested that it would be unwise to raise the question of India with Churchill. '*Marshal Stalin* agreed that this was a sore spot with the British.'[24]

---

[22] W.M. (43) 169th Conclusions, Minute 2, Confidential Annex, 13 Dec. 1943, CAB 65/40.

[23] *Foreign Relations: Cairo and Tehran*, p. 485. For another account of this conversa-tion, see Edward R. Stettinius, *Roosevelt and the Russians: the Yalta Conference* (Garden City, 1949), p. 237–8. See also *F.D.R.: His Personal Letters* ii. 1489.

[24] The rest of the Indian discussion includes this exchange:

The President said that at some future date, he would like to talk with Marshal Stalin on the question of India; that he felt that the best solution would be reform from the bottom, somewhat on the Soviet line.

Marshal Stalin replied that the India question was a complicated one, with different levels of culture and the absence of relationship in the castes. He added that reform from the bottom would mean revolution.

(*Foreign Relations: Cairo and Tehran*, p. 486.)

The two of them felt no similar inhibitions about discussing the French Empire with the Prime Minister. That evening, when the three of them and their advisers met for dinner, Stalin stated that France 'had no right to retain her former empire' and that the French ruling class 'was rotten to the core'. Roosevelt in turn cited strategic points where it would be unsafe to leave the French in control:

> He mentioned specifically the question of New Caledonia and Dakar, the first of which he said represented a threat to Australia and New Zealand and, therefore, should be placed under the trusteeship of the United Nations. In regard to Dakar, *The President* said he was speaking for twenty-one American nations when he said that Dakar in unsure hands was a direct threat to the Americas.[25]

Churchill stated that some strategic bases obviously would have to be controlled by the victorious powers, but that the British Empire did not desire additional territories. This was the line Churchill persistently argued during the conferences, despite Stalin's efforts to draw him out on territorial questions.

When Roosevelt and Stalin next met alone on the afternoon of the 29th, the President expounded his ideas on international organization, which included the 'Four Policemen'. Stalin did not think that the small nations of Europe would like the idea. They would furthermore resent the presence of China, which in his opinion would not be a powerful state after the war. Stalin proposed as an alternative a world-wide organization with regional responsibilities that more closely resembled Churchill's idea of a post-war international organization. After reaching agreement on certain points such as the occupation of the islands in the vicinity of Japan to prevent further Japanese aggression, Stalin said that he still remained sceptical about the Chinese playing such a prominent part in these schemes.

> *The President* replied that he had insisted on the participation of China . . . not because he did not realize the weakness of China at present, but he was thinking farther into the future and that after all China was a nation of 400 million people, and it was better to have them as friends rather than as a potential source of trouble.[26]

Quite apart from this expression of idealism, the Chinese to Roosevelt were vital to the success of his trusteeship schemes.

---

[25] *Foreign Relations: Cairo and Tehran*, p. 509.   [26] Ibid., p. 532.

They would help to hold areas and bases of strategic importance. Though Stalin remained doubtful of the ability of the Chinese to assume these responsibilities, he entirely agreed with Roosevelt about the desirability of creating trusteeship bases in the vicinity of the axis powers. Here the two of them stood in opposition to Churchill, who suspected that some of these bases might fall within the British Empire. That evening at dinner, on the 20th, this exchange took place.

With reference to the occupation of bases and strong points in the vicinity of Germany and Japan, *The President* said that those bases must be held under trusteeship.
Marshal Stalin agreed with the President.

Churchill now made a strong statement in regard to trusteeship bases, going so far as to say that *war* would result if these trusteeship schemes veiled a project for the liquidation of the British Empire.

The *Prime Minister* stated that as far as Britain was concerned they do not desire to acquire any new territory or bases, but intended to hold on to what they had. He said that nothing would be taken away from England without a war. He mentioned specifically Singapore and Hong Kong. He said a portion of the British Empire might eventually be released but that this would be done entirely by Great Britain herself, in accordance with her own moral precepts. He said that Great Britain, if asked to do so, might occupy certain bases under trusteeship, provided others would help pay the cost of such occupation.[27]

With clarity and consistency, Churchill thus stated the position of the British Empire. Egging him on, Stalin stated that he 'favored an increase in the British Empire, particularly the area around Gibraltar'. Stalin for his part refused to be drawn out, though the next day he did mention Russia's lack of an ice-free port in the Far East. Roosevelt thereupon suggested Dairen as a free port under international guaranty. Taken as a whole, Roosevelt's projects for international control as he described them at Cairo and Teheran stretched throughout the entire world and displayed a remarkable optimism in the ability of nations to work together.

On the 30th of November 1943 Churchill asked Stalin

[27] Ibid., p. 554.

whether he had read the proposed press communiqué, shortly to become known as the Cairo Declaration.

Marshal Stalin replied that he had and that although he could make no commitments he thoroughly approved the communiqué and all its contents. He said it was right that Korea should be independent, and that Manchuria, Formosa and the Pescadores Islands should be returned to China.[28]

Though Russia was not at war with Japan, Stalin thus became a silent partner in the Cairo Declaration. It was released to the press on the 1st of December. Like the Atlantic Charter, the Cairo Declaration meant many things to different men. For those concerned with dependent territories, trusteeship plans could now be made on the definite assumption that Japan's Empire would be dismembered.

[28] *Foreign Relations: Cairo and Tehran*, p. 566.

PART III

FROM CAIRO TO YALTA

THE AUSTRALIAN-NEW ZEALAND
AGREEMENT OF JANUARY 1944

IN January 1944 Australia and New Zealand erupted into the general affairs of the Far East and the Pacific.[1] The two governments concluded an agreement partly in dramatic protest against the Cairo Declaration. Churchill and Roosevelt had not consulted the Australians or New Zealanders about the war aims against Japan.[2] On the 29th of January the two antipodean Dominions consequently declared to the world their vital interest in all preparations for the peace in Asia. They insisted on being heard in all future transactions about the Pacific basin. The items of unresolved business included trusteeship. The antipodean view coincided with the American and contradicted the British interpretation of the Atlantic Charter. In the chapter entitled 'Welfare and Advancement of Native Peoples of the Pacific', the agreement read:

The two Governments declare that, in applying the principles of the Atlantic Charter to the Pacific, the doctrine of 'trusteeship'

[1] The basic documentary source on the Agreement is Robin Kay, ed., *The Australian–New Zealand Agreement 1944* (Documents on New Zealand External Relations, Volume i, Historical Publications Branch, Department of Internal Affairs, Wellington, 1972). For evaluations of the Agreement, see especially C. Hartley Grattan, *The Southwest Pacific since 1900* (Ann Arbor, 1963), pp. 184–8, 309–11, 524–5; Alan Watt, *The Evolution of Australian Foreign Policy 1938–1965* (Cambridge, 1967), chs. 3 and 4; Trevor R. Reese, *Australia, New Zealand, and the United States* (London, 1969); for the New Zealand side, especially F. L. W. Wood, *The New Zealand People at War* (Wellington, 1958); and M. P. Lissington, *New Zealand and the United States, 1840–1944* (Wellington, 1972).

[2] The failure to notify the Dominions in advance of the release of the Cairo Declaration was mainly due to the rush of events, though Churchill was not especially eager to consult them (see PREM 4/72/2 and PREM 136/4). The Australian representative in London telegraphed to Canberra on 1 Dec. 1943 that the Dominions Office was 'urgently' sending them the text, and that Churchill had shown 'some signs of grace by saying that he "fears" that arrangements have been made with the President and Chiang Kai Shek for the time of publication'. The telegram and the text of the Declaration did not reach Canberra, however, until after the release of the Declaration. (Bruce to Prime Minister, 1 Dec. 1943, AA A989/43/735/1016/2.)

(already applicable in the case of the mandated territories of which the two Governments are mandatory powers) is applicable in broad principle to all colonial territories in the Pacific and elsewhere, and that the main purpose of the trust is the welfare of the native peoples and their social, economic and political development.[3]

From this time onwards' the Australians and New Zealanders became protagonists in the trusteeship story. Previously regarded by the government in London as minor participants who would acquiesce in the lead taken by the Colonial Office, the two Dominions now made it clear that they expected a voice in decision-making equal to those of Britain and the United States. This development proved to be of cardinal importance. The Australians and New Zealanders helped ultimately to tilt the balance of interpretation of trusteeship more towards the view adopted by the State Department in Washington than that of the Colonial Office in London. The years 1944–5 were critical in the reorientation of external affairs of the two Dominions *vis-à-vis* Britain and the United States. There can be found in the realm of trusteeship all the tensions reflected in other issues such as future security in the Pacific. At a time when the Australians and New Zealanders became acutely aware of the shift in world power from London to Washington, they also found themselves more in agreement with the Americans than with the British about colonial affairs.

The moving spirit behind the Australian–New Zealand Agreement was the Australian Attorney-General and Minister for External Affairs, Herbert Vere Evatt. He was enraged at the Cairo Declaration. '[T]here is no doubt in my mind', wrote the American Minister in Australia, 'that the Anzac Pact . . . was ninety per cent the brain child of Dr. Evatt. . . . I am certain that Dr. Evatt has resented the Cairo Conference more than any other event which has thus far occurred.'[4] Feeling slighted at not having been invited to the conference, Evatt vented his indignation in a variety of ways. He was capable of bluntness to the point of truculence. He indignantly stressed to both the Americans and the British that Australia would not stand idly by while the great powers decided on the future of the

---

[3] The text of the Agreement is printed in full in Kay, *The Australian–New Zealand Agreement*, document 53.

[4] Johnson to Hornbeck, 26 Jan. 1944, Hornbeck Papers Box 262.

Pacific. He abrasively proclaimed his own views on subjects such as trusteeship. To those unaware of his fascination with the Pacific, he appeared to be a self-appointed and egotistical guardian of the islanders. These aspects of Evatt's personality had a definite bearing on the wartime colonial negotiations because the Englishmen and Americans who worked with him on these questions almost without exception regarded him as arrogant, vain, and intolerably ambitious. His Australian critics shared those sentiments. At the same time others admired him for his ambition. He was ambitious not only for himself but for Australia. He championed the cause of the underdog. With a streak of the larrikin, he stood not only for Australia versus the great powers, but also, as later became especially apparent at the San Francisco conference, for small powers throughout the world as they aspired to a greater voice in international affairs. In colonial questions he was a gradualist who favoured thorough preparation for independence. He probably did not envisage independence for New Guinea in this century, though he would not have opposed it. In the wartime controversies about the future of the colonies, he demonstrated a brilliant, searching quality of mind which tenaciously and legalistically clung to problems until he resolved them with sudden clarity. In a word, he was a controversial, outstandingly able man. No doubt he used the trusteeship debate to further his own ambitions, but he possessed a genuine, if flamboyant, sense of outrage at the exploitation of dependent peoples.[5]

To those who had followed Evatt's speeches on the colonial question and the future security of the Pacific, his protest at the Cairo Declaration should have come as no surprise. Over a year earlier, on the 3rd of September 1942, he had stated before the Australian House of Representatives that security and trusteeship were the two bases of future development in which Australia must take the lead. In his view, the Atlantic Charter applied to the peoples of the Pacific and Asia as well as to Europeans. The realization of the goals of the Charter would depend on secure and stable conditions, which first meant the absolute destruction of the system of exploitation created by the Japanese co-prosperity sphere. With a keen sense of the

---

[5] I am especially grateful to Hartley Grattan, W. D. Forsyth, and Sir Alan Watt for giving me their personal recollections of Evatt.

ideological as well as of the military and economic presence of Japan in the Pacific, Evatt argued that the entire future of that part of the world would depend on reconstruction and development that would create prosperity for the inhabitants as well as for the neighbouring and colonial powers.

> In the post-war world the re-organisation of these regions cannot be on the Japanese system. We are now fighting to end that system. Moreover, our post-war order in the Pacific cannot be for the sole benefit of one power or group of powers. Its dominant purpose must be that of benefiting the peoples everywhere. If 'freedom from want' means anything, it means that the age of unfair exploitation is over. ... In short, we must found future Pacific policy on the doctrine of trusteeship for the benefit of all the Pacific powers.[6]

In the debate about the proposed Anglo-American colonial declaration in the winter of 1942–3, Evatt developed his ideas on trusteeship with firmness and lucidity. The Allied powers would have to provide a realistic alternative to the co-prosperity sphere, not mere propaganda. The intrinsic merit of a colonial declaration would rest on a full and frank exploration with the United States of the issues of colonial policy. On the major points mooted between the British and Americans, Evatt flatly stated that there should be *accountability* to an international organization. He had in mind a 'colonial commission' analogous to the Permanent Mandates Commission. Colonial territories would continue to be administered by the 'parent' states, but *all* colonies would be placed under international supervision.[7] Evatt's ideas were thus as advanced or radical as those of the State Department's advisory committees. Throughout 1943 Evatt amplified the goals of trusteeship. He elaborated the details of the regional commissions which would supervise the collaboration of the colonial powers. By October 1943 he could state in the Australian House of Representatives that post-war planning had advanced in detail in regard to specific island groups such as the Solomons, the New Hebrides, New Caledonia, and, of course, Papua and New Guinea. 'I visualize

---

[6] In the Australian House of Representatives, 3 Sept. 1942. The extract was repeated many times in despatches throughout the war as one of the bases of Australian policy.

[7] For the Australian side of the debate on the proposed colonial declaration of 1943, see AA A989 43/735/321.

New Guinea,' Evatt stated, 'both Australian and Dutch, as an integral part of the Pacific zone with which Australia will be vitally interested in collaboration with Britain and New Zealand on the one hand and with the Dutch, French and Portuguese on the other.'[8] Collaborative *zones* for defence and colonial development had become one of Evatt's key ideas.

Evatt was the master of his own policy. With the exception of Lord Hailey, no other statesman in the wartime era demonstrated such a grasp of fundamental principles in the debate about trusteeship. As Paul Hasluck has pointed out, Evatt's staff also served him well.[9] In colonial affairs a key figure in post-war planning (and later Secretary General of the South Pacific Commission), W. D. Forsyth, advised him and provided extensive analysis of the issues of trusteeship. Like Evatt, Forsyth held deep convictions against the exploitation of the peoples of the South Pacific. His orientation in foreign affairs bore the stamp of Labour ideas.[10] While Evatt from time to time would study colonial issues with an intensity that soon put him abreast of immediate problems, Forsyth systematically prepared memoranda and drafted despatches that greatly contributed to the continuity of Australian policy. He clearly outlined Australia's goals in colonial affairs as the Japanese began their retreat. The liberation of the islands would provide the Australians, in Forsyth's view, with a superb opportunity to take the lead in post-war colonial policy and set the example for the other Pacific powers. He wrote in March 1943:

Papua is the first colonial territory from which the Japanese have been completely ejected. . . . this affords an opportunity for the Commonwealth [Australian] Government to give a practical lead towards the kind of post-war settlement it wishes to see in Southeast Asia and the Western Pacific. We are the first colonial power which can yet do this and are thus in a position to influence the colonial settlement in this region.

To take part confidently in discussions concerning the colonies of other powers we need to feel that we have gone as far as possible in the practical implementation in our own colonies of the principles

---

[8] In the Australian House of Representatives, 14 Oct. 1943.

[9] Paul Hasluck, 'Australia and the Formation of the United Nations', *Royal Australian Historical Society: Journal and Proceedings*, xl, Part III (1954).

[10] For Forsyth's background, see W. D. Forsyth, 'The Pre-War Melbourne Group of AIIA: Some Personal Recollections', *Australian Outlook* 28. 1 (April 1974).

we advocate. Moreover, we owe a special debt to the Papuan natives, many of whom earned high praise for the help they gave to our forces in the recent campaign against the invading Japanese.[11]

Forsyth went on to elaborate the colonial issue in relation to Australian security:

In general, the post-war colonial settlement in the Pacific is a vital matter for Australia because the stability of the region in which we live is at stake. Our long-term security depends on the conversion of the Southeast Asiatic area from discord, backwardness, strategic weakness and international rivalry to economic strength, prosperity and political stability.[12]

He concluded that Australia should make every effort to participate in the control of the affairs of South-East Asia and the Pacific following the war. His line of reasoning coincided exactly with Evatt's, but with a much more comprehensive view of the colonial situation.

Forsyth's analysis of Australia's future position in the Pacific and South-East Asia is of considerable interest because he spelled out explicitly the principles on which Evatt implicitly operated in the realm of colonial affairs. As early as the spring of 1943 Forsyth had lucidly outlined the part Australia would play in the affairs of the Pacific *vis-à-vis* Britain and the United States. Both the British and the Americans saw the emerging lines of Australian policy much less clearly. It took the shock of the Australian–New Zealand Agreement for them fully to recognize that New Zealand and especially Australia would follow an increasingly independent path. According to Forsyth, far from merely following the British lead, or submitting to American domination, Australia would take the initiative. He held that the Australians would have to satisfy their own consciences about '"Imperialism" and the future of the colonies', and that a firm Australian stand on the question would not only strengthen resistance against the Japanese but would have some influence in Britain and the United States and even China and India. He wrote in April 1943 that the old colonial regimes had produced instability and consequent insecurity.

Stability in the Pacific Area is essential. . . . Our interests are incompatible with reversion to a colonial system which would be

[11] Memorandum by Forsyth, 29 Mar. 1943, AA A989 43/735/3.
[12] Ibid.

on the one hand a standing challenge to non-colonial powers such as Germany and Japan, and on the other an affront to the colonial peoples, or the growing number of them who inevitably imbibe modern ideas and education.

Further, our special position in the Pacific dictates a long-term interest in the cultivation of political, economic and social strength and maturity among the native communities of South-East Asia and Indonesia. . . . There must be built up in the course of time a self-subsisting Western Pacific system, and the sooner a start is made the better from Australia's point of view.[13]

Forsyth by no means envisaged the immediate end of the colonial system in the Pacific. He rather claimed Australia's right to partake in its eventual termination. 'Western guidance must necessarily remain for a considerable time, but it is vital that administration and development be subject to external supervision, and Australia must insist on this and on full participation in it.'[14]

The planning of the colonies' future in the Pacific was directly linked with the development of Australia's security system. Here the Australian ideas are of interest, among other reasons, because of the way they complemented Roosevelt's 'Four Policemen' scheme which was germinating at the same time. Forsyth wrote in April 1943:

Australia needs and will co-operate in an international police force in the Pacific. But our share in it must be such that we will be in a position—geographically in regard to bases falling to our care, industrially in regard to armament production, militarily in regard to trained and equipped forces of all arms—such that in the event of the system becoming weakened by political, economic or demographic changes, we should be ready to defend ourselves.[15]

The defence scheme thus would be self-sufficient in case the international system collapsed; and Australian participation in the policing of the Pacific would be comprehensive.

It is . . . desirable that we should be given direct responsibility for the police system in the area adjacent to our shores, and whether under mandate or some other arrangement obtain the right to maintain, arm, and man bases in Timor, Dutch New Guinea, New Britain, the Solomons, New Hebrides and Noumea, and that we

[13] Memorandum by Forsyth, 7 Apr. 1943, AA A989 43/735/1021.
[14] Ibid.   [15] Ibid.

should share in the security arrangements covering Malaya, Netherlands East Indies, Japanese Mandated Islands and British Western Pacific possessions, as well as more generally in the Pacific system as a whole.[16]

The danger of this scheme would be that Australia might wind up isolated, by antagonizing the great powers by such far-reaching proposals, or, at the other extreme, might be drawn into responsibilities greater than Australia's manpower or economy could bear. Forsyth emphasized the need for a *balance*:

[O]ur chief difficulty may well be to keep a balance between external security and internal autonomy. This difficulty would be increased if the colonial settlement were such that Britain and the Netherlands lost interest or influence in the Western Pacific. We may in future have use for a European counter-weight to American or Chinese influence in this region. For this reason alone it is not to our interest to advocate international *administration* (as distinct from *supervision*) of colonies or to press for a colonial settlement unduly onerous for colonial powers.[17]

Australia thus had an interest in maintaining British and Dutch authority in the western Pacific in order to counterbalance growing American influence. In this delicate balance, Australia would throw weight behind international supervision, thus encouraging American participation in the security of the western Pacific; but Australia would not urge international administration, which would demoralize the British and other colonial powers. Like Evatt, Forsyth saw accountability to an international organization as the major issue at stake in the future colonial negotiations. Unlike the British, the Australians entirely favoured international supervision.

During the spring of 1943 Forsyth examined at length the ways in which the colonial powers should be held accountable. In summary he outlined the following points which formed the basis of Australia's colonial policy:

(i) The broad principles of the Atlantic Charter should be applied.

(ii) There should be a general system of security, as effective in colonial areas as elsewhere;

[16] Memorandum by Forsyth, 7 Apr. 1943, AA A989 43/735/1021.   [17] Ibid.

(iii) Colonies must share in the benefits of economic collaboration;

(iv) 'Trustee' states should accept accountability to some international body;

(v) Trustee states should promote social, economic and political development;

(vi) Native peoples should participate in government and administration to the fullest possible extent;

(vii) Exclusive economic rights in non-self-governing territories should be relinquished by all powers;

(viii) Administration should remain the responsibility of powers associated with respective territories in the past, subject to changes necessary to general security;

(ix) Colonies should be grouped under Regional Commissions for purposes of international collaboration;

(x) Australia should participate in the control of the affairs of South-East Asia and the Pacific area.[18]

The Australian program of action thus was virtually identical with the State Department's plans, minus only the insistence on independence, and with a greater Australian influence than the State Department had anticipated. The Australian scheme, like the American, embraced an international commission. Under the auspices of the general commission there would be regional commissions. In the western Pacific the Australians envisaged two separate commissions, one for the Indonesian or South-East Asian region, the other for the island groups. Forsyth proposed detailed responsibilities for the commissions, including exchanges of technical personnel, research on economic and social problems, publication of regular reports, and, not least, 'inspection of each territory'. The maps drawn up illustrating the regions of the two commissions made it clear that Australia's voice would be heard all the way from French Polynesia to the Japanese mandated islands and throughout South-East Asia.

By October 1943 Forsyth had completed extensive plans not only for the regional commissions but also for far-reaching reform of the administrations in Papua and the mandated territory of New Guinea. Taking advantage of the opportunities provided by the war, he recommended measures providing amalgamation or at least closer collaboration between the two administrations; a Development and Welfare Act analogous to

[18] Memorandum by Forsyth, 3 May 1943, AA A989 43/735/1021.

the British Act of 1940; and a comprehensive Labour Charter protecting New Guineans against exploitation by the white settlers. These plans are mentioned in passing merely to indicate that Australian officials saw the dawn of a new era in domestic colonial policy as well as in international co-operation. On the domestic side there were similar ramifications in economic and defence planning.[19] The colonial experience in New Guinea, of course, helped to mould the attitudes of Australian planners on the larger colonial issue. They faced a major paradox. On the one hand they were confronted with the New Guinean reality. On the other hand, some of them, at least, were imbued with the ideals of the Labour party. Though Australian officials agreed with the American insistence on international supervision, they found themselves more in sympathy with the British when it came to the ultimate goal of independence versus self-government. No one in the wartime era foresaw self-government, much less independence, as even a remote possibility for New Guinea.

The post-war colonial situation represented only one of several subjects on which the Australians sought New Zealand collaboration. Above all, Evatt wanted to ensure Australian participation in the peace settlement and future security arrangements in the Pacific. It was clear to the New Zealanders that these issues would equally affect their future. The two Dominions began preliminary discussions in October 1943. Little more than a month later, Churchill, Roosevelt, and Chiang Kai-shek issued the Cairo Declaration. The fate of

[19] The following documents give some indication of the scope and substance of administrative reorganization: 'Australian Territories and Australian Colonial Policy', 29 Mar. 1943, AA A989 43/735/144/3; 'The Pacific Territories Association—Memorandum on Post War Reconstruction of Pacific Territories', 13 Aug. 1943, AA A989 43/735/144/3; 'Notes on the Rehabilitation and Reconstruction of New Guinea, Papua and Nauru', 10 Nov. 1943, AA CP 637/1/44, Personal Papers of J. R. Halligan; and, for the defence side, 'The Situation of Australian Colonies as at January 1944', by General T. A. Blamey, Commander-in-Chief, AA A989 43/735/144/3. Of the significant public commentaries, see especially A. P. Elkin, *Wanted—A Charter for the Native Peoples of the Southwest Pacific* (1943), which was discussed extensively within official circles. In this regard Forsyth feared '*possibility of criticism* that there is conflict between *Australian policy* and Australian practice in regard to natives in Australian territories in New Guinea, especially in matters relating to *indentured labour*' (Minute by Forsyth, 16 Jan. 1944, ibid.). Another important pamphlet published at about this time was Julius Stone, *Colonial Trusteeship in Transition* (Australian Institute of International affairs, 1944). Stone was Professor of International Law at the University of Sydney.

Japan's Empire had been determined without even the consultation of Australia and New Zealand. Evatt in particular regarded the Declaration as an affront and a test. He believed that unless Australia and New Zealand acted in concert the great powers would ride roughshod over their interests. These fears were intensified on the eve of the Canberra Conference in January 1944 when Roosevelt at a meeting of the Pacific War Council summarized the results of the Cairo–Teheran meetings and ventured some remarks about the Pacific islands. The President breezily vented his various trusteeship schemes, including specific mention that in his opinion *all* the islands south of the Equator should be included. Since this would directly affect the antipodean Dominions, the statesmen of the two countries were alarmed, even though the President indicated that New Caledonia might 'be transferred to Australia or to Australia and New Zealand'.[20] This bit of generosity on the part of Roosevelt raised disconcerting prospects about the other island groups. The United States did not have a high regard for the claims of Australia and New Zealand to various disputed islands.[21] Indeed there were indications that the President did not take the two Dominions, or at least New Zealand, very seriously. At the same meeting of the Pacific War Council, the New Zealand representative, Walter Nash, stated that his country's interests extended eastward as far as the Society and Tuamotu groups. 'President Roosevelt laughingly suggested that since they were so very ambitious perhaps New Zealand should extend its control to Australia.'[22]

To the New Zealanders the issue of the islands was no laughing matter. To them, as well as to the Australians, the whole

[20] According to the account of the meeting in Kay, *Australian–New Zealand Agreement*, pp. 54–6.

[21] I am indebted to Sir Alister McIntosh (Secretary of External Affairs, 1944–66: Permanent Head of the Prime Minister's Department, 1945–66) for shoving me correspondence dating back to the late 1930s about disputed islands administered by New Zealand but claimed by the United States. To the New Zealanders the high-handed manner of the Americans in their claims to the northern Cook Islands and the Tokelaus still rankled during the war.

[22] Pacific War Council Minutes, 12 Jan. 1944, Roosevelt Papers. Nash also had definite ideas about the disposition of the islands. Here I am grateful to Professor Keith Sinclair for showing me correspondence indicating the exchange of ideas between Nash and the authorities in Wellington on the subject of possible federations and confederations in the South Pacific. (Nash Papers, courtesy of Professor Sinclair.)

question of the future security in the South-West Pacific would depend on the defence guarantees drawn up as part of the peace settlement. In this regard New Zealand as well as the Australian planning encompassed the entire Pacific basin. In a paper drawn up in January 1944, the War Cabinet Secretariat of the New Zealand Prime Minister's Department described the optimal military solution to the problem of the Japanese mandated islands:

We would . . . fully approve the creation of a substantial barrier between Japan, Australia and New Zealand and British territories. This is possible with the cession to the United States of the Island groups to the North of the Equator, i.e. the Carolines, Marianas and Marshalls—which were mandated to Japan by the League of Nations. The occupation of these Japanese fortified Islands by the United States would ensure the creation of a continuous defence line from the mainland of the United States through Hawaii and these islands to the Philippines. In addition, it would create a substantial United States interest in the Pacific and deny the force of the traditional body of isolationist opinion in that country. It should enhance the prospect of close collaboration with the United States in the defence of the Pacific which is essential.[23]

The events of the war had luridly demonstrated the defence dependency of New Zealand and Australia on the United States. The two Dominions had proclaimed eternal thankfulness. By early 1944, however, anxiety now mingled with gratitude as the New Zealanders and Australians contemplated possible post-war American bases in the South Pacific. As Sir Alan Watt has written, the honeymoon was over.[24] The New Zealanders and Australians alike had good reason to combine in an effort to make clear to the United States that post-war defence schemes would be collaborative and not unilateral or decided upon merely by the great powers. Australia and New Zealand would have a voice that counted in the future of the Pacific. This message lay at the heart of the Australian–New Zealand Agreement of the 21st of January 1944.

Like the Atlantic Charter, the Australian–New Zealand Agreement has so many strands of importance for post-war

---

[23] Kay, *Australian–New Zealand Agreement*, p. 60–1.
[24] Watt, *Evolution of Australian Foreign Policy*, p. 77.

foundations that it is easy to lose track of its colonial significance. In this regard there was a meeting of minds between Evatt and the New Zealand Prime Minister, Peter Fraser. They agreed immediately on trusteeship as the basis of future policy. Trusteeship to both of them meant international supervision of colonial territories and accountability to an international organization. Fraser's ideas in their New Zealand context will be discussed later. Here it is important to note that, despite differences in temperament, he and Evatt from the outset formed an effective working partnership. They shared the common ideas of the Labour Party, and both of them felt no hesitation in standing up to either the British or the Americans, though Fraser did so with a good deal more tact than Evatt. Fraser wrote later that, upon arrival in Canberra with the New Zealand party on the 15th of January, he found himself in 75 per-cent agreement with the Australian proposals, which had been thoroughly prepared in advance. In the realm of colonial affairs the consensus was probably even greater because of the careful background papers drafted by Forsyth. The two parties reached agreement in less than a week. Much of this time the New Zealanders spent attempting to soften Evatt's aggressive phraseology. Following his lead the two Dominions took the unprecedented step in British constitutional history of transforming consultative discussions into a formal treaty.

In final form the Agreement still bore the stamp of Evatt's belligerent approach to international affairs. In the case of the post-war territorial settlement, for example, there would be no changes of sovereignty or other adjustments in *any* of the islands of the Pacific without the consent of Australia and New Zealand. Australia would take the initiative in convening an international conference to discuss the affairs of the Pacific and post-war development. They agreed to establish a South Seas Regional Commission. In the security clauses the phraseology read that defence areas *shall* be established.[25] Neither the British nor the Americans were accustomed to such dictation, especially from two remote Dominions in the South Pacific.

The initial British response was one of annoyance. Churchill gruffly noted that the two Dominions had concluded an agreement 'arranged among themselves and published without

[25] Ibid., for a discussion of this point.

consulting us'.[26] Lord Cranborne, now back at the center of the Empire–Commonwealth stage as Dominions Secretary, noted in a memorandum to the War Cabinet that it was 'unfortunate' that the Australians and New Zealanders had made decisions without prior consultation that affected 'our own immense interests in the Pacific'. He especially deplored the Australian urge for 'premature' international discussions. Nevertheless Cranborne on the whole regarded the Agreement as 'extremely valuable'. On their own initiative Australia and New Zealand would now help to relieve that great burden of His Majesty's Government, imperial defence.

From the aspect of defence, it is clearly to the good that Australia and New Zealand should have stated it publicly that they have a primary interest in the defence of the Pacific. This declaration may be extremely valuable when we come to arrangements for the post-war period. Moreover, in advocating the principle of regional collaboration in the Pacific between all the Governments concerned, they have in effect adopted the ideas which we had been considering here and which the Colonial Secretary enunciated in his statement in the House in July last. Finally, so far as the Conference implies closer sympathy and co-operation between Australia and New Zealand themselves, that is all to the good.[27]

Cranborne and his colleagues thus saw a distinct advantage to the Agreement—if Evatt could be kept under control. 'The position is one of some delicacy', Cranborne wrote. 'Dr. Evatt is no doubt delighted with the success of the Canberra meeting and with the lead which Australia and New Zealand have given, and he will be likely to resent anything that he may regard as grandmotherly restraint by the mother country.'[28] Partly not to ruffle Evatt, but mainly because the War Cabinet regarded the Agreement as a genuine landmark in imperial defence, the Australians and New Zealanders received a cordial British response. In Cranborne's words, recording a conversation with Walter Nash, 'we had been delighted with it and . . . we thought that it had initiated a new and valuable inter-Imperial link. We were particularly glad to see the decision of

---

[26] Minute by Churchill, 3 Feb. 1944, DO 35/1989; PREM 4/50/12.
[27] Memorandum by Cranborne, 2 Feb. 1944, W.P. (44) 70; DO 35/1989 PREM 4/50/12. See also *Parliamentary Debates* (Lords), 26 Jan. 1944, c. 555.
[28] Ibid.

the New Zealand and Australian Governments to co-operate in the defence of the Pacific in the post-war period.'[29]

The head of the Far Eastern Department of the Foreign Office, Ashley Clarke, thought that the Agreement embodied principles 'which we ourselves have been discussing, but which have so far not reached any concrete shape'. Though points of detail would have to be settled, there was no reason for the Foreign Office to 'boggle', he wrote.

> In general, I think that this Agreement is to be welcomed. It would have been better if we had been kept somewhat more closely informed by the two Dominions concerned (especially the Australians), but the practical result is on the whole helpful and, from the point of view of the world influence of the British Commonwealth, distinctly encouraging. These two Governments are in a position to say things, e.g. about the post-war set-up in the South-West and South Pacific, which are much less convincing if they come from us in the first instance.[30]

Clarke later noted about the Australian reaction to the Cairo Declaration, 'I am glad that Dr. Evatt brought up the matter of the Cairo communiqué which . . . was sprung on us by the Americans at short notice *after* prior consultation with the Chinese.'[31] Another Foreign Office official, Nevile Butler of the North American Department, found much more fault with Evatt's initiatives and manner, but he also generally agreed with his colleagues about the antipodean motivation.

> It looks as though New Zealand and Australia, as their very real fears of invasion have receded, have now, like most of the Latin American States, grown alarmed of the United States embrace, fostered no doubt by the kind of imperialistic stuff that the [military] services talk, and that they are now more urgently concerned to shake off that embrace than to secure U.S. participation in some Security system.[32]

The Australians now seemed less eager to endorse American planning, but their ideas about regional-defence zones in the South-West Pacific paralleled British thinking.

[29] Memorandum by Cranborne, 14 Feb. 1944, DO 35/1990. See also W.M. (44) 17th Conclusions, 9 Feb. 1944, CAB 65/41.
[30] Minute by Clarke, 2 Feb. 1944, W 2145, FO 371/32681.
[31] Memorandum by Clarke, 2 Mar. 1944, W3317/G, FO 371/42677.
[32] Minute by Butler, 5 Feb. 1944, W2145, FO 371/32681.

In the Colonial Office Christopher Eastwood noted that the Agreement would affect 'almost every department' and concerned them 'very deeply'. He hoped that Lord Cranborne would throw 'cold water' on the idea of an international conference. In general, however, Eastwood regarded the Agreement sympathetically:

[W]hile the two Dominions set about the matter rather tactlessly (the more wary New Zealanders being pushed into it by the Australians), on the whole the agreement between them seems to be rather a good document. It contains one or two oddities. . . . [and] the idea of the International Conference is rather premature. But these and other faults of the agreement may perhaps be attributed to the youthful enthusiasm of the Dominions, the political ambitions of Dr. Evatt, secretarial inefficiency and the haste with which the proceedings were conducted, and I find nothing positively pernicious in the agreement at all. The two countries were speaking as two 'small nations' anxious to keep their end up with the Big Four.[33]

Eastwood also noted later that care should be taken to consult the Australians and New Zealanders in the planning of the regional commissions. '[I]t is clear that Australia, and in a lesser degree New Zealand, are both very sensitive lest "small nations" such as they are should not be consulted before important decisions affecting them are taken.'[34] G. E. J. Gent also stressed the importance of full and friendly collaboration: 'I hope we shall not be too fearful of Australian "Imperialism". . . . I believe that an extension of Australia's practical interest in the South Pacific is of essential importance to the Empire in that hemisphere and our exertions should be in the direction not of curbing it but of doing all we can to promote them and guide it.'[35] The Colonial Office thus saw no reason to be especially alarmed at antipodean initiatives. The exuberant energies of the Australians and New Zealanders would merely have to be channelled in the right direction.

Taking a substantially different view, the British High Commissioner in Australia, Sir Ronald Cross, believed that Australian 'Imperialism' did exist and should not be regarded as

---

[33] Minute by Eastwood, 8 Feb. 1944, CO 968/157/148811/10.
[34] Memorandum by Eastwood, 28 Mar. 1944, CO 968/157/14811/10.
[35] Minute by Gent, 9 Mar. 1944, CO 968/157/14811/10.

a false issue. A close observer of Australian politics, he had reported in 1943 on Evatt's personal ambitions and the secrecy which shrouded Australian plans for 'defence zones' in the Pacific. He evaluated the Agreement in quite different terms from those in London who viewed it as an expression of youthful exuberance. Cross reported in mid-February 1944:

The most important project in the agreement is the 'Security and Defence Zone.' In effect, the two Dominions have drawn a line on the map; a line—somewhat ambiguous in parts—round a large region in which they themselves live, and have proclaimed that they propose that they and the other Governments possessing territories within that area should retain entire possession of their own territories, and that they should manage all their own affairs within that region, including the responsibilities of local defence. They let it emerge clearly that they would object to any outside interference with these indubitable rights, and it is obvious from the drawing of the line and in other ways that it is United States interference with their possessions that they apprehend. . . .

In sum, the Security and Defence Zone declaration amounts to a proposal to establish a Monroe Doctrine covering a large proportion of the territories of the Pacific situated south of the Equator. . . .

A second very important feature of the agreement is the 'South Seas Regional Commission' for the promotion of the welfare of native peoples. It also emerges clearly from the Agreement that the two Dominions are apprehensive lest China should succeed in bringing such pressure to bear upon them that they would be unable to maintain their white immigration policies. . . .

There is thus a bid to set up two political blocs, one primarily in self-defence against the United States, whilst the other might constitute a safeguard against Chinese immigration . . . [Evatt] also desires that the Commonwealth [Australian] Government should take over the administration of the British Solomons, and he no doubt turns a predatory eye towards other islands not in British possession.[36]

The Australian–New Zealand Agreement thus could be read as a far-reaching and systematic plan for Australian expansion and protection of the white immigration policies. It could be interpreted as a definite threat to British possessions, though its main thrust was anti-American.

[36] Cross to Cranborne, No. 73, 18 Feb. 1944, DO 35/1993; W.P. (44) 169; CAB 66/48.

The American response can be summed up as one of suppressed outrage. The State Department officials restrained their indignation because they did not want to give Evatt the satisfaction of knowing the extent of the provocation. The head of the Division of British Commonwealth Affairs, John Hickerson, wrote: 'In our opinion it would be bad tactics to take this Agreement too seriously. We believe that the Agreement goes to lengths which are manifestly ridiculous. We feel that it is largely the result of Dr. Evatt's ego, ambition and feeling of annoyance at being left out of things.'[37] In a memorandum forwarded by Hull to the Joint Chiefs of Staff, the State Department described Evatt as 'anxious to assume a position of leadership in international affairs both for Australia and for himself'. His ambitions could be described in terms usually reserved for the Japanese. 'While he has disclaimed any desire for territorial aggrandisement, he has for some months been talking in terms bordering on a "co-prosperity sphere" for Australia in the Pacific.' The heart of the Australian–New Zealand Agreement, the State Department explained to the Joint Chiefs, amounted to no less than 'an unblushing Monroe Doctrine covering *all* islands of the Pacific'.[38]

With a clear-cut sense of the vital military issue at stake, the Joint Chiefs perceived a threat to the post-war control by the United States of the Japanese mandated islands. An analysis by the Joint Strategic Survey Committee, dated the 4th of March 1944, summarized the strategic significance of the problem.

The relation of these islands to our security will assume a . . . vital character in future, with the increase in the munitioning capacity of Asia that will result from the progressive industrialization of its vast population—approximately one-half the world's total. Their secure defense against a militant Asia can be assured only by the United States. The implication in the Australian–New Zealand Agreement that these countries are capable of defending all or any part of these islands has no foundation in reality.[39]

---

[37] Memorandum by Hickerson, 29 Jan. 1944, USSD 747.47H/21.
[38] Hull to Leahy with enclosures, 5 Feb. 1944, JCS CCS092.2 (2–5–44).
[39] Report by the Joint Strategic Survey Committee, 4 Mar. 1944 JCS CCS092.2 (2–5–44).

Since Australia and New Zealand had ambitions of participating in the post-war defence system, the Joint Chiefs assessed their military capabilities.

Notwithstanding their vast area, their arable regions are so limited that they can support only a small increase in their present sparse population of 8,500,000. Their limited mineral reserves will suffice for only a small munitioning production. These circumstances, coupled with their geographical position, render them incapable of assuring the defense of their territories against any one of the several potentially strong Asiatic Powers.[40]

The Joint Chiefs emphasized the preposterous nature of the antipodean pretensions by pointing out that, far from being able to protect outlying island groups, Australia and New Zealand could not even defend their own home territories.

In April 1944 the Prime Ministers of both New Zealand and Australia passed through Washington on their way to attend the Commonwealth Prime Ministers' Conference in London. Peter Fraser met with Cordell Hull, who proceeded to tell him in lashing words that the United States viewed the Australian–New Zealand Agreement as anti-American in intent. Hull wrote to Roosevelt:

I have told Prime Minister Fraser that this agreement, so far as tone and method are concerned, seems to resemble the Russian action against Great Britain when the Russians, being dissatisfied with the British attitude toward Poland, issued a world-wide statement charging Britain with the intention of negotiating a separate peace with Germany.[41]

Of immediate importance, Hull gained Fraser's acquiescence in postponing the 'international conference' in which Evatt had projected himself as the star. The Secretary of State confirmed the impression that Evatt was the prime mover behind the Agreement. The Prime Minister of Australia, John Curtin, gave Hull a similar account. Curtin had had virtually nothing to do with the actual drafting of the Agreement and, like Fraser, quickly yielded to Hull's demand to forsake the idea of a conference. Hull told Curtin that he had been 'flabbergasted'

[40] Ibid.
[41] Memorandum by Hull for Roosevelt, 22 Apr. 1944, USSD 747.47H/51A. See also memoranda of other conversations with New Zealand officials in USSD NF Box 186.

at the whole affair and did not appreciate 'the attitude of Dr. Evatt'.[42]

On the 25th of April 1944 Roosevelt entertained Curtin for lunch at a country estate in South Carolina. Afterwards they talked for nearly an hour. The Prime Minister began to explain the reasons for the Australian–New Zealand Agreement. 'President Roosevelt said that he thought he had already figured out what had occurred. His guess is that Prime Minister Curtin had had very little to do with the drafting but that Evatt had done most of it and others had merely agreed. Curtin said that was exactly right . . .'[43] Roosevelt directed that a record be kept to indicate 'that it will be best for us to forget the whole incident'.

The tactics of 'the good doctor' (as Evatt was sarcastically called in the State Department) were not forgotten. His aggressive manner detracted from the merit of his argument. In the particular case of trusteeship, the State Department officials had to overcome their aversion to Evatt's personality before they could see that his goal was essentially the same as theirs. Evatt, for his part, had drawn the moral from the Cairo Declaration that the great powers would disregard the smaller nations unless bludgeoned into paying attention. When the Australians learned that the Americans had responded to the Australian–New Zealand Agreement with such righteous indignation, recalls W. D. Forsyth, 'We laughed.'[44]

[42] Memorandum by Hull, 24 Apr. 1944, Foreign Relations, 1944, iii. 192–4; Kay, *Australian–New Zealand Agreement*, pp. 275–7. For comment see especially Lissington, *New Zealand and the United States*, pp. 92–6.

[43] Memorandum dated 25 Apr. 1944, Roosevelt Papers MR Box 168.

[44] As related in a conversation with the author, 17 Aug. 1974.

19

REGIONAL PLANNING IN THE
COLONIAL OFFICE

FOR the Colonial Office, the Australian–New Zealand Agreement acutely raised the issue of future regional commissions as an alternative to international trusteeship. 'The [Australian] Commonwealth and New Zealand Governments', wrote T. K. Lloyd, 'mean to force the pace on the question of a South Seas Regional Commission.'[1] At the same time, the Americans threatened to persist in pressing for the 'freak' (again Lloyd's word) colonial declaration. In the winter and spring of 1944 the Colonial Office thus felt international pressures to proceed with regional post-war planning or forfeit the initiative. If friendly relations with the United States were to be maintained in the realm of colonial affairs, the Colonial Office could not merely do nothing. But it was doubtful whether a colonial declaration would now satisfy the Americans. For all the highflying talk of international trusteeship, the State Department, to the officials of the Colonial Office at least, seemed bent on a much more mundane objective. The United States needed justification for the annexation of the Japanese mandated islands. Though the Joint Chiefs had no qualms in putting forward annexationist claims on grounds of security, to most Americans, including the President, it was heresy to speak of 'imperialism' on the part of the United States, in the Pacific or in any other part of the world.

'Trusteeship', or the opposite of 'imperialism', was the appropriate word. This subtle (or naïve) point did not go unnoticed in British circles. To the officials of the Colonial Office it seemed clear that American 'trusteeship', in the Pacific at least, meant the extension of the American Empire. The words 'cloak' and 'cover' ran through the minutes of T. K. Lloyd and Christopher Eastwood. They had no objection to American aims. Indeed the American presence in the northern Pacific would be necessary

---

[1] Minute by Lloyd, 1 Feb. 1944, CO 323/1877/9086.

to stabilize the region and to create a buffer between Japan and the antipodean Dominions. But American insistence on 'trusteeship' rather than straightforward annexation meant that British planning would have to accommodate an idealistic cover. A colonial declaration alone would not be sufficient. A noble purpose would have to be found for the Americans in specific territorial arrangements that would complement British colonial reorganization. The Colonial Office's grand strategy therefore was designed to deflect the Americans into regional commissions and away from a single international organization which might more directly threaten British authority. To get the Americans down from the clouds of high principles into the realistic planning for the future in definite regions became a major British colonial goal in 1944.

Christopher Eastwood directed the Colonial Office's effort to produce a master plan for regional colonial bodies. He brought to the task a sense of proportion in relation to analogous planning in the Foreign Office and other departments, and in relation to the Prime Minister's ideas on the subject. So vast was the scope of 'regionalism' that he found it helpful intellectually to make clear distinctions. Beginning with the concept in its broadest and fundamental sense, Eastwood wrote that Churchill's notion of regionalism 'follows from the theory that the world is too large to be organised as one unit and must therefore be divided up into a few regions'. Churchill in 1943 had spoken of regional councils for Europe, America, and Asia.[2] Eastwood also noted the regional-defence schemes and world-security plans being developed by the Combined Chiefs of Staff and the Foreign Office.[3] These larger types of regional political and defence planning he distinguished from 'our humbler Colonial sense' of regionalism.[4] Humble it might have been, but it was of central importance. When the planners of whatever ilk established their principles, British colonies in every part of the world would be affected. Thus the Colonial Office was expected to produce 'the major part', in Eastwood's

[2] See Churchill, *Hinge of Fate*, pp. 802–7.
[3] See *The Memoirs of Lord Gladwyn*, ch. 9.
[4] Minutes by Eastwood, 19 Jan., 9 Feb., and 16 Mar. 1944, CO 323/1877/9086. In clarifying his ideas on the subject Eastwood acknowledged as especially helpful the memoranda on regional organization prepared by the Foreign Office Research Department.

words, of the background papers for the Dominions Prime Ministers' Conference in May. This future event in particular gave a sense of urgency to the Colonial Office's regional planning.

Eastwood faced a formidable task. He not only confronted the traditional Colonial Office problem of reconciling local circumstances with general policies but also the difficulty of making the scheme acceptable to other departments in the government, and, beyond that, negotiable with foreign governments. To mention only two difficulties that could be expected to arise within the Commonwealth alone, Canada would probably press for participation in the Caribbean Commission, and South Africa would expect a voice in the affairs of central and possibly eastern Africa.[5] In West Africa the French could not be depended upon to cooperate. In the Pacific, the Colonial Office could only guess how the United States might view possible participation in regional commissions. Eastwood elicited this response from the head of the Western Pacific Department, Trafford Smith, who expressed sentiments that held true of all the area specialists:

We had always imagined that after the war some machinery would be set up to deal with matters of common concern in the South Seas area. It is indeed to the advantage of the various British, French and American Colonial Dependencies concerned that Australia and New Zealand should recognize an obligation to lend their resources, both in material and in expert personnel, towards administrative and economic well being of these territories; and also that they should participate in a regional defence scheme which would presumably involve the other sovereign powers concerned in the area.[6]

Though Trafford Smith recognized the value of international colonial co-operation, he also urged definite limitations. In the Pacific, at least, regional co-operation would be consultative and optional, not mandatory.

It is . . . an undoubted fact that neither New Zealand, Australia, nor the French, nor the Americans have achieved any great success in the administration of their Pacific Island Dependencies,

[5] Lloyd's minute of 1 Feb. 1944, CO 323/1877/9086.
[6] Minute by Trafford Smith, 4 Feb. 1944, CO 323/1877/9086.

compared with that achieved in the Dependencies controlled by the United Kingdom. It is thus the duty of H.M.G. . . . to confine the proposed regional organization to a mutually helpful and consultative one.[7]

If the Western Pacific held promise of fruitful collaboration, South-East Asia, of all the areas, presented the most difficulties. 'There will be a much larger proportion of prognostication' as opposed to actual planning, Eastwood noted about that region.[8]

While the heads of the Geographical Departments analyzed the problem of regional bodies in their particular areas, Eastwood grappled with the central problem of accountability. Were the regional commissions to be merely consultative, without executive authority? Or were they to be responsible to a broader international organization? Eastwood knew that the Americans would press for accountability to an overriding trusteeship authority. Yet he fully perceived the Colonial Secretary's unwavering antipathy to any proposal that savoured of international accountability. Eastwood was intellectually honest. He took account of the arguments in favour of international trusteeship. He found support for the idea in G. F. Seel, one of the very few Colonial Office officials at the time who had anything at all favourable to say about international trusteeship. About an 'International Colonial Commission', Seel wrote:

> Personally I do not understand the objections felt to this. The real difficulty about the P[ermanent] M[andates] C[ommission] was due to the uncertainty of status of the Mandated Territories, not that they had to report each year to an international body. It is true . . . that the value of such a body is not constructive, but in a negative plane. But that is what is needed to ensure that world conscience asserts itself in the government of dependent countries: not to have a world body to carry out their development.[9]

Seel favoured the replacement of the mandates system by an international colonial commission that would represent 'world opinion' and would 'receive reports and bring to light offences against world conscience'.[10] This was the extent to which the

---

[7] Minute by Trafford Smith, 4 Feb. 1944, CO 323/1877/9086.

[8] Minute by Eastwood, 9 Feb. 1944, CO 323/1877/9086.

[9] Memorandum by Seel, no date but *c.* 27 Mar. 1944, CO 323/1877/9086.

[10] Ibid.

trusteeship system of the United Nations received support in its inchoate state in early 1944 in the Colonial Office. Eastwood merely advised the Colonial Secretary that the United States would certainly advocate an international trusteeship authority which would carry with it the right to receive reports and pay visits of inspection. He also pointed out that the acceptance of an 'International Colonial Commission' might be the price the British would have to pay to get rid of the mandates system. The hope in this direction lay in converting the American proposals into an international convention of 'a harmless kind without any supervisory body at all'.[11]

Only the press of events caused the Colonial Secretary to take any action at all. Stanley had procrastinated in coming to grips with the American colonial declaration, hoping that it would die 'a natural death', and in general took the attitude towards the Americans of 'letting sleeping dogs lie'.[12] He had not moved to implement the plan of regional commissions, even though he himself had proclaimed in Parliament that regional development would be one of the main goals of British colonial policy. Like Churchill, he had an extreme distaste for such phrases as 'international trusteeship' or 'international colonial accountability'. Since even some officials in the Colonial Office (notably G. F. Seel and Sydney Caine) clearly demonstrated that British complaints about the mandates system were exaggerated, it could be argued that there was an element of the irrational in the attitude of Stanley—and Churchill—towards international trusteeship, though it could equally be argued that history has proved that they recognized a genuine threat to the British Empire. In any case Stanley responded to Eastwood's mention of an international colonial commission with the words 'I am completely opposed to this'. He thanked Eastwood, however, for the great amount of work put into 'this very difficult & rather nebulous subject'.[13]

The fruits of the Colonial Office's labor can be seen in relation to the four areas where it seemed possible to establish regional commissions. In the *Caribbean* the basis already existed in the

[11] Minutes by Eastwood, 16 and 28 Mar. 1944, CO 323/1877/9086.
[12] Minute by Jebb of 17 Mar. 1944, relating a conversation with Eastwood, U2338/G, FO 371/40749.
[13] Minute by Stanley, 29 Mar. 1944, CO 323/1877/9086.

Anglo-American Caribbean Commission, which could be expanded to include Canada, the Netherlands, France, the independent Caribbean states of Cuba, Haiti, the Dominican Republic, and some of the South American states with economic interests in the area, such as Venezuela. As Eastwood had noted earlier, in the Caribbean 'regionalism is a plant of steady if slow growth'.

In *Africa*, the Colonial Office anticipated the greatest difficulties, in large part because of South Africa. Smuts could be expected, as usual, to press his ideas about all of Africa, which might include a 'regional' commission covering almost all of the continent. In the Colonial Office view such a broad commission would be 'impractical' and its deliberations would be 'largely theoretical'. Above all, South African influence would be extended:

> The inhabitants of West Africa would resent very deeply an association which would appear to bring them under the predominant influence of the Union.

> There would, however, be advantage in a Regional Commission covering Southern and Central Africa. The area would include Northern Rhodesia, Nyasaland, Portuguese East and West Africa and the Belgian Congo. Southern Rhodesia would either be a part of the region or an 'outside Power'. South Africa would also be an outside Power.[14]

The inclusion of Portuguese Africa and the Belgian Congo in a central or southern African commission would lessen the danger of South African domination. For West Africa the Colonial Office would insist on a separate commission covering the four British colonies, French West and Equatorial Africa, the Spanish and Portuguese possessions, and Liberia. The United States would probably be included as having a major interest, though in Stanley's opinion the Americans were unpopular in West Africa. In East Africa the Colonial Office saw little practical use for a regional commission, but granted that it might be necessary to create one eventually in order to include all of the major British colonial territories in some form of regional organization. For the time being Stanley wanted

[14] The quotations follow the project as it appeared in its final form as a War Cabinet paper, 'Regional Bodies in Colonial Areas', W.P. (44) 211, 18 Apr. 1944, CAB 66/49.

East Africa omitted from regional commission schemes. Above all the goal in East Africa would be to prevent South African penetration and *not* to incorporate this region in a larger commission where the South Africans might predominate: 'To include . . . this area in the southern Regional Commission dominated by the Union would undoubtedly increase the Union's political and economic penetration and from our point of view is most undesirable.'[15]

In *South-East Asia* it appeared futile to discuss definite plans for regional organization while the Japanese still occupied the area. Here the difficulties were immense. 'This area before the war had much greater wealth (rubber, tin, &c.) than the other areas discussed, and a much greater population (of the order of 120 millions).' The Colonial Office thought it wise to indicate British willingness to include South-East Asia within the scope of a possible regional commission as otherwise the Americans might think the British blatantly wished to perpetuate the old pre-war imperial order. Within the commission there would be Malaya, the Netherlands East Indies, the British territories in Borneo, Portuguese Timor, Siam, Indo-China, and the Philippines, but the Colonial Office wished to leave open the possible membership of Burma, Ceylon, and Hong Kong. Much of the difficulty involved in establishing a South-East Asia regional commission derived from the economic and strategic interest of several states, including not only the colonial powers but also the United States, Australia, China, India, 'and even possibly Russia'.[16]

In the *South-West Pacific* the Colonial Office officials found, to their surprise, that the opportunities for realistic cooperation were greater than in any of the other regions. The Colonial Office recommended accepting the proposals of the Australian–New Zealand Agreement for collaboration in such policies as health and education, medical services, and labour conditions. 'The region would include Fiji and other United Kingdom islands; New Caledonia and other French islands; the New Hebrides; various United States islands; the Mandated Territories and dependencies of Australia and New Zealand; and the islands at present mandated to the Japanese.'[17] The Colonial Office hoped that the inclusion of the Japanese mandated

[15] Ibid.   [16] Ibid.   [17] Ibid.

islands would help the Americans find sufficient 'cover' for their annexationist projects. In the Pacific, 'it would probably be wise to let Australia and New Zealand take the initiative'.[18]

Stanley had no difficulty in securing the endorsement of the Colonial Office's scheme by his colleagues in the Cabinet. At a committee meeting including Cranborne, Amery, and Ernest Bevin (Minister of Labour and National Service), the Colonial Secretary explained that the United States would probably press 'for some colonial organisation as cover for their plans regarding the Japanese Pacific Islands'. Here Stanley for the first time revealed how far he would be willing to go to meet the American demands on trusteeship. If necessary, he would agree to the creation of an 'international colonial centre'. The Cabinet committee concurred:

> [T]hat the aim should be to get rid, if possible, of the Mandates system and that we should be prepared, if necessary for the achievement of this object to accept the establishment of some form of international colonial centre, attached to the proposed world organisation, to which reports would be made by Colonial Powers and/or Regional Colonial Commissions. The functions of the international colonial centre should be purely secretarial, i.e. it would receive reports and collate information.[19]

Stanley thus hoped to placate the Americans with an international colonial library. As for the regional commissions, he reiterated that they would be 'purely consultative, without executive powers'. When the War Cabinet discussed the Colonial Office's scheme in April, Cranborne commented on Stanley's omission of East Africa from a regional grouping. '[I]f large areas of the Colonial Empire were left outside the Regional Council arrangements, this might cause misunderstanding with the United States.'[20] Apart from this objection, the War Cabinet concurred in the Colonial Office's strategy to deflect the Americans away from international trusteeship and into regional commissions.

To place the problem of regional planning in broader perspective, it is illuminating to trace one particular issue from

---

[18] Ibid.
[19] D.P.M. (44) 3rd Meeting, 12 Apr. 1944, CAB 97/27.
[20] War Cabinet Conclusions 58 (44), 27 Apr. 1944, CAB 65/42.

the beginning of the war. Of all the regions where some sort of co-ordinated program of development could be expected after the cessation of hostilities, East Africa raised the question of trusteeship in its most acute form. The problem had both a national and an international dimension. To pose the issue again in the most basic way, *for whom were these territories being held in trust?* For the white settlers of Kenya? Or for the Africans in Tanganyika? There were further fundamental questions. For example, what of the Indian community in Uganda? During the war the white settlers began to talk once again of closer union. This was an historic controversy. In 1929 the Hilton Young Commission had recommended the appointment of a Governor-General with wide powers of supervision and control. In 1931 a Joint Select Committee of both Houses of Parliament decided that the time was not yet ripe for taking far-reaching steps towards formal union of the three territories.[21] The issue lay unresolved but by no means dormant in the 1930s as the white settlers in Tanganyika uneasily noted Nazi propaganda for the return of the former German colony. Now the war might offer the chance to end once and for all time the tenuous status of the mandate. According to a prominent settler in Kenya, Lord Francis Scott, in late 1939:

> Out here we naturally get infuriated by the various suggestions by armchair professors of the leftist school that after we Colonials have done our bit to help the Empire win this war, as our reward we should be thrown out of the Empire for which we are fighting and handed over to some conglomerate body of Huns and Dagos . . . the British Colonists in Tanganyika want to throw off the shackles of the mandatory system and become a real part of the British Empire.[22]

Such attitudes posed a delicate problem for the Colonial Office. If the issue were mismanaged, the white settlers might be driven into the arms of South Africa. On the other hand the Colonial Office keenly felt the negative injunction of trusteeship: in Tanganyika the interests of the Africans must

[21] For these developments see especially Robert C. Gregory, *India and East Africa* (Oxford, 1971), chs. 9 and 10.

[22] Scott to Halifax, 29 Dec. 1939, copy in CO 847/20/47141, with important C.O. minutes: e.g. 'when the time comes . . . H.M.G. will not be insensitive to the interests and feelings either of the native populations or of those of our own blood in East Africa' (Minute by G. F. Seel, 17 Jan. 1940).

predominate. In the phrase of the time, Tanganyika was a 'native territory'.

The reason for the Colonial Office's anxiety about South African expansion may be made clear from a few quotations. General Smuts, who had taken a large view of the white man's future in eastern Africa since before the turn of the century, said to South African troops in Kenya in 1940: 'The efforts you are making will, perhaps not in our time, bring about a United States of Africa. With the material we have and the chance that is ours, that dream of the future will be realised.' In April of the same year, he developed the theme of pan-South Africanism:

> The time would appear to be both ripe and opportune, as never before, for developing and fostering trade between the Union and her neighbours. . . . The Pan-African idea is more than a dream. . . . The countries of the north are looking to us for guidance. . . . The African idea should become a practical force in the shaping of the destiny of this continent.[23]

By the African idea, Smuts meant the *South* African idea of the eastern part of the continent under South African leadership. In the words of some of his less cautious followers, Dr. Steenkamp and Colonel Reitz respectively:

> I am still hoping to see Jan Smuts' great dream realised when Africa right up to Abyssinia will be one great South African State. . . . An allied victory would change the whole political future of South Africa. A United States of South Africa would be established, and the partners would be countries like Rhodesia, Tanganyika, Kenya and Uganda, who are fighting to-day side by side with South Africa.[24]

> I visualise, some day, a great confederation in Africa, extending from Table Mountain to the Equator . . .[25]

The ideas of Cecil Rhodes were still alive, though not in a way that appealed to Imperialists in London.

South African expansion might take different directions,

[23] Quotations from Smuts's speeches, C.P.P. 96 (44), CO 847/23/47173.
[24] Dr. Steenkamp in the South African House of Assembly, 3 Mar. 1941, and speech to the Empire Group, Cape Town, 10 July 1941, quoted ibid.
[25] Colonel Deneys Reitz (Minister for Native Affairs), speech on the Rand, reported in *Forum*, 2 Nov. 1940, quoted ibid.

informal as well as formal. According to that hard-headed Imperialist, Lord Hailey, in 1941:

I do not believe that South Africa has any idea of establishing control or any form of political federation, but she wishes to get recognition of a sphere of influence in which she would be accounted to be the protector of the interests of white civilisation. South Africa is not interested in Uganda, nor in Nyasaland where there are very few Europeans, but only in the 'white belt'.[26]

Lord Lloyd, the Colonial Secretary in 1940, had made a similar assessment. He was especially pessimistic about the long-range relations between the British and the Afrikaners:

'. . . I am sure that we must reckon with the possibility of South African nationalism taking a strongly anti-British course. . . . The dissident forces in South Africa are inherent and powerful. History and blood will tell, and the fusion of two such obstinate peoples as Briton and Boer is not an easy thing.[27]

Lloyd went on to say that Smuts's moderation should not be allowed to obscure the real danger of Afrikaner nationalism.

As long as Smuts is in charge, there is no immediate anxiety, though even he, whom I know intimately and regard much, is an ardent expansionist as regards the north. But if he should disappear from the scene, we might quickly find ourselves confronted with a situation in which East and Central Africa were subject to powerful anti-British pressure which it was too late to control. The very fact that Smuts is at present in control and that our war interests are leading us to cooperate closely with the Union may, in itself, be a danger in so far as it blinds us to a situation to which we may well wake up too late.[28]

Sir Arthur Dawe (Assistant Under-Secretary of State) posed the basic proposition in a slightly different way. He asked, what about the white settlers in East Africa? Would they drift into the South African camp? 'The real problem is: How far are the people who have migrated to East and Central Africa

---

[26] Note of a discussion at the Colonial Office, 18 Mar. 1941, CO 847/23/47173. Later in the discussion Hailey remarked about race relations in southern Africa: 'The colour bar feeling was just as strong among the British as among the Afrikanders in Northern Rhodesia, though he thought that the war had brought rather more Afrikanders to the Northern Rhodesian mines.'

[27] Lloyd to Sir Henry Moore (Governor of Kenya), 'Most Secret and Personal', 8 Jan. 1941, CO 847/23/47181. [28] Ibid.

from the British Isles beginning to look to South Africa rather
than to Great Britain owing to a reaction against British ideas
on native policy and other matters?'[29] Here was the key issue
as it affected the mandated territory of Tanganyika. Would the
Colonial Office continue to adhere to the principle of paramountcy of native interests? At the same time how could the
Colonial Office reconcile the white settlers?

For the immediate problems of the Second World War period,
a good deal turned on the plans of General Smuts. In 1943 the
Colonial Office feared that he might propose a general conference to discuss the future of tropical Africa. Seizing the
opportunities of the war, the South Africans might make suggestions, for example, about Portuguese Africa and the Belgian
Congo that could prove to be highly embarrassing to the
British. Space does not permit an adequate discussion of the
genesis and debate about this proposed project. In short,
Lord Harlech, the High Commissioner in South Africa, hoped
that a conference might facilitate the post-war planning for the
economic development of southern and eastern Africa. In
London the Imperial statesmen became agitated about the
possibilities and consequences. According to Lord Cranborne:

There are obvious embarrassments in a conference between
belligerents and neutrals in the middle of a world war. . . . This must
cause difficulties for a nation like Portugal, whose collaboration
would be necessary in any international set-up.

There is also the difficulty for us that, in my view at any rate, an
essential feature of our post-war African policy must be to weld our
East African and West African colonies into two great blocks. To
attempt to enter into international negotiations before that stage
had been completed would be to put the cart before the horse, and
might tend to perpetuate the present unsatisfactory position.[30]

Smuts thus appeared to hold out a veritable Pandora's Box of
African troubles for the Imperial government. To stress only
one among many difficulties, Attlee made it clear in the discussions that the Labour Party would not condone any scheme
that might give the white settlers the upper hand. The con-

---

[29] Minute by Dawe, 10 July 1942, CO 847/23/47178.

[30] Cranborne to Attlee, 22 July 1943, CO 847/23/47181. For an illumination of
these issues in regard to the High Commission Territories, see Ronald Hyam,
The Failure of South African Expansion, 1908–1948 (London, 1972), ch. 7.

ference might be restricted to technical economic development. But even that limited scope was objectionable to those in the Colonial Office who attached paramount importance to the African side of the problem. According to G. F. Seel, economic expansion would mean indirect political influence. Smuts might say that he had no intention of interfering politically in East Africa, but such statements were highly misleading.

It is, of course, very convenient for those who wish to force the political pace in *East* Africa . . . to hold out a welcoming hand to South Africa in economic matters while claiming that no political issues need be involved. It is, however, impossible to conceive that if South Africa is encouraged to interest herself financially and economically in East Africa, she will be content to leave the political arena alone.[31]

There were further objections to a conference which might promote South African 'economic assistance' within the international setting of tropical Africa. Sir Arthur Dawe noted, 'it would meet with a storm of criticism from powerful elements in East and Central Africa who do not want to have anything to do with internationalism.'[32]

To their immense relief, the Colonial Office officials discovered that Smuts had not intended to promote a conference to discuss the future of Africa in the middle of the war. In a minute written with uncharacteristic exuberance, Oliver Stanley noted in mid-1943:

I had a talk with Field Marshal Smuts. . . . I found him in very good form and most friendly. . . . His own view appeared to be very much that which we had developed here, viz. that any grandiose conference with wide subjects for discussion would arouse great suspicion and might very well end in complete failure. . . .

I gained the impression that the Field Marshal has no intention of pressing unduly any political connections either in East or Central Africa. Clearly it was his line to develop the closest economic connection so that in the future he would have a very strong hold if he chose to develop the political connection, or in any case, if he decided to leave us with the political headaches in those territories, he would remain in enjoyment of all the economic advantages.[33]

[31] Minute by Seel, 26 June 1943, CO 847/23/47181.
[32] Minute by Dawe, 18 June 1943, ibid.
[33] Memorandum by Stanley, 19 Nov. 1943, CO 847/23/47181.

This was an acute comment. The 'headaches' were indeed severe.

Would the British respond to the challenges and opportunities of the war to set East Africa on a sound future course? Or would British policy *drift*? Lord Cranborne, for one, believed that the time had come to make resolute decisions.

> I am sure that we must find some means of amalgamating Kenya, Tanganyika and Uganda into one block. The present litter of territories is entirely out of keeping with the modern world. What form the new confederation or Dominion should take is still for consideration, and no doubt presents very real difficulties. But, while there must clearly be adequate safeguards for the black population, I would not personally rule out the idea of a white controlled self-governing administration under a Governor General.[34]

Cranborne was writing these lines to Attlee, who in this case persistently upheld the Labour Party view that federation in East Africa should be opposed. From the Tory point of view, it was mandatory that Attlee and the other Labour members of the government be persuaded of the wisdom of solving the East African problem. Otherwise a future Labour government might reverse the course.

Cranborne used all his powers of persuasion. He raised the possibility of a breakaway state (on the lines of present day Rhodesia). 'I fully recognise your preoccupations,' he wrote to Attlee, 'which I know are shared by numbers of people in your party and other parties too.' He went on: 'But we have to face hard facts. The white people of Kenya and Tanganyika are already extremely restive under Whitehall Government. They will not stand it permanently, and we shall, I am convinced, be unable to coerce them, even if we wish to do so.'[35]

Cranborne above all wished to avoid any increase of South African influence. This would have dire consequences for British trusteeship of black Africans.

> Already, Kenya and Tanganyika have moved a considerable way along the road to responsible government, under the guise of machinery set up ostensibly to aid the war effort. It will be impossible to reverse that tendency now, without completely alienating white opinion in the territories concerned, and pushing them to-

---

[34] Cranborne to Attlee, 22 July 1943, CO 822/108/46523.   [35] Ibid.

wards the Union, which would, from the point of view of the black population, be a disastrous development.

I am, therefore, personally in favour of examining sympathetically the possibility of setting up a white controlled responsible government for the two territories of Kenya and Tanganyika, though some other arrangement would have to be devised for Uganda, the three being linked together under a Governor-General.[36]

At the same time Cranborne did not neglect the need for safeguards for the Africans. 'This would no doubt be difficult, but it should not prove insuperable.'[37] He had a Cecilian sense of responsibility to black Africans as well as to those whom he regarded as his kith and kin.

Cranborne favoured a *federal* solution to the problem of East Africa. Sir Henry Moore, the Governor of Kenya, supported a *unitary* solution. The Colonial Office on the whole opposed the unitary scheme because it would mean, in effect, the domination of East Africa by the white settlers. Sir Arthur Dawe once described the 'federal' solution as 'an eventual self-governing Dominion under white settler control'. This was a scheme that would allow autonomy for part of Kenya.

[T]he Kenya Highlands . . . should be granted self-government and the remainder of the three territories [i.e. the remainder of Kenya plus all of Tanganyika and Uganda] would be administered under a High Commissioner under Colonial Office control. Generally speaking the idea would be to divide the territories up into comparatively small areas where self-government by the natives in local affairs would be developed with the intention of larger groupings with greater responsibility for the natives as this became possible.[38]

These proposals formed the subject of intense discussions at the Colonial Office in 1942 and 1943. Sir Henry Moore returned from Kenya to participate in the debate. It is not possible here to pursue all of the ramifications, but it might be noted that in 1942 Harold Macmillan detected a fatal flaw in the 'federal' solution. He wrote that the federal scheme, as presented by Sir Arthur Dawe, was based on two assumptions:

(a) That the Highlands of Kenya are a 'white man's country' in the sense in which other Dominions are to-day or the American

---

[36] Ibid.   [37] Ibid.
[38] Minutes of a meeting in the Colonial Office, 10 June 1942, CO 822/108/46523.

colonies were in the 18th century. By that, I mean a country where
an Englishman can work with his coat off at any time (except perhaps between twelve and three) for a wage: in other words, a
country where—assuming that native and Indian labour were
not available—Englishmen could do the jobs which are now done
by the native or Indian wage-earning artisan or casual labourer,
without fear of physical deterioration.

(b) That on the analogy of the American colonies the claims to
self-government of any substantial number of Englishmen who have
settled permanently in a country cannot be resisted. Sir Arthur
Dawe's plan is to limit their self-government at least to the territory which they propose to inhabit.

Are these two assumptions correct? I accept (b) if (a) is true.[39]

History has vindicated Harold Macmillan's scepticism. Kenya
did not prove to be a 'white man's country' in the sense of
the American colonies or the white Dominions. British trusteeship ultimately led to the creation of Kenya as an African
nation.

The same may be said of Tanganyika, where there were
fewer white settlers. There was also the international influence
of the mandate. In the case of Tanganyika it is possible to see,
perhaps more than in any other mandated territory, the full
meaning of international trusteeship. Even here the idea and
its impact are elusive. Lord Hailey once noted that it would be
of interest to speculate at which point a visitor might become
aware that the territory was governed by a mandatory regime.
Probably one would assume that it was a British colony or
protectorate. Nevertheless there were differences. One of the
outstanding colonial governors of the inter-war period, Sir
Donald Cameron, invoked the purpose of the mandate as a
decisive argument against the entrenchment of a white-settler
regime. The administration took as its guiding principle 'the
material and moral well-being, and the social progress, of its
inhabitants'. European settlements were mainly restricted to
the regions around Mount Kilimanjaro in the north-eastern
part of the territory, and in the southern highlands. In Tanganyika, perhaps as much as in any British African territory, the
district officers believed that they were fulfilling the purpose of

[39] Memorandum by Macmillan, 15 Aug. 1942, CO 967/57 (Private Office
Papers).

Indirect Rule—allowing African societies to develop along their own lines under benign British guidance. There was an *esprit de corps*, according to Lord Hailey, 'which is probably as high as that of any unit in the Colonial Empire'.[40]

Certain Colonial Office officials regarded the development of Tanganyika as an *African* territory as the paramount goal. These included G. F. Seel, the head of the East African Department. 'Tanganyika must remain a predominantly native territory', he wrote in 1943. 'Even if the mandate went,' in other words, if it were abrogated, 'it would presumably have to be taken as axiomatic that the way is kept open for full participation by Africans in the Government as they become capable of taking this responsibility.'[41]

There was a counter-theme in British thought, one championed by Leo Amery. This view held that the interests of the white settlers could be reconciled with those of the Africans, and that Tanganyika was essentially a *British* territory. Again in the words of G. S. Seel: 'For twenty years much ingenuity has been devoted to devising formulae wherewith to avoid a definite answer to the question whether or not Tanganyika is to remain British. A notable example was Mr. Amery's dictum that "Tanganyika is within the framework of the British Empire".'[42] Try as he might, Amery never seemed entirely convincing in this argument. However 'British' Tanganyika might become, the territory was still regarded in England and especially in America as an international mandate.

The future of the Tanganyika mandate was an emotionally charged issue. According to the Governor of the territory, 'In the eyes of the British settler or colonist in East Africa the Mandate is regarded as a root of all evil and there is a strong hope that it may disappear after the war. The very existence of the mandate impeded the union of the three East African territories. To some officials this was not necessarily a bad thing. At every stage of the argument one could stop to ask whether closer union fundamentally was a good idea. If one looked at East Africa as a whole, one striking overall fact predominated.

[40] For Hailey's views on the mandate and the policies of the colonial governors, including Cameron, see CO 847/23/47100, also of value for an indication of Colonial Office response to Hailey's writings.

[41] Minute by Seel, 15 Feb. 1943, CO 822/108/46523.

[42] Ibid.

Again in the words of the Governor of Tanganyika, whose reasoning led him to oppose a union dominated by the white settlers:

The fundamental and over-riding consideration in the whole picture is that the East African territories contain approximately twelve and a half million natives, and at present only from forty to fifty thousand Europeans. . . . I cannot think that any British Government or any Parliament would contemplate accepting a form of union for East Africa which gave a small European minority a predominant influence in the central government or was likely to develop in that direction.[43]

The argument about Kenya not being a 'white man's country' carried ever greater force if applied to all of East Africa. And Tanganyika was not only a 'native territory'; it was also an international mandate. It was not purely 'British', a fact lamented by Amery and the true-blue Tories who wished to conduct regional planning on the premise of an eventual British East African Dominion. The fact was, as G. F. Seel pointed out, that since the First World War 'Britain's position in Tanganyika [has] depended upon an international document'.[44] Whether the mandate would continue in a different form would depend in large part on the attitude of the Americans.

[43] 'Memorandum by the Governor of Tanganyika. Secret and Personal', dated November 1943, CO 822/108/46523.
[44] Memorandum by Seel, dated March 1943, CO 822/108/46523.

20

ISAIAH BOWMAN'S COLONIAL
MISSION TO LONDON, APRIL 1944

IN the midst of the Colonial Office's deliberations about regional planning, Isaiah Bowman arrived in London. He was a member of the mission led by Edward R. Stettinius (now Under Secretary of State) to conduct preliminary conversations on world organization. Bowman had virtually charged himself with the responsibility for discussing the colonial issue. During the briefing of the mission before departure in Washington, on the 17th of March 1944, Bowman asked Roosevelt whether he should pursue the colonial situation. The President replied, 'certainly'. If the British tried 'to push us aside', Bowman continued, should he press them for specific ideas? Roosevelt again answered, 'certainly'. This was the open-ended nature of Bowman's instructions.[1]

Bowman did not receive any specific direction from the State Department, nor did he take with him any definite proposals being debated in the committees.[2] He stressed to the British that his remarks were 'informal' and 'exploratory'. As an eminent geographer and as the chairman of the Territorial Subcommittee, he was perhaps as well qualified as anyone to act as Roosevelt's emissary to discuss general colonial questions; but his academic temperament did not strike the British as giving him particular competence in undertaking detailed negotiations. As a social scientist, Bowman tried to formulate general theories or principles that would be as applicable, to use one of his favourite examples, to the Osage Indians as to the inhabitants of the Russian 'internal colonies'. But

---

[1] Memorandum dated 17 Mar. 1944, Bowman Papers. For a later account given to a meeting of the Subcommittee on International Organization, see I.O. Minutes 54, 12 May 1944, USSD NF Box 42. For the Stettinius mission, see Thomas M. Campbell and George C. Herring, eds., *The Diaries of Edward R. Stettinius, Jr., 1943–1946* (New York, 1975).

[2] See Bowman's memorandum to Hull, 23 Mar. 1944, Bowman Papers. There was to be no exchange of documents nor any negotiations or agreements. The conversations were to be purely exploratory.

ultimately he doubted whether this could be accomplished. Though it might be desirable to devise some sort of blanket colonial formula, he fully perceived the difficulties of generalization. He was temperamentally averse to 'high-falutin' principles that served no particular purpose, and he especially loathed the sermonizing associated with American foreign policy. It did not take much persuasion on the part of the British, therefore, to convince him that the State Department's 'Declaration on National Independence' should be dropped. Bowman attached great importance, however, to one particular point in his discussions with the British: in some way the colonial responsibility of the administering powers should be linked with an international organization.

After their arrival in London at the end of the first week in April, the members of the Stettinius mission were greeted by Churchill. Bowman described his meeting with the Prime Minister as the reason for the Colonial Secretary's eventually adopting a forthcoming attitude. It was not Churchill, however, who stirred up the Colonial Office. The records of the Foreign Office and Colonial Office reveal that Richard Law (now Minister of State at the Foreign Office) took a particular interest in the colonial part of Bowman's mission. Law chaired an inter-departmental propaganda committee on American opinion and the British Empire. He noted especially that Bowman was personally charged 'by the President and Mr. Hull' to discuss trusteeship. In 'Immediate & Personal' letters to Cranborne, Attlee, and Stanley (the members of the inter-departmental committee still giving desultory consideration to the American Declaration on National Independence), Law wrote that, in Bowman's view, Roosevelt and Hull might find it 'embarrassing' if no preliminary thought were given to the colonial question 'before we have to discuss our ideas with the Russians present'. Since Roosevelt usually chose to talk about colonial matters with the Russians, Chinese, or anyone else *before* consulting the British, the Foreign Office viewed this as an opportunity not to be lost. Law further noted that Bowman seemed disposed to admit that the State Department had placed far too much emphasis on 'political independence'. Law wrote:

Dr. Bowman told me that he had been charged by the President with the task of discovering whether there was not some common ground in Colonial questions upon which we could both take our stand. Up till now the Prime Minister had taken one view and the President had taken a diametrically opposed view. He, Bowman, was trying to discover whether there were any means of reconciling the two points of view.[3]

Law also observed that Bowman might be disposed to drop 'high sounding declarations' in favour of more realistic proposals about regional commissions. 'I hope that you will have a talk with Bowman', Law wrote in a postscript to Stanley. 'He seems to be the key-man on this particular question.'

Law and his colleagues believed that Bowman's overture could be explained by American anxiety over the future of the Japanese mandated islands. He, Attlee, Cranborne, and Stanley convened in committee on the 13th of April—before the Colonial Secretary had met Bowman—and speculated that the State Department, if not Roosevelt, wished to revive the negotiations about the colonial declaration in order to justify annexation. Law also conjectured that Bowman's mission might have something to do with Roosevelt's election strategy: 'if no such [colonial] declaration were made, the President would be accused, during the forthcoming Presidential Election in the United States, of being a champion of imperialism.'

The four ministers thought that the United States would do well to follow the strategy pursued by the British Empire on countless occasions throughout the world in similar circumstances: '[I]t was suggested that the United States Administration might justifiably claim that their interest in the Japanese Islands in the Pacific was based solely on strategical grounds and that their annexation was essential in the interests of world security.'[4] Strategic annexation would relieve the Americans from insisting on the cloak of international supervision. On this point Stanley again spoke firmly. He was by no means eager to see the American; but he would make it clear to him that the Colonial Office viewed with intense disfavour any international

[3] Law to Stanley, 11 Apr. 1944, CO 323/1877/9057B; FO 371/40749. In his account of the conversation, Bowman wrote that Law 'seemed a little puzzled at the informality of my relations with the [State] Department, though I tried to clear this up by reference to others with similar status and to the work of the Inquiry in 1918 and my relations with the Peace Conference in Paris in 1919' (Memorandum by Bowman, 11 Apr. 1944, Bowman Papers).

[4] Gen. 32/1st Meeting, 13 Apr. 1944, CAB 78/20.

body with supervisory functions. He would be prepared to support the idea of an international colonial center or bureau if the Americans would accept it in the place of the mandates system. This bureau, Stanley reiterated, would merely function as a distributing center of information. It would mainly 'collate papers'. This bold and imaginative proposal Stanley wanted to hold in reserve in case Bowman sprang some dangerous scheme to resurrect the mandates. With collegial sanction, the Colonial Secretary thus methodically prepared for his meeting with Roosevelt's spokesman.

Bowman met with Stanley on the 18th of April. According to Bowman's account, he tried to make clear to the Colonial Secretary the strength of 'liberal, church, and missionary sentiment throughout the United States with respect to the treatment of dependent peoples'.[5] Stanley did not warm up to these remarks. The Colonial Secretary in his account of the conversation described Bowman's exposition as 'wrapped up in a rather diaphanous cover of the usual idealism'. Though Bowman himself professed dislike of the evangelical element in American policy, he chose to emphasize the moral responsibility of the mandates as he also discursively talked about such topics as the tea market in Tanganyika and the excess of agricultural commodities in the tropics. Only when Bowman mentioned 'a new responsibility' in the Pacific did the purpose of the conversation become clear, at least to Stanley. '[I]t was plain that the real object of any Colonial plan is to enable the United States to get away with the retention of the Marshalls and Carolines. Dr. Bowman, who shifts his ground continually, is not easy to pin down; but so far as I could gather he has two desiderata.'[6] Stanley believed Bowman specifically sought (1) a declaration of general principle; and (2) a section of the future international organization which would deal with dependent peoples.

The Colonial Secretary proceeded to explain the difficulties. He told Bowman of his troubles in communicating with the State Department on the joint colonial declaration and how the British had been 'disappointed' in the unwillingness of the

---

[5] Memorandum by Bowman, 18 Apr. 1944; Bowman to Winant, 28 Apr. 1944, Bowman Papers; a copy of the latter is also in the Taussig Papers.
[6] Memorandum by Stanley, 18 Apr. 1944, CO 323/1877/9057B.

Americans to give any real response. Consequently, he told Bowman, he had taken it upon himself to make a statement in Parliament about regional commissions. This at least had carried the subject forward. At this point Stanley skilfully, though perhaps unwittingly, played on Bowman's frustration at trying himself to devise a general colonial formula. 'In dealing with territories so divergent as the various Colonial Territories,' Stanley observed, 'any general principles had to be the lowest common denominator, with the result that they were apt to look pretty thin.' Bowman did not press the issue of a general colonial declaration, which allowed Stanley to record that what had been said in the Parliamentary statement was sufficient. In regard to the world organization, Stanley flatly told Bowman that it would be 'impossible' for the British to accept any international body with supervisory capacities. The Colonial Secretary did say that it might be possible to create some sort of international office as 'merely a collecting place for information'. The Colonial Secretary thus offered nothing. Stanley could not even guarantee that he could now repeat his promise in Parliament to establish regional commissions because circumstances had now changed. Bowman accurately observed that the Colonial Secretary's response to the general topics of conversation had been 'distinctly chilly'.

Bowman left the Colonial Office an unhappy man. He returned to the Foreign Office, where he had bargaining power. The officials of the Foreign Office keenly wished to reach agreement on the future world organization, and they regarded Bowman as one of the President's key emissaries. Bowman had already made contact not only with Richard Law but also with Gladwyn Jebb, the head of the post-war planning section, and with two fellow scholars, Professors Arnold Toynbee and Charles Webster, both of whom were advising the Foreign Office on world organization. At one of these meetings, Jebb had discovered that Bowman had not seen the British reply to the American Declaration on National Independence. Since the American Ambassador had never forwarded it to Washington, this was hardly Bowman's fault; but it had the dual effect of putting him in a weak position in regard to the Declaration and of making the British more sceptical than ever of American competence in colonial negotiations. Nevertheless Cadogan,

Jebb, and Webster listened sympathetically as Bowman poured out his woes about the interview with Stanley.

'Dr. Isaiah' seemed 'obviously disappointed', Jebb noted, and returned repeatedly to the question of colonial trusteeship.[7] It formed only one part of the general discussion about the world court and other problems of future international organization, but it disturbed Bowman most of all. He was so distressed on this point that Jebb referred to it as a 'King Charles' head'.

He clearly has been under great pressure from the President to obtain some result from it; indeed he practically confessed as much to us. He stressed the fact that public opinion in the United States demanded that something should be said on the subject in connection with the World Organization and that it was not sufficient to leave it to evolve from whatever regional organisations might be set up.[8]

Bowman wanted to be able to say to the President and his colleagues in the State Department that the British would co-operate by at least submitting annual reports to an international organization. At the same time the Americans would agree to submit reports on the Pacific islands. Posed in this way, the problem assumed a vital character. 'Dr. Bowman showed great anxiety on this subject.' In the end Cadogan said that he would have a word with the Colonial Secretary 'on the question of whether Dr. Bowman might have another discussion with him with perhaps a representative of the Foreign Office present'.[9] The Foreign Office thus began to exert considerable pressure on the Colonial Office. Jebb suggested to Cadogan that Stanley might be told 'what importance we attach to getting the Americans into line generally provided we do not give much away in substance and urge him not to shy off the International Colonial Bureau idea'.[10]

[7] See Jebb's minute of 12 Apr. 1944, and Toynbee's memorandum recording a discussion of 14 Apr. 1944, U2344, FO/40749. Memorandum by Bowman, 14 Apr. 1944, Bowman Papers.

[8] Minutes of a meeting of 19 Apr. 1944, FO 37140749; CO 323/1877/9057B.

[9] Ibid.

[10] Minute by Jebb, 19 Apr. 1944, U3587, FO 371/40749. Cadogan's response is of interest: 'If I understood Mr. Bowman aright, he wanted the Power or Powers responsible for a "Region" containing "dependent peoples" to *report* to the World Council (or Assembly). This, of course, is the Mandatory system without the interposition of the Mandates Commission. Whether that Commission was more mischievous than it was helpful, I don't know. I shd. have thought that an unregulated discussion, in a General Assembly, of undigested "reports" would be

Stanley accurately perceived that if he agreed to an international colonial bureau (even if its purpose were merely to 'collate papers') he might be started down the slippery slope towards international colonial accountability. The Americans might try to transform the 'bureau' into another mandates system. He intensely disliked making the concession. Stanley —along with Cadogan—lunched with Bowman on the 24th of April, a few days before the return of the Stettinius mission to America. 'The conversation was lengthy,' Stanley recorded afterwards, 'but, as usual, imprecise.' The Colonial Secretary now succeeded in extracting a commitment from Bowman not to revive the project of a colonial declaration, except in conjunction with plans for a future world organization; and he got an acknowledgement from Bowman that the regional commissions would be without executive authority. Stanley wrote about the one point he yielded:

He [Bowman] is, I think, wedded to the idea that one of the obligations of parent [colonial] States shall be the publication of annual reports which shall be transmitted to a receiving centre attached to the World Organisation. As I gathered it, this organisation would do nothing more than acknowledge receipt and retain the reports available for inspection.[11]

Stanley again had conceded virtually nothing except the possible creation of a library. He elaborated on the regional commissions, causing Bowman to think the negotiations were advancing, but in effect Stanley did not go beyond what he had already said in Parliament.

Bowman felt triumphant. He thought he had persuaded the Colonial Secretary himself that the two countries must work together to solve the problems of dependent territories. In his report, which he put in the form of a letter to the American Ambassador in London, Bowman reviewed his success in convincing the British officials, not least Stanley, of the validity of the American point of view:

What we were all required to do as a result of the war and its vast dislocation of peoples everywhere was to look at dependent peoples

far more dangerous than the former League system. But I may be wrong' (Minute by Cadogan, 19 Apr. 1944, ibid.).

[11] Memorandum by Stanley, 24 Apr. 1944, CO 323/1877/9057B; FO 371/40749. For Bowman's account, memorandum by him dated 24 Apr. 1944, Bowman Papers.

quite closely to see that they who were at our mercy were not neglected in the general settlement to follow the war. The development of their resources by our superior machinery of development, our capital and our technical personnel was a primary obligation.[12]

In the area where Bowman thought he had accomplished the most, the British now knew of the altruistic motives of the United States in the Pacific:

In the Pacific the United States will no doubt assume a new responsibility. One may guess, if not hope, that the responsibility of the United States toward the Japanese mandated islands will be assumed with the approval of the entire world. If we achieve this happy result, it will be because we have some general principles of colonial policy upon which there has been agreement among the colonial powers. We may also suppose that an account of our stewardship will be given to the world. The books of account will be open.[13]

In this Bowman could offer assurance that the British as well as the Americans would publish annual reports which 'would be sent to a central body'. All in all, Bowman's report conveyed the impression that the British now would do more than merely attempt to retain 'every acre of land that the British Empire embraced at the beginning of the war'.

The significance of the Bowman mission is that it gave Stanley and the Colonial Office a momentary sense of false security. The British officials assumed that Bowman represented the President and the State Department, and that agreement had been reached that the parent colonial states would be held accountable only in an extremely minimal way to an international organization (by depositing annual reports in a library). Bowman's influence must therefore have been disappointing to the British. It is true that Charles Taussig took an interest in some of Bowman's ideas about regionalism. Nothing else happened within Presidential circles at this stage. At the State Department, Bowman arrived back when the committees were discussing that most abstract question of all theoretical issues concerning the mandates—where did sovereignty reside? Bowman reported at length to his colleagues—who listened with

---

[12] Bowman to Winant, 28 Apr. 1944, Bowman Papers; Taussig Papers. Bowman incorporated parts of this letter into the report of the Stettinius mission, for which see *Foreign Relations* (1944), iii. 3–30. See also the copy of the report in USSD NF Box 87.   [13] Ibid.

great interest—and then returned to the question of sovereignty and, again, the old question of the general colonial declaration. The bureaucracy continued on its way, drafting and redrafting the future charter of the United Nations' trusteeship system, though Bowman did succeed in shortening the list of injunctions to be presented to the British. The State Department did not budge an inch on the issue of accountability. Far from merely accepting annual reports, the international organization would have the right to hear petitions and make visits of inspection.

Bowman at least helped to dramatize some vital differences between the British and Americans. 'Dr. Isaiah', as the British had called him, returned to Washington convinced that the project for a declaration on general colonial principles should be dropped in order to go full steam ahead with planning for regional commissions. The British officials had persuaded him, among other things, that it was absurd to think in terms of colonial independence, at least for all colonies. He explained to the subcommittee on international organization that he now agreed with the Colonial Secretary: 'You should forget the general principles', Bowman said to his colleagues, 'and should pass on to what you can do about them.' The trouble with us Americans, he went on, is that we talk '*words* instead of figuring out how to deal with *things*'. The British by contrast attempted to come to grips with real problems.

He knew what their reaction was to our previous moral statements and moral attitudes, which did not seem to them to rest on anything concrete and real. The trouble with all these generalized statements was that you did not deal with realities . . .[14]

[I]f you approach the problem of dependent areas from the point of view of general attitudes and moral principles you cannot take adequately into account all of the many diversities of the territories themselves and make allowance for backgrounds that are different, peoples that are different, territories that are different, and rates of progress that are different.[15]

Trying to be more specific, Bowman explained that the British objected to principles of international accountability because

[14] I.O. Minutes 54, 12 May 1944, USSD NF Box 142.
[15] Ibid.

'such a procedure would be like trying to get the Ten Commandments to fit all dependent areas'. He went on:

It simply could not be done, and even if it could be done it would be merely an incitement to riot for agitators all over the world. To meet the need for some kind of international accountability, the British would agree to resume publication of their Colonial Office reports on colonies and other areas and to make these reports available each year at some central place.[16]

Bowman's main point that he tried to drive home to his colleagues can be summed up in his words, 'everything we produced on colonial subjects sounded like the Sermon on the Mount, and everything we said was "just as good as Jesus". Our papers were always awfully good but were awfully unrealistic . . .' One other observation by Bowman deserves special emphasis. The way he reported it to his colleagues was not especially accurate, but it certainly sums up Stanley's attitude towards making the regional commissions accountable to an international organization: 'he would see us in Hades before he agreed to such a proposal.'[17]

[16] Ibid.   [17] Ibid.

21

THE DOMINION PRIME MINISTERS' CONFERENCE OF MAY 1944

OCCASIONALLY in the treatment of a complex subject it is useful to try to view the issues as they were seen by protagonists in the larger story, and not only those involved in the day by day business of, for example, running the Colonial Empire. Such an opportunity exists with the meeting of the Dominion Prime Ministers in May 1944, a few weeks before the Normandy invasion and a few months before the conference on world organization at Dumbarton Oaks. The timing of this illustrious gathering is important because of some of the things *not* said about trusteeship in the spring of 1944. Only the Prime Minister of New Zealand challenged the position of the Colonial Office. Within the British Empire as in the United States, the question of the colonies' future had not yet become urgent, though on both sides it threatened to become divisive. As in the case of the recent negotiations with Isaiah Bowman, the Colonial Office appeared to have the business of trusteeship well in hand. Churchill could sit mainly in silence, preferring as brief a treatment of the subject as possible. The Canadian Prime Minister added nothing. The Australian Prime Minister virtually disavowed the trusteeship policy of Dr. Evatt. General Smuts talked in large strategic terms but showed restraint when referring to South Africa's aims. He said he supported the policies of Churchill and Stanley. Yet it was Smuts only a few months earlier who had uttered words that proved to be an ultimate challenge to the Colonial Office. 'You will have to decentralize from the Colonial Office in London', Smuts had said, 'and give administrative powers of all sorts, and all degrees, sometimes to very small units. . . .' or else redraw the map of Africa in larger units. With this proposition in mind, it is possible to see the problem of trusteeship in larger perspective as of May 1944: the resolution of the colonial issue depended very much on how one viewed the future of the British Empire–Commonwealth and the purpose of colonial reorganization.

To Smuts the Commonwealth, as opposed to the Empire, existed as a separate system and operated on a fundamentally different principle. 'In the Commonwealth we follow to the limit the principle of decentralization', he had said in his famous speech to Members of both Houses of Parliament in November 1943. The Colonial Empire functioned on the opposite principle of centralization.

> To have the Empire centralized and the Commonwealth decentralized, to have the two groups developed on two different lines, raises grave questions for the future. Is this duality in our group safe? . . . I know as a fact that wherever I have gone in the colonial Empire I have found criticism of this situation. Your own British people outside this island, living in crown colonies, are very critical and restive under this system which is centralized in London. . . . The Britisher resents being run by others and from a distance.[1]

Smuts disliked the Colonial Office's system of centralization, but he did not recommend the devolution of power and authority to 'very small units' or to those 'still in a primitive stage of development'. As a solution he offered regroupings and simplification of 'units which have simply arisen as an accident by historic haphazard'. He wanted to reduce the number of 'separate units scattered pell-mell over the colonial Empire'. He made his point clear in regard to Africa.

> You have west Africa, you have east Africa, and you have southern Africa. It is quite possible to group those colonies into larger units, each under a governor-general, and abolish not a few of them that need not continue to enjoy a separate existence. In that way you will overcome the difficulty of the highly centralized system centering in London, which is irksome to the local people, is perhaps not serving their highest interests and their best development, and gives outsiders the occasion to blaspheme and to call the colonial Empire an imperialist concern, run in the economic interest of this country.[2]

Smuts thus summarized some of the main arguments in favour of colonial reform. He implicitly raised the question of trusteeship. For whose benefit would this reorganization take place?

---

[1] The speech is reprinted in Jean van der Poel, ed., *Selections from the Smuts Papers* (Cambridge, 1973), vi. 456–69.   [2] Ibid., p. 466.

Though Smuts sought to ameliorate race relations and hoped for the future collaboration between racial groups, his immediate conception of the Commonwealth was shaped by its history and its status as of 1944. The Commonwealth was composed of Great Britain and the Dominions of South Africa, Australia, New Zealand, and Canada. It was a white man's Commonwealth. The white man would continue to rule in South Africa. In a previous speech Smuts had described 'The Basis of Trusteeship in Africa' as the proper relation between blacks and whites. It was the relation of white guardians and black wards.[3] It was the static type of trusteeship from which Lord Hailey and others had attempted to advance by introducing the concept of 'partnership'. Smuts himself regarded the question of race as 'a root problem in our Empire'. It was one to which he never offered a solution other than the static and perpetual trust held by white guardians over black barbarians.[4]

No one at the time more clearly perceived the basic issues raised by Smuts than did Margery Perham. In a letter to *The Times* which attracted particular notice in the Colonial Office,[5] she asked whether his sharp division of principles was actually true. In her view the position of the imperial government was not static but moving towards the goal of greater local autonomy. In any case the Colonial Office had the responsibility to move in this direction and 'to make up in varying measure for the immaturity or disunity of the dependent peoples'. Moreover, the point about centralization was misleading. Improvement in communication made the colonial Empire in practice a highly *de*centralized Empire with local officials increasingly taking the initiative in consultation with their superiors. As for Smuts's allegation that British people were 'restive' under the present regime, he obviously meant the white settlers in Kenya and Northern Rhodesia, a few thousands among African millions. Did he mean that authority should be transferred to the white settlers? Regional

---

[3] This address of 21 Jan. 1942 is also reprinted ibid., pp. 331–42.

[4] The point is made both forcefully and perceptively by Roland Oliver, 'Blinkered Genius', *Journal of African History* 9. 3 (1968), 491–4, which is a review of W. K. Hancock, *Smuts: the Fields of Force, 1919–1950* (Cambridge, 1968).

[5] See minute by Arthur Benson, 16 Dec. 1943, CO 323/9086. The letter is dated 7 December 1943 and is reprinted in Perham, *Colonial Sequence, 1930 to 1949*, pp. 248–9.

regroupings would turn the white contingents into even smaller minorities. Who but the imperial government should fill the political vacuum? There was force in the argument that the time had come to 'tidy up the show' and abolish artificial colonial units. But this reorganization should not be done at the expense of local progress. 'A premature ironing-out under a regional steam roller of the vitality and rich variety of native groups might fatally interrupt their education in self-government.' Miss Perham congratulated Smuts for having acknowledged in most serious terms the problem of race relations. But she pointed out that he offered no solution. Her own interpretation of equality as the basic goal of trusteeship could not have been more clearly put, and it was the opposite of Smuts's vision. 'Equality is a fact for some of our colonial people, for others it is a test for present policy and a hope for the future . . .'[6]

Whatever might be said of the Colonial Office under the leadership of Oliver Stanley, there did not exist any sympathy for colonial reorganization that would result in greater influence of white settler communities or would satisfy either the economic or political expansionist ambitions of South Africa.[7] The dominant theme in planning the regional commissions in places such as central or southern Africa was to balance South Africa by the inclusion of such colonial powers as Belgium and Portugal. Partly to offset the danger of increasing the white settler voice in East Africa, and partly because of the reluctance to admit South Africa into the region, Stanley had postponed the consideration of an East African regional commission. When the War Cabinet discussed the Colonial Office's plans for regionalism on the 27th of April, however, Lord Cranborne objected to the omission of such a large part of the colonial Empire from regional planning. He feared that the Americans might interpret the British motive as a desire to perpetuate the Colonial Empire. Cranborne's protest carried the sense of the meeting.[8] On the eve of the Prime Ministers' Conference the Colonial Office therefore had to revise the projected regional planning, not so much to accommodate South Africa as to

[6] Ibid.

[7] See Ronald Hyam, *The Failure of South African Expansion, 1908–1948* (London, 1972), ch. 7.

[8] W.M. (44) 58th Conclusions, 27 Apr. 1944, CAB 65/42; and minutes in CO 968/159/14814/1C.

placate the Americans. 'We must "show willing" in regard to an international Regional Commission for East Africa', Stanley told his staff on the 5th of May.[9]

In the view of the Colonial Office, a 'natural' commission in East Africa could include only Kenya, Tanganyika, and Uganda, and, possibly, Zanzibar. The Congo and Mozambique would at least make such a commission 'international' and might accomplish something useful in such areas as research in tropical disease and agriculture. Beyond that British officials could foresee only political, geographical, and racial difficulties. Christopher Eastwood elaborated the scheme and his minutes illuminate the struggle to create a rational regional grouping. The peoples of the southern Sudan, for example, would fit into an East African organization, but the Sudan as a whole 'has always looked to the north for its main contact with the outside world'. Somalia possessed few similarities with most of East Africa and was separated by a desert. Ethiopia, in Eastwood's view 'is no doubt in need of all the good advice she can get and her association on a Regional Council might be to her own advantage'. But how would the membership of Ethiopia be weighed against, say, the white settler voice in Kenya? Of the territories in the India Ocean, the Seychelles, Madagascar, and Mauritius might be included, but, as George Seel noted, their inclusion would hardly make the regions homogeneous and 'would really be no more than a mopping up of areas not included in other more obvious regions'. There would be no way to exclude South Africa because, in Eastwood's words, 'of her major interest in anything that happens in tropical Africa'. In a burst of enthusiasm Eastwood added Egypt, because of the condominium in the Sudan and the waters of the Nile, and India, 'on account of the very large number of Indians settled in East Africa'. Egypt was dropped because it seemed a country more of the Middle East than Africa; and the Indian suggestion caused agitation when Stanley and his advisers considered the question. Eastwood wrote afterwards:

[W]e should resist strongly the suggestion which would be made by *India* that she should be included. . . . it was felt that if she became a member of an East African Regional Commission it might be

---

[9] As related in a minute by Eastwood, 8 May 1944, CO 978/159/14814/1C.

difficult to prevent her becoming also a member of a West Indian Region and South West Pacific Region, on account of the Indians resident in Trinidad, British Guiana and Fiji. . . . The presence of an Indian on an East African Commission would no doubt be very embarrassing to us, and it would also be extremely unpopular with South Africa.[10]

Thus on the eve of the Prime Ministers' Conference the Colonial Office was prepared to proceed with an East African regional commission, including South Africa, if pressed to do so by Smuts, but the Colonial Office would join him in resisting the inclusion of India.

The two other regions that seemed likely to provoke controversy at the Prime Ministers' Conference were South-East Asia and the Western Pacific. In regard to the latter the Colonial Office was now confronted with the plans of the Americans as well as the Australians and New Zealanders. Writing to Cranborne about last-minute Colonial Office calculations, Stanley wanted to make sure that the scheme included both the Americans and the Dutch. The rationale for including the Japanese mandated islands was:

[I]t seemed illogical to have a regional area including some of the Micronesian peoples, e.g. the Gilbertese, and not their near neighbours, the inhabitants of the Marshalls and the other Mandated Islands. It seems from what Dr. Bowman said when he was over here that the United States will want them to be included.[11]

Stanley also saw both ethnological and political reasons why Dutch New Guinea should be included:

I can . . . quite see that since Dutch New Guinea, like the neighbouring Australian possessions, is inhabited by Melanesians, there would be advantage in having it along with other Melanesian lands included in the South Seas Regional Area. Furthermore, Dutch membership of the South Pacific Regional Commission might be an added counter-weight against possible American domination.[12]

In regard to South-East Asia, it seemed best not to be too precise. In the event the Conference took no definite action. To the officials of the Colonial Office this seemed to confirm the

---

[10] Minutes by Eastwood, 29 Apr. and 8 May 1944, and Seel, 29 Apr. 1944 CO 968/159/14814/1C.

[11] Stanley to Cranborne, 5 May 1944, CO 968/158/14814/1B.   [12] Ibid.

wisdom of masterly inactivity. Eastwood wrote shortly after the main colonial business of the Conference had been transacted:

As to the precise area to be covered by a S.E. region I suggest that that is a matter that can safely be left to the future. . . . Certain territories will clearly come within the region, e.g. Malaya, the Netherlands East Indies, Borneo and Indo-China. Exactly how far the region will extend outside this nucleus can, I suggest, be left to circumstances to determine.[13]

Eastwood's colleague, A. E. Benson, who worked with him closely on these questions, wrote with relief that the ministers in the imperial government had all guarded against international accountability in South-East Asia, even though, in his opinion, 'The Foreign Office is riddled with the heresy of international supervision.'[14] He epitomized the attitude of the Colonial Office when he wrote that the heresy of international accountability 'will need a great deal of watchfulness on our part if it is not once more to rear its insidious head'.[15]

The Prime Minister guilty of 'heresy' at the 1944 conference was Peter Fraser. He later became the arch-priest when he chaired the Trusteeship Commission at San Francisco, and for this reason his views of May 1944 are of particular interest. Also later, Dr. Evatt, at the San Francisco Conference and elsewhere, made a great splash in the press as the champion of international accountability, and consequently there has been a tendency to regard Fraser as somewhat of a lesser figure who merely followed Evatt's lead. This definitely was not the case. At the conference of 1944 Fraser stood alone as the spokesman for trusteeship and his views directly contradicted those of his Australian counterpart, John Curtin.

Fraser's attitude towards trusteeship had been moulded long before the outbreak of the war. In the tradition of the Labour Party he opposed 'imperialism'. He read books and pamphlets

[13] Minute by Eastwood, 15 May 1944, CO 968/159/14814/1A.
[14] Minute by Benson, 20 May 1944, CO 968/159/14814/1A. Perhaps a more accurate way of expressing it would be to say that international accountability was not the Foreign Office's *bête noire*, as it was the Colonial Office's. For Foreign Office minutes in preparation for the Prime Ministers' Conference see especially FO 371/42677, FO 371/42678, and FO 371/42681.
[15] Benson's minute of 20 May 1944.

on the subject.[16] He was particularly influenced by Harry Holland, the New Zealand Labour politician who had attacked the Conservatives for their handling of the nationalist movement in Samoa and the uprising of 1929.[17] Fraser's views on trusteeship were his own, as was his attitude towards the imperial government. Though not abrasive like Evatt, Fraser strongly felt that New Zealand should not behave, in the phrase he had used in the aftermath of the Australian–New Zealand Agreement, 'with the humbleness of the Uriah Heep type'.[18]

Fraser's independent views contrasted starkly with those of John Curtin, who, though also of the Labour Party, espoused the cause of closer association with the mother country. It is ironic that Curtin, belonging to the same party and leading the Australian government, held such profoundly different views from Evatt, who was a decided devolutionist. Evatt publicly could not dissent from Curtin, and he paid lip service to collaboration with the British; but in fact Evatt should be regarded as an Australian who hoped his country would be the inheritor of the British Empire in the Pacific.[19] On trusteeship Evatt was at one with Fraser, but the latter pursued his course quite independently.

The Prime Ministers discussed colonial questions on the 9th of May. At Churchill's invitation, Stanley gave a short speech. He welcomed the Australian–New Zealand Agreement as being in accord with the Colonial Office's views on regional organization. He commented on the establishment of regional commissions as the most important development in the colonial field. He believed they would be 'of real practical value' and would be an effective answer to the demand for international control of colonial territories. Leading up to the main point, he made the distinction between two types of criticism: 'So far as

[16] I am greatly indebted to Sir Alister McIntosh for information about Fraser. For Fraser and the subject of trusteeship, see especially Wood, *New Zealand People at War*, ch. 23. For Fraser's own views, Peter Fraser, 'The Work of the Trusteeship Council', *International Conciliation*, No. 445 (November 1948), pp. 651–66.

[17] For the background of trusteeship in New Zealand Labour Party politics, see P. J. O'Farrell, *Harry Holland: Militant Socialist* (Canberra, 1964), ch. 11; and Bruce Brown, *The Rise of New Zealand Labour* (Wellington, 1962).

[18] *New Zealand Parliamentary Debates*, vol. 264, 29 Mar. 1944, pp. 792–9.

[19] On the contrasting attitudes of Curtin and Evatt, I have especially profited from an unpublished essay by Hartley Grattan and from conversations with him about his major work in progress on Evatt.

the British Empire was concerned, we had nothing to fear from criticism, and it was the intention to revert as soon as possible to the publication of full annual reports of our administration. But, while we welcomed constructive criticism, we were anxious to avoid ill-informed and academic interference.' With this allusion to the mandates system, Stanley proceeded to attack it directly. Here is the essence of his objection, noteworthy because it reveals that the question of sovereignty continued to be of paramount concern:

He did not regard the mandate system as wholly satisfactory. It was out of date in the present-day world, being largely negative in character in that its aim was to lay down negative principles, e.g. the prevention of the use of forced labour. The system had served its purpose, but it had become more of a hindrance than an assistance. Large-scale development was generally beyond the local resources of a colonial territory, and *without any guarantee of permanency of sovereignty*, the parent Power was naturally reluctant to provide for large-scale expenditure from its own funds.[20]

Having stated the case against the continuation of the mandates system, Stanley now outlined the positive action the Colonial Office proposed to take by the establishment of regional commissions in various parts of the world. Such a commission existed in embryo in the Caribbean. Australia and New Zealand had made proposals for the Pacific. Though he foresaw great difficulties in tropical Africa, he thought that 'two or three' commissions might be established. Stanley thus outlined the position of the Colonial Office in a general, almost casual way that invited extemporaneous and not detailed responses.

No precise agenda on the subject had been circulated in advance, which made it difficult for the Prime Ministers to reply other than in generalities (a point shrewdly noted by an absent but highly interested observer of the proceedings, Dr. Evatt in Canberra).[21] Fraser responded to Stanley's nonchalant

[20] P.M.M. (44) 10th Meeting, 9 May 1944, CAB 99/28. Italics added.
[21] In a telegram dated 3 May 1944 Evatt had commented on this point and went on to summarize the situation in regard to trusteeship. The telegram is important because Curtin at the conference chose to ignore it and, in fact, temporarily reversed Australia's course. Evatt had telegraphed: 'With regard to colonial policy . . . the present Australian Government has consistently held the view that there should be general agreement to bring all colonial territories under the supervision

presentation, however, by reading verbatim the relevant passages of the Australian–New Zealand Agreement. He emphasized the part stating that the doctrine of trusteeship, already in existence in the mandated territories, should apply to all colonies in the Pacific. Fraser went on to say that the New Zealanders especially welcomed the assistance of the imperial government in that part of the world, particularly in such areas as health services.

The Prime Minister of Australia agreed that welfare and education should be primary objectives of the Pacific regional commission, and he stressed the foundations already laid by excellent Australian colonial administration. Curtin could not give equal praise for Dutch and Portuguese colonial rule. Anticipating the possible demise of the weaker European powers in the Pacific, Curtin went on:

> [H]is information was that in the Dutch and Portuguese territories the position was not so good. The Japanese had received a certain amount of aid from the local inhabitants and he did not think that the same loyalty had been shown to the Dutch and Portuguese authorities as had been the case in British territories. . . . He was not altogether happy about the possibility of allowing large colonial territories to remain the responsibility of weak parent States which had not the resources to provide adequately for defence.

He called attention to American expansion in the Pacific:

> While he—and he thought he could speak for Mr. Fraser too— would welcome the intrusion of United States influence between their countries and Japan, they did not wish this to occur at the expense of British territory, but at the expense of the Japanese and if need be the Dutch and the French.[22]

He made it clear that Australia had no territorial aims. Australia did not have the resources to defend such far-flung islands as the Marshalls and Carolines. Thus he hoped that the United States could be drawn into the area north of the Equator and, equally important, South-East Asia. '[H]e hoped that the

of an international agency. This body should discuss and review the administration of colonies, and its powers should be comparable to those of the Permanent Mandates Commission but extending to all colonial territories.' Evatt's summary was thus unequivocal. Evatt to Curtin, Most Secret, No. 36, 3 May 1944, AA A989 43/735/1021.

[22] P.M.M. (44), 9 May 1944.

United States could be persuaded to undertake definite defence commitments abutting on Malaya.'

When the discussion turned to strategic security, Churchill intervened. 'All over the world', he said, 'there were islands of great strategic consequence.' Here Churchill's remarks reveal his efforts to make his views harmonize with Roosevelt's.

These [islands] would come under the authority of the world organization and be allocated amongst the Great Powers, which would undertake strategic responsibilities to be carried out as a duty on behalf of the United Nations. The Azores and Dakar, for example, might come under the strategic control of the United States.[23]

Churchill said that the United Kingdom would seek no territory, and if asked to undertake strategic responsibilities would do so only if the world organization paid the expense—a theme that began to appear in many of his remarks on the subject for the rest of the war. Whatever the territorial settlement in the colonies, Churchill emphasized that it should be made in accordance with high principles.

On the larger issues of security and strategy, Fraser found himself in agreement with his fellow Prime Ministers. 'As regards the Marshall and Caroline Islands,' he said, 'they fell naturally into the United States sphere of responsibility. This suited New Zealand, as it safeguarded her outermost defence line.' Fraser also made it clear that he was concerned about the future administration of these islands. He pressed Stanley to make an unequivocal statement:

One point on which he [Fraser] sought clarification was the manner in which it was proposed to ensure that a reasonable standard of administration was maintained, particularly in areas like Indo China if restored to their former owners. He felt that there must be some *central international body* to which parent States should be required to report. For our part we had nothing to fear from such supervision, and the local inhabitants in other colonial territories would surely stand to gain.[24]

In reply, Stanley merely explained that he contemplated 'an obligation' to make reports, 'but felt that the question of supervision could best be left on a regional basis'. He did not

[23] Ibid.   [24] Ibid. Italics added.

elaborate. The discussion then turned to Hong Kong. Churchill gave assurance that 'no change was contemplated in our sovereignty'.

Smuts now for the first time entered the discussion. He agreed with the general policies outlined by Churchill and Stanley. Just as Curtin and Fraser had raised the question of the future of the weaker colonial powers in the Pacific, Smuts now pursued the issue in regard to Africa. He called attention to Madagascar 'and its magnificent harbour at Diego Suarez'. The British strategic interests there were as great as the American stake at Dakar—to which Curtin added the analogy of New Caledonia. The future of the French Empire at this time clearly was becoming an increasingly urgent problem. But as to actual transfers of sovereignty in Africa, Smuts pointed out, only the Italian empire would be affected. By no means would the British despoil their weaker allies. Like his antipodean colleagues, however, Smuts showed concern for 'parent States which lacked the resources to develop and defend their Colonial possessions, and instanced Portuguese possessions in Africa'. The imperial government could have only welcomed Smuts's assurance to Churchill that, in regard to the Portuguese colonies, 'South Africa had no territorial ambitions in that direction'.[25]

Curtin again raised the similar point about the Dutch lacking resources to defend their possessions in South-East Asia. To this Fraser observed that the Dutch would be the ones who would most willingly collaborate with the British in colonial questions. Churchill stated that he would be 'most unwilling' to see them dispossessed. He thought that the solution might lie in the regional commissions, through which the various powers would collaborate on matters of defence and economic development. Churchill then added that the work of the regional commissions would be collaborative, not executive. '[H]e could not agree to any unwarranted interference in the affairs of the British Empire.' At this point Fraser returned to the charge for the last time in regard to trusteeship. The key passage of the transcript reads:

Mr. Fraser thought that it was essential to make provision for reports on colonial administration to be submitted to and discussed

[25] P.M.M. (44), 9 May 1944.

by some central international body. Neither *Colonel Stanley* nor *Mr. Curtin* favoured this suggestion.

Mr. Churchill said he regarded the discussion which had taken place as remarkably valuable. A great measure of agreement had been reached.[26]

In his concluding remarks Churchill continued to emphasize the consensus on general issues. On the particular point of trusteeship, however, the discussions were inconclusive.[27] Fraser had made a stand, but he had not pressed his insistence. Stanley had stated clearly that he disapproved of international account-ability. Curtin had agreed with him. Far from having reached a consensus, the conference had left the door open for further controversy.

If the conference had devoted considerable attention to such topics as possible territorial ambitions of the United States, Churchill, for one, did not lose sight of the larger picture. With unwavering persistence he continued to denounce any proposal that might lead to an international body interfering in the internal affairs of the British Empire. He viewed American trusteeship schemes as mainly a cover for annexationist plans in the Pacific. At the same time he saw the trusteeship issue in the perspective of the larger stakes of the war. The colonial significance of the 1944 conference, for the British at least, can be summed up in Churchillian eloquence. He told his fellow Prime Ministers:

The peace and the safety of the world should be our object. . . .

[26] Ibid. In reporting the discussion of the meeting to Canberra, Curtin gave at length Stanley's arguments against the mandates system and his proposals to establish regional commissions. Curtin stated that he had found himself in agreement with the Colonial Secretary, but he did not report that he had opposed Fraser on the issue of accountability, which was a direct repudiation of previous Australian policy as summarized by Evatt in his telegram of 3 May cited in note 21. Though it certainly was his prerogative to do so, Curtin thus did not inform Evatt that a basic point in Australian policy had been reversed. (Curtin to Acting Prime Minister, 16 May 1944, AA A989 43/735/324.) Quite apart from the merit of the case and the relationship between Curtin and Evatt, the effect on the imperial government was baffling. When Evatt again pressed for international accountability later in the year, Australian policy appeared to be totally inconsistent; but from Evatt's point of view there was no inconsistency at all.

[27] The point is clearest from the New Zealand angle, for which see NZ PM 151/2/1. The unpublished New Zealand official account concludes that 'No finality was reached by the end of the meeting'. J. D. O'Shea, 'New Zealand's Part in the Establishment of an International Security Organization' (War History Branch, Department of Internal Affairs, Wellington).

[W]ith the assumption of strategic responsibility, the Power concerned would also have to undertake to maintain certain standards of native well-being. There must be no question of despoiling the weak. The British Commonwealth was the only body of nations still in the struggle which had drawn the sword for honour alone. We must take care not to tarnish it.[28]

[28] P.M.M. (44), 9 May 1944.

22

ROOSEVELT AND THE STATE DEPARTMENT IN THE WINTER AND SPRING OF 1944: THE QUESTION OF A GROWING 'SPIRIT OF IMPERIALISM'

IN January 1944 a perceptive Australian observer of American politics noted that 'there are signs in this country of the development of a somewhat ruthless Imperialist attitude ...'.[1] This change in the public mood manifested itself most clearly two months later, in March, when the Secretary of the Navy, Frank Knox, testified before Congress that, in his opinion, the Japanese mandated islands 'have become Japanese territory and as we capture them they are ours'. In clear-cut fashion he thus resolved the question of sovereignty, and further stated that the mandates should be annexed by the United States for purposes of military security.[2] To most British observers Knox's statement seemed self-evident. To Churchill and Stanley, Roosevelt and Hull merely used the rhetoric of trusteeship as a cover for annexationist ambitions. The question should be directly confronted: did Roosevelt and his advisers consciously devise schemes to conceal motives of imperialism they publicly disavowed?

There is an abundance of evidence, and it is susceptible to different interpretations. To examine the indictment precisely it is useful to consider in detail an elaborate scheme prepared in January 1944 for American control, direct and indirect, of no less than the entire Pacific basin. If any one document could be said to represent a blueprint for American imperialism in the Pacific, this one might qualify. It was drafted for Roosevelt's adviser, Harry Hopkins, by one of the ablest officials in

[1] Alan Watt (Australian Legation, Washington) to W. R. Hodgson (External Affairs, Canberra), 22 Jan. 1944, Evatt Papers.

[2] Quoted in Huntington Gilchrist, 'The Japanese Islands: Annexation or Trusteeship?', *Foreign Affairs*, 22. 4 (July 1944).

the administration, Wayne Coy, at this time Assistant Director of the Bureau of the Budget. Coy described his project modestly as a proposal for 'Organization for Civil Affairs in the Pacific Islands'. In a covering letter, he noted that Hopkins would find interesting the *assumptions* on which the scheme was based. His explicit assumptions, it could be argued, are the ones upon which American officials based their future policy but seldom articulated them so clearly, or, critics would add, so honestly.

(1) The United States is committed to major responsibility for the security of the Pacific coasts of the Americas, the Panama Canal, the Philippine Islands, and the Pacific sea and air trade routes.

(2) The United States will hold by possession, mandate, lease, purchase or agreement general control over Polynesia and Micronesia, adequate participation in Melanesia, and a strong position in Indonesia.[3]

In explanatory footnotes, (a) Polynesia consisted of the 'mid-Pacific triangle' from Hawaii to Easter Island and the North Cape of New Zealand; (b) Micronesia he described as the 'northern island bridge' between Polynesia and Indonesia with a spur north to Japan, including the Ellice, Gilbert, Marshall, Caroline, Marianas, and Bonin Islands; (c) Melanesia, he explained, was the 'southern bridge' between Polynesia and Indonesia and included Fiji, the New Hebrides, New Caledonia, the Solomons, the Bismarck Archipelago, and New Guinea—all territories under sovereignties other than American; (d) Indonesia, for Coy's purposes, meant the archipelagos lying off South-Eastern Asia from Formosa to Australia—'specifically the Philippines and Netherlands East Indies'. The assumptions continued:

(3) The United States will implement its Pacific policy by a chain of naval and air bases stretching westerly through Polynesia and Micronesia to the Philippines and southwesterly through Polynesia and Melanesia to a position north or northeast of Australia, and will continue to base the Asiatic Fleet in the Philippines.[4]

Here, in further explanation, Coy added that it would not be desirable to station large numbers of troops west of Hawaii,

[3] 'Memorandum on Organization for Civil Affairs in the Pacific Islands', enclosed in Coy to Hopkins, 10 Jan. 1944, Hopkins Papers Box 334.
[4] Ibid.

and that in the Philippines the air bases would be operated by the Navy and Marine Corps. In an additional note he quoted the legislation of the 9th of December 1943 which authorized the President to establish and maintain bases for the protection of the Philippines and the United States. The concluding two assumptions read:

(4) The United States will exercise civil authority in its Pacific possessions and mandates; and it will require special representation in civil affairs in all other island groups in which it will maintain bases.

(5) In respect to the Philippine Islands, from the date of expulsion of the enemy through the period of restoration of civil government and democratic processes and until the date of the granting of independence by the United States, the United States will exercise the civil functions set forth in . . . the Philippine Independence Act . . . and thereafter will establish a special form of civil representation appropriate to a protectorate.[5]

Coy thus advocated the establishment of no less than a protectorate in the Philippines and he again precisely described what he meant: 'The functions of civil representation in a protectorate surpass in range and intimacy those commonly performed by an embassy or legation, and include continuous and careful observation, analysis, and report of political, economic and social detail.'[6] The logic, if not the language, is highly reminiscent of British secret discussions about such places as Egypt twenty-five years earlier. The question is, did Coy's scheme, or similar ones, influence Roosevelt?

There is no indication one way or the other that Roosevelt approved, disapproved, or even saw Coy's master plan. It can be said that the scheme represented a more sophisticated type of proposal that often reached Roosevelt's office, of which Admiral Byrd's lengthy personal letter about the future of the Pacific is another prominent example. Roosevelt did not lack advice about the islands. Those who proferred such advice often lacked definite replies. From the occasional direct Presidential responses, such as to the Secretary of the Navy a year earlier, we know that his answers would not always have warmed the hearts of international idealists.[7] Roosevelt usually disassociated

---

[5] Ibid.   [6] Ibid.
[7] For the letters by Byrd and Knox, see above, ch. 16.

himself from schemes that smacked of annexation because he immediately recognized the catchword 'imperialism' as a politically disastrous issue. Moreover, territorial aggrandizement, even if effectively disguised, would be administratively expensive. Yet we know that sometimes he listened sympathetically to proposals which amounted to annexation in all but name. Later in 1944, after the military authorities had thoroughly battered the trusteeship proposals, Roosevelt encouraged Charles Taussig to develop a scheme which would secure responsible civil administration of the islands under the United Nations but would allow the United States 'to maintain full sovereignty'.[8] But in other areas Taussig detected a genuine commitment to the principle of colonial independence. So complex—or devious—was Roosevelt's mentality that it would do him an injustice to underestimate the subtlety of his ideas. Roosevelt publicly espoused trusteeship and opposed imperialism. In fact his interpretation of trusteeship in Micronesia meant American control with full measures for military security. At the same time he persistently rebuffed his military advisers who wanted to disavow trusteeship entirely. The conclusion reached by Willard Range in this regard is balanced and sound: 'For the most part . . . Roosevelt was quite consistent . . . in his desire to see colonialism and spheres of influence replaced by trusteeships and independent states formed on the basis of self-determination. As a practical politician faced with specific problems he was often forced to compromise and accept half a loaf.'[9] As for the relation between the President's public words and his secret actions, he believed his own rhetoric and saw no contradiction between American security and the world's security.

Roosevelt's conception of trusteeship continued to be an eclectic solution for dependent territories and potentially unstable areas. One important strand of his thought was the establishment of military bases for the international police force at such places as Truk, the Bonins, the Tuamotus, Rabaul, Dakar, and Ascension Island. Another element also continued to be the use of trust territories or free ports for political neutralization and facilitation of commerce. Roose-

---

[8] Memorandum by Taussig, 13 Nov. 1944, Taussig Papers Box 47.
[9] Range, *Roosevelt's World Order*, p. 119.

velt wanted to place Hong Kong, Dairen, and a new port at the northern end of the Persian Gulf under international supervision for the benefit of freedom of trade—or, as British observers put it, freedom of American trade.[10] His return from the Cairo–Teheran conferences marked the zenith of his trusteeship proposals. In January–February 1944, for example, he spoke of Morocco: 'I do not think that a population, which is ninety per cent Moors, should be run permanently by France.' His aversion to French colonialism was becoming increasingly emphatic:

[I]f Morocco remains permanently as a French Protectorate, it will tend more and more each year to be thought of as a French Colony. . . . I am inclined to think that . . . [the Moroccan] leaders would like to have the French Protectorate changed into a Protectorate by three Trustees—a Frenchman, an Englishman and an American. They do not want to be exploited and, taking it by and large, they trust the Americans the most.[11]

On the 12th of January the President gave a breath-taking exposition of his ideas to the Pacific War Council. Japan would be stripped of her Empire and the islands would be 'taken over by the United Nations'. The western Pacific would be policed by powers capable of exercising effective military control. Korea would be placed under trusteeship for a forty-year tutelage. Dairen would become a free port. The United States would be willing to act as a 'police agent' in the Marianas, Carolines, and Marshalls. In regard to the New Hebrides the President quoted Admiral Halsey as saying that the French administration 'had been very bad and that they should not be permitted to continue control of the islands'.[12] A couple of weeks later Roosevelt expanded his ideas to Cordell Hull along the same lines, recounting a conversation with the British

[10] Roosevelt's idea was to have equal access and equal rates for international transit but not to permit the carrying of passengers or freight by foreign transport within national boundaries. Leo Amery pointed out in regard to the development of commercial air routes that this would put the Americans at a great advantage, at least in his view, because of the enormous distances of the United States, and the British Empire at a distinct disadvantage over vast stretches in Africa and the Middle East. See, e.g., Amery's letter to Smuts, 18 Jan. 1943, *Selections from the Smuts Papers*, vi. 409–11.

[11] Elliott Roosevelt, ed., *F.D.R.: His Personal Letters*, ii. 1490 and 1493.

[12] Pacific War Council minutes, 12 Jan. 1944, Roosevelt Papers.

Ambassador:

> I . . . told him [Halifax] quite frankly that it was perfectly true that I had, for over a year, expressed the opinion that Indo-China should not go back to France but that it should be administered by an international trusteeship. France has had the country—thirty million inhabitants—for nearly one hundred years, and the people are worse off than they were at the beginning. . . .
>
> I see no reason to play in with the British Foreign Office in this matter. The only reason they seem to oppose it is that they fear the effect it would have on their own possessions and those of the Dutch. They have never liked the idea of trusteeship because it is, in some instances, aimed at future independence. This is true in the case of Indo-China.
>
> Each case must, of course, stand on its own feet, but the case of Indo-China is perfectly clear. France has milked it for one hundred years. The people of Indo-China are entitled to something better than that.[13]

Roosevelt had become more emphatic, but the substance of his ideas was the same. He could multiply the number of cases to which he might apply the panacea of trusteeship, but the basic solution remained the same: international control in which the American voice would be influential if not predominant. Here is the key point: Roosevelt's ideas did not progress. His enthusiasm for trusteeship reached its peak in the winter and spring of 1944, after which time be began to retreat. His large ideas began to crack on the necessity for precise solutions.

Roosevelt's course on the plane of generalities can be illustrated in the case of the Gambia. It was one of the few specific points from personal experience he could bring to bear on the general proposition that the British Empire should be liquidated. He used it repeatedly. He told a press conference in early February 1944:

> Last year I went to a place called Gambia in Africa, at the mouth of the Gambia River. Bathurst is the capital. I think there are about three million inhabitants, of whom one hundred and fifty are white. And it's the most horrible thing I have ever seen in my life. . . . The natives are five thousand years back of us. Disease is rampant, absolutely. It's a terrible place for disease.
>
> And I looked it up, with a little study, and I got to the point of view that for every dollar that the British, who have been there

[13] Hull, *Memoirs of Cordell Hull*, ii. 1597.

for two hundred years, have put into Gambia, they have taken out ten. It's just plain exploitation of those people.[14]

Therefore Roosevelt wanted an international committee to be able to make tours of inspection of such places. '[I]f we sent a committee from the United Nations, to go down to Gambia', and told the British, the President continued, 'if you Britishers don't come up to scratch—toe the mark—then we will let all the world know.' Roosevelt thus stands as a prophet, of sorts, in seeing that the right of inspection would be a vital element in the trusteeship system. He greatly underestimated, however, the element of national sovereignty in colonial territories, of which the flag is the symbol. Charles Taussig recorded this conversation with Roosevelt later in the year, in July, again on the subject of the Gambia.

He [Roosevelt] said that he had pointed out to Churchill that dependent areas, such as Gambia, must in the future be subject to international inspection. The President then, mimicking the voice of Churchill, repeated Churchill's reply: 'We are not going to let any other nation inspect or report on conditions in British territory'. . . .

He then went on to say, still carrying on a conversation between himself and Churchill and replying for Churchill in Churchill's own voice, that Churchill was warped on the idea of sovereignty. The President said he told Churchill so far as he was concerned, he didn't give a damn who had the sovereignty over dependent areas so long as they were subject to international inspection. He said, 'Winston you can keep your old rag flying any place you want'. Churchill's reply, in great indignation was, what do you mean Franklin calling the Union Jack 'an old rag'. The President replied that was perfectly all right, that all flags were made of rags.[15]

At one point Churchill parried that an international team of inspection should be sent to the American South. Roosevelt made jokes in reply, and claimed that a visit would be welcome because things were not as bad as they were painted in the South; but clearly he had not thought out the implication for American dependencies if the inspection proposal were pressed for all of the European colonies. Even for trust territories the right of inspection would be a major innovation in colonial affairs. Anecdotes and generalities were no answer to detailed

---

[14] *Public Papers and Addresses of Franklin D. Roosevelt* (1944–5), p. 68.
[15] Memorandum by Taussig, 13 July 1944, Taussig Papers Box 47.

objections by the European colonial powers and, on the American side, his military advisers. Roosevelt's own progress in developing the implementation of the trusteeship idea became static. It was the State Department that carried the project forward in 1944.

In the spring of that year the problem of trusteeship came under the scrutiny of a State Department committee entitled the 'Informal Political Agenda Group'. The title is misleading. The members were the forerunners of the 'International Organization Group' or, in other words, the corps of senior advisers at international conferences which led to the establishment of the United Nations.[16] Those with a particular interest in the colonial question included Stanley Hornbeck, Isaiah Bowman, and Leo Pasvolsky, Special Assistant to the Secretary of State in charge of preparatory work for international organization. Pasvolsky had already played an important part in the drafting of the Declaration on National Independence.[17] He now took charge of the planning for trusteeship and integrated it into the general strategy for the founding of the world organization. He had gifted organizational ability. From this time on he was the key official who orchestrated both the committee work in the American government on the colonial issue and the negotiations with the British. He was an economist. His profession did not recommend itself to those who believed that questions of diplomacy and international law were best left to diplomats and lawyers.[18] To British eyes he was an improbable figure to be charged with such weighty responsibilities. A newspaper article described him in 1944: 'He is imperturbable, bald, 50 and fat and says he thinks it would be easier to roll than to walk. Hull calls him his "Friar Tuck"'

[16] See Notter, *Postwar Foreign Policy Preparation*, p. 170; and Russell, *United Nations Charter*, p. 220, n. 15.   [17] See above, ch. 14.

[18] Sir Frederick Eggleston, who became Australian Minister in Washington in late 1944, had some particularly sharp things to say about Pasvolsky's handling of the trusteeship question. Eggleston wrote later, at the San Francisco conference, that Pasvolsky was 'an Orthodox economist and has never done any work before in a political sphere' (Eggleston to Zimmern, 3 July 1945, Eggleston Papers 423/10/55). For whatever reason, Pasvolsky impressed the Australians unfavourably. Alan Watt also wrote: 'I think none of us like Pasvolsky whose personality is such that he seems a little inhuman. He never raises his voice or loses his temper and he leaves one with the impression that he is still at heart a Brookings Institute economist whose chief delight is the intellectual pleasure of comparing different sets of statistics' (Watt to J. D. L. Hood, 19 July 1945, Watt Papers 3788).

and trusts to his stout stave when the going gets tough. . . .
Atop the heap sits Leo. He directs, edits and coordinates in
a huge and humble mood.'[19] Pasvolsky had an analytical mind
that went quickly to the essential issues. He made this observation in May 1944 about trusteeship. It sums up what was at
stake between the Americans and the British on the colonial
question. Bowman's interjection served to reinforce his point:

> The danger for the British would be that all of their colonies
> would be drawn into some system of international trusteeship. The
> danger for us would be that we would find all of the detached
> territories reduced to a colonial status.
> Mr. Bowman asked whether this was not in the realm of fancy.
> Mr. Pasvolsky replied that the first point was, but that the second
> point was not.[20]

Pasvolsky clearly saw that the British and other European
powers would never agree to place *all* their colonial territories
under trusteeship. Unless the Americans worked carefully to
preserve a 'special status', the mandates and detached territories might become absorbed into the colonial regimes and the
United States would lose leverage in working for colonial
independence. This was the crucial point which Oliver Stanley,
on the other side, also clearly perceived as he worked for the
abolition of the mandates.

It was in the area of trusteeship that Pasvolsky and his colleagues made the greatest advance in the spring of 1944, but it
should be noted that the Political Agenda Group also reviewed
the two related projects, regional commissions, and the general
declaration. Pasvolsky was greatly aided in this sorting out of
issues and projects by Benjamin Gerig, who had presided over
their drafting in lower committees.[21] Taking the projects in
the order the Agenda Group discussed them, *regional commissions* offered the fewest difficulties. Gerig pointed out that the
commission scheme was designed to stand on its own feet, regardless of its possible future organic relationship with the
international organization. There were five proposed commissions, which corresponded roughly with British plans for regional

[19] *Washington Post*, 13 Aug. 1944.
[20] I.O. Minutes 52, 10 May 1944, p. 3, USSD NF Box 142.
[21] See the minutes of the Committee on Colonial and Trusteeship Problems,
USSD NF Box 56.

bodies in the Pacific, South-East Asia, and in southern, western, and eastern Africa. There still existed differences in opinion about the extent of American participation in, for example, the Africa commissions, and whether Russia should be included in the South-East Asia commission. Whatever the political participation, the commissions would perform a useful service by dealing, on an advisory and collaborative basis, with problems of transport and communication, trade and commerce, health, nutrition, agriculture, labour and education that were of common concern within given regions.[22]

In the second project, *a general colonial declaration*, the contentious words 'National Independence' had been dropped. Nevertheless the committee members quickly found themselves again bogged down in the question of whether independence was the ultimate purpose of self-government. Gerig pointed out that one of the points of the declaration was to reaffirm the concept of the 'sacred trust of civilization' of the mandates system. 'Mr. Hornbeck remarked that we are the only people in the world who think that it is a "sacred trust of civilization" to make everybody independent. It was a big question, he said, whether independence or self-government were really the greatest blessing that all peoples could enjoy.'[23]

Hornbeck had thus retreated from the position he had advocated in 1942, when he virtually had projected the application of the American Declaration of Independence into colonial areas. His reasoning became clear when he mentioned that he had been giving thought to the problem of the Pacific islands. '[T]here were many people in the islands of the Pacific who will never be capable of self-government.' Would we want to foster capacity for self-government, he asked, when ultimate self-government was clearly impossible?[24] Hornbeck wanted to shift the emphasis from 'self-government' to 'self-improvement'. Pasvolsky, however, still wanted a firm, ringing statement emphasizing self-government. He also had helped to draft the original declaration, and he did not want to see it watered down. If the British did not agree, the United States should make a statement of moral principle anyway. Here Pasvolsky collided not only with Hornbeck but also with Isaiah Bowman.

---

[22] I.O. Minutes 52, 10 May 1944. Cf. Russell, *United Nations Charter*, p. 229.
[23] I.O. Minutes 52, p. 14.   [24] Ibid., p. 8.

Bowman had just returned from London and the discussions with Stanley and other British officials were still fresh in his mind. He had been persuaded that the British essentially had the right approach of dealing pragmatically with local problems before jumping into the problems of the universe. Now to his consternation Bowman found his colleagues rehashing the same dialectics of self-government versus independence that they had unsuccessfully debated for two years and, to him at least, were still making no progress. If they were again to propose a colonial declaration, Bowman said, especially one containing 'a large number of general principles', the British would feel 'that they were being asked to read the Old Testament or to examine the Constitution of the United States'. Pasvolsky, who from time to time was slightly cynical in regard to the British, replied that the British themselves were not averse to enunciating principles when it was in their own interest. When Bowman protested that the British felt strongly about American fingers in colonial pies, he drew this rejoinder from Hornbeck:

When Mr. Bowman had said . . . that the British kept objecting that we were always sticking our fingers into their pie, he [Hornbeck] felt like replying to the British that it happened to be their pie which was under our nose and which did not smell too good to us. . . . In other words, Mr. Hornbeck concluded, what becomes of these dependent peoples was everybody's business.[25]

To this discussion of pies and aromas should be added a few spicy comments by Joseph C. Green (Assistant Secretary of State). Green favoured universal principles but wanted to drop the general declaration and apply the principles specifically to the trust territories. He reasoned:

The whole *Declaration of Principles* [the old Declaration on National Independence] . . . should be modified to relate solely to trust territories, so that they would become the principles which the trustee powers would be obligated to carry out under the supervision of the international organization. If this were done, the moral aspirations . . . while applicable only to trust territories, would be reflected throughout the world—in Puerto Rico, in Mississippi, in Malaya, in Burma, and elsewhere. . . . it would then be possible for us to insist upon the application of these principles without being accused of sticking our fingers into other people's pies.[26]

[25] Ibid., p. 15.   [26] Ibid., p. 16.

Hornbeck again objected that all dependent areas were 'everybody's pie', but Green continued to argue that practical application could be given to these profound moral principles if they were limited to specific trust territories. '[I]t would create a standard of conduct for the whole world and would influence such areas as Mississippi and the Navajo territory as well as British and Dutch dependencies.' Gerig observed that the proposal had not been designed to cover 'parts of independent states like our Navajo reservations'. The discussions served the purpose of making it clear that, if the colonial powers eventually agreed to a general declaration, the United States would have difficulty in excluding such territories as Puerto Rico and the Virgin Islands. What is moreover remarkable, the moral earnestness of at least one high American official extended beyond European colonies into backward areas within the United States.[27]

With the third project of *trusteeship and the future international organization*, Pasvolsky and his colleagues made a distinct advance. They did so by definitely resolving, to their own satisfaction at least, the question of sovereignty. The conclusion had far-reaching implications for such vital and concrete issues as the right of petition and visits of inspection. Their judgement had an immediate bearing on the possible annexation of the Pacific islands. By the spring of 1944 this question had become urgent. Hornbeck explained to the international organization group:

[T]his question of sovereignty or title was extremely important because a lot of minds wanted to be satisfied as to exactly where sovereignty resided in the case of the Japanese mandated islands. A lot of good minds in town were also working on this problem and were bothering the Secretary of State. . .[28]

Historically there were four possibilities. (1) Sovereignty might reside in the administering power. This was the extreme case

---

[27] The discussions on the general declaration have a certain air of unreality to them because, despite Bowman's trip to London, the committee members still did not know that the British had replied to the draft Declaration but that the American Ambassador had failed to communicate the British *aide-mémoire*. The committee members were thus operating on the assumption that the British had ignored the Declaration, which was not the case, though some British officials such as Stanley were content to see the issue at stalemate.

[28] I.O. Minutes 54, 12 May 1944, p. 7, USSD NF Box 142.

implicitly and persistently argued by General Smuts in the case of South-West Africa. Ultimately it rested on the right of conquest. This interpretation had been rejected by the Council of the League of Nations. As Gerig explained to the international organization group, no one had ever satisfactorily explained where sovereignty actually resided, but almost everyone did agree 'that sovereignty did not rest in the mandatory power'. (2) Sovereignty might have resided in the League of Nations. Should it therefore reside more definitely in a future world organization? (3) Sovereignty might have resided in the Allied and Associated powers, or in other words those powers who had signed the peace treaties with Germany and Turkey. This was the position taken by the United States because, not being a member of the League, it was the best case to be made for an American vested interest. (4) Sovereignty might ultimately reside with the indigenous inhabitants. Gerig explained that this was a view 'held in liberal circles'. Attractive as this last position might have seemed to the officials of the State Department, there were distinct disadvantages to it because of the Pacific islands. Gerig explained that if sovereignty resided with the inhabitants, ultimately they could claim ownership. 'Mr. Hornbeck agreed, saying that there were not many people who were living on those islands.'[29] The question of sovereignty thus brought them back to the old problem of universal principles which might, in Hornbeck's phrase, 'boomerang'. The exasperation of the committee in dealing with the question is well summed up in Joseph Green's comment, 'it would be well to leave the issue vague and to let the lawyers unscramble the problem for a couple of generations'.[30]

Although immensely complicated, the question of sovereignty could not be avoided because of the impending abolition of the Japanese and Italian colonial empires. The subcommittee on international organization and the State Department's legal adviser, Green Hackworth, had a definite answer.[31] Sovereignty would reside collectively in the members of the international organization, but not in the organization itself. In reaching this solution they had simply put aside the old controversies about

[29] Ibid., p. 8. [30] Ibid., p. 7.
[31] See the 'highly secret' memorandum prepared by the International Organization Subcommittee, USSD NF Box 273.

the mandates in order to break new ground. Hackworth explained to the international organization group:

[I]t was quite unnecessary to talk about title to trust territories at this time. Under the present proposal title would be clearly vested in the members of the international organization and if a member withdrew from the organization it would lose all claim to title in the trust territories.[32]

The reason for vesting title in the collective members of the international organization was to avoid the impression of a sovereign international super-state. They thus would disarm critics of world organization while advancing from the vagueness of the League's position. But Hackworth did not want to be too explicit:

[I]f we thought we were going to give independence to the trust territories as fast as possible it would be desirable not to define the question of sovereignty in very precise terms. In fact, it would probably be easier for these territories to get their independence if the question of sovereignty were left in abeyance.[33]

Here was the stand taken by the State Department: *collective sovereignty shared by the members of the United Nations*. It was not, in Hackworth's words a 'very precise' solution, but it was definite. It placed the State Department in a strong position *vis-à-vis* the colonial powers. If the British, for example, argued against it they would reveal their 'imperialist' colours. If they accepted it, they would acknowledge that they did not claim the same sovereignty in trust territories that they could in their colonies. This had practical ramifications. As Gerig pointed out to the international organization group, 'the mandatories always resisted the idea of inspections by the Mandatory Commission on the ground that such inspections would infringe upon their sovereignty'.[34] The imperial powers would now have less ground to resist tours of inspection. The solution of collective sovereignty also strengthened the hand of the President. Roosevelt had consistently held that the Pacific islands would be administered under the authority of the United Nations. He now had the full legal force and the considered opinion of the experts in the State Department that collective sovereignty would be not only feasible but desirable.

If the State Department moved forward with a definite answer to the question of sovereignty, it can also be said that

---

[32] I.O. Minutes 54, 12 May 1944, p. 6.　　　[33] Ibid., p. 6.　　　[34] Ibid., p. 2.

a change of direction became apparent in May–June 1944 in regard to the general problem of colonial independence as the ultimate American goal. It was directly related to the issue of a 'growing spirit of imperialism' in the Pacific, and the shift of attitude can also be connected with Isaiah Bowman's return from England. Bowman did not believe that the British would listen to a detailed list of moral injunctions. As Joseph Green reiterated the point, which he and others found persuasive: 'If the British, as Mr. Bowman had indicated, were opposed to any kind of Ten Commandments they certainly would object to . . . forty or fifty pious observations.'[35] The State Department's list of proposals became less detailed and more flexible as a result of the Bowman mission. Bowman himself now believed, like the British, that it was futile to try to prepare tribes such as the Hottentots for self-government. He now wanted to exclude not only the word 'independence' but 'self-government' from the American trusteeship proposals. He believed that 'certain tribes would probably never govern themselves democratically'.[36]

Bowman held the extreme position on this point, but others who had been studying the question for the last two years now also backed away from the opposite extreme of independence. The shift is especially apparent in Hornbeck's attitude: '[L]ots of people had not the slightest desire for self-government. . . . lots of groups were intelligent enough to know that by themselves they would get nowhere, but that they might get somewhere if they remained attached to other groups of people.'[37]

Hornbeck meant that the future of the peoples of the Pacific islands lay with the United States. Trusteeship need not necessarily imply independence. In modifying the dogmatic view that independence should be the result of trusteeship, the State Department officials moved closer to common ground with the British. They remained a considerable distance from the Joint Chiefs of Staff, who wanted no question about permanent American authority in the Pacific.

[35] Ibid., 10 May, p. 10.

[36] I.O. Minutes 60, 2 June 1944, p. 2. 'Mr. Hornbeck remarked that Mr. Bowman's dislike of an emphasis upon the promotion of self-government was contrary to the approach of the Secretary [Hull] and he wondered if Mr. Bowman was aware of the fact that the Secretary's speeches emphasized this principle. Mr. Bowman replied that he blamed the advisers of the Secretary for this fact' (ibid., p. 4).

[37] Ibid., 10 May 1944, p. 14.

23

THE AMERICAN MILITARY'S STAND
ON THE ANNEXATION OF THE
PACIFIC ISLANDS

THE United States Navy, like the British Colonial Office, detested the impermanence of trusteeship. If there were any battlefields of the war that needed to be brought into the permanent orbit of the American defence system, in the eyes of the Navy they were the islands of Micronesia. Under Japanese domination they had served, in one of the Navy's favourite phrases, as 'permanent aircraft carriers'. To the officers of the Navy it seemed preposterous that the State Department could envisage these islands as a subject of international debate. Their population was negligible. They served no purpose other than as strategic outposts. They were being won at the high cost of American blood and treasure. Yet the State Department was now preparing to discuss their fate, in another Navy phrase, because of the principle of 'international welfare'. The Joint Chiefs of Staff, who became increasingly interested in the problem in 1944, believed that nothing other than absolute sovereignty in the islands would satisfy the defence requirements of the United States. In the summer of that year the military and the civilian ideas about post-war planning came into direct collision. The whole question of international trusteeship was reopened. If the Joint Chiefs had their way in annexing the mandated islands, then the State Department would have little ground for arguing against 'imperialism' in other detached territories. In this clash the President's position was central but not altogether clear, at least to his military advisers. While encouraging the State Department to proceed with trusteeship plans he had also instructed the military to plan for permanent bases throughout the Pacific and other parts of the world. Though to his own subtle mind these propositions were not contradictory, they led to direct bureaucratic rivalry which challenged even Roosevelt's ingenuity to keep under control.

During the earlier part of the war, the principal officer who communicated the views of the Navy to the State Department was Captain H. L. Pence. He was the Officer-in-Charge of the Occupied Areas Section of the Navy Department. He served as liaison officer, along with Colonel James Oliver of the U.S. Army, on the State Department's Security Subcommittee. Pence was an officer of robust opinions. He believed that the only solution to the problem of the Pacific islands was annexation, pure and simple. In his view the only way peace could be maintained in the Far East would be to encompass Japan permanently with a ring of military bases. Though these military measures might be taken in conjunction with China and possibly Russia, Pence thought it would be simplest and safest to annihilate the Japanese people. His views as expressed to the Security Subcommittee may be taken as the extreme solution to the problem of the Pacific and Far East. In his own words, 'the problem would be simplified if Japan were destroyed'. It was a question of racial survival:

It was a question of which race was to survive, and white civilization was at stake. . . . [W]ar was inevitable and a good thing. When one nation became an international bandit it should be eliminated.[1]

The Japanese would be our enemies for the next hundred years. If any strength is left to them they will seek revenge. The United States must make its position so secure that such a cataclysm shall never arise again. A string of bases was absolutely necessary for our security.[2]

When challenged by the view that a Carthaginian solution would not be permanent because of Japan's recuperative power, Pence reluctantly agreed, giving a highly interesting reason why security would remain fragile. 'Captain Pence replied that this was so', in other words, that Japan could not be permanently crushed, 'because there were not enough naval officers in the world.' A stern call to duty! When asked whether he had views

[1] ST Minutes 17, 12 May 1943, p. 3. For Pence and the establishment of the military government in the Pacific, see Dorothy E. Richard, *United States Naval Administration of the Trust Territory of the Pacific Islands* (Office of the Chief of Naval Operations, Washington, 1957), vol. i. For a study that illuminates stereotyped naval attitudes, see Peter Karsten, *The Naval Aristocracy: the Golden Age of Annapolis and the Emergence of Modern American Navalism* (New York, 1972).

[2] ST Minutes 16, 7 May 1943, p. 4.

on the mandated islands, he replied that he had a great many indeed.

He personally believed that the security of the United States lay in the acquisition of absolute sovereignty over the mandated islands. Control over the mandated islands was closely connected with control over the Pacific Islands in general. The Pacific was 'our lake'; the United States should control a string of islands from Clipperton by way of the Marquesas to the Far East.[3]

These exchanges between Pence and his civilian colleagues were taking place in the spring of 1943, during the time that the General Board was preparing the studies for the President.[4] Pence explained: 'The General Board of the Navy had already given the matter considerable thought. He was dubious about the success of international control, which was a peace treaty solution which did not work in practice. The United States must look to its own security.'[5] Projecting past experience into future probabilities, Pence thought that Japan would continue to remain the American enemy in the Pacific for the indefinite future.

If we proceed on the assumption that our potential enemies will continue to be our enemies, our only security lies in force. The only way to assure our security as a major power in the Pacific is by the acquisition of full sovereignty over the islands. . . .

[T]he attitude of the Navy on this question was that peace would be followed by a period of perhaps ten years when the American people would wish to hold Japan down. But in twenty-five or thirty years Japan would rise again as a force to be reckoned with.[6]

International control would not work. It would mean only compromise and temporary measures. The American people would have to be made aware that in this matter of life and death between the yellow and white races it would be better not to be too idealistic.

The people of the United States must rise above their fear of responsibility. The responsibility for security in the Pacific would rest increasingly on the United States. Every step should be taken to assure the absolute dominance of the position of the white rule in the Pacific.[7]

---

[3] ST Minutes 20, 16 June 1943, p. 2.   [4] See above, ch. 16.
[5] ST Minutes 20, 16 June 1943, p. 2.   [6] Ibid., p. 3.   [7] Ibid., p. 3.

In the phrase Pence used repeatedly, the Navy viewed the Pacific as 'our lake'.

Captain Pence held extreme ideas about the Japanese people, but his views on the mandated islands were in line with the studies made by the General Board. When asked what the Navy's second choice would be if the United States could not acquire full sovereignty, he replied that there should be absolute base rights and administrative control. When asked whether a distinction could be made between key strategic bases and islands of lesser importance, Pence responded that the strategic position would be enhanced if the entire island groups could be held surrounding the strategic bases. Moreover, unless full control could be maintained over all of the island groups in Micronesia, their administration would be difficult. Here Pence as the chief of the occupied areas section had specific questions for the State Department—questions that became pressing as the Navy began to establish military administrations in the winter of 1943–4. In a lengthy series of questions dated the 18th of February 1944, General J. H. Hilldring (Director, Civil Affairs Division, U.S. Army) and Captain Pence asked for specific advice on such basic matters as the nature and purpose of administration in parts of the Japanese Empire: 'Should the administration be punitive, mild, or primarily to safeguard reparations?'[8] Such fundamental questions raised the question of the future American occupation of Japan itself and the status of the Emperor, questions that go beyond the problem of security and trusteeship in the Pacific; but basic assumptions about Japan also affected the Japanese Empire. For example, the Navy wanted to know from the State Department which other powers would participate in the military governments of various parts of the Japanese Empire—in what areas would the British assume responsibilities? Would the Chinese be involved? The Dutch? The Free French? The Russians? What were the basic policies to be pursued in regard to liberated areas? Were the mandated islands a liberated area? 'Does the League of Nations have any residual rights in the mandated islands which must be subserved by the military occupant?'[9] Merely to list a few of the

---

[8] 'Preliminary Political and Policy Questions Bearing on Civil Affairs Planning for the Far East and Pacific Areas', 18 Feb. 1944, USSD 890.014.6.   [9] Ibid.

questions indicates that the Navy fully recognized that, though an absolute stand might be taken on the question of sovereignty, in practice the resolution of these issues would be complicated and would involve some measure of international co-operation if not control.

Within the State Department, the opposite number of Captain Pence was Abbot Low Moffat, Adviser of the Liberated Areas Division. Moffat, like Pence, held strong opinions about the future of the Japanese Empire. He tended to reinforce the Navy's view. Thus from the official most directly concerned with the liberated areas, the Navy did not get an accurate reflection of the ideas of the group of officials who were giving sustained attention to the question of the ultimate future of the mandated islands. Indeed Moffat developed projects which rivalled those of Benjamin Gerig and the Pasvolsky group. Unlike most of his colleagues in the State Department, especially in the Pasvolsky group, he believed that the theory of international accountability, as embodied in the mandates system, 'has been completely discredited' and that the trusteeship proposals were 'another set of platitudes'. Taking a position that had long since been dropped in the advisory committees, Moffat held that international trusteeship should mean international administration or else the United States would be vulnerable to charges of insincerity. '[W]e should determine the policy we consider fundamentally sound for us', he wrote in March 1944, '[and] tell the other nations that this is our position.'[10] He believed in extending the principles of the Atlantic Charter to Asia, in part because the liberation of Far Eastern colonial areas would increase 'our bargaining power' with the Chinese and also because of its value in 'psychological warfare'. '[I]t seems to me that the United States must take an affirmative and aggressive position now, even though this will run counter to the wishes of our British allies . . . our own military and political interests in the Far East must in any event determine our actions.'[11] In short, he favoured taking a unilateral stand, regardless of the international complications.

Moffat's position was very similar to the Navy's. He urged the establishment of long-lease military bases in the Japanese islands. At the same time, however, he proposed thoroughgoing

[10] Moffat to Taft, 7 Mar. 1944, USSD 890.0148/3–744.   [11] Ibid.

international administration in order to make trusteeship a reality and not a sham.[12] These two basic ideas—bases and international administration—of course resembled Roosevelt's thinking and superficially seemed to reconcile the requirements of the Joint Chiefs with the idealism of the President. Moffat had the ear of two high officials who were attracted to his reasoning—Charles P. Taft (Director of the Office of Wartime Economic Affairs) and Joseph C. Grew (Special Assistant to the Secretary of State). Pasvolsky eventually had no difficulty in convincing Taft and Grew that Moffat's plan was hastily conceived and would not withstand close scrutiny (especially the international administration part), but the episode had a chilling effect on some members of the international organization group. It indicated that despite the prolonged and intense attention given to the trusteeship question by acknowledged specialists, someone with half-baked ideas on the subject (from the point of view of the Pasvolsky group) might override or sabotage the trusteeship scheme higher in the administration or in other parts of the government—not least in the Pentagon.

In the spring of 1944 Vice-Admiral Russell Willson and Lieutenant General Stanley D. Embick of the Joint Chiefs Strategic Survey Committee began to meet with the Pasvolsky group.[13] The international relations experts sought military advice on, among other things, the question of an international police force. The time had come to incorporate the scheme into the general proposals for international organization, if the military authorities thought it feasible. Pasvolsky explained that there would be different types of bases, some of which might be under international sovereignty in trust territory. Isaiah Bowman pointed out that the 'international policeman' idea had been tossed about now for over two years and the consensus held that it was not practicable. Stanley Hornbeck, however, spoke in favour of it. He first of all argued that the idea of an international police force appealed to the public imagination (and, though he did not say so, to the President's imagination). He next attacked the view

---

[12] See Moffat's memorandum, 'Proposal for an International Trusteeship System', PWC S248, USSD NF Box 144.

[13] For the background of this representation see JCS 570/3 CCS092 (7–27–42); and Notter, *Postwar Foreign Policy Preparation*, p. 248, which gives the details of other military officers participating in the State Department's committees.

that it would be the international police force alone that would keep the peace. In his view it would *not* have to be superior to all other national forces.

Hornbeck used the analogy of the States of the United States in which state police in any single state were only one in many forces keeping the peace. Using further analogies, he developed this idea: '[T]hese police forces could be scattered in a number of different places like the domestic police forces or like fire-fighters in any American town . . . the council of the international organization acting on behalf of the member governments would have control of the international situation.'[14] Not many of the committee appeared to like Hornbeck's police force, or the analogies, but he refused, in his own words, to be 'sat upon by the rest of the committee'. He continued to elaborate the way in which the international police force would supplement national armies. It would mainly deal with crises of a secondary rather than a primary character:

> He wished to make it clear that he did not conceive of the international police force as taking the place of national armies or seriously affecting the size of national armies. It was, in his opinion, an addition, a force that could be called upon in less serious situations in order to avoid calling upon national armies except in very serious emergencies. Even when it would be necessary to call upon national armies, he said, there would be an advantage in having a small force with which immediately to begin enforcement action.[15]

Hornbeck's police force was thus remarkably similar to the post-war peace-keeping force of the United Nations.

Admiral Willson totally opposed the idea. He denounced it in strong language:

> He said that an international police force was altogether visionary as a practical proposition. Modern warfare was, in his opinion, so complex in operation that the genius of the best brains was tried even to handle national arrangements effectively. He said he could not visualize the possibility of taking people loyal to a number of different nations and welding them into an effective military organization. He considered the idea of a permanent international force absolutely visionary.[16]

---

[14] I.O. Minutes 37, 23 Mar. 1944, p. 7, USSD NF Box 142.
[15] Ibid., p. 8.   [16] Ibid., p. 7.

Willson said that he gave his opinion only individually as a member of the Joint Strategic Survey Committee, but his views coincided with those of the Joint Chiefs of Staff.

Willson and Embick, along with the other member of the Joint Strategic Survey Committee, Major General Muir S. Fairchild, succeeded in blocking, temporarily, the forward movement of the plans for trusteeship in the summer of 1944. They achieved this success by direct confrontation with the State Department and not with the President. There is no indication that Roosevelt paid any attention to the State Department's detailed planning for trusteeship, though he probably assumed that plans were in progress. He knew Cordell Hull could be depended on to continue to harass the British from time to time and that the Secretary's views were not at variance with his own. There is an illuminating contrast in the President's treatment of the military. Whenever the Joint Chiefs raised the issue of trusteeship, Roosevelt responded immediately. On the 4th of July, perhaps as an indication of their regard for the explosive implications of the subject, the Joint Chiefs sent a memorandum to Roosevelt in which they argued in clear-cut fashion that there should be no question about American sovereignty in the Pacific islands.[17] The President let them know straight away that he had not altered his views.

I have your memorandum of July Fourth in regard to policy regarding the Japanese Mandated Islands.

The Joint Chiefs of Staff are right in stating that no other nation should be left even to the partial control of another nation, but they must also realize that we have agreed that we are seeking no additional territory as a result of this war.

I am working on the idea that the United Nations will ask the United States to act as Trustee for the Japanese Mandated Islands. With this will go the civil authority to handle the economic and educational affairs of their many inhabitants, and also the military authority to protect them, i.e., fortifications, etc. It does not necessarily involve a decision on permanent sovereignty.[18]

Once Roosevelt adopted a pet scheme it was exceedingly hard to dislodge him. His ideas were exactly in line with the project of the Pasvolsky group, including even the nuance of indeterminate

[17] JCS memorandum, 4 July 1944, JCS CCS093 (1–8–44) Sec. 1.
[18] Memorandum by Roosevelt, 10 July 1944, Roosevelt Papers MR Box 167.

sovereignty. Though he himself did nothing in particular to see that the project was developed, he would have had no reason to be displeased if he had studied the Pasvolsky group's proposal. Yet he had reassured the Joint Chiefs that he would look after their interests by giving them the authority to fortify the islands. This however did not placate the Joint Chiefs. Frustrated by the President, the Joint Strategic Survey Committee now prepared a broadside for the State Department.

Willson, Embick, and Fairfield presented their views in a study entitled 'Fundamental Military Factors in Relation to Discussions concerning Territorial Trusteeships and Settlements'.[19] The essence of the case was that discussion of trusteeship settlement would prejudice the prosecution of the war. They noted that the civilian members of the delegation to the impending international discussions at Dumbarton Oaks apparently failed to comprehend the way in which trusteeship might affect American security. In their own words, 'The Joint Strategic Survey Committee has noted a lack of appreciation of the implications of fundamental military factors on the part of some of our civil representatives.' They proceeded to make twelve points, all leading to the conclusion that discussions about trusteeship and territorial settlements might adversely affect relations with Russia and should be delayed until the defeat of Japan. Their report was tightly argued and the whole military view, not only of trusteeship but also of the future of the British Empire, is illuminated by following their arguments step by step.

First, the Survey Committee pointed out that, in the territorial settlements, Russian aspirations would conflict with those of the British, on the one hand, and with those of the Chinese, on the other. 'The interests of the United States would undoubtedly be involved, particularly as to the future status of the Japanese Mandated Islands, and British and Chinese interests could be expected to come in conflict, especially as to Hong Kong.' The second part of the case involved the timing of the territorial settlements. Here, they argued, full weight

---

[19] JCS 973, 28 July 1944, JCS CCS092 (7–27–44); USN GB 450. In relation to the earlier General Board studies, the Survey Committee acknowledged the valuable work done by the General Board 'from the naval point of view', but noted that the General Board 'is not closely in touch with the current strategic situation and is not a "joint body"'. JCS 570/3, 10 Jan. 1944.

should be given to American policy both before and after the defeat of Japan. The military situation would change rapidly, and with it the political considerations that would determine American policy in regard to the trusteeship settlements. The timing of the war with Japan led them to consider the broader situation in regard to the war in Europe. In the summer of 1944 the war with Germany was well advanced, but the defeat of Japan was not yet in sight. Russia would emerge from the European war with an 'assured military dominance in eastern Europe and in the Middle East'. Though the United States and Britain would occupy western Europe, their strength there would decline as they continued to prosecute the war against Japan. Despite British assistance, the United States would continue to carry the main burden in the Far East, unless Russia entered the war.

Should Russia promptly and effectively enter the war after the fall of Germany, she would bring her great land and air forces into action directly against Japan, thereby materially shortening the war and effecting vast savings in American lives and treasure.

Should Russia abstain from such action, due to our untimely pressing the subject of territorial settlement—or any other avoidable cause—we must be prepared to accept responsibility for a longer war.[20]

Here the Joint Chiefs laid it on the line to the State Department. If the trusteeship settlements were pressed, it might prolong the war. '[I]t should be clearly recognized by those guiding these prospective discussions that there is an important connection between the timeliness of discussing territorial trusteeships or other forms of territorial settlements and the earliest and least costly defeat of Japan.'

After the defeat of Japan, the timing of the settlements would be less important, but it would be even more important to bear in mind the changing world-wide military situation. Apart from the elimination of Germany and Japan as military powers, and developments in the relative economic strength of the great powers, there were technical and material factors which had brought about this change. 'Among these are the development of aviation, the general mechanization of warfare and the

---

[20] JCS 973, ibid.

marked shift in the munitioning potentials of the great powers.'
After the war there would be only two great powers:

After the defeat of Japan, the United States and Russia will be
the only military powers of the first magnitude. This is due in each
case to a combination of geographical position and extent, manpower and vast munitioning potential. While the United States
can project its military power into many areas overseas, it is nevertheless true that the relative strength and geographic positions of
these two powers preclude the military defeat of one of these powers
by the other, even if that power were allied with the British Empire.

They now commented at length on the decline of the British
Empire:

As a military power, the British Empire in the post-war era will
be in a distinctly lower category than the United States and Russia.
The primacy of the British Empire in the century before World
War I, and her second-to-none position until World War II, have
built up a traditional concept of British military power which the
British will strive to profit by and maintain in the post-war era.[21]

They emphasized the need to regard the British less sentimen-
tally and more realistically:

It is important that, as regards British military power, we clearly
recognize the substantial change that has taken place. Except for
the elimination of Germany as a threat and rival, nearly all the
essential factors of national power in the post-war era will have
altered, to the disadvantage of the British Empire. Both in an
absolute sense and relative to the United States and Russia, the
British Empire will emerge from the war having lost ground both
economically and militarily.

There were additional reasons for the depreciation of the military power of the British Empire.

These are the inroads of aviation and submarine developments
on the former security of her sea lands, and the relative decline
in her munitioning capacity during the past seventy years, from
about fifty per cent to approximately eight per cent of world totals.
A future world conflict may be expected to find British military
resources so strained in the defense of her essential sea lanes that
little, if any of these resources will be available for offensive action
against a land power.[22]

So far as the Joint Chiefs were concerned, the British Empire had ceased to exist as a great power.

In this estimate of national power, France would rank even lower than Britain. China possessed little real military strength. 'Her ultimate munitioning potential, while it may be considerable, will not be developed for a long time and cannot be of the order of magnitude of either Russia or the United States because of the small size of her reserves of iron ore.' Of the other powers, Italy also lacked mineral resources. This left the United States and Russia alone, and for this reason nothing should be done to jeopardize relations with the Russians at least until after the defeat of Japan. The Joint Strategic Survey stated in conclusion: 'From the military point of view, it is highly desirable that discussions concerning the related subjects of territorial trusteeship and territorial settlements, particularly as they may adversely affect our relations with Russia, be delayed until after the defeat of Japan.'[23] Using strong language, the Joint Chiefs accordingly advised the State Department to postpone trusteeship discussions.[24]

The Joint Chiefs' case was unanswerable. Trusteeship controversies might prolong the war. The State Department had no alternative but to acquiesce and to strike trusteeship from the agenda at Dumbarton Oaks. But it was a postponement and not a resolution of the issue. As the war progressed against Japan, the State Department eventually could use the same argument of time against the Joint Chiefs: having fought the war, it would eventually be time to fight the peace.

[23] Ibid.
[24] JCS 973/1; JCS 973/2, Marshall to Stettinius, 3 Aug. 1944; Stettinius to JCS, 5 Aug. 1944, ibid. Notter, *Postwar Foreign Policy Preparation*, pp. 295–6.

24

THE COLONIAL QUESTION AT THE DUMBARTON OAKS CONFERENCE ON INTERNATIONAL ORGANIZATION. THE ADVENT OF HILTON POYNTON AND KENNETH ROBINSON IN TRUSTEESHIP AFFAIRS

NOT knowing the impasse created by the Joint Chiefs blocking the trusteeship plans, the British fully expected the issue to be prominent on the agenda of talks on international organization among themselves, the Americans, Russians, and Chinese at the Washington mansion of Dumbarton Oaks in August–October 1944. In fact the topic of trusteeship was reduced to a blank in the formal discussions, but the larger issue of the future of the colonial empires loomed in the background. More particularly, in 1944 the economic future of the British Empire increasingly preoccupied the minds of those planning the post-war world. Isaiah Bowman, for example, had been especially struck by the mood in London:

> He had been impressed in England by the overpowering fact . . . that at every dinner-table and in every conversation the British talked about their economic situation at the end of the war. This question was a perfect nightmare to them. Mr. Churchill himself had commented that he was constantly being confronted with all sorts of schemes for the post-war world which completely dodged this vital question.[1]

Shortly before the Dumbarton Oaks conference, Richard Law (now Minister of State at the Foreign Office) discussed the general economic situation of the British Empire with Under Secretary Stettinius. How could Britain even begin to repay the wartime debts? According to Law, Stettinius 'asked me whether we had ever considered in London any device such

[1] I.O. Minutes 52, 10 May 1944, USSD NF Box 142.

as giving to the United States some territory'. Merely tossing out the idea, 'he instanced Jamaica'. It would be tempting to draw parallels between similar conversations at the close of the First World War. But it would be misleading. The exchange of ideas between Law and Stettinius is significant because it is *not* representative of the climate of negotiations in 1944. Law's colleagues immediately denounced the proposal. Oliver Stanley wrote to Anthony Eden, 'a proposal to swop bits of the British Empire for financial loans or Lend-Lease is one which we are not even prepared to discuss with the Americans'. Eden replied, 'I entirely agree that there can be no question of us entering into any sort of commitment with the United States Government about bartering British territory against a loan or any other form of financial or economic assistance.'[2] Both Stanley and Eden objected on principle to the swapping of colonial real estate, but the episode also indicated that the Colonial Office fully intended to hold its own.

A. H. (Sir Hilton) Poynton represented the Colonial Office at Dumbarton Oaks. Previously in charge of the defence section, in May 1944, in a reorganization of the Colonial Office's departmental structure, he became head of the Defence and General Department with Kenneth E. Robinson as Principal. These two officials are of great importance in the history of the trusteeship story from this time on. Poynton represented the Colonial Office not only at Dumbarton Oaks but also at the San Francisco Conference, while Robinson managed the London end of the business. After the war Poynton was directly involved in the affairs of the Trusteeship Council of the United Nations and eventually became Permanent Under-Secretary. Robinson became one of the leading post-Hailey academic authorities on trusteeship.[3] They now began to sort out the problems of international trusteeship with a vigour and precision unprecedented in this particular area—with no sympathy towards those who entertained vague

---

[2] Law to Eden, 19 July 1944, No. 3888; Stanley to Eden, 25 July 1944; Eden to Stanley, 27 July 1944, CO 968/156/Pt. 1.

[3] See Kenneth Robinson, *The Dilemmas of Trusteeship: Aspects of British Colonial Policy between the Wars* (London, 1965). For his views on anti-colonialism, 'World Opinion and Colonial Status', *International Organization* 8. 4 (November 1954); an important essay with a similar argument is by Philip W. Bell, 'Colonialism as a Problem in American Foreign Policy', *World Politics* 5. 1 (October 1952).

notions about managing colonial affairs by international committee. In fact their ideas, though quite similar to Stanley's,
were endowed with an intellectual substance and rigour that
the Colonial Secretary never approached.

Poynton believed that it was fallacious to see any connection
at all between the experience of ex-enemy colonial territories,
on the one hand, and colonies under British sovereignty, on
the other. In a memorandum written in July 1944 he analyzed this fundamental distinction. This particular piece of
writing is significant because it reveals a deep antipathy to
international trusteeship and an equally deep commitment
to British colonial responsibilities. Poynton began with the
premise that the mandates did not involve a transfer of sovereignty to Britain, and that the legal precedents of the
mandates system were therefore irrelevant to the problems
of Britain and her dependencies. There was no connection
whatever.

> Nor does 'trusteeship' in respect of Colonies and Protectorates
> imply that we are in some way accountable to the world at large for
> the discharge of our so called trust. That is not the case: our responsi-
> bility is to the people of the dependencies themselves.[4]

This line of analysis led him, like Lord Hailey, to reject
'trusteeship' in favour of 'partnership'. 'The modern conception of "partnership" which is now replacing the idea of
"trusteeship" reflects the true relationship much more clearly.'
The responsibility for implementing the policy of partnership
rested solely with Britain. Poynton espoused the extreme position that all types of British dependencies except mandates
were *British* and nobody's concern but the British.

> A British Colony is every bit as much British territory as the
> United Kingdom itself, and even though this is not literally true of
> Protectorates and Protected States the jurisdiction or treaty alliance
> is with Great Britain and with Great Britain alone. In short the
> dependent status of these territories does not of itself afford any
> grounds for international supervision of their affairs.[5]

To make the distinction even more clear, Poynton pointed out
that France regarded some of her colonies as part of the

⁴ Memorandum by Poynton, ' "International Supervision" and the "Colonial
System",' 26 July 1944, CO 968/156/Pt. 1.   ⁵ Ibid.

metropolitan country. 'It would be quite illogical that these territories should escape international supervision for this technical [French] reason while British territories who enjoy a much larger measure of self-government instead of being administered direct from London would be made subject to international supervision.' In Poynton's view the right of sovereignty was so clear cut that it need not be pursued. 'So much for constitutional theory', he noted, and proceeded to ask whether international supervision actually helped, as some people held, to prevent abuses and exploitation in the colonies. He suspected that strategic views lay beneath humanitarian sentiments, especially in the case of the United States.

The idea [of international supervision] is sometimes represented as a progressive and liberal development calculated to prevent the abuses of exploitation and to promote the well being of the inhabitants. This idea which is widely current among sentimentalists in America is also extremely convenient to the U.S. Administration for reasons which are far from sentimental. There is always a lurking fear among non Colonial Powers that the Colonial Powers will make use of their colonial resources in a manner detrimental to Sovereign Powers which are not so fortunately placed.[6]

After examining the complexities of the British Empire and concluding that international interference would impede the 'perpetual progress' towards self-government, Poynton demonstrated the absurdities of 'independence' and colonial status in Africa, again with specific reference to the United States, this time in regard to Liberia. 'It would be absurd to suggest that Sierra Leone or the Gold Coast should be brought under international supervision while the Republic of Liberia is left to its own devices on the pretext that it is an independent state.' He regarded the Americans as responsible for these misguided and mischievous projects. About American economic policy, Poynton remarked, 'the economic policy of the British Colonial Empire has been far less of an international irritant than the economic policy of the U.S.A.'. Coming back to his central point, British colonies were a British concern.

[S]uch matters as the system of land tenure or the judicial system is [*sic*] a matter of purely domestic concern and while there is no

[6] Ibid.

objection to, and possibly much to be gained from, the inter-change of knowledge and experience with, even, a Central Library of Information attached to the World Organisation, it would be in-tolerable for the United Kingdom Government to be answerable to an international authority for the education policy of the Gambia! In short . . . the conception of a World Colonial Organisation with supervisory powers over the affairs of Colonies, qua-Colonies, must be strongly resisted.[7]

Such were the views of one British official who played such a large part in British decolonization. The British Empire had to be defended against American efforts to vitiate it by inter-national trusteeship. Britain had her own colonial duty and ultimately the British were accountable only to themselves and the inhabitants of the colonies.[8]

With the advent of Poynton the attitude of the Colonial Office, always stiff, became even more rigorous. There was a perceptible hardening of the line not only towards the Ameri-cans but also towards the Foreign Office. On the 26th of July Poynton and Gater met with their opposite numbers at the Foreign Office, Jebb and Cadogan. Cadogan bluntly summed up the situation: the Colonial Office's intransigence on the trusteeship issue might make it impossible for the British to secure future financial aid from the Americans. Gater replied that the Colonial Secretary 'would see the strongest objection to any system which places the present Colonial Empire under any system of international supervision which would derogate from our full jurisdiction'.[9] Gater further pointed out that the Colonial Office, though not wishing to be entirely rigid, took the position that this policy had been approved by the Cabinet (by accepting the Colonial Office memorandum on regionalism of the 18th of April 1944), and therefore any departure would require Cabinet authority. What then, Cadogan asked, might the Colonial Office be prepared to yield? Gater mentioned the

---

[7] Ibid.
[8] Ibid. By contrast, Kenneth Robinson, whose extensive minutes also begin to appear in the trusteeship files at this time, on the whole preferred to leave the premises of his position implicit rather than explicit in the manner of Poynton. At this time the points of his analysis are noteworthy for the perception of the main springs of American policy. For example, he wrote on 4 July 1944, 'American interest in Indo-China . . . is an important part in their whole outlook on "Colonial trusteeship".' CO 968/156/Pt. 1.
[9] Minutes by Poynton of the meeting of 27 July 1944, CO 968/156/Pt. 1.

idea of a colonial library. Cadogan established that before the war the Colonial Office had published annual reports as a matter of course and intended to resume the practice after the war. He said that donating reports to a library 'would be no contribution at all'. He immediately saw through the scheme, especially since the Colonial Office did not even want to have the reports discussed. With the Colonial Office persisting along this line, the Foreign Office would have difficulty in meeting the Americans even half-way on the question. Cadogan again emphasized the larger issue: 'the U.S. approach to the problem would probably be that we were asking them [economically] to "underwrite" the British Empire and that from their point of view it was natural that they should expect to have some say in how the British Empire was run.'

It became clear to Cadogan and Jebb that the Colonial Office above all wanted to avoid international discussion of sensitive British colonial problems. According to the Foreign Office minutes of this meeting: '[S]ome embarrassing situations might arise, for example, if a public discussion took place on the position in Kenya. If the Americans wish to find a cloak for their intentions in the Pacific could they not be met by the acceptance of some form of international trusteeship for ex-enemy dependent territories?'[10] The distinction between ex-enemy dependent territories and normal colonial possessions corresponded with Poynton's views on how to handle the situation; the trouble was, if a trusteeship authority were established for enemy territories, then all of the mandated territories would also probably be included. This in turn was only a short step towards 'meddling' in the affairs of the British colonies. This logical progression of the issues was what Poynton hoped to avoid in Washington and precisely the one he found—with this unanticipated difference: all his discussions on the subject were informal because the Americans had removed the question of trusteeship from the agenda.

When Poynton arrived in Washington, he found that the Chinese, jockeying for advantage in the discussions, had put

---

[10] FO minutes, 27 July 1944, U6284/180/70, FO 371/40749. The day after this meeting Gater wrote to Cadogan that Stanley 'is unable to suggest at the present time any concession which will not, in his opinion, be incompatible with our vital imperial interests'. Gater to Cadogan, 28 July 1944, CO 968/156/Pt. 1.

forward a proposal for trusteeship.[11] It came to nothing because
the State Department officials now had to avoid the issue.
They could talk about trusteeship only informally. Benjamin
Gerig and C. Easton Rothwell sought out Poynton on the 11th
of September. Rothwell was an official who had worked with
Gerig from the beginning of the war on trusteeship problems
and had been involved in the affairs of the Anglo-American
Caribbean Commission. He was now serving as one of Pasvolsky's assistants. Poynton reported to the Colonial Office
that Rothwell immediately 'buttonholed' him on the question of international accountability. He wanted to know from
Poynton whether Lord Hailey's views represented the position
of the Colonial Office. This question went to the heart of the
internal division within the Colonial Office about collaboration with the Americans. During the earlier part of the war
(specifically in his address at the Mont Tremblant Conference
of 1942[12]) Hailey had indicated that an international body
would review progress in colonial territories by examining
reports of the administering authorities. Hailey's views were in
line with those of the Colonial Secretary at the time, Lord
Cranborne, who favoured a much more direct and open collaboration with the Americans than did his successor. With
the advent of Oliver Stanley, Hailey's progressive ideas fell into
disfavour and he was consulted much less frequently. Without
knowing of the extent of this internal transformation in the
Colonial Office, the Americans were left with the impression
that Hailey probably still represented official opinion. Poynton
received instructions from London that Hailey spoke only in
a personal capacity.[13] Poynton did his best to avoid the issue,
and noted with relief that Rothwell merely showed 'slight
signs of disappointment' when told that the British did not
want to make the regional commissions analogous to the
Permanent Mandates Commission. It must have been an uncomfortable moment for Poynton to have to disavow to some
extent Britain's leading spokesman on colonial affairs. The
Americans, not knowing about Poynton's intellectual dilemma,

[11] The Chinese proposed to establish an 'International Territorial Trusteeship
Commission' to administer and supervise trust territories and other 'internationalized' areas. For Colonial Office comment see CO 968/157/14511/A.

[12] See above, ch. 12.

[13] Gent to Poynton, 20 Sept. 1944, CO 968/160/14814/11.

got the impression, in Rothwell's words, that 'Mr. Poynton . . . did not seem to be particularly well informed about Colonial Office attitudes'.[14]

With Rothwell, Poynton discussed problems of regional commissions and the West Indies. Poynton thoroughly believed in the idea of 'functional agencies', in other words, international institutions designed to promote economic and labour policies, social services, and public health control. In his memorandum of the 26th of July, he had analyzed the basis of *legitimate* international interest in colonial areas; it could only be, to emphasize again the key word, *functional*:

> That such international interest is legitimate has long been recognised both by the conclusion of international treaties many of which apply to Colonies as well as to Sovereign Powers, and by the existence of international organisations such as the I[nternational] L[abour] O[organization]. Indeed the functions of the I.L.O. come very near to international supervision over the *execution* of policy. But the I.L.O. does not concern itself simply with Colonies because they are in a dependent status: it rightly concerns itself with labour conditions the world over—sovereign states and Colonies alike.[15]

Poynton thus favoured international cooperation provided it did not interfere in any way with British authority. He discussed the scope of collaboration within the regional commissions at length with Rothwell. They talked about the expansion of the West Indies commission to include other powers. The only point of difference between them appeared to be the American tendency to regard the regional commissions as akin to the Permanent Mandates Commission. On the whole Poynton and Rothwell saw eye to eye.

Poynton also found common ground with Gerig on more general points. The latter freely granted that the mandates system had faults and that the regional commissions would supersede in many respects the Permanent Mandates Commission. 'Poynton readily endorsed this, saying that it was precisely our own [position].' To the British this attitude was

[14] Minutes of a meeting of Pasvolsky, Gerig, Rothwell, and others, on 'Problems of Dependent Territories', 12 Oct. 1944, USSD NF Box 189. Gerig also commented that he 'did not know . . . whether Mr. Poynton was speaking on his own or was reflecting a change of policy on the part of the Colonial Office, but presumably the latter was more the case'.

[15] Memorandum by Poynton, 26 July 1944, CO 968/156/Pt. 1.

surprisingly satisfactory, though Lord Halifax, who reported the conversation to London, also observed that 'we still have the sentimentalists and United States politics to reckon with'.[16] The most important single point that emerged from the conversation between Poynton and Gerig concerned the fate of the Japanese mandated islands and the Italian colonies, which, Poynton had noted earlier, were the 'real crux of the matter'. In London Kenneth Robinson immediately saw the significance of the American insistence: 'I think the most important point . . . is the unlikelihood of our being able to secure the abolition of the Mandates without the regime in the . . . Mandated-territories being assimilated to whatever regime is decided for the Italian and Japanese colonies.'[17]

Thus the Colonial Office officials clearly perceived the interconnection of the issues of ex-enemy colonies and the mandates; they could hardly establish a new trusteeship authority for the Japanese and Italian territories and refuse to place the mandates of the allied powers under the new regime. The issue was gradually becoming one of where the British could hope to draw the line. Nevertheless Poynton held out hope. Gerig and Rothwell appeared to agree at least that 'good points of Mandates and [the] Congo Basin treaties should be universalized and bad limitations rejected'.[18] The Americans were proving themselves to be less dogmatic than Poynton had anticipated.

Far from finding irreconcilable differences, Poynton found a community of colonial interests. In particular he discovered that Henry Villard, the head of the African Division of the State Department, was sympathetic towards the affairs of the British Empire. Poynton submitted a report to the Colonial Office on their discussion of the way in which the Americans and the British might work together in Africa. These excerpts reveal the way in which Poynton foresaw points of agreement. They also serve as a convenient review of the major problems of colonial Africa as seen through Poynton's eyes in September 1944:

1. *Regionalism.* Mr. Villard asked whether there had been any practical developments of the policy announced in Colonel Stanley's

[16] Halifax to Eden, 15 Sept. 1944, copy in CO 968/160/14814/11.
[17] Minute by Robinson, 20 Sept. 1944, CO 968/160/14814/11.
[18] Poynton to Gent, 14 Sept. 1944, CO 968/160/14814/11.

speech of the 13th July, 1943. I said not, but that within the Colonial Office we had devoted a good deal of thought to the possibility of a South Pacific Regional Commission. We had no fixed doctrine but thought that a central permanent secretariat at some suitable point in the Region was an essential feature . . .[19]

Poynton emphasized that the regional councils would be 'functional'. 'The emphasis should be on collaboration and consultation on practical issues—in other words trying to get something positive done—not on supervision and "inquisition".' He granted that there should be some connection between the regional commissions and the future world organization. They next discussed whether the whole system of treaties affecting central Africa should be revised.

2. *Congo Basin Treaties etc.* . . . I said that up to now this problem has been slumbering but the Colonial Office had recently been thinking over the whole position which was to some extent tied up with the provisions of the Mandates. I played my usual 'signature tune' (universalise the good features as far as appropriate and scrap the bad limitations and get rid of the Mandate Terms as such).[20]

Poynton again found that Villard concurred in these points. 'We agreed that a thorough spring cleaning was necessary.' The next item is significant because in discussing it Poynton got his fullest revelation of the controversy between the State Department and the military.

3. *Ex-Enemy dependencies, status of Mandated Territories.* . . . Mr. Villard said that the War and Navy Departments frankly advocated annexation but that the State Department view was divided. Public opinion in the U.S.A. was likely to be against annexation provided (or so I gathered) that security could be assured without direct annexation. The existing Mandates Territories presented a problem. Mr. Villard appeared to agree that there was much to be said from the administrative point of view in aligning them in future with the older dependencies; but public opinion in the U.S.A. would interpret such action as aggrandisement in conflict with the Atlantic Charter.[21]

In conveying the impression that the State Department was 'divided' over whether to place the Japanese mandates under

---

[19] Memorandum by Poynton, 19 Sept. 1944, CO 968/160/14814/11.
[20] Ibid.   [21] Ibid.

trusteeship, Poynton's wish probably fathered the thought. He also exaggerated Villard's willingness to see the mandates assimilated as normal colonies. The significant point is that Poynton acknowledged the force of opinion in Britain against the abolition of the mandates: 'I was bound to agree that there would be a strong body of opinion . . . *in Great Britain*', Poynton stated, that would oppose annexation.[22] On another important topic:

4. *Federation in British West Africa.* . . . Had the Colonial Office ever thought about this? I said it was an old friend. We attached great importance to closer association of the four West African colonies . . . [but] each colony's interests would be in danger of being swamped by the other colonies, except Nigeria which would dominate the rest.[23]

And thus they plunged into a detailed discussion of the future of West Africa. Poynton was very favourably impressed with the head of the African Division.

Mr. Villard was very polite, and obviously keenly interested . . . there was more than courtesy behind his frequent assertion that there was a very great similarity between British and American points of view on the Colonies, and that our two countries would have considerable difficulty in impressing their point of view, for instance, on the French.[24]

As a result of this and further conversations with Rothwell and Gerig, Poynton felt that he had made progress in persuading the Americans that supervision and inspection of the British colonies, at least, would be unnecessary.

I have throughout our discussions tried to impress upon him [Rothwell] that the emphasis we want is not 'Go and see what the British are doing and tell them not to'; but 'Let us all see what each other are doing and together try to do a bit better.' I think this point of view is gaining ground.[25]

In London an official in the Foreign Office wrote to Kenneth Robinson that Poynton 'has been doing some useful educational work during his stay'.[26]

---

[22] Memorandum by Poynton, 19 Sept. 1944, CO 968/160/14814/11. Italics added.   [23] Ibid.   [24] Ibid.

[25] Poynton to Gent, 22 Sept. 1944, CO 968/160/14814/11.

[26] David Owen to Robinson, 6 Oct. 1944, CO 968/14814/11.

Poynton had attempted to perform the difficult task of presenting an essentially traditional position in a manner that would convince the Americans that the Colonial Office was not reactionary but moving forward towards self-government. The Americans did not entirely know what to make of him. On the 12th of October, Gerig, Rothwell, Villard, and others involved in the problems of dependent areas met Pasvolsky to clarify the points of discussion with Poynton. Gerig stated that Poynton 'had shifted ground considerably'. The Far Eastern expert, George H. Blakeslee, concluded that Poynton 'had not thought through his ideas on dependent territories and that he did not represent the highest level of the Colonial Office'. Here Blakeslee was entirely wrong: Poynton's views did reach the highest circles in the Colonial Office, and he had formulated his ideas. They coincided with the Colonial Secretary's own views.

The observations of Pasvolsky and Villard were more perceptive: 'Mr. Pasvolsky remarked that in his opinion the British really wanted to assimilate mandated territories to colonies rather than colonies to mandated territories but they didn't dare to say so. Mr. Villard commented that he had the same impression from Mr. Poynton.'[27] Discussing Poynton's emphasis on 'functional agencies', Pasvolsky 'commented that in his view that was a red herring'. He thought the British were using the regional commissions as a 'false front' in order to get rid of the mandates system. He noted that the idea of a 'false front' was similar to what the Navy might accept in Micronesia. The attitudes of the Pasvolsky group are highly revealing in this regard. They perceived a threat from the Navy, on the one hand, and the Colonial Office, on the other. This exchange between Blakeslee and Pasvolsky goes to the heart of the matter.

Mr. Blakeslee said that . . . it is clear that the Navy wanted the United States to have the Japanese Mandated Islands in full sovereignty. While they would, if necessary, agree that we might hold these islands under the technical authority of the international organization, they could not tolerate any inspection of their bases in the islands. Mr. Pasvolsky pointed out that this was impossible

[27] Minutes cited in note 14, 12 Oct. 1944.

since it was exactly the position taken by the Japanese to which we disagreed so strongly.[28]

Pasvolsky thus identified the attitude of the Navy with the pre-war policy of Japan. From the State Department's point of view it was unacceptable. A 'false front' would undermine the principles of genuine international supervision elsewhere. Fully aware of the danger of a tacit alliance between the Navy and the Colonial Office, Pasvolsky himself now began to try to break down British resistance to trusteeship.

By early October, when Pasvolsky finally decided to deal with the issue, the British colonial expert had already left Washington. Convinced that the Americans were not formally going to discuss colonial affairs at this time, Poynton had received authority to proceed to Jamaica and Trinidad to take up problems of recruitment for the war effort. Pasvolsky approached Gladwyn Jebb, to whom he explained that 'some kind of new system would have to be applied to the Italian and Japanese Empires'.[29] Pasvolsky's intervention roused Lord Halifax, who took the occasion to reiterate his view that, the sooner agreement could be reached on the colonial question, the better. Halifax reasoned as follows:

> We can, of course, tell them [the Americans] politely to mind their own business but if we thus decline informal discussions with them there is nothing to prevent them from circulating their own views. . . . Once they committed themselves in this way it would be much more difficult to influence or modify their views. . . .
>
> Misunderstanding and ill-formed criticism of our colonial policy as you know is one of the most obstinate irritants in Anglo-American relations. The Americans misrepresent us, we rightly resent this, and so it goes on. . . . I submit we have much to gain by retaining [the] initiative as far as we can, and thereby calling the tune ourselves rather than letting the initiative pass entirely to the Americans.[30]

As a result of Halifax's persuasive analysis, the Colonial Office instructed Poynton to return to Washington to discuss trustee-ship informally with Pasvolsky.

---

[28] Ibid.

[29] Jebb to F. O., 7 Oct. 1944, copy in CO 968/160/14816/11. When he returned to London, Jebb told Sir George Gater that he thought 'the Americans would not be too exacting in their requirements'. Minute by Gater, 18 Oct. 1944, ibid.

[30] Halifax to Eden, 7 Oct. 1944, No. 5477, CO 968/160/14814/11.

With a mixture of candour and studied vagueness, Pasvolsky put the American case before Poynton on the 12th of October. Pasvolsky said he had an open mind. Poynton raised familiar British objections to trusteeship, stating in particular that progress towards self-government would be best achieved by the 'parent State' and not by any 'outside body'. According to Halifax, who reported the conversation, Pasvolsky 'surprisingly' seemed to agree. 'Pasvolsky did *not* (repeat *not*) raise the question of supervision.' He would welcome British proposals for a solution. Here is Halifax's commentary on Pasvolsky's tactics:

> On these points vagueness and obscurity of much of what Pasvolsky said appeared to arise largely from the fact that he was evidently groping himself for ideas and phrases; and seemed to indicate that American thinking is still in an embryonic stage where we can do much to influence it. For this reason also, it may well be that eventual State Department policy may not . . . coincide with some of Pasvolsky's embryonic ideas.[31]

Pasvolsky's ideas were far less embryonic than Halifax supposed, but the Ambassador was right in warning of the power of the bureaucracy in the background. From what later transpired it is clear that Pasvolsky hoped the British would now come forward with trusteeship proposals that might aid the State Department against the Joint Chiefs. To the British, who could only dimly perceive this internal confrontation, this appeared to be the decisive opportunity to resolve the trusteeship controversy in their favour, or at least to get a better colonial settlement than if they waited for the Americans to try to impose one.

[31] Halifax to Eden, 16 Oct. 1944, No. 5614, CO 968/160/14814/11.

25

THE COLONIAL OFFICE TAKES THE INITIATIVE. THE POYNTON–ROBINSON PROJECT ON 'INTERNATIONAL ASPECTS OF COLONIAL POLICY'

JUST as the British in 1942 had seized the opportunity to present a colonial declaration when the State Department seemed disposed to accept their views, so they now in the last months of 1944 once again thought that the Americans might be persuaded to abandon international supervision. At least there was nothing to be lost, and a considerable amount to be gained, by having a clearly thought-out program. This idea was in the minds of the Colonial Office officials as they decided to respond positively to the State Department's invitation to submit a proposal on trusteeship as a first step in resolving the differences between the two countries. As Oliver Stanley at the end of the project explained to the War Cabinet, 'It was important that we should take the initiative and should not wait for the Americans to make the first move, lest they should put forward schemes which were unsatisfactory from our point of view, but might attract support.'[1]

The officials who undertook this task were Hilton Poynton and Kenneth Robinson. It was an intense, herculean effort. After Poynton returned from Washington in mid-October, the two of them prepared an initial draft 'On the Future of Colonial Peoples'. They circulated it to the Assistant Under-Secretaries, the Colonial Secretary, and Lord Hailey on the 29th of that month. After two and a half weeks of further intensive effort they produced a second draft, now entitled 'International Aspects of Colonial Policy', which they had revised to take account of extensive criticism. Now a twelve-page printed document, it received another round of criticism, at the beginning

[1] W.M. (44) 172nd Conclusions, 20 Dec. 1944, CAB 65/44.

of December, from within the Colonial Office and from the Foreign Office and Dominions Office. It then went forward to the inter-departmental Armistice and Post-War Committee. Finally in late December it received War Cabinet approval and then went forward to the Dominions. Such was the complicated but systematic development of the single most important British document on colonial trusteeship during the war. It developed into a 'State Paper' in the grand nineteenth-century tradition. It touched on all aspects of colonial rule. It is of fundamental importance in understanding the stance of the British Empire at the close of the Second World War.

Poynton's views, which underpinned the project, have already been described.[2] Robinson's were very similar, though he had a much more open mind on the question of mandates and international trusteeship. Of course he was obliged to follow the line of the Colonial Secretary, which he did vigorously. If the official line were to avoid international supervision, then one could be certain that Robinson had systematically examined every facet of how to proceed. For example, before Poynton left for Dumbarton Oaks, Robinson wrote: 'POINTS WHICH CANNOT BE YIELDED':

(a) Responsibility and power cannot be divorced. We cannot, therefore, accept any scheme which removes power of decision from Parliament and/or the Legislature of the Colony . . .

(b) Any change in the present system must only be made with the free consent of the Colonial people themselves . . .

(c) We must be certain that any concession made as a bargaining factor achieves the purpose for which it was conceded . . .

(d) Any modification of the present system which Britain is prepared to accept must apply equally to other Colonial Empires . . .

(e) A purely Anglo–U.S. declaration about the British Colonial system would give rise to considerable misunderstanding and misrepresentation all over the world, and would be highly injurious to British interests and prestige.

(f) We must also resist any idea that the achievement of self-government by the Colonies can be decided by a time-limit fixed now.[3]

---

[2] See above, ch. 24.
[3] Memorandum by Robinson, 'Territorial Trusteeship', CO 968/156/Pt. 1.

Robinson's views, which for all intents and purposes were identical with Poynton's, will become fully apparent in the development of the project. At its inception, he had clearly in mind one point that had escaped most of his colleagues. If a central international colonial body were effectively resisted, and only a 'library' created, the Colonial Office would lose certain checks over critics of British imperialism. The British would give up these advantages of the Permanent Mandates Commission, again in Robinson's systematic fashion:

(a) opportunity being afforded to the accredited representative of the Government concerned to give oral evidence;
(b) submission of Permanent Mandates Commission report to representative of Government concerned before any publication;
(c) publication of the Government's comments with the report...

In this exhaustive review, only one point did Robinson fail to elaborate. It seemed so obvious that it bordered on the self-evident. It concerned an international *'Colonial Bureau with full powers of investigation and report analogous to the Permanent Mandates Commission'.*[4] So many were the objections that Robinson merely dismissed the proposition. Within a period of months it became one of the most bitterly contested issues between the British and Americans.

The scope of the project can perhaps best be conveyed by following the structure in final form. It consisted of five parts. The first described the objective of colonial policy. It was a restatement of the idea of Lugard's 'Dual Mandate': 'the objective of good colonial administration . . . is to promote to the utmost the well-being of colonial peoples within the world community.'[5] Poynton and Robinson quoted the reaffirmation of this ideal in the Colonial Development and Welfare Act of 1940, and then proceeded to explain how the static concept of 'trusteeship' had given way to the more dramatic notion of 'partnership', which in their view reflected more accurately the increasing part played by dependent peoples themselves in determining their political evolution. This basic premise

[4] Memorandum by Robinson, 'Territorial Trusteeship', CO 968/156/Pt. 1.
[5] Unless otherwise indicated, quotations from the document itself are from the final version presented to the War Cabinet, 'International Aspects of Colonial Policy', W.P. (44) 738, 16 Dec. 1944, CAB 66/59.

caused dissent within the Colonial Office, as indeed did most other parts of the project. Within the Colonial Office alone there existed a wide spectrum of views about the purpose of colonial government and whether self-government should be the ultimate goal. On the point of 'partnership', some officials attached much greater importance than did others to the feelings of the inhabitants of the colonies. One argument against 'trusteeship' was that by giving it international recognition it perpetuated the sense of dependency implicit in a 'trust' relationship. The other school of thought, notably articulated by Sydney Caine, an official who dealt with economic affairs, held that this view was too sentimental and that too much attention given to welfare and political evolution would detract from the part colonies should play in world economic development. The view also persisted that some dependencies *never* could or should achieve sovereign independence, even on the basis of Dominion status. Such were some of the basic divisions of opinion. At the suggestion of Sir Charles Jeffries, the title during the first stage of the project was changed to 'International Aspects of Colonial Policy' in order to convey the immediate problem at hand. As indicated by the division of views, however, much more fundamental issues were at stake and it is important to bear in mind that the original title was 'On the Future of Colonial Peoples'.

Part II was entitled 'A Scheme for future International Collaboration', which broke down into two parts, (A) 'Regional Commissions' and (B) 'Functional Agencies'. The section about the regional commissions explained how social and economic problems of common interest would be dealt with. The commissions would be consultative bodies and would not exercise executive or supervisory powers. They would not concern themselves at all with the constitutional relationship between colonies and parent states. At various stages officials continued to debate, for example, whether Russia would be allowed membership in the South-East Asia Commission, and South Africa's possible membership in the West Africa commission. The most intractable problem continued to be eastern Africa, in part because of the uncertainty of the Italian colonies. The new idea introduced at this stage of the war was the establishment of a commission for north-eastern Africa, embracing the three Somalilands, Ethiopia, and the Sudan. This commission, like the others, was described in detail in terms of 'parent' and dependent states.

In the part dealing with 'Functional Agencies', Poynton and Robinson described how bodies such as the International Labour Organization, which would be attached to the future world organization, would deal with 'the problems of Colonial administration which have a legitimate international interest . . . which arise in similar form in all territories, irrespective of their international status'. Poynton was particularly keen on functional agencies. Like his American counterparts, he wanted some universal means of reaching beyond formal colonial territories into areas of 'internal colonies'. A later exchange makes Poynton's view on this basic issue very clear. In February 1945 the Colonial Office commented on a Canadian telegram to the Dominions Office which stated that functional agencies of the world organization would operate throughout the world in sovereign states containing dependent peoples. International agencies would affect the Indian tribes of Canada as they would those of the United States. 'That's exactly why they're so relevant', Poynton commented.[6] Functional agencies such as the International Labour Organization were a means of at least calling attention to universal standards without in any way interfering with sovereignty. For this reason Poynton attached great importance to them.

Part III in final form was entitled 'Measures to Ensure Publicity in Colonial Administration'. It dealt with the possible creation of an 'International Colonial Centre' and the problem of international accountability. In the original draft this was the weakest section. To Poynton and Robinson's critics within the Office, it appeared to be window dressing for the abolition of the mandates system, which contained an element of truth. They had followed Stanley's basic idea of creating a library that would merely collate papers and make reports available. T. K. Lloyd, an Assistant Under-Secretary, put his finger on the crucial point:

The proposal . . . for the creation of an international Colonial Centre seems to me to be . . . merely for the sake of filling an apparent gap in a theoretical system. The Centre, as I understand its functions, will be little more than an international library with no initiative even in the field of colonial research . . .

I do not think that it will satisfy American and other critical opinion. The ineffectiveness of the Centre will make it almost valueless in their eyes.[7]

During late November, Poynton and Robinson spent much time trying to close the gap in their theoretical plan by making the international colonial center a meaningful international body.

In Part IV Poynton and Robinson dealt with the mandated territories and the Italian colonies. In the intial draft they gave full vent to their objections to the mandates system. It had been designed to protect the interest of the great powers as much as to promote the development of the inhabitants. Its treaty obligations were negative in character. The terms of the trust were 'reactionary'. Uncertainty of international status did not encourage long-range development. The requirements of equal access of economic opportunity worked to the detriment of the inhabitants and economic planning. The mandated territories were victims of sterile internationalization. If ever there existed a succinct and powerful condemnation of the mandates system, this was it. Almost everyone thought that Poynton and Robinson had over-argued their case. 'There is a general consensus of opinion that the case against the mandates is overstated', Robinson wrote on the 13th of November.[8] Here, and in the concluding section, Part V, the two authors softened the criticism of the mandates system and attempted to prove that the Colonial Office stood to gain by genuine international collaboration. They walked a tightrope held by those, on the one side, who (like Sir William Battershill), deprecated international schemes because they might impinge on British sovereignty and administration, and those on the other side, who (like Lord Hailey) wanted more and not less international collaboration.

Sir William Battershill was Deputy Under-Secretary of State. He is of particular interest in the context of trusteeship because he became the first post-war Governor of the Trust Territory

[7] Minute by Lloyd, 9 Nov. 1944, CO 968/162/14814/11A.
[8] Memorandum by Robinson, 13 Nov. 1944, CO 968/160/14814/11.

of Tanganyika. He came straight to the point in a memorandum to Poynton of the 9th of November:

The main object is to get rid of the mandates. I hold no brief for mandates but I think it is possible to pay too big a price for their abolition. I regard this price as too big. There will be likely to be even more intervention (and possibly interference) in matters which rightly are the province of the S[ecretary of] S[tate] and the Colonial Governments by outside bodies than there ever was under the mandates system.[9]

Battershill objected especially to possible visiting missions of inspection.

It is not proposed that these bodies should have the right to inspect or indeed to visit the territories though I should see great difficulty in refusing visits. Inevitably a visit, made even with the purest of motives will result in an inspection; and the body visiting will at once become the focus for every disgruntled individual and body of individuals. . . . I feel that the authority of the local Government is likely to be considerably reduced by visits which as I have said I should find it very difficult to refuse. Also it seems to me that these bodies would in time inevitably reduce the power of the S.S. to be master in his own house.[10]

Above all he protested on constitutional grounds:

It seems to me that we are getting on to dangerous ground from the point of view of political theory here. . . . We are proposing to set up a very complex organisation which though comparatively harmless in theory will be apt to become dangerous in practice— dangerous in that they seem to be interposed between the local legislature and Government and the Secretary of State and Parliament . . .[11]

He entirely agreed with Poynton and Robinson on the weakness of the mandates system, but pointed out that if the mandated status were abolished, this would by no means solve the problems of the territories involved. He drew examples comparing Palestine and Tanganyika.

The difficulty lies largely in the plural community. Palestine is an example of the plural community. It is a hopeless proposition from this point alone even if you had no mandate. . . . the abolition

[9] Memorandum by Battershill, 9 Nov. 1944, CO 968/162/14814/11A.
[10] Ibid.   [11] Ibid.

of the mandate by itself would not really solve anything in Palestine.

In Tanganyika Territory you get something of the opposite. Omitting the settler problem it is fair to say that there you do not really get a plural community. The reason why the country is rather backward cannot wholly be put down to the iniquities of the mandate system. The reason is rather that when we took it over it was under capitalised and certainly did not have enough working capital. If the mandate there was abrogated tomorrow and the place proclaimed a British Colony that would not alter the place much in its essentials. Your main difficulties would still persist [12]

In other words, the mandates system should not be made a scapegoat. On the whole, Battershill was willing, reluctantly, to go along with Poynton and Robinson's project, but, as Robinson noted, 'Sir W. Battershill is evidently very uneasy about the danger of infringement of sovereignty.'[13]

Lord Hailey was asked for his opinion, apparently on the initiative of Sir George Gater. Hailey always had a disposition to look at documents with an eye for their intended effect. If the purpose were to abolish the mandates, then in his view Poynton and Robinson were on the way to achieving the opposite of what they wished. Producing a proposal for the Americans that included the abolition of the mandates would have the same result as waving a red flag before a bull. Poynton and Robinson were working against the idealism of both the founding of the mandates system in 1919 and the Atlantic Charter. Inadvertently, they had exposed the Colonial Office to charges of 'Imperialism'.

[I]t raises the issue whether the abolition of the Mandates would involve the charge that the Powers now holding them were aggrandising themselves. The Mandates system was created in 1919 largely to avoid that charge; the circumstances have since then only altered in so far that the principle of non-aggrandisement has been reinforced by the Atlantic Charter. Will the mere qualification of control, by the creation of Regional Commissions, dispose satisfactorily of the imputation of aggrandisement?[14]

[12] Ibid. Many contemporary observers would have taken issue with his description of Tanganyika lacking the components of a plural society. Apart from the white settlers, the Arab, Indian, and African societies seemed to make it almost a classic case.

[13] Memorandum by Robinson, 13 Nov. 1944, CO 968/160/14814/11.

[14] Memorandum by Hailey, 10 Nov. 1944, CO 968/162/14814/11A.

This is not to say that he favoured continuing the mandates system. Hailey wanted to *by-pass* idealistic debate by concentrating on the establishment of the regional commissions. '[I]f we could get the Regional Commissions accepted first, on a suitable basis, we should then be in a stronger position to come back on to the question of the existing Mandates.' His analysis touched on many points, but foremost among them was the belief that, if the regional commissions could be made to work, then the issue of the mandates would become theoretical and fade in importance. He thought that the question of publicity would be essential in convincing the Americans of their good faith. By encouraging the glare of publicity into their colonial affairs, the British would, in effect, be demonstrating their accountability.

This is not the place to explore all the implications of the doctrine of 'accountability,' but I think that we might succeed in by-passing the more idealistic theories on the doctrine by concentrating on a practical interpretation of it, namely, that Colonial administration can best be subjected to the influence of outside opinion by giving the largest measure of publicity to its content.[15]

Hailey's criticisms were clearly reflected in the redrafting of the project. The passages attacking the mandates system were toned down and those dealing with publicity were bolstered. The result was a much more positive proposal emphasizing regional commissions and acountability through publicity.

Of the responses of the geographical Departments to the project, the most interesting came from the one which previously had the least to say about trusteeship. The Middle Eastern Department now gave its views, which included the reason why Palestine and Trans-Jordan, though under mandate, had *not* been discussed along with the other mandated territories. The following passage written by E. B. Boyd of the Palestine Department was flagged as having 'special secrecy' and not to be circulated outside the Colonial Office:

I notice that . . . [the project] makes no specific reference to the 'A' Mandates, and this is, I think, as it should be. The future of Palestine and Trans-Jordan is an entirely separate problem . . .

[P]lans are now well advanced for the announcement of a new

[15] Memorandum by Hailey, 10 Nov. 1944, CO 968/162/14814/11A.

policy whereby the Mandate for Palestine and Trans-Jordan will be abolished and the existing Palestine divided into a Jewish State, a Jerusalem State, and an 'Arab' residue which will be fused with the present Trans-Jordan to form a new state of Southern Syria. The two former units will be independent states in treaty relations with Great Britain; the Jerusalem State will be an autonomous state under the protection of Great Britain (or of the United Nations if any appropriate association of the latter comes into being after the war).[16]

Palestine thus provided a guide to possible solutions of the other mandated territories. If they ever reached an advanced stage of political development, incipient nation-states could form treaty arrangements that would prove just as satisfactory as Dominion status, at least to some officials of the Colonial Office. For the other mandated territories, however, even self-government seemed ages away. Since the matter of treaties and protected states had been raised, Sir Arthur Dawe, who supervised the Middle Eastern Department, ventured these remarks:

I think on this point that it would be best to avoid any suggestion that mandated territories . . . absorbed would become 'protectorates'. The Protectorate status is in many ways antiquated and anomalous, and my own view is that where practicable, having regard to treaty and other factors, we should, as a general policy, aim at transforming protectorates into Colonies.

If therefore we took over Tanganyika as a British possession, it should, in my opinion, become a Colony like Kenya and not a protectorate like Uganda.[17]

Dawe's remarks were exactly in line with the Colonial Office views of 1919. In this sense the much celebrated continuity of the British 'official mind of imperialism' has yet a different meaning.[18]

One other commentary on the project deserves special attention because it alone of the critiques challenged the premises of Poynton and Robinson and expressed radical sentiments— radical at least in the sense of basic ideas shared more by critics of British imperialism than by those attempting to preserve the

[16] Memorandum by E. B. Boyd, 6 Nov. 1944, CO 968/162/14814/11A.
[17] Memorandum by Dawe, 9 Nov. 1944, ibid.
[18] 'The Official Mind of Imperialism' is the sub-title of *Africa and the Victorians* (London, 1961) by Ronald Robinson and John Gallagher.

Empire. It serves as a dissenting opinion by which the project can be seen in relief. The author, Sydney Caine, did not believe that Poynton and Robinson had clarified the nature of the colonial problem. They had emphasized the words of Article 22 of the League Covenant (the mandates charter), colonial peoples 'not yet able to stand by themselves'. Caine asked, 'are there any peoples in the world who can stand by themselves, except perhaps the Russians and the United States? Even if one does not take the phrase quite so literally, there are many countries, such as Liberia and Siam, which are very close to Colonial status in this sense.' The thought reveals clearly what many at the time perceived but few so succinctly expressed: in relation to the emerging super-powers of the United States and Russia, almost all other parts of the world could be viewed as essentially a colonial situation. 'Colonial status', if the phrase were to have any meaning at all, probably made best sense, in Caine's view, as being governed by someone else.

This at least was one way of looking at the heart of the colonial problem. Another was to look at motives. The Americans talked much about welfare and development in the colonies, but if one looked at their idealism in relation to their economic investments the problem assumed another dimension. Caine, writin gas an official especially concerned with economic affairs, observed: 'The Americans themselves are not really interested only in the welfare of Colonial peoples but also in the exploitation of natural resources in colonial territories.' He went on to challenge some of the common economic assumptions about the mandates:

Play is made [in the project] with the deterrent to development produced by the uncertain tenure of the Mandates. It is extremely doubtful whether there is anything significant in this complaint. The popular allegation was that capital investment was prevented by insecurity, but somehow or other Palestine, whose political future was at least as uncertain as that of any other mandated territory, succeeded in attracting a capital investment probably greater than that of any other country in the world during the inter-war period, and there was quite a lot of capital investment in Tanganyika, where the allegation was most frequently made.[19]

[19] Memorandum by Caine, 9 Nov. 1944, CO 968/162/14814/11A.

On the attack on the mandates system generally by Poynton and Robinson, Caine wrote: 'No mention is made of one of the real weaknesses of the Mandates Commission, i.e. that its members had no right to visit or inspect the territories in question.' Here of course he was expressing diametrically opposite views to those of almost everyone else in the Colonial Office. Taking the question of inspections and infringement of sovereignty head-on, he continued:

If we really want any future international organisation to be effective, I think it is essential that, whether under that name or not, there should be some provision for inspection. That would undoubtedly be distasteful to national sovereignties, but I think that we ourselves could concede a right of inspection with very little loss, because in fact we do not prevent people going to our Colonies and finding out what they can and publishing the results. Some other Colonial powers do, and it would be helpful to us to be able to discover more of what is going on in them than we can at present.[20]

This was not a new argument. Hailey, among others, saw the advantage of inspection in the colonial territories of other Empires, and he was prepared in the last resort to grant visits of inspection. Hailey also minimized the significance of 'sovereignty'. What is refreshing about Caine's view is the tone of scepticism (which Hailey also shared in his more philosophical moments): ultimately the question of sovereignty did not make much difference to Caine (and the same can be said in the end about Hailey). In contrast, to most others in the Colonial Office the issue of sovereignty seemed linked with the preservation of the Colonial Empire, which made a good deal of difference. Caine's was a lonely, dissenting view.

Consensus and not dissent characterized the proceedings of the Armistice and Post-War Committee on the 18th of December when Stanley presented the project for approval as a paper to be submitted to the War Cabinet. Attlee, Bevin, Amery, and Cranborne, among others, all attended and none ventured comments of substance. Stanley, who prided himself on his ability to guide papers through committee, adopted Hailey's tactic of explaining that, since the Americans attached such great importance to 'accountability', the British would be accountable 'to world opinion' by the publicity given by the

[20] Ibid.

'International Colonial Centre'. He frankly described the centre as 'a sop to the Americans'. No one objected. The only point of interest is a query made by Sir Alexander Cadogan, who wanted to know about the relation of the center to the General Assembly of the future international organization. '[D]id we, for example, mean that if the Assembly wanted to consider the status of Negroes in Jamaica they would not be able to do so unless the United States agreed that they would discuss the status of Negroes in Virginia?' Was that what the Colonial Office meant? Colonel Stanley said 'that he did not want the General Assembly to discuss, for example, the constitution of Malaya, any more than the constitution of the United Kingdom. . . . The purpose . . . was to ensure that a Colony as such was not singled out for discussion rather than an independent sovereign State.'[21]

Securing the approval of the Armistice and Post-War Committee, Stanley now brought the project before the War Cabinet.[22] Perhaps because of the press of other business, Churchill made no objections. Cadogan recorded in his diary:

> Cabinet at 6. We meant to deal—amongst other things—with Dumbarton Oaks and Territorial Trusteeship.
> Talked till 6.45 about military situation. . . . Then a wrangle about Local Govt. till 7.50. Then World Organisation! A complete madhouse—P.M. knows *nothing* about it. . . . Just as utterly futile on Territorial Trusteeships. The old P.M. is failing.[23]

Whatever the cause of the lapse of interest at this particular time, Churchill continued to erupt periodically on the colonial question, so the remark about 'failing' was not entirely accurate, at least in regard to trusteeship. In any event, the Poynton–Robinson project for Regional Commissions (and the abolition of the mandates) was now the policy of the United Kingdom Government and was now ready to go forward to the Dominions.

Events had long overtaken the Colonial Office's initiative. Among other things, the Australians and New Zealanders had again taken an independent stand on the colonial question. This will be discussed in the next chapter. Here it is impor-

[21] A.P.W. (44) 23rd Meeting, 14 Dec. 1944, CAB 87/66.
[22] W.M. (44) 172nd Conclusions, 20 Dec. 1944, CAB 65/44.
[23] *Diaries of Sir Alexander Cadogan*, pp. 688–9.

tant to conclude with the responses of the Dominions to the Poynton–Robinson project, though it means moving beyond the chronology of the trusteeship problem at the end of 1944. It is an indication of the difficulties in long-range planning in wartime that the Colonial Office did not learn of the reactions of the Dominions until the time of the Yalta Conference in February of the next year. The replies nevertheless clarify the general position of the imperial government and the Dominions. They reflect a continuity of basic attitudes.

By the time the Dominions Office circulated the Poynton– Robinson project—by airmail[24]—to Ottawa, Cape Town, Canberra, and Wellington, it was the product of many hands and a polished document. In the consensus of opinion expressed by Gladwyn Jebb in the Foreign Office, the paper set out 'in convincing language an admirably constructive policy'.[25] At the specific requests of the Foreign Office and Dominions Office, and prompted by criticism within the Colonial Office, Poynton and Robinson had toned down the diatribe against the mandates system. Nevertheless the document as a whole still conveyed the general impression of a Colonial Office fixation on this particular point in relation to international supervision and American criticism. This comment was written by a Foreign Office official at a later stage, when the question arose whether the document should be submitted to the Americans:

In reading this memorandum it is very difficult to avoid being influenced by . . . the Colonial Office's bugbears. . . . The Colonial Office's bugbears are (1) opposition in principle to international administration (an opposition authoritatively supported by many disinterested and experienced persons); and (2) opposition to outside interference in constitutional relations (which is the very thing the Americans cannot keep their tongues and pens, if not their hands, off); and (3) an intense dislike of the mandates system . . .[26]

Such was the general flavour of the document on which the Dominions were invited to give their opinions.

---

[24] The Dominions Office refused to telegraph the contents of the document on grounds that it was 'quite impracticable' because of the length. Minute by Poynton, 15 Dec. 1944, CO 968/160/14814/11.

[25] Jebb to Poynton, 16 Nov. 1944, CO 968/14814/11.

[26] Minute by H. J. Harvey, 31 Jan. 1945, FO 371/50807.

The responses from Canada and South Africa did not discourage the Colonial Office. The Canadians apparently feared that the encouragement of functional agencies of the world organization working in such areas as human rights might have some bearing on their own 'dependent peoples'.[27] But on the whole they were content to leave the initiative in the matter with the imperial government. The South Africans showed a similar concern for the possible encroachment of the regional commissions into the 'domestic aspects of South African native policy, e.g. control of native labour . . .'.[28] They also acquiesced. The South Africans could be expected to support the imperial government. As Lord Cranborne later summed up, bringing in the other two Dominions: 'Australia and New Zealand favoured the Mandate system, whereas South Africa was violently opposed to it. Canada would support anything that suited the Americans.'[29]

From Australia the reply was far more favourable than the Colonial Office had anticipated. It was not belligerent. Writing as though Australia were the center of the universe, Dr. Evatt congratulated Colonel Stanley on bringing the Colonial Office round to a position more in line with the Australian–New Zealand Agreement of January 1944. The Colonial Office had made 'a definite advance', in Evatt's view. Like Poynton and Robinson, Evatt had a rigorous and precise mind, and perhaps for this reason in part he liked the document. He was particularly pleased about passages that dealt with functional agencies such as the International Labour Organization.[30]

---

[27] Canada to Dominions Office, 3 Feb. 1945, WR213/27, DO 35/1902; minutes by Robinson and Poynton, 5–7 Feb. 1945, CO 968/161/14814/11 Pt. 1. On the passage pertaining to the functional agencies, Robinson noted that it was 'essential' and 'I think we should resist any attempt to remove it'. Poynton concurred, adding, 'Most important.'

[28] C. Heaton Nicholls (High Commissioner) to Cranborne, 6 Feb. 1945, WR213/27, DO 35/1902.

[29] A.P.W. (45) 5th Meeting, 5 Mar. 1945, CAB 87/69.

[30] Australia to Dominions Office, 5 Feb. 1944, WR213/30, DO 35/1902. In his draft Evatt had included a passage about the functional agencies that illuminates his thought in this regard: 'Organisations such as the I.L.O. or other functional bodies of an international character not only admit the duty of member States to improve labour conditions but provide a specific means for such improvement by the gradual adoption of domestic legislation which is designed to effect such improvement. Similarly, it may be contended in relation to similar bodies exercising their functions in relation to dependent territories.' Draft of 30 Jan. 1945, AA A1066/H/45/1021.

Though Evatt made it clear that he still supported the doctrine of accountability, in general he applauded the effort of the Colonial Office to find common ground for agreement. In the Colonial Office, Poynton found Evatt's response 'very satisfactory'. He noted that the Australians wanted to retain the mandates system; but he clearly was encouraged by Evatt's suggestions about functional agencies as a means of imposing universal standards. 'Very sound', Poynton wrote, and further noted that the Australian response was 'certainly a great deal nearer acceptance of our proposals than we had some reason to believe'.[31] This was because Evatt had chosen to emphasize the points where he thought the Colonial Office had moved forward. Evatt alternated his tactics of bludgeoning and praise, and in this particular instance he found much to commend in the Colonial Office's effort.

From New Zealand the Colonial Office received a veiled rebuke. The reply included this passage:

> To the New Zealand Government the issue of self-Government is as important to the full development of the native peoples as that of health or labour and is in equal measure a matter of international concern.[32]

Far more was involved in this mild comment than met the eye. The New Zealander who had analysed the Colonial Office document and prepared the draft was F. H. Corner, an official of particular interest for the subject of trusteeship because he later served as Ambassador to the United Nations and New Zealand's representative on the Trusteeship Council. On point after point Corner took issue with the Colonial Office, not least on the question of self-government. In initial form part of his comment had read: '"The development of self-government *within the British Commonwealth"* repeats the old confusion. As the United States well knows, self-government is self-government.'[33] He described two axiomatic New Zealand positions:

   (a) That provision should be made for the international community to a parent State's administration of dependent territory...

---

[31] Minute by Poynton, 7 Feb. 1945, CO 968/161/14814/11 Pt. 1.

[32] New Zealand to Dominions Office, 14 Feb. 1945, WR213/32, DO 35/1902.

[33] Memorandum by Corner, 31 Jan. 1945, NZ PM 151/2/1. For his general views on trusteeship, see F. H. Corner, 'The Trusteeship Council', in *The United Nations* (United Nations Association, New York, 1965).

(b) That provision should be made for the international community to determine whether a dependent people are ready for self-government.

Both these ideas the United Kingdom rejects as interference with sovereignty and with a purely internal constitutional issue.[34]

These ideas were in line with Peter Fraser's position.[35] They reflected a fundamental dissatisfaction with the British Colonial Empire. Corner brought out his feelings dramatically. He quoted the Colonial Secretary's words, giving them emphasis: 'The real test is . . . not only the actual political advances that we make but it is also, *and I think more important,* the steps that we are taking, economic and social as well as political, to prepare the people for further and future responsibilities.'[36] One official commented, '*This could be close to Hitler talk.*'[37] Those words would have come as a profound shock to the officials of the Colonial Office. No doubt they were deliberately exaggerated for effect. Yet they bear passionate witness to the New Zealand attitude towards international trusteeship. Just as much as the fire-eating American critics of British imperialism, those in the Labour tradition of New Zealand believed that self-government was the proper end of colonial rule.

[34] Memorandum by Corner, 31 Jan. 1945.

[35] In the ellipsis of point (a), Corner had included the idea that if necessary it would be possible to 'transfer the administration', which went beyond Fraser's views.

[36] The excerpt is from Stanley's Parliamentary statement of 13 July 1943. Corner's italics.

[37] The name of this official is withheld at the request of the New Zealand Ministry for Foreign Affairs.

26

THE AUSTRALIAN–NEW ZEALAND
CONFERENCE OF NOVEMBER 1944

URING the same time that the Colonial Office was preparing the definitive case on the colonial problem, in early November 1944 Australia and New Zealand again combined and arrived at exactly the opposite solution. According to the Australians and New Zealanders, there should be not less but more international supervision of colonies. 'Accountability' should be the watchword guiding the development of dependent peoples. To be sure, colonial welfare was not the sole motive of the conference. Representatives of the two countries met technically to implement the machinery of the Australian–New Zealand Agreement and to formulate their ideas about the proposed international organization. Beyond that, Dr. Evatt, above all, feared another 'Big Three' decision such as the Cairo Declaration which would have even more far-reaching consequences for Australia. By late 1944 an armistice with Japan, if not total defeat, seemed a much more real possibility than earlier in the year because of the rapid changes in the Pacific war. The details of the entire Far Eastern settlement might soon be at stake. Independent action to reinforce the Australian–New Zealand Agreement might at least forestall arrangements for a peace in the Pacific dictated by the United States. Such was Evatt's reasoning.[1] He had failed to interest Britain and the United States in an international conference to discuss the affairs of the Pacific, and he had no reason to abandon his theory that the great powers would ignore Australia and New Zealand unless coerced into paying attention. On the other hand he could hardly hold a conference to discuss subjects such as territorial settlements without raising suspicion of 'imperialism' on the part of Australia. For this reason such topics as trusteeship and the South Seas

[1] This interpretation is based on a reading of the relevant parts of the Evatt Papers at Flinders University and the files of the Ministry for External Affairs (see especially AA A989 44/655/27).

Commission were conspicuous on the agenda of the Wellington Conference of November 1944.

W. D. Forsyth prepared the background papers on trustee-ship from the Australian side, and F. H. Corner for the New Zealanders. Setting out the two cardinal points of Australian policy, Forsyth wrote:

(a) that the post-war colonial settlement in the Pacific is a vital matter for Australians because the stability of the region in which they live is at stake; and

(b) that the possession of colonial territories imposes a trust on the guardian states to be exercised for the benefit of and cooperation with the colonial peoples concerned.

Specifically, '*Trustee states should accept accountability to an international body*.'[2] In demonstrating the consistency of Australian policy towards this goal, Forsyth quoted at length the major telegrams on trusteeship that had passed between Canberra and London.[3] Repeatedly Evatt had emphasized the key point that trustee states should accept 'the principle of accountability for their trust to some International Colonial Commission operating through machinery analogous to the Permanent Mandates Commission'. The New Zealanders had shared this outlook both generally and in detail. They now brought with them in their meeting with the Australians their own specific proposals. As framed by Corner, the New Zealand position was just as insistent on the same paramount issue. Like Forsyth, he identified international supervision as the crux. Supervision would be the means by which accountability would be enforced. Summing up the entire proposition of trusteeship, Corner observed:

This principle asserts that colonies are not to be used as pawns in the game of international politics, that the well-being and development of native peoples is the first consideration and forms a sacred trust of civilization. The principle has been so long and so well argued as to be no longer questioned. But the application of the principle is contested, the crucial point being supervision.[4]

---

[2] Memorandum by Forsyth, 'Summary of Views of Various Governments on Colonial Policy', Wellington Conference Paper No. 3, AA A989 44/655/27. Italics added.   [3] See above, Ch. 13.

[4] Memorandum by F. H. Corner, 'Colonial Policy: Mandates', 28 Oct. 1944, NZ PM/151/2/1.

Corner, like Forsyth, stressed accountability. The two officials responsible for preparing the trusteeship question for the agenda of the conference thus held identical views.

The proceedings of the conference reveal that Dr. Evatt at this stage was more interested in some of the larger issues of power politics than the administrative supervision of trusteeship. In a speech marked with points of self-congratulation, he argued that the Australian–New Zealand Agreement had checked American imperialism in the Pacific:

I think one effect of the Australian—New Zealand Agreement is that America today is not prepared to seek for new sovereignty or share of sovereignty south of the equator. I think it is more and more the plan that American future control should be limited to the ex-Japanese mandated islands.[5]

Evatt admitted frustration in obtaining a full voice in post-war plans. Australia and New Zealand had not been invited to Dumbarton Oaks. He told the New Zealanders:

You have tried, and we have tried, to get some effective voice in the organisations which are being set up in Europe to deal with the plans for the European settlement. We have not succeeded. It has not been for want of trying. I feel unless New Zealand and Australia work together, and pretty strongly, the same thing may occur in the Pacific. The stage might come when we will have to speak up on these matters.[6]

Collaboration between Australia and New Zealand, according to Evatt, should be axiomatic. The louder the antipodean voice, the better.

Peter Fraser addressed himself directly to the question of trusteeship. He recounted his experience at the Prime Ministers' Conference. No doubt thinking of the historic connection between the Stanley (Derby) family and British colonial policy, he elevated the Colonial Secretary to appropriate status.

On the question of the Pacific, I agree that matters have gone in the direction of our ideas and ideals better than they appeared to go at one time. . . . I am not sure whether I got much support at the Prime Ministers' Conference. I agree with the proposal put forward some months ago by the Americans in regard to the possibility of

---

[5] Record of Conversations annexed to Proceedings of the 4th Meeting of the Wellington Conference on 6 Nov. 1944, NZ PM 153/21/1 Pt. 1.   [6] Ibid.

international trusteeship and reports to an international body. But Lord Stanley would not agree to that at the moment.[7]

Fraser was content to see the Americans as permanent residents in the northern Pacific. On the whole, everything by late 1944 seemed to be satisfactory: 'The Marshalls and the Carolines are now being controlled by the Americans, and our right of way to the Philippines is assured, and really that is the outer rampart of the Pacific, and immediately everything else dwindled in importance.'[8]

The New Zealand Deputy Prime Minister, Walter Nash, also had much to say about the general affairs of the Pacific, especially in regard to the United States and trusteeship. In a rambling speech he made these points:

[I]n essence I think the Southern Pacific in the future means more power and voice to Australia and New Zealand than to any other power . . . we can gain a lot of support in the United States from the trusteeship idea. It is not thrown overboard, there, and they do not want to dominate in general. . . . The feeling now with regard to the South Pacific is that they [the Americans] are willing to co-operate with the peoples of the South Pacific, which in the main means Australia and New Zealand.[9]

Thus one of the significant features of both the Australian and New Zealand speeches was a much less suspicious attitude towards American imperialism than had existed at the time of the Australian–New Zealand Agreement. The visit to Washington by the two Prime Ministers had contributed to an atmosphere of better understanding, and the Australians and New Zealanders were not unaware of the controversy within the American government about the future of the Pacific islands.[10]

Expressing the cordial agreement of both parties, the following passage of the conference proceedings endorsed trusteeship. It went far beyond merely reaffirming the principle.

Powers responsible for dependent territories should accept the principle of trusteeship, already applicable in the case of mandated

⁷ Ibid.   ⁸ Ibid.   ⁹ Ibid.
¹⁰ The despatches of Walter Nash during the time he served as New Zealand's representative on the Pacific War Council provide many insights into the workings of the American government in wartime. This subject has now received full treatment by Keith Sinclair, *Walter Nash* (Oxford University Press, 1976), Ch. 18.

territories. In such dependent territories the purposes of the trust is the welfare and advancement of the native peoples. Colonial Powers should undertake to make regular reports to an international body analogous to the Permanent Mandates Commission, set up within the framework of the General Organisation. This body should be empowered to publish reports of its deliberations *and to inspect* dependent territories.[11]

As best he could, the British High Commissioner in Wellington, Sir Harry Batterbee, had followed the semi-secret proceedings of the conference that led up to the inclusion of the word *inspect*. He pleaded with Fraser and Evatt to substitute the word *visit*. Evatt stood firm.[12] The Australians and New Zealanders now were on record as holding the view consistently opposed by Churchill and almost everyone else in the imperial government—*the right of inspection* of the British Colonial Empire.

Lord Cranborne at the Dominions Office was extremely angry when he learned of the conference's proceedings. 'I think . . . that we ought to take the strongest objection to the declaration which they have made on the subject of Colonial administration.' Cranborne now had cause to relive his nightmare of a motley crew of Eastern Europeans and Latin Americans prying into the affairs of the British Empire. He told his colleagues in the War Cabinet that he wanted to rebuke the Australians and New Zealanders in emphatic language.

I might observe . . . that the two Governments describe the proposed international supervisory body as being analogous to the Permanent Mandates Commission. In fact, the Permanent Mandates Commission did not exercise such wide powers of supervision and inspection as are involved in the present proposal . . .

In general, I think the time has come when we should speak frankly to the two Governments. . . . It seems to me essential that we should make clear to them the deplorable results which are likely to ensue.[13]

In contrast, the reaction within the Colonial Office was

---

[11] The conference conclusions are printed in Kay, *The Australian–New Zealand Agreement*, pp. 229–35. Italics added.

[12] Batterbee's telegraphic reports are printed in W.P. (44) 630, CAB 66/57. Batterbee had managed to persuade Fraser to substitute 'visit' for 'inspection' in the closing speech of the conference, but Evatt had insisted on 'inspection' remaining in the printed transcript.

[13] Memorandum by Cranborne, 10 Nov. 1944, W.P. (44) 641, CAB 66/57.

mild. Kenneth Robinson warned against driving the Australians and New Zealanders into an intransigent position. 'The "Colonial question"', he wrote, 'is one in which the general background of the Dominions in many ways closely resembles that of the U.S., and it would be very unfortunate if . . . the Australia[n] and New Zealand Governments were to be driven into taking up an unyielding attitude.'[14] Robinson's lines indicate what in fact happened. When Fraser and Evatt received the Dominions Office's complaint, they were aggrieved. Cranborne's offending words, sent with the approval of the War Cabinet on the 14th of November, were: 'We have learnt with considerable surprise and concern . . . [that] the Australian and New Zealand Governments . . . declare their support for the idea of an international supervisory body with power to visit dependent territories and publish reports of its deliberations.'[15] Using indignant language, Cranborne went on to say that the imperial government had 'very strongly the view' that international supervision would 'be contrary to the interests . . . of the British Empire'. He pointed out that the Australian Prime Minister in May had shared that view. 'This matter is of vital importance to the United Kingdom', Cranborne stated, and the stand of Australia and New Zealand would cause 'serious difficulty and embarrassment' in future discussions with the United States. If the Dominions had had the courtesy to consult the imperial government, they would have learned that the Colonial Office was about to circulate an extensive set of proposals (the Poynton–Robinson project). Instead the Australians and New Zealanders had declared their views 'without any prior consultation with or warning to us'. In short, the position adopted by the two Dominions was totally unacceptable in manner, tone, and substance.

The Prime Minister of New Zealand, who had an obstinate streak in him, refused to be cowed. 'My own views on this question were made very plain at the Prime Ministers' Conference,' he telegraphed to Cranborne, 'and since they reflect the opinions of the New Zealand Government, I consider it

[14] Minute by Robinson, 15 Nov. 1944, CO 968/157/14811/10A. Stanley did not record his opinion.
[15] Dominions Office to New Zealand, 14 Nov. 1944, NZ PM 153/21/3, Pt. 1; DO 35/1898 and 1995; Kay, *Australian–New Zealand Agreement*, pp. 239–43. W. M. (44) 155th Conclusions, CAB 65/44.

my duty to state them publicly.' Fraser expressed 'surprise' that the principles which the New Zealand and Australian governments upheld as 'fundamentally sound' should cause embarrassment in London. He then pointed out that Cranborne had responded impetuously. Reading the worst into the Australian–New Zealand Conference, the Dominions Office in the rebuke had mentioned 'control by a central international body'. Fraser rejoined that 'nothing in my statement . . . is inconsistent with the exercise of full governmental authority by Colonial Powers'. Addressing himself to the question of accountability, Fraser gave a clear exposition of the colonial philosophy of New Zealand and the way to fulfil it.

[I]t would, in our opinion not only be right, but in the highest degree politically wise and expedient, for countries owning Colonies to accept the principle of accountability to the international authority for the welfare and advancement of native people. In the case of British Commonwealth territories I feel that we have much more to gain than to lose by conceding this point.

The enlightened and liberal administration by the Colonial Office should in particular ensure the fullest support of any responsible authority, and the acceptance of trusteeship and accountability would seem essential if action is to be taken through publicity to improve the lot of natives in Colonial areas outside the British Empire and Commonwealth.[16]

On the issue of visits of inspection, New Zealand would support such a proposal. The positions of New Zealand and the imperial government were poles apart. So divergent were the two positions that Fraser challenged the wisdom of Britain's colonial course:

I do most earnestly suggest that the British Commonwealth as a whole would be committing a profound error if it did not take a lead in this question of accountability in the interest of the welfare of Colonial peoples, and for this reason I think it advisable to make quite clear what the attitude of the New Zealand Government would be in this matter in any international discussions.[17]

Far from extracting an apology, Cranborne had stiffened Fraser's attitude. New Zealand now even questioned the moral earnestness of the imperial government.

[16] New Zealand to Dominions Office, 19 Nov. 1944, ibid.   [17] Ibid.

The New Zealand response left no doubt about basic disagreement, but Fraser's reaction was mild compared with
Evatt's. Evatt was 'surprised and indignant', he telegraphed to
Fraser.[18] For reasons in part connected with Evatt's intrigues
with his colleagues, he first directed his wrath towards the
Australian High Commissioner in London, S. M. Bruce, who,
in Evatt's view, had taken the side of the imperial government.
Bruce had telegraphed to the Australian Prime Minister—in
a telegram marked 'Prime Minister. *Top Secret.* Personal—himself only' (but which nevertheless reached Evatt)—that the
Australian–New Zealand Conference had 'put the cat among
the pigeons'. Bruce had commented in particular on Curtin's
remarks agreeing with the Colonial Secretary at the Prime
Ministers' Conference. Now, the High Commissioner reported,
there was a certain 'bewilderment' about Australian inconsistency. There was 'electricity in the atmosphere'. The imperial
government had not even been consulted. He hoped that the
proposal for international colonial supervision might be quietly
dropped.[19] To Evatt this amounted to no less than sabotage
of one of his main policies. In one of his drafts lambasting
Bruce, Evatt denounced the High Commissioner's 'violence of
expression and obvious lack of sympathy with and concern
for success of [an] integral part of Australia's external policy'.
To Bruce he also made his indignation quite clear about the
Dominions Office telegram. Someone in London may have
misunderstood Australian policy, Evatt stated, 'but no ap-
prehension, however genuine, can excuse the tone of the Dominions Office telegram'. He blamed the Colonial Office. In
another draft of the same cable, he stated:

It is evident that the Colonial Office is under a serious misappre-
hension of the consistent views of the Government on this matter.
. . . It is impossible for us to believe that this had Cabinet approval,
still less that of the Prime Minister. Please inform us as soon as
possible who are really responsible . . .[20]

Evatt did not press the point, but if he had he would have
learned that it was Lord Cranborne himself who had sent the
telegram with the approval of Churchill and the War Cabinet.

[18] Evatt to Fraser, 16 Nov. 1944, AA A989/44/630/5/1/11/22.
[19] Bruce to Curtin, 13 Nov. 1944, ibid.
[20] The drafts are in AA A989 44/630/5/1/11/22.

In the drafting of the reply to the Dominions Office, Evatt especially revealed his sensitivity to attacks on what he considered to be the vital issue of trusteeship. He yelped like a wounded coyote (or rather, dingo). The following passages are taken from progressive stages of the draft:

[W]e have noted the tone of your telegram with pain and surprise, and cannot think that it is calculated to lead to the fair and objective examination of this matter, which is clearly necessary in the circumstances . . .

We are at a loss to understand why you should think that supervision by an authority set up within the framework of the proposed General International Organisation would be contrary to the interests of dependent peoples and parent nations . . .

The recognized international status of the self-governing Dominions entitles us to act on our own views in external relations and any attempted veto would be disastrous to the whole concept of a Commonwealth of autonomous nations.[21]

What galled Evatt above all was the charge that Australian policy was *inconsistent*. Since he had Prime Minister Curtin's words at the Prime Ministers' Conference thrown in his teeth, he studied the transcripts. Attacking the problem with the intensity of a brilliant lawyer making the best of a bad case, he argued that the Australian Prime Minister had merely expressed his personal views and had by no means repudiated the formal state document of the Australian–New Zealand Agreement which explicitly affirmed the trusteeship principle. As if warming up to his case, Evatt then launched a legalistic attack on Cranborne's use of the phrase international 'control' of colonies. 'Such a term misrepresents our view, in the expression of which we have been careful to use the term "supervision", as indicating a very limited and special function, interfering in no substantial way with the sovereignty and control by the parent States.' Evatt toned down the final draft sent to the Dominions Office, but it was impenitent.

Cranborne now had to decide whether to prolong the controversy or to placate the two Dominions. He decided definitely in favour of the latter course. 'The two Governments argue in defence of their action', Cranborne wrote to his

---

[21] Ibid. Australia to Dominions Office, 19 Nov. 1944, DO 35/1898 and 1995; W.P. (44) 677, CAB 66/58.

colleagues in the War Cabinet. 'Their replies raise a number
of debating points which it seems unnecessary to pursue.'
Australia and New Zealand seemed to ignore the basic objection by the imperial government of publishing a policy
statement without prior consultation (which from the antipodean vantage point appeared to be a strange argument
since the imperial government had not consulted them about
the Cairo Declaration); but at least, in Cranborne's words,
'they explain that they had not meant to support the setting
up of an international body in relation to colonial territories
which would interfere with sovereignty and control by the
parent States'.[22] Cranborne therefore despatched a conciliatory
telegram to the two Dominions:

> We feel that there has been some misunderstanding. . . . It was
> never in our mind to question the right of the Australian and New
> Zealand Governments to make any declaration which they think
> proper on Colonial as on other aspects of public policy. But we were
> seriously perturbed as to the practical results which were likely to
> flow from the procedure that has been adopted . . .
> In particular we are glad to note that you had not contemplated
> an international body which would interfere with the sovereignty
> and control by the parent states in relation to colonial territories. . .[23]

With characteristic candour, Cranborne explicitly said that
he regretted the misunderstanding. At least the positions were
now entirely clear. Australia and New Zealand favoured international supervision as a means of promoting colonial accountability, though without any interference with existing national
sovereignties.

Despite the atmosphere of controversy which clouded the
relations between the two Dominions and the imperial government, the Australian–New Zealand Conference did make
limited progress towards the establishing of the South Seas
Regional Commission. Australia and New Zealand reached
further agreement on the basis of cooperation in health and
medical services and education; for the improvement of
labour conditions; in research in the fields of economics and

---

[22] Memorandum by Cranborne, 22 Nov. 1944, W.P. (44) 677, CAB 66/58; DO
35/1995.
[23] Dominions Office to Australia and New Zealand, 24 Nov. 1944, NZ PM
153/21/3 Pt. 1; AA A989 44/630/5/1/11/22.

social anthropology; and in communications. The commission would be advisory and consultative, with no executive authority. Its functions did not extend as far as some officials in New Zealand and Australia would have liked. F. H. Corner wrote in late November: 'We have stripped the commission of any political functions or relation to any scheme of international supervision or control that might or might not be set up. It is a purely cooperative welfare body.'[24] While the Australians and New Zealanders laid these bases of the future post-war Pacific, the imperial government refused to move ahead at this time. For a variety of complicated reasons, including the part British colonies in the Pacific would play in the commission and the relation of the Pacific regional commission to those in other parts of the world, the Colonial Office declined to enter into advanced planning at this stage. Above all, it was the question of accountability that, in the Colonial Office's view, needed to be resolved before further progress could be made with the regional commissions. If international supervision were established as part of the future world organization, then other countries might press for its extension into the regional commissions. Stanley and Cranborne explained in a joint memorandum to the War Cabinet:

[T]he suggestions for the establishment of a South Seas Regional Commission are satisfactory . . . but we think it desirable to avoid committing His Majesty's Government in the United Kingdom definitely to participating in such a scheme until the wider question of international supervision and inspection has been satisfactorily settled.[25]

Despite the refusal of the imperial government to proceed at this time, the Australian–New Zealand Conference of November 1944 stands as a landmark in the creation of the South Seas Commission in 1947.[26]

For the immediate wartime controversies about trusteeship and the future of the colonial empires, the significance of the conference is that it polarized the position of the two Dominions,

---

[24] Minute by Corner, 27 Nov. 1944, NZ PM 151/2/1.
[25] Memorandum by Cranborne and Stanley, 23 Nov. 1944, W.P. (44) 681, CAB 65/67. See the extensive minutes in CO 968/158/14814/1B.
[26] See T. R. Smith, *South Pacific Commission: an Analysis after Twenty-Five Years* (New Zealand Institute of International Affairs, 1972).

on the one hand, and that of the imperial government on the other. Evatt and Fraser made it clear that Australia and New Zealand would eventually take sides with the State Department if proposals for international supervision were introduced at an international conference. Cranborne revealed that the imperial government would continue to resist international accountability at almost any cost. The controversy surrounding the conference is especially illuminating in regard to Cranborne's attitude. One of his friends, Lord Croft, wrote him a letter deploring the conference. It fairly represents true-blue Tory thought on the subject of trusteeship as of late 1944. Croft described himself as 'more Australian minded than even the Australians', and as one whose political life had been devoted to promoting Imperial unity. He wrote to Cranborne, congratulating him that he had resisted the antipodean proposal for international supervision.

Trusteeship has always hitherto meant that the British Parliament acts as Trustees for the inhabitants in the Crown Colonies which are in its trust rather than seek material gain for the Sovereign power and its own nations.

It has never involved accountability to international busybodies, who had no part, lot, share, or responsibility in purely British territory.

That the Dutch, French, Belgians, and possibly the Portuguese might be able to share experience and assist each other and ourselves in combatting tropical diseases or fighting pests etc., is eminently sound, but that any country without Colonial experience should butt in much less 'supervise' would seem to invite the conditions of Bedlam.[27]

Cranborne entirely agreed with those sentiments. And he not only objected to international accountability but also specifically to the way in which the colonials had pursued an independent course. 'Australia and New Zealand were present at the Prime Ministers' talks in May last,' Cranborne wrote

[27] Croft to Cranborne, with copy and covering letter to Stanley, 28 Nov. 1944 CO 968/157/14811/10A. For a further example of Croft's views, see his essay, 'Thi is Germany Lying!', in W. A. Wells, ed., *How the Colonies Joined the Empire* (pamphlet, London, 1941). 'It can confidently be stated that no single territory of the Empire fell to us as a result of pre-meditated aggression. . . . The British Colonial Empire differs from all others in history, past or present, in that almost in its entirety it fell into our sphere of influence without conquest and without design, and frequently against the desire on the part of our Government.'

to Croft, 'and their Governments should have known perfectly well that we, in the United Kingdom, were opposed to continuation of the Mandate system. It was, therefore, I feel particularly unjustifiable on their part to make a public declaration in favour of a continuation of Mandates without prior consultation with us.'[28] Since Cranborne only a half-year later became the British spokesman on the colonial issue at the San Francisco Conference, it is especially significant that he regarded *imperial unity* as one of the essential issues at stake. In November 1944 Evatt therefore had made a perceptive remark about Cranborne's telegram protesting against the Australian–New Zealand Conference when he noted that it sounded like 'a voice from the distant past'.[29]

[28] Cranborne to Croft, 1 Dec. 1944, CO 968/157/14811/10A.
[29] This was a phrase in one of Evatt's draft replies to the Dominions Office in AA A989 44/630/5/1/11/22.

WASHINGTON IN THE WINTER OF 1944–1945. THE ADVENT OF SIR FREDERICK EGGLESTON AS AUSTRALIAN MINISTER. ARTHUR CREECH JONES AND THE INSTITUTE OF PACIFIC RELATIONS CONFERENCE AT HOT SPRINGS

THE latter part of 1944 was marked by polarization on the colonial question both within the British Empire–Commonwealth and within the government of the United States. The intervention of the Joint Chiefs, by blocking discussion of the trusteeship issue at Dumbarton Oaks, had paralyzed the decision-making process in the State Department, but had not brought about a change of policy. The Australian–New Zealand Conference fully revealed the opposite approaches of the two antipodean dominions and the imperial government. Thus there were not merely two, but four, major collision courses. If the military emerged victorious in the confrontation with the State Department, then this outcome might influence the Colonial Office's showdown with the Australians and New Zealanders, and vice versa. If the State Department won out, then the hand of the two Dominions might be strengthened. The same could be said from the vantage-point of the struggles within the Empire–Commonwealth. As if this were not complicated enough, it was becoming quite clear that the Allies with colonial possessions, especially the French and the Dutch, would also demand a voice in the eventual colonial settlement, and that Far Eastern affairs would have to be sorted out with the Chinese—with one of the key figures, Roosevelt, believing that the colonial question involved no less than the future of the white and yellow races. It is therefore fortunate for the historian that at this crucial time a participant arrived in Washington who possessed a keen interest in the trusteeship issue and systematically recorded the events and his impressions in detail in his diary and despatches. It was Sir Frederick Eggleston, the first Australian Minister in China, who in November 1944 assumed his Ministerial responsibilities in the United States.

Eggleston had served on the Australian staff at the Paris Peace Conference. One of his favourite anecdotes was about Clemenceau's placing the colonial question high on the agenda, knowing that the British Dominions would lead the race in picking up the pieces of the German overseas Empire and would thus indirectly help France in Europe. 'When I was in Paris,' Eggleston would relate, 'the Mandate System was forced on us by the British Government.'[1] Now the opposite was occurring, with the Australians attempting to impose trusteeship on the British. Eggleston had a rich background from which to relish these historical ironies. He had legal as well as historical training and was a recognized authority on international relations—facts which explain his appointment as Minister in Chungking in 1941. He had written essays on social philosophy, was the author of *State Socialism in Victoria*,[2] and had edited a symposium on *The Australian Mandate for New Guinea*.[3] Shortly before the war he had served as chairman of a governmental committee considering the amalgamation of Papua and New Guinea. He had also served as chairman of the Australian delegations to the Institute of Pacific Relations conferences in 1927, 1929, and 1936. There was probably no other Australian with a greater knowledge of the mandates system (with the exception of Evatt, who had an unrivalled grasp of the *principles* involved). Physically Eggleston was a large, heavy-set man who suffered from arthritis and had great difficulty in moving about. His physical incapacity is important because it limited his political effectiveness.[4] His part was important as much for his observation and reflection as for his influence. He was referred to as a 'Buddha', which aptly describes his ponderous, philosophical approach to the question of trusteeship. He was definitely committed.

---

[1] This particular version is Eggleston's story as related later to Lord Cranborne at the San Francisco Conference. He recorded Cranborne's reaction: 'He didn't like this very much.' Diary, 21 May 1945, Eggleston Papers 423/10/1287.

[2] London, 1932.   [3] Melbourne, 1928.

[4] See *Australian Diplomat: Memoirs of Sir Alan Watt* (Sydney, 1972), pp. 59–60.

Summarizing his interpretation of the significance of the Australian–New Zealand Conference, he wrote to Evatt: 'It must not be forgotten that the Wellington resolution proposes a universalisation of the Mandate System—its application to all Colonial dependencies. I have for years advocated this . . .'[5]

On the 14th of November, Eggleston presented his credentials to the President. Roosevelt let him know straight away that he did not like that 'stormy petrel, Dr. Evatt'. 'With a snap of the jaw', the President said that he knew Evatt was responsible for the Australian–New Zealand Agreement and was the source of discord in Australian–American relations. Then they talked about the colonial issue. Roosevelt remarked that the British 'were attempting to get some sort of hold over the Netherlands East Indies'. He would support the Dutch, he said, in part because he believed that they were sincere in saying they would bring democracy to South-East Asia.[6] He wished the British would do the same for Malaya and Burma. But he had little hope. His suspicions of British imperialism had not been allayed. Turning to China, for example:

He [Roosevelt] said that he had numerous discussions with Winston about China and that he felt that Winston was 40 years behind the times on China and he continually referred to the Chinese as 'Chinks' and 'Chinamen' and he felt that this was very dangerous. He (Roosevelt) wanted to keep China as a friend because in 40 or 50 years' time China might easily become a very powerful military nation.[7]

Only a few days later Roosevelt spoke in similar vein to Stanley Hornbeck, who was now assuming duties as Ambassador to the Netherlands. Now the President embellished his suspicions about British imperialism by saying that the Australians shared them.

The President said that the Australians are apprehensive about an indicated intention of the British to gobble up business in Sumatra,

---

[5] Eggleston to Evatt, 19 Dec. 1944, Eggleston Papers 423/10/640.
[6] For F. D. R.'s attitude towards the Dutch, see below, p. 437. The day after Eggleston's interview, on the 15th of November, Roosevelt made a major intervention in the colonial issue by directing the State Department to proceed with trusteeship planning. This is discussed below in ch. 28 as part of the prelude to the Yalta Conference.
[7] Eggleston Diary, 14 Nov. 1944, Eggleston Papers 423/10/1378.

Java and Borneo. He mentioned the effort of the Dutch to improve their political system as regards the position in the kingdom of the colonial areas. He mentioned his own concern regarding Indochina. He said that he did not intend to lay down a policy regarding Indochina, but that he felt strongly that there must be made provision looking toward preparing the people of that area for independence . . .

He said that we must be on guard against the possibility of the formation of a combination among the orientals in antagonism or opposition to us (meaning I [Hornbeck] inferred, the Occident).[8]

The record of this conversation is important as an indication of Roosevelt's thought on the colonial issue at this time, especially since it shows that he was still keen on preparing Indo-China for eventual independence. But on one point the account should be corrected. Neither Eggleston nor any other Australian at this time, at least according to the available records, had told Roosevelt that Australia shared suspicions of British imperialism in the Dutch Indies. As in the case of telling Churchill earlier that Chiang Kai-shek supported trusteeship, Roosevelt played fast and loose with the truth. His general views, however, were quite consistent. As Eggleston observed, the President was strongly critical of the British and 'wanted them to give up Malaya and Burma unconditionally as he was giving up the Philippines'.[9]

Eggleston arrived in Washington at a time of transition in American foreign affairs. Cordell Hull's resignation as Secretary of State and the appointment of his successor, Edward R. Stettinius, Jr., raised the question, especially in the minds of foreign observers, whether the State Department would now acquire a more decisive voice in foreign policy, or whether the President and his advisers would continue to predominate. Eggleston is a particularly valuable source on this subject because in this transitional period he obtained interviews with both White House officials and with those at the State Department and interrogated them specifically on the colonial question. He first sought out Harry Hopkins, who earlier in the year had taken an especial interest in the Pacific islands by having Wayne Coy prepare a highly sensitive memorandum

---

[8] Memorandum by Hornbeck, 20 Nov. 1944, Hornbeck Papers Box 367.
[9] Eggleston to Evatt, 11 Dec. 1944, Evatt Papers; AA A1066 P45/153/3.

on the subject.[10] The Australian Minister's letters and diary reveal Hopkins's thoughts in late 1944. Eggleston wrote on the 5th of December:

> I saw Mr. Harry Hopkins this morning. . . . He referred to the Japanese Islands and I said that we would be only too glad for the Americans to take them over. He said, well Roosevelt won't do that. He said Churchill is always suggesting to him that he take them over, knowing that if he did so we would be committed to annexation and the President would not be caught by this. . . .
>
> He said the President had a curious idea of sovereignty. He said he believed in sovereignty with these dependents being in the United Nations and repudiating it to someone to manage it for them. I said that was rather in accord with our own ideas. . . .[11]

In emphasizing these familiar views, Hopkins gave Eggleston the notion that the President and his advisers were still the pre-eminent voice in the colonial issue.

From the new Secretary of State, Eggleston got the impression of a mouthpiece, and not an especially accurate one. Eggleston detected a confusion of thought about trusteeship. When Stettinius asked him whether he thought each trust territory should be adminstered by a single power, Eggleston replied, 'one power shall be responsible as mandatory'.

> He [Stettinius] said, 'well, there is where you will come into conflict with the President.' He said he was speaking quite confidentially but the President's view was that the Sovereignty was to be in the United Nations as trustee and that it should govern through an international organisation. He was not very clear here and he said that three or four nations might be associated in the joint government.[12]

Stettinius, in other words, had not yet grasped that Roosevelt espoused indeterminate sovereignty but administration by a single power under the auspices of the United Nations. The Secretary of State was quite firm, however, in saying that this was a matter in which the President took such a personal interest that the State Department would merely carry out his policy. '[T]he Secretary of State had no set opinion of his

---

10 See above, ch. 22.
11 Eggleston Diary, 5 Dec. 1944; Eggleston to Evatt, 5 Dec. 1944, Evatt Papers.
12 Eggleston to Evatt, 11 Dec. 1944, Evatt Papers; AA A1066 P45/153/3.

own; this was a matter on which the President had views and he would only act as his mouthpiece.'[13]

One other of Eggleston's interviews at this time merits special attention because it illuminates some of the tone and substance of the discussion at the Institute of Pacific Relations meeting at Hot Springs, Virginia, in January 1944, as well as the thinking of a high official in the State Department. In the restructuring of the Department, Joseph C. Grew had become Under Secretary of State. To him the Australian Minister developed forcefully the consequence of the American policy of self-determination, especially in the basin of the Pacific. As Grew perceived the argument, it could be summed up as '*the Balkanization of the Pacific*'.[14] At the meeting of the Institute of Pacific Relations, which was again attended by government officials in an unofficial capacity, some of the American delegates had reaffirmed the view that independence should be the proper end of self-government. This reopening of the basic colonial question of the whole wartime era caused foreign observers to wonder whether the dogmatic insistence on independence now characterized the new regime at the State Department. For this reason Eggleston's conversation with Grew is of particular interest. Eggleston said that at the conference several American delegates 'had expressed themselves very emphatically in favour of immediate independence for Colonies'. According to Eggleston's diary:

I said one of them had said, 'You mustn't sand-bag independence by self-government.' He [Grew] laughed and said, 'Are my boys talking like that? We are not in favour of immediate independence, but we like the pattern that was adopted in the Philippines, of giving independence as soon as possible and fixing a date.'[15]

Here Eggleston emphasized his key point:

I said that in my opinion that to terminate the Western Empires in the Pacific where they were part of the strategic structure would be a great mistake; it would Balkanise the Pacific and I said the mere possession of bases in the area would not be sufficient.[16]

[13] Ibid.
[14] Memorandum by Grew of a conversation with Eggleston, 15 Jan. 1945, Grew Papers (Harvard University). Italics added.
[15] Eggleston Diary, 15 Jan. 1945. [16] Ibid.

Eggleston feared that American enthusiasm for independence would destroy the political structure of the Pacific basin, and with it any chance of post-war security.

Of the Americans who attended the Institute of Pacific Relations Conference, those who were most vocal on the subject of independence were members of the State Department's Committee on Dependent Areat, the realm of Benjamin Gerig. The views of this group of international relations experts and scholars are especially illuminating on the difference between this conference and the previous one held at Mont Tremblant in 1942. At both conferences the future of the Colonial Empires had been vigorously debated, but with an important difference. The discussions of 1942 were, on the whole, characterized by friendly exchanges by men sympathetically listening to other points of view. The members of the Dependent Areas Committee now noted a distinct change: '[T]he recent IPR Conference had been characterized by considerable acrimony, especially in the discussions of dependencies. This contrasted with the attitude at Mont Tremblant in 1942 where there had been keen discussion but no bitterness.'[17]

They noted that the positions had polarized: '[O]n general colonial questions the British, French, and Dutch delegations had been like peas in a pod. The anti-imperialistic forces had been the delegations of Canada, the United States, Australia, and New Zealand in about that order.'[18]

The American group had been especially sceptical about the announcement of a Dutch delegate that the Netherlands intended to make a 'Commonwealth' out of the mother country and the colonies, and therefore colonial discussions had no relevance to the Dutch. The Americans, in comparison, were regarded with equal scepticism by the other delegates. One of the Englishmen, Arthur Creech Jones, showed great curiosity, for example, about the Committee on Dependent Areas. Did it deal with American dependent territories as well? Specifically Creech Jones asked, did it deal

---

[17] CDA Minutes 93, 30 Jan. 1945, USSD NF Box 183. For the conference see *Security in the Pacific: A Preliminary Report of the Ninth Conference of the Institute of Pacific Relations, Hot Springs, Virginia, January 6–17, 1945* (New York, 1945).
[18] CDA Minutes 93.

with the 'fifteen million dependent peoples in the United States proper', in other words, the American Negro? *Touché!* The question was all the more pointed because Creech Jones directed it to the American Negro member of the Committee on Dependent Areas who later became so prominent in United Nations affairs, Ralph Bunche.[19] This was only one point among many on which the Labour spokesman on the colonial issue antagonized the Americans with whom he came into contact in early 1945.

Creech Jones's advent to the post-war Colonial Office has been aptly described as 'rather like making a theoretical prison reformer a prison governor'.[20] He possessed an unrivalled specialist knowledge of colonial affairs and a dedication to the principle of eventual independence for the colonies. Therefore one might have supposed that he shared common ground with American critics of British Imperialism. Such was not the case. Creech Jones was also a British patriot who resented American interference in the affairs of the British Empire. He opposed international arrangements because he believed that nationalist groups could make more rapid progress towards self-government under British rule. He was unenthusiastic about regional commissions. According to the minutes of the Dependent Areas Committee in January 1945, which record Creech Jones's views at the Institute of Pacific Relations Conference, he deprecated cooperation with the Americans in the Caribbean Commission because of 'racial attitudes prevalent in the United States'. He declared that a regional commission in West Africa would be 'impossible' because 'Nigerian and Gold Coast nationalists would not tolerate international interference'. His attitude towards the mandates system was also negative. The British already accepted the principle of 'accountability', and in any case the post-war colonial systems would not be based on 'the principles of imperialism'.[21] Since he had such definite opinions, and because he was Oliver Stanley's opposite number in the Labour Party, Creech Jones was invited to meet with the Dependent Areas Committee at the State Department.

[19] Memorandum by Bunche, 7 Jan. 1945, Taussig Papers Box 48.
[20] Quoted in Goldsworthy, *Colonial Issues in British Politics*, p. 50, which contains a good discussion of Creech Jones, pp. 16–23.
[21] CDA Minutes 90, 9 Jan. 1945.

The Dependent Areas Committee greeted Creech Jones on the 23rd of January as a statesman of 'great popularity with the natives'. In his introductory remarks he noted that he had always tried to stimulate public interest in colonial questions in the hope that the Colonial Office would pursue 'a more vigorous policy'. He had been, he said, 'a thorn in the side of the British Government'. He assured the committee members that his approach to the problems of dependent territories would not be the same as Oliver Stanley's. 'His approach would rather be that of a Socialist.' His following remarks, however, indicated to the committee that there was much less of a difference between Labour and Tory colonial policies than was commonly believed. Creech Jones even congratulated Stanley on doing 'a reasonably good job'. Both political parties in England, he said, were now 'walking together' on the colonial issue. Both recognized the need for more systematic economic development. He outlined points of progress in education. He talked about problems of development in water resources, soil erosion, and public health. He noted that there had been some agitation about 'economic imperialism', and he assured the committee that attention was being given to this question. Rather than attacking the Colonial Office for misguided economic policies, as he had frequently done in Parliament, he now stressed the positive aspects of British colonial policy, which seemed very positive indeed if compared with retrograde French imperialism:

It had been British policy to insure that each territory must stand on its own. This, it was declared, was directly opposite to the French conception of colonial policy. In order that the colonies might develop toward self-government, the British Government, Mr. Creech-Jones declared, had attempted not to tie in the colonial economy with the English economy. . . . British policy had been designed to 'prime the pump' in the direction of self-government and a more developed economy.[22]

Despite the emphasis on economic and social development, British policy had not neglected constitutional progress. He cited advances towards self-government in Ceylon, Burma,

[22] CDA Minutes 92, 23 Jan. 1945.

Malta, and West Africa. Turning at last to the question of mandates, he disappointed his audience:

[B]ritish policy with respect to the mandates had not been universally good. In the Cameroons, for example, little money had been spent and very little had been done in the way of public works because British capital and government could not be certain the Cameroons would not be returned to Germany with a consequent loss of British holdings.[23]

Without indicating any enthusiasm at all for international accountability, Creech Jones at least assured his listeners that he would like to see the mandates system modified rather than abolished, though he was not too clear about the modifications. In his view Stanley had confused thoughts on the subject. This was the impression that Creech Jones also left with the State Department's committee. 'Mr. Creech-Jones' views on accountability boil down to establishing an agency to receive reports, leaving everything else to public opinion.'[24]

In the aftermath of the Institute of Pacific Relations Conference, Creech Jones's talk helped to crystallize in the minds of the American colonial specialists the general situation as of early 1945. The colonial powers were combining into a united front against the anti-colonial powers. At the colonial settlement, France, the Netherlands, and Belgium could be expected to line up with the British. Canada, Australia, and New Zealand would take the same side as the Americans. Within England, Creech Jones would support Stanley. In particular Creech Jones's visit to Washington brought home to the State Department's specialists the amount of resentment building up in the ranks of the imperial powers against American intervention in the colonial world. Creech Jones had specifically asked Ralph Bunche why the Americans did not tend to their own 'dependent peoples'. The Dependent Areas Committee pondered this question with indignation. The charge was, as the members of the Committee formulated it on the basis of the discussions at Hot Springs, that the United States 'had no moral right to criticize the workings of empire' until 'Negroes were treated equally with all others in the United States'. The

[23] Ibid.
[24] CDA Minutes 93, 30 Jan. 1945.

Dependent Areas Committee rejected this moral indictment as totally misguided:

[T]he Negro problem was a domestic minority question and not a colonial issue. What the American Negroes wanted was equal rights as American citizens. They did not wish separation from the United States as most of the colonial nationalists wished separation from their metropoles. Moreover, the American Negroes did not want to be identified with colonial peoples, for they considered themselves to be entirely different from and much above the status of those peoples.[25]

Perhaps ultimately it was a case of the British pot calling the American kettle black, and vice versa. But one thing is conspicuous on the American side, quite apart from the self-righteous tone and the presumption of speaking for the Negro population. It is the absence of any observation that, for example, British colonial subjects, in the British view at least (again leaving aside the presumption), might have wished for eventual self-government within the British Empire as much as Negroes in America hoped for equal status. It was the same pattern of thought that led to talk of American 'trusteeship' while calling British ventures of the same sort 'imperialism'. It probably would have given British critics such as Creech Jones a sense of satisfaction to know that the indictment about the American Negro at least hit a very raw nerve.

[25] CDA Minutes 93, 30 Jan. 1945.

28

PRELUDE TO YALTA
THE COLONIAL SECRETARY'S VISIT
TO WASHINGTON IN JANUARY 1945

LITTLE over a month before the conference at Yalta, Churchill wrote the following minute on the trusteeship issue. If any one document can be singled out as evidence of the explosive nature of the colonial question, this is probably the one:

How does this matter stand? There must be no question of our being hustled or seduced into declarations affecting British sovereignty in any of the Dominions or Colonies. Pray remember my declaration against liquidating the British Empire. If the Americans want to take Japanese islands which they have conquered, let them do so with our blessing and any form of words that may be agreeable to them. But 'Hands off the British Empire' is our maxim and it must not be weakened or smirched to please sob-stuff merchants at home or foreigners of any hue.[1]

Churchill wrote these lines in response to a telegram from the Embassy in Washington. Leo Pasvolsky was pressing the British to come forward with proposals for a colonial settlement, which, from the State Department's point of view, would at least serve to get the trusteeship issue on the agenda of problems to be resolved. The question of enemy colonial territory could not be postponed indefinitely, but the Joint Chiefs had blocked the State Department's progress. For this reason, Pasvolsky said to Halifax, the ball was in the British court.[2]

Although Churchill had chaired the War Cabinet meeting that had given perfunctory approval to the Colonial Office memorandum on 'International Aspects of Colonial Policy' (the Poynton–Robinson project), he certainly had not read it, nor had he followed the reasons why both the Colonial Office

---

[1] Minute by Churchill, 31 Dec. 1944, PREM 4/31/4; CO 968/161/14814/11 Pt. 1; FO 371/50807; DO 35/1900.
[2] Halifax to Eden, No. 6901, 30 Dec. 1944, FO 371/50807.

and Foreign Office felt it necessary to take the initiative at this time.[3] With the Americans now raising the question, Churchill demanded to know why the Foreign Office appeared to be acquiescing in the liquidation of parts of the British Empire. Pasvolsky, hoping to take advantage of a trip by Oliver Stanley to the West Indies, had proposed that the Colonial Secretary on his return might stop in Washington to talk about matters that the Prime Minister regarded as not open to discussion. The Foreign Office was the intermediary. Eden now had to explain himself to Churchill.

The Foreign Secretary reassured the Prime Minister that the British Empire would not be frittered away. He recapitulated for Churchill's benefit the gist of the Poynton–Robinson project—'a constructive policy of international co-operation in colonial development which fully safeguards the sovereignty and administrative authority of the responsible metropolitan Powers concerned'. This was War Cabinet policy, which Churchill himself had approved. According to Eden:

There is not the slightest question of liquidating the British Empire. On the contrary, we are anxious to persuade the Americans not to go in for half-baked international régimes in any ex-enemy colonies they may take over, nor to advocate them for others, but to accept colonial responsibilities on the same terms as ourselves.[4]

The purpose of Stanley's talks with Pasvolsky, Eden further explained, would be 'to retain the initiative and possibly forestall some embarrassing American move'.[5]

Despite Eden's comforting message, Churchill nevertheless sensed that the British Empire was 'being jockeyed out or edged nearer the abyss'.[6] He now gave the matter careful consideration. On the 18th of January he wrote to Eden that he understood the purpose of discussion with the Americans would be exclusively aimed at these two objectives (in Churchill's own words):

(1) to secure international agreement to the termination of the Mandate System and avoid its extension to enemy territories conquered in the present war, and

---

[3] But see the brief prepared for Churchill in PREM 4/31/4; for a description of the War Cabinet meeting, *Diaries of Sir Alexander Cadogan*, pp. 688–9.
[4] Eden to Churchill, 8 Jan. 1945, PREM 4/31/4; FO 371/50807; CO 968/161/14814/11 Pt. 1; DO 35/1900.   [5] Ibid.
[6] Minute by Churchill, 10 Jan. 1945, PREM 4/31/4.

(2) to allow foreign powers a means of expressing their reasonable and legitimate interest in Colonial territories *without* affecting our sovereignty and executive authority, or entitling them to meddle in constitutional questions, or establishing international bodies possessing powers of interference divorced from responsibility.

If you are satisfied that this is so and that these proposals involve no danger to our Colonial Empire, I have no objection . . .[7]

Churchill's view could hardly have been made more explicit. By the time he wrote those lines, the Colonial Secretary was already in Washington on his way back from Jamaica. But he needed no instructions. His views were only slightly less rigid than Churchill's, and he had every intention of keeping the British Empire as free from international interference as possible. It is a measure of Stanley's urbanity that the Americans regarded him as far less reactionary than Churchill. In fact Churchill could not have picked a more able official to hold the line. No one was less willing than Oliver Stanley to give up a single inch of the British Empire.

The Colonial Secretary's official duties in the West Indies consisted of the inauguration of a new constitution in Jamaica and the tending of affairs of the Anglo-American Caribbean Commission. Because of the latter business it naturally fell to Charles Taussig, as the American Joint Chairman, to make the arrangements for Stanley's visit to Washington. Taussig continued to hold a unique position in the colonial affairs of the two countries. As the Commission's Joint Chairman, he was part of the State Department's bureaucracy. He served on numerous committees, including the one on Dependent Areas. Despite his seniority and political connections with the President, he worked on a collegial basis with Pasvolsky and Gerig. The Commission was his specific business, but during the war he had become, increasingly, the highest official in State Department–White House circles to take a consistent interest in the general colonial question, especially as it affected Anglo-American relations. At periodic intervals he arranged to see Roosevelt on the subject. In early November 1944 he had told the President 'that the colonial matter was beginning to crystallize'.[8] Now in January

---

[7] Churchill to Eden, 18 Jan. 1945, PREM 4/31/4; FO 371/50807; CO 968/161/ 14814/11 Pt. 1; DO 35/1900.

[8] Memorandum by Taussig, 10 Nov. 1944, Taussig Papers Box 47.

of the next year it appeared to be coming to a head. The Colonial Secretary would meet with the President. In this encounter Taussig would play a key part both as Roosevelt's right-hand man on colonial issues, and, apparently, as one of the few Americans Stanley respected socially and intellectually.

The visit got off to an awkward start. When Stanley arrived in Washington on the 15th of January, Taussig and his welcoming party went to the wrong airport. To make amends, Abe Fortas (at this time Under Secretary in the Department of the Interior) suggested that they should present the Colonial Secretary with a bottle of whiskey. Whiskey being short in wartime, Taussig jokingly suggested that they give him the island of St. Croix instead.[9] The next day Taussig called at the British Embassy at 11.45 a.m. and escorted Stanley on a courtesy visit to Secretary of the Interior, Harold Ickes. They then proceeded to the White House for luncheon with the President. The State Department had made careful preparation for the visit and had sent Roosevelt a seven-page background paper for him to peruse so that the main points at issue—especially trusteeship—would be fresh in mind. Unfortunately the memorandum was misplaced in a clutter of papers on the secretary's desk. When it was finally found the luncheon was twenty minutes behind schedule. With Stanley waiting in another part of the White House, Roosevelt asked Taussig for a one-and-a-half minute résumé of the briefing paper. Taussig suggested that the affairs of the West Indies were less urgent than the question of mandates and trusteeship. On the way to meet the Colonial Secretary, Taussig told Roosevelt that Stanley was the son of the Earl of Derby. 'This struck a responsive cord [sic] with the President.' On greeting Stanley in the private dining room, Roosevelt opened the conversation by saying that years ago as Assistant Secretary of the Navy he had been in Paris when the Earl of Derby was Ambassador. It did not make a happy beginning. Stanley said his father was eighty years old and in poor health.[10]

Roosevelt's conversations were usually entertaining, and the

[9] Memoranda by Taussig, 16 Jan. 1945, Taussig Papers Box 49. Taussig wrote two memoranda recording Stanley's interview with Roosevelt, one for limited distribution within the State Department, and the other for his own record, which will be referred to as (1) and (2). The St. Croix anecdote is in (2).

[10] Ibid. (2).

record of this one is no exception. It is important to separate the points of particular significance, on the one hand, and, on the other, Presidential poppycock, as Stanley might have put it. There are three items which are especially illuminating as to Roosevelt's frame of mind on the colonial question in the month before Yalta. The first is Indo-China. Roosevelt told Stanley that there would be 'trouble' at the meeting with Churchill and Stalin. 'French Indo-China must not be turned back to the French. It should be administered by a group of nations selected from the United Nations.' To this the President added a remark that must have struck Stanley as presumptuous in the extreme: 'As to Burma, that is a somewhat different situation. I don't know yet just how we will handle that situation.'[11] The second point concerns the Pacific islands. 'The United States doesn't want any of the islands that it does not already have', Roosevelt said. But he added casually, 'except a few of the northern mandated islands over which we will act as "guardian"'.[12] The President only touched on this point in passing, but it was highly significant for Stanley, because he believed that almost everything else the President said was a smoke-screen designed to cover this particular aim. The other point is important in a more general way. Roosevelt recounted his conversation with Queen Wilhelmina. He told Stanley that the Dutch expected to attain commonwealth status for Java and Sumatra in the near future, and also for Borneo— 'when the headhunters were educated—an estimate of about 100 years'. Roosevelt also inquired about Dutch New Guinea, which he himself described as having 'the lowest form of civilization in the world'. He told Stanley that he had asked the Queen for a *timetable*.[13] He now re-emphasized his request for the benefit of the British Colonial Secretary. No other specific point so well illuminates the real difference between Roosevelt's approach to the colonial question and that of the British and Europeans.

The Colonial Secretary more than held his own in conversation with the President. Fortunately Taussig recorded the exchanges in detail. In discussing Hong Kong, Roosevelt said he thought Churchill had made a mistake in making the speech conveying the message that 'what we have we hold'.[14] He told

[11] Ibid. (1).   [12] Ibid. (1).   [13] Ibid. (1).   [14] Ibid. (2).

Stanley about Chiang Kai-shek's offer to make Hong Kong a free port. Among other points, the British would not be deprived of property rights as of the period prior to the Japanese invasion. Chiang had given him a personal guarantee that he would keep Hong Kong open 'to the entire world on equal terms'. Here is Taussig's account of how Roosevelt, on this occasion, met his match:

The President interpolated his talk on Hong Kong with the following, 'I do not want to be unkind or rude to the British but in 1841, when you acquired Hong Kong, you did not acquire it by purchase.' Stanley's instant rejoinder was, 'Let me see, Mr. President, that was about the time of the Mexican War.'

The President said that Chiang had confirmed in a letter his willingness to make a free port of Hong Kong. Stanley's only comment on the Hong Kong narrative was, 'It will be a long three days [of official visit], Mr. President.'[15]

Checked in this direction, Roosevelt trotted out again the case of the Gambia. He told Stanley that he had been shocked at the conditions he had found there. Had Winston mentioned this, perhaps in a Cabinet meeting?

Stanley's reply was that plans for considering improvement of conditions in Gambia had already been under discussion by the Cabinet before your talk with Winston. However, your talk served a useful purpose for which I owe you my thanks as it was as a result of this that I was able to carry on.[16]

Next the President plunged into another of his favourite anecdotes, this one about Churchill and the Sultan of Morocco at the time of the Casablanca Conference. Roosevelt recounted the advice he had given to the Sultan, to keep the oil money and build irrigation projects.

The President said that the Sultan seemed amazed at the advice that the President gave him, and said do you really mean that, Mr.

[15] Ibid. In the other memorandum (1) Taussig recorded that Roosevelt repeated his protest at Churchill's attitude to the Chinese: 'The President said, "Winston calls the Chinese 'pig-Tails' and 'Chinamen'. The Chinese don't like that. The Chinese are vigorous, able people. They may acquire Western organization and methods as quickly as did the Japanese".'

[16] Ibid. (2). Afterwards, however, Stanley told Taussig that he had 'exaggerated a little to the President as to the effect of his talk with Churchill although the President's talk had proven of some assistance'.

President; do you really mean to give me such unselfish advice? The President said he looked at Winston who had gone very red in the face, and replied that he very definitely and seriously meant to give him that unselfish advice. He said the Sultan then turned to Winston and asked him if his advice would be the same. The President said all that Winston could do was to 'splutter'.[17]

In a highly discursive fashion, Roosevelt jumped from topic to topic, including the Australian–New Zealand Agreement. He said 'Evatt had written a "rude" document. . . . "We will completely ignore it."' Roosevelt also talked about post-war Germany. He meandered on the subject of colonial economics. He repeated what he had said before about the West Indies. He digressed on the Philippines. By this stage of the luncheon Taussig was beginning to wonder whether any business would be transacted at all.

Stanley finally managed to steer the conversation on to the West Indies and the Caribbean Commission. He told the President that the Colonial Office hoped to establish several regional commissions along the same lines. They would lead the way in post-war colonial development. This was precisely the direction which Taussig did *not* want the conversation to take. Stanley would later be able to argue that Roosevelt had shown interest in the regional commissions and was silent on trusteeship and international supervision. Taussig therefore broke in and asked directly whether the commissions would include mandated territories. 'The purpose of this question was to present the question in the event he [Roosevelt] wanted to discuss mandates and trusteeships.'[18] Stanley merely replied 'yes' to the question and Roosevelt did not pursue the issue. 'The President did not bring the matter up directly during the entire conversation', Taussig recorded ruefully. So far as making progress with trusteeship was concerned, Roosevelt's meeting with Stanley, in Taussig's view, was a disaster.

Since Taussig had directly reminded Roosevelt of the trusteeship issue, it certainly did not pass by unnoticed. The President was probably sizing up the Colonial Secretary. Having received a polite but quite firm rebuff on the Hong Kong overture (which Roosevelt by this time must have had doubts on), he quickly gathered that Stanley was, in Taussig's phrase,

[17] Ibid. (2).   [18] Ibid. (2).

'hardboiled'. Whether deliberately or not, Roosevelt did not run the risk of receiving an unequivocal *non possumus* on the question of international supervision, nor did he play into Stanley's hands by listening to the Colonial Office's proposal for a library dressed up as an 'International Colonial Centre'. Roosevelt may not have been consciously aware of the choice he made at this stage in not presenting trusteeship directly now to Stanley and saving it later for Churchill, but if this is true, then he demonstrated an uncanny awareness that it would be better to put it forward as part of a bargain package when he could expect Stalin's support. To have raised international supervision with Stanley would have put the British on guard and would have ensured a Colonial Office representative at Yalta. Wittingly or not, Roosevelt made the right choice. Stanley returned to London hoping the President might *not* raise the issue and thinking that he might have done some useful work. He left a favourable impression on the President. 'I liked Stanley', Roosevelt later told Taussig. 'He [Roosevelt] thought that Stanley was more liberal on colonial policy than Churchill.'[19] Since the Colonial Secretary no less than the Prime Minister believed that the affairs of the British Empire were no business of the Americans, it was a good performance on Stanley's part.

The luncheon with the President was only the beginning of a rigorous three days for the Colonial Secretary. Apart from exacting discussion in the State Department, Stanley also found himself on a goodwill mission. In the view of Lord Halifax, the Colonial Secretary himself now could be given the opportunity to present British colonial policy in a favourable light. On the 17th of January Halifax gave a dinner for Stanley. The American guests included Taussig, Stettinius, Vice President-Elect Harry Truman, Justice Felix Frankfurter, and Walter Lippmann. After the meal Halifax had all of the chairs put in a circle and suggested that they have a round-table discussion. He wanted everyone to be 'indiscreet'. He explained that the Colonial Secretary had come to Washington on Caribbean business and turned the meeting over to him. Stanley talked briefly about the Caribbean Commission and generally about British colonial policy. Among other things he emphasized the

---

[19] Memorandum by Taussig, 15 Mar. 1945, Taussig Papers Box 49.

positive goals that could be accomplished through regional commissions and the negative aspects of the Permanent Mandates Commission. After a few words by Stettinius, Harry Truman said he would like to ask a question. Suppose Puerto Rico were a British colony, and were treated the way the Americans treated it—what would be the American reaction? This led to some interesting comments by Frankfurter, who had been involved in Puerto Rican affairs following the First World War. It was now twenty-four years later, he said, and exactly the same problems were still being debated. Later in the discussion Frankfurter provided one of the most trenchant remarks about trusteeship in the whole evening—and indeed in the entire wartime era. At the mention of the word, Stanley had indicated, with 'intonation', according to Taussig, that he did not believe it to be a satisfactory concept. 'Just what is meant by trusteeship?' Stanley asked. He clearly expected to get no answer, or at least an unsatisfactory one. Here is Taussig's account of the Colonial Secretary getting far more than he had bargained for in trying to browbeat an American audience. With analytical acumen and entirely sure of his ground, Frankfurter went to the heart of accountability:

. . . Justice Frankfurter took over. *The Justice pointed out that trusteeship had a very definite meaning in Anglo-Saxon law; that the basic principle of trusteeship was that a trustee did not judge its own acts.* He reiterated this several times as Stanley tried to make a case that the British were the trustees of their own colonies. Stanley for the first time appeared to be on the defensive. He evaded direct questions of Frankfurter and appeared to be purposefully evading the issue.[20]

Thus the Colonial Secretary nearly found himself hoist on his own petard of accountability. It must have been a rare moment. But it was short-lived. Walter Lippmann thought that such discussion served no useful purpose because it had nothing to do with the reality of power politics. Taussig lamented in his concluding remark about the dinner, 'Walter Lippman did not help the United States cause with his remark that it is quite all unimportant and merely an argument in semantics.'[21]

Unfortunately for Stanley, he found himself embroiled in a comparable open-ended debate the next day. This one

---

[20] Memorandum by Taussig, 16 Jan. 1945 (2). Italics added.   [21] Ibid.

resembled a family quarrel. Late in the afternoon of the 18th of January, Halifax invited all of the Dominion representatives to the Embassy. For Stanley, who usually liked exacting discussions, this one was too precise. Sir Frederick Eggleston wanted to know whether reports on colonial administration would be submitted to the future international organization. Stanley replied that this would be 'most undesirable' because the majority of the members would be 'completely ignorant' of colonial administration. 'The Latin American States for example would represent about a third of the total.'[22] This was not what Eggleston had in mind. He persisted. He referred to the mandates system and reminded his peers that he had been present at its creation at the Paris Peace Conference. He wanted to know whether Stanley envisaged a similar body in the new international organization to which all governments would be accountable for their colonial administrations. Stanley thereupon expressed his 'strong conviction' that the Permanent Mandates Commission had contributed 'nothing of value'. Here he was much more frank than he had been with the Americans about his real objection to the mandates system:

In his own experience of West Africa the most backward of the territories administered by the Colonial Office had been the two mandated territories of the Cameroons and Togoland: the personnel there had always had the feeling *that they were doing a temporary job* and the feeling of *impermanence* engendered by the mandates themselves had not unnaturally resulted in major schemes of development being concentrated in Nigeria and the Gold Coast where all concerned knew that they were working for the future.[23]

Eggleston directly took issue with him. He said that Australia's experience in New Guinea with the mandates system, far from being a hindrance, had been a help. The New Zealander, C. A. Berendsen, broke in saying that he agreed. He in fact

---

[22] 'Note of a Meeting' at the British Embassy, 18 Jan. 1945, copies in CO 968/161/14814/11 Pt. 1; FO 371/50807; and DO 35/1901, the last containing a revealing covering letter dated 27 Jan. 1945. The Embassy in Washington had encouraged Alan Watt, Secretary of the Australian Legation, to attend in order to act 'as a brake on Eggleston, and in order to ensure that if Eggleston reported on the meeting to his Government he should at least send out as fair a report as possible'. Eggleston reported the meeting accurately in a telegram to Evatt of 19 Jan. 1945 (AA A1066 H45/1021) but in his diary he complained that Halifax had tried to discredit his views.

[23] 'Note', 18 Jan. 1945. Italics added.

had been the New Zealand official responsible for administration in Samoa and for the reports to the Permanent Mandates Commission. Each year he had found it a useful exercise in stocktaking to draw up the annual report. 'The experience of New Zealand was that the Permanent Mandates Commission had been helpful rather than the reverse.'[24] The South African representative, Dr. S. F. N. Gie, now disagreed with the Australian and the New Zealander. He came down on the side of the Colonial Secretary, agreeing about 'the adverse affect [sic] of impermanence'. The Germans in South-West Africa had exploited the mandates system to prevent its assimilation into the Union. Now Stanley agreed with the South African. Strange bedfellows!

Eggleston returned to the charge. Halifax thought that the Australian was becoming distinctly tiresome. In the British Ambassador's opinion such areas as New Guinea, Malaya, and the Dutch East Indies, had so little in common that it would be 'futile' to expect one international body to supervise all of them. Trying to shift the discussion away from Eggleston, Halifax asked Stanley whether the Americans had revealed any of their ideas on the subject. Stanley replied that American thinking still seemed to be at a formulative stage. Eggleston would not remain silent. To the contrary, he stated:

He had discussed the question with Mr. Grew, Mr. Hopkins, and the very highest quarters and he had been told that the President had it very much in mind that there ought to be some declaration to the effect that independence was the goal so far as dependent territories were concerned.[25]

Halifax again tried to minimize Eggleston's argument, this time saying that it would be a mistake to draw any definite conclusion from a conversation with the President—Roosevelt 'would express a view in order to crystallise it in his own mind and to hear the comments of others. It did not necessarily represent a final or even a considered opinion.'[26] Stanley,

---

[24] Ibid.

[25] Ibid. A memorandum by Escott Reid of the Canadian Embassy reveals some of the acrimony of the discussion: 'Colonel Stanley indicated in some of his replies his belief that the Australian Minister did not know very much about the subject he was talking about.' Memorandum by Reid, 19 Jan. 1945, CAN 180(S).

[26] 'Note', 18 Jan. 1945, CO 968/161/14814/11 Pt. 1.

however, decided to meet the issue head-on. Since they were talking about fundamentals, he would give them his opinion about the American insistence on independence as the ultimate goal of colonial rule. Here the discussion is revealing because it is one of the few times he condescended to talk about time-tables.

· Colonel Stanley thought that anything in the way of a pledge of ultimate independence was fantastic, let alone a series of dates. The Philippines had been under some sort of European administration for 300 years, but it would be incredible that the countries of the world should pledge themselves to the ultimate independence of New Guinea or Papua.[27]

Eggleston agreed that independence was out of the question for New Guinea. Berendsen also concurred: 'the idea of ulti-mate independence of all dependent territories was impossible of acceptance.'[28] Thus Stanley at least managed to get the Dominions representatives to reach a consensus that indepen-dence was not a panacea.[29]

Eggleston attempted to tell Halifax and Stanley that, on the basis of conversations with Roosevelt, Hopkins, and Grew, the Americans might insist on measures aimed at promoting uni-versal independence for the colonies. Therefore Stanley had better go slow in throwing cold water on the proposition of international accountability. Better to negotiate a renewed mandates system, in Eggleston's view, than to push the Ameri-cans into more drastic measures. Halifax had not warmed up to this suggestion. In his opinion, which Stanley shared, the time had come for a showdown.

Earlier that same day, Stanley had put his cards on the table at the State Department. The other participants were Pasvolsky, the master strategist; Taussig, the practical minded representa-

---

[27] Note', 18 Jan. 1945, CO 968/161/14814/11 Pt. 1.   [28] Ibid.
[29] The Canadian Minister, Escott Reid, spoke of the issue of independence at the Institute of Pacific Relations conference: 'The fact that independence had been promised the Philippines in a year resulted . . . in a conviction of self-righteousness that . . . had proved very trying to the British delegates, who had reacted strongly. So had the French delegates who had said that [the] United States could complain about the way other countries treated negroes when they had set their own house in order and had had a negro in the United States cabinet.' For this and other material of considerable interest from the Canadian vantage point, see CAN 180(S).

tive of Rooseveltian idealism; and Gerig, the expert.[30] A later account of this encounter had it that Pasvolsky apparently struck Stanley as almost Russian-like in his mannerisms and technique of rephrasing propositions abstractly and impersonally as a means of a.non-commitment.[31] The discussion was lengthy but the main points can be starkly described. Stanley did an effective job of arguing against the mandates system by pleading a positive case. He wanted to profit from the valuable contribution of the Permanent Mandates Commission in colonial affairs, notably in the realm of publicity. But he also wanted to dispose of the purely negative obligations of the mandates system by replacing them with co-operative arrangements. In the British view this could best be done through the regional commissions. In bringing forward the idea of reporting to an international body through the commissions, Stanley now even went so far as to say that he would agree that the international organization could draw up a questionnaire on which the reports would be based. In an effort to help the Americans solve their problem of how to dispose of the Pacific islands, he stated that each administering power would assume voluntary responsibility to participate in the regional commissions and make reports. If they did not assume these obligations, they would have to withdraw from the region. Throughout he stressed the word 'voluntary'. He clearly opposed any obligation to sit in judgement by an international body, or, in Churchill's phrase, to be put 'in the dock'. Stanley also made his position perfectly clear on two other key points.

[30] P. H. Gore-Booth of the British Embassy accompanied Stanley. The record of the conversation on 18 January, with a covering note by Gore-Booth, is in CO 968/161/14814/11 Pt. 1; FO 371/50807; and DO 35/1901. The American record is in USSD NF Boxes 185 and 273. The latter is much more detailed.

[31] In a letter dated 9 Feb. 1945, Sir John Macpherson, Taussig's opposite number as Joint Chairman of the Caribbean Commission, reported Taussig's *post mortem* of the meeting to T. K. Lloyd at the Colonial Office. 'He [Taussig] realises that the Secretary of State felt that . . . he was made to do all the talking and he senses that this evoked understandable irritation. He insists, however, that Pasvolsky was not trying to hold back, though his queer Russian manner made it appear as if he were. Instead of directly expressing views on any suggestion voiced by Colonel Stanley, Pasvolsky, according to Taussig, would indulge in a long analysis of the pros and cons, leaving his views to be inferred. Taussig was often tempted to butt in and say "what Mr. Pasvolsky means is that the U.S. view on that is so-and-so", but he didn't feel that he could.' Macpherson to Lloyd, 9 Feb. 1945, CO 968/161/14814/11 Pt. 1.

On the question of *inspections*, he thought they would be 'unwise and impracticable'. 'Such inspections would weaken the position of the administering authorities in the eyes of native peoples and could only create confusion.' On the question of *petitions*, he also thought that 'petitioning by natives over the heads of the administering authorities was not helpful or practicable'.[32] As in the case of the Caribbean Commission, he believed that the other colonial powers should be brought into the discussion on this matter since they would be vitally affected as well.[33] Towards the end, Stanley took a definite stand on the ultimate issue of self-government versus independence. He told the Americans that the British goal was self-government or, in some cases, Dominion status within the Empire. He gave a reason that later, in the era of decolonization, gave both Americans and Englishmen cause for reflection: 'There should not be too many small independent entities scattered around the world, most of which could not exist alone . . . in the British conception, dominion status meant the right to secede, but it was hoped this would not happen.'[34]

Pasvolsky's main strategy during the encounter was to maintain a sharp distinction between mandates and detached enemy territories, on the one hand, and colonies, on the other. Stanley did not like these distinctions. He attempted to blur them by arguing that in the case of mandated Togoland and the colony of the Gold Coast, for example, 'there was no point in preserving a distinction which had no practical meaning'.[35] Pasvolsky insisted that there was a real meaning, because ultimately it touched on the question of sovereignty. The United States argued that sovereignty in the mandated territories resided in the Allied and Associated powers who had signed the peace treaties at the close of the First World War, while

[32] American minutes, 18 Jan. 1945, USSD NF Box 273.

[33] In the discussions about the Caribbean Commission Stanley had pressed hard for the inclusion of the French and the Dutch. He told Taussig, 'the other colonial powers were already suspicious of the United States, and . . . he was afraid if we delayed too long, they would become suspicious of his government.' Taussig memorandum (2), 16 Jan. 1945, Taussig Papers Box 49. To the Americans it seemed clear that Stanley's plan included the other European powers because they would support the British position. The memoranda of the talks on Caribbean affairs during Stanley's visit are in USSD NF Box 185.

[34] American minutes, 18 Jan. 1945.

[35] British minutes cited above, note 30.

Stanley held that sovereignty resided in the administering powers. At one of the few times that he spoke at length, Gerig emphasized that this point was 'fundamental'. It raised the whole question of annexation. The United States opposed aggrandizement. If the colonial settlement now consisted of veiled annexations, then it would prove to cynics everywhere that the mandates system had been, in his phrase, 'a fraud'.[36] Of course he could have just as well directed his remarks towards the United States Navy as to the British Colonial Secretary. So far as Stanley was concerned, he left Washington knowing that the State Department, at least, would fight to the end to preserve the principles of the mandates system.

Stanley had been exasperated by some of the idealistic talk, but on the whole he had no reason to be displeased. From neither the President nor the Pasvolsky group did he get the impression that the trusteeship issue would be resolved quickly and basically. On the contrary, he thought he had agreement that papers would be exchanged between the two governments so that the differences could be thrashed out before discussing them at an international conference. He had made clear the British position on inspection and petitions. He had urged that the other colonial powers be allowed to have their say in the matter. On this last point Stanley perhaps overplayed his hand. He drew the immediate rejoinder from Pasvolsky that the Russians and the Chinese would also have to be consulted. In a paper on points that needed to be resolved at Yalta, Pasvolsky drew this major conclusion as a result of Stanley's visit:

The British position is clearly designed to win support from other states with colonies in order to offset the support which, they anticipate, the United States will receive from the Soviet Union and China.[37]

At Yalta the Americans jumped to gain the advantage of Russian support. It transformed the 'colonial question' of the wartime era.

[36] American minutes, 18 Jan. 1945.
[37] *Foreign Relations: The Conferences at Malta and Yalta (1945)*, pp. 81–5.

29

YALTA: AGREEMENT ON THE TRUSTEESHIP FORMULA

IN his manœuvrings in the months before he met with Churchill and Stalin in the Crimea in early February 1945, Roosevelt demonstrated a consummate handling of the colonial issue. Whatever effect his failing health may have had in other matters, his trusteeship policy was deft.[1] He was tenacious in purpose, though his breezy talk sometimes disguised his persistence. He did not raise the issue with the Joint Chiefs. With the British Colonial Secretary he deliberately avoided the subject. Well before Stanley's visit, however, he had given specific instructions to Pasvolsky to prepare the case on trusteeship for discussion with Churchill and Stalin. On the American side, the genesis of the Yalta colonial decision is to be found in Roosevelt's remarks to his advisers on international organization on the 15th of November 1944.

[T]he President said that it was his definite desire that the principle of international trusteeship be firmly established and that the international organization should provide adequate machinery for that purpose.

He said that the Army and Navy have been urging upon him the point of view that the United States should take over all or some of the mandated islands in the Pacific, but that he was opposed to such a procedure because it was contrary to the Atlantic Charter. Nor did he think that it was necessary. As far as he could tell, all that we would accomplish by that would be to provide jobs as governors of insignificant islands for inefficient Army and Navy officers or members of the civilian career service.[2]

Roosevelt's contempt for petty military bureaucracy is a recurrent theme in his conversations. He believed the military

---

[1] On the question of Roosevelt's health, Anthony Eden commented: 'I do not believe that the President's declining health altered his judgment, though his handling of the Conference was less sure than it might have been.' (*The Reckoning*, p. 593.) This judgement is endorsed by the leading scholarly authority, Diane Clemens, *Yalta* (New York, 1970), p. 104.

[2] *Foreign Relations: The Conferences at Malta and Yalta (1945)*, p. 57.

had no business in civil administration. The defence of the United States was an entirely different matter. Roosevelt also instructed the State Department to coordinate trusteeship planning with the Joint Chiefs. He wanted the Pacific islands fortified and capable of defence. This directive led to the creation of a high-powered inter-departmental committee that discussed trusteeship with considerable intensity during the winter and spring of 1945. During this time the Secretary of State for War, Henry L. Stimson, began to marshal heavy artillery against trusteeship. The interaction between the State Department and the Pentagon will be considered in a later chapter as prelude to the colonial settlement. Shortly before the San Francisco conference the objections by Stimson and the Joint Chiefs nearly succeeded in defeating the trusteeship proposals. For the Yalta conference the military protests came too late.

The President's interest in trusteeship schemes as a means of stabilizing unsettled areas and opening the door to American commerce remained constant. He had begun to retreat, however, from some of his more grandiose and impracticable ideas. The case of Iran is particularly striking because on this issue Roosevelt gave way on the eve of the Yalta conference. In early December the President wrote to the Secretary of State that he still hoped to see a free port and international railway at the head of the Persian Gulf. '[T]hree or four Trustees [should] build a new port in Iran at the head of the Persian Gulf (free port), take over the whole railroad from there into Russia, and run the thing for the good of all.'[3] The proposal received detailed examination in the State Department. Superficially the idea appeared to be a good one. Russia would be assured of an economic outlet to the Persian Gulf and might be persuaded to avoid force; Iran would be assisted economically; and international co-operation rather than rivalry would be encouraged. Unfortunately the scheme flew in the face of Iranian realities. The Russians could not be expected to internationalize any part of Iran under their control; a traditional element of British policy had been to deny Russia access to the Persian Gulf; and, not least, the Iranians themselves were highly suspicious of internationalization. 'No matter how drawn up or

[3] Memorandum by Roosevelt, 8 Dec. 1944, ibid., p. 333.

proposed, the plan would appear to Iran, and doubtless to the world, as a thinly disguised cover for power politics and old-world imperialism.'[4] In the judgement of the State Department, a trusteeship regime could be imposed on Iran only by force of arms. Thus did the State Department dissuade Roosevelt from discussing trusteeship for Iran with the British and Russians at Yalta.

Roosevelt was well served by the officials who subjected his ideas to such scrutiny. Though some of his schemes did not sustain close examination, others did. In the briefing book that accompanied the American delegation to Yalta, the section on dependent territories contained separate entries on the three projects of a general colonial declaration, regional commissions, and trusteeship—in other words, summaries of the three major policies of the State Department towards colonial areas during the entire war. The word *accountability* was underlined. Since the Joint Chiefs had objected to territorial discussions that might prolong the war, the briefing book put forward the principle and the machinery of trusteeship without reference to specific territories. Nearly three years of labour on the part of Benjamin Gerig and the specialist committees were summarized in a single paragraph entitled '*A Trusteeship Mechanism*'.

A trusteeship mechanism should be provided by which the international organization would succeed to the rights, titles, and interests of the Principal Allied and Associated Powers, and to the rights and responsibilities of the League of Nations with respect to the mandates. It should also be given authority over certain territories which may be detached from the present enemy states, and over any other territories which by agreement may be placed under its control.[5]

The State Department thus offered a solution to immediate problems that had to be resolved before an international organization could be established. This was the stage of the war when the arduous drafting of the State Department's specialists began to have a specific impact on momentous decisions.

It was the question of the future of the Japanese mandated islands and the Italian colonies that forced Churchill's hand.

---

[4] State Department memorandum on Iran, 6 Jan. 1945, *Foreign Relations: The Conferences at Malta and Yalta (1945)*, p. 345.

[5] Briefing Book excerpt, ibid., p. 92.

Something had to be done about them. Frustrated in his attempt to persuade Roosevelt simply to annex the islands, Churchill responded negatively to alternative solutions. With a suspicious eye on the Foreign Office, the Prime Minister had written on the 18th of January that he would concur in trusteeship proposals only if they involved 'no danger to our Colonial Empire'. He noted specifically that he would object to the extension of the mandates system to enemy territories.[6] His views were identical with the Colonial Secretary's, except that Stanley now knew that it would be impossible to persuade the Americans to terminate the mandates system. After Stanley's return from America in late January, Eden consulted him about Churchill's minute. Stanley thought it would be an appropriate time to advise Churchill on how to proceed with the Americans. In part because of the interview with Roosevelt, he believed that the President would not press the issue and that in any case the State Department would not act until the Colonial Office could present the Poynton–Robinson project (which was gaining the approval of the Dominions at this stage). Stanley's attitude therefore was to hope that Roosevelt would not raise the issue, and, if he did, to suggest postponement until the State Department received the Colonial Office proposals. He still hoped to retain the initiative with regional commissions. With Stanley's concurrence, Eden sent this assuring message to Churchill on the eve of the Yalta conference:

[W]e both feel that our proposals [the Poynton–Robinson project] cannot possibly involve any danger to our Colonial Empire. On the contrary, it seems to us that if they are generally adopted, the position of our Colonial Empire would not be endangered but rather buttressed and reinforced.

A further great advantage in our now agreeing to present them to the Americans would lie in the fact that we should thereby gain the initiative and possibly succeed in preventing the Americans from circulating schemes of their own which, if adopted, would endanger our Colonial Empire.

. . . [I]f the President should revert to this question during the forthcoming conference (and only of course if he does) you might very suitably say that we hope very shortly to present to his Government a well-considered plan for international collaboration in these

---

[6] See above, p. 434.

problems. You might add that you would greatly hope that the Americans for their part would not circulate any papers on this subject until they had carefully studied our proposals.[7]

Thus the combined opinion of the Foreign Secretary and the Colonial Secretary did not lead Churchill to believe that the trusteeship issue would come to a head at Yalta. Nor did the preliminary discussions between the British and American delegations in the Mediterranean, at Malta, from the 30th of January until the 2nd of February, cause him to be alarmed about the colonial question. No member of the Colonial Office accompanied the delegation. While Roosevelt's advisers served him well on trusteeship, Churchill's Foreign Office officials performed less than zealous service on an issue that the Colonial Office—and the Prime Minister himself—considered to be of vital importance.

Eden, Cadogan, and Jebb all had a hand in the trusteeship negotiations, and all of them tended to subordinate the issue for the sake of smoother relations on the larger question of the future international organization. They also had one particular new development fresh in mind. On the 18th of January Eden had circulated to the Armistice and Post-War Committee a memorandum written by Sir William Malkin, the legal adviser at the Foreign Office. Malkin dealt with the termination of the mandates system as a question in international law. In his own words, it was an 'extremely difficult one'. He pointed out that no one actually knew where sovereignty resided.[8] He did not believe that the dissolution of the League would terminate the mandates system. The clearest and simplest solution would be annexation. But even a lawyer could see that 'this might be objected to as savouring of "imperialism"'. He noted in particular that the United States had treaty rights safeguarding American interests in the 'A' and 'B' mandated territories. In short, there could be no agreement

---

[7] Eden to Churchill, 24 Jan. 1945, FO 371/50807 (with important minutes in this file); CO 968/161/14814/11 Pt. 1; PREM 4/31/4.

[8] 'The question where sovereignty in mandated territories now resides is one about which lawyers have argued for 25 years without any definite conclusions being reached, but few hold that it resides in the Mandatory, though the Union of South Africa apparently hold this view as regards their own C. Mandate.' Memorandum by Malkin with covering note by Eden, 18 Jan. 1945, A.P.W. (45) 7, CAB 87/69; FO 371/50630.

about the future of the mandates without American concurrence. Eden noted that the Americans could block British proposals for the future of Palestine if the disposition of the other mandates displeased them.[9] When the question of trusteeship arose in the preliminary discussions at Malta, Eden, Cadogan, and Jebb were fully aware of this quagmire in international law. All three of them also genuinely deplored the possibility of a recrudescence of old-fashioned imperialism. They were much more committed to international organization and keeping the peace than they were to the preservation of the British Empire, at least in the style of the Prime Minister.

At Malta, Alger Hiss entered the trusteeship story. At that time serving as Deputy Director in the State Department's Office of Special Political Affairs (with particular responsibilities for international organization), he demonstrated a quick and firm grasp of the principles as set out in the briefing book, and a persistence in keeping after the British until they responded. He and another member of the delegation, James F. Byrnes (Director, Office of War Mobilization, and later Secretary of State) told Eden and Cadogan that the Americans wished to reach agreement on a trusteeship 'formula'. Cadogan as a result drafted a telegram to London, but he did not send it because Eden wished to raise the question with Churchill. The Colonial Office thus remained in ignorance. Eden in fact did not report the American overture to the Prime Minister. Nothing on the British side was done until Hiss raised the issue again on the 4th of February at Yalta, this time with Jebb. Hiss vigorously put forward the American case. According to the British record:

He [Hiss] said that the American Administration were firmly of the opinion that to assimilate the existing mandates to existing territorial empires—even if this was part and parcel of some larger deal for the Colonies as a whole—would be a 'retrograde step'. He further argued that for such areas as the Japanese mandated islands and, notably, Korea, it would almost certainly be necessary to set up some kind of new machinery as a result of this war and that the British idea of having one State solely responsible for every dependent area could not therefore in practice work.[10]

---

[9] Eden's note, ibid.
[10] Memorandum by Jebb, 4 Feb. 1945, with minutes and marginal notations by

Jebb merely adopted the line already agreed upon in London, and told Hiss that the Colonial Office was preparing a set of proposals. Hiss insisted on a formula. As Hiss presented it (or at least as Jebb recorded it), this was the language:

[T]he three powers are agreed that there should be considered at the United Nations Conference the subject of territorial trustee-ships and Dependent Areas and that provision should be made in the Charter covering these points.[11]

Even in this innocuous form, Jebb saw exactly what was at stake. '[I]f we accept their present formula it would be evident that we shall come near to committing ourselves to the principle of mandates both existing and possible, which we particularly want to avoid.' Jebb accordingly argued against the proposal, using the powerful observation that if the Americans, British, and Russians agreed on colonial trusteeship, 'the French would immediately conclude that the whole World Organisation scheme was some kind of plot designed to deprive them of their colonial possessions'. Hiss and Byrnes admitted that there was force in this argument. They also agreed that, in Jebb's words, 'sticky though we [the British] might be on territorial trustee-ship, the French were likely to be ten times stickier'.[12] But Hiss and Byrnes were not diverted by the red herring of French colonialism. They persisted in the quest for a formula.

For the trusteeship controversy, the significance of the Yalta conference can be summed up by stating simply that the Americans succeeded in getting their formula. Since the Colonial Office regarded this development as close to a sell-out, it is illuminating to trace in detail the British side of the American triumph. The key lies in the action (and inaction) of the Foreign Secretary and Permanent Under-Secretary. Although Eden resisted Churchill's unabashed attitude of 'we mean to hold our own', he took care not to flout the Colonial Office. He made it clear that in principle he opposed a continua-

Cadogan, FO 371/50807. Apparently there is no American record of this conversa-tion. For the Malta conversation, see also Stettinius, *Roosevelt and the Russians*, p. 236.

[11] Ibid. Jebb underlined the 's' in 'trusteeships' to denote a nuance in American and British usage. 'Trusteeships' to the Americans could mean individual regimes of a makeshift or temporary nature. 'Trusteeship', in the singular, to the British meant a system or set of principles. The ideological dimension was always present in British usage, but not necessarily in the American.   [12] Ibid.

tion of the mandates system. But he did not vigorously oppose trusteeship. Cadogan shared all of Eden's sentiments and he reacted in the same way. He merely regarded it as a bother that 'someone in the U.S. Administration (I'm not quite sure who) . . . is pushing this question into the discussions'.[13] Neither Eden nor Cadogan believed that Roosevelt would press the issue—at least not seriously. Their immediate estimate of the President's intentions at Yalta was shaped by Harry Hopkins. Cadogan noted on the 5th of February that Hopkins advised Eden 'to wait until the President raised the matter, and rather hinted that the President might not go so far in this as some of his subordinates'.[14] Cadogan further noted that Churchill at least should be warned. Accordingly he drafted this minute, which was given to Churchill under Eden's signature.

PRIME MINISTER.

[1.] You should know that at Cricket [code name for Malta] and here the Americans have raised with us the question of 'Territorial Trusteeship'.

2. . . . [T]heir idea was that agreement should be reached here that a provision on this point should be included in the Charter of the World Organization.

3. I expressed my doubts about this as it might commit us to a continuation, if not an extension of the Mandates system.

3. [sic] They have now suggested that we should here agree to include in the records of this Conference an (unpublished) Protocol to the effect that this question 'should be considered at the United Nations Conference'. I am against this.

4. I have a line from Harry Hopkins that the President himself may not press this too hard, and I suggest we wait to see what proposal he makes, if any . . .

(SGD.) A. EDEN
5th February, 1945[15]

Eden and Cadogan thus sized up the trusteeship issue at Yalta. Their view miscalculated the power of the American bureaucracy, which made its voice heard through the briefing book. They also misread Roosevelt's intentions and underestimated his commitment to trusteeship. Eden's minute served as Churchill's

---

[13] Minute by Cadogan, 5 Feb. 1945, FO 371/50807. [14] Ibid.
[15] The memorandum is in 371/50807, with minutes by Cadogan and Jebb.

only briefing on the subject before the trusteeship question arose in the conference on the 9th of February.

The day before, during the afternoon of the 8th, Roosevelt met privately with Stalin. Among other topics, they discussed the political conditions under which Russia would enter the war against Japan. Roosevelt stated that there would be 'no difficulty whatsoever' in regard to the southern half of Sakhalin and the Kurile Islands going to Russia at the end of the war. They reverted to the problem of a warm water port, already mentioned in their discussions at Tehran. Saying that he had not discussed the matter with Chiang Kai-shek, Roosevelt explained to Stalin:

> [T]here are two methods for the Russians to obtain the use of this port; (1) outright leasing from the Chinese; (2) making Dairen a free port under some form of international commission. He said he preferred the latter method because of the relation to the question of Hong Kong. The President said he hoped that the British would give back the sovereignty of Hong Kong to China and that it would then become an internationalized free port.[16]

After further exchanges, Stalin said that he would not object to an internationalized free port.[17] This was the context of the discussion that followed on trusteeship.

Roosevelt proposed trusteeship for Korea and Indo-China. Stalin readily endorsed it as a solution for unstable areas. Roosevelt emphasized the temporary nature of the trusteeship regimes. He described them as a sort of experiment in preparation for independence, with definite timetables.

> He [Roosevelt] said he had in mind for Korea a trusteeship composed of a Soviet, an American and a Chinese representative. He said the only experience we had had in this matter was in the Philippines where it had taken about fifty years for the people to be prepared for self-government. He felt that in the case of Korea the period might be from twenty to thirty years.
> Marshal Stalin said the shorter the period the better, and he inquired whether any foreign troops would be stationed in Korea.

---

[16] *Foreign Relations: Yalta*, p. 769.

[17] For discussions of the Far Eastern question, see Clemens, *Yalta*, ch. 7; George A. Lensen, 'Yalta and the Far East', in John L. Snell, ed., *The Meaning of Yalta* (Louisiana State University Press, 1956); and Ernest R. May, 'The United States, the Soviet Union and the Far Eastern War', *Pacific Historical Review*, 24. 2 (May 1955).

The President replied in the negative, to which Marshal Stalin expressed approval.[18]

Roosevelt now solicited Stalin's advice about what position the British should hold in Korea. The President described it as a 'delicate' point.

He personally did not feel it was necessary to invite the British to participate in the trusteeship of Korea, but he felt that they might resent this.

Marshal Stalin replied that they would most certainly be offended. In fact, he said, the Prime Minister might 'kill us'. In his opinion he felt that the British should be invited.[19]

The conversation then turned to Indo-China. Roosevelt had in mind a trusteeship regime for that area also.

The President . . . added that the British did not approve of this idea as they wished to give it back to the French since they feared the implications of a trusteeship as it might affect Burma.

Marshal Stalin remarked that the British had lost Burma once through reliance on Indochina, and it was not his opinion that Britain was a sure country to protect this area. He added that he thought Indochina was a very important area.

The President. . . . added that France had done nothing to improve the natives since she had the colony.[20]

Whatever Stalin might have thought about the President's concern for welfare in Indo-China, he probably assumed that the United States aimed at post-war control of the area. Roosevelt himself seemed to reveal this point when he told Stalin in conclusion that de Gaulle hoped shortly to send French troops to Indo-China. Stalin asked where de Gaulle planned to get the troops. 'The President replied that de Gaulle said he was going to find the troops when the President could find the ships, but the President added that up to the present he had been unable to find the ships.'[21] Stalin and Roosevelt found themselves in general agreement about the Far East and trusteeship. The next day Stalin aligned himself with Roosevelt in the trusteeship controversy with Churchill.

Since the beginning of the war, Churchill had regarded trusteeship schemes as a cover for American ambitions. In this

[18] *Foreign Relations: Yalta*, p. 770.　　[19] Ibid.　　[20] Ibid.　　[21] Ibid.

sense he needed no briefing. The mention of the very word 'trusteeship' triggered an emotional response. The topic got on the agenda innocently enough. Alger Hiss was the ubiquitous official in the background who kept pushing the subject into the discussions.[22] At a meeting of the Foreign Ministers at noon on the 9th, Stettinius, using Hiss's notes, suggested to Eden and Molotov that the five governments that would have seats on the Security Council should consult about trusteeship before the conference in the spring on international organization. Stettinius made it clear that particular islands or territories would not be mentioned. He deferred to Eden's suggestion that the matter should not even be mentioned in the invitation to the conference, but that it would be taken up diplomatically. The three foreign secretaries agreed on this procedure.[23] The subject thus appeared in their report to the 'Big Three' that afternoon at 4 p.m. It was in this session that Churchill erupted with his famous line that under no circumstances would he ever 'consent to forty or fifty nations thrusting interfering fingers into the life's existence of the British Empire'.[24]

Fortunately Byrnes took a verbatim account in shorthand of Churchill's explosion. Rhetorically it must rank high in the annals of British imperialism as an extemporaneous and uninhibited defence of the Empire. Stettinius merely reported that there would be consultation on trusteeship before the conference on international organization.

Mr. Churchill: I absolutely disagree. I will not have one scrap of British territory flung into that area. After we have done our best to fight in this war and have done no crime to anyone I will have no suggestion that the British Empire is to be put into the dock and examined by everybody to see whether it is up to their standard. No one will induce me as long as I am Prime Minister to let any representative of Great Britain go to a conference where we will be placed in the dock and asked to justify our right to live in a world we have tried to save.[25]

Roosevelt interrupted at this point and requested Churchill to let Stettinius finish his statement, since it had nothing to do with the British Empire. Churchill was hardly pacified.

[22] *Foreign Relations: Yalta*, pp. 793–4. [23] Ibid., pp. 810–13. [24] Ibid., p. 844.
[25] James F. Byrnes, *Speaking Frankly* (New York, 1947), p. x.

Mr. Churchill: . . . As long as every bit of land over which the British Flag flies is to be brought into the dock, I shall object so long as I live.

Mr. Stettinius: The only thing contemplated as to territorial trusteeship is to provide in the Charter of the world organization the right to create a trusteeship if it desires to do so. Later on, we have had in mind that the Japanese mandated islands be taken away from the Japanese. We have had nothing in mind with reference to the British Empire.

Mr. Churchill: So far as the British Empire is concerned, we ask nothing. We seek no territorial aggrandizement. If it is a question solely of dealing with enemy territory acquired during the war, it might be proper to put them into some form of trusteeship under the United Nations.[26]

Slightly assuaged, Churchill thus accepted Stettinius's explanation. As if grasping for aid, the Prime Minister asked Stalin how he would feel 'if the suggestion was made that the Crimea should be internationalized for use as a summer resort'. Stalin replied that he would be glad to give the Crimea as a place to be used for meetings of the three powers.[27] Stalin had in fact been delighted with the outburst. The British and the Americans were divided. Roosevelt was embarrassed. According to Eden's account, Stalin 'got up from his chair, walked up and down, beamed, and at intervals broke into applause'.[28]

They briefly adjourned. Hiss prepared a short statement of trusteeship. Working from the briefing book, he noted the following three points that became the 'trusteeship formula':

Territorial trusteeship would apply only to:

(1) Existing mandates of the League of Nations.
(2) Territory to be detached from the enemy as a result of this war.
(3) Any other territory that may voluntarily be placed under trusteeship.[29]

Churchill obviously did not study the formula closely. He had been assured specifically that it applied only to detached enemy territories. It is clear that the Prime Minister reluctantly agreed to it only because the Secretary of State said explicitly that the proposal had nothing at all to do with the British Empire.

[26] Ibid.
[28] Eden, *The Reckoning*, p. 595.
[27] *Foreign Relations: Yalta*, p. 844–5.
[29] *Foreign Relations: Yalta*, pp. 858–9.

But the written formula now included mandated areas, including *British* mandated territories. Neither Eden nor Cadogan protested. Both of them believed anyhow that it would be necessary to assimilate the mandates into the new trusteeship system, if only to resolve the legal difficulty of the termination of the mandates. It is doubtful whether Stettinius grasped the distinctions. He had innocently bamboozled the Prime Minister. In any case Churchill accepted the formula. He had fallen into the trap. He had given the future international organization the basis for putting the British Empire 'in the dock'. In the Tory view, that bastard child of the United Nations organization, the Trusteeship Council, was thus conceived at Yalta.

PART IV

THE COLONIAL SETTLEMENT
OF 1945

30

THE AFTERMATH OF YALTA
LONDON

THE colonial consequences of the Yalta accord were not as sharply apparent at the time as they are in retrospect. When Churchill returned to London, he demanded to know from the Foreign Office how the trusteeship decision affected the British Empire. The matter was by no means clear in his own mind. It is significant that he pressed the Foreign Office, as if Eden and Cadogan were responsible for a distasteful development in imperial affairs. The Colonial Office learned of the trusteeship formula with exasperated dismay. Aggrieved that important colonial business had been transacted without even consulting them, the Colonial Office officials again confirmed their own view that the spirit of appeasement lingered on in the Foreign Office. Now the Americans were being placated by giving way on issues that vitally touched the Colonial Empire.

Precisely how did the American trusteeship schemes threaten British colonial rule? In the long run the answer lies in the detailed negotiations that established the Trusteeship Council of the United Nations and the influence of the trusteeship system during the subsequent era of decolonization. The more immediate answer is the Colonial Office's loss of momentum as a result of Yalta. In late 1944 the Colonial Office had put forward a far-reaching and imaginative set of proposals (the Poynton–Robinson project) by which the colonial world would develop along British lines and according to British ideals. Regional development was the watchword. Economic and social progress would first be emphasized. Then sound political growth would come as a matter of course. The goal was strong, interdependent units within the existing colonial empires. There would be limited but real international collaboration. In retrospect the Yalta endorsement of the American concept of trusteeship helped to set the colonial world on a different course towards self-determination, independence, and fragmentation. Though no doubt an exaggeration, there is some truth in the view that the British post-war colonial vision died at Yalta. In any event the Colonial Office henceforth adopted a defensive but by no means passive posture.

The official British response to the Yalta colonial formula can be seen as a struggle between the bureaucracies as well as individuals attempting to defend their particular policies. One looks in vain for the ideological element—the clash between the Tory and Labour views on the future of colonies. It is missing, despite the central part played by Attlee. At this stage of the war Attlee again enters the trusteeship story, this time as Chairman of the Armistice and Post-War Committee, the ministerial body that thrashed out the colonial problem before it reached the War Cabinet. If Attlee had followed his Labour instincts, he at least would have attempted to ensure that the project of international supervision of colonies got a fair hearing; instead he fell into line with his Tory companions and applied his administrative talent to promoting consensus. Like his colleague Creech Jones, Attlee on the colonial issue stands out far less as a Labour ideologue than as an Englishman who chose to close ranks against the Americans. Eden, by contrast, can be viewed as the embodiment of a Foreign Office tradition. Colonial issues could and should be subordinated to larger ones of good foreign relations and the world's peace. Eden was responsible for the transaction at Yalta. He minimized its importance. He argued that in fact he had given away nothing. This line pleased Churchill, who suspected that international trusteeship might damage the Empire but hoped that as little harm as possible had been done. Oliver Stanley keenly resented the dénouement at Yalta. The granting of the premises of American trusteeship appeared to cancel at one stroke his progress in international colonial affairs. Taking exactly the opposite line from that of Eden, Stanley argued that substantial concessions *had* been made and that British colonial policy would have to be adjusted accordingly. It is a measure of the Colonial Secretary's realism (and, his critics would have added, his apathy) that he was able to abandon the Colonial Office's elaborate scheme for international collaboration through regional commissions and change course to accommodate the Americans.

Like other documents conceived in haste at international wartime conferences, the colonial section of the Yalta protocol appeared ambiguous after the event. In a minute for the Prime Minister dated the 22nd of February 1945, Eden in cavalier fashion attempted to clarify the meaning. He stated that there could be 'no doubt' that ' "territorial trusteeship" (whatever that may be) will continue to apply to the existing mandates of the League of Nations . . . '.[1] Eden argued that since something had to be done about the termination of the mandates, the protocol signified 'only the recognition of a fact'. He also reminded the Prime Minister that territories detached from the enemy as a result of the present war might be subject to trusteeship, but to the Foreign Office this clearly did not mean that *all* colonial territories would be placed under international supervision. Finally he pointed out with considerable verbosity that, at the conference on the future international organization to be held in San Francisco, only general principles would be discussed, not specific territories. With similar vagueness Cadogan discussed the matter with Sir George Gater, Permanent Under-Secretary at the Colonial Office. He assured him that nothing important in colonial affairs had transpired at Yalta. In part because Cadogan was a persuasive talker and Gater not an especially forceful personality, the Foreign Office's initial contact with the Colonial Office seemed to be reassuring. Cadogan's entry in his diary is revealing:

After a Conference, one always has to spend a lot of time explaining to those who have no experience of Conferences why one has not been able to obtain 101% of what they set out to demand. However, Gater was not unreasonable and I enveloped him in clouds of warm and woolly words.[2]

Thus Eden and Cadogan dealt with the American trusteeship scheme as they felt it deserved to be treated—as little more than hot air.

Things might have gone smoother for the Foreign Office had there not been a bureaucratic blunder. The Colonial Office, having been excluded at Yalta, now learned that the Foreign Office was conducting a private correspondence with

[1] Minute by Eden to Churchill, 22 Feb. 1945, FO 371/50807; PREM 4/31/4.
[2] David Dilks, ed., *The Diaries of Sir Alexander Cadogan* (New York, 1972), p. 719.

the Prime Minister about trusteeship. The Foreign Office had sent the minute of 22nd February to Churchill without, in Poynton's words, 'consulting or informing the Colonial Office'. When Poynton learned of this it came as a 'revelation'. He wrote about 'embarrassing developments'.[3] Not least, he noted, the Prime Minister had 'returned to the charge' as a result of the Foreign Office minute. Assured that nothing important had been sacrificed, Churchill wanted to make this clear to Parliament (and thereby to the Americans and the entire world). He asked Eden what he should say. The Foreign Office now had to turn to the Colonial Office for help. The previous failures to consult them hardly increased the Colonial Office officials' love for the Foreign Office. But collaboration came easily. No one wanted a Churchillian proclamation on colonial trusteeship. If the Prime Minister early in the war had stated that there were unequivocal British pledges about self-determination in regard to the Atlantic Charter, what might he say now? So urgent did the Colonial Secretary regard the matter that he considered it during tea on a Saturday afternoon. Stanley combined with Eden cogently to prevent the Prime Minister from erupting publicly on the subject. Churchill remained silent. At least Stanley and Eden had prevented another 'we mean to hold our own' type speech.[4]

In rendering account to Stanley about Yalta, Eden adopted a nonchalant line in the extreme. Disingenuously, and with a good deal of rhetorical dexterity, the Foreign Secretary attempted to convince the Colonial Secretary, as he had the Prime Minister, that nothing had been yielded to the Americans. Stripped of verbosity (or, to repeat Cadogan's phrase, 'warm and woolly words') Eden argued simply that the British could not be committed to 'territorial trusteeship' because no one knew what it meant. It was a clever tactic. It diverted the argument from what had actually happened at Yalta to rather academic discussion about the meaning of trusteeship. Eden even told Stanley that, since the Americans themselves had no

---

[3] See Poynton's minutes of 24 Feb. 1945, CO 968/161/14814/11; the blunder was that of Gladwyn Jebb, who prepared the minute for Churchill. See his minute of 24 Feb. 1945, FO 371/50807. 'Mr. Jebb was very apologetic', Poynton wrote; but the C.O. was hardly appeased.

[4] See minutes and memoranda in CO 968/161/14814/11; FO 371/50807; PREM 4/31/4.

precise idea about trusteeship, there was nothing to prevent the British from carrying on with their original plan of abolishing it. This specious reasoning was greeted with incredulity even within the Foreign Office.[5] Stanley saw through it immediately. Whatever the meaning of trusteeship, the British were now committed to it. He resolved to get a clear-cut explanation from Eden by convening the Armistice and Post-War Committee. 'No doubt the Foreign Secretary can say', he wrote to the members of the committee about the Yalta accord, 'whether its effect is to commit us to the continuation of the Mandates system, or . . . whether it is still open to us to advocate the abolition of the Mandates . . .'[6]

At the meeting of the Armistice and Post-War Committee on the 5th of March, Stanley came bluntly to the point. Did or did not the Yalta protocol bar the British from raising a fundamental question? Could they still propose to abolish the mandates system? 'He hoped that the Foreign Secretary would be able to say what interpretation should be attached to the Protocol.' One might have thought that such an unequivocal phrasing of the proposition might have forced Eden to acknowledge that the British at Yalta had committed themselves in principle to trusteeship, which in effect meant the continuation of the mandates system in modified form. Instead Eden attempted to argue the opposite. He came armed with a legal opinion which gave force to the point that not even lawyers, still less the Americans, knew the meaning of trusteeship. Then in an audacious move he implied that the Prime Minister might have made a political deal at Yalta that might determine the British commitment. Here is Eden's response to Stanley's direct challenge.

MR. EDEN said that a great deal depended upon what the Americans meant by the words 'Territorial Trusteeship'. They had been constantly asked to explain what they meant, but had so far not made any reply. One would probably be safe in surmising that they felt the need for some system which would enable them to take control and fortify the Japanese islands in the Pacific without incorporating them in United States territory, and thus without running counter to public opinion in the United States.

[5] See Jebb's minute of 24 Feb. 1945, FO 371/50807.
[6] Memorandum by Stanley, A.P.W. (45) 24, 27 Feb. 1945, CAB 87/69.

His own personal view was that it was still open to us to argue the case for the abolition of the Mandate system. The Legal Adviser for the Foreign Office had given the opinion that the wording of the Protocol could not be strictly interpreted as debarring us from doing so. It would be necessary, however, to get the Prime Minister's confirmation that nothing had passed in discussion which would make this impossible.[7]

The number of false hares released by this statement is remarkable. As the committee members chased them down, Eden himself wriggled free from any blame that might have been attached to him for carelessly yielding vital points to the Americans.

Stanley, for one, saw that the Yalta accord had transformed the situation. The British had accepted the premise of international trusteeship. He pointed out that it would be absurd to argue that they themselves did not understand its meaning.

COLONEL STANLEY thought that it would be very difficult to go ahead on the old basis in view of the Protocol. We could hardly argue that we did not know what territorial trusteeship meant, as if we did, it would be open to the Americans to inquire why in that case we had signed the Yalta Protocol. He was inclined to think that the Americans meant by territorial trusteeship something on the lines of the old Mandate system, but modified to make supervision more strict.[8]

A little later Stanley further clarified what the Americans meant by trusteeship: 'there was no doubt that the Americans intended to convey supervision. In conversation they frequently used the word "accountability".' He emphasized that they were now committed to an international agreement. It would be bad tactics, he said, to lay themselves 'open to a charge of breach of faith in the light of our signature at Yalta'. Ernest Bevin supported Stanley on this point and expressed the consensus of the committee. There could be little doubt, Bevin said, 'that the Yalta Protocol committed us to a continuance of some kind of Mandate system, and that a frontal attack on the latter was thus ruled out'.

Stanley also emphasized that the attitude of the Dominions no less than the Yalta agreement had a bearing on British

---

[7] A.P.W. (45) 5th Meeting, 5 Mar. 1945, CAB 87/68.   [8] Ibid.

political strategy. Lord Cranborne pointed out that until the Dominions made clear their reaction to the Yalta agreement Britain could hardly approach the United States again about the meaning of trusteeship (as Eden apparently wanted to do). So far the Dominions did not even know what had transpired in this regard. It was agreed to send them the secret protocol. With remarkable foresight Cranborne gave a preview of the difficulties of the San Francisco Conference. He stated:

> The Dominions themselves were not at one. Australia and New Zealand favoured the Mandate system, whereas South Africa was violently opposed to it. Canada would support anything that suited the Americans.[9]

As if the problem were not sufficiently complicated, Eden had suggested that the Prime Minister might have made a political bargain at Yalta in a way that would prejudice British action on trusteeship. This was an extremely clever move on Eden's part. He simply passed the responsibility on to the Prime Minister, who he knew would absolutely minimize the concessions made at Yalta. Attlee, writing on behalf of the committee, asked Churchill the meaning of the Yalta accord in this regard. 'Does it commit us to the continuation of a Mandate system?'[10]

When he received Attlee's minute, Churchill learned that Eden 'felt . . . that an authoritative interpretation of the extent to which we are committed should be sought from you'.[11] Churchill of course was blameless in the business of giving way to the Americans. He could protest innocently. Thanks to Eden he now had the chance to make clear his views. He weighed his words carefully. Just as he had found an acceptable meaning to the self-determination clause in the Atlantic Charter, so he now ingeniously made the best of an objectionable part of the Yalta protocol.

> The expression 'Mandate system' was only used at Yalta to limit territories which would come within the scope of discussions affecting 'territorial trusteeship'. This is necessary in view of the disappearance of the old League of Nations on whose authority the mandates were held.[12]

---

9 Ibid.   10 Ibid. Attlee to Churchill, 5 Mar. 1945, PREM 4/31/4.
11 Ibid.   12 Minute by Churchill, 10 Mar. 1945, PREM 4/31/4.

So far Churchill had stated facts with which almost anyone would agree. He now included a sentence that the Americans, at least, would have considered as a breach of faith. The colonial section of the Yalta accord, Churchill wrote, '*in no way governs any arrangement that may be made for the future*'.[13] Since the whole purpose, from the American side anyway, was to replace the mandates by a trusteeship system, this was a highly debatable contention.

Churchill now was merely following Eden's lead. Accordingly, the whole question of the mandates remained open.

We are certainly not committed to the maintenance of the mandate system; but there is no question of subjecting any non-mandated British territories to any form of territorial trusteeship unless we choose to do so of our own accord. I should myself oppose such a departure which might well be pressed upon nations like Britain, France, Holland and Belgium, who have great colonial possessions, by the United States, Russia and China who have none.[14]

Eden and Stanley were probably relieved that Churchill had not voiced these sentiments in Parliament. Such a speech would have raised questions about the motives and good faith of the British Empire. For Eden, things could not have turned out better: he had been able to appease the Americans, and Churchill had defended the colonial section of the Yalta protocol, but not publicly. Stanley at least had the assurance that the position was stronger than one might have assumed from a straightforward reading of the protocol. But he also saw that there was considerable wishful thinking on Churchill's part. The Americans obviously would not interpret the agreement in the same way. While Churchill continued inflexibly to defend the Empire by pure Tory standards (or, in the eyes of his critics, reactionary standards), Stanley now began an orderly retreat.

Unlike Eden, Stanley could not be content with facile arguments to the effect that the Americans did not know what they were talking about, or that the matter should not be taken seriously. To the Colonial Secretary the Yalta accord came as a climax of other important developments. He now fully apprehended that any move to adjust the mandates would

[13] Minute by Churchill, 10 Mar. 1945, PREM 4/31/4, italics added.
[14] Ibid.

be fraught with difficulties in international law. He perceived the violent clash of opinion between the Dominions. His talks in Washington had led him to the opposite conclusion from Eden's: far from having glib ideas on the subject, trusteeship appeared to be one matter to which the Americans had given sustained and serious thought. Above all, events seemed to be moving much more rapidly than he had anticipated. Unless the British moved quickly, they might be caught off guard on the colonial question at San Francisco as they had at Yalta. In March 1945 the Colonial Secretary therefore made a searching reappraisal. It brought about a wrenching readjustment in the direction of British colonial policy in its international dimension.

Churchill had stated categorically that nothing decided at Yalta should prevent the British from carrying out their own colonial plans. It was therefore on other grounds, not those of Yalta, that Stanley decided that the time was not ripe for a forward policy. This was a weighty decision. The deliberations of the Colonial Office in 1944 had led to the systematic plan of the Poynton–Robinson project whereby the British would not only seize the initiative in international colonial affairs but would also provide an overall coherence to post-war British colonial policy. 'The Colonial Office memorandum . . . was the product of a long and careful examination', Stanley wrote in a paper laying his views before the War Cabinet.[15] 'I thought then, and I still think, that it represents the best policy for our Colonial Empire.' International collaboration would be achieved through regional commissions, in Africa, in South-East Asia, and in other parts of the world. Stanley now concluded that this grand scheme could not be realized, at least at the present time. In his judgement the various issues had all become hopelessly entangled with the future of the mandates. He again stressed the negative reaction he had experienced in Washington. He recounted how he had outlined some of the main points of the Colonial Office project to the Americans.

The reception was most disappointing. No real attempt was made to appreciate its effects upon Colonial administration as a whole, but it [the Poynton–Robinson project] was viewed entirely in relation to the occupation by the United States after the war of the

[15] Memorandum by Stanley, 'International Aspects of Colonial Policy', A.P.W (45) 38, 19 Mar. 1945, CAB 87/69; CO 968/161/14814/11, PREM 4/31/4.

Japanese islands. For this purpose, the one thing that matters is that the United States, while occupying the islands, should not appear to have a theoretical sovereignty over them (for that would be Imperialism).[16]

Any attempt to replace the mandates system by regional commissions would be regarded as British 'Imperialism'.

This view was shared even by Australia and New Zealand, and to some extent by Canada. South Africa was the only Dominion from whom the British could now expect support. It was impossible to predict the reaction of the other colonial powers, but one thing was now certain that had not been clear a few months earlier. Instead of leisurely and restricted discussion of regional commissions with the Dominions and the United States, colonial problems would now be debated at San Francisco. As a result of the Yalta protocol, the future of the mandates would appear on the agenda. The British plan to liquidate the mandates had involved the substitution of regional commissions that would touch all of the Colonial Empire. Here was one of the main reasons for shelving the Poynton–Robinson project. 'If we had to do that at San Francisco,' Stanley wrote about a general debate on colonial problems at the conference, *'it would mean throwing the whole Colonial Empire open to discussion by this motley assembly, a procedure which I should regard as hazardous in the extreme.'*[17] Aversion to the 'motley assembly'—where British colonial rule might be criticized—provides one of the key reasons why the Colonial Office proposals were, in the phrase of Gladwyn Jebb of the Foreign Office, 'still-born'.[18]

The alternative to the British program was to accept a modified version of the mandates. If this course were adopted, the British would, in Stanley's words, 'insist on their revision in order to eliminate their worst features'. This possibility caused the Colonial Secretary to re-examine the Colonial Office's bugbear of international control, which turned out to be less horrendous than commonly assumed. The chief objection of the Colonial Office to the mandates system was not, as many people thought, the amount of supervision. According to Stanley, international supervision 'on the whole did little harm, although some people may question whether it did much good'.

[16] Ibid.   [17] Ibid., italics added.
[18] Minute by Jebb, 24 Feb. 1945, FO 371/50807.

The real complaint of the Colonial Office was the sense of impermanence. This could not be resolved short of changes in international title, which would certainly raise the cry of British 'Imperialism'. There was no alternative but to live with indeterminate sovereignty. Other objectionable features of the mandates system might be corrected. Representatives serving on the international body would represent their governments and would not be chosen for their individual qualifications (the meticulous criticism of Lord Lugard still needled the official mind). Among other points, the defence prohibitions of the mandates now seemed obsolete. The territories should have the right to defend themselves. Above all, the open-door economic provisions would have to be abolished and the territories left free to adjust their own economic policies. Another caveat should be mentioned because the issue later became so important in the post-war years. If the British were clear on any one point, it was that there should be no rights of visitation by an international authority. Here they sensed a danger which proved to be real. On a last point they were led astray. The Yalta protocol included a passage saying that territories might 'voluntarily' be placed under trusteeship. The Colonial Office feared that the United States might immediately place *all* of her colonial possessions under international trusteeship and thereby establish a dangerous precedent. 'We shall be continually under pressure from some elements in the United States', Stanley wrote, 'to take advantage of this proposal to bring the whole of our Colonial administration under international review.'[19] This was a false danger. After the war, no one, not even the Americans, volunteered to place territories under trusteeship that had not been mandates or ex-enemy colonies.

Romanticists of the British colonial era might pause to wonder about the possible consequences of the grand colonial design if it had been implemented in 1945. It might have contributed to sounder regional development in places such as Africa, and might have prevented some of the extreme

---

[19] Memorandum by Stanley, 19 Mar. 1945. For a full appraisal of the mandates system at this juncture, see memorandum by Kenneth Robinson, 9 Mar. 1945, CO 968/161/14814. For approval of Stanley's views by the War Cabinet, see W.M. (45) 38th Conclusions, 3 Apr. 1945, CAB 65/50.

fragmentation of the independence era. But Stanley's decision to hold the line rather than launch a forward policy has stood the test of time as a realistic action. A British effort to liquidate the mandates system in 1945 by replacing it with regional commissions would almost certainly have been interpreted as 'imperialism', especially in American circles. As events transpired, the British found that they would do well to prevent the Americans from transforming the mandates system into a strong international authority, with rights of inspection as only one among many objectionable features. The fear of a 'motley assembly' interfering in the affairs of the British Empire became increasingly a real one. In the months following Yalta, from time to time it appeared to the British that in the struggle within the American government the military might triumph over the State Department, thus undermining the trusteeship scheme. On the whole, however, the news that reached London hardly reassured the British about modest American intentions. One report to the Foreign Office from the Embassy in Washington in late March said that the State Department intended to plunge into a full-scale campaign to 'tighten up' the trusteeship proposals. Instead of merely giving a questionnaire to the colonial regimes, for example, the international authority would send out technical representatives, doctors, sanitary experts, economists, and social analysts. They themselves would investigate conditions in the colonies. Churchill grumbled suspiciously in regard to this possibility: 'I do not like it. It goes beyond what I was assured at Yalta.'[20]

[20] Halifax to Eden, No. 162 tel., 23 Mar. 1945, FO 371/50807; minute by Churchill, 29 Mar. 1945, ibid.

31

THE AFTERMATH OF YALTA
WASHINGTON

IN Washington the reaction to the colonial section of the Yalta protocol quickly developed into a struggle, to use the description of Secretary of State Edward R. Stettinius, between the 'Hottentots and Crusaders' of the State Department and the 'hard boiled realists' of the Navy and War Departments.[1] In this bureaucratic contest the Department of the Interior lined up with the State Department and, thanks to Abe Fortas (then an Under Secretary in that Department and later a Supreme Court Justice), contributed to the legal and moral dimension of the controversy. It is indeed the legalistic flavour of morality that distinguishes the American debate from the British. In London the discussions were remarkable for straightforward concern with British power and the integrity of the British Empire. In ministerial circles Stanley, Eden, and Cranborne defended the interests of their departments and combined, as they had done since the beginning of the war, to resolve their differences in committee. British Ministers drew strength from their civil servants, who had long-standing expertise in such areas as Africa and Asia.

By contrast many of the American personalities involved in the trusteeship controversy had legal or military background. Though there were a few civil servants such as Benjamin Gerig whose careers were dedicated to such causes as international organization or dependent peoples, most had only an ephemeral interest in trusteeship. The debate was none the less just as intense as in British circles. The bases of decision constantly shifted, both within and between governmental agencies. It is noteworthy that only in the last months of the war did the Secretaries of State, War, and Navy actually meet together to attempt to shape a common policy. Whereas in

---

[1] As related in Halifax to Eden, No. 2233, 3 Apr. 1945, copy in CO 968/161/14414/11.

London Churchill participated in the debates as first minister among equals, in Washington Roosevelt remained aloof. The key to the struggle was to catch the President's ear. It is a measure of Roosevelt's personality as well as the American political system of the time that the warring factions would accept his decision as final. The President's death on the 12th of April 1945—at the very time the trusteeship controversy reached its peak—transformed the situation and caused the Secretaries of State, War, and Navy to arrange their own compromise. Until then it was open bureaucratic warfare.

The ambiguity (or lack of clarity) in Roosevelt's views enabled both civil and military authorities to argue that they represented the President's 'true' position. Shortly before and after the Yalta conference, the confrontation occurred in a newly created inter-departmental Committee on Dependent Areas.[2] The Departments established this body of high ranking officials in part to settle the unfinished business of a complicated problem, and perhaps also to prevent one bureaucratic group from getting the upper hand. The military representatives were Admiral Willson and Generals Embick and Fairchild of the Joint Chiefs Strategic Survey Committee. Fortas sat on the committee for Interior. State Department members included Nelson Rockefeller (at this time Assistant Secretary) and authorities on the trusteeship question such as Taussig and Gerig. Pasvolsky chaired the group.

The committee first met on the 2nd of February 1945, the day before the beginning of the Yalta conference.[3] Their deliberations thus had no influence at all on the Yalta proceedings.

[2] The formal title was 'Committee on Dependent Area Aspects of International Organization', not to be confused with the State Department's Dependent Areas Committee. The minutes of this committee are in USSD NF Box 189. For other important documents see JCS CCS092 (7-27-44), which includes proceedings of the State–War–Navy Coordinating Committee, a body that acted as a clearing committee of the Departments but did not assume a prominent role in trusteeship affairs. For its formal function in this regard see e.g. *Foreign Relations, 1945: United Nations*, pp. 93–5. On these committees and the trusteeship question in 1945, see Notter, *Postwar Foreign Policy Preparation*, pp. 387–90; and Russell, *United Nations Charter*, ch. 23.

[3] The State Department initiated the correspondence leading to the establishment of the committee on 30 Dec. 1944. For the reaction of the War and Navy Departments, see JCS CCS092 (7-27-44). Cf. Russell, *United Nations Charter*, p. 573. The members are listed in Notter, *Postwar Foreign Policy Preparation*, pp. 387–8, which gives an accurate account of the committee's genesis.

But the minutes of the committee are of considerable interest for the meaning of Yalta; and they also reveal the workings of the American government at this particular time. Some of the committee members had never before been involved in trusteeship affairs. At the first meeting Rockefeller, for example, wanted to know 'what kind of real estate' they would be talking about. Embick stated flatly that the War Department opposed *any* discussion with foreign governments about dependent areas. Little progress had been made in resolving bureaucratic disagreement, or even in getting high officials to study the problem. Some of the initiates knew nothing about the scope of the trusteeship proposals. Rockefeller, again for example, asked whether Puerto Rico would be placed under trusteeship—a question that would have caused sardonic laughter in the Colonial Office. Pasvolsky replied negatively. Admiral Willson returned to Rockefeller's query about 'real estate'. The Navy, he said, for reasons of security happened to be very interested in this question, especially in regard to certain islands in the Pacific. Rockefeller's mind quickly linked the two concepts of 'real estate' and 'security'.

Mr. Rockefeller said that he did not see how trusteeship could be applied to any island on which we would have military bases. He did not see how it would be possible to maintain such bases if the members of any international organization body could wander about and discover their secrets. Admiral Willson commented that this was exactly the view of the Joint Chiefs of Staff, which felt that special provision had to be made for islands in which we had special security interests.[4]

Thus there emerged the proposition that certain conditions should be attached to the fate of the Japanese mandated islands. This was by no means a new idea. It was implicit in security discussions within the government since early in the war, and in the public debates on the subject.[5] It was during the meetings of the inter-departmental Dependent Areas Committee in February 1945, however, that the concept of the 'strategic trust' emerged in the form that found its way into the United Nations Charter.

The Dependent Areas Committee met at weekly sessions that

[4] D Minutes 1, 2 Feb. 1945, USSD NF Box 189.
[5] See, e.g., Huntington Gilchrist, 'The Japanese Islands: Annexation or Trusteeship?', *Foreign Affairs* 22.4 (July 1944).

lasted up to three hours. The verbatim transcripts run up to thirty single-spaced typewritten foolscap or legal-sized pages. It is impossible here to relate much more than some of the high points of the proceedings. To establish clearly the military and civilian sides of the argument, it is perhaps helpful to isolate the remarks of the two most lucid and forceful spokesmen on the respective sides, Admiral Willson and Abe Fortas.

Admiral Willson had studied the President's memoranda on the mandated islands to the Joint Chiefs. He rightly believed that Roosevelt had no intention of weakening the American strategic position in the Pacific. The phrases 'exclusive control', 'all the attributes of sovereignty', and 'the substance of sovereignty but not sovereignty itself' recurred in the Admiral's comments to the committee. He took a distinctly unsentimental attitude towards the islanders. 'Did we have any reason to believe', he asked, 'that international standards for the administration of native peoples would be any higher than the standards which the United States maintained in its own territories?'[6] Since everyone agreed that the answer was 'no', Willson failed to see the force of the argument of 'international trusteeship'. In questions of native welfare as in defence, he believed that Americans should look after their own interests first. At one point he referred sarcastically to the 'international welfare boys' at the State Department. He contemptuously dismissed 'the church vote'.[7] The inhabitants of the islands were, after all, 'pretty small potatoes', numbering only 103,000 (a figure his colleague General Embick, by omitting the Japanese, reduced to 50,000 natives, which gave greater force to the argument).[8] In territorial extent, the islands amounted to only 830 square

[6] D Minutes 2, 8 Feb. 1945, USSD NF Box 189. For comment on the Navy's attitude at this time see Raymond Dennet, 'United States Navy and Dependent Areas', *Far Eastern Survey* xiv. 8 (April 1945).

[7] Ibid. On this point General Embick expanded: 'he did not want to appear irreligious but that he did want to take exception to some of the things that these church groups had been doing for the past thirty years. The church people had been utterly indifferent to our national defense. They had got us into the Kellogg Pact and they had reduced our army to zero. He had no sympathy with these religious organizations which hadn't learned anything despite all their mistakes in the past which are costing us such heavy loss of lives today.' In his opinion, General Embick concluded, 'they were the most meddlesome people in the world.'

[8] Ibid. Other members of the committee quickly pointed out the disadvantages of this argument—e.g. Charles P. Taft stated that '50,000 people were all that you needed to get the Church groups and the missionaries against you'.

miles (though they extended over an immense area of the tropical North Pacific). Willson jokingly 'wondered whether the President couldn't say that each country was entitled to annex 830 square miles only!' Point by point he met the civilians on their own ground. He doggedly followed the technical details and made persistent challenges on grounds of international law and common sense. Before Yalta he proposed to solve the problem of the strategic islands in the Pacific by a ninety-nine-year lease. Having made progress in convincing the committee members of the virtue of this solution, Willson on the 13th of February learned of the terms of the Yalta agreement as Pasvolsky read a communication from the Crimea. It ruled out the possibility of a ninety-nine-year lease. The islands of the Pacific along with the other mandates would be held under international trusteeship. Willson remarked that the committee was 'just about back where it had started from'.[9]

The Admiral now worked to ensure that at least there would be *two different types* of trust territories—strategic and non-strategic. For the American strategic territory in the Pacific he demanded absolutely no restriction on military requirements. He failed to see why this should pose any difficulty. After all, he said, 'the American public had already swallowed the partition of Poland and the suppression of states on the Baltic Sea'.[10] In Willson's view the real trouble was sitting in committee debating 'ands' and 'buts' and then having American representatives arrive at conferences 'and agree to everything that the Russians want'.[11] If it were absolutely necessary that the mandated islands be placed under a trusteeship regime, then they should be designated a 'strategic territory' and *not* a 'trust territory', as the State Department would have it. The distinction appeared to be crucial to the members of the committee. Regardless of the trusteeship system, the islands might be held either as a 'strategic territory' that would minimally satisfy the military authorities, and consequently would be denounced abroad as a sham, or as a 'trust territory' which would appear to compromise American security.

These issues seemed momentous in 1945. The United States was fighting the war against Japan for security in the Pacific.

[9] D Minutes 3, 13 Feb. 1945, ibid.   [10] D Minutes 4, 22 Feb. 1945, ibid.
[11] D Minutes 5, 27 Feb. 1945, ibid.

At the same time there was a magnificent opportunity for American leadership on the political and moral issue of dependent peoples. It was Abe Fortas who played the key part in attempting to reconcile the two parties. Since he represented the Department of the Interior, his stand is also significant as revealing the American attitude towards dependent peoples under the jurisdiction of the United States. He saw the problem of the Pacific islands as similar to that of the Virgin Islands. There was little chance that either group of islands would ever become even autonomous. He wanted to see the same standards of administration applied to one region as to the other. For that reason, in part, he welcomed the trusteeship proposals as an extension of benevolent American rule. He did not fear visiting missions of an international organization, provided they would not be 'inquisitional'. They would probably be less embarrassing than the Congressional committees that already plagued the Interior Department.[12] At the same time he responded entirely sympathetically to the demands of the Joint Chiefs for military security. Fortas therefore tried to find middle ground between the State Department and military positions. He found Admiral Willson and his two colleagues unyielding. Every time he attempted a compromise, Fortas lamented, the representatives of the Joint Chiefs 'jumped all over his poor lily-white body!'[13] He did not understand why they should do this since he was attempting to come to their aid. His solution was to accept the demands of the military representatives but to make them, in his phrase, more '*palatable*' to the world at large by reconciling them to the humane principles of trusteeship.

Fortas's keen legal mind saw the heart of the difficulty as the creation of two different types of control. One would be a genuine trusteeship, the other a variant—in fact a unique

---

[12] Fortas did object to the right of petition. 'Receiving petitions would be incompatible with the idea of colonial status and would result in a hopeless mess. It was bad enough now for the people of our territories to be able to submit petitions to Congress.' (D Minutes 1, 2 Feb. 1945, ibid.) On the question of visiting missions, Ralph Bunche later stated that the colonial powers in Africa would resist this innovation and that the consequences would have to be made clear. 'The Belgians, for example, would not want any investigation in Ruanda-Urundi, if they could help it. But you would be perfectly sure that they would accept this provision if they had to in order to keep Ruanda-Urundi.' (D Minutes 6, 2 Mar. 1945, ibid.)   [13] D Minutes 6, 2 Mar. 1945, ibid.

exception—because of its military character. 'The plain fact', Fortas stated, was that their trusteeship scheme 'did not place strategic areas under any real trusteeship system.' The committee members would provide 'an elastic escape clause' whereby the American military could do anything they wanted. How could this be justified, or, to repeat Fortas's phrase, made more palatable to the American public? He provided a simple argument. It was the same argument that ran through the debates on the defence of the British Empire since the late nineteenth century. The case had to be made, not on grounds of *national* security, but on grounds of *world* security. 'There was', according to Fortas, 'an important basic principle involved here. When we take over the Marianas and fortify them we are doing so not only on the basis of our own right to do so but as part of our obligation to the security of the world.'

Admiral Willson agreed with the argument of world security. 'The more powerful the United States is,' he stated, 'the better off the [international] organization will be.'[14] The *only* problem, the Admiral stated, was that it would be necessary to know whether a particular territory would be a strategic territory. The Navy demanded an absolute distinction between 'closed' areas and 'open' areas. The closed areas would be exempt from international agreements. The State Department wanted assurance that the trusteeship welfare provisions would apply to the peoples of the closed as well as open areas. The compromise proposed by Fortas amounted to at least keeping the door open for 'real trusteeship' even in closed areas. Here they came to loggerheads. On the 2nd of March Fortas made this plea.

[T]he Government would be missing a bet if it failed to take a clear-cut stand on this issue. It was perfectly obvious that strategic areas were being given a special status that was in no way a trust status and that special reservations were being made. . . . These reservations were being made in the interest of world security rather than of our own security . . . what was good for us was good for the world.

It was terribly important to say to people . . . that these strategic areas were being set up in a circumscribed way because they were to be operated in the interest of world security and for the security

[14] D Minutes 5, 27 Feb. 1945, ibid.

of everyone. Only on this ground could these reservations be justified.[15]

Moreover, the administering authority even of strategic areas should guarantee the humane principle of trusteeship. To make this point absolutely clear, Fortas insisted on the phrase 'strategic *trust* territory'. Admiral Willson refused to give way. He argued that the word 'trust' would detract from the military and strategic nature of the territory. *All* the strategic territory should be a *closed area*. When asked whether the concept of the 'strategic trust' would be unacceptable to the Joint Chiefs, the Admiral replied 'yes' and said that it would be 'even more unacceptable to the Secretary of War and the Secretary of the Navy'.[16]

At least the inter-departmental Committee on Dependent Areas clarified the central problem. In Fortas's clear-cut words, this was the *status* of a strategic territory *within* a trusteeship system. No doubt all of the many hours of discussion of this point were eventually helpful in the technical drafting of the trusteeship agreements. In March 1945 however it appeared that this dedicated labour would be fruitless. The Secretaries of War and Navy, Henry L. Stimson and James Forrestal, rebelled against the idea of trusteeship itself. Stimson's first major blast had in fact occurred shortly before Yalta. In a well-known memorandum to the Secretary of State, he developed what might be called the Stimson doctrine of 'strategic outposts'. His logic and that of Admiral Willson were identical, but Stimson's analysis contained a historical dimension unusual in official American writing. He discussed the League of Nations' lack of a 'foundation of security' and concluded that the basis of American security must be laid before entering into the 'needless mazes' of international trusteeship. It would be

---

[15] D Minutes 6, 2 Mar. 1945, ibid.

[16] Ibid.; and the minutes of 27 Feb., especially for his argument about the strategic trust. Willson objected specifically to a commitment to fulfil the 'trust'. The wording of the technical point on which they reached an impasse was: 'in the case of strategic areas, a statement of the additional rights and responsibilities which the administering authority should assume in exercising its trust in the interest of security'. Other more general points of disagreement included the Trusteeship Council of the General Assembly versus the Security Council as the body responsible for strategic areas. The military representatives argued for the Security Council in order to have veto power. For a discussion of these and other points, see Russell, *United Nations Charter*, pp. 576–81.

a mistake, Stimson wrote, to include the Japanese islands in a trusteeship system. Here is Stimson's classic formulation of the problem:

Acquisition of them [the Japanese mandated islands] by the United States does not represent an attempt at colonization or exploitation. Instead it is merely the acquisition by the United States of the necessary bases for the defense of the security of the Pacific for the future world.

To serve such a purpose they must belong to the United States with absolute power to rule and fortify them. They are not colonies; they are outposts, and their acquisition is appropriate under the general doctrine of self-defense by the power which guarantees the safety of that area of the world.[17]

With that judgement the Secretary of the Navy whole-heartedly concurred.[18] As Stimson recorded in his diary—with words that proved true for the entire episode—'Jim Forrestal proved to be a very vigorous supporter of my views.'[19]

Stimson's admonition left no lasting impression on Stettinius. The Secretaries of War and Navy had no direct influence on the Yalta trusteeship proceedings. Stimson warily noted these developments and, after the return of the Crimean delegation, on the 3rd of March raised the trusteeship issue with the President himself. He pointed out to Roosevelt that the situation in regard to the mandated territories differed entirely from the time of the First World War. Now there existed 'no population to be imperialized' and the islands should be disposed of in accordance with the paramount security interests of the United States. Stimson easily got Roosevelt to follow the argument.

He [Roosevelt] evidently had the thing in his mind, but I took the occasion to state it as clearly as I could to him again, and *he agreed with me*. I told him that the important thing now was that when they form the categories of the kinds of trusteeship in the discussions prior to and at San Francisco they should put the

---

[17] Stimson Diary, 23 Jan. 1945, Stimson Papers; *Foreign Relations: Yalta*, pp. 78–81. For Stimson's general views see Henry L. Stimson and McGeorge Bundy, *On Active Service in Peace and War* (New York, 1947), pp. 599–605.
[18] For Forrestal's views see Walter Millis, ed., *The Forrestal Diaries* (New York, 1951). An indication of Forrestal's initial awareness of the mandates question occurs in his diary entry of 7 July 1944 when he noted 'that it seems to me a *sine qua non* of any postwar arrangements that there should be no debate as to who ran the Mandated Islands'. Forrestal Diary, Forrestal Papers; Millis, *Forrestal Diaries*, p. 8.   [19] Stimson Diary, 22 Jan. 1945.

Pacific islands in an entirely different category from colonies. *He agreed.*[20]

Roosevelt had a marvellous ability to assure people that he sympathized with their views. In this case he simply did not go on to say to Stimson that his own idea of international trusteeship did not contradict that of national security. A few days later at a Cabinet meeting on the 9th of March, Roosevelt again displayed a gift not only of being agreeable but also for solving difficult political problems and reconciling opposite parties.[21] He stated that the sovereignty of the Pacific islands would be vested in the United Nations. He thus disposed of the potentially embarrassing issue of direct annexation. He then said that the United States would be requested by the United Nations to exercise 'complete trusteeship'. He thus assured the State Department. He then added that this trusteeship would be for the purpose of 'world security' (and incidentally made the same point as Abe Fortas was making before the inter-departmental committee, that the case should be argued on grounds of world and not national security). He thus attempted to pacify the War and Navy Departments. With a few words Roosevelt, on his own, expressed the consensus of hours and hours of committee work. However, his comments were, as usual, general and imprecise. Different people could interpret the President's remarks in various ways, depending in part on his degree of candour.

To say that Roosevelt was imprecise is by no means to say that he did not know what he wanted. Fortunately there is a frank record of his ideas on the colonial question little less than a month before his death. On the 15th of March Roosevelt talked at length with Charles Taussig. Of all of his advisers, it was Taussig with whom Roosevelt confided most candidly about the politics of his trusteeship schemes. The record of the conversation is especially significant in that it is the last full account of Roosevelt's views on the subject. Taussig related the developments in the inter-departmental Dependent Areas Committee (which incidentally is of interest for students of the American bureaucracy because it indicates a particular way in which committee work may have been significant after all).

[20] Stimson Diary, 3 Mar. 1945, italics added.
[21] See *Forrestal Diaries*, p. 33.

Only in the previous week had the committee reached dead-lock. Taussig posed the question of the 'strategic trust' area and related how the military representatives insisted that *all* the strategic territory should be a closed area. Roosevelt responded by saying that he favoured the *two* categories of open and closed areas, and that the open areas 'should be subject to inter-national agreements'. The President thus desired more than lip-service to the ideal of international trusteeship in the Pacific. Not losing sight of American security, Roosevelt also said 'that if the military wanted, at a later date due to change in strategy, to make all or part of the open area a closed area, it should be provided that this could be done with the approval of the Security Council'.

There followed an exchange about the ambitions of the United States Navy in which Roosevelt revealed, as he had previously, a scepticism about the Navy's administration of dependent peoples.

The President then asked me [Taussig], 'What is the Navy's attitude in regard to [these Pacific] territories? Are they trying to grab everything?' I replied that they did not seem to have much confidence in civilian controls. The President then asked me how I accounted for their attitude.

I said that I thought that the military had no confidence in the proposed United Nations Organization. The President replied that he thought that was so.[22]

Taussig related Admiral Willson's crack about 'the inter-national welfare boys' at the State Department, and then recorded Roosevelt as saying 'that neither the Army nor the Navy had any business administering the civilian government of territories; that they had no competence to do this'.[23] Roosevelt may have had superficial ideas about the 'natives' of the non-western world, but at least according to his own lights he proved himself to be a staunch guardian.

The conversation between Roosevelt and Taussig expanded into larger subjects. The President recounted various stories, though Taussig managed to prevent him repeating the one about Churchill and Hong Kong. His repertoire now included an encounter with King Ibn Saud of Arabia, whom he had met

[22] Memorandum by Taussig, 15 Mar. 1945, Taussig Papers; *Foreign Relations: United Nations*, pp. 121–4. [23] Ibid.

on his return from Yalta. Roosevelt had told him that Arabia needed irrigation projects. More seriously, at least for the purpose of international history, there recurred in Roosevelt's monologue the theme of the necessity of the white races of the world accommodating the yellow or brown races.

The President said he was concerned about the brown people in the East. He said that there are 1,100,000,000 brown people. In many Eastern countries, they are ruled by a handful of whites and they resent it. Our goal must be to help them achieve independence —1,100,000,000 potential enemies are dangerous. He said he included the 450,000,000 Chinese in that. He then added, Churchill doesn't understand this.[24]

The question of the future of the peoples of Asia led specifically to the issue of the future of the French colonies. Here again the persistence of the President's ideas is remarkable, though on the question of Indo-China he now reluctantly granted that France might be restored as the colonial power.

He [Roosevelt] said ... he had not changed his ideas; that French Indo-China and New Caledonia should be taken from France and put under a trusteeship. The President hesitated a moment and then said—well if we can get the proper pledge from France to assume for herself the obligations of a trustee, then I would agree to France retaining these colonies with the proviso that independence was the ultimate goal.[25]

Roosevelt's words in regard to *independence* as the ultimate goal might be read as his last will and testament for dependent peoples.

I [Taussig] asked the President if he would settle for self-government. He said no. I asked him if he would settle for dominion status. He said no—it must be independence. He said that it is to be the policy and you can quote me in the State Department.[26]

---

[24] Ibid.   [25] Ibid.

[26] Ibid. In an annex to the memorandum marked 'Top Secret' and 'For Mr. Taussig's Files Only', Taussig related how he asked Roosevelt to include him in the San Francisco delegation. 'The President said that he wanted me to go to San Francisco, and that he felt I would be extremely useful in matters pertaining to the negotiations on colonial matters.' Taussig further recounted some bizarre anecdotes which are of interest in illuminating some of the by-ways of the colonial question during the war. For example, they discussed the problem of birth control in Puerto Rico, which had recently experienced the highest birth-rate in its history. Roosevelt jokingly said: ' "I guess the only solution is to use the methods

No one can say whether, if Roosevelt had lived, his trusteeship schemes might have altered such basic propositions as the nature of post-war American intervention in South-East Asia. It can be said that he persistently championed eventual *independence* of the colonies. For this Roosevelt has a fair claim for recognition as one of the great architects of the post-war world.

Just as in England the individual attitudes of Churchill, Eden, and Stanley played such an important part in the shaping of British international colonial policy, so in the United States the personalities of Roosevelt (with Stettinius as his subordinate) and Stimson left a distinctive imprint on American trusteeship policy. Roosevelt demonstrated an intuitive vigilance in keeping departmental policies in line with his own aims. It can be said in this particular case that he was more effective than Churchill in manipulating the bureaucracies. With Stettinius as Secretary, Roosevelt controlled the State Department, at least to the extent that any bureaucracy could be kept in check. In this the Secretary of War was certainly not oblivious to the Presidential weight behind trusteeship, despite Roosevelt's assurances about the islands. As his diary indicates, Stimson felt that unless he moved quickly, the War and Navy Departments would be faced with an accomplished fact of trusteeship in the Pacific.

Only two days before Taussig's conversation with Roosevelt, the American delegation to the San Francisco Conference convened on the 13th of March in a preliminary meeting in Washington. They approved of the policy of trusteeship as one of their basic projects.[27] The inter-departmental committee held its last meeting on the 15th.[28] Stimson began to give full

which Hitler used effectively." He [Roosevelt] said that it is all very simple and painless—you have people pass through a narrow passage and then there is the brrrrr of an electrical apparatus. They stay there for twenty seconds and from then on they are sterile.' They also discussed the 'race problem' in Panama. Roosevelt related 'that the Jamaicans in Panama were dangerous; that each Jamaican man slept with three women every week'. Not to be outmatched by Roosevelt in racy stories, Taussig 'told the President that I thought he did the Jamaicans an injustice; that sleeping with only three women in a week was a sign of impotence'.

[27] See *Foreign Relations: United Nations*, pp. 116–17.
[28] See ibid., pp. 135–8, for the committee draft of trusteeship arrangements, dated 17 Mar. 1945. The strongly worded section on the powers of the Trusteeship Council included these rights:

    a. to call for and examine reports from the administering authorities;

consideration to the problem on the 18th.[29] Since the committee worked within the frame of reference of Yalta (and thereby a positive action on trusteeship), it looked as though a giant machine had been set in motion which even the Secretaries of War and Navy might be powerless to stop. The military representatives on the inter-departmental committee had done their best to hold the line, and Stimson and Forrestal could at least expect a reasonable hearing on the issue of 'closed' and 'open' areas. What else could be done? Stimson's strategy was to play for time. He was convinced that he and Forrestal could build a persuasive case that trusteeship was a bad idea from the very beginning, at least in regard to the Pacific islands. To do so he first needed to prevent the discussion of trusteeship at San Francisco. He therefore set about persuading Stettinius that postponement of the entire issue was the wise course. And Stimson still held out hope for annexation.

The struggle against trusteeship at this juncture essentially was Stimson's. This is not to say that Forrestal did not have equally strong feelings or less interest. Forrestal supported Stimson to the hilt. Stimson himself emerged as the moving force in part because of his personality, intellect, and stature. As Sir John Simon had ruefully discovered during the Manchurian crisis, Stimson could match wits with any statesman of his time. As a former Secretary of State and now again Secretary of War (a position he had first held before the First World War), his voice carried unrivalled authority on matters of international security. He was a forceful personality. His colleagues regarded him as a gentleman and a man of honour. During the trusteeship crisis, Stimson managed to challenge Roosevelt's control of the issue and, following the President's

> b. to interrogate representatives of those authorities;
> c. to review periodically the financial position of each trust territory;
> d. to conduct periodic inspections in the trust territories.

The escape clause read: 'in the case of strategic areas, to such provisions in the respective trusteeship arrangements as may be required for security purposes . . .' This left open the entire question of the extent to which strategic areas would be bound by the general provisions of trusteeship. Since the military representatives had prevented the inclusion of a statement of the responsibilities binding the administering authority in a strategic area, the State Department took the view that only the President could resolve this point. See Gerig's memorandum of 12 Mar. 1945, USSD NF Box 186.

[29] See Stimson's Diary entry of 18 Mar. 1945.

death, took the lead in subordinating the rivalry of the departments to the higher interest of national unity.

Such high-minded purpose did not characterize all of the controversy. Stimson in fact was extremely irritated that Roosevelt had compromised American security in the Pacific. Forrestal noted on the 30th of March, after a meeting between the two of them and their aides, that Stimson expressed 'great concern' over the drift of talk about trusteeship. 'He [Stimson] said he was fearful that in the commendable effort to advance the idea of trusteeship we might be tempted into making quixotic gestures the net result of which might be that we would surrender the hardly won islands which we had taken in the Pacific to the principle of trusteeship whereas the British, Dutch and French would not.'[30] Stimson himself recorded in his diary, in summary of the new Stimson doctrine:

My point was that we had always stood for freedom and peace in the Pacific and we had waged this war to throw out an aggressor and to restore peace and freedom and everybody knew it; that these bases had been stolen by the aggressor who had used them to attack us and destroy our power; that we had fought this war with much cost of life and treasure to capture these bases and to free from the threat of aggression all of the peace-loving nations of the Pacific.[31]

Venting his anger against Roosevelt, Stimson continued:

The President has apparently devised this whole subject of trusteeship for the purpose of making a magnificent American gesture which will enable him to persuade the British to 'trustee' India and Hong Kong, the French to 'trustee' Indo-China, and the Dutch to 'trustee' the Netherlands [East Indies]. Each of these nations is now coming out and violently opposing any such idea, and the whole thing bids fair to make a tremendous row.[32]

Stimson had initially drafted a letter to Roosevelt expressing these protests. On reflection (and after a conversation with John J. McCloy, at this time Assistant Secretary of War) he did not send it. He thought that a letter would give the President a chance to retort that trusteeship was a *fait accompli*. Therefore Stimson now chose to attack the weakest party. He proposed to Forrestal that they should meet with Stettinius.

---

[30] Forrestal Diary, 30 Mar. 1945, Forrestal Papers; cf. *Forrestal Diaries*, p. 37.
[31] Stimson Diary, 30 Mar. 1945, Stimson Papers.   [32] Ibid.

The meeting occurred on the 2nd of April. Stimson made the various points in his new doctrine. The task turned out to be much easier than he had anticipated. 'Stettinius said he agreed absolutely with me and of course Forrestal, with whom I have gone over it before, backed me up.'[33] Stimson proposed that the three of them should combine to write a letter to the President advising postponement of the entire issue. James Dunn (Assistant Secretary of State and Chairman of the State–War–Navy Coordinating Committee), who accompanied Stettinius, pointed out that, if there was to be postponement, then it should be *complete* because otherwise piecemeal discussion of trusteeship would raise other issues. 'This having been already the view of the War and Navy Departments,' Forrestal recorded, 'there was immediate agreement.'[34] What a satisfactory outcome for Stimson! Discussion of trusteeship now would be postponed, and he would have the time to prepare the case for annexation.

Stimson's elation was short-lived. Within a matter of days Stettinius reneged. The explanation of his behaviour is less a question of weakness or incompetence than eagerness to please. Trusteeship proved to be a matter on which he could not please everyone, even with the best of will (which even his critics conceded to him). On the one hand he faced pressure from the Department to produce the report of the interdepartmental committee for review by the President. Stettinius probably had still not fully comprehended the strength of Roosevelt's feelings on the subject, though he would shortly learn. On the other hand he was persuaded by the powerful arguments of Stimson and Forrestal. On the 6th of April he reported to his staff committee the 'very serious difference of opinion' between the Departments.[35] He now hoped to stay neutral, letting the President make the final decision. About the same time Harold L. Ickes, Secretary of the Department of the Interior, wrote Stettinius a letter urging him 'steadfastly [to] hold the line' of the Interior-State position. It was the opposite of the advice Stimson and Forrestal had given him. Ickes enclosed a copy of a memorandum to the President (actually

---

[33] Stimson Diary, 2 Apr. 1945.   [34] Forrestal Diary, 2 Apr. 1945.
[35] See *Foreign Relations: United Nations*, extracts from Stettinius's diary, 18 Mar.–7 Apr. 1945, pp. 140–1.

written by Fortas) which stated that the Secretary of the Interior was 'considerably disturbed' by the attitude of the Army and Navy.[36] Now *Roosevelt* sent Stettinius a *copy* of Ickes's memorandum. It is possible that in connection with these developments Roosevelt told Stettinius to rally to trusteeship. When Forrestal asked him why he had changed his 'mind, Stettinius responded that he was 'under orders'.[37]

In any case Stettinius was not so dull-witted as some of his critics supposed. He certainly felt the pressures being exerted on him. It must have caused anguish to have to choose between the President and 'the Colonel'. Stimson recorded in his diary on the 6th of April, when he was enjoying himself in the country:

. . . [P]oison has crept into even this Garden of Eden. Harvey Bundy [Special Assistant to the Secretary of War] called me up to tell me that Ed Stettinius had suddenly turned over 180 degrees . . . and doesn't want to go on with the problem of trusteeship which he and Forrestal and I have been working out. . . .

It was enough to upset me. . . . It made me feel that it is so futile at this time to have such instability in one's associates.[38]

Stimson was thus checked. There was now nothing left for him and Forrestal to do but to submit a joint protest to the President. They could still hope to block the trusteeship arrangement by obstructionist tactics. Stimson and Forrestal therefore drafted a letter declaring the position of the War and Navy Departments. In a confrontation with the President, they would bring with them the Joint Chiefs. The lines were drawn for a battle royal.

Poor Stettinius! The good Secretary was caught in the middle of a fracas not of his own making. The experts of the State Department quickly reasserted their command of the technical points. For example, Gerig—via Taussig—was one of the few officials who knew Roosevelt's true views on trusteeship and that the President would support the State Department's

---

[36] Ickes to Stettinius, 5 Apr. 1945, ibid., pp. 198–9.

[37] *Forrestal Diaries*, p. 38.

[38] Stimson Diary, 6 Apr. 1945. For an account of the staff meeting of representatives of the Departments, see memorandum by Gerig, 7 Apr. 1945, *Foreign Relations: United Nations*, pp. 204–6. When asked why the Secretary of State had reversed his stand, one of the State Department representatives said that Stettinius 'had taken the advice of a number of officers'.

position.[39] He helped to produce the memorandum for the President which summarized and strongly pleaded the Department's position. One point in particular stood out, and it indicates one of the advantages held by the State Department over War and Navy. It probably appealed to Roosevelt because he was responsible: trusteeship had repeatedly been raised at international conferences on American initiative. To postpone the issue now would disrupt the entire San Francisco Conference. It was a good case.[40] But Stettinius read it with dismay. Thanks to his subordinates, he now found himself taking a vigorous stand against Stimson and Forrestal. He telephoned Forrestal and asked him 'if he would explain to Colonel Stimson' that the Secretary of State 'disassociated' himself from his own memorandum. He lamely explained, '*I was out of town when the memorandum was prepared.*'[41] Here was a case of the policy of the State Department being executed despite the Secretary of State.

Roosevelt read the State Department's memorandum at his retreat in Warm Springs, Georgia. On the 10th of April the White House received the following message for Stettinius. It was Roosevelt's last instruction on the colonial question. 'Your message on International Trusteeship is approved in principle. I will see your representative and that of the Army and Navy on the 19th. That will be time enough.'[42] Cavalier to the end, Roosevelt confidently planned on waiting until the very eve of the San Francisco Conference to make the final plans. With other governments planning to discuss trusteeship pursuant to the Yalta protocol, the American military authorities would indeed find themselves faced with a *fait accompli*.[43]

At the time of Roosevelt's death on the 12th of April, the opposing military and civilian sides appeared more equal than

[39] Copies of Taussig's conversation with Roosevelt of 15 March were given only to Gerig, Pasvolsky, and Dunn (as the supervising Assistant Secretary). A copy was also later given to Alger Hiss. Stettinius at some stage also read it.

[40] See *Foreign Relations: United Nations*, pp. 211–13.

[41] Extract from Stettinius's diary, 8–14 Apr. 1945, ibid., p. 210. Italics in the original.   [42] Ibid., p. 211, n. 52.

[43] According to the Yalta agreement, the British, Soviet, Chinese, and French governments would participate in discussions about trusteeship before the San Francisco Conference. By early April all of them had accepted the State Department's invitation. For summary of these developments, see memorandum by Pasvolsky, 13 Apr. 1945, *Foreign Relations: United Nations*, pp. 288–9.

it might seem in retrospect. For the civilians who had devoted a large measure of their wartime efforts to the colonial question, the fate of trusteeship now seemed to hang in the balance. Charles Taussig, for one, made extraordinary efforts. First he had kept pressure on the Secretary of State and, through Fortas, had then drawn the Secretary of the Interior into the controversy against the Secretaries of War and Navy.[44] Now, on the 12th of April, he happened to be talking to Mrs. Roosevelt about trusteeship at the very time of the fatal attack in Warm Springs. He had gone to see her because the President's message ('Trusteeship is approved in principle') did not seem decisive enough for the Department. He wanted Mrs. Roosevelt to get in touch with her husband to send another, more firm, instruction. Taussig told her about the background of the controversy and gave her the record of his recent conversation with the President, 'which she read slowly and carefully'. He explained that he was worried. '[A]ll of the work the President had done with Churchill over the last few years on this subject and the plans that the President had made will be nullified if we did not handle this situation properly now.' Taussig was quite frank about the personalities involved:

> I told Mrs. Roosevelt that the position taken in the Department . . . was one of vacillation and hesitancy . . . that Stettinius seemed unwilling to make a decision; that Pasvolsky, who favoured keeping trusteeship on the agenda, was obtuse in his presentation of the case and that Jimmy Dunn definitely opposed it.[45]

Mrs. Roosevelt said it was clear that 'Franklin has given the green light . . . to keep trusteeship on the agenda for San Francisco'. She agreed to help by telephoning her husband,

[44] e.g., the day after Stettinius met with Forrestal and Stimson on 2 April, Taussig called to see whether it was true (as he had learned from Gerig) that the Secretary had caved in. Stettinius euphemistically replied that the results of the meeting were 'cloudy' and reassured Taussig that 'I believe that the colonial problem is perhaps the most important to come up at San Francisco'. Memorandum by Taussig, 3 Apr. 1945, Taussig Papers. In the same memorandum Taussig described a conversation with Fortas, who said 'that he would bring Ickes into it immediately and arrange for him to contact the President'.

[45] Memorandum by Taussig, 12 Apr. 1945, Taussig Papers. The telephone call from Warm Springs had probably occurred five minutes before their talk. 'In retrospect', Taussig noted, 'it was apparent that Mrs. Roosevelt was totally unaware of what was happening, at Warm Springs, during the thirty minutes of our conversation.'

but, by the time they had finished talking, word had reached the White House that the President had suffered a stroke.[46] Nevertheless the conversation had a consequence for the American delegation at the conference. Stettinius found out about the meeting with Mrs. Roosevelt and was indignant at the intervention. He probably also concluded that Taussig did not have much confidence in his ability. The two men were estranged. 'It just broke my heart when I heard what you had done at the White House', Stettinius told Taussig a few days later.[47]

Roosevelt's death had a sobering impact on everyone involved in the trusteeship controversy, and it especially influenced Stimson. He wrote in his diary on the 12th of April:

I have never concealed the fact that I regarded his [Roosevelt's] administrative procedure as disorderly, but his foreign policy was always founded on great foresight and keenness of vision, and coming at this period when the war is closing and will I feel sure be succeeded by a period of great confusion of ideas in this country, the loss of his leadership will be most serious.[48]

In this time of national crisis, Stimson concluded, 'there is nothing to do but to close in and make a solid phalanx'. On this point he found common agreement with Forrestal and Stettinius. From here on they pulled together and the trusteeship issue reached a quick resolution.

Stimson provided the leadership. To summarize a complex problem, together with Forrestal he yielded the military position of a 'strategic territory' in the Pacific to one of a 'strategic *trust* territory'. They withdrew the joint War–Navy paper drafted for the President and agreed to work in unison with the State Department. Stimson did not find the task congenial. He wrote of a meeting at the State Department with Forrestal and Stettinius and their aides on the 16th of April: 'Stettinius has not got a firm enough hand on his affairs and with all his pleasantness and briskness he does not make his machine go.'[49] Nevertheless they made progress. Again to summarize a complex series of exchanges between the Departments, the State Department accommodated War and Navy by shifting the priorities

[46] Memorandum by Taussig, 12 Apr. 1945, Taussig Papers.
[47] Memorandum of telephone conversation between Taussig and Stettinius, Stettinius Papers Box 244.   [48] Stimson Diary, 12 Apr. 1945.
[49] Ibid., 16 Apr. 1945; and Forrestal Diary, same date.

from trusteeship to security, or, to put it in the form endorsed by the new President, making it clear that American security stood number one on the list. In the formula that became the policy of the United States, the trusteeship system would provide:

(1) the maintenance of United States military and strategic rights,

(2) such control as will be necessary to assure general peace and security in the Pacific Ocean area as well as elsewhere in the world, and

(3) the advancement of the social, economic, and political welfare of the inhabitants of the dependent territories.[50]

The general points were deliberately vague. When Stimson on the 17th talked to the delegates to the San Francisco Conference, he stressed that the intent was to give the United States '*full control*' over the Pacific islands. 'I emphasized these two words when it was sought later by some of the State Department underlings to pin me down as to the methods of fortification, etc., which we desired to put in. I told them that that could not be foreseen in the changing conditions of warfare.'[51]

The meeting at which Stimson and Forrestal addressed the delegation to the San Francisco conference will be considered in a later chapter. Here it seems appropriate to conclude with merely a few of Stimson's observations at that time, if only because they convey a sense of the agonizing spirit of the military concessions and also the sense of reassurance Stimson and Forrestal received from the delegates. The Secretary of War began by saying that he and Forrestal felt that there 'must be no cleavage' among the three Departments. Thus they met in a spirit of compromise. After guiding the delegates through the points in his 'strategic outpost' doctrine, he said that he believed 'that we could under proper conditions introduce the trustee system even into these [closed] bases, but it must give us full control and full strategic rights for the protection of them'.[52] Forrestal followed with an effective speech on the need to provide adequate defence in the Pacific. '[T]hose who hate

[50] These are the three points in the 'Recommended Policy of Trusteeship' approved by Truman on 18 Apr. 1945. See *Foreign Relations: United Nations*, pp. 350–1.
[51] Stimson Diary, 17 Apr. 1945. Italics added.
[52] Ibid.

war must have the power to prevent it.'[53] Stimson then emphasized that the two of them had 'gone to the last limit' in making
concessions to the State Department. At least he felt a sense of
gratification by the response:

The delegation asked questions, all of which seemed to be thoroughly on my side and most of which seemed to wish to go further
in giving the United States sufficient bases and sufficient power over
them. . . . I felt that I had implanted in the minds and feelings of the
delegation seeds for a proper defense of the Pacific against the frailty
of treaties and the danger of relying upon them alone.[54]

Stettinius, for his part, was greatly relieved.

On the next day, the 18th of April 1945, the three Secretaries met with President Truman. Stimson's diary again illuminates a sense of historic occasion as well as the change of
regimes. 'There were no long drawnout "soliloquies" from the
President', and the meeting moved so briskly that they finished
more business than anticipated. On the subject of trusteeship,
Stettinius asked Stimson to explain to the President the nature
of the compromise. Stimson assured Truman that the United
States would hold the bastions of the Pacific for the benefit of
'freedom-loving countries' and not for purposes of 'imperialism'.
The President, Stimson recorded in his diary, 'followed me
intelligently and sympathetically. . . . and then signed his
approval of the recommended policy of trusteeship'.[55]

[53] Forrestal Diary, 17 Apr. 1945; *Forrestal Diaries*, p. 45; *Foreign Relations: United Nations*, pp. 350–1.
[54] Stimson Diary, 17 Apr. 1945.
[55] Ibid., 18 Apr. 1945. *Foreign Relations: United Nations*, pp. 350–1.

32

THE INTERNATIONAL CONFERENCE BEFORE SAN FRANCISCO: THE COMMONWEALTH MEETING IN LONDON, APRIL 1945

THE spring of 1945 holds a place of distinct importance in the history of that phenomenon known as British 'Imperialism'. It came under siege in a manner that set the pattern for the post-war years. American idealists attacked it. British Fabians attempted to reform it. Commonwealth statesmen (or 'Empire Statesmen', depending on one's point of view) debated what to do about it. British officials denied its existence—but they found themselves facing that dreadful prospect envisaged by Oliver Stanley, defending the Empire, in his phrase, in a motley international assembly. In various ways not only the Americans but also the Australians and eventually the Egyptians and even the Guatemalans expressed their dissatisfaction. This chapter will examine mainly the Commonwealth controversies about the panacea for imperialism—trusteeship—on the eve of the San Francisco Conference. British officials faced dissension within the Commonwealth as well as attacks in the United States and in England. The problem of how to preserve a united front provides one of the keys to British official thought at this time.

The extreme form of American criticism persisted. To those who regarded the war as a struggle for freedom throughout the world, colonial liberation should follow in the wake of the destruction of Axis power. Sumner Welles, for example, believed that there would be a surge of post-war 'oriental nationalism'. His views are of particular interest in this regard, even though he now spoke in retirement and in no official capacity. British officials noted his championing of the anti-imperial cause. In late March 1945 Welles wrote an article in the *New York Herald Tribune* pleading a powerful case for trusteeship in colonial areas. He believed that the San Francisco Conference would offer the opportunity to write a resounding conclusion to the Atlantic Charter. This revived with full force the old controversy of whether the freedom guaranteed to Europe also pertained to the non-western world. 'The peoples of the Orient', he wrote, 'are not going to be satisfied . . . with unimplemented promises. Nor will some of them submit for more than a very brief time longer to any form of alien control.' To Welles there was only one practical method to safeguard the world against 'a general and violent upheaval' of colonial peoples: international trusteeship must be securely established. Every colonial power should be made directly responsible to an international body which would exert final authority over dependent peoples.

Where alien governments control dependent peoples who are not yet ready for the enjoyment of autonomy, those colonial powers should demonstrate to the international trusteeship that they are administering such regions for the benefit of the native inhabitants and that they are preparing their wards for autonomy or independence.[1]

Welles thus restated the case for international trusteeship as vigorously as he had in the early years of the war.

The British responded to the arguments with equal robustness. The indignant reaction of Gladwyn Jebb is especially interesting because of his subsequent participation in the San Francisco conference. He marked up Welles's article as if in a running debate. Welles wrote: 'Immediately after the end of this second world war a far more powerful surge toward freedom among the peoples of the East will be inevitable.' Jebb noted caustically, 'And, I suppose, a far more powerful repression!'[2] According to Welles, 'Many of the dependent peoples are fully aware that they are strongly supported by public opinion in the Western democracies.' Jebb asked, 'Will there then be revolts in Puerto Rico, Hawaii & Alaska?' Welles seemed to be oblivious to the American side of the colonial question. The former Under Secretary observed that Egypt 'has already announced her intention to secure the abolition of all semblance of British control'. Would Panama now seek to abolish American control, Jebb asked? Welles could see no reason 'why the

---

[1] *New York Herald Tribune*, 28 Mar. 1945.
[2] Ibid., marginal notes by Jebb, FO 371/50808.

peoples of the Orient who are fitted for self-government should not at once be accorded the same right'. 'E.g. the Dyaks of Borneo', was Jebb's repartee. In Welles's view, colonial peoples 'are unable to comprehend how the terms of the Atlantic Charter, which are clearly universal in their scope, can logically be interpreted as applying only to the West and not to the East'. 'Clearly', Jebb noted ironically. At one point Welles touched on India:

If the United Nations Conference at San Francisco fails to deal with this great problem in the same spirit in which this war for freedom has been waged, Gandhi's prophesy [*sic*] that unless the peoples of the East obtain their fundamental liberties, another and a bloodier war will be inevitable, will bid fair to be realized.[3]

'What about Alaska?' Jebb retorted, perhaps a little irrelevantly. Welles claimed that international trusteeship would be the only effective way to safeguard against a violent colonial revolution. Jebb now gave full reign to his sarcasm. 'Instead of being governed by one white race the wretched people must be governed by several.' Welles believed that the colonial powers should demonstrate accountability. Jebb thought that this was preposterous. 'Must *we* demonstrate to the Haitians & the Portuguese?' In peroration Welles wrote: 'the powers administering dependent peoples shall be held responsible by the public opinion of the world. . . .' Public opinion, Jebb underlined with contempt. Whose public opinion? That of the U.S.S.R.? China? Saudi Arabia? Argentina?[4] Clearly there was as little agreement on these basic issues as there had been at the beginning of the war.

How should such criticism be answered? In Washington Lord Halifax doubted whether it should be attempted unless a 'dynamic and forward' explanation could be given about the future direction of British colonial policy.[5] 'Otherwise silence', Halifax advised. The Foreign Office pressed on the Colonial Office the need not to be put on the defensive at San Francisco and to provide 'some stunning examples of our progressive beneficence and striking statistics for the American mind, to show our unselfishness etc., etc.'. 'Education and social welfare go down

---

[3] Ibid.   [4] Ibid.
[5] Halifax to Eden, No. 2437, 12 Apr. 1945, FO 371/50808.

well', the Foreign Office observed, and urged the Colonial Office to make the defence of the Empire 'as rousing as possible!'[6] The Colonial Office did not respond enthusiastically to this Foreign Office solicitude. Indeed the reaction was almost the opposite of the forward-looking attitude that would appeal to foreign critics. The Colonial Office saw no need to be apologetic. So far as appeasing ignorant critics was concerned, too many concessions had already been made. Instead of a 'rousing statement', the Colonial Office defiantly proposed to offer these words for foreign consumption: '[M]andated territories are as much a part of the British Empire as any other colonial territories and His Majesty's Government have no intention of surrendering to any other Power the responsibilities with which they have been charged for their administration.'[7] On this statement a Foreign Office official noted 'very provocative'. This was certainly an accurate observation. Had the declaration been made publicly (which it was not, due to the difference of departmental attitudes) it would have confirmed suspicions not only in America but also in England that old-fashioned Imperialism lingered on in the Colonial Office.

The Fabians wondered whether the earth-hunger of First World War times still existed. Rita Hinden, the Secretary of the Fabian Colonial Bureau, asked in an article in the *New Statesman*, 'will Britain and France and Belgium merely annex their Mandates in spite of the fine phrases of the Atlantic Charter?' She pointed out that these matters had been secretly discussed at Yalta. 'In this mood the Great Powers are approaching San Francisco.' Secret diplomacy again threatened to veil the intrigues of Imperialism. The Fabians were determined not to lose sight of the fundamental issue:

> When the Mandates system was introduced after the last war, it was hailed as a most significant step towards the recognition of an international conscience regarding backward lands. No longer were Colonies which had belonged to a defeated enemy to be handed over, like chattels, to the victors. They were to become 'the sacred trust of civilisation' . . .[8]

Would the same principle be embodied in the trusteeship

---

[6] Campbell to Gater, 10 Apr. 1945, CO 968/161/14814/11.
[7] Gater to Campbell, 11 Apr. 1945, FO 371/50808.
[8] Rita Hinden, 'Colonies at San Francisco', *New Statesman*, 21 Apr. 1945.

system? Or would the Colonial Office succeed in pouring 'cold water' on the mandates and 'jettisoning' international trusteeship? The Colonial Office's true feelings thus were no secret to the Fabians. 'A clear principle is at stake', Rita Hinden wrote. She urged her readers to remember that trusteeship was only a means to an end. Here she posed the issue in an incisive way. 'Above all, let us not forget, in making these plans, that the *real* object of colonial policy is to end the colonial system—all the rest is a mere stop-gap.'[9] *To end the colonial system*: even if this premise could be agreed upon, the method and pace were certain to cause controversy. It was a proposition that some Commonwealth leaders felt just as strongly about as some American and English Labour critics of the Empire. Some statesmen and officials in the imperial government rejected it just as vehemently.

The first meeting of the Commonwealth conference on the 4th of April 1945 marks the ascendancy of Lord Cranborne on the British side of the trusteeship controversy. As much as any statesman of the era, he would have scoffed at the idea of the end of the British Empire. At the San Francisco conference he became one of the key figures in the colonial settlement. Though not possessing an especially original mind, he certainly was a competent Dominions Secretary. With confidence in himself and in the Imperial mission, he treated his fellow Empire Statesmen as if they were members of an extended family or a select club. His friendly disposition and aristocratic charm contributed to a spirit of unity that might otherwise have been missing. In his introductory remarks to the conference he emphasized that they would not want to give the impression of 'ganging up' on the other nations at San Francisco. 'We are not entering this world organization merely for what we can get out of it', Cranborne told his colleagues.[10] They hoped to

---

[9] Ibid. For another trenchant commentary, see *The Economist* of 31 Mar. 1945, which concluded: 'it looks as if the colonial problem, which was not, as at one time seemed possible, a factor in the outbreak of war, might well become a bone of contention at the peace conference.'

[10] Minutes of the British Commonwealth Meeting, B.C.M. (45), 1st Meeting, 4 Apr. 1945, CAB 99/30. An Australian representative, Paul Hasluck, commented on Cranborne's chairing of the meetings: 'I gained a completely new conception of the arts of chairmanship in watching Viscount Cranborne handle all sorts of situations, generally in a way that imperceptibly brought the meeting to the solution he wished it to reach.' Paul Hasluck, 'Australia and the Formation of the

contribute to international security and world peace. To Cranborne's mind this meant the peace and security of the British Empire, in much the same way his grandfather, the great Lord Salisbury, had conceived it. To Cranborne it seemed the natural outcome of events that 'Hitler's invincible legions are at this very moment being chased across the length and breadth of Germany'. The Empire now faced new problems of the peace settlement, and Cranborne confidently hoped to resolve them in the same Imperial tradition of Lord Milner in 1919.

The Commonwealth conference revealed sharp differences about the general colonial question and about the specific issue of trusteeship. The Canadian Prime Minister did not attend. Hume Wrong of the Ministry of External Affairs successfully managed to keep the Canadians from becoming embroiled. The Australian Deputy Prime Minister, F. M. Forde, stated in his introductory remarks that the Australians 'are satisfied that, in the Pacific the mandates system has operated successfully and that the native peoples affected thereby have derived substantial benefit from that system'.[11] Forde also emphasized the equal status of Australia as an autonomous nation within the Commonwealth. He might have said the same about the factions within the Australian delegation itself. There were in fact *two* Australian delegations. One was led by Forde, the other by H. V. Evatt. At San Francisco they split into two camps, each occupying a separate floor of the same hotel and treating the other as a foreign delegation. Evatt in his introductory remarks began to elaborate the theme he presented at San Francisco and later as President of the General Assembly of the United Nations: 'middle powers' such as Australia would bear some of the major responsibilities of the world organization. The New Zealand position generally was in line with the Australian, though as previously Peter Fraser steered an individual and independent course. As if in ironic reassurance, he stressed to Cranborne that there would be no intention to form 'ourselves into a British *bloc*'.[12]

General Smuts reinforced the same idea. 'No one has any right to think that we are "ganging-up"', he told the conference.

United Nations', *Royal Australian Historical Society: Journal and Proceedings* 40. 3 (1954), 165.   11 B.C.M. Minutes, ibid.   12 Ibid.

Unlike Evatt, Smuts believed that the future of the world now rested with the great powers rather than with the small or 'middle' nations:

> On the Big Five will rest a terrible responsibility for peace. If they cannot keep together, the position of the smaller nations, who cannot defend themselves, will be hopeless, because this war has shown that the smaller States are helpless children, absolutely helpless before the new weapons and the new forms of war power. . . .
> If San Francisco fails then I see nothing but stark disaster before mankind. . . . World war to-day means quite a different thing. . . . If we want to do good, if we want to save our race, and if we want to perpetuate this human race divine, the glory of our world—we shall have to eliminate war from our programme.[13]

In this eloquent, extemporaneous speech, Smuts went on to describe the Commonwealth as a group comprising 'all cultures, all stages of civilisation, the group which has matured in human wisdom and . . . developed a technique of human government such as no other group possesses'. The British therefore had a special responsibility at San Francisco. Unlike Cranborne, Smuts did not view the prospect all that confidently. The world situation as well as that of the Commonwealth was changing:

> [W]e have internal difficulties, we know how scattered we are all over the world, we know that our sea power is not supreme, our former unique sea power is no longer the sure shield, and the oceans do not keep us together any more . . . we are in a somewhat insecure position.[14]

Thus Smuts with moving words summed up the state of the British Empire–Commonwealth on the eve of the San Francisco Conference as they and the other victorious powers approached the 'greatest crisis of humanity'.

Sir Firoz Khan Noon then spoke on behalf of India. He stressed that India had achieved Dominion status in practice if not yet in theory. Then in ludicrous contrast to the lofty words of General Smuts he made this forecast: 'I liken the San Francisco Conference to a man who is trying to put a large number of frogs into one basket, and all the frogs keep trying to jump out one after the other, and he is constantly putting

[13] Ibid.   [14] Ibid.

them back into the basket. That is what I foresee is going to be the case in San Francisco.'[15]

Trusteeship arose first on the agenda as an item of urgent business. If, in accordance with the Yalta protocol, preliminary discussion were to be held prior to San Francisco, then the Dominions would have to agree with the imperial government at once on what line to take.[16] Oliver Stanley attended the meeting to explain the position of the Colonial Office.[17] Probably it was a great annoyance to him to have to go through the entire business again, but he explained patiently how the purpose of the Poynton–Robinson project had been to get rid of the mandates. He now stressed how the situation had changed and how the Americans 'were primarily concerned to seek ways and means of acquiring Japanese islands in a manner which would not adversely affect their own public opinion'. After considering the American attitude and the views of the Dominions, and because of the Yalta protocol, the imperial government now would acquiesce in the continuance of the mandates system by some form of international trusteeship. But Stanley pointed out that the United Kingdom delegation would 'strongly' resist international accountability that went *beyond* the mandates system. He concluded his remarks by making it quite clear that the Colonial Office would have nothing to do with any form of an extended mandates system: 'It was certainly not the intention of the United Kingdom Government to agree that the Mandatory system might be extended to territories under its sovereignty.' When Peter Fraser asked him whether this hard line was a 'considered opinion', Stanley firmly replied that indeed it was.[18]

The situation now differed radically from that of the meeting of the Commonwealth Prime Ministers in the previous spring, when Fraser had offered the only resistance to the Colonial

[15] Ibid.

[16] In the event the pre-conference discussions were reduced to an exchange of views between Hilton Poynton and David Owen of the Foreign Office, and, on the other side, Benjamin Gerig at the State Department on 10 and 14 April. See Halifax to Eden, Nos. 2240 and 2544, 12 and 15 Apr. 1945, FO 371/50808; CO 968/161/14814/11. After Roosevelt's death the project of preliminary discussion was abandoned.

[17] For departmental background, see CO 968/161/14814/11; FO 371/50808; DO 35/1906.

[18] B.C.M. Minutes, 2nd Meeting, 4 Apr. 1945, CAB 99/30.

Office. Now *Evatt* was present. He plunged into the sea of the trusteeship controversy like a hungry shark. His comments fill nearly five of the twelve pages of the meeting's minutes. With an unrivalled mastery of the legal aspects of the mandates, he traced the history of the system and interpreted President Wilson's intention. He addressed himself to broad questions of international law and native welfare. He spoke legalistically and aggressively. He discussed the reports to the Permanent Mandates Commission and asked whether the new body should be empowered 'to cause dependent territories to be visited'. He considered at length the Colonial Office's proposals for regional organization. He presented eight detailed arguments for a general recognition of trusteeship for *all* dependent peoples. In the course of this presentation he supported his points by reference to scholarly works on the subject. Since historians of international trusteeship have often wondered about possible academic influence in trusteeship affairs, it is of interest to note that Evatt referred to J. S. Furnivall, L. P. Mair, and M. F. Lindley.[19] Evatt knew these and other works backwards and forwards. There was no question of his merely following a brief prepared by one of his subordinates.[20] Here was one of the world's authorities on international law and dependent peoples. He did not stop with mere analysis. He further demonstrated that Australia and New Zealand were committed to the implementation of trusteeship by virtue of the resolution of the Australia–New Zealand Conference of November 1944. He then hammered on the theme of *British* commitment to trusteeship through the Colonial Development and Welfare Act. He stressed the obligation that now existed in international law and diplomacy as a result of the Yalta Conference. He buttressed

[19] L. P. Mair, *Welfare in the British Colonies* (Royal Institute of International Affairs, London, 1944); J. S. Furnivall, *Educational Progress in S.E. Asia* (Institute of Pacific Relations, London, 1943); M. F. Lindley, *The Acquisition and Government of Backward Territory in International Law* (London, 1926). The other work which virtually all students of the mandates system had read was Quincy Wright, *The Mandates Under the League of Nations* (Chicago, 1930).

[20] I am grateful to W. D. Forsyth for discussing with me this and other points in regard to Evatt. Hasluck observes that Evatt arrived in London with only a vague knowledge about the preliminary planning for the world organization and mastered the material virtually on the spot. Hasluck, *Australia and the Formation of the United Nations*, p. 164. For the background of Australian policy at this time, see AA A1066 H45/1021 and P45/153.

all of these points by expanding on the Labour Party's position on native welfare. He made it clear that he opposed international administration. But he could not see why the Colonial Office should fail to take the lead in a proposal that after all represented British principles. He did not think it too much to ask for support for the principle of protecting native welfare and submitting annual reports. He hoped that voluntarily the British might do much more by placing British colonies under international trusteeship. 'He could imagine nothing less onerous in the case of Powers such as the United Kingdom, Australia and New Zealand, which discharged their colonial obligations honestly and in the best of their ability. If they refused to do so it would set the worst possible example for others.'[21] If Cranborne and Stanley had still hoped to gain the active support or at least the acquiescence of the Dominions, that hope now vanished after Evatt's speech.

Peter Fraser supported Evatt. He was at a loss to understand why Great Britain of all countries should object to the principle of trusteeship. 'A bold and generous gesture in the direction which Dr. Evatt suggested would not only serve as a lesson to other countries, but would be highly acceptable to public opinion both in the United Kingdom and in the Dominions.'[22] He favoured reports submitted to an international body. In particular he hoped an international regime might improve conditions in the French islands. He wondered in fact whether it would be in the best interests of the inhabitants to restore certain islands to France. The French territories in the Pacific were badly administered. '[T]heir Social Services were neglected and the native population exploited . . . [and] it was a matter for serious consideration whether such territories as New Caledonia and Tahiti should automatically be restored to their former owners.'[23] Fraser emphasized native welfare. Here was a chance to prove to the world that the British Empire–Commonwealth had no ulterior motives.

This matter was a world question. In the Atlantic Charter certain promises had been made which it was necessary to find means to

---

[21] B.C.M. Minutes, 2nd Meeting, 4 Apr. 1945.

[22] Ibid. For Fraser's published thoughts on trusteeship, see Peter Fraser, 'The Work of the Trusteeship Council', *International Conciliation*, No. 445 (November 1948). For the background in New Zealand, see NZ PM 151/2/1.

[23] B.C.M. Minutes, 2nd Meeting, 4 Apr. 1945, CAB 99/30.

implement . . . . and the present vacuum could best be filled by setting up an international body to which reports were sent. There was no question of colonial territories being *administered* by such a body or of infringing in any way the present sovereignty of colonial territories.

He earnestly hoped that the United Kingdom Government . . . would see their way to making a bold and generous gesture in the direction which he had indicated.[24]

Fraser thus saw himself in agreement with Evatt and the two of them thus found themselves in diametric opposition to the Colonial Office on the issue of voluntary trusteeship.

The frontal attack by the two Australasian statesmen may have been overwhelming. Immediately after the meeting, Oliver Stanley's doctor ordered him to bed. In any case Stanley suffered from nervous tension and Evatt and Fraser's powerful defence of international trusteeship must have been disconcerting.

The response of the imperial government should be studied in conjunction with that of General Smuts. The views were similar. Smuts desired the abolition of the mandates system just as much as the Colonial Office. At the third meeting on the 5th of April, he took account in a negative way of the contribution of the Australasian representatives and ignored their positive suggestions about voluntary trusteeship. Smuts thought that everyone would agree that no one wanted to surrender the present mandates, to an international authority or anyone else. He took it for granted that the mandates system needed to be improved. He admitted that disagreement existed as to procedure. While the antipodean representatives apparently desired a free-wheeling talk with other powers on colonial matters, Smuts wanted to keep existing mandates out of the discussion. Even though the British might desire alteration of the terms of the mandates, how could the Commonwealth presume to dictate to sovereign powers how to control or administer colonial dependencies? 'In his view the furthest we of the British Commonwealth could go would be to say "we for our part are acting on this [trusteeship] principle". To go further would risk encountering the opposition of other Powers.'[25] All in all, a more conservative disinclination to extend responsibilities of trusteeship would be difficult to

[24] Ibid.   [25] Ibid.

conceive, and the position is quite understandable in view of South Africa's aim to absorb completely the South-West Africa mandate.

The outlook of the imperial government corresponded with Smuts's view. Cranborne also followed tactics of negative consensus. At least there were certain possible developments that none of the Commonwealth members favoured. These included the creation of multi-national trusteeship territories. Sir Firoz Khan Noon, for example, stated on the 5th of April that 'single-Power mandates' were preferable to 'international mandates'. He compared 'the former to a cow belonging to one person and the latter to the cow which was communally owned by the village, milked by all and fed by none'.[26] The Canadian delegation also contributed to the negative consensus by stressing the need not to alienate American public opinion. It had to be taken into account, even though it was, in Hume Wrong's words, 'often ill-informed and . . . suffered from misconceptions and confusion of thought'. Any attempt to 'muzzle' discussion of the colonial question at San Francisco would antagonize Americans otherwise friendly to the Commonwealth.[27]

With such points in mind, Cranborne presented the results of the conference to the War Cabinet on the 12th of April.[28] He explained that agreement could be reached on what ought *not* to be done, but that Australia and New Zealand urged voluntary extension of the trusteeship principle, especially in regard to islands that did not belong to them. 'The Australian and New Zealand representatives laid stress on this in connection with the return to France and Portugal of territories now occupied by Japan.'[29] Cranborne was perfectly aware of the *Realpolitik* of this position, whereby Australia and New Zealand would extend their influence through an international regime. He thought it would be dangerous for the imperial government to agree to it because then the United States might seize upon the trusteeship system to interfere with British colonial rule. He thought that the representatives of Australia and New Zealand

---

[26] B.C.M. Minutes, 3rd Meeting, 5 Apr. 1945, ibid.

[27] Ibid. For the Canadian background to these comments, see CAN 180(S).

[28] See memorandum by Cranborne, W.P. (45) 228, 10 Apr. 1945, CAB 66/64; FO 371/50808; DO 35/1906; CO 968/161/14114/11; PREM 4/31/4. For the War Cabinet discussion, WM (45) 42nd Conclusions, CAB 65/50.

[29] Ibid.

should be 'frankly' informed that the imperial government had no intention of extending the scope of trusteeship.

The War Cabinet concurred. Churchill himself outlined the strategy to be followed.

As regards the line to be taken at San Francisco, THE PRIME MINISTER thought that the great Colonial Powers such as France and the Netherlands would certainly object to arrangements for placing their Colonies under voluntary trusteeship; and that as a matter of tactics we should be well advised to let them take the lead in this matter and then lend our support to their arguments.[30]

Churchill thus clearly saw the larger political configurations already beginning to take shape. Confident that the French, Dutch, and Belgians would beat down the Australian and New Zealand proposals, he saw no danger in letting the antipodeans press their point of view. As a further sop he was even willing to concede to Australia and New Zealand the principle of 'voluntary trusteeship', whereby any nation could place territories under international control if it so desired. It was not much of a concession, but at least it would help the cause of imperial unity.[31]

Cranborne explained the position of the imperial government on the 13th of April 1945, the day after Roosevelt's death. He opened by paying tribute to the dead President—'one of the greatest friends of world peace and, he thought, of the British Commonwealth also'. Cranborne then turned again to the problem of trusteeship. He emphasized the unity and consensus of the Empire–Commonwealth. The United Kingdom government agreed that the mandates system should be continued. There would have to be certain modification of the terms of the mandates, especially in the clauses on defence and freedom of trade. The imperial government hoped that at San Francisco the discussion would avoid detail. He said that Australia and New Zealand had pressed for the extension of the mandates system, and he stated that the War Cabinet gladly now accepted the principle that non-mandated territories voluntarily could be placed under international trusteeship. The United Kingdom did not, however, 'intend to apply this principle to their own

[30] Ibid.
[31] Here Churchill followed Cranborne's recommendation. See memorandum of 11 Apr. 1945, PREM 4/31/4.

colonial territories', since everyone seemed to be of one mind 'that to do so would have a deplorable effect by encouraging agitation and a sense of impermanence of British rule'.[32] Cranborne hoped that the conference would agree that the United Kingdom had gone to great lengths to meet the wishes of Australia and New Zealand.

Far from agreeing, Fraser and Evatt both protested. Fraser stated that trusteeship would be a major element in the world settlement and warned that the imperial government would be placed 'in an isolated position and stigmatised as reactionary'. Evatt entirely concurred. 'He thought it would be better for the United Kingdom Government not to accept the principle of trusteeship at all than to accept it and refuse to apply it to their own territories.'[33] Sir Ramaswami Mudaliar of the Indian delegation now came down firmly on the side of Fraser and Evatt. He invoked that most powerful reason of all why the principle of trusteeship should be fully employed—the prevention of war. 'By accepting this principle we should . . . remove a fundamental cause of future wars.' Since territorial ambition did not motivate British policy, why did the imperial government hesitate? Moreover, in the Indian view, if Britain took the lead, the 'pressure of world opinion would oblige such States as France, Belgium and Portugal to follow suit'.[34]

As if an omen of things to come in the debates of the United Nations, the discussion threatened to get out of hand. Moreover it grew acrimonious. Cranborne said that after all the United Kingdom in a spirit of compromise had accepted the continuation of the mandates system, which otherwise might have been abolished. Evatt disagreed. Having begun with the premise of continuation, he thought the United Kingdom government had conceded very little. Fraser admonished Cranborne that the position of the imperial government would alienate the United States. He feared there would be no 'bar of world opinion' to judge 'countries which treated their native colonial populations badly'. Smuts observed that the United States, not being a colonial power, could criticize without facing the problems involved. The mood of the meeting shifted against the imperial government. Recriminations were ex-

---

[32] B.C.M. Minutes, 12th Meeting, 13 Apr. 1945, CAB 99/30.
[33] Ibid.   [34] Ibid.

changed. Cranborne, for example, told the Australian and New Zealand representatives that the 'C' mandates in their charge were easier to administer than the British 'B' mandates. He tried not to be 'too despondent' about the limited scope of the consensus. His only support had come from General Smuts. At least Cranborne could take consolation that the nations of the Commonwealth would not give the impression to the world at large, in his phrase, that they were 'ganging up'. The trusteeship discussions ended on that note.[35]

The Commonwealth meeting of April 1945 stands out as the time when Evatt and Fraser emerged together as the champions of the type of trusteeship that remains today the basic principle in the Pacific basin. They emphasized to their colleagues that the welfare of the inhabitants of the islands had to be taken into consideration as well as the security of the great powers. As in the history of colonial trusteeship during the First World War, cynics might retort that it is surprising that the well-being of the ruled seemed always to be identical with the control and benefit of the British Empire–Commonwealth. There can be no doubt, however, that Evatt and Fraser believed the record of Australia and New Zealand to be in advance of the performance of other powers in the Pacific, and that they regarded the renovation of the mandates system as a chance to improve administrative conditions generally. As for the immediate importance of the Commonwealth conference, it demonstrated that the Australians and New Zealanders would express their own views at San Francisco regardless of the imperial government. The colonial question had cracked the façade of the Commonwealth.

[35] Ibid.

33

SAN FRANCISCO: THE RESOLUTION
OF THE 'STRATEGIC TRUST'
CONTROVERSY AND THE FOUNDATION
OF COLONIAL ACCOUNTABILITY

ABOUT a month before the opening of the San Francisco Conference on the 25th of April 1945, Walter Lippmann wrote an article which appeared in American and British newspapers entitled 'Pandora's Box'.[1] The box was the colonial issue. Perhaps more than any other contemporary commentator, Lippmann put into sharp perspective, on the one hand, the problems facing the American delegation, and, on the other, the way in which many Englishmen regarded the general colonial question but seldom saw it so expressed from an American viewpoint. 'Our own colonial empire,' he wrote, 'though a small one, is exceedingly complex. Yet it is fairly simple as compared with a great structure like the British Commonwealth and Empire or with that of the French Empire.' He warned that this fact would constantly have to be borne in mind at San Francisco, especially if the American delegates were to introduce a general colonial declaration. 'For any declaration we sponsor must fit our own ideals and practice in the Philippines, in Alaska, in Puerto Rico, in the Canal Zone, in Guam and in the Virgin Islands.' What was the purpose of colonial rule? Independence? Lippmann himself expressed doubt about the wisdom of this goal, though as will be seen his scepticism was not shared by some members of the American delegation. 'I doubt whether the mind of man is capable of composing a declaration which covers all these specific colonial territories', Lippmann continued. In his view this did not mean that the United Nations organization should not be concerned with colonial questions, but that it would be a mistake to go too far in the direction of colonial accountability.

[1] *Washington Post*, 20 Mar. 1945; *Sunday Times* (London), 25 Mar. 1945.

[W]e should be very chary indeed of proposing great generalizations which cannot be applied to all the particular cases. . . . It just is not in the cards to make the Governor of Alaska, the Governor of Bermuda or the Governor of Tunis legally answerable to an assembly in which Saudi Arabia, Iraq, Iran, Liberia, Ethiopia, Dominica and Haiti sit as sovereign judges.

There was also a related problem at San Francisco, that of security. Here again Lippmann's remarks were perspicacious:

What should be done with Pantelleria, for example, cannot be determined intelligently until Britain, France and the United States know where they stand with respect to one another on all sea and air bases in the Atlantic Ocean. What should be done with the islands in the Pacific cannot be determined until there is among all the Powers concerned a specific security agreement for the Pacific.[2]

The word 'security' sums up the dominant concern of the protagonists of the era. If there were any lessons to be learned from history, surely one of them was the futility of non-fortification schemes, as in the case of the Japanese mandated islands.

The history of the colonial question at San Francisco can be viewed as an attempt to resolve the two issues of security and colonial accountability, on the one hand, and the larger question of the future of dependent peoples on the other. This chapter and the succeeding one will examine the two problems in that order, in accordance with their approximate chronological development. Of course all of these matters were interdependent and in turn were only a few among many great issues such as the controversy of the great powers' veto, the creation of the Security Council, the function of the General Assembly, and the jurisdiction of the International Court of Justice. Within a period of approximately two months, the delegates to the conference created the basis of what we know today as the post-war system of international organization. Fortunately the complexity of the situation can be followed through the lengthy, detailed account of the conference from the angle of the United Nations, Ruth B. Russell's *A History of the United Nations Charter*. The reader is referred to it for the workings of the commissions, the technical drafting, and

[2] Ibid.

general perspective. This account proceeds on the assumption that the colonial settlement had a logic of its own and an independent intrinsic interest.

To some contemporary participants the colonial issue appeared vital. It certainly did to some members of the American delegation such as Isaiah Bowman and Charles Taussig. It is indeed helpful to regard the American delegation as the key to the whole situation. Had there not been an American commitment, there would have been no 'colonial problem'. Or, to phrase the proposition differently, had the Americans not pushed trusteeship to the fore, the Australian and New Zealand initiative would have been less effective. The British contribution should be viewed as one of response, as should that of the other colonial powers. As the debate gained momentum, representatives of the other powers, many of them anti-British, attempted to twist the issues to their own advantage. Thus with the founding of the trusteeship system there existed a microcosm of the world of the later colonial debates of the United Nations.

The American delegation was a masterpiece of political composition. As a Senior Adviser, Cordell Hull represented a bi-partisan support of the future international organization, though Hull himself did not attend the conference because of illness. Senator Tom Connally of Texas was the Democratic Chairman of the Foreign Relations Committee. Senator Arthur Vandenberg of Michigan also served on that same key committee and represented an internationalist Republican policy. Representatives Charles A. Eaton of New Jersey and Sol Bloom of New York, Republican and Democrat respectively, both were members of the House Committee on Foreign Affairs. The other two delegates were Virginia Gildersleeve, Dean of Barnard College, and Commander Harold Stassen, a former Governor of Minnesota now on active service in the United States Navy.[3] Great care had thus been taken not to repeat the mistakes of the Versailles period. It was a balanced group which could expect Congressional support. There was also a certain amount of familiarity with the specific issue of trusteeship because Connally, Eaton, and Bloom had partici-

---

[3] For the American delegation and the conference, see especially Robert A. Divine, *Second Chance: The Triumph of Internationalism in America During World War II* (New York, 1967), ch. 11.

pated in the State Department Advisory Committee discussions of 1942–3. It was not as if they were unfamiliar with the issues. Stassen was charged with the responsibility of the colonial question at San Francisco, and Vandenberg displayed a particular interest in the security aspects of the problem. The real powers on the delegation were Vandenberg, Connally, and Stassen. Stettinius acted as Chairman of the Delegation with Leo Pasvolsky serving in the capacity of Adviser. Other Advisers who played important parts in the colonial settlement were Isaiah Bowman and Charles Taussig, the latter representing what might be called the Roosevelt tradition in colonial affairs. One other figure should be given prominent mention. Benjamin Gerig attended as one of the three 'Chief Technical Experts' of the delegation. He served as Stassen's right-hand man. The continuity of the State Department's trusteeship policy found its voice in Gerig. Almost as if in a delicate system of checks and balances, the members of the Joint Chiefs Strategic Survey Committee also attended the conference, with Admiral Willson keeping an especially vigilant eye on the security of the Pacific.

The question of trusteeship first came to the attention of the delegation when they met with Stettinius, Forrestal, and Stimson on the 17th of April.[4] The delegates all sympathized with Stimson's plea for 'full control in strategic areas'. Vandenberg recorded in his diary:

> The Army and Navy are insistent that we must *keep* full control of most of the Pacific bases taken from the Japs. The State Dept. is afraid this will set a bad example to the other great powers. Secretary of War Stimson made a particularly moving speech. . . . (We all agree with him.) He said he didn't care so much about the 'title' to these Islands *if* we have *absolute*, undisputed control over our base needs.[5]

Representative Eaton stated during the discussion that 'it would never be possible to get anything through Congress that didn't protect American interests in the Pacific'.[6] Stassen commented that the island bases 'are as essential a part of our

[4] See above, ch. 31.
[5] Arthur H. Vandenberg, Jr., *The Private Papers of Senator Vandenberg* (Boston, 1952), p. 169.
[6] *Foreign Relations: 1945: United Nations*, p. 317.

armament as guns and ships'. But he clearly saw the force of
the argument of accountability: the United States did have an
obligation, he said, 'to protect the native population and not to
exploit selfishly the economic resources of the area'. Thus from
the beginning Stassen held an equally poised position on the
issue of strategic security and colonial accountability. Senator
Connally, by contrast, said that he saw no objection 'to taking
Japanese territory'. Miss Gildersleeve emphasized that 'we
don't intend to grab, but we do intend to hold what is necessary
for our security'. The debate seesawed in the way it had since
the beginning of the war. Vandenberg stated 'that Congressional opinion is totally in sympathy with the position of the
Secretaries of War and Navy'.

On this occasion it was Isaiah Bowman who provided the
counterweight of the argument for trusteeship. His comments
serve to illustrate the logic of the State Department's position
on the eve of the San Francisco Conference.

We have been led into a situation in which the world expects us
to do something on trusteeship. We are faced with such questions
as whether we wish Somaliland to go to the British. We will have
to participate in its disposition. What in this situation is our safeguard? It is in the fact that we have set up a principle—a principle
of trusteeship in the interests of the natives.[7]

No one would disagree with the military requirements, Bowman continued, but it was quite important to make clear one
salient point in favour of trusteeship:

[I]t is important to nail down the position . . . that no matter how
few the people in a particular territory, to insure that our obligation
to those people will be discharged, because if this should be given
up there would be no defense at all in dealing with Britain and Russia. We would be at the bar of opinion, and if we accept the trusteeship system we will be able to say that we have taken a position.[8]

This was an eloquent expression of the idealism of trusteeship.
But it caused anxiety that accountability might be implemented
at the expense of American security. As was to happen many
times at San Francisco, Stassen steadied the debate. He stated
that he had no intention of abandoning the responsibilities of
trusteeship, 'but there must be a distinction in the degree or in

---

[7] *Foreign Relations: 1945: United Nations*, pp. 318–19.   [8] Ibid.

the terms of the trusteeship in the strategic areas on the basis of military requirements'.[9] At this time Stassen was widely regarded as a possible future Presidential candidate. In part because of this, his immersion in trusteeship affairs attracted considerable attention in the press. By all accounts he performed outstanding service at the conference.

For Australia Evatt was the spokesman on trusteeship, as on all else. No other single individual stands out so strikingly against the background of the San Francisco Conference. With that mixture of ambition, pride, and driving energy that characterized his personality, he now attempted to organize the United Nations according to his general precepts of international law and his specific objectives of eliminating the veto power of the Security Council and the strengthening of the General Assembly. Evatt arrived in San Francisco as practically an unknown politician representing a British Dominion in the Pacific; he left with an established reputation of an international statesman. An excerpt from the unpublished autobiography of the Australian Minister in Washington, Sir Frederick Eggleston (who attended the conference as a delegate), provides insight into this complex and ambitious man. Like everything else concerning Evatt, Eggleston's comments could probably be disputed, but they are none the less interesting:

Dr. Evatt proved himself master of the documents as no other member was and a true internationalist. It was a laudable ambition to become a great international figure. He was genuinely behind all the idealist international philosophy. He had had a checkered career, was unpopular in Australia and not very popular in his party. He had the psychology of the poor boy who had had a series of frustrations which embittered him but only stirred his determination to succeed. This was his chance and he took it and in spite of the immense difficulties before him, made up his mind to fight. When he did so, he used every instrument and found his main assistance from the representatives of the smaller powers, who came in behind him and made him their hero.[10]

[9] Ibid., p. 319.
[10] Eggleston's unpublished autobiography, Eggleston Papers. Another passage reads: 'As compared with the Paris Conference [of 1919] the San Francisco Conference was tame. The most prominent figure was certainly Dr. Evatt. Commander Stassen was popular and persuasive but compromised his reputation for idealism. Senator Vandenberg increased his reputation for shrewd political sense. Connally did not improve his, he only showed how Dr. Evatt's arguments hit him in the

However one might evaluate Evatt's motives, he did emerge as the leader of the small nations against the great powers.

Evatt's aggressive personality and lack of tact often provoked a sense of outrage.[11] But no one denied his ability. Here was an Australian dynamo. Those working in the realm of trusteeship affairs felt the impact of his abrasive personality no less than in other areas—despite a concerted effort on the part of the British and Americans which prevented him from becoming chairman of the trusteeship commission.[12] Evatt proclaimed the Australian position in the press as well as in the conference: *all* colonies should be placed under international trusteeship. Of course he already knew the impossibility of this goal, but it gave him a superb platform from which he could rally the anti-colonial nations that helped to form his international constituency. He seized opportunities as they arose. 'The United States was expected to lead the conference in demanding that the dependent territories be prepared for eventual self-government', a newspaper article reported him saying in early May. 'The fact that the American delegation hasn't even offered a phrase concerning independence has given other interested nations an unanticipated opportunity to step in and take the credit for liberal leadership.'[13] Evatt did not hesitate. With his taking an aggressive stand on the issue of colonial independence, the Americans as well as the British found themselves on the defensive.

Peter Fraser became chairman of the conference's trusteeship committee, technically known as Commission II/4 (the fourth committee of the commission on the General Assembly).

raw. The ablest man on the machine was undoubtedly Mr. John Foster Dulles. . . . Mr. Stettinius was a disappointment, his thought was as thin as his smile was wide and his chairmanship of United States Steel evidently taught him nothing as to the conduct of meetings.'

[11] See especially *Australian Diplomat: Memoirs of Sir Alan Watt* (Sydney, 1972); and by the same author for an account of Evatt's policy at San Francisco, *The Evolution of Australian Foreign Policy* (Cambridge, 1967), ch. 4.

[12] At least so the British and Americans thought. The initial proposal was to appoint Deputy Prime Minister Forde as chairman of the trusteeship committee. The British interpreted this as a plot by Evatt to get himself appointed. Halifax consequently told Stettinius, 'Australia would certainly mean Evatt and that he could have made no worse personal selection if he wished to carry a mixed team along. Stettinius warmly agreed and said that he would certainly get it changed.' Halifax to Eden, No. 2430, 11 Apr. 1945, copy in CO 968/161/14814/11.

[13] *New York Post*, 4 May 1945, clipping in the Evatt Papers.

A newspaper columnist remarked at the close of the conference, 'Working shoulder to shoulder with Evatt was New Zealand's Prime Minister Peter Fraser. To the stuff-shirt Tories of the British Foreign Office these two are considered the terrors of the Empire.'[14] This statement was only partially true, as we now know from the diary of a stuff-shirt Tory of the Foreign Office, Sir Alexander Cadogan. He referred at one point to 'Old Fraser, the New Zealander, [who] is almost equally tiresome [as Evatt], but mainly from silliness: he's rather a dear old thing really, and at heart quite friendly.'[15] By silliness Cadogan perhaps meant Fraser's insistence that everyone be allowed to express his point of view provided he stuck to the subject. Fraser chaired severely whenever anyone violated his sense of parliamentary propriety.[16] He incurred a good deal of criticism because of his handling of the trusteeship commission. For example, in Eggleston's words, 'He oozed goodwill, was solicitous that everybody should understand everything and be satisfied so that his various inter-positions sensibly lengthened the discussions instead of shortening them which was his expressed desire.'[17]

At least by all accounts Fraser, in contrast to Evatt, was a gentleman. He was as equally committed as Evatt to the same type of trusteeship, but not abrasively. During the Commonwealth conference in London he had reported to New Zealand that he was 'anxious not to embarrass the United Kingdom Government at the San Francisco Conference but that if the matter [of voluntary trusteeship] was raised there we would feel it necessary to state our views quietly but firmly'.[18] Fraser and Stassen got on well together (in fact Stassen was the only prominent American statesman with whom the New Zealander became well acquainted at the conference), while at the same time—and again in contrast with Evatt—he was friendly with Lord Cranborne. In a sense it was entirely appropriate that Fraser became chairman of the trusteeship committee. He was the *only* Prime Minister who actually visited a mandated

---

[14] Drew Pearson in the *Washington Post*, 30 June 1945.

[15] *Diaries of Sir Alexander Cadogan*, p. 745.

[16] For a valuable account of Fraser at the conference, see Eugene P. Chase, 'Peter Fraser at San Francisco', *Political Science* (Wellington), 11. 1 (March 1959).

[17] Eggleston's unpublished autobiography, Eggleston Papers.

[18] Fraser to External Affairs, 15 Apr. 1945, NZ PM 151/2/1.

territory during the war. In December 1944 Fraser had gone to Samoa. It was more than a perfunctory tour. He spent several days discussing problems of health, education, agriculture, and administrative affairs with the Samoan leaders and took the opportunity to give them advice on various things. 'The ravages of strong drink among many races and countries are well known in history,' he told the Samoan leaders on one occasion, 'and the Bible warns against it.'[19] Fraser himself sustained the ordeals of the San Francisco conference with hot tea and buttered toast.[20] He was the object of much good-natured and some spiteful banter, but according to his own lights the elderly New Zealand Labour politician had genuine concern for the welfare of dependent peoples.

Lord Cranborne commanded the British side of the trusteeship issue, with Hilton Poynton and Brigadier Ian Jacob as his respective colonial and military aides. With considerable urbanity he attempted to co-ordinate the efforts of the Empire representatives. Evatt proved to be the only openly defiant one. Fraser at least offered his goodwill. The Canadian Prime Minister, Mackenzie King, showed little interest in trusteeship. General Smuts served as the chairman of the commission on the General Assembly, which occupied most of his energies, though he kept a sharp eye on trusteeship whenever it threatened to impinge on the status of South West Africa. Eden telegraphed to Churchill on the 30th of April:

> On the whole we are a pretty good Empire party here. Smuts has been most helpful at every point and we are giving him the chairmanship of the most important commission. Mackenzie King has intermittent colds in head and feet, brought on by the imminence of his general election, but on the whole he is in good heart and very helpful. Evatt is the most tiresome and Fraser the most woolly. But between them they are making clear to the Americans and all concerned that we do not control their votes. Bobbety [Cranborne] manages most ably to get his mixed team along somehow.[21]

Because of the extreme position of the antipodeans, especially Evatt, a greater degree of collaboration sometimes existed

---

[19] For Fraser's visit to Samoa, see NZ EX 1/67/1.
[20] I am indebted to Sir Alister McIntosh for relating to me his recollections of Fraser at the conference.
[21] Eden to Churchill, 29 April 1945, PREM 4/31/7.

between the British and American representatives than among those of the Commonwealth.

Effective collaboration developed in another way as well. It was the first time that the experts on the colonial question had all met together. Gerig, Poynton, and W. D. Forsyth of Australia, for example, had all spent a good deal of the wartime era studying the same problems. There was a meeting of minds and mutual respect despite divergent aims. The Americans helped to break down barriers of suspicion or reservation about the position of the United States in the Pacific by candidly explaining to their foreign colleagues the crisis between the military and the State Department. For the antipodeans one meeting at the beginning of the conference was particularly significant. John Hickerson of the British Commonwealth Division of the State Department talked with certain Australian and New Zealand representatives. Fraser, Carl Berendsen, and Alister McIntosh were present on the New Zealand side, Forsyth on the Australian. Hickerson said that he wanted to give them 'a complete & truthful "off the record" account' of the American position.[22] He said that the Americans genuinely wished to promote the principle of trusteeship. But at the same time he explained that the United States wanted complete control over the Japanese mandated islands. He told them about the dramatic compromise between the State Department and the military authorities, who had demanded outright annexation. Peter Fraser replied that he wanted to see the United States responsible for the security of the northern Pacific and that he hoped the Americans would take the lead in instituting a system of reporting on all colonial areas. Evatt, though he was not at the meeting, also agreed on the need to make the United States the master of the northern Pacific.[23] On this fundamental issue the Americans managed from the outset to win the sympathy of the Empire–Commonwealth group (though the United Kingdom delegation withheld support for bargaining purposes). No doubt everyone regarded American ascendancy in the northern Pacific as inevitable; but the linking of military security and trusteeship was not clear-cut. By taking

---

[22] Memorandum by Forsyth, *c.* 1 May 1945, Forsyth Papers.
[23] Memorandum by Evatt, 10 May 1945, Evatt Papers. Evatt stressed the point several times at press conferences.

their foreign colleagues into their confidence the State Department officials helped to prove that they sincerely hoped to establish genuine trusteeship and not a façade.

It is Anglo-American collaboration that explains the resolution of the two issues of the strategic trust territory and colonial accountability. Throughout the conference Stassen and Gerig worked effectively with their British counterparts, Cranborne and Poynton. On the whole the Americans held the upper hand. The draft of their proposal had been years in the making. The best the British could produce was a warmed-over version of Article 22 of the League Covenant, understandably enough, since they were prepared to go no further than a renewal of the mandates system.[24] It was in the interest of both the British and the Americans to try to reach agreement on fundamentals; despite the divergence of views on the general issue of the future of colonies, they now had similar ideas about the limited function of the trusteeship system. During the first week and a half of the conference, the trusteeship commission made very little progress and showed 'signs of restlessness'.[25] During this time, in fact, intense secret discussions were being held between the American and British groups, and between the British delegation in San Francisco and the authorities in London. During the first half of May, Cranborne and Stassen successfully worked towards a concord that carried the conference and laid the basis of the trusteeship system.

The military problem arose first. The Americans made it the basis of their position that they would hold the Japanese mandated islands as a strategic trust territory. It was a clear, determined stand, with even the military advisers within the American group assuring the delegates that this was the only

[24] For Poynton's ideas, submitted in a memorandum written by him and A. D. K. Owen of the Foreign Office of 13 Apr. 1945, see CO 968/161/14814/11; FO 371/50808.

[25] Russell, *United Nations Charter*, p. 809. For an acute contemporary review, see Huntington Gilchrist, 'Colonial Questions at the San Francisco Conference', *American Political Science Review* 39. 5 (October 1945). Gilchrist had served as one of the first members of the League's Secretariat as Assistant Director of the Mandates Section. His other works include: 'Dependent Peoples and Mandates' in *Pioneers in World Order: An American Appraisal of the League of Nations*, ed. Harriet E. Davis (New York, 1944); and 'The Japanese Islands: Annexation or Trusteeship?', *Foreign Affairs* 22. 4 (July 1944).

solution to an otherwise hopeless problem.[26] To General Jacob, reporting to the Chiefs of Staff in London, the American purpose seemed merely to escape 'the odium of becoming classified as an imperialist power'.[27] Should the British protest? By asking for instructions on this point Jacob brought into play the strategical calculations of the British Empire, as formulated by the imperial government. There already existed a careful report on the Japanese islands prepared by the War Cabinet's Far Eastern Committee in consultation with the Chiefs of Staff, the Minister of Civil Aviation, and the Imperial Communications Committee.[28] This report advised that the United States should assume sole responsibility for the mandated islands and that no limits should be placed on fortification. British security in this part of the world would depend entirely on American defence. The question now merely arose whether the British should object to classification of the islands as a 'strategic trust'.

The planning staff of the Post-Hostilities Planning Committee responded to Jacob's request for instructions by concluding that the American scheme was strategically *objectionable*. So also did the Colonial Office, but for political reasons. The military logic held that the Americans could designate the islands 'strategic' because there was a clear-cut future enemy, the Japanese. But what if the British also wanted to designate all or part of a territory 'strategic'? They would have to substantiate their case by making clear the potential enemy. This would be both politically embarrassing and strategically difficult. The diverse geography of the British tropical African mandates differed from the obvious strategic position of the Japanese islands. The Colonial Office pointed out that if part of a colony were administered as 'strategic' and the other part 'non-strategic' the natives would be confused as to the purpose of British rule. In any case this line of reasoning did not appeal to the Americans and made for difficult bargaining on the part of the British delegation. Cranborne pointedly telegraphed to Stanley that none of the British proposals would stand a chance of acceptance by the Americans 'unless we cater for what they

[26] See e.g. the minutes of the American delegation, 26 Apr. 1945, *Foreign Relations: United Nations*, pp. 445–52.
[27] Jacob to Chiefs of Staff, 28 Apr. 1945, FO 371/50808; CO 968/161/14814/11.
[28] A.P.W. (45) 50, 4 Apr. 1945; for this report in relation to Colonial Office political strategy, CO 968/154/18404/1.

conceive to be their strategic requirements'.²⁹ Jacob informed
the military authorities that 'nothing would induce the American Chiefs of Staff to abandon a proposal which evidently had
been arrived at after a great struggle with the State Department'.³⁰ To the British delegation in San Francisco, it became
increasingly evident that there were genuine political and
strategic reasons for the classification of the Japanese mandates
as a 'strategic trust'. In London Oliver Stanley held out. To
him it appeared preposterous that the Americans should foist
trusteeship upon the conference and then seek to escape its
obligations by designating their own territory 'strategic'.

When Stanley learned of the details of the American plan
(which Stassen circulated to the trusteeship committee on the
30th of April and released to the press on the 3rd of May) he
telegraphed to Cranborne that from the Colonial Office's
standpoint it was *'unacceptable'*. 'Our territories are not small
islands but large and populous countries', the Colonial Secretary advised. If parts of the territories were classified 'strategic' then different administrative conditions would be created
(Stanley did not specify which 'large and populous' territory
he had in mind—Tanganyika?—or why it might fall into a
'strategic' category). The Colonial Secretary had also hoped to
restrict trusteeship activity to a specialized commission (along
the lines of the Permanent Mandates Commission, but with
official representation) operating under the narrow auspices of
a social and economic council. He now learned that the General
Assembly would exercise trusteeship authority. '[O]ur object is
to minimize functions of [the] General Assembly in this rather
special field', Stanley telegraphed. With the motley international assembly now becoming a reality, Stanley pointed out
that this meddlesome band would 'seek outlet for its energies
in quite undesirable directions'. On one point he indicated
especial concern. It is of particular interest because of the
consequence for the decolonization era. Stanley deprecated the
possibility of petitions and visiting missions.

[T]he proposal that both Assembly and Trusteeship Council should
be empowered to accept petitions, [and] to institute investigations

²⁹ Cranborne to Stanley, No. 71, 30 Apr. 1945, FO 371/50808; CO 968/161/
14814.
³⁰ Jacob to Chiefs of Staff, No. 271, 12 May 1945, FO 371/50809; CO 968/161.

... is *wholly unacceptable*. This would apparently involve the complete freedom of the Assembly to intervene actively in all matters of administration of such territories and you will be fully alive to [the] impossible situation which this would create for us *in all cases* and especially Palestine.[31]

Stanley correctly sensed that the Arab states might attempt to exploit the trusteeship issue, which, as will be seen in the next chapter, they did. With considerable anxiety the Colonial Secretary contemplated the formation of an anti-British bloc, including Russia and China as well as the United States and her Latin American satellites.

Lord Cranborne fully recognized the danger of an anti-British movement, and he was just as concerned as Stanley to make no concession that would jeopardize the Empire. On the 3rd of May the British delegation submitted a counter-proposal for trusteeship. It had been prepared by Poynton and Jacob in consultation with London. It essentially re-endorsed the principles of the mandates system without extending them. The British plan made no distinction between strategic and non-strategic territories. At a press conference on the 4th of May (the day after Stassen's meeting with the press) more than 500 reporters listened to Cranborne as he tried persuasively to argue the British case; but the American press took the opportunity to emphasize, as in the bold print of the *New York Herald Tribune*, that the '*British Oppose U.S. Proposals on Trusteeship of Seized Areas*'. The British were portrayed as objecting to American plans for the Pacific islands which might be 'vital to the defense' of the United States.[32] Nor did the British counter-proposal find a favourable reception within the trusteeship commission. Stassen reported to the American delegation that the British paper was 'unacceptable'. 'It was weaker than ours, there was no spelling out, and there was no division of strategic and non-strategic areas.'[33] With particular dismay the British noted that the French representatives favoured the American scheme. Until the French archives are accessible the reason for this strategy will not be known, though Cranborne observed

[31] Stanley to Cranborne, No. 267, 2 May 1945, FO 371/50808; CO 968/161.
[32] *New York Herald Tribune*, 4 May 1945.
[33] Minutes of the American delegation, 4 May 1945, *Foreign Relations: United Nations*, p. 597.

that the French appeared to think that the sloppy American wording was 'more elastic' and that in general the French were nevertheless extremely suspicious of the American plan. The New Zealanders responded more favourably than the British expected, but in fact the only whole-hearted support came from South Africa. The British delegation thus faced the prospect of becoming politically isolated.[34]

With a keen awareness of the advantage of working within a consensus, Cranborne now surveyed the issues at dispute with the Americans. He especially wanted to reach agreement with them, if at all possible, before the Chinese, Russians, and others might submit proposals that would be to the British disadvantage. In particular Cranborne had good reason to fear an initiative by Evatt. The impact of the Australian's forensic power was being felt in the conference. On the release of the American and British papers Evatt complained that he had not been given ample opportunity for advance preparation. He might now transform or replace the proposals for the cause of radical trusteeship. Cranborne therefore looked at the situation with an eye towards bringing British policy into line with the American. On the 8th of May he drew up a list of points on which the British might yield or stand firm. The one advantage the British held was the possibility of giving way on the issue of the strategic trust territory. This after all could have no adverse effect on the British Empire. The American Navy representatives were making no secret about their desire to use the Pacific islands as bases. General Jacob pointed out that a word of sympathy informally in this regard would carry the British a long way in building up a spirit of goodwill.[35] This was accordingly done. It cost the British nothing, and it helped immensely in bringing the two parties together.

The British resisted several proposals that appeared to be much more important at the time than they do in retrospect. The Colonial Office, for example, deplored the free-trade obligations of the mandates. The Americans were equally determined to have non-discriminatory provisions. Here the British tried to hold out, though they finally gave way. Cranborne was more willing to yield to the American insistence that

---

[34] Minutes of the British delegation, 4 and 5 May 1945, CO 968/162.
[35] Ibid., 8 May 1945.

the trusteeship council should report to the General Assembly. There was also a question of providing reports on all dependent territories. On this point Attlee carried the British delegation. 'We have nothing to hide', he said, and argued that they should make a virtue of the customary British practice of publishing reports on colonial territories and making them generally available.[36] One other point that could be yielded, in Cranborne's view, was the right of petition by the natives to the trusteeship council. The Americans were insistent on this right, and, though it would be an annoyance, it was not vital. This was an important concession because with the benefit of hindsight it did emerge as one of the important differences between the trusteeship system and the mandates system. On the major point where Cranborne thought they should hold their ground, *there must be no unconditional right of inspection.* Even here Cranborne was prepared to make concessions. He would be willing to grant that visits of inspection might be made under appropriate circumstances and with the assent of the trusteeship power.[37] To the arch-Tories of the British Empire, in retrospect this represented one of the landmarks in the beginning of the descent down the slippery slope of decolonization.

Cranborne calculated the British retreat against the background of the trusteeship commission. He had no reason to be pleased with the drift of the discussion. By the 10th of May the Russians as well as the French announced support of the American scheme. The South African representative did not help the British cause by arguing for the termination of the South-West Africa mandate, thereby raising suspicions that this was the course the British also secretly favoured for their mandates. The Chinese suggested that the word 'independence' be introduced—a harbinger of the bitter controversy of the second half of the conference. The Filipino representative made what Cranborne described as 'odious comparisons' between

[36] Ibid.

[37] Poynton telegraphed to Kenneth Robinson, who was in charge of the London end of the transactions in the Colonial Office: 'Lord Cranborne has made it clear that in some circumstances arrival of investigating body might have disastrous results on tense political situations, and therefore unconditional right of investigation cannot be granted. Nevertheless, he personally . . . would not entirely rule out possibility of investigation where circumstances seemed appropriate, with consent of administering state.' Poynton to Robinson, No. 173, 6 May 1945, CO 968/161/18414/11; FO 371/50808.

the situation in the Philippines and that of other dependent territories.[38] There was nothing surprising in these varied remarks. Anti-colonial sentiment had to be expected in a 'motley international assembly'. On the 10th of May however Evatt leaped into the discussion with a detailed program. He systematically drew together the main points of a forward and inspirational trusteeship scheme. 'I see no reason why the progress of these [colonial] peoples should be of [*sic*] any less a matter of international concern than the progress and welfare of peoples of territories taken from our enemies', Evatt stated. He pointed out that the conference was 'morally bound' by the Atlantic Charter to assure 'all the men in all the lands' freedom from want as well as freedom from fear. He urged the application of trusteeship for *all* colonial territories. He trusted that this plea would appeal to all enlightened men. He concluded his remarks for universal trusteeship by pointing out that it was 'very close to the heart of him whose service to the world every delegate to this Conference has so recently recognized—Franklin Roosevelt'.[39] According to the *New York Herald Tribune*, 'Dr. Evatt pulled no punches in his effort to persuade colonial powers that they should be required to put their present colonies under trusteeship in addition to the lands wrested from enemy nations.'[40] On the 12th of May Evatt's stand was widely reported in the press.[41] On the same day Cranborne urgently telegraphed to Stanley that the mood of the conference was turning against the British.

Unless the British could make concessions to bring their scheme into line with American thinking, Cranborne explained, then they would 'run the risk of being outvoted into something worse'. He thought that a compromise was possible. After long discussion with Stassen and Gerig, Cranborne and Poynton proposed to throw their weight formally behind the American scheme for a 'strategic trust' territory. They also compromised on numerous points of drafting, of which one in particular

---

[38] Minutes of the British delegation, 12 May 1945, CO 968/162. See also *Documents of the United Nations Conference on International Organization San Francisco 1945*, x, pp. 428–34.

[39] 'Territorial Trusteeship Statement', 10 May 1945, Evatt Papers, and ibid.

[40] *New York Herald Tribune*, 12 May 1945.

[41] There is an extensive press cutting collection in the Evatt Papers which is invaluable in studying the public response to trusteeship.

should be mentioned. The Americans insisted on the phrase 'states directly concerned' as the formula by which the technical agreement would be reached about which power would be the administering authority. Cranborne objected to this phrasing because any power, not least Russia, could argue direct concern. Cranborne accurately predicted that it would give rise to lengthy disputes, but he nevertheless proposed to give way in order to reach agreement.

The Americans also proved to be adamant about the free trade clauses. Most important of all, the British found Stassen absolutely immovable on the question of visiting missions.[42] Cranborne recommended a compromise whereby visiting missions would be received only at the invitation of the administering authority. 'I appreciate [that] these proposals are not all you or I would have wished,' he summed up for Stanley, but 'they are the result of long drawn out and extremely hard bargaining.'[43] In a subsequent telegram Cranborne stressed the political danger. The British found themselves in a situation in which they faced no alternative but to yield on the colonial issue or to abandon the United Nations. In a 'Most Immediate' and 'Top Secret' telegram Cranborne asked the War Cabinet to take the 'delicate' situation into account:

Our difficulty is political. We cannot count on carrying any point which may be pressed to vote in Committee unless United States supports us. We are therefore in dilemma that if we feel so strongly on any point that we cannot meet United States views and must force the issue, almost certain result will be that we lose altogether.

The British horror was that the motley international assembly was also an anti-colonial assembly: 'States which are not personally affected in these matters would naturally vote against Colonial powers on principle, quite apart from Latin-American tendency to support United States. So far as we can see we have no redress except refusal to sign Charter which appears unthinkable.'[44] Cranborne thus brought out the reason for capitulation in a way that could not fail to have its impact on

---

[42] Cranborne to Stanley, No. 268, 12 May 1945, FO 371/50809; CO 968/161.
[43] Ibid.
[44] Cranborne to Stanley, No. 300, 14 May 1945, ibid.; PREM 4/31/7.

Stanley, Churchill, and the War Cabinet. '[*T*]*o refuse to sign the Charter would be unthinkable.*'[45]

In London Stanley in exasperation wrote in a memorandum for the War Cabinet that the Americans were securing a territory 'free from any trusteeship "strings"', thereby removing 'the one incentive the United States have to take a sensible and realistic view of trusteeship provisions in other mandated territories'. But Stanley also noted that Russia, France, and China had all indicated support of the American proposal. If the British failed to go along, then the initiative would pass to even more distasteful personages, namely the Australians and specifically Evatt. With heart-wrenching groans, Stanley thus resigned himself to yielding to the Americans, even on the 'most objectionable' proposal to accept visiting missions. Cranborne could at least make sure that the inspections would take place only '*at the invitation* of the administering State'.[46]

At a meeting of the War Cabinet on the 14th of May 1945, Stanley repeated his protest and stated that in the last resort His Majesty's Government could simply refuse to alter the terms of the existing mandates (in effect the position taken by the South Africans). Obviously this was not an appealing argument to those who attached value to getting along with the Americans and who did not wish to jeopardize the establishment of the United Nations because of minor colonial issues.

Churchill carried the sense of the meeting. He had always taken the line that the Americans should be allowed to dispose of the Pacific islands as they saw fit. He now was willing to take a moderate stand on the specific colonial issues. If he had lingering objections to the British Empire being put 'in the dock', at least he now had assurance that international supervision would be quite limited. The examination of annual reports by the Trusteeship Council represented no more than a disagreeable hangover from the mandates system. And the point about the visiting missions, after all, was not much of a concession, especially if the circumstances of the visit could be controlled by the administering power.

THE PRIME MINISTER said that in his view the proper course was to refuse to accept any compromise in respect of our

45 Minutes of the British Delegation, 14 May 1945, CO 968/162. Italics added.
46 Memorandum by Stanley, 14 May 1945, W.P. (45) 300, CAB 66/65.

present mandated territories; but, subject to that, to allow the United States to have their way over the special category of 'strategic' areas in which they would wish to place all the Pacific Islands which they might capture from the Japanese. He thought it would be better tactics to postpone pressing even for the improvements which we were justifiably anxious to see in the conditions of the present mandates.[47]

The other members of the War Cabinet concurred. Cranborne accordingly received authority to bring the British proposals in line with the American. No doubt Stanley keenly resented the concessions, but to almost everyone else they appeared negligible in comparison with the risk of wrecking the conference. The Americans and the British accordingly fused their schemes, and provided the working basis on which the trusteeship system was elaborated. The Trusteeship Council would be empowered to examine annual reports, to receive petitions, and to despatch visiting missions at the invitation of the administering authority.[48] The focus of controversy in mid-May then shifted to the issue of the ultimate purpose of trusteeship and whether it should be independence. As this transition was taking place Hilton Poynton wrote a poignant letter to Kenneth Robinson at the Colonial Office summarizing, in his view, the disastrous course of events. His postscript expressed the feeling of despair of those who thought the British Empire had already yielded too much: 'I am . . . disheartened over the whole thing. I'm afraid we've got ourselves into a ghastly jam. I expect you are all seething with rage in London.'[49]

[47] W.M. (45) 61st Conclusions, 14 May 1945, CAB 65/60.
[48] For further details, see Russell, *United Nations Charter*, ch. XXXI.
[49] 'I'm sorry,' Poynton added, 'but I've done my best.' Poynton to Robinson, 18 May 1945, CO 968/161/14814/11.

34

SAN FRANCISCO: THE QUESTION OF COLONIAL INDEPENDENCE

ONLY 'a miserable attempt', according to an Australian delegate looking back on the results of the conference, was made 'to settle the Colonial questions'.[1] This negative judgement of Sir Frederick Eggleston is of particular interest in view of his experience a quarter of a century earlier, when he had followed the colonial settlement at the Paris Peace Conference. He shared a disillusionment with those who had idealistic hopes that the San Francisco Conference might advance the position established in 1919. In a formal sense the settlement of 1945 represented only a narrow improvement. The colonial powers, including the United States, scarcely granted any more authority to the new international organization than the League had possessed. The rights of visitation and petition were important exceptions, but the significance seemed debatable at the time. Nor did the general declaration —with which this chapter will be concerned—inspire much confidence in the liberal intentions of the colonial powers. To those who wanted to end old-fashioned Imperialism, the responsibility for failure to take a bold stand rested in large part with the United States. The Americans had raised expectations that they might unfurl an anti-imperial banner. Therein lies a story of conflict. They were by no means agreed as a delegation about the future of the colonies. In one sense, the question of colonial freedom can be seen as coming to a head in May 1945 as the anti-colonial nations lined up against the imperialists. For no other delegation perhaps was the choice more excruciating than for the American. When it came to the test, the United States sided with the colonial powers.

The colonial settlement can also be interpreted in a different and more positive way. Apart from the various territorial issues which will be dealt with in the next chapter, the powers

[1] Eggleston's unpublished autobiography, Eggleston Papers.

represented at San Francisco reached agreement on three chapters in the United Nations Charter. Going from the particular to the general, Chapter XIII specifies the institutional structure and function of the Trusteeship Council. Chapter XII establishes the general principles of trusteeship and includes the distinction between strategic and non-strategic territories. To conclude formal agreement on these controversial areas required long and difficult bargaining, as the reader will have concluded from the preceding discussion. Chapter XI of the United Nations Charter is entitled 'Declaration regarding Non-Self-Governing Territories'. One of the passages which created the most controversy restates the obligation of the 'sacred trust', a concept now left implicit:

> to develop self-government, to take due account of the political aspirations of the peoples, and to assist them in the progressive development of their free political institutions, according to the particular circumstances of each territory and its peoples and their varying stages of advancement.

Like the drafting of the chapters on trusteeship which proceeded simultaneously, this related chapter on non-self-governing territories evolved against the background of profound ideological differences.

At one extreme the Russians argued for *full national independence and self-determination in all colonial areas.* At the other extreme the British argued that there should be a distinction drawn between independence and liberty. Many colonial subjects, according to Lord Cranborne, enjoyed far greater liberty than those of some independent states in Europe. During this long and sometimes bitter debate, Cranborne granted that in the evolutionary process of political development, *independence might be the outcome of self-government.* Whether independence on the whole is preferable to self-government within the jurisdiction of the metropolitan country remains, then as now, a debatable point.

For the British and the other colonial powers to have formally acknowledged that their duty lay in the direction of progressive self-government of the colonies can be interpreted as a significant step forward on behalf of dependent peoples throughout the world. For those who might denounce the chapter as mere rhetoric, it can be said that the issues of self-government and independence seemed real at the time. To the representatives of the powers assembled at San Francisco, there was a sense that they were setting a course that would affect the future of colonial subjects everywhere. Once inscribed in the Charter of the United Nations, the pledges could not be erased. In view of the gravity of the issues at stake, what is surprising is not the cautious endorsement of the goal of self-government —with the possibility of independence—but the fact that the colonial and anti-colonial powers could finally reach agreement.

The ideological split developed on the 12th of May.[2] The Chinese and Russian representatives wished to include the word *independence* in the declaration. The French representative immediately objected. He said that the scope of trusteeship should be strictly defined and that there must be no intervention in the internal affairs of member states. The Dutch spokesman held that the imposition of a general declaration on the 'advanced' colonial states would be 'a backward step'. The South African protested against any alteration of the terms of the mandate, saying that it would be 'a breach of faith'.[3] According to the Indian representative, K. S. Menon, who gave one of the most vivid descriptions of the reactions to the word 'independence', the most 'ominous' feature of the debate was 'Russia's newborn interest in colonial affairs. . . . She has imported the magic words full national independence and self-determination into her statement of the objectives of colonial policy.'[4]

It was against this background—with the colonial powers arrayed against Russia and China—that Stassen made an extemporaneous speech of fundamental importance. He stated simply and clearly that the United States would vote against Russia and China because the subject of independence was not one on which the great powers could expect to reach agreement. He argued that the phrase self-government was encompassing enough, since self-government might lead to independence.

[2] See *Documents of the United Nations Conference on International Organization* (hereafter *UNCIO Documents*), x. 433–41.

[3] The South African delegate went on to argue the case for incorporation of South-West Africa into the Union, at which time Fraser declared him out of order. The South-West Africa question is discussed in ch. 35 below.

[4] In U.K. Delegation to Foreign Office, No. 333, 16 May 1945, FO 371/50809.

He gave as an example the American experience in the Philippines. Then—with words that would have comforted Christopher Eastwood and others in the Colonial Office—Stassen stressed that the future of the world lay with *interdependence*, not independence. He spoke of the American forty-eight states, 'whose strength is based not on their complete independence as separate entities, but on their unity and interdependence'. Lord Cranborne did not intervene to say so, but of course the same case could have been argued for the constituent parts of the British Empire. Stassen even compared the colonial empires with the federal system of the United States.[5] To those in the Roosevelt tradition of colonial affairs, his speech represented no less than an abandonment of colonial independence as the historic goal of American policy.

Stassen's speech may have been extemporaneous but it was logically consistent and clear. He explained to the American delegation that 'progressive development toward self-government' would be the only formula which would command the assent of the colonial as well as the anti-colonial powers. Self-government might lead to independence. On the other hand the word 'independence' was provocative. Did the United States moreover really intend to promote independence throughout the world? It was a large question. Again he stressed the phrase 'progressive development toward self-government', which implied possible independence, but not necessary independence in all cases. He did not want to go beyond endorsing self-government. 'If one goes beyond that phrase there was danger that we would be interpreted as butting in on colonial affairs.'[6] Stassen was a cogent speaker, thoroughly in control of the complexity of the problem. He seemed moderate while at the same time he took a firm stand. Representative Bloom, who had listened to the speech before the trusteeship committee, called it 'the best he had ever heard'.[7] Despite Stassen's persuasiveness, the issue of colonial independence caused sharp dissent within the American delegation.

When the Americans discussed the question of independence on the 18th of May, everyone at the meeting sensed a critical

---

[5] See *Foreign Relations: 1945: United Nations*, p. 790, n. 14.
[6] Minutes of the American delegation, 18 May 1945, ibid., pp. 792–3.
[7] Ibid., p. 793.

decision. Would they stand with Russia, China, and the Asian and colonial peoples? Or would they decide that their true interests lay with their western allies, above all with the British Empire? However one phrased the proposition, it was difficult to avoid taking a position one way or the other. The issue evoked keen interest even from those not usually involved in colonial affairs. Harley Notter, a State Department expert on international organization and a scholar of Woodrow Wilson's foreign policy,[8] began the discussion. He felt that both the British and the Russians, for different reasons, would take advantage of the United States if the Americans did not explicitly espouse 'independence'. The Russians would exploit the situation in Asia. 'This position [of self-government] would be very unpopular in the Far East', he stated. 'To take any position short of independence simply would not satisfy the colonial peoples.' Moreover, to follow Stassen's line of self-government would be to play into the hands of the imperialists. In Notter's view the issue was clear–cut. 'If we maintained the present position [of self-government] we would be spearheading for the British, Dutch and Belgian colonial empires.' Perhaps because of his study of Woodrow Wilson, Notter was apprehensive of the United States being duped by the imperialists. He used strong language. '[I]n opposing independence we were putting ourselves in the position to be played for suckers.'[9]

Of all of the members of the delegation, Charles Taussig reacted most vehemently. To him Stassen's speech in favour of self-government was a tragic blunder. To repudiate 'independence' meant a rejection of the ideals of Franklin D. Roosevelt and Cordell Hull. Taussig now attempted to rectify the damage done by Stassen. He prepared a memorandum protesting the goal of self-government. He circulated it to key members of the delegation such as Isaiah Bowman who he hoped would lend support as a colonial authority.[10] Taussig then stated the case before the delegation. He stressed that the colonial issue had 'serious implications' throughout the world and especially in the Far East. He urged support for the Russian and Chinese

---

[8] See Harley Notter, *The Origins of the Foreign Policy of Woodrow Wilson* (Baltimore, 1937).

[9] Minutes of the American delegation, 18 May 1945, pp. 793, 796.

[10] Memorandum dated 18 May 1945, Bowman Papers.

position. He gave the following reasons. They indicate the still powerful influence of the ideas of the dead President:

(1) Independence as a goal for all peoples who aspire to and are capable of it has been the traditional and sacred policy of this Government. It has been exemplified in our policy in the Philippines, and it has been reiterated on numerous occasions by President Roosevelt and former Secretary of State Cordell Hull.

(2) An excellent opportunity is afforded to make a profitable gesture on behalf of the peoples of the Orient as well as those in Africa and the Caribbean.

(3) The Russians especially and the Chinese will be able to capitalize on their stand for 'independence' against the opposition of the non-Asiatic peoples of the West unless we take a strong position.[11]

Stassen immediately defended his position by pointing out some of the flaws in the logic of self-determination and independence. Did the United States wish to give independence to Puerto Rico? He believed that American policy could be vindicated by the example of the Philippines. There was, moreover, an important fundamental reason why the United States should not endorse 'independence': '*we . . . did not wish to find ourselves committed to breaking up the British empire.*'[12] With incisive clarity Stassen thus identified the American dilemma, not only in the colonial debate at San Francisco but also in the postwar era. The more firm a stand on the colonial question, the more irreversible a direction the United States would take in global alignments.

There followed an exchange between Stassen and Taussig, the latter making an emotional as well as a rational appeal to the ideals of President Roosevelt, the former coolly appraising the disadvantages of 'independence' as a universal goal. Stassen reiterated his belief that 'interdependence' rather than 'independence' was the word of the future. He furthermore pointed out that, if the American delegation insisted on 'independence', the trusteeship committee would reach an impasse. 'If we sided with the Chinese and the Russians on this issue, there probably would be no trusteeship system since the British will never accept that position.'[13] At this point Stettinius

---

[11] Minutes of the American delegation, 18 May 1945, pp. 793–4.
[12] Ibid., p. 794. Italics added.   [13] Ibid., p. 794.

broke in and proclaimed that there was no question 'where we stood as a nation'. As if it were perfectly obvious, he said that the United States supported human rights and self-determination. The Secretary of State swung his weight behind Stassen. Taussig now made his last significant protest. He told the delegation about his last meeting with Roosevelt on the 15th of March. He said he had asked the President specifically 'whether he would settle for self-government'. Roosevelt's reply, of course, was that 'he would settle for nothing less than the objective of independence'. Taussig continued:

[I]n talks with the President it was clear that he felt that the word 'independence' rather than progressive self-government would alone satisfy the Oriental people. To deny the objective of independence, he [Roosevelt] felt, would sow the seeds of the next world war. The President had felt that we should take the leadership and indicate to the Oriental peoples that we do not back the imperial role of the handful of non-Asiatics.[14]

Taussig thus provided an accurate account of Roosevelt's views, including the belief that 'the next world war' could be brought about because of the colonial question.

With dispassionate scepticism, Stassen refused to be drawn into a philosophical debate on the virtues of independence. He merely challenged the proposition by again going to the heart of the matter, at least from the American point of view. '*Mr. Stassen asked whether it was our intention to give complete independence to Hawaii.*' He continued by emphasizing the importance of looking to the future rather than to the past. 'Independence, he felt, was a concept developed out of the past era of nationalism. It suggested, and looked in the direction of, isolationism. We should be more interested in inter-dependence than in independence and for this reason it might be fortunate to avoid the term "independence".'[15] With such persuasive reasoning Stassen began bringing the other members of the delegation around to his side, one by one.

John Foster Dulles was among the first to say he was convinced by Stassen's presentation of the case for self-government. He believed that independence 'might not assist in the establishment of future peace'. Dulles added that 'the church

14 Minutes of the American delegation, 18 May 1945, p. 794.
15 Ibid., p. 795. Italics added.

groups with which he was associated were satisfied in all their statements with self-government or autonomy as objectives of the trusteeship system and had never insisted on independence'.[16] Dulles may have had a moralistic tendency to see things in black and white, but in this instance he shrewdly perceived the difficulties in which the Americans would find themselves if they took a righteous stand on the side of independence. He said that he supported Stassen.

Isaiah Bowman was asked for his views. Since he had discussed the colonial issue with the British at great length in London a year earlier, his position on the question appeared to Taussig to be crucial. Bowman said that they confronted a real problem. As had been apparent in other committee discussions, he was becoming increasingly preoccupied with Russia. He now saw the crux of the colonial question as 'the problem of Russia promising to do one thing and doing another'. In Bowman's view Russia was attempting to sow 'the seeds of independence' throughout the world. 'Russia, he felt, was trying to substitute what she wanted in the areas now dominated by the Netherlands and Britain.' As if with a premonition of the cold war, Bowman foresaw the danger of alienating the British. 'Russia now faced one of her greatest opportunities. When perhaps the inevitable struggle came between Russia and ourselves the question would be who are our friends. Would we have as our friends those whom we had weakened in the struggle or those whom we had strengthened?'[17] Taussig interrupted to say that this view was entirely misguided. He did not see how abandoning the objective of independence would strengthen the American position. On the contrary, Taussig thought that rejecting independence would 'play directly into Russian propaganda', especially in the Far East. Bowman retorted that the United States was establishing the trusteeship system in order *not* to play into anyone's hand. And he ultimately thought that British friendship was worth more than the abstract ideal of independence. With a sense of betrayal, Taussig later recorded that Bowman and even Benjamin Gerig failed to support the goal of independence as the historic policy of the United States.[18]

---

[16] Ibid., p. 795.   [17] Ibid.
[18] Undated memorandum (post-San Francisco) in the Taussig Papers.

Bowman's analysis of a Russian colonial plot raised cataclysmic suspicions among some of the other delegates. Representative Eaton felt that it all boiled down to 'who was going to be master of the world'. He saw it as a struggle 'as to whose ideals were going to dominate'. He stated that he for one would not vote 'to put Russia in control of the world'.[19] On this and similar comment Stassen refused to take an alarmist view. He believed that there was 'plenty of room for both the ideals of this country and of Russia if they competed on a proper basis'.[20] Other members of the delegation had been turning over the issue as they saw it from their particular vantage points. Nelson Rockefeller for example noted that backward peoples faced a basic conflict. 'If they achieved independence, the assistance, which they needed from the larger states to advance their economic and social status, would collapse.'[21] He thought that this conflict was handled as satisfactorily as it could be in Stassen's formula. Dean Gildersleeve said that she supported Stassen. Connally thought that Stassen's position was 'entirely satisfactory'. The Texas Senator was afraid, he said, that 'if the word "independence" was put in, there would be a good deal of stirring up of a desire for independence and the orderly procedure in the direction of self-government would be interrupted'.[22] Senator Vandenberg and Representatives Eaton and Bloom also concurred. With a steady hand, Stassen had carried the delegation in favour of self-government as the goal of American policy. The question of the American dependencies had loomed in the background of the debate. Even Taussig eventually acknowledged that American 'dependent peoples would prefer their integrity under the United States to the proclamation of Russia that it favored their independence'.[23]

A few of the State Department officials acquiesced only reluctantly in the solution of self-government. Harley Notter, for example, pointed out that there was no fundamental difference in the goal of self-government or independence because the former implied the possibility of the latter. But he observed that there was a world of difference in the approach to the problem. He felt that the Americans, to repeat his

---

[19] Minutes of the American delegation, 18 May 1945, p. 797.
[20] Ibid., p. 797. [21] Ibid., p. 796.
[22] Ibid., p. 797. [23] Ibid., pp. 796–7.

phrase, were being 'played for suckers'. This was a charge to which the American delegates were especially sensitive. In concluding the discussion, they emphasized the importance of not being portrayed as *opposing* independence. Here Pasvolsky played an important part. During the debate, he had intervened from time to time to emphasize the desirability of reaching a compromise between the two positions of self-government and independence. He wanted to 'dress up' Stassen's stand so that the Americans would *appear* to support independence, whereas in fact they would be supporting self-government. He devised a formula whereby independence might be acknowledged as a possible outcome of self-government. It was agreed to urge this possibility on the British. The outcome was that the word 'independence' eventually found its way into the trusteeship chapter (XII) but not in the declaration on non-self-governing territories (ch. XI). The British viewed 'independence' with repugnance, but they were so relieved that the Americans had sided with them on the *general* colonial declaration that they were prepared to make the concession for the *specific* trust territories. For the Americans, Stassen's steadfast moderation preserved British friendship without rejecting the possibility of liberation. In his subsequent public statements, Stassen made it clear that self-government might lead to eventual independence.

With the Americans and the British in agreement about the two major issues of the strategic trust territory and the limitation of the word 'independence' to the trusteeship chapter, Stassen and Cranborne were able to work together to bring the colonial business to a conclusion. Anglo-American collaboration forms one of the main themes of the rest of the conference. The two delegations had a powerful reason to collaborate: unless they solved the colonial problems, Evatt might do it for them. The combination of the two powers proved effective in eventually bringing the smaller nations as well as China and Russia into line. The Chinese responded to American pressure, for example, in withdrawing the word 'independence' from the general colonial declaration. The Russians took a generally compliant line in order to be assured of a seat on the trusteeship council.

It was the oratory of the smaller powers that caused the

United States and Britain the most difficulty, mainly because of the annoyance and embarrassment. The precursors of the 'Third World' bloc of the United Nations exposed the gap between the idealistic rhetoric and the actual practice of the colonial powers. During one of the sessions the Filipino representative, General Carlos P. Romulo, for example, made an impassioned speech in favour of absolute independence. He denounced the phrase 'self-government' as meaningless. He emphasized that excluding 'independence' from the general declaration would confirm the intention of the colonial powers not to liberate millions of colonial peoples throughout the world. Romulo was eventually 'squared' by Stassen (as Cranborne described the political process of silencing him), but not before the Filipino had made it clear that the colonial declaration hardly measured up to the expectations aroused by the Atlantic Charter.

To the British a similar annoyance came from the delegate of Guatemala. On one occasion he delivered a rousing speech on the subject of Guatemalan claims against British Honduras. He argued that under no circumstance should Belize (British Honduras) be placed under trusteeship because this would prejudice claims of Guatemalan sovereignty. Since trusteeship was not a real issue in this regard, almost everyone regarded the speech as an attack on British Imperialism. The Guatemalan spoke in Spanish. When the speech was translated into English, Peter Fraser angrily declared him out of order. But the protest against British Imperialism had been read into the record, to the extreme exasperation of the British delegation. The Argentine delegate followed with a similar declaration in regard to the Falkland Islands. At the time these episodes appeared farcical to some observers, but the British took them seriously (and the issues have persisted). The British Empire was under attack in the motley international assembly. Despite the Anglo-American combination, the smaller powers could not be controlled. It was a good foretaste of the later colonial debates of the United Nations.[24]

For both the British and the Americans the last crisis of the conference concerned the future of the Middle East. Like the

[24] The most candid accounts of these debates are in CO 968/161/14814/11. For the published version see *UNCIO Documents* x.

Latin Americans, the Iraqis and Egyptians seized the opportunity to denounce western imperialism. With fiery conviction they proclaimed that 'self-determination' was a fundamental human right. In the words of the Indian representative, reporting a speech by the Iraqi, 'There were certain countries which regarded liberty equality and fraternity as fit for home consumption only and not for export. Peoples of mandated territories who had been promised independence had now to suffer bloodshed and see their cities bombed and destroyed in order to achieve it.'[25] He referred to the French expedition to Lebanon and Syria, which with maladroit timing had been sent on a 'pacification' mission at the very time of the San Francisco conference. In the view of the Arabs, the western powers needed to bring their own concepts of civilization up to date. Here it can be said that an advance was made in relation to Article 22 of the League Covenant. The United Nations Charter did not carry over the anachronistic phrases of 'A', 'B', and 'C' peoples of different stages of civilization and progress. Who after all should be the judge of whether nations were 'not yet able to stand by themselves'? When the western nations spoke of a 'sacred trust of civilization', *whose* civilization did they have in mind? With the Iraqi delegate in the vanguard against these Eurocentric concepts, the conference adopted such awkward but politically and ideologically neutral phrases such as 'non-self-governing territories' in place of the old phraseology which suggested that these peoples were *unable* to govern themselves.

Beneath the surface of these verbal clashes lay the problem of Palestine. It was not mentioned in the formal sessions, but in the meetings of the delegations the subject was, in Stassen's phrase, 'a hot potato'. The Arab states feared that the colonial powers would tilt the balance in Palestine in favour of the Jews. The Egyptian delegate introduced a resolution that, in regard to the mandate–trusteeship negotiations, would in effect maintain the *status quo* in Palestine. For the British, who above all were anxious to keep on good terms with the Arabs without exacerbating the Palestine problem, this was an explosive situation. If the Arabs (or the Russians) attempted to promote the principle of self-determination it would be, according to

[25] Menon to Caroe, No. 538, 1 June 1945, FO 371/50810.

Lord Cranborne, 'disastrous'.[26] For the Americans the question was equally delicate. One mis-step would have the Jews as well as the Arabs in an uproar at one or the other being given the advantage. It is a measure of Stassen's leadership that the Jewish delegate Sol Bloom congratulated him for doing 'an excellent job' of keeping the lid on (and he further stated to the delegation that Stassen 'had been the only delegate on the [Trusteeship] Committee who had taken an intelligent position and who had been sincerely interested in establishing a worthwhile trusteeship system'.)[27] The key to the stand-off between the Jews and Arabs in regard to the trusteeship issue was the so-called conservatory clause sponsored by the Egyptian delegate, who by all accounts was one of the outstanding Arab statesmen at the conference. Jewish rights in Palestine were not diminished while the Arab states received the assurance that they were not increased. The *status quo* was frozen. In this respect the United Nations Charter did not add to or detract from the League of Nations Covenant.

If the Australians had had their way, the colonial chapters would have been much more rigorous. Towards the beginning of the conference, on the 10th of May, Evatt had submitted an alternative draft trusteeship proposal that provided for universal trusteeship, or what he called trusteeship for 'new' as well as 'old' mandates. It was not even discussed. Evatt made no secret of his resentment at the British and Americans blocking his schemes. In the struggle for control of the trusteeship committee, Evatt lost to Stassen, who was not only in league with Cranborne but also emerged as a leading personality at San Francisco as a result of his able handling of the trusteeship business. At the close of the conference a poll taken among newspapermen revealed that Stassen tied with Evatt in an 11–11 vote as to the statesman 'who made the best impression on the Conference'.[28]

Though Evatt's main contribution to the founding of the United Nations is not to be found in the realm of trusteeship (despite his later claims that the colonial chapters were due to Australian initiative), nevertheless he can rightly be identified in

---

[26] Minutes of the British delegation, 30 May 1945, CO 968/162.
[27] Minutes of the American delegation, 5 June 1945, p. 1170.
[28] Described in Eggleston to K.K. Officer, 5 July 1945, Eggleston Papers.

a general and a specific way with the ingredients of the colonial settlement. Generally he contributed greatly to what he called *the moral tone* of the declaration on non-self-governing territories.[29] More specifically he kept up persistent pressure for *accountability*. He demanded that the colonial powers submit reports on all dependent territories. This feature of the trusteeship negotiations did not constitute much of a concession for either the Americans or the British (since reports were submitted to Congress and Parliament anyway), but to have regular reporting established through an international agency was an important step. The Indian representative, for example, regarded this part of the accord as among the most significant achievements of the conference:

The most important innovation now made is to institute a limited system of reporting on all dependent territories. The administering authorities have undertaken an obligation to transmit regularly to the Secretary General for information purposes statistical and other information of a technical nature relating to economic, social and educational conditions in the territories for which they are responsible . . .[30]

At the closing session the Dutch representative said that the decision to request reports for dependent territories represented an 'historic moment'. There was a consensus that Australia deserved credit for many of these 'liberal' features of the settlement, if only because Evatt had continually pressed for concessions from the colonial powers. He did not, however, take a stand on the side of 'independence'. Like virtually all the representatives of the western powers, Evatt was a gradualist who believed that self-government or independence would be achieved only after decades and even centuries of economic and social progress. His contribution, above all, amounted to his constant reminder to the colonial powers that they had a moral responsibility to their dependent peoples. That he succeeded, moreover, in making clear in a painful and abrasive

---

[29] As Evatt described his purpose in late May in a telegram to Canberra, 'To give more moral appeal to what is so far a very barren and arid documentation . . .', Evatt to Canberra, 28 May 1945, AA A1066 H45/771/3. For a discussion of Australian policy at San Francisco, see W. J. Hudson, *Australia and the Colonial Question at the United Nations* (Honolulu, 1970), ch. 1.

[30] Menon to Caroe, No. 781, 20 June 1945, FO 371/50810.

way that Britain no longer dominated Australia is evident
from an acid comment by Sir Alexander Cadogan: 'Evatt, the
Australian . . . [is] the most frightful man in the world; he
makes long and tiresome speeches on every conceivable subject,
always advocating the wrong thing and generally with a view
to being inconvenient and offensive to us.'[31]

At the closing meeting of the trusteeship commission on the
21st of June 1945, the delegates attempted to surpass each
other in assessing their achievement. It is noteworthy that
Stassen paid an especially warm tribute to the Russian representative, who had not proved to be obstructive. Though the
Russians would have liked further explicit endorsement of the
principle of self-determination and national independence in
all colonial areas, these sentiments found eloquent expression
in the voices of other delegates, especially those of the Arabs.
The French representative stated that his country was the home
of liberty, equality, and fraternity, and that therefore France
welcomed the trusteeship chapters. The Iraqi retorted that
liberty, equality, and fraternity should be proven by deeds and
not mere words. The Egyptian noted that the colonial settlement was by no means perfect but at least it was a step in
the right direction. Australia regarded the colonial declaration
as 'the most important and far reaching joint declaration of
Colonial policy in history'. Peter Fraser stressed that the goal
was to help dependent peoples to help themselves. The Belgian
emphasized that the motto in the Congo was 'to rule in order
to serve'. General Romulo described every word in the charter
as representing the blood of the brown man as well as the white.
'God fulfills himself in many ways,' the Filipino said, 'sometimes by granting self-government and sometimes independence.' The word 'independence' evoked many emotions. At
San Francisco it became abundantly clear that the word would
be used increasingly throughout the colonial world. In a sense
the San Francisco conference thus can be seen as marking the
flow into independence that characterized the post-war era.

'Independence' certainly lay heavy on the mind of the representative of the greatest colonial power in the world at that
time, Lord Cranborne. He told the conference in his parting
words that it had never been the intention of the British to deny

[31] *Diaries of Sir Alexander Cadogan*, p. 745.

the possibility of independence. But he said that he should sound a warning note. 'We are all of us in favour of freedom,' Cranborne said in this eloquent statement, 'but freedom for many of these territories means assistance and guidance and protection.' In retrospect his words may appear highly paternalistic, but they were quite characteristic of the times and of the conviction of the British of their colonial mission. Cranborne likened the development of the colonies to an evolutionary ladder. Up this ladder moved the colonial peoples as they attained 'a higher measure of self-government'. Here was Cranborne's view of how 'independence' fitted into this evolutionary process:

Do not let us rule out independence as the ultimate destiny of some of these territories. It is not ruled out. . . . But to have it as the universal goal of colonial policy would, we believe, be unrealistic and prejudicial to peace and security. Nor am I sure it is in the minds or desires of the vast majority of colonial peoples themselves.

What do these peoples want? They want liberty. Let us give them liberty. They want justice. Let us give them justice. . . . Let us help them to climb the rungs of the ladder of self-government. That is the purpose . . . so that ultimately dependent or independent they may play their full part in a peaceful, prosperous and independent world.[32]

No doubt some of the representatives of the non-colonial powers dismissed Cranborne's words as mere rhetoric of British Imperialism, but he certainly struck a keynote of post-war colonial policy when he stated that it was the duty of the colonial powers gradually to train the colonial peoples 'in the management of their own affairs so that should independence ultimately come they will be ready for it'.

---

[32] For the formal record of this speech, see *UNCIO Documents*, viii 158–9.

35

STRATEGIC SECURITY AND THE COLONIAL SITUATION IN 1945

'IT is not only in Europe that we are likely to have our troubles!' wrote a Foreign Office official in January 1945.[1] The exclamation brings to mind the problems at the close of the First World War as well as those of the second. At both times the fate of the British Empire seemed bound up with the questions of non-western nationalism and American anti-imperialism. These forces were clearly recognized in 1919 and they now appeared magnified perhaps a hundredfold in 1945. Another British official wrote: 'The Americans do not wish us to recover our previous position in Asia, confuse this wish in their minds with the principle of self-determination (alias 'freedom') & so see in every move to recover lost property a sinister desire to enslave native peoples.'[2] Churchill, for one, continued to believe that it was outrageous for the Americans to take such a distorted and sentimental view. He again made it absolutely clear that the British meant to hold their own. He recorded a conversation with the American Ambassador to China, General Patrick Hurley in March 1945, writing that the General 'seemed to wish to confine the conversation to civil banalities. I took him up with violence about Hong Kong and said that never would we yield an inch of the territory that was under the British flag.'[3] Churchill's sentiments seemed like an echo from the nineteenth century to some of his contemporaries, and it is true that his views were more characteristic of the close of the First World War period than of the Second. But the issues were essentially the same.

In 1945 British statesmen calculated the defence of the Empire in exactly the same way as their predecessors a quarter of a century earlier: British lines of communication to the East would have to be made secure against any possible

[1] M. E. Dening to Sterndale Bennett, 17 Jan. 1945, FO 371/46325.
[2] Minute by J. Thyne Henderson, 14 Jan. 1945, ibid.
[3] Note by Churchill, 11 Apr. 1945, ibid.

aggressor. At both times the defence of the Empire involved British expansion. In 1919 most of the German colonies and much of the Ottoman Empire became British mandates. Now the question was whether parts of the Italian colonial empire would become British trust territories. Churchill's successor as Prime Minister, Clement Attlee, regarded international trusteeship as a continuation of the old story of British Imperialism. He wrote in September 1945:

> After the last war, under the system of mandates, we acquired large territories. The world outside not unnaturally regarded this as a mere expansion of the British Empire. Trusteeship will appear to most people as only old mandates writ large.[4]

With the objections of a Labour politician who opposed Imperialism on ideological grounds, Attlee also sensed that the basis of power of the British Empire was being transformed. Above all the development of air technology and the advent of the atomic age probably marked the beginning of the Empire's decline and fall in a way just as distinct as the rise of the nationalist movements in Asia and Africa. Since this watershed is more apparent in retrospect than it was at the time, it is of considerable interest that Attlee saw it clearly in 1945. The British Empire, he wrote, was the creation of sea power.

> Quite apart from the advent of the atomic bomb which should affect all considerations of strategic area, the British Commonwealth and Empire is not a unit that can be defended by itself. . . . With the advent of air warfare the conditions which made it possible to defend a string of possessions scattered over five continents by means of a Fleet based on island fortresses have gone. . . . In the air age the neutrality, if not the support, of all countries contiguous to the route are needed.[5]

Throughout the world the old basis of strategy and political order was changing to British disadvantage.

In the Far East the restoration of the British Empire depended on American accommodation as well as the general situation in Asia. Old antagonisms and suspicions marked the last stage of the war. 'Everything at present points to the fact

---

[4] Memorandum by Attlee, 1 Sept. 1945, C.P. (45), 144, CAB 129/1.
[5] Ibid.

that the United States intend to take a leading part in settling the future of the Far East', wrote M. E. Dening, the Foreign Office official attached to the South-East Asia Command. 'If they were not so ham-fisted in their conduct of international affairs, this might be all to the good.' But in his opinion the Americans would find themselves in a head-on collision with Russia. The American conception of a Far Eastern settlement, in British eyes, might not lead to the stability envisaged by the planners in Washington. Dening's lines convey some of the bitterness felt by British officials who resented the anti-colonial American attitude in Asia.

> One of our major tasks will be to convince the United States that it is not in their interests to undermine the stability of the British Empire in Asia and the Pacific or to upset the equilibrium in Siam, Indo-China or the Netherlands East Indies. At present American imperialism is in the forefront in the conduct of affairs in the Far East, and not only is there a tendency to try to elbow us out but there is also [a] smearing campaign which not only attributes to us the meanest motives but also seeks to belittle everything that we do.[6]

His portrayal of an American anti-British campaign may have been overdrawn, but Dening was accurate in saying that the Americans wished to alter the 'equilibrium' in Asia. They did not want a return to the pre-war *status quo*. For this reason in part the United States had proposed trusteeship for such territories as Indo-China and Korea. Whether trusteeship regimes were in fact feasible became increasingly doubtful. In both areas China would be one of the principal trustees. As the war in the Far East approached its climax, British officials, at least, saw that the post-war political configurations of Asia would not fulfil the hopes of Roosevelt and other Americans who had put faith in China as a future world

---

[6] Dening to Sterndale Bennett, 17 Jan. 1945, FO 371/46325. For an important assessment by an American scholar in 1945, which also emphasizes a resurgence of Anglophobia, see Jacob Viner, 'The American Interest in the Colonial Problem', in Jacob Viner and others, *The United States in a Multi-National Economy* (New York, 1945), p. 2: 'Some of the anti-colonialism in this country is primarily a manifestation of Anglophobia rather than, or more than, a genuine sympathy with the natives of the colonial areas, and much of the avowed anti-colonialism is in reality motivated more by the desire to check the growth of close ties of friendship and collaboration between the English and ourselves than by a genuine interest in the plight of the Hindus or of the West Africans.'

power. According to Geoffrey Hudson in the Foreign Office in March 1945: 'The idea that China after the war would be the Great power stabilising the Far East in America's interest now seems to have been fatally undermined by hard facts . . .'[7]

The 'hard facts' of the situation in Indo-China made Roosevelt's trusteeship scheme seem more and more like a pipe-dream. He himself must have recognized the political and military reality when he said to Charles Taussig on the 15th of March that he would settle for French recognition of the obligations of a trustee. If Roosevelt had lived, he might have succeeded in extracting concessions from the French, though they certainly would have demanded that the same conditions should apply to other colonial territories such as British Malaya and the Netherlands East Indies. Though Roosevelt no doubt would have welcomed such general principles of trusteeship, this explains only part of his response to the problem. As much as Roosevelt genuinely disliked French imperialism, he had also been treating it as a sensitive political issue. To the American public it would have been less easy for him to justify restoration of French colonies than those of Britain or the Netherlands. Despite the Brazzaville Conference, the French did not have the reputation of enlightened imperialists. Thus Roosevelt talked nonchalantly about the desirability of having a Filipino, a Chinese, and a Russian as well as an American involved in the trusteeship regime. Even if he had had his way, there would have been no question of an international administration. There might have been some degree of international supervision. If the post-war history of the other trust territories is any indication, there would have been no direct intervention except in the form of visiting missions. It is therefore difficult to accept the view of some writers who have discussed trusteeship in relation to the origins of the war in Vietnam. Arthur Schlesinger, Jr., for example, has written that if Roosevelt's scheme had been carried out, 'the world might have been spared much bloodshed and agony'.[8] This is a highly optimistic judgement.

In any case when Roosevelt died the spirit of the trusteeship

---

[7] Minute by Hudson, 19 Mar. 1945, ibid.

[8] Arthur Schlesinger, Jr., *The Bitter Heritage: Vietnam and American Democracy, 1941–1966* (Boston, 1966), p. 3.

proposal for Indo-China departed with him. No one had been able to answer the question posed by Geoffrey Hudson in the previous year: when the French eventually sent warships to Saigon or Haiphong, who would prevent the reassertion of French authority?[9] Certainly not the British, who had every reason to want the restoration of a stable French Colonial Empire as well as a strong metropolitan France. 'We want to see French Indo-China restored to France,' wrote the head of the Far Eastern Department of the Foreign Office, 'not merely as part of our general policy of building up a France friendly to us, but in the interests of stability in the Far East. The present uncertainty is not only dangerous in itself but casts doubt on the future of other territories awaiting liberation, including our own.'[10] He went on to say that the British would regard sympathetically any request for aid to French forces in the reoccupation of Indo-China, even though this might bring the British 'into head-on collision with the Americans'. With considerable relief the British noted the American acquiescence that occurred in the spring of 1945. General de Gaulle pressed on President Truman the 'very important political, moral and military consequences' of American opposition.[11] At San Francisco Stettinius told the French representatives that the United States had never 'even by implication' questioned French sovereignty in Indo-China, though he added that certain elements of American public opinion condemned French actions there.[12] Later in the year Dean Acheson in the capacity of Acting Secretary of State declared that the United States had 'no thought of opposing the reestablishment of French control'.[13] Trusteeship for Indo-China thus died a natural death with the restoration of French authority.

Trusteeship had also been proposed for Korea. There the situation differed fundamentally from the one in Indo-China. Korea was part of the Japanese Empire. The Koreans had never been under western sway. At Yalta Roosevelt had told Stalin that he thought Korea might be ready for independence

[9] Minute by Hudson, 8 Sept. 1944, FO 371/41720.
[10] Sterndale Bennett to Dening, 14 Apr. 1945, FO 371/46304.
[11] De Gaulle to Truman, message conveyed in French Note of 15 May 1945, *Foreign Relations* (1945), vi. 308–9.
[12] Grew to Hurley, 2 June 1945, ibid., p. 312.
[13] Acheson to Robertson, 5 Oct. 1945, ibid., p. 313.

after a period of tutelage of twenty to thirty years. Stalin probably regarded the trusteeship proposal merely as a means of dismembering the Japanese Empire. In view of the American plans for the Pacific islands, why should he object to a similar scheme for Korea?[14] The sudden end of the war brought about an improvised arrangement whereby the Japanese troops north of the 38th parallel surrendered to Russian authorities, those to the south to American (the capital, Seoul, thus falling into the American zone). During this time the Americans received powerful statements from various Korean groups that a trusteeship regime would be unacceptable. For example, Syngman Rhee, the Chairman of the Korean Delegation at San Francisco (and later President of South Korea) wrote in May that the Yalta accord would contradict the pledge of the Cairo Declaration for independence and warned against making Korea 'the victim of secret diplomacy'. Later in the year he stated that the Korean people were 'unanimously against a joint trusteeship or any other measure short of complete independence'.[15] Of these various statements reaching Washington in opposition to trusteeship, one in particular grasped the issues at stake in terms of the historical development of the West. According to the Acting Chairman of the Korean Commission, Ben C. Limb, Korea's domination by Japan should not prejudice her immediate self-government. 'Other nations have amply proved their ability to administer themselves as exemplified by Bulgaria after the War of 1877 and by Poland after the World War.' He pointed out that Korea had maintained independent nationhood for forty centuries and had contributed to the world's civilization. 'Any idea calculated to apply international trusteeship over Korea is destructive to the true interests of the Korean people, for such a trusteeship by its very nature will divide up the people and country and make unity and independence impossible.'[16]

Despite an abundance of similar Korean protests, plans for a trusteeship regime continued to gain momentum in late 1945. The Commonwealth nations supported the proposal for

---

[14] I am indebted to Professor Herbert Dinerstein for his views on Stalin and the trusteeship proposals.

[15] *Foreign Relations* (1945), vi. 1028, 1111.

[16] Ibid., Limb to John Carter Vincent, 7 Nov. 1945, pp. 1115–16.

a four-power-trusteeship regime of the United States, China, Russia, and Britain—the Australians adding the proviso that Australia must be included.[17] The governing consideration of the western powers was the belief that unless agreement on a trusteeship regime could be reached, the next war might find its origins in international rivalry in Korea. On the 27th of December the Moscow conference of Foreign Ministers announced agreement on a proposal to establish a four-power trusteeship 'for a period up to five years'. They had seriously underestimated the mood in Korea. In the words of General Douglas MacArthur, 'In the minds of all Koreans, "Trusteeship" hangs over them as a sword of Damocles. If it is imposed now or at any future time it is believed possible that the Korean people will actually and physically revolt.'[18]

If there was any one issue in Korea on which all Koreans could agree, it was opposition to a trusteeship regime. Quite apart from resentment at foreign tutelage, the Koreans believed that they were being treated in the same way as 'the uncivilized aborigines of the South Seas'. With an explosive combination of racial pride and nationalism, the Koreans rejected trusteeship with a vehemence that seemed to threaten the peace in East Asia.[19] The question has been given exhaustive treatment on the Korean side in a work which observes: 'The advocates of trusteeship, whatever their political complexion, had good reason to fear for their lives.'[20] In Korea the proposal for trusteeship ended in large part because of the overwhelming opposition of the Koreans themselves. This complicated issue belongs more to the history of the origins of the cold war than to trusteeship (except in the limited sense of a makeshift device in power politics), though in one sense the post-war controversy in Korea yields an insight, from the Korean point of view, into the general problem of cultural relativity in regard to trusteeship. 'The Koreans

[17] See CAB 96/9.

[18] MacArthur to JCS, 16 Dec. 1945, *Foreign Relations* (1945), vi. 1146.

[19] e.g., the commanding officer in Korea, Lieutenant General John R. Hodge, forwarded a message from Korean leaders in December 1945: 'Any trusteeship applied to Korea will eventually destroy peace in the Far East.' Ibid., p. 1154.

[20] Robert A. Scalapino and Chong-sik Lee, *Communism in Korea* (2 vols., Berkeley, 1972), i. 279. This distinguished work deals in detail with the trusteeship issue in Korean politics and in relation to other issues such as the Communist movement, Russian tactics, and the psychological reaction of the Koreans.

feel, and with some justice,' wrote an American official in Korea in 1946, 'that their cultural level and history entitle them to different treatment at the hands of the United Nations from that applicable to peoples of mandated territories in Africa and backward races in southeast Asia which have not yet made any contributions to mankind or history.'[21]

At the Potsdam Conference in July 1945, President Truman rejected the possibility of American trusteeship for the Italian colonies. 'We have enough "poor Italians" to feed in the United States', he told Churchill and Stalin.[22] At this time Stalin demonstrated a great interest in the fate of the Italian colonies. 'Who gets them?' he asked. When Churchill pointed out that Britain alone had conquered the Italian Colonial Empire, Stalin retorted that the Red Army had taken Berlin. The Russians put forward a claim for membership in a tripartite-trusteeship regime composed of Britain, the United States, and the Soviet Union. Possible Russian intrusion into northern Africa brought about a shift in American policy in support of Italy as the trusteeship power in Libya and Somalia. Like the subject of Korea, this topic belongs more to the era of the cold war than to trusteeship during the Second World War, but it is illuminating for present purposes to examine briefly one particular aspect of the voluminous British files. Ernest Bevin, Eden's successor as Foreign Secretary, emerged as a Labour statesman who sensed his imperial responsibilities just as keenly as his Tory counterparts. At the time, some sceptics doubted whether a change from Tory to Labour would alter British Imperialism. If they had been privy to the secrets of the British government they would have confirmed the impression of Bevin as the inheritor of the imperial legacy from Churchill. In a memorandum for the Cabinet written together with G. H. Hall, the new Colonial Secretary, Bevin stated in August 1945 that Britain could not 'disinterest' herself in the Italian colonies:

They flank our main line of Imperial communication by sea and

---

[21] Langdon to Secretary of State, 8 May 1946, *Foreign Relations* (1946), viii. 671–2.

[22] Conference Proceedings, 22 July 1945, *Foreign Relations: Conference of Berlin* (1945), ii. 265. The editors of *Foreign Relations* note that Truman may have referred to the 'poor Italians' in Italy rather than in the United States.

air to India, Australia and New Zealand through the Mediterranean and the Red Sea and provide bases from which Egypt, the Sudan and Kenya could be attacked. We must therefore ensure that they do not come under the control of any State which is potentially hostile or incapable of providing for the maintenance of orderly conditions and for their defence in peace and war.[23]

These were words that could have been written just as well by Lord Curzon in 1919. The reasoning was identical. Apart from adjustments in the Mediterranean islands and Eritrea, there could be no alternative but to place Cyrenaica and Somalia under British trusteeship. Bevin regretted that the Americans might resent 'the painting of any further red on the map'. But since the United States refused to accept responsibility for the Italian colonies, he intended to twist the situation to British advantage.

The Italian colonies were just as vital to British imperial defence as the Pacific islands were for American security. Unless the Americans supported the British in the Mediterranean and Red Sea, according to Bevin, 'we shall certainly be unable to join them in resisting Russian claims to trusteeship responsibilities, whether alone or in co-trusteeship with them, in Korea and the Pacific islands'. In some ways the story of the fate of the German colonies repeated itself, at least in the logic of imperial defence:

> It may be argued that the United Kingdom is undertaking unnecessary burdens, or conversely, is obtaining the lion's share. This seems to be unavoidable. The maintenance of our position in the Middle East remains a cardinal feature of British policy and in consequence we must be prepared to undertake the commitments and expenditure inherent in maintaining that position. Strategic facilities in Cyrenaica are essential and the proposal for a united Somalia is far the best solution for the future of this area.[24]

There was, moreover, a powerful humanitarian reason why most of the Italian colonies should be placed under British trusteeship. The Colonial Office argued that the unification of Somalia by Britain would be in the best interest of the inhabitants. Would Somalia fare as well under someone else? In the phrase of one Colonial Office official, this was 'the acid

[23] Memorandum by Bevin and Hall, 25 Aug. 1945, O.R.C. (45) 21, CAB 134/594.   [24] Ibid.

test'. Could Britain honestly and honourably avoid the responsibility? 'What reason is there to suppose that the French would not exploit and misgovern Somalia as they did Syria?'[25] The close of the war thus rejuvenated Britain's sense of Imperial mission.

The future of the Italian colonies proved to be a bitterly divisive issue within the British Cabinet. If Bevin's views represented the continuity of the Imperial tradition, Attlee's sentiments were similar to those of the Little Englanders who had denounced Imperial adventures in the nineteenth century. Believing that the strategic basis of British power had altered adversely, Attlee held the view that the Empire could only be defended within the framework of the United Nations organization. 'If the new organization is a reality, it does not matter who holds Cyrenaica or Somalia or controls the Suez Canal. If it is not a reality we had better be thinking of the defence of England, for unless we can protect the home country no strategic positions elsewhere will avail.'[26] Apart from strategic considerations, Attlee believed that there were practical disadvantages to trusteeship responsibilities. 'They involve us in immediate [financial] loss. There is no prospect of their paying for themselves. The more we do for them the quicker shall we be faced with premature claims for self-government. We have quite enough of these awkward problems already.' With words that could just as easily have been uttered by Sir William Harcourt in the 1890s, Attlee continued:

Cyrenaica will saddle us with an expense that we can ill afford. Why should we have to bear it? Why should it be assumed that only a few great Powers can be entrusted with backward peoples? Why should not one or other of the Scandinavian countries have a try? They are quite as fitted to bear rule as ourselves. Why not the United States?

British Somalialand has always been a dead loss and a nuisance to us. We only occupied it as part of the scramble for Africa. . . . The French are on the spot in French Somalialand. Why not let them have it if they like? It will be a sop to their pride, and may help them to put up with the loss of their position in the Levant. There would, of course, be the sentimental objection to giving up a piece of the

[25] C.O. memorandum, n.d. but *c.* 1 Sept. 1945, FO 371/50792. For the C.O. views see CO 968/153.
[26] Memorandum by Attlee, 1 Sept. 1945, C.P. (45) 144, CAB 129/1.

Empire, but otherwise it would be to our advantage to get rid of this incubus.[27]

Attlee's views by no means silenced those who believed, for example, that 'the Red Sea area is a vital link' in the chain of imperial defence.[28] But his ideas are representative of the new thinking of some members of the post-Churchill government. On the whole it *did* make a difference that a Labour government assessed the meaning of British Imperialism in the immediate post-war years and that it was Attlee, not Churchill, who began the liquidation of the British Empire.

There were three Italian colonies whose future was at stake: Libya, Eritrea, and Somaliland. The last was the only one to become a trust territory. Eritrea, though divided between Muslims and Christians, was eventually absorbed into Ethiopia in 1954. A major post-war controversy developed over Libya. At the London conference of September 1945 the United States put forward a scheme for collective trusteeship. The Soviet Union favoured individual trusteeship, with the breaking up of Libya into its constituent parts of Fezzan, Cyrenaica, and Tripolitania. The British then began to favour Italian trusteeship over parts of the former empire as a means of checking Russian expansion into the Mediterranean. At the Paris conference of April 1946, the Russians swung around in support of Italian trusteeship as a consequence of the growing strength of the communists in Italy. Two years later, by April 1948, the East and West had reversed their positions. The Soviet Union, again in response to the political situation in Italy, now favoured the original plan of collective trusteeships. At least the Russians hoped to keep a foot in the door. The Americans and British now supported trusteeship by the

[27] Memorandum by Attlee, 1 Sept. 1945, C.P. (45) 144, CAB 129/1.
[28] Minute by Lord Hood, the Foreign Office official in charge of planning the future of the Italian colonies, 3 Sept. 1945, FO 371/50792. He argued as follows: '[T]he advent of air power has in no way altered the fact that the first vital interest of this country is not merely the defence of the shores of these islands, but also the security of communications between this island and the outer world, from which our food supplies and other vital war materials are derived. . . . There must inevitably be an element of reinsurance in our present attitude towards the World Organisation. If it fails, we may again have to fight a war and our victory may again turn on our success in the Western Desert. The maintenance and strengthening of our position in the Middle East must thus remain a cardinal feature of Imperial policy.'

Italians, but reserving Cyrenaica for the British for strategic reasons. At this point, in the summer of 1948, the matter was handed over to the General Assembly, in accordance with the Treaty of Peace with Italy, after the great powers failed to . reach agreement. In the General Assembly, of course, veto power could not be exercised.

For the purpose of conveying some idea of the consequence of the wartime controversy, the following table indicates the complexity of the Libyan situation as of September 1948.

Australia	Trusteeship under Britain. If Libya is divided, parts should be placed under similar systems of trusteeship.
Belgium	No specific recommendation. Guiding principle should be wishes of population and satisfaction of legitimate claims.
Brazil	Settlement of British commitments and trusteeship under Italy.
Byelorussia	Trusteeship under Italy. No partition.
Canada	Trusteeship under Britain, whether or not territory is divided.
China	Immediate independence.
Czechoslovakia	Trusteeship under Italy. No partition.
Egypt	Independence or trusteeship under an Arab state.
Ethiopia	Against return to Italy.
France	Possible partition with special French rights in Fezzan.
Greece	No recommendation but concerned with rights of Greek nationals in Libya.
India	Trusteeship under direct U.N. administration.
Iraq	Immediate independence.
Italy	Trusteeship under Italy.
Netherlands	Trusteeship under Italy.
New Zealand	Trusteeship under Britain.
Pakistan	International control with Egyptian participation.

Poland	Trusteeship under Italy. No partition.
Soviet Union	Direct United Nations administration under trusteeship.
Ukraine	Trusteeship under Italy. No partition.
Union of South Africa	Partition. Tripolitania under British trusteeship; Fezzan under French trusteeship; Cyrenaica under British trusteeship.
United Kingdom	British trusteeship for Cyrenaica, postponement of decision on remainder of Libya.
Yugoslavia	Trusteeship under Italy.[29]

It is highly doubtful whether even Roosevelt would have sustained his enthusiasm for trusteeship under such exasperating circumstances of small as well as great nations voicing their opinions. In the event, the position of the United States shifted to check the Soviet Union. With the Russians supporting collective trusteeship, the Americans again reversed their position and favoured speedy independence. After an interim administration by the United Nations, Libya emerged in the vanguard of newly independent nations in 1951. Whatever the machinations of the great powers, the case of Libya provides a memorable example of how the trusteeship issue indirectly worked in favour of independence.

To General Smuts the problem of the Italian colonies was inseparably linked with large questions of global security and the future of the British Commonwealth and Empire. In September 1945 he urged that the United States be given Eritrea with the port of Massawa as a strategic base. 'It is to our interest to associate the United States of America with the British Commonwealth in this all important line of communication.'[30] Britain—or the Commonwealth—should acquire a comparable strategic base in Cyrenaica in order 'to safeguard the communication lifeline to India, Australia and New

---

[29] Reproduced in modified form from Benjamin Rivlin, *United Nations Action: Italian Colonies* (New York, 1950), pp. 22–3. For the Libyan question see especially Adrian Pelt, *Libyan Independence and the United Nations: A Case of Planned Decolonization* (New Haven, 1970).

[30] *Aide-mémoire* by High Commissioner for South Africa on conversation with Smuts, 3 Sept. 1945, GEN 88/1, CAB 78/37.

Zealand'. By securing these two bases together with the Americans, the British would effectively eliminate one of the causes of the two world wars. Here is the way in which Smuts read one of the major lessons of the war: 'The strategic plan of the Axis powers was to seize Egypt between the twin jaws of its military power in Libya and Eritrea. The plan very nearly succeeded. It was finally defeated by a Commonwealth army at El Alamein. . . . the future control of both strategic bases in Cyrenaica and Italian Somaliland should contain an effective guarantee to the Commonwealth that the danger it had to fight against in 1914 and 1939 shall not occur again.'[31]

Unless the British once and for all established absolute control over the short route to the East, then major wars might again occur in that part of the world. Smuts developed this argument in relation to the changing character of the Arab world, the Jewish problem in Palestine, and the expansion of Russia in Eastern Europe. The scope of his analysis was quite similar to the breadth of his interpretation of the balance of power at the close of the First World War—with one major exception. He now took account of that unique development, the atomic bomb. In this regard Smuts's views are of particular interest because he wanted to create a storage base for atomic weapons in Cyrenaica. He based his argument on the premise that the advent of atomic warfare did not alter the need to defend the traditional British lines of communication. He then discussed the possibility of an atomic stalemate:

If Washington suspected that Moscow could as easily drop an atomic bomb on New York as she could on Moscow, would America dare to use it? And in such a case would not the final test of power lie with that country which was prepared to use the bomb and pay the least regard for human life and the destruction which it would create? Again, is not the menace of the bomb greatest to the densely populated countries, where liberal ideals prevail, while being of lesser concern to those more sparsely populated countries of great area, where authoritarianism is in force?[32]

This line of reasoning led Smuts to conclude that the desert wastes of Cyrenaica might be of crucial importance to British defence in the post-war era.

[31] 'The Italian Colonies, and British Interests in the Mediterranean–Red Sea Route', 25 Sept. 1945, C.P. (45) 189, CAB 129/2. [32] Ibid.

With the recent air developments, and particularly with a few atom bombs stored away in the vast regions of the uninhabited desert, it can truly be said that Cyrenaica is the key to all the Near Eastern defences. It provides, moreover, the only real answer to any attempted raids by a future rapacious European Power, heedless of consequences; for if the fear of reprisals by densely populated Western European countries should operate against the use of the atomic bomb to their detriment, and if Washington and New York should fear their fate too much to come to the rescue, no such fear would prevent its use from the deserts of Cyrenaica. . . . Only the fear of certain punishment inflicted in the capital and towns of his own country would restrain the aggressor. The remote desert would offer that threat without fear of reprisal and act as a safety valve for the world.[33]

Since Cyrenaica was mainly desert and contained only a sparse nomadic population, the British could put forward an argument for a 'strategic territory' in the same way the Americans had for the Pacific islands. Had the British Commonwealth emerged from the war as a potent, cohesive force in international affairs (as Smuts and others such as Leo Amery hoped it would), the bi-polarity of the Soviet Union and the United States might have been offset by British power in such places as Cyrenaica.

Smuts would have liked to have had international recognition of South-West Africa as a 'strategic area' of South Africa. If his views on such questions as the atomic stalemate seem prophetic, his ideas on the particular issue of South-West Africa appear obsolescent. If South Africa had simply annexed South-West Africa during the war (in the manner that the Soviet Union appropriated the Baltic states) perhaps the vexed question of South-West Africa might not have arisen before the United Nations and the International Court of Justice.[34] This remains speculation. In the event, Smuts chose to request incorporation on grounds of geographical proximity, ethnic kinship, defence, and self-determination. According to the South African government at the close of the war, the white

[33] Ibid.
[34] W. K. Hancock, *Smuts: The Fields of Force* (Cambridge, 1968), p. 467. For the South-West Africa question, see Solomon Slonim, *South West Africa and the United Nations: an International Mandate in Dispute* (Baltimore, 1973). See also especially John Dugard, ed., *The South West Africa/Namibia Dispute* (Berkeley, 1973).

population of South-West Africa and the Africans—as indicated by their chiefs—wanted incorporation. Whatever the merit of the case, the South Africans thought that the principle of self-determination would work in their favour. They believed that they had discharged the obligation of the League's Covenant.

Smuts held that the South-West Africa mandate had been a success, as indeed had all of the British mandates. Many prominent figures in the English-speaking world at that time would have agreed. His thoughts as of September 1945 provide an illuminating survey of the mandates in relation to the general colonial situation.

The Japanese did abuse their trust both militarily and economically, and they did not make the interest of their subject populations paramount. But to whom else does this indictment apply? To Australia in her mandate over New Guinea or to New Zealand in her mandate of Western Samoa? These two countries would be the first to repudiate such an allegation. Certainly the charge [of violation of the mandates] cannot be laid against the British, whose record of trust is beyond reproach . . .

Smuts went on to assess the British achievement in the African mandates:

Tanganyika is regarded by all unbiassed observers as a model of advanced native administration in which the native authority is encouraged and directed to the uplift of the people. South-West Africa under the Mandate held by the Union shows a material political and social advance of a truly commendable character. It has its own Executive Committee, elected by the Legislative Assembly, which governs its own concerns. Its population of all races has increased by 40 per cent. since the Mandate was granted. Its trade and industry have prospered exceedingly, and it has ministered to the needs of its native population in a manner comparable with any other country in Africa.[35]

This was a distinctly South African way of viewing the colonial question. Smuts's ideas about South-West Africa had not found acceptance in 1919 and they now appeared increasingly anachronistic in a world of emerging nations.

When Smuts made his plea before the United Nations in 1946 for incorporation and termination of the mandate, he

[35] 'The Italian Colonies', 25 Sept. 1945, cited p. 561, n. 31 above.

rested his case ultimately on the legal argument that South Africa had fulfilled the terms of Article 22 of the League's Covenant. No doubt from the South African point of view that was true. But with the benefit of hindsight it was almost certain that the argument would be rejected in an assembly where a substantial number believed that *independence* should be the natural outcome of the colonial relationship. South Africa refused to place South-West Africa under trusteeship. After lengthy proceedings at the International Court, the General Assembly of the United Nations in 1966 terminated the mandate. In the case of South-West Africa can be seen, above all, the transformation of the colonial question. The legalistic assembly of the League of Nations evolved into the political forum of the United Nations, where 'trusteeship' became synonymous with preparation for independence.

From the vantage point of Australia and New Zealand, the paramount issue in the colonial question was gradual preparation for self-government within a defence structure for the South-West Pacific and South-East Asia.[36] Neither Evatt nor Fraser championed the goal of independence, though probably neither would have resisted it. With a vision characteristic of the times, they foresaw self-government as an evolutionary process to be achieved after solid economic and social advance over a period of many decades. Here the Australians and New Zealanders proved themselves to be the staunchest supporters of 'trusteeship' in practice as well as theory. The South Pacific Commission became the most conspicuously successful of the regional schemes for colonial development that had its origins in the wartime years.[37]

[36] For the defence aspects, see especially Roger Bell, 'Australian-American Discord: Negotiations for Post-War Bases and Security Arrangements in the Pacific 1944–1946', *Australian Outlook* 27. 1 (April 1973). For an important contemporary Australian assessment of the trusteeship system (by one of the Australian representatives at the San Francisco Conference), see K. H. Bailey, 'Dependent Areas of the Pacific: An Australian View', *Foreign Affairs* 24. 3 (April 1946). See also A. H. McDonald (ed.), *Trusteeship in the Pacific* (Sydney, 1949). For a contemporary Canadian view of particular significance, Sir Robert Holland, 'Trusteeship Aspirations', *Foreign Affairs* 25. 1 (October 1946). Lord Hailey noted on his copy, 'Useful. Points of difference between Covenant & Charter. Estimate & value of some of generalization in Charter (Not found elsewhere).' (Hailey Papers.)

[37] See T. R. Smith, *South Pacific Commission: an Analysis after Twenty-Five Years* (New Zealand Institute of International Affairs, 1972). W. D. Forsyth, the former Secretary of the South Pacific Commission, looks back with satisfaction on the out-

New Zealand pioneered the way in the Pacific by granting independence to Western Samoa in 1962.[38] The fact that Samoa was a trust territory probably accelerated the pace. Above all the visiting missions helped to create a sense of national consciousness within the international community.[39] New Guinea achieved independence in 1975, several centuries earlier than the wartime statesmen had anticipated.[40]

Apart from South-West Africa (Namibia), which remains in dispute, the only remnant of the mandates system today is Micronesia, or the United States Trust Territory of the Pacific Islands.[41] The charges of 'Imperialism' so frequently levelled against the colonial powers are now directed towards the Americans as the nations of the 'Third World' and the Communist bloc in the United Nations periodically denounce the United States as an expansionist and assimilationist power. Nor is the impression of American imperialism restricted to former colonial peoples and cold war rivals. From the beginning of the post-war era British and Commonwealth statesmen, above all, perceived the irony of the American anti-colonial stance and simultaneous emergence of the United States as a global or quasi-imperial power. 'The Americans . . . are very keen on this elision of strategic area,' Sir Frederick Eggleston

come of the trusteeship controversy: 'Ah Christ, what fun it was—and we won, too!' (letter to the author, 20 Aug. 1974). This sentiment is distinctly in contrast with the English feeling as expressed by Arthur Creech Jones, who wrote in 1956 about his dealings with the Trusteeship Council: 'It was a miserable & disappointing experience—& I suppose, inevitable after all the propaganda about imperialism & colonialism.' (Creech Jones to Fox-Pitt, Secretary of the Anti-Slavery and Aborigines Protection Society, 21 Jan. 1956, Anti-Slavery Society Papers.)

[38] See especially Mary Boyd, 'The Record in Western Samoa since 1945', in (ed.) Angus Ross, *New Zealand's Record in the Pacific Islands in the Twentieth Century* (New Zealand Institute of International Affairs, 1969).

[39] See J. W. Davidson, *Samoa mo Samoa: the Emergence of the Independent State of Western Samoa* (Melbourne, 1967).

[40] For a perceptive account of New Guinea's independence and other recent historic events in the Pacific, see Deryck Scarr, 'The Pacific Islands since 1919', in (eds.) William S. Livingston and Wm. Roger Louis, *Australia, New Zealand and the Pacific Islands since the First World War* (in press). On the general question of dependencies, see especially David W. Wainhouse, *Remnants of Empire: The United Nations and the End of Colonialism* (New York, 1964).

[41] British and French Togo and French Cameroons received independence in 1960. Italian Somaliland was united with British Somaliland and granted independence in the same year. Tanganyika and British Cameroons achieved independence in 1961. Western Samoa and Ruanda–Urundi followed in 1962.

wrote about the creation of the new American territory in the Pacific in 1945, 'and it gives a lie to the lot of their absurd criticism of the colonial system before the war.'[42] In the words of another writer in 1947: 'The United States have been the cradle of modern Anti-Imperialism, and at the same time the founding of a mighty Empire.'[43]

If foreign loans and economic assistance are considered as vehicles of economic imperialism, then, especially from the vantage point of the British, the post-war era can be seen as one of American 'informal empire'.[44] There are many analogies between the nineteenth century Victorian and the post-war American empires. Perhaps it is partly true that Americans sought economic and to some extent political domination of the world in much the same way as their British predecessors. There was certainly the same complexity of human motive. It is illuminating to take into account the comment of a perceptive French observer, shortly after the close of the war. He had no particular love of American imperialism and, as a Frenchman, good reason to resent it. His observations are of value because they were contemporary and because they portray the richness of American reaction to the phenomenon of 'Imperialism' in 1945. Maurice Levallois, Head of the Third Division of Political Affairs in the Ministry of Overseas France, wrote in October of that year:

As far as can be gathered from the press and religious and political statements, Americans strongly disapprove of colonialism because they consider it wicked, anti-Christian, anti-democratic, and anti-liberal. Furthermore they believe that it constitutes a perpetual threat to world peace because the possession of colonies engenders constant rivalry between nations. In short, they condemn it because they regard it as one of the most hypocritical forms of imperialism.

He pointed out a fallacy of the theorists of economic imperialism:

It would be easy to fall into the error of thinking that this repro-

[42] Eggleston to K.K. Officer, 5 July 1945, Eggleston Papers.
[43] M. J. Bonn, 'The U.S.A. and British Imperialism', *Political Quarterly* 18.1 (January–March 1947).
[44] e.g., Leonard Woolf wrote in 1947: 'high priority should be given to the effort to disentangle ourselves from U.S.A. domination'. *The Labour Party's Dilemma* (pamphlet, London, 1947).

bation is only a mask and equally unfair to suspect that this ideal serves only as a cloak for sordid, economic designs.

On the contrary, Levallois wrote, the American response was extremely complex:

... [O]ne would have to be very naive not to realize that interest and moral principle are not here in contradiction. But it would be a grave psychological mistake to believe that only self-interest enters into question. The good faith and generosity at the source of as powerful a current of opinion as this, are not suspect even if less admirable interests also figure in it.[45]

Levallois concluded that most Americans did not favour immediate independence for colonial peoples, who would require a period of educational and political development. It was a balanced judgement of the general post-war American attitude. Americans in general may have held anti-colonial sentiments, but they did not believe in precipitous decolonization.

To what extent did anti-colonial sentiment in the United States contribute to the decolonization of the British Empire? During the war some American officials and even the President hoped to liquidate the Empire, in part through international trusteeship; but, in fact, from about 1943 into the period of the cold war the general policy of the American government, in pursuit of security, tended to support rather than break up the British Imperial system. It was an awareness of changing times rather than demands from Washington that led the British progressively to decolonize the Empire. Ronald Robinson has written: 'official pressure for colonial independence might be off [as of 1943–4]; but the slightest agitation of profoundly anti-colonial public in the United States might force the administration in Washington to turn it on again at any moment. A fitful and most uncomfortable sleeping partner now shared the Empire's bed; unless the British put on clean linen and purified the imperial house, he would awake and

---

[45] Maurice Levallois, 'Anti-Colonialist Tendencies in the U.S.A., U.S.S.R. and China', *Renaissances* (October 1945). For a Belgian view of these problems, Pierre Orts, 'La Charte de San-Francisco: un tournant de la colonisation,' *La Revue coloniale belge* 16 (1 June 1946).

wreck it.'[46] It is ironic that the inclination of the American government in the immediate post-war period to acquiesce in the colonial *status quo* was frustrated by British estimates of anti-colonialism in the United States, Britain, and elsewhere. These assessments in part prompted the British to democratize colonial rule. American anti-colonial sentiment (combined with a new and overwhelming British sense of dependence on the United States) powerfully affected the state of British morale and also changed the judgements of colonial nationalists about the balance of power in the colonies.

During the wartime period few predicted the speed or scope of the subsequent colonial revolution. When Sumner Welles in 1942 intoned 'the age of imperialism is ended', he and most other Americans probably had little inkling of the consequences. The swift political fragmentation of the colonial world was an outcome which the United States neither planned nor welcomed. But it was a triumph of those Americans, including Roosevelt, who believed that 'independence' was a natural and desirable goal. When the threat of Russia became ominous, the watchword 'security' began to eclipse 'independence'. In the colonial question this transformation is especially noticeable in the spring of 1945, though certainly there were earlier signs. Instability in post-colonial areas increasingly became a preoccupation in the American government. If it was true for Lord Curzon and others in 1919 that the sun never set on the crises of the British Empire, then the year 1945 must have marked a similar moment of truth for the Americans.

It would be a mistake to place too much emphasis on 'security' as the American priority in the colonial world. The American delegation at the San Francisco conference formally went on record in favour of 'self-government' as the goal of colonial rule, but they also carefully stated that self-government might lead to independence. 'Independence' and 'security' were not seen as contradictory concepts. It was hoped that the former colonies would align themselves in foreign affairs and in defence treaties with the United States, Britain, and the other western

---

[46] Ronald Robinson, 'Andrew Cohen and the Transfer of Power in Tropical Africa, 1940–1951', unpublished paper presented at the Anglo-French Colloquium on Independence and Dependence: the Relations of Britain and France with their Former Territories (Paris, 6–8 May 1976).

powers, that the new nations would have stable political regimes, and moreover that they would be democratic. When these hopes were progressively shattered, there developed among the American and British liberal designers of decolonization a sense of bitterness—and a complaint from the latter that the Americans had too quickly accelerated the pace.[47] The repercussions of the cold war worked in favour of a swift transfer of power.

The overriding significance of the trusteeship issue during the war was a concern for the future of dependent peoples. It is entirely understandable that Americans conceived of independence as the ultimate goal because it was within their national tradition to remember their own break with the British Empire. It is equally easy to see why those within the British Empire and Commonwealth spoke of eventual self-government, with less emphasis on the political future and more on the economic and social development of the colonies. To British officials with experience in Africa it seemed far-fetched to speak of future self-government, still more so of independence; the immediate need appeared to be the raising of standards of living by providing more wage-earning jobs and better health services. The problem of the Pacific islands seemed similar to those of Africa. The Americans of this era no more thought of independence for the Marianas than the British did for Tanganyika. It seemed monstrously unjust for the British and others to suggest American insincerity merely because the former Japanese islands would be held as a 'strategic' territory. To all Americans who followed the battles of the Pacific, 'Iwo Jima', 'Tinian', and 'Saipan' were emotional words. The strategic character of the islands by the end of the war had become so exclusive that Americans no more questioned it than the British did Gibraltar's. Perhaps there is an important conclusion to be drawn from this. Strategic calculations with emotional origins can become absolute. When they carry over into a different era, they can become irrational.[48]

---

[47] 'Americans have asked me,' writes the last Governor-General of Nigeria, Sir James Robertson, '"Why did you leave so soon before the colonial territories were ready to rule themselves?" and when I have replied, "Partly, I am sure, because of your pressure on us to go", have answered that they did not know then what they now know and that we should have resisted their pressure'. Sir James Robertson, *Transition in Africa: From Direct Rule to Independence* (London, 1974), p. 253.

[48] On this point see especially Pomeroy, *Pacific Outpost*, p. xix. Of course the

For the British it seemed emphatically unjust for the Americans to impose standards of international trusteeship on British territories. The British were convinced of the superiority of their colonial administration. There was a certain element of humiliation conveyed by the idea of international supervision, as if there were a *question* of accountability. This was an argument, however, that cut two ways. Since the British regarded their Colonial Empire as a source of pride, then why not codify British colonial policies through international conventions in order to raise standards throughout the world? If one pursues this line of argument there quickly arises a fundamental question. It is one at which the Europeans as well as the British waxed indignant. *Why should the question of dependent peoples be restricted to the European overseas empires?* Why should trusteeship not apply to the Indian tribes of North America? Or for that matter to the dependent peoples within Russia? In the post-war period this proposition became known as 'the salt-water fallacy' as British representatives at the United Nations pointed out that dependent peoples throughout the world should be the proper concern.[49] According to this powerfully stated view, the debate should not be restricted, as it frequently has been in the United Nations, to the European overseas empires.

Of all the protagonists of the wartime trusteeship controversy, Lord Hailey perhaps saw most clearly the paradoxical and ultimately irrational nature of the issue. Indeed he emerges as a philosopher of world affairs with the stature of J. C. Smuts and A. J. Balfour. In the Hailey Papers there is a memorandum,

constant strategic theme can be argued as well. Apart from use as testing sites, the Pacific islands will probably always have a 'denial value' to the United States. How to reconcile national security with possible independence of the island groups might become just as great a challenge to American statesmen as the questions of independence were to the British in the late 1950s and 1960s. For a discussion of these points by officers of the United States Naval War College, see Louis, *National Security and International Trusteeship in the Pacific*. See also especially Donald F. McHenry, *Micronesia: Trust Betrayed* (Washington, 1976); James H. Webb, Jr., *Micronesia and U.S. Pacific Strategy: A Blueprint for the 1980s* (New York, 1974); and Carl Heine, *Micronesia at the Crossroads* (Honolulu, 1974).

[49] The phrase is usually associated with Sir Hilton Poynton, to whom I am indebted for discussion of these problems and for allowing me to read his unpublished essay on decolonization. For a cogent argument similar to that of 'the salt-water fallacy', put forward by the Belgian representative at the United Nations, see F. Van Langenhove, *La Question des aborigènes aux Nations Unies: La Thèse belge* (Brussels, 1954).

apparently written merely to clarify his own thoughts, in which Hailey pondered the meaning of 'trusteeship', probably at the time of the San Francisco Conference. He noted that it represented his 'personal' views and that he had never fully discussed them at the Colonial Office. It puts many of the themes of the present book into the perspective of a wise and learned British Imperialist. Here follows, then, the testament of Lord Hailey.

Unlike those who argued that the British were accountable only to Parliament, Hailey was prepared to admit the principle of international accountability, if only because international conventions would merely embody minimal British standards. They would do no harm (here of course Hailey like most others did not anticipate the transformation of the Trusteeship Council into a political instrument). International colonial standards might help to improve general colonial practices. Nevertheless he saw a paradox. 'No one apparently demands that Russia or China should be held "accountable" for the peoples whom they have, by various means, absorbed within their boundaries.'[50] No one would propose that South Africa should be held accountable to any outside body for the 8,000,000 black Africans who were politically dependent on 2,000,000 whites. Ethiopia was not accountable for the social advancement of the provinces held in something like serfdom by the ruling caste, nor were the Creole rulers of Liberia to be summoned into the court of international opinion for their treatment of the tribes in the hinterland. In this respect Hailey was anticipating 'the salt-water fallacy' of the post-war period. 'It is only the Colonial powers, i.e. powers possessing *overseas* territories, that are to be held accountable . . .'[51]

There was a further paradox. Many of the 'dependent peoples' in the colonies were not the indigenous communities. The original populations of the West Indies, for example, had been absorbed into communities established by the British through the slave trade or indentured labour. Mauritius was similar. Hong Kong was a British creation. The majority of the population of Malaya consisted of immigrant Chinese and Indians. In India or in China they certainly would not be

[50] Memorandum by Hailey, no date but spring or summer of 1945, Hailey Papers.
[51] Ibid.

subject to international control. There were still more paradoxes. What was the test of 'backwardness'? In British colonies
there were standards of justice, and economic and social conditions in advance of those in areas of 'sovereign' rights. 'Are
the conditions in Siam comparable with those in Ceylon?
Is the individual liberty or social justice greater in Ethiopia
than in Malta? Are conditions in some of the South American
Republics so immeasurably superior to those in the British West
Indies?'[52]

To these considerations Hailey added a final point. Had the
advocates of international control stopped to ask themselves
whether the colonial peoples themselves would care to be
internationalized? Rightly or wrongly Hailey himself believed
that the 'natives' in British colonies would protest vigorously.
It could be taken as a certainty that the white settlers, whether
it be the French in New Caledonia or the Belgians in the
Congo, would oppose international control with a vengance.
And what after all was a 'colony' or 'dependent peoples'?
Were the white settlers in Kenya any less 'African' than the
black Africans? At the time such questions were not merely
dialectical.

Hailey noted the need for moderation in all these complex
and emotional issues. With words that surely are as relevant
now as then, he wrote that those who offered sweeping solutions
'must not assume that because they feel a strong moral sentiment on the subject, all the logic is on their side, and that
they will find before them an unlimited field for the practical
application of their conception . . .'. Like A. J. Balfour, Hailey
mastered the art of the dialectic to the extent that he could
push the ultimate argument in the direction he wished it to go.
In his case the thrust was sceptical but humane. He recognized
the need for a new vision. He saw the real problem as economic
development. It was up to the British, he thought, to do their
part in closing the gap between the western and the non-
western world. But it was a job not only for the British but
for all of the colonial powers. Hailey was under no illusion
that this task might be accomplished, and he recognized the
danger that *political independence* would by no means resolve the
problem of *economic dependence*. Would colonies that become

[52] Ibid.

politically independent truly increase their freedom? Ultimately Hailey was prepared to disregard the paradoxes that today remain unresolved. He found no final answers. The only course for the British was to carry on as well as they could.

The trusteeship issue of the Second World War brought out the best efforts of that generation of statesmen and civil servants concerned with the future of colonial peoples. The politicians who took definite stands for and against international trusteeship, such as Roosevelt and Churchill, were responding in their own way to a sense of guardianship as well as what they believed to be national interests. Perhaps they learned, respectively, the limits of American idealism and British power. Behind the politicians stood the civil servants who created the trusteeship system, including Sir Hilton Poynton and Kenneth Robinson in England, W. D. Forsyth in Australia, and Benjamin Gerig in the United States. Like Lord Hailey, they pursued a course that they hoped would raise the standards of living and contribute to social justice in the colonies. Ultimately they were concerned, as Sir Keith Hancock recognized at the time, with the profound question of human freedom.[53]

A slightly different emphasis may also be valid. In the meeting-room of the Trusteeship Council at the United Nations, there is a sculpture of a young woman releasing a bird. The bird symbolizes the trust territories on their flight to independence.[54] The bird is proud and determined, yet will it be truly free? There was an illuminating exchange of ideas on precisely this subject during one of the many discussions on trusteeship at the State Department during the war. It gives insight into the American commitment to colonial independence. Isaiah Bowman commented to Leo Pasvolsky that the American plan for decolonization was 'like setting a bird free, but putting a little salt on its tail'. Pasvolsky replied with a slightly more charitable explanation: 'it was like setting a bird free, but only in the garden.'[55]

[53] Hancock, *Argument of Empire*, p. 8.
[54] F. H. Corner, 'The Trusteeship Council', *The United Nations: Twenty Years* (20th Anniversary Commemorative Book, New York, 1965), p. 74.
[55] I.O. Minutes 60, 2 June 1944, USSD NF Box 142.

INDEX

Abyssinia *see* Ethiopia
Acheson, Dean, 552
Aden, 49, 126, 127
Advisory Committee on Foreign Policy (including Subcommittee on Political Problems of the Advisory Committee on Post-War Foreign Policy), debate on colonial issues 1942, 159–74; and Declaration on National Independence, 232–42; 68, 159
Alamein, significance of battle, 50, 259, 561
Alaska, 47, 165, 166, 272, 498, 499, 512
Aleutian Islands, 264
Altrincham, Lord *see* Sir Edward Grigg
American Air Lines, 269
American Export Airlines, 269
Amery, L. S., and imperial preference, 24; views about the British Empire, 32–4; on Palestine, 53; and Italian colonies, 63; scorn for international trusteeship, 89; dislike of economic clauses of mandates, 90; and Atlantic Charter, 126, 127, 129; and future of Hong Kong, 190; refuses to abandon any territory, 192; appalled at idea of international colonial administration, 194; and regional commissions, 215, 316; and abortive Anglo-American colonial declaration, 218, 222; mandates a 'relic', 224; and future of Tanganyika, 325; and post-war air routes, 355 n.; 403, 562
Angell, Sir Norman, 20–1
Anglo-American Caribbean Commission *see* Carribean Commission
Angola, 171
Appeasement, and British colonies, 36–7, 63, 66, 151
Armistice and Post-War Committee, 403–4, 464, 467
Ascension Island, 272, 354
Atlantic Charter, applicability to colonial territories, 20–1, 223–4, 247, 254; and trusteeship in Palestine, 62; and Italian colonies, 64, 67; and Pacific islands, 85; Article II (self-determination), 121–33, 161; supplement recommended, 140; possible extension into colonial charter, 141, 177–8, 231; Welles stresses universality of, 155; Smuts appeals to, 209; and territorial changes proposed by U.S. Navy, 266; compared with Cairo Declaration, 274–5, 286; and Australian–New Zealand Agreement 1944, 289, 291; and colonial problems at Dumbarton Oaks, 387; and Poynton–Robinson project, 399; 469, 499, 500, 506, 528, 542
Atomic bomb, 561–2
Attlee, Clement, attacks imperialism and proposes international administration, 33; as intellectual heir of 'Little England' tradition, 48–9, 557; describes Red Sea areas as 'incubus', 49; dissents from Middle Eastern policy, 67; on Atlantic Charter, 125; proposed international control in the colonies, 192–5; and abortive Anglo-American colonial declaration, 212, 214, 250; opposes white settler schemes, 320, 322; and Isaiah Bowman, 329; helps to close ranks against the Americans after Yalta, 464; and San Francisco conference, 527; and trusteeship as a continuation of imperialism, 549; on the atomic bomb and the nature of the British Empire, 549; on Cyrenaica and Somalia, 557
Attu Island, 272
Austin, Warren R., 174
Australia, policy towards mandates, 18, 107, 502; as trustee in Pacific, 167, 196, 292–8, and regional commissions, 216, 315–16; and abortive Anglo-American colonial declaration, 221, 223; and Pacific Peace settlement, 228; and Nauru, 240; air routes to, 269; post-war planning in, 289–99; security in the Pacific, 294–6; and aftermath of Australian–

Australia (*cont.*):
New Zealand Agreement, 301–8; 'Monroe Doctrine' of, 305–6; and South-East Asia regional commission, 315; responds to Poynton–Robinson project, 406–7; and New Zealand, conference, 1944, 409; trusteeship policy similar to State Department's, 420, 422; and Hot Springs Conference 1944, 428; and aftermath of Yalta, 472; and the Commonwealth Meeting 1945, 502; record as a colonial power, 511, 564; 431, 469, 559

Australian–New Zealand Agreement 1944, concluded 300–1; international reaction to, 302–8; checks American imperialism in the Pacific (according to Evatt), 411

Australian–New Zealand Conference 1944, 409–21, 505

Azores, 272, 347

Bahrein, 239
Balfour, A. J., 34, 570, 572
Barbados, 250
Batan Island, 264
Batterbee, Sir Harry, 413
Battershill, Sir William, and a new Scramble for Africa, 65; deprecates international trusteeship schemes, 397; criticizes Poynton–Robinson project, 398–9; 57
Beaverbrook, Lord, and imperial preference, 32 n.
Becker, Carl, 125
Beer, G. L., 6
Belgium (and Belgian Congo), estimate of Congo's decolonization 'more than a hundred years', 237; and regional commissions, 197, 314, 340, 341; comment by Lord Croft, 420; danger of trusteeship system to, 470; 44 n., 89–90, 151, 170, 171, 387, 431, 509, 536, 546, 559, 572
Benson, A. E., 343
Berendsen, C. A., 442–3, 521
Berle, Adolph, on air routes in the Far East, 80–1; on Palestine, 169; on Japanese mandates and Italian colonies, 241
Berlin Act 1885, as precedent for mandates system, 89–90, 95
Bermuda, 85, 127, 272

Bevin, Ernest, and regional commissions, 215, 316; and Italian colonies, 555–6; 403
Bidault, Georges, on France as her own trustee, 46
Bikini Island, 115
Bizerta, 228
Blakeslee, George, member of Territorial and Security Subcommittees and Chairman of Interdivisional Area Committee for the Far East, 71–2; on self-determination, 79; on the Japanese mandates, 81; relates history of North Pacific, 83; on sovereignty in the Pacific, 85; and influence of committees, 86–7; assesses historical accuracy of Cairo Declaration, 281 n.; on U.S. Navy aims in the Pacific, 389
Bloom, Sol, 237, 514, 515, 535, 544
Bonin Islands, 78, 261, 264, 265, 272, 352, 354
Bora-Bora, 269
Borneo, 127, 135, 191, 248, 315, 343, 437, 499
Borton, Hugh, expresses Wilsonian consensus 1943, 81; on decisions of Cairo Conference, 87, 275; 72
Bowman, Isaiah, mission to London 1944, 54–6, 327–34; on work of Territorial Subcommittee, 71; on colonial evolution, 170; redrawing the map of Africa, 171; development scheme for Portuguese colonies, 172; on shortcomings of mandates, 174; and trusteeship planning 1942–3, 183, 238–41; reports to State Department on results of mission to London, 334–6; on self-government and independence, 361; on preparing the Hottentots for self-government, 365; and international police force, 371; comment on British preoccupation with economic questions, 378; and San Francisco conference, 514, 536, 539; articulates State Department policy, 516; 69, 160, 227, 358, 359, 573
Boyd, E. B., 400–1
Brazil, 264, 272, 559
Brazzaville Conference, 28, 43–6, 551
Bretton Woods, 24

British Empire, Churchill on, 5, 8, 10, 14, 16; Milner on, 5; and common culture with U.S., 6; Roosevelt's ideas about, 9; as distinguished from Commonwealth, 9; Hailey a godsend of, 12; sense of moral revival in, 15–16, 103; and economic autarchy of, 22; and the U.S. in 1941, 24; economic resources of, 25; power in relation to U.S. and Russia, 25, 51; problem of security in Middle East, 48–51; different types of in Middle East, 49; evolution of, 99; Article III of Atlantic Charter used to attack, 124; racial situation in, 127, 138; 'colour bar' in, 127 n., 137; new era initiated by fall of Singapore, 145; as one of the 'Four Policemen', 148, 228; and Pacific islands, 156; Americans not fighting to hold together, 198; criticized by Wendell Willkie, 199–203; goal defined as development of self-governing institutions, 207; and regional commissions, 215–16; British evaluated as colonial administrators, 237; and international police force, 260, 263; and question of decentralization, 338; nature of, 339; decline of military power, 376; economic policy of, 381; and Hot Springs Conference 1944, 428; defended by Churchill at Yalta, 458–9; compared with American colonial empire, 512; and transformation caused by atomic bomb, 561–2

Brussels Act 1890, 89 n.

Bunche, Ralph J., analyzes Brazzaville Conference, 45–6; encounter with A. C. Jones, 429; and petitions, 480 n.

Bundy, Harvey, 491

Burke, Edmund, on trust, 88

Burma, as affected by Atlantic Charter, 130; F. D. R. on, 437; 135, 165, 168, 248, 315, 361, 425, 430, 457

Butler, Nevile, views on U.S. and mandated territories, 63; complains about Oliver Stanley, 256; comment on Australian–New Zealand Agreement, 303; 247 n.

Byelorussia, 559

Byrd, Admiral Richard E., leads expedition to South Pacific, 269–70;

reports to F. D. R. on result of mission, 270–1; 353

Byrnes, James F., 453–4, 458

Cadogan, Sir Alexander, analyzes F. D. R.'s trusteeship policy, 40; drafts self-determination article of Atlantic Charter, 123; doubts whether Declaration on National Independence can be translated into English, 232; timetables for independence 'silly', 246–7; and Cairo Conference, 278, 281–2; and Isaiah Bowman's visit 1944, 331, 333; on U.S. underwriting British Empire, 383; inquiries about colonial investigative powers of international organization, 404; subordinates mandates question at Yalta, 452; brief for Churchill, 455; acquiesces in trusteeship formula, 460; uses 'warm and woolly words' with C.O. after Yalta, 465; at San Francisco Conference, 519, 546

Caine, Sydney, views on economic problems of Middle East, 52–3; and international trusteeship, 313; emphasizes world economic development, 395; challenges common assumptions about mandates, 402–3

Cairo Conference 1943, decisions taken 'by chance, not design', 87; summary of significance of, 274–5; business transacted at, 279–82

Cairo Declaration, interpreted by David Lawrence and Walter Lippmann, 274; drafted by Harry Hopkins, 280–1; revised by Cadogan and Churchill, 281–3; approved by Stalin, 285–6; Australia and New Zealand protest against, 289, 298–301; 418

Cameron, Sir Donald, 324

Cameroons, 116, 172, 173, 442, 565 n.

Canada, takes little part in trusteeship debate, 17; and abortive Anglo-American colonial declaration, 220–1, 223–4; and regional planning 1944, 311, 314; and question of human rights, 406; and Hot Springs Conference 1944, 428; and aftermath of Yalta, 472; 431, 469, 559

Canal Zone *see* Panama Canal

Canton Island, 272

Caribbean, regional planning in, 313–14
Caribbean Commission, creation of, 180; 'model' for future commissions, 181; 197, 311, 313–14, 345, 429, 435, 440, 446
Caroline Islands, 76, 81–4, 265, 300, 346, 347, 352, 355, 412
Ceylon, 315, 430
Chamberlain, Joseph, 100
Chapter XI of U.N. Charter (non-self-governing territories), 175, 230, 533, 541
Chapter XII (trusteeship system), 175, 230, 533, 541
Chapter XIII (trusteeship council), 533
Chiang Kai-shek, ideas about trusteeship, 157; discusses trusteeship schemes with F. D. R. 1943, 273, 425; aims at Cairo Conference, 275; confers with F. D. R. at Cairo Conference, 278–80; and Hong Kong, 438; 28, 33, 38, 456
China, and trusteeship schemes, 28–9, 32, 167, 228, 236, 559; as a great power, 74, 275, 280, 551; as a xenophobic power, 76; and Formosa and Manchuria, 79; as one of the 'Four Policemen', 148, 227–9; and regional commissions, 185, 215–17, 315; and Hong Kong, 188–90; extraterritorial rights in, 206; and International Police Force, 260, 263, 264; and Cairo Conference, 280–1, 282, 284; military potential of, 377; and support of U.S. in trusteeship proposals, 447; as member of anti-British bloc, 525; and San Francisco Conference, 527, 530, 534, 536, 541
Christmas Island, 272
Churchill, Winston S., ideas about the British Empire, 5, 14; views of Hong Kong and China, 7; and trusteeship as a cloak for American expansion, 8; First Minister Speech of November 1942, 8, 200; regards F.D.R.'s ideas on India as fatuous, 9; 'keep a bit of India', 10; Tory view of the Empire, 15; anecdote about Empire and Commonwealth, 16, 110; grand strategy of according to Angell, 20; and American 'indirect' imperialism, 26; and de Gaulle, 27; and Indo-

China question, 28, 40–1; and Palestine, 53–4, 57–8; directs inquiry into Eritrea and Tripolitania as possible Jewish colonies, 58; and territorial aggrandizement in Middle East, 62; contempt for international trusteeship, 89; refuses to place British Empire 'in the dock', 99; discusses Atlantic Charter with F. D. R., 121–3; and Burma, 125; speech of September 1941 on Atlantic Charter, 129–31; believes F. D. R.'s thought belongs to time of George III, 147; erupts over F. D. R.'s ideas about India, 149–50; and the Washington monument, 181; and Wendell Willkie, 199–200; Hailey's position not far removed from, 209; relies on Stanley to hold the line, 211; and the abortive Anglo-American colonial declaration, 217–19, 256; discusses trusteeship schemes with F. D. R. 1943, 273; aims at Cairo Conference, 275; does not respond to colonial overture at Quebec, 277; and Cairo and Teheran Conferences, 280–5; reacts to Australian–New Zealand Agreement, 301–2; on regionalism, 310; meets with Stettinius mission, 328; and Dominion Prime Ministers' Conference 1944, 337, 344, 347–8; denounces international body interfering with British Empire, 349; vows not to despoil the weak, 350; 'trusteeship' used to cover expansionist ambitions, 351; and the flying of the Union Jack, 357; described as 'failing' on trusteeship question, 404; 'Hands off the British Empire', 433; instructions on trusteeship issue, 434–5; and Sultan of Morocco, as related by F. D. R., 438–9; and Japanese islands and Italian colonies at Yalta, 450–1; receives less than zealous guidance on colonial question, 452; briefed, 455; defends British Empire, 458–9; acquiesces in trusteeship formula, 460; after Yalta demands explanation, 463; responds to post-Yalta situation 466, 469–70, 474; and Common, wealth Meeting 1945, 509; guides policy at time of San Francisco,

530–1; British Empire will never yield 'an inch', 548; and Italian colonies, 555; sense of guardianship, 573

Clarke, Ashley, debates 'economic imperialism' with Stanley Hornbeck, 31; comment on Australian–New Zealand Agreement, 303

Clauson, Gerard, objects to high-handed F.O. practice, 56–7; and Japanese banks 'playing merry hell with Malaya', 67 n.; believes Hancock's views to be 'great nonsense', 105

Clipperton Island, 75, 261, 269, 270, 272, 368

Cohen, Andrew, 105

Colonial Charter *see* Atlantic Charter

Colonial Development and Welfare, fundamentals of, 99–103; bibliographical note, 100; 1929 Act, 100–1; 1940 Act, 100–1, 298, 394, 505; 1945 Act, 101

Colonial Office (*see also, e.g.*, Cranborne, Stanley), similarities of ideas with U.S. Navy and Joint Chiefs' Strategic Survey Committee, 6–7, 108, 390, 422; administration of the dependent Empire, 10; centralized system of administration criticized by Smuts, 17, 337–8; reaction to American 'economic imperialism', 31; and appeasement in the colonies, 37, 63, 66; tendency to be pro-Zionist, 49; and economic development of Middle East, 52; and Palestine, 53; and solution to problem of Italian colonies, 65–7; distaste for mandate obligations, 90; indignation at Permanent Mandates Commission, 93; fears impact of visitations, 96; and Sir Frederick Lugard on the Permanent Mandates Commission, 98; and Colonial Development and Welfare, 100–3; not responsible to world opinion, 107; and Australian–New Zealand Conference November 1944, 414; and racial problems, 127; advanced and unconventional views of, 128; interprets Atlantic Charter, 129, 131–3; insists on administrative control regardless of international arrangements, 191, 258; under Oliver

Stanley persistently rejects international trusteeship, 211; 'amateurish and uncooperative', 256; and regional planning, 309–26; tension with F.O. over visit by Isaiah Bowman, 332; and international accountability, 343; intends to hold its own, 379; controversy in over trusteeship and partnership, 395; bugbears of, 405; in ignorance of events at Yalta, 453; responds to Yalta with exasperated dismay, 463; post-war vision affected by Yalta, 464; responds to F.O. advice on colonial question, 499–500; objects to American 'strategic trusteeship', 523; and free trade clauses of the mandates, 526, 529; and Somalia at end of war, 556–7

Columbia, 269

Committee on Dependent Areas (Benjamin Gerig), reconciles idealism and realism of trusteeship system, 115; invites Arthur Creech Jones to speak on British policy, 429–31; agitated on question of American Negro, 432; 114

Committee on Dependent Areas (interdepartmental), formation of, 476, discusses problem of Pacific, 477–82

Commonwealth Conference 1945, 497–511

Congo *see* Belgian Congo

Connally, Tom, 235, 514, 540

Corner, F. H., analyzes C.O. policy early 1945, 407–8; outlines N.Z. policy late 1944, 410; on South Pacific Commission, 419

Coupland, Reginald, 103–4

Coy, Wayne, 352–3, 425

Cranborne (Lord Salisbury), and future of South-East Asia, 29; views about the British Empire, 34–5; deplores American intervention, 53 n.; sums up C.O. position in relation to Atlantic Charter, 133; discourages idea of 'Colonial Charter', 142; colonial policy in 1942, 187–97; and abortive Anglo-American colonial declaration, 212, 215, 222–4, 249–50, 252; and Australian–New Zealand Agreement, 302, 304; and regional commissions, 316, 340; and future

Cranborne (*cont.*):
of central and eastern Africa, 320, 322–3; and Isaiah Bowman 1944, 328–9; angered by Australian–New Zealand Conference November 1944, 413–18; reveals that imperial government will resist accountability, 420; regards imperial unity as essential, 421; assesses position of Dominions after Yalta, 469; and Commonwealth Meeting 1945, 501–2, 506, 508–11; and San Francisco Conference, 519–20, 522–9, 533, 535, 541; and the evolutionary ladder of colonial progress, 546–7; 384, 403, 475
Croft, Lord, 420
Cross, Sir Ronald, comment on Australian–New Zealand Agreement, 304–5
Cross, Samuel H., 156
Cuba, 176, 314
Curacao, 29
Curtin, John, meets with Hull and Roosevelt, 307–8; at Dominion Prime Ministers' Meeting 1944, 337, 344, 346, 348–9; 417
Cyprus, 49, 65, 127
Cyrenaica, 59–61, 65, 556–62

Dairen, 280, 285, 355, 456
Dakar, 228, 264, 284, 347, 348, 354
Danzig, 208
Davis, Norman H., 173
Dawe, Sir Arthur, on problems of central and eastern Africa, 319–21; and amalgamation schemes for East Africa, 323–4; advocates transformation of mandates and protectorates into colonies, 401
Declaration on National Independence, 177–9, 182, 230–2, 242–5, 328–31; British response to, 250–8; dropped in favour of 'general colonial declaration', 360–2
De Gaulle, Charles, preservation of colonial empires a link in common with Churchill, 27; attitude towards American trusteeship schemes, 28; and Indo-China, 41, 552; and Brazzaville Conference, 43–6; discussed by F. D. R. and Stalin at Yalta, 457
Dening, M. E., 550

Djibouti, 64, 234
Dodecanese, 65
Dominican Republic, 314
Dominion Prime Ministers' Conference 1944, 311, 337–50
Dulles, John Foster, 125, 518 n., 538–9
Dumbarton Oaks Conference, reason colonial issue not formally discussed, 377; China puts forward trusteeship schemes, 384 n.; discussion about regional commissions, 385; regionalism, 386; Congo treaties and mandates, 387; federations, 388
Dunn, James, 41, 490, 493
Dutch East Indies *see* Netherlands East Indies

Easter Island, 268, 352
Eastwood, Christopher, and Jewish settlement schemes, 60–1; analyzes Atlantic Charter, 126–8; 131–2; on 'independence' and 'interdependence', 247, 253, 535; suspicion of U.S. ambitions, 248; and the abortive Anglo-American colonial declaration, 253, 277; comment on Australian–New Zealand Agreement, 304; and regional planning 1944, 310–13, 341–3
Eaton, Charles A., 234, 237, 514, 540
'Economic imperialism', 22, 26 n., 31, 51, 67, 68, 74, 86, 90, 144, 206, 402, 566
Ecuador, 269, 272
Eden, Sir Anthony, and F. D. R.'s trusteeship policy, 40; critical of Walter Lippmann, 134; and Hong Kong, 189, 191–2; and abortive Anglo–American colonial declaration, 212, 246, 250, 256; discusses colonial issues in Washington 1943, 227–9; colonial issue at Quebec Conference, 276; and Cairo Conference, 282; reassures Churchill on trusteeship question, 434; on F. D. R.'s health, 448 n.; advises Churchill on eve of Yalta, 451; subordinates colonial question, 452; takes care not to flout C.O., 454; brief for Churchill, 455; acquiesces in trusteeship formula, 460; defends Yalta accord, 464–70; and San Francisco Conference, 520
Eggleston, Sir Frederick, on Pasvolsky, 358 n.; background, 423; interview

with F. D. R., 424; interviews with Hopkins and Stettinius, 424–7; and argument of 'Balkanization of the Pacific', 427–8; interrogates Stanley on trusteeship, 442; firm view that 'independence' is the goal of American policy, 443; urges a renewed mandates system, 444; at San Francisco Conference, 517, 532; on American imperialism, 565–6

Egypt, 49, 51, 65, 163, 234, 341, 498, 546, 556, 559

Embick, General S. D., memorandum on 'Fundamental Military Factors', 374; on the 'Church group' in the U.S., 478 n.; 260, 371, 373, 476, 477

Emerson, Rupert, 151, 153–4

Emrys-Evans, Paul, 192, 196

Eniwetok Island, 115

Eritrea, as possible Jewish colony, 58–9; 64, 253, 556, 558, 560–1

Ethiopia, and Eritrean problem, 59, 64; and Jewish settlement schemes 61 n.; discussed in American committee 1943, 233–5; 341, 559; 572

Evatt, H. V., attitude towards mandates, 18, 564; personality and background, 107–8; and international accountability, 221, 410; and Australian–New Zealand Agreement 1944, 290–3, 301, 411; regards Cairo Declaration as affront, 299; and 'grand-motherly restraint' by Imperial government, 302; ambition of, 305; annoys U.S. government, 307–8; policies disavowed at Dominion Prime Ministers' Meeting 1944, 337; summarizes Australian policy, 345 n.; a devolutionist, 344; responds to C.O. policy early 1945, 406–7; motives of in regard to Australian–New Zealand Conference November 1944, 409; indignation at Imperial government, 416–17; described by F. D. R. as 'stormy petrel', 424; at the Commonwealth Meeting 1945, 502, 505–6, 510–11; at the San Francisco Conference, 517–18, 520, 528, 544–6; 421, 423, 502, 564

Fabian Colonial Research Bureau, bibliographical note, 16; and inter-national accountability, 107; and trusteeship and partnership, 145; 14–15, 500

Fairchild, General Muir S., memorandum on 'Fundamental Military Factors', 374–7; 260–73, 476

Fezzan, 59, 558–60

Fiji, 127, 315, 342, 352

Forde, F. M., 502

Foreign Office (*see also*, *e.g.*, Eden, Cadogan), and colonial appeasement, 36–7, 63, 66; analyzes F. D. R.'s trusteeship policy, 38–40; tendency to be anti-Zionist, 49; and Palestine, 53, 55–6; solution to problem of Italian colonies, 64–7; tension with C.O. over visit by Isaiah Bowman, 332; and 'heresy' of international accountability, 343; advises C.O. on colonial questions, 499–500

Foreign Office Research Department, on Italian colonies, 59; and Jewish settlement schemes, 60, 62

Formosa, 72, 76, 79, 80, 227, 264, 282, 286

Forrestal, James, supports Stimson, 483, 488; meeting with Stimson and Stettinius, 489–90; cooperates in resolving trusteeship issue, 494–6; 482

Forsyth, W. D., and post-war planning for Australia, 293–7; and Australian–New Zealand Agreement 1944, 301, 308; outlines Australian policy late 1944, 410; and San Francisco Conference, 521; reflects on outcome of trusteeship controversy, 564 n.; 573

Fortas, Abe, participates in post-Yalta trusteeship debate, 476; attempts to reconcile military and civilian factions, 480; and strategic security, 481–2; 436, 484

'Four Policemen' scheme, 148, 160, 284, 295

France (and French Colonial Empire), and question of independence of colonies, 19; conditions in, 27–8; and Brazzaville Conference, 43–7; representation on regional commissions, 196; French evaluated as colonial administrators, 237; discussed at Teheran Conference, 283–4; and regional planning, 314–16;

France *(cont.)*:
denounced by F. D. R., 355;
military strength of, 377; comment
on by Lord Croft, 420; and Hot
Springs Conference 1944, 428; possibility of trusteeship conspiracy
against, 454; danger of trusteeship
system to, 470; Peter Fraser critical
of colonial administration, 506;
colonial empire compared to that of
U.S., 512; and San Francisco Conference, 525–6, 534, 546; and Indo-
China at end of war, 551–2; 428,
431, 509, 559
Frankfurter, Felix, on Anglo-Saxon
law and trusteeship, 441; 440
Fraser, Peter, attitude towards trusteeship, 18, 564; background and personality, 107–10; and Australian–
New Zealand Agreement 1944, 301;
interview with Cordell Hull, 307;
at Dominion Prime Ministers' meeting 1944, 337, 343–9; on security in
Pacific, 411–12; retort to Imperial
government November 1944, 415;
at Commonwealth Meeting 1945,
502, 504, 506–7, 511–12; visit to
Samoa, 520; chairs Trusteeship
Commission at San Francisco, 518–
19, 520, 542, 546; hopes Americans
will be responsible for security in
northern Pacific, 521; 408
Furnivall, J. S., 136, 505

Galapogos Islands, 261, 263, 268, 269,
272
Gambia, 126, 127, 226–7, 250, 356–7,
382, 438
Gater, Sir George, attitude towards
colonial appeasement, 37–8; annoyed
at F.O., 66; visit to Washington,
181; interview with F. D. R., 182;
observations on Declaration on
National Independence, 248–9; C.O.
does not wish to be entirely rigid,
382–3; C.O. prepared to yield on
colonial library, 383; discusses Yalta
accord with Cadogan, 465; 214,
258 n.
General Board of the United States
Navy, study of International Police
Force and Pacific islands, 262–9;
disclaims motives of imperialism,
265, and Atlantic Charter, 266;

blueprint for an 'American lake',
267; and security in the Pacific,
368–9
Gent, Gerard, and question of economic imperialism, 30; and colonial
appeasement, 37; attitude towards
Hong Kong, 37 n.; and Italian
colonies, 65; analyzes Declaration
on National Independence, 248;
comments on Australian–New Zealand Agreement, 304
Gerig, Benjamin, background, 91;
bibliographical note, 92; and Dependent Areas Committee, 114;
and trusteeship planning 1942, 183;
reviews proposals 1944, 359–60, 362;
and question of sovereignty, 363–
4; discussions at Dumbarton Oaks,
385–6; impression of Poynton, 389;
and Stanley–Pasvolsky encounter,
445; raises question of sovereignty in colonial territories, 447; and
trusteeship mechanism, 117 n., 450;
and Stettinius–Stimson controversy,
491–2; Stassen's right hand man at
San Francisco, 515; and the colonial
issue at San Francisco, 521, 522,
528
Gibraltar, 126, 127, 285, 569
Gie, S. F. N., 443
Gilbert and Ellice Islands, 264, 266,
272, 342, 352
Gildersleeve, Virginia, 514, 516, 540
Gold Coast, 381, 442, 446
Green, Joseph, proposals for security
in the Pacific, 78; on general colonial declaration extending throughout backward areas, 361–2; on ques-
tion of sovereignty, 363; 365
Greenland, 264, 272
Grew, Joseph C., not in favour of
immediate independence, 427; 371,
443
Grigg, Sir Edward, views on Middle
East, 50–3; responds to American
criticism, 203–4
Guadalcanal, 259
Guam, 76, 83, 84, 111, 165, 264, 265
Guatemala, 272, 542

Hackworth, Green, on question
sovereignity, 363–4; 182, 230
Haden Guest, Dr. Leslie, attacks policy
of partnership, 144–5

Hailey, Lord, key figure in colonial question, 10–11; and Mont Tremblant Conference, 11–13, 205–9; influence during war, 13–14; bibliographical note, 13; meets with Hamilton Fish Armstrong and Wendell Willkie, 14; anticipates political and social change, 97; and Carlton Hotel Meeting 1939, 103–4; deprecates view of Walter Lippmann, 134; objects to comparing Philippines with Malaya, 135 n.; champions 'partnership' versus 'trusteeship', 139–43, 339; addresses A.S. and A.P.S. 1942, 142; ideas on 'partnership' criticized by Fabians, 145; meets F. D. R., 218; and abortive Anglo-American colonial declaration, 253–4; views on South African expansion, 319; and trusteeship in Tanganyika, 324–5; representative of C.O. views in 1944? 384; on trusteeship and international accountability November 1944, 399; emphasizes publicity as positive aspect of international trusteeship, 400; on sovereignty, 403; summary of thoughts on colonial question, 571–3; 69, 204, 252

Haiti, 314

Halifax, Lord, and use of phrase 'Empire' and 'Commonwealth', 16, 110; and the abortive Anglo-American colonial declaration, 229; and National Declaration on Independence, 232, 243, 250, 252–3; discredits importance of timetables for independence, 246; urges keeping the initiative in colonial affairs, 390; on Pasvolsky, 391; discussion of trusteeship with Stanley, 440–1; minimizes significance of F. D. R.'s utterances on trusteeship, 443; 176, 356, 499

Hall, G. H., 555

Hall, H. Duncan, 110–12

Hancock, W. K., and colonial development, 103–5; themes of *Argument of Empire*, 112–13; and question of human freedom, 573

Harlech, Lord (W. Ormsby-Gore), 106, 320

Harrod, R. F., describes American myth about British Empire, 22; ideas about a prosperous world, 24

Hart, Admiral Thomas C., 262

Havana Convention, 151–2

Hawaii, 165, 166, 236, 261, 265, 352, 498, 538

Hepburn, Admiral A. J., 267

Hickerson, John, 306, 521

Hilldring, General J. H., 369

Hinden, Rita, views on British Empire, 15–16; bibliographical note, 16; urges publicity in the colonies, 107; exhortation on eve of San Francisco Conference, 500–1

Hiss, Alger, and trusteeship formula at Yalta, 453–4, 458–9

Hitler, Adolph, and British Empire, 33, 129; 502

Hobson, John A., 23

Holcombe, Arthur N., 151–2

Holland, Harry, 344

Honduras, 126, 127, 184, 542

Hong Kong, as an issue of contention between Churchill and Roosevelt, 7; freedom of trade in, 30; created by British, 35, 571; future of, 37, 127, 188–92, 229; key point in post-war defence arrangements, 206; discussed at Cairo Conference, 279–80, 285; F. D. R. on, 437–8; discussed at Yalta, 456; 135, 165, 168, 248, 315, 348, 355, 374, 489

Hood, Lord, critical of Jewish settlement schemes, 61 n.; and international supervision of colonies, 67; and imperial defence, 558 n.

Hopkins, Harry, drafts Cairo Declaration, 280–1; sums up F. D. R.'s ideas on sovereignty, 426; at Yalta, 455; 155, 228, 351, 425–6, 443

Hornbeck, Stanley K., debates 'economic imperialism' with Ashley Clarke, 31; on economic controls to keep Japan disarmed, 77; and influence of committees, 86–7; believes in 'moral suasion', 161; views about South-East Asia, 162; high minded principles might boomerang, 165–6; on racial implications of trusteeship, 174 n.; and Declaration of National Independence, 177–8, 182, 230; on Nauru, 240; visit to London 1943, 278 n.; on self-government and independence, 360–2, 365; on question of sovereignty, 362–3; and international police force, 371–2; interview with F. D. R. November

Hornbeck (*cont.*):
1944, 424–5; 84, 160, 168, 205, 232 n., 358
Hoskins, Colonel Harold, 55
Hudson, Geoffrey, analyzes F. D. R.'s trusteeship policy, 39; 69, 551
Hughes, William M., and creation of mandates system, 92–3; final jab at Wilson, 93 n.
Hull, Cordell, and free trade, 24; and trusteeship planning, 175–7, 180, 182, 185–6; and debate about 'Parent States', 186, 212, 218; and question of colonial independence, 225, 229–30, 232–5; meets with Eden 1943, 227–8; gives Halifax draft of Declaration on National Independence, 232; and policy of 'continual preachment', 242; and Quebec and Cairo Conferences, 276; excoriates Fraser on Australian–New Zealand Agreement, 307; tells Curtin he is 'flabbergasted', 307; 246, 355–6, 373, 425, 514, 537
Hurley, General Patrick, 548
Huxley, Julian, 103–4

Iceland, 264
Ickes, Harold, 436, 490–1
Imperial Preference, 32
India, crisis in 1942, 8, 11; eventual Dominion status of, 10, 179; as affected by Atlantic Charter, 130; Smuts on, 209; and regional commissions, 215–17, 315, 341–2; discussed by F. D. R. at Teheran Conference, 283 n.; 162, 165, 180, 489, 499, 556, 559, 560, 571
Indirect Rule, cardinal principle of, 96–7; 93, 128
Indo-China, and trusteeship schemes, 9, 38–9, 167–8, 225, 228, 347; F. D. R.'s views on, 27, 157, 356, 425; and Brazzaville Conference, 44, 46; discussed at Cairo Conference, 277–8, 283; F. D. R. says will cause 'trouble' with Stalin and Churchill, 437; discussed at Yalta, 456–7; prospects had trusteeship schemes been realized, 551–2; 28, 152, 162, 164, 165, 196, 248, 266, 315, 343, 489, 550
Indonesia, 352
'Informal Empire', in the Middle East,

49–51; in the Pacific, 78; American, 566
Informal Political Agenda Group (International Organization), 358
Institute of Pacific Relations, conference at Mont Tremblant, 11–13; 1944 conference at Hot Springs, 427–8
Interior Department, 480, 490
International Labour Organization, 385, 396
International Organization Subcommittee, 183–4
International Police Force, zones, 260, 371–3; bases and evolution in time, 261; 259
Internationalization, as a solution to the 'colonial problem', 95, 152–3, 157, 167, 168, 173, 245
Iran, trusteeship scheme for Persian Gulf, 449–50
Iraq, 49, 51, 169, 543, 546, 559
Italian colonies, and Jewish settlement schemes, 58–62; fate of, 233, 248, 395, 555–62; at Yalta, 450; 386, 397
Ituaba Island, 265

Jacob, General Ian, 520, 523, 524, 525
Jamaica, 132, 379, 390, 435
Japan *and* Japanese Empire (including mandated islands), U.S. Navy seeks to prevent British claims on, 18–19; future debated in State Department committee, 68–87; and mandates system, 90; question of island fortification, 114 and n.; F. D. R.'s ideas about, 156, 227–8, 355; imperialism in Korea, 164–5; discussed in C.O., 248; discussed by Joint Chiefs' Strategic Survey Committee, 260–1; and Cairo Conference, 275, 281–4, 286; and Australian security, 296; discussed by Isaiah Bowman in London 1944, 334; J.C.S. estimate, 374–5; U.S. to act as 'guardian' over islands, 437; at Yalta, 450, 453, 459; and aftermath of Yalta, 467; discussed in Dependent Areas Committee 1945, 477, 482–3; at San Francisco, 523–4, 531
Jebb, Gladwyn, analyzes National Declaration on Independence, 244–5; and Isaiah Bowman 1944, 331–2; and discussions with C.O., 382–3;

evaluation of Poynton–Robinson project, 405; subordinates mandates question at Yalta because of quagmire in international law, 452–3; indignation at Sumner Welles's article on colonial liberation, 498–9; contempt for public opinion, 499; 217, 390, 472

Jeffries, Sir Charles, 395

Joint Chiefs of Staff (and J.C.S. Strategic Survey Committee), see reason for continued existence of British Empire, 6; oppose international supervision, 19; estimate decline of British power, 25; and International Police Force, 259–61, 372–3; survey of U.S. military requirements, 271–2; analysis of Australian–New Zealand Agreement, 306–7; urge annexation of Pacific islands, 309; and controversy with State Department, 366; memorandum on 'Fundamental Military Factors in Relation to . . . Territorial Trusteeships', 374–7; protest ineffective for Yalta, 448–9; and San Francisco, 515; 365, 477, 480, 482, 491

Jones, Arthur Creech, bibliographical note, 11; at Mont Tremblant Conference, 11–12; indignant at critics of British Empire, 15; on Colonial Development and Welfare, 100–1; and international accountability, 107; and Atlantic Charter, 131; on trusteeship and partnership, 145; and question of American Negro, 428–9; speaks before Dependent Areas Committee, 429–32; 258, 464, 565 n.

Kenya, and tradition of trusteeship, 108–9, 317–18; discussed after fall of Singapore, 136–7; and amalgamation schemes, 322–3; and regional commissions, 341; 98, 339, 383, 556, 572

Keynes, John Maynard, 22, 34

Khan Noon, Firoz, 503–4, 508

King, Admiral E. J., an Anglophobe, 18; on significance of battles in the Pacific, 84; on British sea power, 260

King, Mackenzie, on Churchill and British Empire, 14; on the 'imperialist idea', 17; and San Francisco Conference, 520

Kirk, Grayson, views on peace with Japan, 73–4; voices moderate opinion, 76; on bases in the Pacific, 78, 86; on trusteeship for Korea, 80; 72

Knox, Frank, urges F. D. R. to annex Japanese islands, 262; testifies that Japanese islands should be annexed, 351

Korea, and trusteeship schemes, 9, 72, 185, 225, 228, 235–6, 453; airbases in, 76; and principle of self-determination, 79; reaction to trusteeship schemes, 80; Japanese imperialism in, 165; and Cairo Conference, 282, F. D. R. on, 355; discussed at Yalta, 456–7; at end of war, 553–6; 233, 253, 286, 550

Kurile Islands, 74, 80, 81, 456

Labour Party, and the Empire, 14–15; policy towards colonial territories, 18, 173

Labrador, 272

Lampedusa, 63

Law, Richard, dissents from Palestine Committee, 54; analyzes Declaration on Independence, 243, 276–7; and Isaiah Bowman's mission, 328–9, 331; conversation with Stettinius about colonial compensation, 378–9; 181, 196

League of Nations (*see also* mandates, Permanent Mandates Commission), 90, 263

Leahy, William D., 259

Lebanon, 169, 543

Leopold II, 89

Levallois, Maurice, 566–7

Liberia, 'a great independent state . . . and happy as a clam', 171; 95, 264, 314, 381, 402

Libya, as possible Jewish settlement colony, 58–61; fate of, 64–5; at end of war, 555, 558–60; 183, 253, 561

Life magazine, 'Open Letter . . . to the People of England', 198–9; Smuts interview, 209–10

Limb, Ben C., 553

Lindley, M. F., 109, 505

Line Islands, 266

Linlithgow, Lord, 217–18

Lippmann, Walter, on the post-Singapore war, 134–5; trusteeship 'merely an argument in semantics', 441; 'Pandora's Box', on the eve of the San Francisco Conference, 512–13; 440
Listowel, Lord, 140
Litvinov, Maxim, 155, 157
Lloyd George, David, 122
Lloyd, Lord, 319
Lloyd, T. K., analyzes Declaration on National Independence, 248; criticizes Poynton–Robinson project, 396–7; 309
Long, Walter, 90
Loyalty Islands, 266, 267
Lugard, Sir Frederick (Lord), and the tradition of trusteeship, 96–8; on reform of mandates system, 106; responds to Churchill's 'First Minister' speech, 200–1; 473

MacArthur, General Douglas, 134, 554
McCloy, John J., 489
McCormick, Anne Hare, on non-western civilization, 170; mandates 'hypocritical', 172; 160, 168, 173, 193
McIntosh, Alister, 521
MacMichael, Sir Harold, proposals for Palestine, 53 n.
Macmillan, Harold, analyzes consequences of Atlantic Charter, 132–3; thinks 'trusteeship' obsolescent, 139; advocates 'partnership', 143–4; and amalgamation schemes for East Africa, 323–4
Madagascar, 341, 348
Madeira, 272
Mair, L. P., 505
Malaya, future of, 30, 37, 191; and trusteeship schemes, 32; and the lessons of fall of Singapore, 134–8; and Australian security, 295–6; 127, 152, 165, 189, 216, 248, 315, 343, 347, 361, 425, 443, 551, 571
Malkin, Sir William, 452
Malta, 49, 127, 276, 431, 572
Manchuria, 79, 227, 282, 286
Mandates (*see also* Permanent Mandates Commission *and* Trusteeship), as a sacred trust of civilization, 3; as a type of formal empire, 49; stink in the nostrils of Arabs, 60; system

established 1919, 90, 92; free trade clauses, 90–1; 'A', 'B', and 'C' types, 92, 152; annual reports, 93, lacking in powers of inspection and visiting missions, 95; and Article 22 of League Covenant, 97; treated as British colonies, 99; a check on South African expansion, 106; principal clauses, 114; Hailey assesses value of, 143; F. D. R. unenthusiastic about, 153; criticized by Isaiah Bowman, 174; reform of 184; compared with regional councils, 214; discussed at Dumbarton Oaks, 387–8; Stanley gives frank views on, 442; Stanley argues case against at State Department, 445; Sir Frederick Eggleston urges renewal of, 444; legal position of, 452, 468; C.O. on, 501; discussed at Commonwealth Meeting 1945, 504
Manila, 75
Marcus Island, 265
Mariana Islands, 81–4, 264, 265, 300, 352, 355, 412, 481, 569
Marquesas Islands, 75, 228, 264, 266, 267, 269, 270, 272, 368
Marshall Islands, 81–3, 115, 264, 265, 300, 342, 346, 347, 355, 412
Massawa, 64, 560
Massey, William F., and creation of mandates system, 93
Mauritius, 127, 341, 571
Menon, K. S., 534, 543, 545
Mexico, 272
Micronesia (*see also* Japanese Empire), 'native welfare' in, 86; Rooseveltian trusteeship in, 354; future debated in State Department committee, 68–87; discussed by Joint Chiefs' Strategic Survey Committee, 260–1; U.S. to act as 'guardian' in, 437; discussed in Dependent Areas Committee 1945, 477, 482–3; 81–4, 116, 165, 342, 352, 565
Middle East Supply Centre, 49
Milner, Lord, as representative of enlightened British Imperialism, 5; 502
Mississippi (state of), 361–2
Moffat, Abbot Low, 370–1
Molotov, V. M., 155, 157, 276, 458
Mont Tremblant Conference 1942, 205–9; contrasted with Hot Springs

Conference, 428
Mook, H. van, 29
Moore, Sir Henry, 323
Morocco, 355, 438–9
Morrison, Herbert, and the 'jolly old Empire', 14
Moyne, Lord, assassination of, 57; and self-government in the Empire, 126; interprets Atlantic Charter, 128; deprecates view of Walter Lippmann, 134
Mudaliar, Sir Ramaswami, 510
Murray, Wallace, 54, 56, 169

Nash, Walter, 299, 302, 412
Natal, 264
Nauru Island, 116, 240
Navajo reservations, 362
Navy (U.S.) *see also* General Board, sees reasons for continued existence of British Empire, 6; in tacit agreement with Colonial Office on question of mandates, 18, 108, 390, 422; distrusts international supervision, 18; believes ultimately that the peace would rest on military security, 68; dislike of impermanence in Pacific islands, 366; no confidence in future international organization, 485
Netherlands (and Netherlands East Indies), and question of independence of colonies, 19, 29–30, 111, 152, 155, 168; investment in, 153; and representation on regional commissions, 196, 215, 342, 343; Dutch evaluated as colonial administrators, 237, 346; and Australian security, 295–6; comment by Lord Croft, 420; F. D. R. believes will bring democracy to South-East Asia, 424; British imperialism and N.E.I., 425; and Hot Springs Conference 1944, 428; danger of trusteeship system to, 470
New Britain, 272, 295
New Caledonia, 266, 267, 284, 292, 315, 348, 352, 506, 572
Newfoundland, 264, 272
New Guinea, head-hunters to be educated in, 30; independence of, 92, 298, 444; F. D. R. on future of, 437; 116, 291–3, 352, 423, 442, 443, 563, 565

New Hebrides, 38, 169, 194, 208, 264, 267, 292, 295, 315, 352, 355
New Zealand, policy towards mandates, 18, 107; representation on regional commissions, 196, 216, 315–16; and abortive Anglo-American colonial declaration, 219–20, 223; and Pacific peace settlement, 228; and Nauru, 240; post-war planning in, 300–1; and aftermath of Australian–New Zealand Agreement, 301–8; hostile response to C.O. policy early 1945, 407–8; convenes with Australia in conference November 1944, 409; trusteeship policy similar to State Department's, 420, 422; and aftermath of Yalta, 472; record as a colonial power, 511, 564; 431, 469
Nigeria, 388, 442
Nile, 234, 341
Non-self-governing territories (Chapter XI of U.N. Charter), 92, 115, 230, 533, 543
Northeast Airlines, 269
Notter, Harley, 536, 540
Noumea, 295
Nyasaland, 314, 319

Office of Strategic Services, 70, 124
Oil, importance of in British Middle East policy, 48, 50–1
Olive, Colonel James, on lines of communication, 75–6; on islands in Pacific, 86; 72, 367
Orts, Pierre, 97
Ottawa tariff system, 22–4

Pacific Charter *see* Atlantic Charter
Pacific War Council, 277, 299
Pakistan, 559
Palestine, as part of Middle Eastern Empire, 49; mandatory rights in, 51; national home in, 53; Ministerial Committee on, 54–7; discussed in American committee, 169; and problems of the plural society, 398; the mandate and partition, 400–1; capital investment in, 402; and the San Francisco Conference, 543–4; 525
Panama Canal, excluded from trusteeship schemes, 168; 32, 263, 268, 352, 498, 512
Pan American Airways, 269
Pantelleria, 63, 513

Papua *see* New Guinea

Paramaschiru, 272

Partnership, concept debated 1942, 135, 137, 139–46, 207; wartime idea distinguished from later usage in connection with central Africa, 139 n.; defined in Poynton–Robinson project, 394

Pasvolsky, Leo, and Declaration on National Independence, 230–1; and general colonial issues, 241; key official co-ordinating trusteeship efforts, 358–9; on general colonial declaration, 360–1; on question of sovereignty, 362; on British using regional commissions as false fronts, 389; identifies attitude of Navy with pre-war attitude of Japan, 390; discusses colonial issue with Poynton, 391; arranges for Stanley's visit to Washington, 433–4; discussion with Stanley about colonial issues, 444–7; chairs inter-departmental Dependent Areas Committee, 476; adviser at San Francisco, 515, 541; 371, 479, 493, 573

Pence, Captain H. L., believes that 'the Japanese should be destroyed', 73; on lines of communication, 74–5, 86; on possibility of racial war, 76; on economic controls over Japan, 77–8; proposes scheme of American 'informal empire', 78; places security over idealism, 85; on permanently crushing Japan, 367; on means of achieving white rule in the Pacific, 368; on policies of administering liberated areas, 369; 72

Perham, Margery, and Carlton Hotel meeting 1939, 103, 105; assesses American criticism of British Empire, 113, 124, 201–3; analyzes post-Singapore state of the Empire, 135–9; criticizes Smuts on issue of decentralization, 339–40; on equality as the goal of trusteeship, 340

Permanent Mandates Commission, composition of, 93; compared with Trusteeship Council, 95, 99, 117; and Sir Frederick Lugard, 97–8; and Havana Convention, 152; compared with regional commissions, 197, 385; chief value of publicity, 208; evaluation by G. F. Seel, 312;

Kenneth Robinson on, 394; 410, 413, 524

Persian Gulf, trusteeship scheme for, 449–50; 355

Peru, 272

Pescadores Islands, 280, 282, 286

Peterson, Sir Maurice, 55–7

Phelps-Stokes Fund, 14, 202

Philippines, after Singapore, 134–5; excluded from trusteeship schemes, 168; plan for quasi-protectorate in, 353; representative at San Francisco Conference, 527–8; 84, 176, 178, 180, 206, 261, 264, 265, 272, 315, 352, 425, 444, 512, 537

Phoenix Islands, 266

Polynesia, French, 267, 352

Port Arthur, 280

Portugal (and Portuguese colonies), believed to be morally debauched, 185; representation on regional commissions, 197, 314, 340; colonial rule criticized, 346; comment by Lord Croft, 420; 95, 151, 165, 168, 171

Post-Hostilities Planning Committee, 523

Poynton, A. H. (and Poynton–Robinson project), background, 379; analyzes issue of 'trusteeship', 380–2; and Dumbarton Oaks, 383–91; begins Poynton–Robinson project, 392–3; on partnership and trusteeship, 394; elaboration of project, 395–7; attack on mandates system, 397; and criticism by Battershill, 398–9; and Lord Hailey, 399–400; and Sir Arthur Dawe, 401; and Sydney Caine, 402–3; and Armistice and Post-War Committee, 403–4; Foreign Office response to project, 405; reaction of Canada, South Africa, Australia, and New Zealand, 406–8; on eve of Yalta, 451; and aftermath of Yalta, 466, 471; at Commonwealth Meeting 1945, 504; at San Francisco Conference, 520, 521, 522, 525, 528, 531; 573

Puerto Rico, 47, 95, 111, 236, 361–2, 441, 477, 498, 512, 537

Rabaul, 78, 354

Regionalism *and* regional commissions (*see also* Caribbean Commission *and*

South Pacific Commission), discussed by Hailey, 143, 207–8, 400; discussed in American committees, 171, 173, 185; in the Far East, 189, 191; proposed by Cranborne, 195–6; compared with mandates system, 197; in West Indies, 180–1, 210, 213; commissions debated in London 1942, 214–16, 219; in British *aide-mémoire* 1943, 251; in Stanley's policy statement July 1943, 258; planning in the C.O. 1944, 309–26; discussed at Dumbarton Oaks, 385–7; and federations in West Africa, 388; and question of aggrandizement, 399; and Australia–New Zealand Conference 1944, 418–19; in F. D. R.–Stanley talk, 439; after Yalta, 463, 471, 473–4

Reid, Escott, 443 n.; on Philippines' independence producing American self-righteousness, 444 n.

Rhee, Syngman, 553

Rhodesia, Northern, 132, 314, 339

Rhodesia, Southern, 314

Robinson, Kenneth E. (and Poynton–Robinson project); background, 379–80; on Italian and Japanese colonies, 386; begins Poynton–Robinson project, 392–3; general views of, 393–4; on partnership and trusteeship, 394; elaboration of project, 395–7; attack on mandates system, 397; and criticism by Battershill, 398–9; and Lord Hailey, 399–400; and Sir Arthur Dawe, 401; and Sydney Caine, 402–3; and Armistice and Post-War Committee, 403–4; Foreign Office response to project, 405; reaction of Canada, South Africa, Australia, and New Zealand, 406–8; warns against driving Australians and New Zealanders into intransigent position, 414; on eve of Yalta, 451; and San Francisco Conference, 531; 573

Rockefeller, Nelson, 476, 477, 540

Romulo, Carlos P., 542, 546

Ronald, Sir Nigel, 64

Roosevelt, Eleanor, 493–4

Roosevelt, Elliott, and *As He Saw It*, 19–21; recounts F. D. R.'s views on French colonies, 27; account of Atlantic Charter meeting, 121; account of Casablanca Conference 226

Roosevelt, Franklin D., and imperialism as a cause of war, 3, 226, 538; a gradualist, 4; and independence for the colonies after a period of tutelage, 4; as father of the post-war world of politically independent nations, 5, 487; Hong Kong becomes a major issue with Churchill, 7; and India, 8–9, 149–50; trusteeship regimes a concrete way to alter the colonial *status quo*, 9; and Russia and Britain (Elliott Roosevelt's interpretation), 20–1; anti-colonial attitude (according to Norman Angell), 21; and comment to Churchill about rock and sand bar, 26; and French colonial empire (*see also* Indo-China), 27–8, 40–1, 155; and the Dutch educating head-hunters, 30; and South-East Asia, according to Amery, 32; as enemy of British Empire, 33; expounds on trusteeship schemes on return from Cairo–Teheran Conferences, 38–9; megalomania of compared with that of Wilson and Lloyd George, 38; proposes a Christian, an Arab, and a Jew as Trustees in Palestine, 55; and territorial aggrandizement in Middle East, 62; ignores work of committees, 86–7, 275, 281; discusses Atlantic Charter with Churchill, 121–3; assessed by Harold Macmillan, 133 n.; on trusteeship as a replacement of imperialism, 147–8; address to people of Philippines 1941, 148; offers advice on India, 149; reflects American public opinion, 150; and future of Japanese Empire, 151; and Woodrow Wilson, 122, 153; circumspect about territorial aggrandizement, 154; discusses colonial questions with Molotov, 156–7; favours internationalization, 158; and the 'Four Policemen', 160; does not want British West Indian 'headaches', 182; believed by British to be ill-informed about Far East, 191; responds to Willkie, 199; Atlantic Charter applies to 'all humanity', 200; dislikes phrase 'Parent State', 218, 223; colonial

Roosevelt (*cont.*):
system means war, 226; meets with Sultan of Morocco, 226–7; discusses Pacific islands with Eden 1943, 228–9; instructs J.C.S. to plan for International Police Force, 259–60; restrains Navy on Japanese mandates question, 262; geopolitical ideas about Polynesia, 267–9; curtails Navy's ambitions, 267; critical of General Board's reports, 267; directs Admiral Byrd to investigate South Pacific, 269; pleased with J.C.S. survey 1943, 272; acquires precise military information before Cairo Conference, 273; aims at Cairo, 275; business transacted at Cairo and Teheran, 275, 278–86; relates results of Cairo–Teheran Conferences to Pacific War Council, 299; meets with John Curtin 1944, 308; instructions to Stettinius mission 1944, 327; motivated by 'imperialism'?, 353–4; refines concept of trusteeship, 354–5; believes British Empire should be liquidated, 356; says international inspection team would be welcome in American South, 357; trusteeship ideas become static, 358; receives State Department support on notion of sovereignty, 364; holds central position in controversy between State Department and military, 366; rebuffs J.C.S., 373; assures military he will fortify islands, 374; and future of yellow and white races, 422, 425; quotes Churchill on 'Chinks' and 'Chinamen', 424; and the British and Dutch in South-East Asia, 425; interview with Stanley, 436–40; on Indo-China, Burma, the Pacific islands, New Guinea, and timetables for independence, 437; ignores trusteeship issue, 439; good performance with Stanley, 440; Halifax on forming opinions, 443; directive on the Pacific islands late 1944, 448–9; meets with Stalin at Yalta, 456–7; and Churchill's defence of British Empire, 459; able to control bureaucratic factions, 476; and strategic outposts doctrine, 483–4; directive on Pacific islands March 1945, 484; last interview with

Taussig on colonial affairs, 484–7; sceptical about Navy's aptitude to administer dependent areas, 485; on future of 'brown peoples in the East', 486; emphasizes *independence* as goal of American policy, 486; control over State Department, 487; and Stimson, 483–4, 488–9; last instruction on trusteeship from Warm Springs, 492–3; Stimson pays tribute to, 494; Taussig evokes Rooseveltian ideal of independence at San Francisco, 537–8; final thoughts about Indo-China, 551; sense of guardianship, 573
Rothwell, C. Easton, 384–6, 388
Ruanda–Urundi, 44 n., 116, 171, 173, 480 n., 565 n.
Russia, power of in relation to British Empire and United States, 25, 51; possibility of remaining peaceful after the war, 74; as a foe, 75; and Korea, 79; 'internal colonies' in, 111, 232, 238–9, 241–2, 570; as one of the 'Four Policemen', 148; as trustee in Pacific area, 167, 185, 196, 228, 236; and International Police Force, 260, 263, 264; and South-East Asia regional commission, 315, 360, 395; entry into Far Eastern War, 375; and support of U.S. with trusteeship proposals, 447; and Persian Gulf trusteeship scheme, 449; as member of anti-British bloc, 525; policy at San Francisco Conference, 527, 529, 530, 533, 536, 539–41, 546; and the Italian colonies, 555–6, 558–60
Ryckmans, Pierre, 44
Ryukyu Islands, 80, 280

St. Helena, 250
Sakhalin, 227, 456
Samoa (American), 47, 111, 264, 266, 272
Samoa (Western), 96, 109, 116, 264, 266, 272, 344, 563, 565
Samuel, Lord, 204–5, 211
Sarawak, 135, 248
Schlesinger, Arthur, Jr., review of *As He Saw It*, 20–1; 551
Scott, Lord Francis, 317
Security Subcommittee, tension between civilian and military rep-

resentatives in, 85–6; and Cairo Conference, 275; 68–87

Seel, George F., views on Italian colonies, 62, 66; and international trusteeship, 312–13; on South African expansion, 321; on trusteeship in Tanganyika, 325–6; on regional commissions, 341

Self-determination, principle of, 3–4, 79, 81, 99, 165, 166, 183, 223, 533, 546

Senussi, 60, 65

Seychelles, 127, 251, 341

Shanghai, 264, 279

Shotwell, James T., historical perspective on British and French colonialism, 162–3; 160

Siam, 315, 402, 550, 572

Sierra Leone, 381

Singapore, fall of 15 February 1942, 7; and trusteeship schemes, 32; created by the British, 35, 189; and consequences of disaster for colonial affairs, 134–46; catastrophe at initiates new era of British Empire, 145; 76, 168, 285

Smith, Trafford, 311–12

Smuts, J. C., definition of Commonwealth, 17; and South-West Africa, 17–18, 562–4; wants to abolish mandates system, 18; views on 'satellite settlements' for Jews, 58; believes that mandates system has outlived its time, 106; interviewed in *Life* 1942, 209–10; on evolution of Commonwealth and Parent States, 219; and South African aims in central and eastern Africa, 318–21; at Dominion Prime Ministers' Conference 1944, 337, 348; and decentralization of Empire–Commonwealth, 338; basis of trusteeship, 339; rests claim to South-West Africa on right of conquest, 363; at Commonwealth Meeting 1945, 502, 507, 510–11; and San Francisco Conference, 520; and Italian colonies and strategic security, 560–2; postwar review of trusteeship, 563

Society Islands, 266, 267, 270

Solomon Islands, 264, 269, 272, 292, 295, 352

Somalia, 49, 58, 64, 66, 116, 341, 516, 556–8, 561, 565 n.

South Africa, policy towards mandates system, 18, 108, 116; representation on regional commissions, 197, 314–15; and abortive Anglo-American colonial declaration, 219, 223; expansionist aims of, 317–21; concern for regional commissions in relation to domestic policies, 406; and aftermath of Yalta, 472; 98, 172, 469

South-East Asia, regional commission in, 215–16, 315, 360, 395; and Australia, 294–7; 29–30

South Pacific Regional Commission, 301, 305, 309, 311, 410, 418–19, 564

South-West Africa, and international control, 17–18, 116; 'C' type classification, 92; annexation urged by Smuts, 106; incorporation endorsed by American committee, 172; Smuts and, 210, 219, 363, 508, 520; at San Francisco Conference, 527; 165, 443

Sovereignty in colonial areas, problem of the former Japanese Empire, 81, 85, 151; in relation to international supervision, 197; F. D. R. on, 357, 484; International Organization committee, attempts to resolve, 362–4; Caine and Hailey on, 403; Hopkins sums up F. D. R.'s ideas on, 426; discussed by Stanley and Pasvolsky, 446–7

Soviet Union *see* Russia

Stalin, Joseph, and Teheran Conference, 283–6; meets with F. D. R. at Yalta, 456–7; aligns himself with U.S. in trusteeship controversy, 457, 459; and Italian colonies, 555; 28, 33, 38, 448, 553

Stanley, Oliver, views about the British Empire, 35–6; pique at Foreign Office, 56; and the F.O.'s 'Xmas spirit', 66; regards idealism of mandates as cant, 90; detests free trade clauses of mandates, 91; deplores impermanence of mandates, 98; on the 'motley international assembly' 99; and CD&W, 102–3; and international accountability, 107; sets out to abolish mandates system, 211–14, 359; proposes regional commissions, 214, 216–17; and abortive Anglo-American colo-

Stanley (*cont.*):

nial declaration, 222–4, 250–1, 253; aghast at National Declaration on Independence, 244; *On Stanley On!*, 252; objects to Hailey's approach to colonial questions, 255; Parliamentary statement of July 1943, 256–8; extreme distaste for international trusteeship, 313; and regional planning 1944, 316, 341; writes with uncharacteristic exuberance about Smuts, 321; meets with Isaiah Bowman 1944, 328–31, 333; pressure by F.O. on, 332; Bowman's impression of his reaction to trusteeship: 'he would see us in Hades', 336; no sympathy with South African expansion, 340; attacks mandates system at Dominion Prime Ministers' Conference 1944, 344–5, 347; disapproves of international accountability, 349; 'trusteeship' used to cover American expansionist ambitions, 351; policies discussed at Dumbarton Oaks, 386–7; attempts to take the initiative, 392; guides Poynton–Robinson project through Armistice and Post-War Committee, 403; described by Creech Jones as doing 'a reasonably good job', 430; purpose of talks in Washington, 434; views only slightly less rigid than Churchill's, 435; interview with F. D. R., 436–40; believes F. D. R. sends up a smoke-screen, 437; holds his own with F. D. R. on Hong Kong, 438; on regional commissions, 439; not put on guard by F. D. R., 440; confronted with incisive statement on trusteeship by Frankfurter, 441; explains to British Empire group that trouble with mandates is *impermanence*, 442; uncharacteristically frank views on 'independence', 444; argues against mandates with Pasvolsky, 444–5; takes stand on self-government versus independence, 446; leaves Washington knowing Americans will fight to the end for the mandates, 447; advises Churchill on eve of Yalta, 451; resents Yalta accord, 464; controversy with Eden after Yalta, 466–8; begins retreat and adjusts to 'trustee-ship', 470–1; again on the 'motley assembly', 472; reassesses international supervision, 472–4; realistic action in not attempting to liquidate mandates system, 474; and Commonwealth Meeting 1945, 504, 506, 507; at time of San Francisco Conference objects to strategic trusteeship, petitions, and visiting missions, 524–5; yields to Americans on trusteeship issues, 530–1; 379, 384, 431, 475, 497

Stassen, Harold, at San Francisco Conference, 514, 515–16, 519, 522, 525, 528, 534–42, 543; performs outstanding service, 516–17; does not wish to commit U.S. to breaking up of British Empire, 537; on question of Hawaiian independence, 538

State Department (*see also, e.g.*, Hull, Welles, Pasvolsky, Gerig), in agreement with Australia and New Zealand on question of mandates, 18, 420, 422; and European reoccupation of colonies, 18; ambivalent attitude towards British Empire, 19; and universal application of trusteeship doctrine, 19; reaction to Dutch plans for colonies, 29–30; believes in a peace based on international organization, 68; trusteeship planning, 177–9, 182–6; stand on sovereignty, 364; and question of independence, 365; and controversy with J.C.S., 366; yields to J.C.S. and strikes trusteeship from Dumbarton Oaks agenda, 377; and F. D. R.'s directive on Pacific islands late 1944, 448–9; and Persian Gulf trusteeship scheme, 449–50; and briefing book at Yalta, 450, 459; F. D. R.'s control over, 487; policy at San Francisco, 116–17, 516

State–War–Navy Coordinating Committee, 476 n., 490

Stettinius, Edward R., mission to London 1944, 54, 327; conversation with Richard Law about colonial compensation, 378–9; interviewed by Sir Frederick Eggleston, 425; erroneous grasp of F. D. R.'s ideas about trusteeship, 426; a 'mouthpiece', 427; at Yalta, 458–60; meeting with Stimson and Forrestal on trusteeship, 489–90; turnabout on colonial issue, 490–3; and row with Taussig, 494; works together with Stimson and Forrestal to resolve trusteeship issue, 494–6; at San Francisco Conference, 538, 552; 440, 475, 515

Stilwell, General Joseph, discusses Hong Kong with F. D. R., 280 n.

Stimson, Henry L., and post-war France, 41; protests too late for Yalta, 449; doctrine of strategic outposts, 482–3; presses doctrine on F. D. R., 483–4; attempts to prevent discussion of colonial issue at San Francisco, 487–90; works together with Forrestal and Stettinius to resolve trusteeship issue, 494–6, 515

Strachey, John, 34

Straits Settlements, 135

Sudan, 341, 556

Surinam, 29

Suva, 272

Syria, 169, 543, 557

Taft, Charles P., 371

Tahiti, 272, 506

Tanganyika, question of permanence as British possession, 98; and tradition of trusteeship, 317–20, 324–6; and amalgamation schemes, 322–3; and regional commission, 341; problems of economic development, 399; capital investment in, 402; 96, 116, 171, 172, 173, 563, 569

Tangier, 169, 194

Taussig, Charles W., and Anglo-American Caribbean Commission, 180–1; description of political connections, 435; with Stanley at F. D. R. interview, 436–40; and Stanley–Pasvolsky discussion, 444–6, especially 445 n.; most intimate adviser of F. D. R. on colonial affairs, 484; last interview with F. D. R., 484–7; interview with Mrs. Roosevelt, 493–4; row with Stettinius, 494; and San Francisco Conference, 514, 539–40; invokes spirit of F. D.R. supporting independence, 536–8; 213, 354, 357, 476, 551

Teheran Conference, 283–6

Territorial Subcommittee, and eco-

nomic control of Japan, 77; and Japanese islands, 80–1; and Cairo Conference, 275; 43, 71

Timor, 165, 228, 237, 295, 315

Togo, 116, 172, 173, 442, 446, 565 n.

Toynbee, Arnold J., 60, 69, 331

Transcontinental and Western Air, 269

Trans-Jordan, 49, 51, 400–1

Treasury, and CD&W, 102–3

Trinidad, 272, 342, 390

Tripolitania, 59, 61–2, 65

Truk Island, 76, 85, 264, 354

Truman, Harry, query about Puerto Rico, 441; approves of trusteeship policy of U.S., 496; and Indo-China, 552; and Italian colonies, 555; 440

Trusteeship (*see also* mandates *and* Trusteeship System of United Nations), as antithesis of imperialism, 3; as a principle of colonial administration, 12, 18–19; as a cloak for American expansion, 8, 30–1; economic element of, 25–6; 30–2, 48, 51–2, 59, 67, 68, 74, 86, 90–1; and strategic considerations, 26; and ethics of Empire, 31; and the French colonies, 27–9, 38–47; and the Dutch colonies, 29–30; as distinguished from make-shift in international politics, 43; as a means of continuing paramountcy, 51; as extension of mandate in Palestine, 55; essence of accountability, 57, 88, 114, 292, 301, 382, 409; and Jewish settlement schemes, 62; and American security in the Pacific, 86; bibliographical note, 88; national versus international concepts, 88–90; distinction between international *administration* and international *control*, 95; associated with sterile legalism of League of Nations, 139; denounced as old-fashioned, 140; and the American Negro, 166; racial implications of, 174; purpose of to facilitate decision by indigenous peoples, 238; discussed at Cairo and Teheran Conferences, 280, 285; and the Australia–New Zealand Agreement 1944, 289–92; and Australian conceptions of, 292–8; F. D. R. believes all Pacific islands should be

Trusteeship (*cont.*):
regulated by, 299; C.O. regards as American 'cloak' and 'cover', 309; in Tanganyika, 324–6; as a solution to unstable areas, 354; as a panacea, 356; defined in Poynton–Robinson project, 394; Hailey emphasizes publicity as positive aspect, 400; conception of endorsed by Australia–New Zealand Conference November 1944, 412–13; formula agreed upon at Yalta, 459; 'strategic' trust concept developed, 477, 479, 522, 528; F. D. R.'s application to specific areas, 489; idealism of expressed by Bowman at San Francisco Conference, 516; as a continuation of imperialism, 549

Trusteeship*s*, nuance in American and British usage, 454 n.
Trusteeship System of United Nations, independence explicit goal of, 92; contrasted with mandates system, 95, 99, 117; visiting missions a distinguishing feature, 96, 357, 527; 'strategic' territory of, 115–16; authority of council, 116; designed to promote security, 237; established at San Francisco, especially 531
Trust Territory of the Pacific *see* Micronesia
Tuamotu Islands, 228, 266, 267, 269, 270, 354
Tubuai Islands, 266, 267

Uganda, tradition of trusteeship in, 317; and amalgamation schemes, 323; and regional commission, 341; 171, 319
Ukraine, 560
Union Islands, 266
United Nations (Organization), sovereignty of Pacific islands to reside in, 85; and colonial questions, 160–1 (*see also* Trusteeship System)
United States (*see also* Joint Chiefs of Staff, Navy, and State Department), anti-colonial attitude, 3, 9, 11, 22; resources of in relation to British Empire and Russia, 51; heir incumbent of the British Empire, 79; expansion of not characterized by over-all clarity of policy, 87; and

mandates system, 90–1; fighting for independence in Asia, 134–5; as one of the 'Four Policemen', 148; as trustee in Pacific, 167, 196, 228, 236; believed by Lord Cranborne to be responsible for war in the Pacific, 35, 189; and regional commissions, 215; interested in natural resources as well as native peoples in the colonies, 402; imperialism of checked in the Pacific (according to Evatt), 411; to act as 'guardian' over Pacific islands, 437; significance of Yalta Conference for, 454

Vandenberg, Arthur, particular interest in security problem at San Francisco, 515, 516; 514
Venezuela, 314
Villard, Henry S., 170, 386–9
Virgin Islands, 47, 95, 236, 362, 480, 512
Volcano Islands, 265

Wake Island, 264
Wallis Islands, 267
Watt, Sir Alan, 442 n.
Webster, Charles, 331–2
Welles, Sumner, and free trade, 24; describes Oliver Stanley as a 'most narrow, bigoted, reactionary Tory', 35; fire-eating ideas about international trusteeship, 95, 173; *Time for Decision*, 111, and Atlantic Charter, 123; Memorial Day address 1942, 154–5; proclaims end of imperialism, 158; and future international organization, 160; advocates liberation, 161, 163; comments on European colonialism, 164–5; and principle of self-determination, 166; views on South-East Asia, 167; contempt for Portuguese colonialism, 168; 'Negroes are in the lowest rank of human beings', 170; wishes South Africa to incorporate S.W. Africa, 172; refuses to place colonies in western hemisphere under international supervision, 184, 236; and question of colonial independence, 225, 233; meets with Eden 1943, 227; elaborates trusteeship ideas 1943, 235–8; article on colonial liberation in *New York Herald Tribune* March

1945, 497–9; 182, 568
West Indies, 127, 182
White, Freda, 146
Wilhelmina, Queen, and declaration of political union, 29; F. D. R.'s conversation with, 437
Willkie, Wendell, views on imperialism, 8; round-the-world tour, 199; criticism of British Empire, 200–3, 212; 277
Willson, Admiral Russell, denounces International Police Force, 372; memorandum on 'Fundamental Military Factors', 374–7; argues case for annexation before Dependent Areas Committee, 478–9; and strategic security, 481–2; on the 'international welfare boys', 478, 485; and San Francisco Conference, 515; 260, 371, 476, 477, 480
Wilmot, Chester, 19, 21
Wilson, Woodrow, on imperialism as a cause of war, 3; and principle of self-determination, 4; and the Pacific islands, 83; ghost of haunts F. D. R.,

122; compared with F. D. R., 133 n.; ideas of in relation to trusteeship system, 238; influence at San Francisco Conference, 536
Winant, John G., and abortive Anglo-American colonial declaration, 249–51; fails to forward British *aide-mémoire*, 255
Woolf, Leonard, abandons idea of internationalization, 94; hostile to South Africa, 106–7; 22–3, 34, 109, 566 n.
World Charter *see* Atlantic Charter
Wrong, Hume, 502, 508

Yalta Conference, and principle of international trusteeship, 67; accord influenced by State Department's briefing book, 70, 450, 459; negotiations, 448–60; significance of, 463–4
Yemen, 65
Yugoslavia, 560

Zanzibar, 341